CONFRONTATION IN CENTRAL EUROPE

CONFRONTATION
IN CENTRAL EUROPE
Weimar Germany
and Czechoslovakia

F. GREGORY CAMPBELL

The University of Chicago Press
Chicago and London

F. GREGORY CAMPBELL is assistant professor of history at the
University of Chicago.

Library of Congress Cataloging in Publication Data

Campbell, F   Gregory.
    Confrontation in central Europe.

    Bibliography: p.
    Includes index.
    1. Czechoslovak Republic—Politics and government.
2. Czechoslovak Republic—Foreign relations—Germany.
3. Germany—Foreign relations—Czechoslovak Republic.
4. Germans in the Czechoslovak Republic. I. Title.
DB215.2.C35   327.43'0437   74-11618
ISBN 0-226-09251-8

THE UNIVERSITY OF CHICAGO PRESS, CHICAGO 60637
THE UNIVERSITY OF CHICAGO PRESS, LTD., LONDON
© 1975 by The University of Chicago
All rights reserved. Published 1975
Printed in the United States of America

For Barbara

Contents

Acknowledgments

Initial research for this project was made possible by grants from Yale University and the Inter-University Committee on Travel Grants at Indiana University. I am also indebted to the staff of the Joseph Regenstein Library at the University of Chicago for their willingness to acquire research materials, and to augment their already impressive holdings in Central European history.

I appreciate the cooperation of the staffs of the various archives whose holdings are discussed in the bibliographical essay. For invaluable help in preparing the manuscript for publication, I wish to thank Rita Hinckley, Monica Schaeffer, Rose Watson, and particularly Robert Smith.

A number of colleagues, teachers, and friends have read the manuscript. For their praise, but especially for their criticisms, I am grateful to William H. McNeill, Akira Iriye, and Václav Laška of the University of Chicago; Josef Anderle of the University of North Carolina; and Hanna H. Gray, Hans W. Gatzke, Piotr S. Wandycz, and Henry Ashby Turner of Yale University. Other historians in Czechoslovakia and Germany have read all or part of the manuscript. They realize my gratitude to them.

The late Hajo Holborn first aroused my interest in this topic. His dedication to high scholarly standards and his strong-willed commitment to humanistic principles were an inspiration to two generations of students. If this book is a fitting addition to the others that he helped to inspire, I shall be satisfied.

Introduction

The fourteen years between October 1918 and January 1933 were a unique period in Central European history. The defeat of both Russia and Germany and the dissolution of the Habsburg Empire in the First World War created a rare opportunity for the various nationalities of Central Europe to live in independent nation-states beyond the dictates of outside forces. This book deals with two of those nationalities—the Germans and the Czechs—and specifically with the diplomatic relations between the two republics founded in their names.

Historians continue to debate various interpretations of the nationality conflicts in the Habsburg Empire. Hitler's attacks on Czechoslovakia and the Munich decisions of 1938 are well-known to all. The expulsion of the Sudeten Germans from Czechoslovakia in 1945-46 has been the subject of much controversy. But the period between 1918 and 1933 has received scant attention. In the absence of major diplomatic crises, it is customarily assumed that the relations between the Weimar and the Czechoslovak republics were harmonious and that national frictions were of diminishing importance. But did the republican period really offer an interlude of harmony in the long history of Czech-German rivalries? Was there not a basic continuity in Czech-German relations, from the Czech national revival in the late eighteenth century through the middle of the twentieth century? In this book I shall argue that the national conflict continued undiminished, although relatively concealed, between 1918 and 1933 and that the focus of that conflict was the diplomatic relationship between Weimar Germany and the Czechoslovak republic. While concentrating on the 1918-33 period, I have considered it necessary to include opening and concluding chapters that attempt to place the republican period into the longer history of Czech-German rivalries.

The competition between the Czechoslovak and the German republics was also a significant aspect of international relations in the interwar years. What were the prospects that Germans and Czechs, the Weimar and the Czechoslovak republics, could function as independent yet interdependent members of a free community of nations? The answers depend on the responses to many other much more specific inquiries. It is with such questions that this study is concerned—questions of potentially vital import for the peace settlements of 1919 as they applied to Central Europe.

In this study I have tried not to create and dwell in a rarefied atmosphere of high diplomacy. In attempting to investigate all factors that might have influenced the relations of the two republics, I have discussed certain domestic political, social, and economic conditions in the two countries as well as the broader issues in international relations. The domestic history of Weimar Germany has been and continues to be the subject of much analysis by able historians. Their work eases the task of placing German foreign policy in a larger context. On the other hand, less has been known in the English-speaking world about domestic conditions in the first Czechoslovak republic. I have considered it necessary to devote particular attention to Czechoslovakia because the nationality disputes within the country influenced Czechoslovak-German relations. Moreover, Germany occupied a larger place in Czechoslovak diplomatic calculations than did Czechoslovakia in Germany's foreign policy orientation. Domestic factors influencing Czechoslovak policy toward Germany therefore merit special emphasis. But this book is not a narrative of the domestic political histories of the republics, nor is it an analysis of the socioeconomic structure of society either in Germany or in Czechoslovakia. Such studies, particularly for the successor states to the Habsburg Empire, still should be done, for they could add significantly to our knowledge about Central Europe in the twentieth century. But in this book the determining factor has been simply the influence of any domestic situation on the foreign policy of one republic toward the other. Whenever there was a discernible and significant relationship, I have tried to discuss the interaction of foreign and domestic considerations. When there was none, I have avoided adding inconsequential detail to the narrative.

I have used the word *interaction* in discussing the relationship of foreign and domestic concerns. The question concerning the *primacy* of foreign or of domestic policy in the political history of a country is rhetorical. No general philosophical answer to that question would facilitate our understanding of any particular chain of historical events. Obviously, both foreign and domestic factors should be considered by policymakers in the formulation of a political program, but the relative weight of the various components in any decision depends on the merits of any given case and the men making the decision. Particularly in diplomatic history it is essential to be precise. The viable alternatives that confront policymakers often differ only in nuances, but those are differences that can be crucially important in the histories of nations. In other types of historical study it is possible to analyze statistically the actions of large masses of people and thereby to gain useful insights into the behavior of various social groups. But a diplomatic historian must deal with a relatively small number of people who must be understood as individuals if their decisions and policies are to be comprehended. In a broader perspective it is perhaps possible to develop workable models of ways in which international relations operate. But a diplomatic historian must still investigate the particulars if he is to explain how a given relationship developed. In short, in diplomatic history there is no substitute for specificity. That does not necessitate a horde of factual details. It does mean that any analysis must be conducted on the grounds of the subject matter itself. Only by analyzing the historical events themselves is it possible to discern the major problem areas and to understand the forces operating, for example, in the contacts between Weimar Germany and the Czechoslovak republic.

An emphasis on domestic considerations is particularly pertinent for Czechoslovak-German relations in view of the national minorities in both countries in the years between 1918 and 1933. The relationship of the Sudeten Germans to the government in Berlin, as well as to the one in Prague, is one of the major focuses of this study. What attempts were made by the Czechoslovak government to reconcile the minority nationalities to the new republic? How legitimate were the complaints of the minorities, particularly those of the Sudeten Germans? To what extent and in what ways did Weimar governments hope or seek to exploit the influence of the Sudeten Germans within Czechoslovakia? Germany also had its minorities. In what ways, if any, did the Czechoslovak authorities attempt to profit by the presence of the Lusatian Sorbs in Prussia and Saxony? The nationality disputes, as they affected the diplomacy of the two countries, will be one of the major topics demanding our attention.

Another focus of this study will be regional problems in "Central Europe." In loose political usage, particularly in Germany, that geographical designation has often applied to all the territory from Germany to the Soviet borders and from the Baltic through the Balkans. During the past generation, historians have rightly emphasized the tendency in German foreign policy since the nineteenth century to regard *Mitteleuropa* as a special sphere of German influence. That tradition seemed to culminate temporarily in Germany's annexationist war aims during the First World War. Did the collapse of the German army and the revolution of 1918-19 snuff out Mitteleuropa ambitions in Berlin? Was Weimar German policy toward the other Central and Southeast European states in any way colored by Mitteleuropa thinking? The area between Germany and the Soviet Union remained fragmented and weak and eventually became an easy prey for Hitler. Were there no fears in the successor states, and particularly in Czechoslovakia, of a possible revival of the German grasping for hegemony in Central Europe? If those fears existed, why was so little done to build a buffer against German expansionism? These are crucially important questions for an evaluation of the roles of men like Gustav Stresemann and Edvard Beneš in Central European diplomacy.

That area of Central Europe with which we are most immediately concerned includes Austria and Poland as well as Germany and Czechoslovakia. The fate of Austria in particular was of crucial significance for Czechoslovak-German relations throughout the interwar period. Indeed, Austria occupies almost as large a part in the narrative as Czechoslovakia and Germany. In view of experiences during the Weimar years it is not at all surprising that the Munich decisions of 1938 followed the *Anschluss* by only six months. We shall have to examine the role that Austria played in the relations between Berlin and Prague, and the ways in which various Austrian leaders attempted to exploit Austria's unique situation. And the relationship between Czechoslovakia and Poland cannot go unregarded. Although the French encouraged cooperation between Warsaw and Prague, it may well be that the French could never construct an eastern alliance system out of their various eastern allies. The effect of Czechoslovak-Polish rivalries on German policy will be another theme in our treatment of Central European diplomacy.

In addition to a consideration of domestic conditions in the two countries and of regional affairs in Central Europe, a third and final focus will fall on the broader issues of international affairs and the way in which they influenced Czechoslovak-German relations. The Czechs owed their independence primarily to the support of the Western powers during the latter stages of the First World War. How was it possible that a small group of political emigrés were able to achieve formal diplomatic recognition from the great powers and then enjoy their extensive support at the peace conference? How reliable did Czechoslovakia's friends and allies remain through the Weimar years? How far into the past can we trace anti-Czech attitudes among the Western powers, such as were displayed during the Munich crisis of 1938? We shall pay particular attention to the roles that Czechoslovak diplomacy played in the debates on disarmament and security and on reparations, and to the effects of those issues on the relations between Berlin and Prague.

Finally, the first Czechoslovak republic has long basked in widespread historical repute as a bastion of stability and democracy in a politically chaotic area of Europe. The two chief leaders of the republic have also enjoyed illustrious personal reputations. Tomáš G. Masaryk has gone into history in Western countries as a democratically minded philosopher-president, as a humanist committed to the social welfare of all the citizens of the republic. Although he has not been treated so well in official historical writing in Czechoslovakia since 1948, his reputation remains much the same in the Czech popular mind. Edvard Beneš has been credited with similar values, and with great diplomatic finesse as well in Western historical writing. To what extent are those reputations merited? Our investigation of Czechoslovakia's German policy should necessarily have bearing on the historical reputations of those men and their republic, for the German question lay at the heart of almost all their political calculations.

As a diplomatic history, this study relies in large part on the archives of various foreign ministries. Most of the primary evidence comes from the memoranda, telegrams, reports, and instructions that are left in the wake of international relations and that are the normal tools of a diplomatic historian's craft. The major German Foreign Office documents are readily available on microfilm, and I have supplemented those microfilms with research in the Political Archive of the Foreign Office in Bonn. They are the most important sources for the German side of the narrative.

The archives of the Czechoslovak Ministry of Foreign Affairs are generally closed for the period after 1918. Various Czech and Slovak historians have had access to selections from the archives, and I have used their works as an indirect source for Czechoslovak documentation. But in this research project I have tried to demonstrate the futility of keeping an archive closed after a number of other countries with whom a government maintained diplomatic relations have opened theirs. I think that I have been able to put together a fairly complete picture of Czechoslovak policy by sifting through the diplomatic reports from Prague that are contained in the French, British, Austrian, German, and American diplomatic archives. The French documents for the period through 1929 were opened for historical research in 1972. France was the best ally of Czechoslovakia, and Beneš was more candid in discussions with French statesmen than with those of any other country. The French harbored deep sympathies for Czechoslovakia, and their documents afford a positive and optimistic view of the country and its policies. The British documents are available for the entire interwar period. From a pro-Czech bias in the early 1920s, the British documents reveal an emerging critical view of Czechoslovakia and the growth of attitudes that ultimately culminated with the Munich policy of 1938. The Austrian archives are officially closed for the period after 1925, but the Austrian government obligingly gave me permission to read the pertinent files for the years 1926 through 1933. The Austrians, who should not be equated with the Germans in their attitudes toward Czechoslovakia, had the clearest perception of domestic political and social issues in Czechoslovakia. That should not be surprising in view of the centuries of association of Czechs and Austrians in the Habsburg Empire. The American reports are of value mainly for Beneš's occasional comments to the American minister in Prague about international issues. I have used the German documents in order to investigate the ties between Berlin and the Sudeten Germans and the use that German diplomacy hoped to make of the Sudeten German minority. I have tried not to allow my view of Czechoslovak domestic problems to be determined simply by German reporting. In investigating Czechoslovak policy toward Germany and the Sudeten Germans I have selected and interwoven evidence from the various archival sources. I believe that by analyzing the information in the archives in Vienna, Paris, London, Bonn, and Washington I know quite well what must be in the Czechoslovak archives. There should not be too many secrets left in Prague.

Among the best sources for domestic histories of the two republics are reports about their internal affairs by certain knowledgeable diplomats in Prague and Berlin. Through their informants, the ambassadors and ministers often knew much more about the background of political decisions than appeared in newspapers. Political intrigues in the capital cities became the subject of in-depth reporting. The analyses of experts stationed as attachés in the diplomatic missions afforded succinct appraisals of military, social, and economic conditions in the republics. In short, I have exploited the standard sources for diplomatic history in order to obtain valuable information about much more than diplomatic negotiations themselves. Diplomatic documents, like any other source material for historical research, obviously have liabilities. Diplomats can be charged with rumormongering, with reporting only what their governments want to hear, or simply with negligence and stupidity. But in any large-scale research project the shortcomings of those men and their reports soon become obvious. When a diplomatic historian is confronted with mounds of evidence, his primary problem is one of selection, and suspect sources can easily be discarded.

In addition to the research in the diplomatic documents, I have worked for several months in the newspaper archives in Prague. The newspapers were a particularly important source for the first two or three years of the existence of the Czechoslovak republic, when power relationships were being established and confirmed in political practice. Along with the memoirs, diaries, and governmental publications that are cited at various points in the narrative, the newspapers complete the primary source material for this study. Lest the emphasis on primary documentation become misleading, I obviously do not believe that the writer of a historical monograph can ignore other secondary literature. The first chapter, which traces the nationality conflict through more than a century, necessarily relies largely on secondary sources. A number of those works contain information that has not been made generally available in English. Throughout the narrative and the analysis I have tried to digest the insights of other historians and to integrate their findings into the information gained from the primary sources. But whatever new knowledge or understanding this work may contain is derived largely from the documentary sources. So far as I know, no historical work has yet exploited the particular files of the French, Austrian, and British archives that I have consulted. Portions of the American and German documents have appeared in other books with emphases and interpretations different from those in this work.

In what ways was there a confrontation between Weimar Germany and the Czechoslovak republic? What were the broader implications of their relationship? These are questions to which we now can turn.

1   *Before the Republics*

For Czechs, triumph; for Germans, defeat: October 28, 1918, was Czechoslovakia's day of independence. Early in the morning the news arrived in Prague that the Austrian foreign minister had accepted the conditions for an armistice laid down in President Wilson's latest note. The Austrian capitulation opened the way for the independence of the Czechs and the Slovaks. The Czech National Committee in Prague deliberated through the day, and then in the late afternoon proclaimed the independence of Czechoslovakia. As the news spread through Bohemia and Moravia, it unleashed joyful demonstrations among the Czechs, who paraded through the streets tearing down German statues and shop signs. The members of the Czech gymnastic and cultural society, Sokol, took over the police duties and themselves participated in the celebrations of national independence. The news of independence spread more slowly through Slovakia, but already on October 30 the Slovak National Committee proclaimed the unity of Slovakia with Bohemia and Moravia in the new Czechoslovak state. In the middle of November the National Assembly met in Prague and elected Tomáš G. Masaryk president of the country. Credited more than anyone else with the achievement of independence, Masaryk began his return from America in November and arrived in Prague just before Christmas. As his train pulled into Wilson Station—newly renamed from Francis-Joseph Station—and as he rode through the streets of Prague, he was hailed as the father of his country and the symbol of the new state. He took up residence on Hradčany in the ancient castle of German emperors and Bohemian kings, over which now waved the flag of the Czechoslovak republic.

THE NATIONAL REVIVALS

The Czechs

Those events had been long in coming, but their roots did not sink so deeply and so firmly into the past as many people thought. By 1918 popular opinion tended to view the history of the lands of the Bohemian crown in terms of traditional national rivalries. Manuscript sources across the centuries indeed attested to frictions between Czechs and Germans in Bohemia, Moravia, and Silesia. The chronicle of Dalimil in the early fourteenth century, accounts of the Hussite wars, records from the Thirty Years' War, and the reforms of Maria Theresa and Joseph II supplied evidence of earlier national antagonisms. Precedents for almost any historical event can be traced far back into the past, but the further one goes the more forced one's judgments are likely to become. Extant records of nationality disputes in the Bohemian crown lands before the nineteenth century are episodic in nature, and they do not document an unbroken continuum of rivalry and friction. When they occurred, national conflicts were usually mixed with other kinds of issues such as religious controversies or power struggles between emperor and estates. And there were also periods of fruitful cooperation between Czechs and Germans in the Bohemian crown lands. Over the centuries, daily life in Bohemia was surely characterized by mutual toleration more than by open conflict. Although a higher proportion of Germans than of Czechs lived in towns and worked in industry and commerce, the majority of Germans, like the majority of Czechs, lived on the land. Intermarriage between the nationalities was a frequent occurrence, and a blurring of nationality distinctions was a logical result. At the top levels of society, questions of nationality hardly arose before the nineteenth century. In the dynastic state to which Bohemia, Moravia, and Silesia belonged after 1526, the Habsburg house shared power with a cosmopolitan aristocracy. Whatever the practical effect of Habsburg policies, the emperors never adopted "germanization" programs out of nationalistic motivations. The culture that has made Prague a monument of European civilization reflected Italian and French styles, which were adapted by receptive Central Europeans. It was an exaggeration to attribute the creation of the Czechoslovak republic, as many contemporaries did, to centuries of national rivalries.

The foundation stones of Czechoslovakia were quarried directly from various national revivals of the late eighteenth and nineteenth centuries. The political philosophy and the socioeconomic evolution of that period were preconditions for politically significant nationality conflicts in the Habsburg Empire. If one searches for the origins of Czechoslovakia, one must examine the national movements among Czechs, Slovaks, and Germans in the lands that were to make up the new state.

Historians have traditionally emphasized that the Czech national revival in its early stages was largely a cultural movement. The earliest public manifestations of a Czech national spirit appeared in literary undertakings in the late eighteenth century. The greatest names were those of Josef Dobrovský and Josef Jungmann. Dobrovský published his *Geschichte der böhmischen Sprache und Literatur* already in 1792, but his most important work was his grammar of the Czech language that first appeared in 1809. It was this grammar that established the foundations for literary Czech in the nineteenth century.[1] Jungmann followed in 1825 with his own history of Czech literature, which, in contrast with Dobrovský's, was written in the Czech language itself. Jungmann's most notable contribution was his five-volume Czech-German dictionary that appeared between 1835 and 1839. Hand in hand with efforts to rationalize the language went attempts to give Czechs a literature of their own. Jungmann translated classics from Western languages into Czech. Josef Kajetán Tyl wrote romantic nationalist novels that were highly popular in the 1830s and 1840s. Václav Hanka forged manuscripts of supposedly ancient Czech poems and succeeded for decades in convincing many people that the Czech language possessed some of the oldest literary treasures in existence. A more analytical and critical mind belonged to the journalist Karel Havlíček. Havlíček's *Pražské noviny* supplanted German newspapers in Prague's coffeehouses around 1846. He called for an abandonment of sentimental nationalism and pan-Slav dreams in favor of hard work for national self-improvement.[2] By 1848 the acknowledged leader of the Czech nation was František Palacký, whose work as editor of the *Časopis českého musea* had placed him at the heart of the national movement. The earliest leaders were men of letters.

Mention of some of the more eminent Czechs should help illuminate rather than obscure the deep intellectual and social currents that were propelling the national revival. In its broader context the Czech phenomenon was only one of innumerable national movements in the nineteenth and twentieth centuries, and the Czechs shared many common experiences with other peoples. Viewed in its own specific terms, the movement was, in part, an expression of the romantic, cultural nationalism of the early 1800s. The intellectual elite owed many of their ideas to the German philosopher Johann Gottfried Herder, who had taught that every culture reflects humanity in its own distinctive way and who had called upon the Slavic peoples to regain their glorious national past. Several of the early Czech (and Slovak) leaders studied at Jena, where they came directly under Herderian influence.

More mundane forces were also at work in the society at large. In the last half of the eighteenth century the reforms of Maria Theresa and Joseph II helped to establish a social basis for the Czech national revival. The agrarian reform patents of 1781 abolished some of the worst abuses of serfdom, and allowed peasants to conclude their own matrimonial contracts, to select their own vocation, and to migrate at will across the countryside. The new mobility meant that Czech peasants were free to move to towns and cities, where a slowly growing Czech middle class eventually became a pillar of the national revival.[3] The royal reformers also abolished the *robota*, or forced labor, exactions on peasants living on estates owned by the state. That reform had the effect of breaking up the manorial system and creating communities of small independent farmers. Joseph's attempts to abolish robota on private estates as well met the fierce opposition of the seigneurs and had to be abandoned. Yet even on private estates the material welfare of peasants was better than it had been before the reigns of Maria Theresa and Joseph II.[4] In the next half-century the robota obligations were often commuted to monetary payments, thereby creating a more nearly independent existence for the peasantry.[5] Nevertheless, a host of anachronistic feudal dues remained in force, and the robota itself was not formally abolished until the revolutions of 1848.

An independent Czech peasantry, whose prosperity mounted with the growth of sugar-beet cultivation in the nineteenth century, became the all-important economic basis for the national movement. Into the twentieth century, Czech political and intellectual leaders were seldom more than a generation removed from the soil. The agrarian reforms of Maria Theresa and Joseph II made contributions to the establishment of both a Czech middle class and an independent peasantry, a development which formed the social basis for the national revival.

The education and language policies of Maria Theresa and Joseph II also helped to spur the reawakening. In the 1780s the number of elementary schools in Bohemia doubled as a result of royal encouragement and local initiative. The consequent growth of at least a semiliterate Czech-speaking population inevitably created a demand for materials such as readers and almanacs in the Czech language.[6] The education reforms therefore encouraged the development of a literary Czech language even though Joseph designated German as the state language of the empire. Already in the mid-1770s German was the language of instruction in the elementary schools and the gymnasia in Bohemia, and a mastery of German was essential for higher education. Joseph's language ordinances failed to arouse the same degree of opposition in Bohemia as in Hungary, in part because germanization had already proceeded further in the Czech lands. The growth of early Czech nationalism has been explained in part as a reaction against Joseph's germanization policies.[7] But Czech never completely disappeared from use in the meetings of the estates, and even after Joseph's decrees officials continued to publish ordinances in Czech when it was necessary to communicate with the public at large. Czech was a threatened but never a dead language. Certainly by 1918 hatred of Joseph was intense, as nationalist Czechs demonstrated by destroying his statues throughout Czechoslovakia. But his germanization efforts were merely part of his attempt to centralize and to rationalize the govern- mental structure of the state. The quintessential enlightened despot of a cosmopolitan age was hardly motivated by nationalist emotions.

Joseph was anathema to the local Bohemian nobility, whose privileged position in society his reforms threatened to destroy. They became exponents of Bohemian particularism and actually helped to cultivate a Czech national consciousness which could be exploited against Vienna. Most notable of their achievements was the founding of the Bohemian

Museum in 1818. The Czech-language journal of the museum, *Časopis
českého musea*, specializing in literary and scientific articles and book
reviews, became the preeminent learned organ for the Czech public. In
1831 the museum sponsored the establishment of the *Matice česká*, an
organization that immediately assumed the role of the prime sponsor for
Czech cultural projects.[8] Most subscribers to the magazine and con-
tributors to the *Matice česká* were clergymen, burghers, or seigneurial or
government officials. Most came from an urban environment, although by
mid-century more sons of peasants were manifesting interest in the
achievements of Czech culture.[9]

The Czech national movement first appeared as a political force in the
revolutions of 1848. Palacký's refusal to attend the German National
Assembly in Frankfurt and the Czech advocacy of a decentralized Austrian
Empire foreshadowed the future political conflicts between Czech and
German nationalism. Much of the propaganda of 1848 adopted a
stridently nationalistic tone on both the German and the Czech sides. The
first formal Czech political program appeared in the March Petitions,
which demanded equality of nationalities, the union of Bohemia and
Moravia, and autonomy for the two provinces within the Austrian Empire.
Although the autonomous union of Bohemia and Moravia was never
realized until 1918, certain practical achievements such as the introduction
of the Czech language into secondary schools and universities were gained.
Larger groups were brought temporarily into the political process. The
most lasting achievement of 1848 was the freeing of the peasantry from
the robota obligations, which signified the disappearance of the last
vestiges of serfdom. By 1848 the potentially dangerous conflict in the
countryside was between the landed peasants, who were living a
reasonably comfortable existence, and the cottagers and landless agricultural laborers.[10] The landed peasantry attempted with little success to
exclude the cottagers from the franchise. The basically conservative
outlook of the emancipated Czech peasantry was reflected in the Bohemian
and Moravian diets as well as in the Czech delegation to the Imperial
Parliament, meeting first in Vienna and then in Kroměříž [Kremsier].[11]
In the towns the small Czech middle class evinced the same kinds of fears
of an attack on property rights, and the threat of a "communist uprising"
haunted their imaginations in the early days of the March revolution.[12]
The specter of social conflict among Czech nationals therefore appeared
briefly during 1848-49 before the Habsburg armies put an end to popular
participation in the political process. But the modernization of society
over the ensuing decades meant that those social conflicts would inevitably
reassert themselves in more enduring form.

Although the political compromise of 1848 disappeared with the
triumph of Habsburg arms and the attempts to reestablish royal absolutism

in the 1850s, Czech cultural achievements grew at an even faster pace in the last half of the nineteenth century. Writers like Božena Němcova and Jan Neruda found their subject material in the daily lives of Czech peasants and the lower middle class. With the easing of censorship in the 1860s the Grégr brothers began publishing in 1861 the *Národní listy*, the most prestigious and influential of Czech newspapers. In the following year Miroslav Tyrš and Jindřich Fügner organized a gymnastic and cultural society that they named *Sokol*, or "Falcon." Like the German *Turnverein*, to which it bore striking resemblances, the Sokol idealized classical values of a "sound mind in a sound body" and sought to instill a proud nationalism into its members. Enduring international fame came to the composers Bedřich Smetana and Antonín Dvořák, who adapted folk melodies and extolled the Bohemian landscape in their symphonic compositions. The great symbol of the cultural renaissance became the construction of the imposing Czech National Theater in Prague with money raised largely from popular donations. In view of the competition with the Germans, whose culture had more readily survived the vicissitudes of history, the new cultural attainments were indispensable for bolstering the national self-image of Czechs.

The simultaneous demographic and economic development of the Czech nation also strengthened its competitive position with the Germans. At no time had the distinctive Czech character of some towns completely disappeared. Small marketing centers in Czech agrarian areas, in particular, had retained their Czech identity across the centuries. Nor was there ever a clear-cut dichotomy between German town-dwellers and Czech rural inhabitants. In a preindustrial society most people, whatever their nationality, earned their living on the land. Nevertheless, rapid urbanization and industrialization improved the relative position of the Czechs in the late nineteenth century. Between 1843 and 1910 the city of Prague with its suburbs quadrupled in size to over six hundred thousand, and Plzeň (Pilsen) grew from a town of under ten thousand to a city of over one hundred thousand.[13] Czechs repeatedly claimed that Austrian censuses exaggerated the number of Germans living in the cities and towns.[14] Whether or not Austrian census statistics were completely reliable, the migration of Czechs from the countryside to towns and the rapidly growing national consciousness of Czechs already living in those towns clearly altered the traditional national character of many urban centers. In the last half of the nineteenth century towns that had once appeared to be typical examples of German culture assumed a Czech identity. Prague was the most notable example.

In economic development the Czech peasantry enjoyed growing prosperity until the mid-1880s. A key factor was the rapidly expanding sugar-beet production of Bohemia and Moravia, which accounted for one-quarter of the entire European output by 1880. The money that was painstakingly accumulated in the villages helped to finance Czech participation in new industrial enterprises.[15] Whereas the traditional glass and textile industries were largely in the hands of German or German-Jewish entrepreneurs, Czech finance had a considerable interest in the new heavy industry. In Plzeň Emil Škoda, starting with a small machine shop, became the preeminent arms producer in the empire. Later, in Moravia, Tomáš Bat'a founded what was to become the largest shoe and leather company on the continent. The financing of Czech economic expansion was made possible by the founding of numerous banks and credit institutions, foremost of which was the *Živnostenská banka.* Investments were made for national as well as profit motives, and the structure of Czech financial and industrial power took on aspects of a closed economic system.

In the political life of the Austrian Empire the Czech national movement developed from a peripheral phenomenon into a key locus of power in the last half of the nineteenth century. The Austrian military defeats in northern Italy in 1859 signaled the end of the absolutist programs of Prince Felix von Schwarzenberg and Alexander Bach and inaugurated a period of constitutional experimentation. The October Diploma of 1860 briefly aroused hopes for greater local autonomy, which were quickly disappointed by the February Patent in 1861. The February constitution of 1861 did reestablish local provincial diets, but it provided that those diets were to elect representatives to an imperial parliament where real political power would lie. Moreover, the local diets themselves were to be elected by a curia system, representing particular socio-economic groups. In the lands of the Bohemian crown that electoral system was designed to favor the German over the Czech element.[16] But by far the greatest disappointment for Czech political leaders was the Compromise of 1867, which was concluded in the aftermath of the Austrian defeat in the Seven Weeks' War. In the compromise the Habsburg authorities acceded to Magyar demands and divided the empire into two separate halves, united in personal union under the crown and sharing only a common foreign and defense policy. The compromise represented a resounding victory for the Magyars, who henceforth ruled supreme in their half of the state. In Austria the constitutional laws of December 1867 represented an attempt to adapt the February constitution of 1861 to the new conditions. The 1867 constitution continued the system of an imperial parliament and local provincial diets in Cisleithania, formally espoused the principle of the equality of all nationalities, and declared the basic rights of man and citizen in good liberal tradition. But it also retained a highly centralized political structure and an electoral system that discriminated against the Czechs.[17] With their appetite for equal political rights and local autonomy whetted by the Magyar success, Czechs protested in mass demonstrations, and their leaders boycotted the Vienna Reichsrat until 1879.[18]

Until the late 1880s the political leadership of the Czech national movement remained in the hands of a party that came to be known as the Old Czechs. The now venerable Palacký, until his death in 1876, and his son-in-law, František L. Rieger, were the major leaders of the party. At the time of the Austro-Hungarian Compromise, the party was essentially an assemblage of local notables, representing mainly the interests of the landholding peasantry. The Old Czechs cooperated closely in the Bohemian Diet with the aristocratic Conservative party led by Count Jindřich Jaroslav Clam-Martinic. Their mutual opposition to political centralization in Vienna and the common economic interests of aristocratic landowners and small peasant holders imparted an enduring stability to the coalition of Conservatives and Old Czechs.[19] In response to the Compromise of 1867 the Old Czechs, supported by the Conservatives, enunciated the theory of Bohemian state rights (*státní právo, Staatsrecht*). Essentially they demanded the same concessions for themselves that had been accorded the Magyars in 1867. They claimed that the lands of the Bohemian crown enjoyed historic privileges similar to those of the crown of St. Stephen. The historical basis for the theory of Bohemian state rights was tenuous at best, and it met particularist opposition even in Moravia and Silesia.[20] Until the First World War, however, it remained the primary legal and historical basis of Czech claims for local political autonomy. And the autonomy of the Bohemian crown lands was the ultimate political goal of nationally minded Czechs.

Until 1879 the German Liberals ruled supreme in Vienna. After 1867, except for a few brief months in 1871, the Czechs could have little hope of realizing their constitutional goals in the face of a dominant German element in the Austrian half of the monarchy. Their leaders began more openly to look abroad for support against German and Magyar influence in Central Europe. Palacký and his associates demonstratively participated in the Slav Congress in Moscow in 1867. Before the Franco-Prussian War, Rieger tried to interest Napoleon III in the Czech question, even as negotiations were underway for an alliance between France and Austria-Hungary.[21] During the war itself Czechs openly sympathized with the French while Germans celebrated with the news of the Prussian victories. This impulse to seek support from France and Russia makes it possible to trace the roots of Czechoslovakia's alliance policy in the 1920s and 1930s at least as far back as the 1860s. In the 1870s the evolution of Austrian foreign policy posed a further challenge to Czech national interests. After the founding of the German Empire, the Austrian government abandoned the hope of reversing the decision of 1866 and began to make its peace with Bismarck's Germany. Ultimately the result was the conclusion in 1879 of the Dual Alliance. Formally a mutual defense pact against Russia, it was actually the diplomatic basis for German dominance in Central Europe. For the Czechs the whole rationale of Austro-Slavism was that they would support the multinational empire in order to have protection against German influence. For them, therefore, the Austrian constitutional and diplomatic decisions between 1867 and 1879 inevitably weakened the very raison d'être of the Habsburg Empire.

In the 1870s the Old Czech boycott of the political process was barren of results. Under increasing pressure from a younger generation the Old Czechs responded positively in 1879 to the invitation of Count Eduard Taaffe to return to the Reichsrat and to join his new government, which excluded the German Liberals. That decision left the Old Czechs in a difficult theoretical position, however, for they were actively cooperating in a political system whose constitutionality they did not formally recognize. The very same dilemma was to confront the Sudeten Germans in the 1920s. Whatever their difficulties in theory, practical advantages did come to the Czechs as a result of their cooperation with Taaffe's coalition of German clericals, aristocrats, Poles, and Czechs. The policy of trading concessions among the various groups resulted in the designation of the Czech language as one of the "outer" languages of the bureaucracy. This reform meant that an average Czech could more easily use his own language in dealing with officials, and it tended to increase the number of Czechs in bureaucratic positions. In 1882 the Czechs also succeeded in dividing Prague's Charles University into separate Czech and German institutions, with the Czech university soon becoming preeminent. Revisions in the electoral laws introduced lower tax qualifications and enfranchised more Czech voters.[22] But among a younger and more radical generation of Czechs there had been a growing dissatisfaction since the 1860s with the conservatism of the Old Czechs. The discontent of the younger element with the policy of trading concessions and making compromises increased in the 1880s. By the late 1880s another political movement—the young Czech party—began rapidly to displace the Old Czechs.

The differences between Old Czechs and Young Czechs were largely of temperament. Although the Young Czechs were more inclined toward political democracy, both groups held to the doctrine of Bohemian state rights and aimed at the acquisition of political autonomy within the Habsburg Empire. Both considered themselves representatives of the entire national movement, comprising Czechs of widely varying socioeconomic circumstances. For Young Czechs, as for Old Czechs, the issue of nationality was the important element in their identity. But the rhetoric of the Young Czechs was more inflammatory and their patience more easily exhausted. In their attacks on the Habsburg Empire they ran the risk of completely abandoning the Austro-Slavism of Palacký, and they drew warnings from the Old Czech camp that the only alternatives to a multinational Danubian empire were either German or Russian domination. The small nationalities themselves were incapable of preserving their own independence.[23] In response to such criticism Josef Kaizl, a former Old Czech who was to become a leader of the Young Czechs in the 1890s, attempted to develop a rationale for the existence of competing political groups in what was ideally a united national movement. In 1889 Kaizl argued that the task of the Old Czechs was to work for gradual improvement through the political process, while the function of the Young Czechs was to keep the opportunist policy in bounds and "to spur it on to a quicker, more energetic tempo."[24] In the 1920s some Sudeten German political leaders were to attempt the same justification for their own radical and moderate parties. After a long period of prosperity, an agricultural crisis hit Bohemia in the mid-1880s in the form of rapidly falling grain prices and a drop in sugar-beet cultivation. The Young Czechs exploited agrarian discontent and scored resounding victories in the provincial elections of 1889 and in the Reichsrat elections of 1891.[25] Although Taaffe retained the Old Czechs in his coalition, his own government fell in 1893, and the Old Czechs lost whatever remained of their political significance.

In victory the Young Czechs eventually adopted the opportunistic policies of the older generation. After remaining in parliamentary opposition and employing obstructionist tactics in the early 1890s, the emerging leaders of the party, Josef Kaizl and Karel Kramář, maneuvered the party into support of the government of Count Casimir Badeni between 1895 and 1897. But the party had a radical element that demanded fundamental constitutional reform, in the sense of Bohemian state rights, before agreeing to support any Austrian government. As a result of the party's accommodationist policies with Badeni, some of the radicals left to found new splinter parties. Badeni needed Young Czech votes in order to renew the Ausgleich legislation of 1867, and he was willing to buy their support. At the urging of the Young Czechs, Badeni issued new language ordinances for Bohemia and Moravia in April 1897, making Czech an "inner" language within the administrative bureaucracy. This meant that Czech was put on an equal plane with German within the administration of Bohemia and Moravia, and the law required all civil servants within the provinces to possess a command of both languages by July 1, 1901. The effect of these ordinances, had they remained in force, would have been to alter radically the national composition of the bureaucracy, which traditionally had been overwhelmingly German. Few Germans bothered to learn Czech, whereas almost all Czechs had some knowledge of German. The storm of protest that erupted among the Germans in the provinces eventually forced Badeni's resignation and the rescinding of the language ordinances. The confrontations of 1897 launched a period of nationalist agitation during which all other issues took secondary rank, and the deep divisions within the Reichsrat forced later prime ministers to appoint bureaucratic cabinets of "experts" and rule by emergency decree.[26]

But even when nationalism appeared to triumph, other signs began to strengthen hopes for the ultimate viability of the multinational state. Socioeconomic modernization had made national political parties such as the Young Czechs obsolete by the beginning of the twentieth century. The Young Czechs had reached the height of their power in the 1890s, and their continuing, though declining, influence thereafter was largely the product of national inertia. Parties representing various class interests made their appearance in Czech politics in the 1890s, and their influence continued to grow with the approach of universal manhood suffrage. For national reasons the Young Czechs continued to champion a broader franchise even as it threatened to undermine their own political position. A cautious reform of the electoral system took place in 1896 with the introduction of a fifth curia to be elected by universal manhood suffrage, in addition to the four existing ones, representing socioeconomic groups. That compromise failed to satisfy anyone, however, and debates in the following decade resulted in the abolition of the curial system itself. The revolution in Austrian electoral history came in 1907 with the intro-duction of universal manhood suffrage for Reichsrat elections in the Austrian half of the monarchy. The new franchise, by removing some of the devices that had afforded disproportionate political influence in Vienna to the Germans, represented a victory for the non-German nationalities.[27] On the other hand it encouraged the political expression of diverse socioeconomic interests and confirmed the social fragmentation of the national movement.

Of the various new political movements, the Czech Agrarian party did the most serious damage to the Young Czechs. The Young Czechs had supplanted the Old Czech party as a result of defections of landowning peasants into their ranks, and various agrarian associations remained political allies of the Young Czechs in the mid-1890s. But the founding of the Agrarian party in 1899 offered small landowners an alternative to the Young Czechs, who came to be regarded as advocates of urban industrial interests. In the 1907 and 1911 elections the Agrarians emerged as the strongest single Czech party in the Reichsrat, and in their chairman, Antonín Švehla, they boasted one of the most effective Czech political leaders.[28] While Agrarians were establishing themselves as the dominant political force in the countryside, the enfranchisement of industrial workers nourished the growth of the Social Democrats. Formally founded in 1889 as a supranational movement, the Austrian Social Democratic Workers' party adopted in 1899 a program advocating a federal empire and local "national-cultural autonomy."[29] But national antagonisms undermined class unity in the same way as class conflicts created fissures in the Czech national movement. In 1911 the Czech wing of the party declared its independence and established itself as a separate political party. In addition to the Czech Agrarians and Czech Social Democrats, other parties also made their appearance in the last two decades before the First World War. In 1898 the Czech National Socialist party appeared as a populist movement among the lower middle class, who disliked the internationalism of social democracy. Along other ideological lines, Catholics organized a Citizen's Conservative party. After bolting from the Young Czechs, Tomáš G. Masaryk used his moral and intellectual prestige to found a small but influential party that called itself the Realist, or People's, party. The Czech population was therefore represented in the Reichsrat by a multiplicity of parties representing a wide range of socioeconomic interests or ideological commitments.

The significance of the political fragmentation of the Czech national movement is open to debate. The appearance of parties representing various interests and ideologies was a logical concomitant of socioeconomic modernization. The same process was occurring among the Germans. Yet the parties also retained the designation of their nationality, and it would be difficult to demonstrate that national rivalries were actually diminishing by 1914. The most that can be said with assurance is that ideological and socioeconomic interests were more formally represented in the political process than had previously been the case. Given the challenge that the nationality conflicts posed to the Habsburg Empire, the crucial question by 1914 was whether other interests could or would dilute the strengths of the national confrontations. With the outbreak of the First World War and the resulting demise of the empire, the question remained unanswered. But it is sufficiently suggestive that historians should not simply dismiss the multinational empire as inevitably doomed by its national rivalries. The same set of problems rose again with the founding of the Czechoslovak republic. The interaction of the conflicting claims of national loyalties, socioeconomic interests, and ideological commitments determined the internal viability of the new republic.

The republic itself was not foreseen in the prewar years. Except for a handful of radicals, Czech political leaders from the various parties continued to press for local political and cultural autonomy in the lands of the Bohemian crown. They did not advocate the dissolution of the Habsburg Empire. It is therefore necessary to look to the war years themselves in order to discover both a reversal of the trend toward political fragmentation among the Czechs and a radicalization of their national program. The significance of the war itself for the founding of the Czechoslovak republic can hardly be exaggerated.

The Slovaks

Before turning to the war, however, it is necessary also to discuss the national movements among the Slovaks and the Germans in the nineteenth century. The Slovak national revival demands relatively little space in this account. The major British authority on the Slovak question estimated that in 1918 there was a maximum of one thousand educated and nationally conscious Slovaks among a population of more than two million.[30] He was never seriously contradicted. The meager number of potential Slovak leaders after 1918 reflected the success of magyarization policies over the preceding century. Slovak members of the gentry had long since assumed Magyar loyalties. Magyarization policies had encountered only weak resistance among the Slovak population both in the countryside and in the towns, where the national revival had never proceeded beyond its nascent stage. In comparison with the lands of the Bohemian crown, Slovakia was placid in the last decades before the First World War. By the time of the war itself there was probably more national consciousness among Slovak emigrants to the United States than there was in Slovakia itself.

A basic division within the Slovak national movement compounded its weakness. Most Slovak leaders, like their Czech counterparts, thought in terms of Slavic unity and the necessity of mutual support among the Slavic peoples in the struggle for the preservation of their national existence. The Czechs were the most readily available champions of the Slovaks. Across the centuries the two nationalities had exerted a mutual cultural influence over one another, and along the Moravian-Slovak frontier nationality distinctions had become quite blurred. Yet the philological work of the first half of the nineteenth century kindled a controversy as to whether Slovaks ought to adopt Czech as their literary language or to develop a separate language of their own. Predictably, the latter alternative prevailed. When Slovak political activity began to revive at the turn of the twentieth century, differences were again discernible between those Slovaks who thought in terms of close cooperation with the Czech movement and those who concentrated on a distinctly Slovak political program. Given the weakness of the Slovak revival, the two tendencies were never mutually exclusive. The few Slovaks who were conscious of their national identity were interdependent, and they could not afford the luxury of excommunicating one another. Both traditions—the Czechoslovak orientation and the philosophy of Slovak distinctiveness—coexisted for a century and survived the First World War. As conflicting interpretations of the meaning of Slovak nationality, they were to play a vital role in the first Czechoslovak republic.

In the nineteenth century Lutheran pastors were predominant in the leadership of the Slovak revival. Their numbers were particularly striking inasmuch as Protestants constituted less than a fifth of the Slovak population. The Slovak Lutherans were an alien element in Catholic Austria, and they were closely associated with Czech culture. Until the reign of Joseph II they had been subjected to a vigorous campaign of proselytism and discrimination. From the time of the Reformation they had read the Czech *kralická* translation of the Bible and had used the Czech language in their liturgy. Young Slovak Protestants more typically went abroad to study than did their Catholic counterparts, and the experience of foreign study tended to heighten their national consciousness. Upon returning home they were less easily absorbed into a Magyar intellectual and cultural milieu.[31]

Perhaps the greatest nineteenth-century poet in the Czech language was Ján Kollár, for thirty years the pastor of the Slovak Lutheran church in Budapest. His monumental epic, *Slavy Dcera,* gained immense popularity when it first began to appear in 1824. As the model for his "daughter of the Slavs," Kollár chose his German wife, whom he had met while studying in Jena and imbibing Herderian influence. The poet meets her on the banks of the Saale, loses her, and wanders through Central Europe in search of her. The places the poet encounters remind him of the real or imagined glories of the Slavic past, and the poem becomes an appeal for the unity and liberty of all Slavs. *Slavy Dcera* reflected Kollár's theories about the nature of nationalism and the interrelatedness of the Slavic tongues. Drawing a sharp distinction between the concepts of a state and a nation, Kollár defined a nation in linguistic and cultural terms and insisted on the essential unity of all Slavic tongues and peoples.[32] A kindred spirit was Pavel Jozef Šafařík. Šafařík's Lutheran background and Jena education closely resembled Kollár's. A close friend of Palacký, Šafařík settled in Prague in 1832 and published archaeological studies that greatly stimulated interest in the early history and culture of the Slavic peoples.[33] Kollár and Šafařík became the leading Slovak spokesmen for Czechoslovak mutuality in the first half of the nineteenth century.

However impassioned were the calls for Czech-Slovak community, the emphasis on the distinctiveness of Slovak nationality and language won wider acceptance in Slovakia. Already in the 1780s the stirrings of national sentiment appeared particularly among Slovak Catholic theological students at the Bratislava General Seminary. The Josephinian reforms, which aimed at the cultivation of a useful priesthood employing local languages, doubtlessly encouraged the young theological students to develop the

Slovak dialects into a literary language. In fact by the 1780s there already existed a debate as to whether Slovak was a language distinct from Czech. Antonín Bernolák and his fellow seminarians responded that it was. In 1787 Bernolák published his *Dissertatio philologico critica de litteris Slavorum*, followed in 1790 by his *Grammatica slavica*, which attempted to codify the language on the basis of a Western Slovak dialect.[34] During the next half-century, Bernolák's language won widespread acceptance among the Catholic clergy while Protestants continued to use liturgical Czech.

It was for the purpose of healing the religious split and unifying the national movement that Ludovít Štúr developed in the 1840s a new literary language that became the foundation of modern Slovak. The challenge of Hungarian nationalism propelled the development of a Slovak consciousness in the first half of the nineteenth century. From the 1790s the Hungarian diets passed successive laws replacing Latin with Magyar as the language of public life in Hungary. By the 1840s the liberal and tolerant spirit of Count Stephen Széchenyi lost ground to chauvinist attitudes whose chief spokesman was Louis Kossuth. A law of 1840 attempted to establish the dominance of the Magyar language in the churches and provoked a formal protest by a Slovak delegation that traveled to Vienna for audiences with Metternich and his chief rival, Count Kolowrat. That was one of the first occasions of open political activity by a Slovak national group.[35] In 1844 Ludovít Štúr lost his teaching position in the Protestant lyceum in Bratislava because of his resistance to magyarization programs. He then began to publish a newspaper, *Slovenskje narodnje noviny*, in a language whose grammar he formally codified in 1846. Štúr's prime objective in introducing a new version of literary Slovak was to heal the language division between Protestant and Catholic Slovaks and thus enable them to stand united against magyarization efforts. In that goal he received hearty support from two Slovak Lutheran pastors, Jozef M. Hurban and Michal M. Hodža. Leaders of Catholic Slovaks welcomed his efforts as well, and Štúr's codification eventually won common acceptance.[36] Inasmuch as it was based on the dialect of Central Slovakia, it was actually further removed from Czech than Bernolák's version had been, but Štúr and his friends calculated that their newly codified language could be more easily understood throughout Slovakia.

The effort to establish a distinctive Slovak literary language unleashed a storm of bitter protests from the leaders of the Czech national revival in Prague. Those Slovaks of Czechoslovak orientation such as Kollár joined in the condemnation of Štúr and his circle. Štúr's critics were more concerned about a rupture between Czechs and Slovaks than they were about divisions among Slovaks themselves. They feared that a permanent split could only weaken the national efforts of both groups, and from a Czechoslovak point of view their concern was legitimate. Czechs tradition- ally had a difficult time discerning in the Slovaks anything more than a variation on Czech nationality. Men like Palacký, Rieger, and Havlíček displayed an insensitivity toward Slovak desires for a distinctive national identity akin to the attitudes that many Germans had adopted toward Czech ambitions. Amidst personal recriminations, Havlíček labeled the new Slovak literature "Tatar," and Štúr retorted in kind by refering to Czechs as "Germanized ghosts."[37]

The controversy continued until the revolutionary year of 1848, when Štúr and Havlíček briefly laid aside their differences in favor of political cooperation. Štúr came to Prague, published articles in Havlíček's newspaper, and acted as one of the guiding spirits behind the Slav congress. Štúr and his Slovak colleagues enjoyed a warm reception in Prague, particularly from the Czech radicals. Yet even in 1848 and 1849 neither the Czechs nor the Slovaks, either in their petitions to the crown or in their formal programs, actually advocated the political union of the two nationalities. When Palacký eventually suggested the idea, Štúr and his colleagues reacted negatively in the fear that such a union would establish Czech hegemony over the Slovaks. As conflicts between Slovaks and Magyars intensified in 1848 and 1849, the Slovak leadership finally demanded a complete separation of Slovakia from Hungary. But they requested that Slovakia become a crownland administered directly from Vienna, and they said nothing about a union with the Czech lands.[38] With the failure of the revolutions, the language recriminations returned once again; the mutual interests of Czechs and Slovaks gradually waned, and the two nationalities followed diverse paths of development during the next half-century.

Before 1867 Slovaks could look to the Habsburg crown for a measure of protection against magyarization efforts in Hungary. They won a few rewards for their loyalty during the struggles between the Habsburgs and Magyar nationalists in the early 1860s. Most notable was the establishment of three Slovak high schools and, particularly, the founding of the *Matica slovenská* as an organization for the patronization of Slovak cultural undertakings.[39] But the compromise of 1867 left Slovakia completely under the domination of the Magyars, who proceeded to stifle the development of Slovak national consciousness by all imaginable means. Little or no help could be expected from Vienna. By the mid-1870s the high schools and the *Matica slovenská* were disbanded. Thereafter, the Slovaks possessed no high schools, no technical institutes, and no teacher-training academies. Of the more than four thousand elementary schools in Slovakia, fewer than 10 percent conducted instruction in Slovak by 1913, and even their Slovak character was nominal.[40] Part of the magyarization program was the encouragement of permanent Slovak emigration abroad in the hope that Slovak emigrants would melt into the "Anglo-Saxon race" in the United States.[41] Insofar as transportation and industry in Slovakia were improved, the purpose was to unify and strengthen Hungary vis-à-vis its Austrian partner in the Habsburg monarchy. The Hungarian government artificially stimulated industrialization in Slovakia through a policy of protective tariffs and state subventions in order to be in a stronger position in the decennial trade negotiations with Austria.[42] Nevertheless, most Slovaks remained impoverished peasants, many of whom streamed into the Hungarian plain in harvest season and then retired northward into their valleys in the winter. Even topography divided the Slovaks and helped to unify them with the inhabitants of the Hungarian plain. From the Carpathian mountains along the northern border of Slovakia, ridges extended southward and obstructed east-west communications across Slovakia. The Hungarian rail network consisted of spokes radiating from the central hub at Budapest, and, in the case of Slovakia, following the river valleys northward into the Carpathians. Except for one east-west railway line, communications across Slovakia were left undeveloped.

Despite the magyarization policies, or perhaps stimulated by them, stirrings of renewed Slovak political activity appeared at the turn of the century. But again the Slovak national movement was characterized both by its weakness and its potential internal divisions. In the late 1890s young Slovak students, who were influenced by Masaryk's lectures at Charles University, founded the *Československá Jednota* for the purpose of working for the national unification of Czechs and Slovaks. Two of their number, Vavro Šrobár and Pavel Blaho, established in 1898 the periodical *Hlas* to voice their views. From their circle eventually came the earliest and most dedicated Slovak advocates of Czechoslovak unity during the first republic. At the same time that the "Hlasists" were making their appearance, a group of Catholic priests began more actively to assert Slovak rights. Under the leadership of Father Andrej Hlinka, they first cooperated with the Hungarian Catholic People's party but then in 1901 founded their own Slovak National Party. Basic differences in values and commitments distinguished the clericals from the "Hlasists," and the latent antagonisms later blossomed into a bitter rivalry during the first republic. Before the war, however, the very weakness of the Slovak movement militated against fragmentation. Hlinka actively worked for Šrobár in the parliamentary election of 1906 and received a prison sentence from the Hungarian government as a reward.[43] The persecution of Hlinka made him the most popular prewar leader among the Slovaks.

The most effective prewar Slovak politician was Dr. Milan Hodža. A member of the Budapest parliament, Hodža became a close advisor to

Francis Ferdinand, the heir to the throne. Francis Ferdinand's antipathy for the Magyars was well known. Between 1902 and 1906 the relationship between the Habsburg crown and the Magyars was particularly strained because of the demands of the Hungarian Independence party for a Hungarian national army using Magyar as the language of command. According to his memoirs, which should be used with caution, Hodža and other minority politicians proposed the introduction of universal suffrage in Hungary as the best means of destroying Magyar dominance and creating a conservative peasant democracy. Along with universal suffrage he advocated land reform in order to afford the peasantry an economic livelihood and, it was hoped, to instill a desire for property in the urban working classes. Ultimately he hoped for the "federative rebuilding of the Habsburg Empire," which would allow for closer Czech-Slovak political cooperation.[44]

Briefly in 1905 and 1906 it appeared that the conflict between the crown and the Magyars might afford the minorities greater freedom for their own national development. Even as the Austrian half of the empire was moving toward universal suffrage, the crown used the threat of a broader franchise to force the Magyars into concessions in the army dispute. It is interesting to note that universal suffrage in Austria was aimed at diluting the nationality conflicts by affording greater voice for conflicting class interests, whereas in the less modernized society of Hungary universal suffrage could promote nationality conflicts and mitigate Magyar extremism. After 1906, with the apparent approach of at least a wider suffrage system and more nearly honest elections in Hungary, Magyar officials intensified their magyarization policies in an effort to complete their work of the previous half-century. The success of the magyarization programs, particularly among urban, educated Slovaks, led many observers to believe that the Slovaks were on the verge of national extinction. The Slovak national movement remained a weak and peripheral phenomenon, lined with fissures that had the potential of widening into chasms.

The Germans

Although Germans were scattered throughout the Czech and Slovak lands, the principal concentrations of Germans were in western and northern Bohemia, northern Moravia, and Silesia. Their ancestors had lived in those areas for several hundred years. By the late nineteenth century debates raged between German and Czech publicists concerning historical claims to the territory. On the one extreme, Germans considered themselves the autochthonous element in the country. German tribes had lived there for several centuries before the Slavs had arrived in the early Middle Ages, and the Germans of the twentieth century therefore enjoyed an older and more valid claim to the territory. On the other extreme, Czechs emphasized that the early Germanic tribes had been displaced by the Slavs and that the current German residents were descendants of settlers who had appeared no earlier than the twelfth or thirteenth centuries. Many Germans had arrived much later than that. The current inhabitants of Bohemia, Moravia, and Silesia were therefore to be regarded merely as guests who might be tolerated as long as they caused no trouble.[45] The persuasiveness of such historical arguments was minimal, inasmuch as both nationalities had inhabited the territory for generations. But the illusory nature of these historical claims reflected the extent to which national rivalries had dulled reason and exacerbated emotions.

The Germans of Bohemia, Moravia, and Silesia did not experience a national revival to the extent that the Czechs and eventually the Slovaks did. The Germans enjoyed the immense advantage of being part of a much larger cultural community that could boast distinguished accomplishments in every field of artistic endeavor. They had no need to recodify a literary language or to make special exertions to develop a distinctly German form of literature, art, or music. Despite strong French and Italian influences in Central Europe, there was no question that the lands of the Bohemian crown lay within a German cultural sphere. That had been true since the Middle Ages. The Czechs had confronted difficult obstacles in developing and maintaining a distinctive cultural identity even in the days of Charles IV and the Hussites, and their efforts had practically collapsed in the Counter-Reformation. After the battle of the White Mountain in 1620, the new Bohemian nobility—of international origin and loyal to the Habsburgs—did become germanized. To be sure, the Czech language still had not disappeared from the debates of the Bohemian diet by the late eighteenth century, and the cultural values of the aristocracy were cosmopolitan rather than narrowly nationalistic. But the foreign influences that the new nobility introduced to Bohemia came with a German accent. Ironically enough, the Czech national revival continued the tradition and contributed to the survival of German cultural dominance in the nineteenth century. It was largely through the medium of German that foreign influences were introduced into Czech culture. For that reason the compilation of a Czech-German dictionary was an indispensable assignment in the early stages of the national revival. With the spread of cultural awareness and the growth of national feeling by the early twentieth century, many Germans of Bohemia, Moravia, and Silesia took special pride in the accomplishments of their own local artists and intellectuals. But the great strength of German-Bohemians vis-à-vis Czechs was that seventy million other Germans in Central Europe were setting the cultural tone of the entire area.

From a political and social standpoint, also, there was no doubt that the Germans were the dominant nationality in the empire. Their position resulted in part from centuries of political association between the Habsburg lands and the German states of Central Europe in the Holy Roman Empire of the German Nation. More concretely, the dominance of Germans as a group can be traced directly to the reforms of Maria Theresa and Joseph II. Even as the innovating monarchs helped to stimulate the Czech national revival, their reforms also established the foundations for German preeminence until the end of the empire. The designation of German as the basic language of administration and the requirement that instruction in the schools be in German afforded Germans an immense advantage over other nationalities in the empire. In the nineteenth century most politically minded Germans continued to support the Josephinian precedent of a highly centralized administrative system. Many also hoped for German national unity, and the Austrian German Liberals emerged in 1848 as spokesmen for the *grossdeutsch* idea of including the Germans of Austria in a single German nation-state. The German Liberals were the chief architects of Austrian policy in the 1860s and 1870s, and liberalism remained the dominant political current among Austrian Germans until the 1880s. It has been seen that their centralizing impulses collided with the interests of the old feudal nobility and the minority nationalities, who sought refuge in particularistic and federalistic policies. But the German Liberals never thought of themselves as rabid nationalists, and indeed they did not need to be in view of their power position in the empire.

Militant German nationalism was a phenomenon of the late nineteenth century, and it attained its most radical form in the lands of the Bohemian crown. In large part it was a reaction to the increasingly serious challenges of the Czechs during the last decades of the century. The boom in coal-mining and industrialization in the German border areas attracted young Czechs from the interior of the provinces. Czechs had relatively more to gain from socioeconomic modernization than Germans, whose occupations already reflected a more diversified economy in their areas of settlement. Czechs were therefore more geographically mobile than the Germans. It is estimated that between 1880 and 1900 half a million Czechs migrated to areas that had previously been 80 percent German.[46] Although some of them went to Vienna and Lower Austria, the majority settled in the German areas of Bohemia, Moravia, and Silesia. German townspeople in general grew increasingly restive at Czech infiltration into their villages and towns. The frictions of urban life found expression in cultural rivalries. Parents strove to maintain the national identity of their children. Certainly there was no such thing as a purely German or Czech national culture, but the very intermixture of nationalities contributed to cultural rivalries. It became a popular sport to list Czech leaders who bore

German names and Germans with Czech names. The founders of the Czech
Sokol movement itself were of German origin.[47] In debates over census
techniques Czechs insisted that the maternal language, not the paternal, be
used to determine nationality. They were conscious that Czech fathers
were more likely to come under German influence at their work than the
mothers were at home. In the attempt to establish and maintain a national
identity the schools became a primary battleground between Germans and
Czechs. The language of instruction, the content of the curriculum, the
composition of the teaching staff were issues of bitter controversy. In the
last two decades of the century, both nationalities founded numerous
self-help cooperatives, many of which were dedicated to educational and
cultural activities. Among the Germans the most significant organization
was the *Deutscher Schulverein,* which within a year of its founding in
1880 boasted 120,000 members.[48]

The German Liberal party became a spawning ground for other parties
that tried in various ways to represent the ideas and interests of lower
classes of the population. The Liberals maintained their support among
professional and upper middle-class elements, but with the trend toward
universal suffrage Liberal electoral strength declined proportionately. It
has often been noted that Karl Lueger, Victor Adler, and Georg von
Schönerer all emerged from the left wing of the Liberal party to found
political movements of their own, each attempting to deal with socioeconomic problems more directly and effectively than Liberal ideology
allowed. Lueger and his Christian Socials gained control of Vienna. Adler's
Social Democrats eventually became the largest party in Austria. But the
German-nationalist organizations of Schönerer found their main strength
in the German areas of Bohemia. Those Germans whose economic position
was most directly threatened by the Czech migrations were the same
Germans who were least attracted by principles of laissez-faire liberalism.
Among miners, industrial workers, and artisans the challenge of Czech
competition for jobs provoked defensive responses that often found
expression in a nationalist vocabulary. German nationalist trade unions
charged that employers were using Czech migrants as strikebreakers and
sources of cheap labor. The unions tended to characterize Germans as a
reservoir of skilled labor and Czechs as raw, unskilled workers.[49] It has
already been seen that national rivalries ultimately destroyed the attempts
of the Austrian Social Democratic party to build a supranational
working-class movement. The majority of German and Czech workers
remained loyal to their respective socialist parties, but some were
fundamentally dissatisfied with the international emphasis of Marxian
socialism. Just as the Czech National Socialist party made its appearance in
1898, so also did former disciples of Schönerer organize a German
National Socialist Workers' party in 1904. Other group and confessional

interests such as the agrarians and the Catholics founded their own political movements. By 1914 the Germans possessed a full spectrum of political parties, just as the Czechs did.

The political conflicts between Germans and Czechs fundamentally influenced the attitude of both nationalities toward the Habsburg monarchy. It has been seen that Czech political leaders demanded autonomy for the lands of the Bohemian crown because in Austria as a whole Germans outnumbered Czechs. For the same reason German Bohemians, Moravians, and Silesians opposed local political autonomy because they in turn would be outnumbered by the Czechs. German leaders began to insist upon a division of Bohemia into separate German and Czech parts. That plan was adamantly resisted by Czechs, however, who insisted upon the indivisibility of all the Bohemian crown lands in the knowledge that, if the German areas were detached, little of much worth would remain. Although various compromise proposals to the constitutional impasse were offered, no solution ever won popular support among both nationality groups. Increasingly, the crown was forced into the position of acting as an arbiter between the nationalities, and in that role it lost prestige and support among both groups.

The sharpest confrontations between the two nationalities broke out in 1897 with Count Casimir Badeni's abortive attempt to make language reforms in the bureaucracy of Bohemia and Moravia. The Badeni ordinances tried to establish Czech as an internal language of the bureaucracy, thereby forcing German officials to learn and correspond in Czech as well as German. Although the ordinances threatened to give Czechs a competitive advantage over Germans in the struggle for jobs, that was not their basic significance. Czechs were already being attracted to the bureaucracy in greater numbers than the Germans.[50] In fact, by 1915 only about 10 percent of the provincial civil service positions in Bohemia were held by Germans.[51] The real significance of the Badeni ordinances was that they were viewed by both sides as an implicit recognition of the Czech program for provincial autonomy and therefore as a denial of the German demand that the provinces be separated into distinct administrative areas.[52] With fears of falling under Czech dominance rife among the Germans, Schönerer and his followers took the lead in organizing mass demonstrations that threatened to dissolve into political and social chaos. The ordinances were withdrawn, and Badeni resigned. Various historians have pointed to the events of 1897 as the launching point for an era of nationalist confrontations in Austria. The historian who has done the most exhaustive study of the Badeni reforms argues that they marked the point where the local national conflict in Bohemia spread throughout the Austrain half of the empire.[53] Certainly it is true that nationalist propaganda intensified and that many Austrian Germans began to look to

Berlin more than to Vienna for aid against the Slavic menace. Yet Austria-Hungary's position as the only reliable diplomatic ally of Germany meant that officials in Berlin could hardly favor attitudes that would weaken the domestic authority of the Habsburgs. Because of both domestic and foreign political factors, therefore, the Germans of Austria had no place else to go. The majority of them were more intent on maintaining their inherited privileges in Austria than in agitating for more radical solutions.

In a discussion of national revivals and rivalries the Jews of Bohemia deserve special attention. With the intensification of the nationality conflicts by the 1890s, Jews found themselves in a dilemma. Austrian census standards did not allow for a Jewish nationality, and Jews came under pressure to declare themselves either Germans or Czechs. Inasmuch as assimilationist thinking dominated in Jewish circles, that was not in itself a hardship. But the question of which nationality to choose did create problems. In the 1900 census, 11,346 Prague Jews declared themselves German whereas 14,145 opted for Czech nationality. The Jews who designated Czech as their nationality came largely from lower economic strata whereas the wealthier professional classes considered themselves German. Indeed, the German Jews made up almost 40 percent of the entire German population of Prague and its suburbs by 1900.[54] Jewish prominence in the professions and in publishing German-language newspapers in Prague encouraged the identification of Jews and Germans in the minds of many Czechs. That development was ironic in view of the rising anti-Semitism in German nationalist groups. But Jews, particularly of educated circles, contributed to the Czech attitudes. Until the war the vast majority of Jewish university students continued to enroll in the German university rather than in the much larger Czech university in Prague. When anti-Semitic attitudes excluded Jewish students from German student fraternities, they formed fraternities of their own and paraded their colors through the streets of Prague in much the same fashion as their anti-Semitic German colleagues.[55] Thus, whereas the majority of Prague Jews were declaring Czech nationality, the activities of socially prominent and visible Jews promoted the identification in Czech minds of Jewishness and Germanness. The consequences were potentially dangerous.

CZECHS AND SLOVAKS DURING THE FIRST WORLD WAR

The outbreak of war in 1914 caught Czech politicians and the Czech population as a whole by surprise. Among political leaders there was no general agreement concerning attitudes toward the war itself or the political goals that the Czechs as a nationality ought to adopt in the war. The rivalries in the Czech political parties contributed to that situation, and some parties were visibly relieved that they could avoid taking an open stand on the war inasmuch as the Austrian Reichsrat was not in session. Among the Czech population as a whole there was no equivalent of the "August Days" mentality of national rejoicing and release that swept over some European populations. A quiet and subdued response to the war reflected both popular ambivalence toward Austria and distaste for fighting other Slavic peoples such as Russians and Serbs. Although there was widespread discontent from the early stages of the war, Czech resistance openly assumed a political dimension largely in the latter stages. The year 1917 marked a turning point, and in the course of 1918 Czech spokesmen spoke more openly about complete independence from Austria. In the early stages of the war the independence movement rested largely on the work of the Czech exiles abroad. The diplomatic recognition of Czechoslovak independence by the Western powers in 1918 was almost exclusively their accomplishment. The exiles and the political leaders who remained at home attempted to maintain contacts and coordinate their activities, but the physical difficulties of keeping lines of communication open in wartime and the diversity of opinions they represented meant that the two movements proceeded essentially independently of one another. Both the foreign and the domestic movements played essential roles in determining the character of the Czechoslovak republic as it emerged in October 1918.

Trains carrying Czech recruits to the war in 1914 were chalked with antiwar slogans. Ironic songs and jokes drifted from the cars. Already in the early stages of the war Czech troops sang *Hej Slované* at midnight, and the Russians held their fire while the Czechs crossed no-man's-land.[56] Mass desertions followed in 1915. The military command resorted to breaking up the Czech regiments, interspersing German and Hungarian troops among them. At home the assiduous Austrian bureaucracy reported all kinds of antiwar and anti-Austrian remarks, and political repression grew much more severe.[57] Czechs refused to support the Austrian war loans to the extent that the Germans of the empire did.[58] A handful of prominent Czech leaders formed a secret conspiratorial group that they dubbed the "Maffie" and that aimed at detaching Bohemia from Austria. In May 1915 the Austrian police arrested the major leaders of the group, the most famous of whom was Karel Kramář. As leader of the Young Czechs since the 1890s, Kramář had acquired a reputation as the foremost Czech advocate of Neo-Slavism, and during the First World War he still hoped to see a Russian prince wearing the crown of St. Wenceslas. Kramář's popularity had declined, however, and only his arrest and death sentence by the Austrian authorities restored him to his former appeal among the Czech population. The activities of Czech soldiers, civilians, and political leaders demonstrated antiwar and anti-Austrian attitudes from the early stages of the war.

Yet it is easy to exaggerate the extent of Czech resistance. The majority of Czech soldiers fought loyally in the Austrian army throughout the war. Until the closing stages of the war most of the complaints of the civilian population focused on economic concerns and were not translated into antistate activity.[59] And the leaders of the various Czech political parties continued to issue declarations of loyalty to the Habsburg Empire until 1918. The "activist" course of the Czech political parties represented an opportunist attempt to garner political concessions within the Austrian state. The basic demand of the parties remained the recognition of Bohemian state rights, which was tantamount to a federalization of the empire. None of the parties openly espoused the cause of national independence until 1918. In January 1917 the exiles won their first major victory when the Entente included a demand for the "liberation of Czechoslovakia from foreign rule" in its statement of war aims. Czech parliamentary delegates responded with a specific declaration of loyalty to the empire, and they repeated those sentiments when the Austrian Reichsrat reopened in May 1917. Although the Austrian government dealt harshly with political dissension until the closing months of the war, the political loyalty of the Czech political parties cannot be explained simply by the fear of reprisals. It was the privations of the extended war and the growing vulnerability of the Austrian government that gradually radicalized the parties. Only in the winter and spring of 1918 did the Czech parties omit their declaration of loyalty to the Habsburgs and begin to speak openly in favor of independence.[60]

It is possible to argue that the professional politicians were more cautious than the Czech population in general. If one searches for an expression of more radical sentiments, one can do no better than the manifesto signed by more than two hundred Czech writers and intellectuals in May 1917. While phrased in sufficiently general language to pass censorship, the manifesto clearly warned Czech parliamentary delegates in the Viennese Reichsrat to restrain their declarations of loyalty to the Habsburg state. The writers succeeded, up to a point. The parliamentary spokesmen strengthened their language and demanded the union of Slovakia with the lands of the Bohemian crown within a federal empire.[61] Despite historians' claims to the contrary, it is not certain that Czech popular opinion supported the radical stand of the writers more than the moderate approach of the political representatives.[62] In the absence of elections, and before the age of mass opinion polls, there was no reliable way of determining the breakdown of public opinion in various stages of the war. But bureaucratic reports of Czech political offenses tended to document the same general evolution of attitudes that was to be found among the political parties.[63] Moreover, it was not the case that all Czech intellectuals were radically opposed to the Habsburg state. The professors at the university, who, after all, had a considerable stake in the system, were seldom to be found among the radicals. The two most accomplished Czech historians of the late nineteenth and early twentieth centuries—Jaroslav Goll and his pupil, Josef Pekař—actively supported the monarchy during the war. In 1915 Goll keynoted a demonstration marking the sixty-seventh anniversary of Francis Joseph's accession to the throne, and in 1917 Pekař loyally prepared an oration for the projected visit to Prague of Emperor Charles.[64] Attitudes toward the Habsburg Empire varied among the nation's intelligentsia just as they did among the political leaders. The idea of a nation united behind a specific political program is a myth.

Until the latter stages of the war, the movement for Czechoslovak independence rested in the hands of a small group of political emigrés (they obviously could not work openly in Austria-Hungary). Tomáš G. Masaryk led the way into exile in December 1914. At the age of sixty-four, Masaryk had long enjoyed an international reputation for high intellectual and political standards as a professor in Prague's Czech University and as a deputy in the Austrian Reichsrat. Masaryk himself embodied both the cultural and political phases of the Czech national revival. He was a sincere believer in cultural nationalism as originally expressed by Herder; at the same time, he was an able practitioner of the political "plebiscitarian" nationalism that had its origins in the French Revolution. As of 1913 Masaryk had continued to proclaim his loyalty to the empire, but the outbreak of the war seemed to furnish conclusive proof that the Austro-Hungarian authorities had relegated the empire irrevocably to the status of a junior partner with Imperial Germany. Instead of being a protector of the minority nationalities and a barrier to German domination of Central Europe, the Dual Monarchy was to become the instrument of German expansionism. Masaryk therefore made his radical decision to abandon the monarchy and to work for the independence of the Czechs.[65] In the early stages of the war he was still not certain what kind of state the Czechs ought to have. He inclined toward a monarchy with possibly a Russian, but preferably a Belgian or Danish, prince on the throne.[66] But his ideas evolved in the West, and long before the war was over he and his colleagues had become convinced that the times demanded a democratic republic. In September 1915 Masaryk was joined by a thirty-one-year-old university lecturer named Edvard Beneš. Unknown at the time, Beneš's political personality and reputation still had to develop. The other outstanding personality among those working in the West for independence was Milan Štefánik. A Slovak, Štefánik had well-placed friends in Parisian political circles, and he eventually was commissioned a general in the French army. If it had not been for his untimely death in an airplane crash in 1919, he probably would have played an important political role in the republic.

The exiles established contact with the Czech emigré colonies and some Czechophiles in the West—notably Wickham Steed, foreign editor of the London *Times;* R. W. Seton-Watson, a young British historian specializing in Central European affairs; and Ernest Denis, professor at the Sorbonne. But in the early years of the war their contacts with top political leaders were few and insignificant. The Entente powers by no means advocated a dissolution of Austria-Hungary. The British and the French traditionally favored the existence of a Danubian monarchy, and the Romanovs could hardly assume the role of empire-breakers. When the United States entered the war, it waited for more than eight months before declaring war on Austria-Hungary; and when Wilson pronounced his Fourteen Points in January 1918 he spoke of "autonomous development" for the peoples of the empire, but he did not mention independence. Throughout 1917 Emperor Charles undertook peace initiatives. The Western powers were receptive to the idea of breaking the Austro-German alliance, and obviously the Austrians would not agree to a peace that meant the dissolution of the empire. Therefore the Entente refrained from extensive support of the claims of the various nationalities. The Czech leaders at home were justifiably cautious.

The exiles were in a difficult position. The country that they were attempting to destroy seemed to have the support of the majority of Czech leaders. The governments whose support they needed in order to achieve independence had no desire to break up an historic state in the European state-system. Masaryk and his followers therefore had to content themselves with limited propaganda activities—delivering lectures and publishing pamphlets and periodicals. In Britain, the most influential of the publications was a weekly entitled *The New Europe.* Launched in 1916 and edited by Seton-Watson, it contained a number of articles by Masaryk, and it eventually helped to mold British thinking in favor of the Czech cause. By the time of the peace conference much of what younger British leaders knew or thought about Central Europe came from *The New Europe.*[67] While Masaryk spent most of his time in London, Beneš concentrated his activities in Paris. There Beneš guided the daily work of the Czechoslovak National Council after its organization in 1916. With Ernest Denis he helped to found or edit the reviews *Nation tchèque* and *Monde slave.* The contributions of Denis's circle of friends from the university to those journals augmented the prestige of the Czechoslovak movement. But the Czech exiles needed something tangible to offer the Entente powers. The only thing they had was the large number of Czech prisoners of war, the vast majority of whom were in Russia. At the beginning of the war the Russians agreed to the formation of a Czech legion to be composed of Czech emigrés in Russia, but the Romanov government did not wish to encourage national revolts against another dynasty and therefore prevented the large-scale employment of prisoners of war in the legion. It was only after the outbreak of the revolution in 1917 that the Czech legion grew into a powerful fighting force.

The first diplomatic success for the Czech exiles came in January 1917. When the Entente powers answered Wilson's request for a statement of war aims, they included the "liberation of the Italians, Slavs, Romanians, and Czechoslovaks from foreign rule" among their conditions for peace. Entente statesmen were at least aware that Czechs and Slovaks were Slavic. The redundancy in the phrasing resulted simply from a last-minute decision to make special mention of the "Czechoslovaks" while simultaneously indicating a general interest in other Slavic peoples.[68] But "liberation" did not necessarily mean "independence."[69] A new opportunity for the Czechs came in March 1917 with the Russian Revolution. The foreign minister of the new provisional government, Paul Miliukov, was a friend of Masaryk, who made immediate preparations to go to Petrograd. Before Masaryk arrived, however, Miliukov was out of office, and Masaryk spent most of his time in Russia organizing the Czech legion. The provisional government was committed to the continuation of the war effort. With Russian resources at the point of exhaustion, the government agreed to the wholesale participation of Czech prisoners as a separate fighting unit on the front. The Czechs fought bravely in the summer and autumn of 1917. But after the Bolshevik Revolution Masaryk was mainly interested in withdrawing the Czechs from Russia; the effort to evacuate them through Vladivostok led to their famous exploits along the Siberian railway in 1918. Smaller units of the Czech legion were formed on the French and the Italian fronts, but they never approached the military and political importance of the legionnaires in Russia.

The real turning point for the Czech exiles came only in the spring and summer of 1918. Various considerations finally provoked the decision of the Entente countries to recognize the independence of Czechoslovakia before any revolution had occurred and while the Habsburg authorities still exercised control over the territory of the new state. The military situation of the Western powers was precarious between March and July of 1918. Even before the formal exit of the Soviet Union from the war, with the signing of the Treaty of Brest-Litovsk in March, General Erich Ludendorff began a wholesale transfer of troops to the western front for his spring offensive. The purpose of that offensive was to force Britain and France out of the war before the fresh American armies could become effective. The grave danger that the offensive posed to the Allies and associates compelled them to grasp for means of keeping German forces away from the front, and they finally seized upon the idea of encouraging unrest among the national minorities of the Central Powers. In April Georges Clemenceau published the secret correspondence from 1917 between the Austrians and the Allies about a separate peace for Austria-Hungary. The effect of that publication was to force the Austrian government irrevocably into the arms of the Germans, and the Allies abandoned hopes of detaching the Habsburg Empire from Germany. They no longer had any reason to court the favor of the Habsburg authorities rather than that of the national minorities. The military situation also constrained the Italian government to modify its previous stance against Serbo-Croatian demands for a South-Slav state, and in April representatives of the various nationalities of the Habsburg Empire staged a mass demonstration in Rome in what they termed a "Congress of Oppressed Nationalities." Beneš was one of its chief organizers. In private conversations with Western statesmen Beneš magnified the revolutionary sentiment among the Czechs in Bohemia and Moravia and argued that a clear statement by the Western powers favoring independence for the Czechs could provoke violent upheavals against the Habsburg authorities.[70] Leaders of the West were increasingly willing to listen to Beneš and to hope that he was right.

In American eyes the recognition of Czechoslovak independence graphically implemented the Wilsonian principle of national self-determination. In the spring of 1918 Masaryk left Vladivostok, sailed across the Pacific, and then journeyed through the United States to Washington. In June he had his first talks with President Wilson and Secretary of State Lansing. Much has been made of Masaryk's persuasive abilities in direct conversation, and over the years many people came away from audiences with him deeply impressed with the moral force of his character. Masaryk and Wilson were very similar personalities in their interests and values, and there can be little doubt that Wilson was influenced by Masaryk's political opinions. Moreover the Czechs and Slovaks seemed to be made to order for the application of the principle of national self-determination. Weak and in need of help, they were easy to idealize as democratic fighters for freedom. But the overwhelming reason for extending recognition to the Czechs was the fact that after June 1918 the Czech legion controlled Siberia.

At the time of the rebellion along the Trans-Siberian railway, few Western statesmen knew very much about the Czechs or their cause. The man who was later to become the first British minister to Prague began a Foreign Office memorandum in late 1917 with a remark, "A Mr. Beneš came to see me today."[71] Beneš, of course, was urging independence for the Czechs, but Foreign Office sentiment was captured in this comment by a high official: "It would be difficult to give more than an expression of sympathy with Czech aspirations on the basis of self-government of minor nationalities. The geographical position of Bohemia is an almost insurmountable stumbling block."[72] Through 1918 the general unfamiliarity with the Czechs was reflected in the British documents in a myriad of small but significant ways—for example, by gross misspellings of the names of Masaryk, Beneš, and Štefánik; by references to the legionnaires as "Czech-Slovenes"; and by the inquiry of the member of parliament who was friendly to the Czechs but who evidently believed that they lived along the Adriatic.[73] In March 1918 British military intelligence was still uninformed about the size or the quality of the Czech legion in Russia and was quite skeptical about the military value of the legionnaires.[74] The French had better information, however, and they pressed for an agreement that the legionnaires should be transported from Vladivostok, and perhaps from Murmansk and Archangel as well, to France in order to help defend the western front against the German offensive. The Supreme War Council agreed to the French proposal at Abbeville on May 1 and 2 and reconfirmed that decision at Versailles in early June.[75]

It was the responsibility of Britain to provide shipping to transport the legionnaires to France, but the British had no vessels available for the purpose. The only possibility was that the Japanese might be persuaded to make some ships available, but British diplomacy took only hesitant steps in that direction. By late April dominant opinion in both the Foreign Office and the War Office strongly opposed a Czech evacuation of Siberia. It was argued that even if the shipping problems could be overcome the legionnaires could not arrive in France in time to be effective in the campaign season of 1918. On the other hand, they were providentially in a position to resist German encroachments into Siberia and to prevent any exploitation of the area by the Central Powers. British Foreign Secretary Arthur James Balfour considered the decision of the Supreme War Council "absurd," and his chief assistant, Lord Robert Cecil, was one of the most outspoken advocates of military intervention in Russia.[76] The question of commitments in Siberia was deadlocked in May 1918 because of Wilson's opposition to intervention. Neither Britain nor France had the forces with which to intervene, and the Japanese were willing to commit troops only in conjunction with the Americans. Initial British efforts to persuade Wilson to support intervention had reached a fruitless climax in February, and in the weeks thereafter the question had lain dormant.[77] But as British policymakers became aware of the existence and the value of the Czech legion in Siberia, they recognized a new tool for the implementation of their purposes.

The objectives of Allied intervention in Russia have long been the subject of vehement debate. Although British policymakers such as Balfour and Cecil supported intervention, they usually adopted a studied vagueness even in their internal memoranda about the exact nature of their goals. They emphasized the supposed menace of German prisoners of war operating in Siberia, but information from the area was so sketchy that such fears were largely the product of vivid imaginations in London and other capitals. Whereas British officials made every effort in their written communications to deemphasize any involvement in the internal political affairs of Russia, they also called for action against the German "allies" in the country. Those allies could only be the Bolsheviks, who had taken Russia out of the war and who were delivering supplies to the Germans during their western offensive. In the Allied military situation of May and June 1918 the Bolsheviks could qualify as enemies regardless of ideological considerations. Any intervention against German influence in Russia or any attempt to reestablish an eastern front could only be an intervention against the Bolshevik government as well. The two themes ran parallel in the documents, as in the telegram from the British diplomatic representative in Moscow when he learned of the Czech revolt along the Siberian railway: "Fate has given us in Czechs last chance of regaining Russia and of re-creating in her new source of strength against Germany."[78] The British government went into the intervention deliberately and with at least the secondary purpose of combatting the Bolshevik government. But they seemed motivated initially not so much by fear of Marxist revolutions as by the seeming dictates of military strategy.

The people in charge of the British Foreign Office had already contemplated the use that was eventually made of the Czech legion weeks before the actual Czech revolt along the railway. In May they launched an effort to persuade the French government that the Czechs were more valuable in Siberia than they could be in France. Clemenceau responded in a vehement letter to Lord Robert Cecil that the issue of the war would be decided solely along the western front and that every available man was required there. He noted that the Czechs were more than eager to fight against Germans. He added that their leaders had consistently maintained that the legionnaires would not become involved in internal affairs in Russia.[79] Clemenceau's adamant stance prevented any change in official policy, but the British government did little to find means of actually transporting the legion to France. Cecil, in his comments on Clemenceau's letter, emphasized the military necessity of creating a diversion in the east and added: "if they [the Czech legion] can be employed in order to produce effective intervention by the Japanese in Siberia, with or without the consent of the Americans, they would be fulfilling a far more important service to the Allied cause. . . . There is no means of obtaining Japanese help without American approval, unless we can start intervention by some other force, which will cause the Japanese to intervene lest their position on the Pacific coast of Asia should be injured."[80] At the very time that Cecil was writing those lines, the legionnaires revolted against Bolshevik attempts to disarm them and within two weeks extended their control over thousands of miles of the railway. Charges that the revolt was planned from abroad flattered the conspiratorial proficiency of the West and exaggerated the ability even to communicate between Siberia and the Western capitals. But nothing could have been more opportune from the standpoint of British policy.

With Czech detachments strung along the railway, there appeared to be a real danger that Bolshevik forces could break the Czech lines of communication, thereby dividing and defeating the legionnaires. A fresh wave of importunities flowed in from London and Paris pleading with Wilson to intervene so as to save the Czechs from a possibly dreadful fate. The evident need to rescue the Czechs brought a reversal in Wilson's policy in early July, and in the next month the first American and Japanese troops landed in Vladivostok. As subsequent events were to demonstrate, the legionnaires were quite capable of defending themselves, and it may well be that the danger in which they had supposedly found themselves had been purposely exaggerated. But there is every reason to believe that Wilson acted in good faith on the basis of the information supplied to him.[81]

By the summer the Allies were deeply in debt to the Czechs. Masaryk and Beneš realized that the time had come when they could press for open diplomatic recognition by the Western powers, and they exploited with dexterity the opportunities afforded them by the deeds of the Czech legion. The French needed the least persuading. The outlines of French postwar foreign policy were already forming, and a series of successor states with strong Slavic influence seemed to offer a more reliable barrier to German domination of Central Europe than a Danubian empire under Austrian and Magyar leadership. In April 1918 Clemenceau's exposure of the Austrian peace feelers of 1917 destroyed all chances for a separate peace with Austria-Hungary at a time when the British and American governments still hoped for an agreement with Vienna. At the end of May during the British-French debate about the employment of the Czech legion, Clemenceau told Beneš: "I want to have all your men in France. We consider them soldiers of the best order. You will have a declaration from us, and we will recognize your independence. You will be independent, you merit that. You can count on me; I will go with you all the way."[82] By the end of June Foreign Minister Pichon sent Beneš a formal letter recognizing the Czechoslovak National Council as "the first core of the future Czechoslovak government."[83] After the German offensive ground to a halt in July and the Western armies began their counteroffensive in August, there was no longer any need for Czech troops on the western front. Competition then developed between the British and the French governments for influence over the legion in Siberia. At the end of September Pichon and Beneš signed a secret treaty in which the French government recognized the National Council as the de facto government of the Czechs and pledged French support for Czech claims to the historical boundaries of Bohemia, Moravia, and Silesia, and their union with Slovakia.[84] In that treaty the French undertook territorial commitments that had been scrupulously avoided by the British and the Americans.

British policy toward the Czechs underwent a radical reversal in the spring and summer of 1918. During April and May Beneš emphasized the desirability of having a recognized authority capable of giving orders and commanding the respect of the legionnaires in Siberia. In fact, events in Siberia more or less proceeded along their own course regardless of instructions arriving from London or Paris, but the theoretical logic of Beneš's argument found resonance in London. On June 3 the British government sent Beneš a letter stating British readiness "to recognize the Czecho-Slovak National Council as the supreme organ of the Czecho-Slovak movement in Allied countries, and ... to recognize the Czecho-Slovak Army as an organized unit operating in the Allied cause."[85] That declaration stopped short of formal recognition of Czechoslovak independence. Specialists on Central European affairs such as Lewis Namier and Harold Nicolson as well as higher officials believed that the British government had already gone far enough in its commitments.[86] The reluctance to witness a political and economic fragmentation of the Danubian area persisted. Moreover, the government had no desire to take on added obligations in its war aims at a time when the ultimate issue of the conflict was still very much in doubt. But it was only a matter of weeks before Beneš approached the British again with fresh requests. In mid-July he urged that the British government extend formal diplomatic recognition to the National Council as the "true government" of the Czechs and Slovaks. Beneš suggested that the recognition coincide with the landing of Allied forces in Siberia.[87] Opinion in the Foreign Office was almost unanimously negative toward this "novel" proposal, and both Nicolson and Namier pointed out the analogy with the Irish situation. If the Western powers could sponsor on their soil provisional governments for dissatisfied minorities, so could Germany and Austria-Hungary.[88] Yet in late July and early August the British government did indeed decide to extend formal recognition to the Czechs. It is clear from conversations between Foreign Office officials and Beneš that the price of that recognition was Czech agreement to put the legionnaires at the disposal of Entente policy in Siberia.[89]

The path by which the Czechs attained recognition from the American government was similar to that followed in London. Like the British, American policy had aimed at the detachment of Austria-Hungary from Germany and the maintenance of the empire essentially in its then-current boundaries. In May 1918, however, Wilson and Lansing reversed themselves after what they regarded as Clemenceau's "ill-conceived" exposure of the Austrian peace correspondence and announced that "the nationalistic aspirations of the Czecho-Slovaks and Yugo-Slavs for freedom have the earnest sympathy of this government."[90] Their primary purpose was to create internal dissension in the Habsburg Empire in much the same way as they thought the Germans had done in Russia. The question of Czechoslovak (or Yugoslav) independence was not their chief concern. Masaryk had already arrived in Washington in early May, but he did not receive an interview with Wilson for more than five weeks. When they did meet on June 19, Wilson was interested not in the Czechs and Slovaks but in Masaryk's impressions of the situation in Russia. The romantic fight of the legionnaires did focus American attention on the Czech question, however, and public opinion appeared to become increasingly sympathetic toward the national minorities of Central Europe. After the decision to intervene in Siberia, Masaryk began to press for formal recognition of Czechoslovak independence in July. By that time he found a sympathetic response from Wilson and Lansing, and the American government formally recognized the "National Council as a de facto belligerent Government" on September 3. American policy was explained to the public not on the grounds of national self-determination but by the contribution of the Czech armies to the war effort.[91]

The unavoidable conclusion that follows from a discussion of these diplomatic maneuvers is that Western recognition of Czechoslovak independence had little or nothing to do with the actual situation in Bohemia, Moravia, Silesia, and Slovakia. Czech and Slovak public opinion may have favored independence, but Western statesmen had no way of knowing for sure, and the question was not of primary importance to them. Their decision to recognize Czechoslovak independence was tantamount to a decision to withdraw diplomatic recognition from Austria-Hungary and to contribute to the complete dissolution of a traditional great power in the European state-system. Border territories could have been detached from the empire and given to Italy or to Polish or Yugoslav states without destroying the basic integrity of the empire. But it was impossible to remove Bohemia, Moravia, and Silesia from the heart of the empire and have anything left worthy of the name. By recognizing Czechoslovak independence Western statesmen helped to undermine the Habsburg Empire not primarily because of conditions within that state but because of military and diplomatic considerations arising from the war situation in 1918 and Western intervention in the Russian civil war.

Diplomatic recognition of the Czechoslovak national movement was more important for the future of Czechoslovakia than for the fate of Austria-Hungary. By the summer of 1918 the empire was on the verge of collapse. The effects of food shortages, malnutrition and illness, monetary inflation, labor strikes, and growing unrest among the national minorities were compounded by a political leadership incapable of taking timely and decisive actions.[92] But even a resolute leadership would have faced problems that were practically insurmountable. Western recognition of Czechoslovak independence therefore came at a time when the movement toward independence was already far advanced within the empire. An undisputed effect of diplomatic recognition, however, was that it enormously increased the prestige of the exiled leaders, particularly Masaryk, Beneš, and Štefánik. Before the war Beneš and Štefánik had been practically unknown among their countrymen, while Masaryk had acquired the reputation of a controversial loner in politics whose prestige was greatest in intellectual circles. Their successful diplomatic activity abroad, however, eclipsed the more mundane and opportunistic efforts of the Czech and Slovak leaders who remained at home during the war. Masaryk, primarily, and Beneš, secondarily, reaped personal popularity which they successfully translated into political power in the interwar years. Štefánik, also, could have exercised great influence had he not been killed when the airplane bringing him home in 1919 crashed almost within sight of his destination. The prestige of Masaryk and Beneš augmented the power of liberal democratic forces in the new country and helped to determine the constitutional structure and political development of the first Czechoslovak republic. Such was the primary historical significance of the early recognition of Czechoslovak independence.[93]

In view of the leading roles that Masaryk and Beneš played in the first republic, it is instructive to note the way in which they handled delicate political negotiations already in 1918. A key issue concerned the employment of Czech legionnaires in Siberia. Masaryk's and Beneš's attitudes toward the intervention were highly ambivalent. Masaryk could have little faith in the claim that the purpose of the intervention was to combat German prisoners of war in Siberia. Upon arriving in Tokyo from Siberia in April 1918, Masaryk addressed a memorandum through the American diplomatic service to Wilson in which Masaryk noted: "Nowhere in Siberia did I see armed German and Austrian prisoners of war." Masaryk advocated a de facto recognition of the Bolshevik government and pointed out that the Bolsheviks were at least no worse than the other factions in the Russian political struggles. Moreover, he supported the disarming of the Czech legionnaires because, as he pointed out, they could be rearmed anyway upon arriving on the western front.[94] At the same time Beneš was working in Paris and London to bring the legionnaires to the western front where he believed their presence would produce greater political benefits for the Czech cause. He agreed to their temporary use against German prisoners of war in Siberia but opposed support of one Russian faction against the other.[95] As the Western powers moved toward intervention, however, Masaryk and Beneš modified their stance considerably. By summer, in Washington, Masaryk was much more critical of the Bolsheviks, and he approved of the legionnaires defending themselves by any means available if the Bolsheviks were "disloyal."[96] In August, when Cecil handed Beneš the British declaration recognizing the Czechoslovak National Council, Cecil wrote: "I asked him whether the Czech-Slovak troops would be kept in Russia, and he said that they would do whatever the Allies thought right." By that time it was apparent that the intervention would be more anti-Bolshevik than anti-German, and, given Masaryk's firsthand observations, it is doubtful that Beneš could have had illusions about that fact. Beneš was tacitly agreeing to the employment of the legionnaires in the Russian civil war in exchange for a recognition of Czechoslovak independence. Beneš thought that the government in Russia should be conducted provisionally by Admiral Kolchak and Generals Kornilov and Denikin.[97]

The political benefits that accrued to the Czechs from the Allied intervention in Russia continued after the achievement of Czechoslovak independence. The presence of the legionnaires in Siberia during 1918 and 1919 and the fact that they functioned as instruments of Allied policy in Russia strengthened the Czech position at the peace negotiations. Moreover, the fears of Western statesmen that Bolshevism might spread through Central Europe made them anxious to establish stable nation-states that could successfully resist social revolutions. The threat of Bolshevism as much as the possibility of a German resurgence explains the highly favorable treatment that the Czechs received at the peace conference. Moreover, Austria and Hungary were exhausted and could offer no effective resistance. Yet, as the months wore on, pressure mounted within Czechoslovakia to bring the legionnaires home, and the legionnaires themselves became increasingly restless and disenchanted with the intervention. Friction between their commanders and Admiral Kolchak sparked interminable disputes. The Czechoslovak government began to press the Western powers for a quick withdrawal of the troops from Siberia, which was finally accomplished in the early months of 1920.[98]

Masaryk and Beneš had opportunistically exploited the best means available for the creation of an independent Czechoslovak state, and they had therefore cooperated with the interventionists. But they had never become strong proponents of the intervention as such. Masaryk retained a healthy skepticism about the utility of the intervention, and both he and Beneš always wanted to avoid obstacles to an eventual Czechoslovak-Russian rapprochement. Any suggestion by historians that the Czech leadership was party to the initial uprisings along the Siberian railway in

June 1918 grossly exaggerates the ability to make effective communications between the West and Siberia. Moreover, the authority of the Czechoslovak National Council was not so absolute that it could order the legionnaires to stage a general insurrection throughout Siberia. Nor did Masaryk and Beneš have any personal influence in the Allied decisions to intervene in Russia. They simply responded to an existing situation. In an exchange for a recognition of their own authority to speak for the Czechs and Slovaks and then for a recognition of Czechoslovak independence they raised no objection to attempts by the great powers to use the Czech legion for the political purposes of the Western alliance.

Another political challenge that confronted Masaryk in the United States was the problem of maintaining the full support of the Czech and the Slovak emigré colonies. It was hoped that their political influence would enhance Masaryk's authority and promote American recognition of Czechoslovak independence. But there were problems in tapping that source of power. At the outset of the war deep divisions appeared in the American Czech and Slovak communities, considerable portions of which remained loyal to Austria-Hungary.[99] Only in the course of the war did support for the exiles increase among American immigrants, who became the chief source of funds for the Czechoslovak National Council.[100] The support of American Slovaks was particularly important in view of the political passivity of most Slovak peasants in the home country. In May 1918 Masaryk began a speaking tour calculated to demonstrate the enthusiasm of American Czechs and Slovaks for Czechoslovak union and independence. In Pittsburgh, the headquarters of the Slovak League of America, he met with leaders of the immigrant groups and came to an understanding that was to become famous as the "agreement of Pittsburgh." The Slovaks wanted an autonomous position for Slovakia within a federal republic inasmuch as they feared assimilation by the stronger Czech group. Already in Cleveland in October 1915 the leaders of the Slovak League had agreed with Czech groups to support the founding of just such a republic.[101] From Masaryk they sought—and thought that they obtained—the promise of Slovak autonomy. The relevant passages from the Pittsburgh agreement read:

> Slovakia shall have her own administrative system, her own diet and her own courts.
> The Slovak language shall be the official language in the schools, in the public offices and in public affairs generally.[102]

Masaryk negotiated and signed the agreement, which was dated May 30, 1918.

The Pittsburgh agreement had no official significance for the founding of Czechoslovakia. Besides Masaryk, the contracting parties were only

American Czechs and Slovaks, not residents of the territories in question. The immediate purpose of the agreement was to demonstrate the support of the immigrant colonies for the efforts of the Czechoslovak National Council to achieve complete national independence. Yet the Pittsburgh agreement became the focus of bitter controversy between the central government in Prague and Slovak autonomists in the interwar years. In response to repeated accusations that Masaryk had reneged on his promises of Slovak autonomy, Masaryk even branded the agreement a "forgery" by 1929.[103] The controversies between Czech centralists and Slovak autonomists will command some attention in the study of Weimar German-Czechoslovak diplomatic relations, but the significance of the Pittsburgh agreement at this point is the evidence that it affords of Masaryk's political opportunism. Masaryk and his chief lieutenant, Edvard Beneš, subordinated everything else to their vision of an independent Czechoslovak state. In 1918 they exploited the immigrants in the United States and the legionnaires in Siberia in order to attain their goal. They succeeded in their tactics, but both actions aggravated problems that were to confront the republic through most of its existence.

In Bohemia, Moravia, and Silesia the radicalization of the Czech population and its leaders belonged to the last year and a half of the war. In that period the Austrian police reported a growing number of arrests for political reasons, and Czech leaders voiced their grievances against the monarchy ever more openly. Economic privations had steadily mounted through the war, but the winter of 1918 brought fatal shortages of foodstuffs and fuel supplies. Particularly among the working classes, deaths from malnutrition and tuberculosis multiplied. Although labor unrest was already manifest in 1917, nothing could match the general strikes that spread through both Austria and Germany in mid-January 1918. In Austria the immediate occasion was the reduction of the flour allotment from 200 to 165 grams per day. But the strikes occurred largely among German workers, and their Czech counterparts were slow to join in, although the Czechs did stage mass demonstrations on January 22.[104] The general tendency in this period of crisis was that Czechs of various social classes and ideological persuasions coalesced and acted politically as a unified national body. It was easy to place the responsibility for the privations of the war on German leaders in Vienna and Berlin. The war temporarily reversed the movement discernible in the two decades before 1914 toward the political fragmentation along socioeconomic lines of the Czech national movement. Thus a crisis situation that could have encouraged a social revolution in a nationally homogeneous state actually helped to provoke a Czech national revolution in the multinational empire.

The coming of that revolution was clearly visible in Czech political activity during 1918. Still, as of the summer of 1917, Czech politicians

and intellectuals had proclaimed their loyalty to the empire while urging
the establishment of a confederation in which Slovakia would be united
with Bohemia, Moravia, and Silesia. But in January 1918, in their
Epiphany declaration, the Czech political parties for the first time omitted
an avowal of their loyalty to the empire or of their desire for a federal
state. By April and May Czech propaganda openly promoted the founding
of independent successor states to the empire. Partially in response to the
urgings sent by Beneš from Paris, Czech political leaders refounded the
National Committee (*Národní výbor*) in July and again demanded national
independence. It was this National Committee that eventually ruled the
country in the early days after the revolution. The Catholic political forces
were traditionally the most loyal to the Habsburgs, but by September 29,
in response to a Viennese order to divide Bohemia into separate German
and Czech administrative areas, the Catholics proclaimed their complete
identification with the Czech national movement. The socialists, while
participating in the basic trend toward national consolidation, attempted
to maintain their own unique identity by founding the Socialist Committee
at the beginning of September. The socialists even promoted a revolution
against Habsburg authority on October 14, which was abortive but
demonstrated socialist power nonetheless. Therefore, while the exile
leadership garnered diplomatic victories abroad, the political leadership at
home increasingly asserted Czech independence from Austrian authority
and laid the basis for the revolution.[105]

Signs of discontent and unrest appeared in Slovakia in the last year of
the war as well. Before 1918 the Slovak countryside was calm; indeed,
until the end of the war there were few disturbances or demonstrations. In
1914 Father Ferdis Juriga, one of the two Slovak representatives in the
Hungarian Diet, affirmed the loyalty of the Slovak people to the
Hungarian government. During the war, Slovak politicians such as Milan
Hodža tried to prepare for any eventuality that might arise from the
military encounters, but few Slovaks believed that the Central Powers
would be so thoroughly defeated that Hungary would dissolve. The most
that might be gained, therefore, was an autonomous existence for the
Slovaks within the Magyar half of the empire. The tendency to look to
Prague for effective assistance against Magyar domination was not yet
widespread. Insofar as Slovak leaders hoped for support from the great
powers, most turned toward Russia. The Russian military debacle in 1917
instilled a defeatist spirit and further encouraged political passivity.

By the spring of 1918, however, the general unrest of the last year of
the war did spread to Slovakia. Some of the returning prisoners of war
from Russia brought with them radical ideas imbibed in the revolutionary
situation in Russia, and they helped to spread discontent in Slovakia as
elsewhere among the Central Powers. The first important manifestation of

the new spirit was the May Day demonstration of 1918 in Liptovský Svätý Mikuláš. The man who inspired the workers' pro-Czech resolutions was Vavro Šrobár, a former student of Masaryk and already for two decades a leading Slovak spokesman for the Czechoslovak orientation. Despite the May Day demonstration, most Slovak activity in 1918 was confined to a relatively small group of political leaders. The Slovaks simply did not possess large urban centers of their own where they could develop a more active political awareness. Most Slovaks active in the professions or commerce had become "magyarones" and were lost to any Slovak national movement. In political consciousness, the Slovaks were decades behind their Czech kinsmen. At the end of May the leaders of the Slovak National party met in the village that served as the center for the national movement, Turčiansky Svätý Martin. There a split became obvious between those who favored union with the Czech lands and those who only hoped for Slovak autonomy within Hungary. But it was in that meeting that Father Andrej Hlinka emerged as a spokesman for the Czechoslovak orientation, with his famous statement: "The thousand-year marriage with the Magyars has not succeeded. We must dissolve it."[106] Yet in the following months the political situation remained dormant in Slovakia, and only in October did Slovak leaders follow the example of other minority nationalities in the empire and form their own national council. It was composed of a handful of party leaders. The Slovak National Committee convened in Martin on October 30 and demanded the right of self-determination for the Czechoslovak nation, of which the Slovaks were an essential part. When news of the Austrian capitulation and the proclamation of the Czechoslovak republic arrived hours later, Slovak leaders generally regarded the declaration as a statement of the Slovak desire to join in the new republic. In view of later Czech-Slovak conflicts, it is important to note that there was no Slovak opposition to the creation of Czechoslovakia.[107]

The final chapter in the demise of the Habsburg Empire began in the last half of September 1918 with the collapse of the Bulgarian front. After that time the Austro-Hungarian military situation was completely hopeless. On October 4 Vienna joined with Berlin in an appeal to Wilson for an armistice on the basis of the Fourteen Points. Wilson simply referred the Austrians to the military authorities in Europe and took his time about formulating an answer. On October 16 Emperor Charles attempted to stave off disaster by declaring the federalization of the Austrian half of the empire, but events had outstripped that concession. Masaryk had foreseen Charles's move, and on October 18 he issued in Washington a Declaration of Independence for Czechoslovakia. Modeled closely on the American Declaration of Independence, it was actually written by an American lawyer who at the time was in the service of the War Department.[108] On

October 21 Wilson finally answered the Austrian armistice appeal with a reminder that the situation had changed since he had first formulated the Fourteen Points. Specifically, the United States recognized the Czechs and Slovaks as a belligerent nation and sympathized with the Yugoslav aspiration for independence. That answer snuffed out the last hope for the preservation of the empire, yet peace had to be made. On October 27 Count Julius Andrássy—the son of the Andrássy who, with Bismarck, had first launched the Dual Alliance almost forty years previously—accepted Wilson's note as the basis for an armistice. Andrássy's note meant that independence for the national minorities was available for the taking. And so it came about that members of the National Committee in Prague finally proclaimed the independence of Czechoslovakia on October 28.

That proclamation was the work of younger men. As of October 28 a delegation of senior political and economic leaders was in Geneva conferring with Beneš about steps to be taken in the establishment of a new republic. It was the first collective meeting in more than three years between the emigrant and the domestic political leadership. In the Geneva meeting they agreed on the composition of the new government. The preeminent role of the exile leadership was recognized by the fact that Masaryk became president, Beneš foreign minister, and Štefánik minister of war. But among the domestic leaders Masaryk's old rival, Karel Kramář, won the premiership, and representatives from the various Czech political parties controlled the other ministries. The cabinet included three Slovaks. It was agreed that a German-Bohemian would be invited to join the government "in order to protect the interests of the Germans in Bohemia."[109] At the same time there was common agreement about the necessity of a Czech military occupation of the entire country, including the predominantly German areas. The Czechs and the Slovaks had emerged from the war with achievements for which few had dared to dream in 1914.

GERMANS DURING THE FIRST WORLD WAR

The Germans of Bohemia, Moravia, and Silesia supported the war more heartily and suffered more severely than their Czech countrymen. Catholics, socialists, or nationalists, Germans of the various political groupings closed ranks in the August days of 1914 and loyally watched their young men march enthusiastically off to war. In the next four years German-Bohemian soldiers were killed at more than twice the rate of their Czech counterparts. At home, their parents and relatives bought Austrian war bonds much more avidly than the Czechs and therefore suffered more severe financial losses when the empire collapsed.[110] As the war dragged on and food shortages became more desperate, the Germans of the industrial border districts hungered more than the Czech peasant farmers in the hinterland. The relative Czech passivity toward a war for which Germans were making great sacrifices created widespread resentment among German-Bohemians and aggravated the national conflict. On the German as on the Czech side the war exacerbated national rivalries.

In view of the party conflicts in the interwar years, it is important to note wartime attitudes among various German political groupings. German nationalist forces particularly welcomed the outbreak of the war. In it they discerned an opportunity to reverse the trends of preceding decades and to reestablish German dominance in the Austrian half of the empire. The fact that Imperial Germany and Austria-Hungary fought together against most of the rest of Europe seemed to vindicate the anti-Schönerer nationalists, who in the prewar years had supported the Habsburg Empire as the best friend of Germany. During the war German nationalists developed a project of constitutional reform that culminated in their "Easter Program" of 1916. In order to achieve German numerical dominance in the Reichsrat, they demanded the political separation of Galicia from the rest of Austria. They insisted on the confirmation of German as the state language throughout Austria and on an even closer diplomatic alliance with Imperial Germany. Until basic constitutional changes could be dictated by the crown, they opposed the convocation of the Reichsrat. With that program, in 1915 and 1916 they seemed to have some chance for success. Fears of precisely such developments had, after all, driven Masaryk into exile. But the war situation was such by 1917 that the young emperor avoided nationalistic policies and tried to conciliate the national minorities. His decision to reopen the Reichsrat in May 1917 was therefore a defeat for the German nationalists.[111] The war had lasted too long and had ultimately weakened central authority too seriously for the nationalist program to remain a viable political policy.

Equally as loyal to the empire at the beginning of the war and more moderate in their attitudes on the nationality issue were the Catholic and the socialist political forces among the Germans. After Lueger's stormy battles with imperial authorities in the 1890s, the Christian Social party had become a central pillar of the empire. Throughout the war the loyalty of German political Catholicism was never in doubt, but voices arose from German Catholic ranks advocating appeasement of the national minorities. The most notable theoretical work of a Catholic spokesman on the nationality question came from a young prelate and theologian in Salzburg, Ignaz Seipel. In *Nation und Staat,* which appeared in 1916, Seipel drew a sharp distinction between the concepts of nation and state and argued that a multinational state represented a higher form of polity than did the nation-state. He was convinced that the multinational federal form was more practically suited for conditions in Central Europe. In the last two years of the war Seipel became increasingly active in a group dedicated to international peace and imperial reform, a group whose most notable members were Heinrich Lammasch and Josef Redlich. As late as October 1918 the Christian Social party continued to advocate a multinational federal state. By October 25, however, when Lammasch agreed to form a new government including Redlich and Seipel, they could only preside over the final dissolution of the empire.[112]

The German socialists also entered the war with a tradition of loyalty to the empire. Since the Brünn program of 1899 the Social Democrats had advocated a federal empire, and in Karl Renner and Otto Bauer they had supplied two leading theoreticians on the nationality question. Renner and Bauer supported the Austro-Marxist concept that socialism could best be achieved in a large state and that the empire was desirable for that reason. When war broke out, Austrian German socialists, like their counterparts in the Reich, remained loyal to their government, although there was some discontent on the left. But the trials of the war eventually caused growing numbers of socialists to weaken in their support of the empire. Friedrich Adler, the son of the party leader, Victor Adler, assassinated the Austrian prime minister as a protest against the war in October 1916. The Russian revolutions of 1917 helped to radicalize socialist thought, and the socialist party congress of October 1917 issued a call for peace on the basis of no annexations, no indemnities. At the congress Renner continued to advocate the reconstitution of Austria in a federal form. The left wing of the party under the leadership of Bauer, however, came out for the creation of national assemblies in order that the various nationalities might determine their own political futures. By the last months of the war the party defended the right of self-determination for all nationalities, which meant in effect that it renounced its previous loyalty to the Habsburg Empire. But the Austrian German socialists were careful to note that the right of self-determination applied to the Germans as well as to the other nationalities. Maintaining their belief in the efficacy of a large state in promoting socialism, they insisted by the autumn of 1918 that the Germans of Austria, including those of Bohemia, Moravia, and Silesia, should have the privilege of joining the Reich.[113] Therefore, the socialist abandonment of Austro-Marxism in favor of national self-determination paradoxically heightened tensions between Germans and Czechs.

In Austria as in Czechoslovakia the transition from empire to republic was a bloodless enterprise confined essentially to the activities of high political leaders. Emperor Charles's manifesto of October 16, 1918, calling for the restructuring of the empire along federal lines prompted the convocation of national assemblies for the various peoples of the empire. When the German Reichsrat deputies met on October 21, the Christian Socials and the German Nationalists remained loyal to the monarchy, but the Social Democrats advocated the founding of a democratic republic, which would become an autonomous part of Germany. Despite the differences in their sympathies the three leading German political groups directed the revolution in concert. Charles renounced his participation in state affairs on November 11, and on the following day the national assembly proclaimed German-Austria to be a republic.[114] Renner became the head of the first republican government, and Bauer the foreign minister. But the emphasis was on reconciliation, not revolution, and a coalition of major parties ruled the Austrian republic for almost the first two years of its existence. The birth of the Austrian and the Czechoslovak republics was similar in many respects. In the course of the First World War the major German and Czech political parties, except for the radical nationalists on both sides, had trod parallel paths. Loyal to the empire during the first three years of the war, they recognized the mounting signs of dissolution in late 1917 and 1918 and proceeded to salvage what they could for their respective nationalities. The basically national character of the revolutions was underlined by the fact that political parties representing various ideologies and socioeconomic interests cooperated in founding the republics.

The national revolutions and the creation of the independent successor states transferred to the sphere of international relations disputes that had previously been confined within the Habsburg Empire. Matters that had involved administrative boundaries, domestic economic policies, or parliamentary politics became questions of international frontiers, commercial treaties, and diplomatic alliances. It was inevitable that Germany through its normal diplomatic activities should become more directly involved with Danubian problems than it had been when those problems were internal concerns of the Habsburg Empire. Germany was not unique in that respect, for the diplomacy of other great powers, particularly of France and Britain, also concentrated more attention on Danubian affairs after they became matters of international dispute. It has been possible to trace the rise of Czech-German conflicts before 1918 largely in terms of political and social-economic evolution within the Habsburg Empire. After 1918, the focus of the national conflict became the newly created diplomatic relationship between Berlin and Prague. If that shift was not at once obvious, it certainly became so within a few years of the armistice. To be sure, Czechoslovakia confronted internal nationality disputes very similar to those of the old empire, for the new republic was also a multinational state. The rivalries within Czechoslovakia necessarily influenced the diplomatic relations between Berlin and Prague, but it was the diplomatic relationship itself that was the new and fundamental aspect of the national conflict.

In view of the key role of diplomacy in the interwar years it is important to survey German policies in Central Europe before 1918. From a Czech standpoint the major challenge was the potential creation of a Germanic Mitteleuropa. Already in the middle of the century Czech interests were fundamentally affected by the drive for German national unification. If a German nation-state had to emerge at all, the Czech leadership much preferred the *kleindeutsch* solution, which would exclude Austria and therefore themselves from a German political union. In that respect, there was a real community of interests between Czechs like Palacký and Prussians like Bismarck. Of all the non-German nationalities within the Habsburg Empire the Czechs were the most immediately endangered by the *grossdeutsch* alternative to national unification. The grossdeutsch program would have divided the Habsburg Empire and have included the German lands of Austria in a German nation-state. Bohemia, Moravia, and Silesia were part of the Germanic Confederation, and Germans tended to consider those lands to be as much German as Czech in character. The grossdeutsch solution, therefore, threatened to include the Czechs as a very small minority in a German political union. Bismarck's successful expulsion of Austria from Germany in 1866 temporarily removed the danger, even though the growth of a powerful and united Germany along the borders of Bohemia, Moravia, and Silesia hardly pleased nationally minded Czechs. But the creation of the Dual Alliance between Germany and Austria-Hungary in 1879 laid the foundation for German political and economic penetration into the Habsburg realm. The rapid industrial expansion and demographic growth of Imperial Germany strengthened its capacity to dominate the region. By the time of the First World War a Germanic Mitteleuropa was well on the way to becoming a reality. As far as ambitions in Central Europe were concerned, Germany had more to lose than to gain from a war.

In recent years historians have engaged in bitter debate about the nature of German aims during the First World War. The controversy has centered on questions such as the personality and goals of Chancellor Theobald von Bethmann-Hollweg, the relative influence of various circles and philosophies in the formation of German policy, or the degree of consistency in Germany's aims abroad in the years before and during the war.[115] But there is no question that in the war years the German government under Bethmann-Hollweg hoped for a political and economic consolidation of Central Europe. A Germanic Mitteleuropa was to become the basis of Germany's political power in the twentieth century. That was an essential war aim even of liberal and moderate forces in German politics.[116] In 1915 Friedrich Naumann's book, *Mitteleuropa*, popularized and gave moral ornamentation to the idea. Naumann argued for the creation in Central Europe of a closely knit military, political, and economic entity under German leadership. He wisely never specified the exact boundaries of his Central Europe, but his rhetorical questions hinted that it would stretch from Belgium past the Vistula and from the Baltic through the Balkans. Naumann's popularized version did not differ substantially from the actual plans of Germany's political and military leaders. Whereas the Czech exiles aimed at breaking up the Austro-Hungarian Empire in order to achieve their national independence, the German government hoped to merge the two empires and their war gains into one great military, political, and economic area under German leadership.

The fortunes of war temporarily brought gains for Germany far beyond Central Europe. The Russian revolutions of 1917 and that country's military collapse allowed the German high command to dictate peace terms at Brest-Litovsk more ambitious than even the most extreme annexationists had thought possible in 1914. While the German army attempted to insure the victory in the east through its western offensive in the spring of 1918, German diplomats turned their efforts toward consolidating German hegemony in Central Europe in a formal diplomatic agreement. Negotiations between Berlin and Vienna about a Central European federation began in earnest. The Germans naturally dominated the talks, particularly as Emperor Charles was at pains to demonstrate his loyalty to the alliance after Clemenceau's disclosure of Charles's secret correspondence for a peace settlement in 1917. Through the summer of 1918, negotiations for a customs union between the two empires were held in Salzburg. The military collapse in August and September undermined those plans, and the final outcome of the war was far different from what had been so confidently expected. But insofar as those negotiations seemed to reflect demographic and economic realities in Central Europe, even the debacle of 1918 did not destroy ideas that extended back at least as far as Friedrich List and Karl, Baron von Bruck. As long as the objective situation remained essentially unchanged, Germans could continue to dream of a Mitteleuropa organized and led by Germans.[117] The German revolution of 1918 did not necessarily alter the basic tenets of German Central European policy, for circles that had espoused Mitteleuropa ideas helped to found the Weimar republic.

2 German Bohemians or Sudeten Germans? 1918–1921

The first three years after the declaration of Czechoslovak independence and the end of the war distinctly showed the pattern of relations that was to prevail in Central Europe until the rise of Hitler. It was a formative period during which problems arose for which statesmen were unprepared because of the sudden, surprising outcome of the war. At the beginning, it was by no means certain what attitudes the authorities in Berlin and Vienna would take toward the new government in Prague, nor was it clear to Germans and Austrians what the policy of the Czechoslovak government would be toward its neighbors. By the middle of November 1918 the governments in all three capitals based their claims to authority on a successful revolution, and it was to their advantage to appear free of old imperial traditions. But almost immediately there arose the inevitable questions about potential nationality conflicts, territorial disputes, and trade and tariff policies. Nor could the larger questions of international politics leave the relations among the Central European countries unaffected.

The first three parts of this chapter focus on the period between October 1918 and the summer of 1919. The early postwar conflicts between Czechs and Germans in Bohemia, Moravia, and Silesia; the initial diplomatic contacts between Berlin and Prague; and the political struggles at the Paris peace conference reflected the uncertainty about the territorial extent of the new Czechoslovak republic. After the conclusion of the peace treaties of Versailles and St. Germain in June and September 1919, respectively, the consolidation of the new political order in Central Europe became the primary concern of the day. The last three parts of the chapter treat the efforts to establish a stable political and socioeconomic order in Czechoslovakia, the creation of new alignments among the Danubian states, and the impact of international disputes on Central European diplomacy. In each case, those topics are approached from the standpoint of their effect on Czechoslovak-German relations. It should become apparent that Czechoslovakia enjoyed strong political leadership with clear concepts of foreign and domestic policies. There was more fluidity in postwar German diplomacy, however, and many Germans within Czechoslovakia faced basic questions about their identity. Although a certain measure of stability had been achieved by the end of 1921, the title of the chapter should illustrate the many uncertainties of the early postwar years.

THE GERMAN-BOHEMIAN GOVERNMENT

Responsible Czech politicians undoubtedly preferred to have at least token German cooperation in the founding of the republic. The meeting between Beneš and domestic Czech leaders in Geneva in late October 1918 resulted in a decision to include a German in the cabinet, and Masaryk also favored recruiting Germans for responsible political positions. It was clearly in Czechoslovak interests to present an image of unity and tranquility to the outside world, particularly at a time when decisions were being made about the postwar map of Europe. The German-Bohemians therefore had a valuable commodity to sell in a voluntary acquiescence to the republic. It is conceivable that through active participation they could have helped fashion a constitutional order more to their liking than was the one that eventually emerged.[1] Yet it should be remembered that the revolution came quickly and that most German-Bohemians were not psychologically conditioned for an abrupt change in the power relationships among the nationalities. The founders of the new republic were firmly resolved to establish a bureaucratically centralized Czechoslovak nation-state. German-Bohemian leaders feared Czech dominance in such a construct. They fought to detach the predominantly German areas from the new republic.

On the day after the proclamation of Czechoslovak independence the German-Bohemian delegates in the Austrian Reichsrat announced the separation of their lands from the Czech areas and their inclusion as an autonomous province within the Austrian state. They chose Liberec (Reichenberg) as the capital, began the formation of government administrative organs and a *Volkswehr*, and elected Rafael Pacher the head of the government.[2] Pacher never filled that position, accepting instead the more sedate job in Vienna as State Secretary for Education.[3] The role of *Landeshauptmann* for German-Bohemia therefore came in early November to Rudolf Lodgman von Auen, who as a member of the Austrian Reichsrat and Bohemian Landtag had advocated a federalization of Austria during the war. After the military debacle, Lodgman attempted to salvage what he could for the Germans, and he remained for years one of their more irreconcilable leaders.[4] The German-Bohemian delegates, aware of their extreme vulnerability, concluded their resolution of separation from Bohemia with a warning that was prophetic, if tragic: "The forceful denial of the right of self-determination to the German people in Bohemia would inevitably lead to a situation when force would have to decide the struggle between the peoples."[5] The right of national self-determination remained the watchword of the Germans for years, but the threat of force in the future mirrored simply the current weakness of the Germans.

German-Bohemia was only one of four areas that proclaimed their separation from Bohemia and Moravia in the post-October 28 days. There were as well the Sudetenland, German Southern Moravia, and the Bohemian Forest District. The Sudetenland, taking its name from the Sudeten mountains along the Silesian frontier, was second to German-Bohemia in political and economic importance. It also had its own separate administration and *Landeshauptmann.* German Southern Moravia and the Bohemian Forest District did not have the size, the population, the natural resources, or the industry that the German areas in the north possessed. The political movements in these areas failed to establish so well-developed an administration as German-Bohemia and the Sudetenland, and the main goal of their activities was simply inclusion in Lower and Upper Austria. Together, these four areas included most of the frontier districts of Bohemia, Moravia, and Silesia.[6]

The potential danger to the new Czechoslovak state of having Germans in almost complete control of the areas bordering Germany and Austria was obvious. On the other hand, the fact that the German settlements were strung around the frontier areas made it practically impossible for them to constitute a unified state or to be incorporated as a separate province into either Germany or Austria. The people had never thought of themselves as a unified folk, and over the centuries of their settlement in Bohemia, Moravia, and Silesia they had come from separate German states and tribes. In short, there was no such thing as a *Sudetendeutscher Stamm.*[7] The political situation in 1918 and 1919 dictated cooperation among the Germans. Lodgman, Josef Seliger, the local head of the German Social Democratic party, and Robert Freissler, the *Landeshauptmann* for the Sudetenland, acted as their main spokesmen. However, this was a political expedient and not an expression of a close historical or geographical union among the German peoples in Bohemia, Moravia, and Silesia.

Almost until October 29 it was not clear that the Germans could compromise their differences and agree on common policy. Only at the beginning of October did the representatives of the German Nationals, the Christian Socials and the German Social Democrats in the Austrian Reichsrat meet together and agree on the formation of a German bloc dedicated to achieving national self-determination for the Germans in Bohemia, Moravia, and Silesia.[8] That action was at least partly due to the formation of a similar parliamentary bloc by the Czechs a few days earlier. The initiative for cooperation among the Germans came from the Social Democrats, who had previously held themselves aloof from the German bourgeois parties while cultivating friendly relations with their Czech counterparts. With the old Habsburg realm in dissolution, both the Czech and the German Social Democrats abandoned their internationalism, at least temporarily, in order to seek refuge with their fellow nationals in the new nation-states of Central Europe. The Social Democratic resolution, to which the other German parties agreed, recognized the right of national self-determination of all the peoples of the empire. It demanded the same rights for the Germans and strongly opposed the inclusion of German territory in the new non-German states.[9]

If the German Social Democrats had long sought to cooperate with their Czech counterparts, many German industrialists remained less than enthusiastic about a division of the historic provinces. German industries in the border areas depended on the Czech lands for markets, and there was justifiable fear of the destruction of these industries should they be separated from Bohemia. The German industrial areas could not exist separately as an economic unit; geography prevented them from being economically a part of Austria if the rest of Bohemia and Moravia were not; and the competition of Reich-German industries might ruin them if they became a part of Germany. German businessmen were caught between their national loyalties and their economic interests. As early as October 14 the German ambassador in Vienna, Count Wedel, reported that the German industrialists of northern Bohemia were not enthusiastic about an incorporation of the area into the Reich.[10] Even the more nationalistic of Prague's two major German newspapers, the *Deutsche Zeitung Bohemia,* printed an editorial on October 19 entitled "Doubting Is Not Betrayal," in which it pointed out the economic disadvantages of separating the industrial areas from Bohemia and Moravia and including them in the Reich. The newspaper did not argue that the German areas ought to become part of a new Czechoslovak state, but it did call for a fair hearing for legitimate economic concerns.[11]

From the standpoint of German industrial interests, the economically sensible solution was to remain a part of Czechoslovakia and to work for some sort of customs confederation among the successor states. The thought of becoming a national minority in a Slavic state, however, did much to counteract the economic sense of German industrialists, who were accustomed to being a dominant force in the old empire. On October 24 the leading German industrialists met in Reichenberg and adopted a resolution calling for the right of national self-determination for the Germans. They wanted inclusion in Austria, but, should the Czechs obstruct the policy, they called for a joining of German-Bohemia with the Reich. In adopting their resolution they protested that their national loyalty was just as true as that of Germans of other economic classes.[12] They took that position largely because of the pressure of the moment and the feelings of their fellow Germans. At best, however, they remained lukewarm to the idea of separation from Bohemia and Moravia, and if they did not oppose the separation movement they also did not actively support it. When the Czechs occupied the German areas during the next two months, the industrial interests were among the first to make their peace with the Czech authorities.

The situation at the end of October found the Czechs with a national council in Prague laying claim to all of Bohemia, Moravia, and the formerly Austrian part of Silesia, while the Germans were establishing governments in the border areas and proclaiming their separation from the Czech lands. The Czechs were in much the stronger position. They had twice the population; they possessed a respectable police and military force in the form of the Sokol members, augmented by the legionnaires returning from the front; and they were exhilarated by their triumphant declaration of independence from the old Habsburg authorities. Moreover, with the approach of winter in a Central Europe racked by the Spanish influenza and starved by the war and the blockade, the Czechs possessed a greater store of foodstuffs than did the German-Bohemians. Czechs dominated the agricultural central portions of Bohemia and Moravia and traditionally supplied foodstuffs to Germans in the industrial border areas. During the course of the war, however, there had been a growing tendency among Czech peasants to horde their produce; and, as the Germans had made sacrifices for the war effort, they had found themselves increasingly weaker and dependent on the Czechs. In the face of the Bolshevik menace that seemed to haunt Central and Eastern Europe in the winter of 1918-19, the Americans and the Western Allies delivered food shipments to those authorities whom they were trying to support; and the young Czechoslovak government enjoyed the full blessing of Wilson and the Allies.[13] It was the Czechs who would distribute the food relief. On the other side, the German-Bohemians and German-Moravians could count on no help from Austria or Germany, which were themselves impoverished and torn by revolution. Dire necessity forced the Germans to take the initiative in seeking an understanding with the Czech authorities.

In early November German representatives came to Prague in order to confer with the Czech National Committee.[14] The Germans sought a modus vivendi by which each nationality would rule in its own area until the peace conference drew new international boundaries—and they wanted the delivery of food supplies to the German areas of the country. The Czechs were willing to send foodstuffs to the Germans, but at a price, and that price was German recognition of the National Committee as the legal government over all Bohemia, Moravia, and Silesia. On all sides nerves were frayed and emotions at a fever pitch. Alois Rašín, one of the more brilliant but volatile of the Czech leaders, supposedly greeted Josef Seliger, the head of the German Social Democratic Party, with the remark: "We don't negotiate with traitors!"[15] A few days later Seliger related the insult in a fiery speech to a German audience, and throughout the interwar years nationalist orators always succeeded in arousing deep resentment among Germans with a reminder of Rašín's words. At the meeting in Prague, the German delegates remained unwilling to exchange political concessions for economic advantages. With the Czechs claiming the whole of the historic lands and the Germans insisting on a division, the demands of the two groups were irreconcilable. The German delegation left with no agreement.

Things did not long continue in a stalemate. In the middle of November the Czech National Committee began to send legionnaires into the German areas to occupy the towns and cities. They met with little effective resistance. Only occasionally were there clashes with small bands of German youths, and there were few injuries or deaths. The hasty efforts of the German-Bohemian government to organize a militia had come to naught. The German population was simply too demoralized and exhausted from their sacrifices in a losing war to be willing or able to respond to the challenge of the Czech authorities. Moreover, it was by no means certain that the majority of the German-Bohemians actually wanted to be detached from Czechoslovakia. The German consul-general reported to Berlin that a plebiscite among the German-Bohemians would not necessarily yield a majority in favor of joining the Reich.[16] The German-Bohemian government was never able to rely on the active support of the German population; and, with the impending occupation of Reichenberg, Lodgman and his government fled into exile on December 11. By the end of the month the Czechs were in complete control of the German lands. Lodgman and his friends went to Zittau in Saxony, across the border from Reichenberg. They met with a cool reception from Saxon officials, who refused them permission to conduct their government-in-exile, as planned, in either Zittau or Dresden.[17] Finding a similar attitude in Kurt Eisner's Bavaria, they continued around the borders of Bohemia until they reached Vienna, where they were free to conduct their propaganda.

In the chaotic weeks after the revolutions and the armistice, it was natural that the Austrian government took more interest in the fate of the German-Bohemians than did Berlin. Whereas the Czech leadership showed little or no desire for former Imperial German territory, Bohemia, Moravia, and Silesia had been the most valuable provinces of the Habsburg Empire. The Germans inhabited the richest sections of those lands and controlled most of the industries and the mines. If Austria could have retained just the German-Bohemian areas, it would have salvaged much of its former industrial capacity. The wealth of German-Bohemia helps to explain why even a Social Democratic minister of defense in Austria attempted to supply the German-Bohemians with arms in their fight against the Czechs and tried to persuade the Bavarians to do likewise.[18] As the Czech legionnaires occupied the German lands in November and December, the

Austrian government submitted repeated protests to Prague. The Czechoslovak government ignored the protests and refused to recognize any diplomatic representative of Vienna so long as the Austrians laid claim to Bohemia and Moravia. The Czechs declined to place the German-Bohemian question before an arbitration commission, as the Austrian Foreign Secretary, Otto Bauer, had suggested. Confident of Western support, they informed the Austrians that the Entente would settle the dispute shortly by notifying Vienna that German-Bohemia was to be included in Czechoslovakia.[19] Austrian authorities, in turn, welcomed Lodgman and the German-Bohemian exile government and cooperated with them in their propaganda activities.

The most striking success of Lodgman's exile government came in February 1919 at the International Socialist Congress in Berne. In their attempt to revive the Second International, the founders of the Congress hoped that their meeting would aid Wilson's efforts toward achieving a liberal peace settlement in Paris. For them, the keystone of the new territorial settlements should be the principle of national self-determination, which, to be effective, would have to be applied impartially to all nationalities. Over the bitter opposition of the Czech socialist delegates, the congress endorsed the right of German-Bohemians to national self-determination.[20] That was precisely the principle on which Lodgman's government was basing its separatist movement. If most German-Bohemians supported Lodgman, it was only through a violation of national self-determination that the Czechs could hope to establish a viable state. After the meeting at Berne there was temporarily a new buoyancy among the German separatists, who imagined that their representatives would continue on to Paris in order to sway the peace conference even as they had carried their point among the socialists. But as of mid-February Western statesmen were by no means prepared to receive representatives from the enemy powers, and the German delegation was forced to return to Vienna, there to continue its ultimately futile agitation.

For tactical reasons, Lodgman and his exile government maintained little open connection with Berlin. But even as he was leaving Vienna for the socialist congress, Lodgman had met with a German diplomatic representative and had discussed ways in which the Berlin government could support his cause. Preferably, it could concentrate detachments of troops on the frontier and, upon the invitation of the German-Bohemian government, march them in as police forces. If, however, Berlin should fear such overt action, it could simply build up weapons supplies along the border so that the German-Bohemians could cross over and get them for an uprising against the Czechs.[21] Even Lodgman could not have taken those ideas seriously in February 1919. It was obvious that the German-Bohemian population had no desire for a struggle with the Czech legionnaires. Nor could the leaders of the young German republic, as they were preparing for the opening of the Weimar National Assembly and as the peace conference was holding its initial sessions in Paris, become involved in any way in an armed conflict with the Czech authorities. Caution ruled supreme in Berlin; there was no possibility for effective military support for the German-Bohemians; and Lodgman therefore counseled against verbal pronouncements of support by the Weimar National Assembly.[22] If military power sufficient to wrest control of the German-Bohemian areas from the Czechs was not available, the German-Bohemian government preferred to stand alone, relying on the moral influence of their plea for national self-determination.

Open cooperation with Berlin was impolitic at the moment, and any attempt to tie the German-Bohemian areas with Austria would have resulted in an utterly unviable geographical monstrosity. The exile government therefore aimed officially at the establishment of an independent German-Bohemian state. But Lodgman and his associates had no intention that that state should continue to survive indefinitely even if such were possible. They regarded German-Bohemia simply as a temporary construction until the time when it could break up and join the neighboring states within the Reich. With their claim to national self-determination, they calculated that they could more easily win the agreement of the peace conference for an independent state than for an immediate inclusion within Germany. But once they had established their state and after wartime animosities had begun to fade, they believed that the Western powers could do nothing if the new German state voluntarily elected to join the Reich.[23] The doctrine of national self-determination had won acceptance only at a very late date among the German-Bohemian nationalists, who had steadfastly opposed the national claims of the Czechs in the Habsburg Empire. These German-Bohemian nationalists then used the doctrine not primarily in the interests of insuring their own independent existence but rather in the hopes of realizing the old nationalist ideal of a Great-German state.

Although the pan-Germans had achieved their greatest political successes before the war in the German-Bohemian areas, it was by no means the case that all German-Bohemians had embraced their doctrines. The temporary unity among the German-Bohemians in the months after the war arose only from the circumstances of the moment. As time went on, and as it became obvious that the German territories would indeed remain a part of the Czechoslovak republic, the political factions among the German-Bohemians began to reassert themselves.

National hopes and aspirations branched into many different directions, and few Germans could quickly reconcile themselves emotionally to their existence in a Czechoslovak state. But many did continue to look to

Vienna rather than Berlin. Some were romantics who harbored fond memories of the culture of the Danubian empire. Many members of the upper levels of society wistfully remembered the cosmopolitan social life of the old imperial capital. Others were devout Catholics who looked to Vienna as the defender of Catholicism in Central Europe. Still others were Jews who had gained influential positions and occasionally nobility in the Habsburg Empire. The leading German newspapers in Prague, *Deutsche Zeitung Bohemia* and *Prager Tagblatt*, in which Jewish influence was considerable and even dominant, were more inclined to Vienna than to Berlin.[24] German industrialists and businessmen hoped to retain their commercial ties with Vienna and therefore with the Danubian area despite the new national boundaries. Those people could only have mixed emotions about coming under Berlin.

Yet for the German nationalists the question "Vienna or Berlin?" was pointless in 1919. They aimed not only at the incorporation of the German-Bohemian areas within the Reich but also at the Anschluss of Austria as well. And again their plea was national self-determination. The demonstrations in various parts of Austria in support of an Anschluss gave weight to their case, and a consistent application of Wilson's principle pointed toward Austria's inclusion in the Reich. From a pan-German viewpoint, whether or not the German-Bohemian government ostensibly aimed at establishing an independent state, whether or not the emotional ties of many German-Bohemians were still with Vienna rather than Berlin, the prospects for the future were that a Great-German state would arise in Europe. Incorporating the German Austrians and the German Bohemians, it would find the moral justification for its existence in that ultimate expression of triumphant nationalism—national self-determination.

The power to effect such changes, however, lay solely in the hands of the peacemakers in Paris. In the winter and spring of 1919 the members of the German-Bohemian exile government in Vienna could only wait and hope for an opportunity to present their case before the peace conference. Meanwhile, politicians and diplomats in Berlin and Prague were actively seeking a new relationship in the postwar world.

INITIAL ENCOUNTERS BETWEEN BERLIN AND PRAGUE

Lodgman and his German-Bohemian exile government represented the intransigent attitudes that never completely disappeared at any point in the interwar period. But from the very beginning there were also many moderate voices among the Germans that urged accommodation and cooperation with the Czechs. Even before the end of the war when it became obvious that the Czechs and Slovaks were going to succeed in establishing their own state, divided councils ruled among Imperial

German diplomats concerning policy toward an independent Czecho-slovakia. Some were as irreconcilable as Lodgman; others were impres-sively realistic and levelheaded. In the middle of October, with the Habsburg Empire in obvious dissolution, the German ambassador in Vienna, Count Wedel, called a conference with his Saxon and Bavarian counterparts as well as with Reich-German military representatives in Vienna. The purpose was to agree on a strategy toward Austrian problems, and uppermost in Wedel's mind was the German-Bohemian question. He argued that the Reich should start preparing for a military intervention on behalf of the German-Bohemians in the event of the establishment of an independent Czechoslovakia. The German-Bohemians would otherwise be submerged in the new Czech state, for their geographical situation made it impossible for them to rely on the Austrian Germans. In addition to stressing the need to protect fellow Germans against Slavic domination, he pointed out that the northern Bohemian coalfields would be a major acquisition for the German economy. Wedel found support among his listeners, who agreed to coordinate policy toward Austria and the German-Bohemians.[25] In the following weeks Wedel continued to argue that, if Czechoslovakia was weakened economically by the loss of the border areas, the Czechoslovak government might eventually be willing to enter into "tolerable relations" with Germany.[26]

There is actually little evidence that officials of the Foreign Office in Berlin agreed with Wedel's opinions or desired an intervention in Bohemia and Moravia. In October 1918, Prince Max's government was wrestling with the myriad problems called forth by the collapse of the German war effort. Faced with urgent demands from the supreme command for an immediate armistice, with Wilson's increasingly stringent armistice notes, with the task of quickly democratizing Bismarck's authoritarian state— haunted by the prospect of revolution and civil war—the politicians and bureaucrats in Berlin could devote scant attention to problems that in more peaceful times would have received top priority. For that reason the archives of the German Foreign Office contain many more reports coming from abroad than instructions emanating from Berlin. On the day that the Czechs proclaimed their new state, the state-secretary for foreign affairs, Wilhelm Solf, did inquire of the high command at Spa concerning the possibility of sending troops to German-Bohemia.[27] Hindenburg answered on that same day that some forces could be sent but that they would be suitable only for police duties and not for combat against front-line Czech soldiers.[28] In any case, the rush of events quickly made such ideas utterly fanciful.

A much more moderate and conciliatory voice was coming from Prague at the same time that Wedel was urging intervention from Vienna. In the week before the proclamation of the Czechoslovak republic, the Imperial

German consul-general, Baron Friedrich von Gebsattel, warned that the Czechs, determined to retain all Bohemia and Moravia, would never reconcile themselves to German annexation of the border areas. German-Bohemia and German-Moravia could easily become a new Alsace-Lorraine in the east. Even if Germany successfully acquired and kept those areas, Czechoslovakia and the other Slavic states would surely retaliate by disrupting German trade relations in Central Europe. In Gebsattel's opinion, it was better that the Reich not add to its troubles by becoming involved in a dispute about the border territories.[29]

Gebsattel believed that a peaceful, conciliatory policy was also in the interests of the Germans in Bohemia and Moravia. He wanted the German-Bohemians, for their own welfare, to reach a compromise agreement with Czech leaders as quickly as possible. In view of conditions in Central Europe and Allied support of the Czechs, a conflict with the Czechs would be a hopeless venture for the German-Bohemians. On the other hand, from the Czech viewpoint, it would be wise to conciliate such a large and potentially powerful segment of the population as the German-Bohemians represented. The more stable and peaceful Czechoslovakia appeared from the very beginning, the stronger would be its diplomatic position with the Western powers. Gebsattel therefore hoped that Czech authorities would be willing to grant more concessions to the German-Bohemians the earlier the Germans reconciled themselves to an existence in the new Czech state. Each side stood to benefit by being moderate and cooperative with the other from the outset.[30] Such were the views of the Imperial German consul-general in Prague on October 25, three days before the actual proclamation of the Czechoslovak republic. The split between Wedel and Gebsattel concerning policy toward the Czechs was simply an early example of the diverse currents that continued to characterize German attitudes toward Czechoslovakia for years to come.

In the dying days of the German Empire Gebsattel was left to deal largely on his own with the Czech National Committee after the proclamation of the Czechoslovak republic on October 28. On October 29—the very day of the founding of the German-Bohemian government—Gebsattel visited the National Committee on his own initiative, primarily in order to express his concern for the safety of the Reich Germans in Czechoslovakia.[31] The Czechs received him in friendly fashion, and the next day the German consul in Brno (Brünn) followed Gebsattel's example and established initial contacts in Moravia as well.[32] But military preparations for a possible intervention in Bohemia had not yet been abandoned by Imperial German officials, who claimed to be "free of all aggressive tendencies."[33] Imperial Germany came closest to active military intervention in Czechoslovakia in the first week of November, when food riots broke out in the

German-Bohemian border areas. Reich-German authorities prepared to dispatch troops to act as police forces in quelling the disorders but soon desisted as a result of pressure from Vienna and Prague. The foreign secretary in Vienna, Victor Adler, appealed to Berlin not to intervene, fearing that the Czechs would respond by occupying all the German areas of Bohemia and Moravia. Gebsattel quickly warned that an intervention would destroy his efforts to establish good relations with the Czech National Council.[34] In any event, Berlin was powerless to undertake serious military initiatives in November 1918, and the plan was dropped.

In Prague Gebsattel was convinced that Entente troops would occupy Bohemia and Moravia in the immediate future. He feared especially for the welfare of the Reich Germans in Czechoslovakia, and on November 2 he again visited the National Committee in order to get assurance concerning the safety of the Germans. In contrast with their earlier attitude, however, the Czech leaders reacted coolly and inquired whether any news had come from Berlin. Gebsattel understood them to be referring to formal recognition by Imperial Germany of the new Czechoslovak state and went back to his consulate to think matters over. He then made the decision to return to the National Committee and to announce on his own authority that the Imperial German government would welcome a Czech diplomatic representative in Berlin and that formal recognition was thereby being extended to the Czechoslovak republic. The members of the Czech National Committee immediately reacted in the friendliest fashion and gave Gebsattel all the assurances he desired concerning the safety of the Reich Germans.[35] Rumors subsequently spread about a supposed remark by Gebsattel that Germany desired not a square inch of Bohemian or Moravian territory. He made no mention of such an assertion in his report to Berlin; but the rumor did help to inflame the passions of the German-Bohemian leaders, for it undercut their claims to the right of national self-determination.

That a local consul-general could attempt to make the decision concerning diplomatic recognition of a new state was further testimony of the chaotic conditions in early November 1918. Fearing for the safety of the Germans in Czechoslovakia and believing that the formal recognition was unavoidable anyway, Gebsattel nevertheless far exceeded his authority, as he himself admitted. On November 7, Foreign Secretary Solf informed Gebsattel that it was impossible to extend recognition to Czechoslovakia while refusing to recognize Austrian independence (after all, the question of the Anschluss was very much up in the air), and he developed an interpretation of Gebsattel's action that stopped short of formal diplomatic recognition. Solf admitted that good relations with Czechoslovakia were desirable, and he observed that the lack of diplomatic recognition would not prejudice "the territorial question." The clear implication of that statement was that Berlin had no designs on the German-Bohemian border areas. However, he advised "cautious aloofness from the Czech authorities until events could take a more definite direction."[36] But it was Prague rather than Berlin that had time on its side. Two days after Solf dispatched his telegram, revolution swept away the imperial regime, and the German republic was proclaimed.

Friedrich Ebert's government soon demonstrated its desire to exchange diplomatic representatives with Prague, and it was thereby less cautious about recognizing the Czechoslovak republic than the government of Prince Max had been. But, like their predecessors, the Social Democratic leaders confronted many worries more pressing than the situation in Bohemia and Moravia, and day-to-day administration proceeded much as it had during the imperial regime. Only gradually did changes come in the German diplomatic service after the revolution of November 9. The same men stayed initially in the same posts, writing reports for the republican government similar to those that they had written for the emperor. On their printed stationery they did cross out the word *Kaiserlich* but sometimes forgot to do even that. In Prague, Gebsattel continued his policy of conciliation under increasingly difficult circumstances. As the Czechs prepared to occupy the German-Bohemian areas in late November, Gebsattel warned Berlin not to assist the German-Bohemians and urged that German policy not alienate the Czechs, who would be influential at the peace conference and who were destined to assume the leadership of the Slavic nationalities.[37] Gebsattel's recommendations seem to have been in accord with such thinking as there was about Bohemia and Moravia in the German Foreign Office.

Until Masaryk's return to Prague at Christmastime, the leading political figure in Bohemia was Karel Kramář, who served until July 1919 as the first premier of Czechoslovakia. Kramář's conversations with German representatives during November accented his overweening confidence in the strength of the Czech position. Kramář reminded the Germans that their two countries were still formally at war; that the Czechs must remain loyal to their Western allies by not sending any official representative to Berlin; that the Germans were beaten to a worse degree than they themselves realized; and that there was a universal hatred of Germans and things German, which would take years to overcome. Only in a provisional trade agreement might there be an early understanding between the two countries. But there did exist a common danger for both peoples, and that was the threat of Bolshevism. As the German representative paraphrased Kramář's remarks,

[Between Czechoslovakia and the Soviet Union] there is formally a state of war, and this state of war will be used to deport all undesirable elements who can be shown to be engaging in Bolshevik propaganda.

The struggle against Bolshevism is a question that concerns both Germany and the Czechoslovak republic. It can in no way be in Germany's interests for the Bolshevik movement to spread to Bohemia. I pointed out that in my opinion both states should support one another in the fighting of Bolshevism. The premier handled this question in a very lively manner and with obvious interest.[38]

The Ebert government's most useful diplomatic tool was the threat of a Bolshevization of Central Europe; for, if nothing else, the creation of a common enemy might help the German republic break out of its diplomatic isolation. Its desire to see a Czech representative in Berlin reflected the hope of casting off the liabilities of the Imperial German legacy and of being treated like one of the successor governments to the old empires. Acceptance by the Czechs might be a step toward acceptance by the Western powers. The Ebert government was already incurring the enmity of the Bolsheviks in any case, and Ebert and the Majority Socialists genuinely feared the Bolshevik threat within Germany itself.

Kramář was among the most extreme anti-Bolsheviks in Prague, where it was not difficult to arouse animosity toward the Bolsheviks in view of the fact that the Czech legionnaires had been fighting along the Trans-Siberian railway for months. A wealthy man with conservative bourgeois tastes, Kramář had a Russian wife, had been one of the foremost neo-Slavists before the war, and had advocated placing a Russian prince on the throne of St. Wenceslas. All the more bitter was his reaction, therefore, as he witnessed the Bolshevik revolutionaries seizing control of the country on which he would have most liked to rely. But Kramář was also an ardent nationalist, and if he despised the Bolsheviks he feared the Germans. Long a leader of the Czech national movement, Kramář's imprisonment and death sentence by the Austrians during the war had made him an abiding enemy of all things German. There could be little hope for genuine understanding between Prague and Berlin so long as Kramář influenced Czech policy.

With the election of Tomáš G. Masaryk as the first president of Czechoslovakia on November 14, 1918, followed by his triumphant return to Prague on December 21, foreign representatives had a considerably more sophisticated and levelheaded man with whom to deal. The sixty-eight-year-old Masaryk's reputation as an idealist and a humanist was already well established. Widely credited among his countrymen with having achieved Czechoslovak independence by his work in the Western capitals during the war, he was held in such reverence that throughout the first Czechoslovak republic it was political suicide to attack him directly. Masaryk, too, was a nationalist, as his lectures and articles during the war amply demonstrated, but with his nationalism he combined a sensitivity and a perspective that enabled him to understand and appreciate the legitimate aspirations of other nations and peoples. Masaryk and Kramář differed not only in the breadth of their vision in foreign affairs but also in their attitudes on the fundamental social problems created by an industrial society. Besides his national loyalties Masaryk retained a social commitment that put him on the moderate left in the Czechoslovak political spectrum—more sympathetic toward the "socialist" than toward the "bourgeois" parties, although, as president, he remained officially above political party strife. Almost three decades earlier Masaryk had broken with Kramář's Young Czech party and had formed his own political party, which had remained numerically weak but had nevertheless been influential because of Masaryk's reputation. With conflicting personalities and varying political and social attitudes, Masaryk and Kramář could hardly be expected to work closely together. After his initial contributions toward founding the republic Kramář and his National Democratic party retained only secondary significance during the interwar period, while Masaryk wielded ultimate political authority in the republic until 1935.

Although the German consulate continued to exist and to function during the first months of 1919, the Czechoslovak government refused to recognize it as an official representation of the German republic. The new German foreign minister, Count Ulrich von Brockdorff-Rantzau, therefore chose Professor Samuel Saenger to be his personal representative in Prague. The reasons for that choice were not hard to find. Saenger and Masaryk had long been personal acquaintances, and the two professors shared similar political and social attitudes.[39] Saenger went to Prague in January 1919 and served as minister in every way except in name, although diplomatic relations were not formally begun for more than a year. On February 6 he reported about a conversation with Masaryk in which Masaryk insisted on the historic borders of the Bohemian crown yet promised lenient treatment of the German minority, mentioning English local government as a pattern. In economic matters, Masaryk thought that it would be necessary to establish some sort of Eastern European confederation in which Austria and Hungary would be included. Although the claim to the historic boundaries was nothing new, Masaryk's espousal of the idea of an economic confederation in Eastern Europe was to gain added significance in the light of the subsequent opposition of Czechoslovakia to any such plan. Other reports emanated from Prague in the winter and spring of 1919 that confirmed Masaryk's receptivity to proposals for international economic cooperation in the Danubian area.[40] Apparently, nothing was ever spelled out, nor were any concrete plans formulated. The pervasive concern about the possible spread of Bolshevism tinged that conversation between Masaryk and Saenger, who were certainly not among the more fearful or reactionary politicians at the time. They agreed on the mutual interests of their states in combatting the spread of Bolshevism, for any daily newspaper told of strikes, riots, and attempted assassinations in the chaotic aftermath of the war.[41] One of the first tangible signs of cooperation between the two countries was the collaboration of their police forces in tracking down communist agitators.[42]

Just as significant as Masaryk's remarks was the advice that Saenger appended to his message to Berlin. Far from encouraging a German irredentist program in Czechoslovakia, Saenger counseled the Foreign Office to urge the German-Bohemians to cooperate with the Czech majority. If by working with the Czechs the German-Bohemians could acquire a political influence commensurate with their numbers and economic strength, they would be a potent force in the new state. Berlin could use them in order to bend Prague toward a friendlier attitude toward Germany. Relations with Vienna should be cultivated so that Austria could serve as "the bridge to the southeast and especially to the so-decisive Czechoslovak state."[43] Saenger was aware that this policy required patience and delicate diplomacy, but he thought that the rewards were worth the effort. His more sophisticated policy, which could claim a peaceful intent and might eventually yield higher rewards, found more resonance in Berlin than the irredentism of Lodgman and the German-Bohemian government.

THE PEACE SETTLEMENTS

The countries of Central Europe had little influence at the Paris peace conference. As defeated powers, Germany, Austria, and Hungary could not participate in inter-Allied negotiations. For the German-Bohemians this meant that they had no effective opportunity to present their case to the peacemakers. Czechoslovakia was eventually recognized as a belligerent power from the day of its independence, but despite its formal status as a partner of the great powers the young republic was in fact a suppliant for their favors. Beneš remained in Paris until September 1919 and acted as the chief spokesman for Czechoslovakia. In presenting the Czechoslovak case his strategy was twofold. He tried to picture the country as an island of calm and order in Central Europe where the peacemakers need not worry about the dangers of social revolution. At the same time he encouraged authorities in Prague to stage a series of faits accomplis in order to occupy and control those territories upon which Czechoslovakia was making a legal claim at the peace conference.[44] The fundamental issues for Czechoslovakia involved territorial questions. Disputes over border territories led to open fighting between the Czechs and Poland and Hungary. In contrast, Berlin's refusal to exploit the discontent of the German-Bohemians was indicative of the way in which German policy toward Czechoslovakia would develop in the Weimar years.

From the day of independence the Czechs had seemed confident that their new state would include all of the historic lands of the Bohemian crown. Not only were they able to establish their control throughout Bohemia, Moravia, and Silesia, but they also enjoyed the firm support of the Western powers—or so they alleged. When the Austrians protested in December against the Czech occupation of the German areas, the Czechs curtly retorted that the Entente would soon inform Vienna that Czechoslovakia was to possess the historic boundaries of Bohemia and Moravia.[45] Such news was not forthcoming from the West. On the contrary, in early January the London *Times* published an officially inspired editorial that aroused panic in Prague. The *Times* castigated the nationalities of Eastern Europe for their chauvinism in trying to seize every bit of territory available. The newspaper warned that the peace conference would not tolerate any fait accompli in the area and proclaimed that the final settlement should be based on the principle of national self-determination.[46] The idea that the only way by which Czechoslovakia could possess its historic boundaries was by a departure from general Allied policy and the thinly veiled accusation that the Czechs, among others, were trying to present the peace conference with a fait accompli inspired an early retort from Prague.

On January 14, Karel Kramář revealed in the National Assembly the reasons for the previous Czech optimism about the borders. He read aloud passages of a formerly secret treaty concluded in Paris on St. Wenceslas's Day (September 28) 1918 between France and the Czechoslovak National Council. The last part of the second article of the treaty read:

> The French government obligates itself to support the reconstitution of an independent Czechoslovak state within the boundaries of its former historic lands.[47]

Kramář also read an excerpt from a note of Foreign Minister Pichon in which, in the midst of diplomatic niceties, Pichon promised French support for Czech acquisition of the historic boundaries.[48] The mere promise of diplomatic support by the French failed to impress either the German or the Austrian representatives in Prague, who noted a growing anxiety among the Czechs as the time of decision approached in Paris. At the end of February Czech authorities arrested the German vice-consul on charges of espionage and accused the Austrian government of planning military attacks against Czechoslovakia. The authorities temporarily forbade the publication of Prague's *Deutsche Zeitung Bohemia,* which was allegedly implicated in the case. In fact, both of Prague's major German newspapers had secretly offered to publish articles for the Austrian government. Officials of the *Bohemia* claimed subsequently, however, that the real reason for the shutdown was that the Czechs had not wanted its voice in support of self-determination for the Germans to be heard at a time when the peace conference was making its decision on the issue.[49] There was reason to censor the news coming from Czechoslovakia in view of Beneš's efforts to portray the country as an island of calm and order. On March 14, 1919, German-Bohemians staged mass demonstrations protesting the denial of their right to national self-determination. The Czech occupation had prevented their participation in the election of the Austrian parliament, which was convening on that day. In several different towns, nervous Czech police fired on the demonstrators, killing fifty-two Germans and wounding eighty-four others.[50] This was the worst incident of its kind in the short history of the young republic.

In the early stages of the peace conference it appeared that a struggle was developing between those who gave precedence to the idea of national self-determination and those who insisted on historic boundaries for strategic and economic reasons. It pitted the French against the Americans and the British, who claimed to stand for national self-determination. President Wilson's consternation at learning of the three million Germans living in Bohemia and Moravia was supposedly mirrored in his remark, "Masaryk never told me that."[51] The article in the *Times* reflected the disquiet in London concerning the potential fragmentation of Eastern Europe, and at the peace conference David Lloyd George quickly became impatient with what he considered to be the nationalistic claims of many Eastern Europeans.

A potentially dangerous situation for Czechoslovak diplomacy arose in the Teschen dispute with Poland. Located by the Silesian-Polish frontier, the duchy of Teschen covered approximately 850 square miles with a population of around 350,000. Its significance lay in the fact that it contained large supplies of coking coal, the possession of which could help make Czechoslovakia the dominant supplier of coal for other Danubian countries. Teschen had been part of the Czech crown lands since the fourteenth century, and the major railway connecting the Czech lands with Slovakia ran through the duchy. But Poles outnumbered Czechs approximately two to one, and there was a significant German minority as well. The Polish government claimed the area on the grounds of national self-determination, while the Czechoslovak government based its case on historical and economic arguments. On November 5, 1918, local Czech and Polish authorities in Teschen agreed to divide the duchy temporarily along ethnographic lines, leaving most of the territory under Polish administration. Prague was never willing to accept that solution, and on January 23, 1919, Czech troops crossed the demarcation line and occupied most of the economically valuable portion of Teschen. The armed conflict between Czechs and Poles created a sensation at the Paris peace conference and exposed the Czechoslovak government to bitter criticism. The diplomats in Paris continued to wrestle with the rival claims through most of 1919 and solved the problem only temporarily by agreeing to hold a plebiscite in the near future.[52] The Teschen dispute seemed to raise the possibility of an alliance between Germans and Poles in Czechoslovakia, both groups appearing to be discontented minorities. A few weeks after the occupation of Teschen, Lodgman claimed that a common struggle of Poles and Germans against Czechs was "envisaged very seriously."[53] In fact, however, the national minorities suffered from too many internecine rivalries to be able to construct a common front against the Czechoslovak authorities.

Despite the attacks on Czechoslovak policy in Teschen, the Czechoslovak government remained in a very strong diplomatic position during the peace conference. In Teschen, as in German-Bohemia, possession was nine points of the law. Although the conflict was embarrassing to the French, they fully supported the Czechoslovak position, partly because they feared that they might otherwise drive Czechoslovakia into a rapprochement with Germany.[54] Despite the tarnish on their image, the Czechs still afforded Wilson an opportunity for indulging his predilection for protecting small and exploited nations. In Masaryk, the Czechs had a leader after Wilson's own heart. More important, of course, were the services that the Czech and Slovak legionnaires were performing along the Trans-Siberian railway. In presenting the Czechoslovak case for Teschen, Beneš argued that "it would be a badly chosen moment to hurt too much their [the legionnaires'] national feeling."[55] Throughout the months of the peace conference the great powers remained dependent on the Czech legion for support in the Russian intervention. The basic góod will of the Western powers and the Czechoslovak services in Siberia were ably exploited by the two official Czechoslovak representatives at the peace conference.

Besides Beneš, the other Czechoslovak delegate at the peace conference was Karel Kramář, the first premier of the republic. Although the two men were destined to become bitter rivals in Czechoslovak politics, at the peace conference the personalities of Kramář and Beneš complemented one another and thereby strengthened the presentation of the Czechoslovak case. Kramář was the uncompromising one of the two, insisting always upon the maximum claims of the Czechs. Beneš was the more reasonable, willing to make concessions in the extreme positions of his government but using Kramář as the example of home opinion that prevented him from compromising essential issues.[56] That situation worked out well for the Czechs. The only two significant claims that the Czechs did not attain—a Czech protectorate for the Lusatian Sorbs and a land corridor between Austria and Hungary to Yugoslavia—were the two that the realist Beneš could have had little hope of achieving.[57] In the process, Beneš acquired a reputation for being a reasonable and moderate statesman.

From his wartime days in Paris Beneš had excellent contacts with French officials, and he also had an understanding of the kinds of arguments that were likely to impress Entente leaders. He appreciated the need to keep his points simple and his claims clear and direct. In the eleven memoranda that he submitted to the peace conference, he portrayed the Czechs as a peaceful people who had for centuries struggled for freedom against a dominating neighbor. He added that the Czechs were historically dedicated to democratic political and religious ideals, pointing out the Hussite struggles and the Thirty Years' War. The third memorandum was entitled "Problems Touching the Germans of Bohemia." Here Beneš argued that the 1910 Austrian census exaggerated the number of Germans in the country, there not being more than eight hundred thousand to a million in Bohemia, that almost nowhere was there such a thing as a purely German area, that from a historical viewpoint the Germans were only relatively recent "colonists," and that the new Czechoslovak government would be sure to establish a liberal administration, perhaps "on the order of Switzerland."[58] This memorandum and the others in the series did not in themselves have much effect on the decisions of the peace conference (the influence of the French representatives was decisive), but they did have significance in the interwar years. In October 1920 the *Bohemia* somehow acquired a copy of the memorandum on the Germans in Bohemia and proceeded to publish it in installments together with comments on what it considered to be Beneš's falsifications.[59] In the late 1930s the Nazis did the same thing with the entire series.[60]

At the peace conference the task of drawing the frontiers between Czechoslovakia and Germany fell to the Commission on Czechoslovak Affairs. Here, and in its subcommission, the French delegates emerged as the staunchest defenders of the Czechoslovak cause. They freely accepted the Czech claim to the historic boundaries of Bohemia, Moravia, and Silesia and supported minor border rectifications in favor of Czechoslovakia. Openly, they pursued a balance-of-power policy; they were adamant that no Germans should be transferred from previously Austrian territory to the Reich, and they followed the general line of rewarding friends and punishing enemies. The American members of the commission, Professor Charles Seymour of Yale University (later succeeded by Professor Archibald Cary Coolidge of Harvard) and the twenty-five-year-old Allen Dulles, were no match for the French in either diplomatic experience or knowledge of Central-European problems.[61] They lodged some protests in favor of the nationality principle but to no avail. The report of the commission recommended the maintenance of the historic boundaries with a minor adjustment by which Czechoslovakia would acquire some of the territory of the Glatz salient in return for German acquisition of the area around Friedland.[62]

The commission completed its work in February and March, and on April 1 its report came to the Council of Ministers for debate.[63] With some support from Arthur James Balfour, the British foreign secretary, Lansing launched a strong attack on the practice of drawing boundaries according to strategic considerations without regard for the principle of national self-determination. The American members of the commission had filed a minority recommendation that favored the transfer of the territory around Rumburg and Asch to Germany, and Lansing attempted to expand these suggestions into a general attack on the historic-strategic boundary. Lansing's criticisms finally elicited an exclamation from Pichon that expressed the essence of French policy:

> M. Pichon said that on behalf of France, he also had reservations to make. He could not allow Germany to be fortified by populations taken from what had been Austrian Dominions, taken, moreover, from Bohemia, which, he trusted, would remain an Ally of France, and handed over to Germany, which, as far as he was concerned, still remained a country to be feared. If America refused to take into account considerations of national defense, France was not in a position to neglect them.[64]

The meeting thus ended, having accomplished only a straining of tempers and having failed to reach a recommendation from the ministers for presentation to the Council of Four.

On April 4 the question of German-Czechoslovak boundaries came finally to the Big Four.[65] At the meeting Colonel House represented Wilson, who was ill. Clemenceau opened the discussion by remarking that the commission's recommendation of minor adjustments in the border was unnecessarily complicated and that it would be better simply to maintain the historic boundaries. Lloyd George and House immediately agreed to this, and the frontier between Germany and Czechoslovakia was settled. After the negotiations of the previous two months the almost offhand manner in which the final decision was made was certainly anticlimactic. The decisions concerning the borders of Bohemia and Moravia were made before the German representatives ever appeared at the conference and without the direct participation of the Czechs.

In his remarks on April 4 Clemenceau observed that any border rectifications could be left for Germany and Czechoslovakia to decide at a later date.[66] At the peace conference only minor modifications were eventually made in the historic frontier. The only ones of any significance were Hlučínsko (Hultschin), a small farming district along the Moravian-Silesian frontier, which Czechoslovakia received from Germany; Vitorazsko (Gmünd), a railway point, and Valtice-Poštorná (Feldsberg-Temenau), which came to Czechoslovakia from Austria.[67] Despite the talk about the historic boundaries it was not certain that all Czechs would resist minor cessions of territory to Germany. It was obviously dangerous

to include three-and-a-quarter million Germans in a state in which the
Czechs themselves hardly constituted a clear majority. If by small border
rectifications one could reduce the German minority, the stability of the
Czechoslovak state might be enhanced. Already in October 1918 the
Czech vice-president of the Austrian Chamber of Deputies, Vlastimil
Tusar, intimated that the Czechs might be willing to compromise on the
boundaries issue.[68] In early February Professor Coolidge reported to the
American delegation at the peace conference about a conversation with
Masaryk in Prague. Masaryk remarked that the Czechs would be willing to
fight to maintain the historic boundaries even against an unfavorable
decision of the Entente. Under questioning by Coolidge, however, Masaryk
admitted that some alterations could be made without impairing the
security or the economy of the country.[69] Word filtered to the Germans
that Beneš might be receptive to minor territorial adjustments; and in the
postwar years Beneš repeated on several occasions that at the peace
conference he had offered to cede several border areas to Germany.[70]

Actually, there was little support on the Reich-German side for an
exchange of territories or for the acquisition of small parts of Bohemia,
Moravia, and Silesia. Industrial interests in Prussian Silesia were reluctant
to face the added competition of German manufacturing in Moravia and
the formerly Austrian part of Silesia. The refusal of Saxon officials in the
winter of 1918 to give either political or military support to the
German-Bohemian government mirrored a disinclination in Dresden to
include the "less than delightful" German-Bohemians in the Saxon state.[71]
And many Germans living in the Czech lands actually feared the cession of
small amounts of border territory to Germany. The exiled representatives
of the Sudetenland opposed any partition of the German territories that
would diminish the power of the German minority in Czechoslovakia or
that would cut the age-old cultural ties among the Germans in Moravia.
Either the Germans ought to be accorded the right of national self-
determination, by which all the German-inhabited lands would join the
Reich, or the entire area should remain a part of Czechoslovakia.[72] A
minor exception to the general reluctance to see a division of the German
territories was constituted by the representatives of the Egerland, who as
late as August 1919 still hoped to break away from Bohemia and join
Bavaria.[73] But, given the existence of a German minority in Czechoslovakia, German-Bohemian leaders in general wanted to keep that
minority as large as possible.

As far as the peace settlement with Germany was concerned, the period
of greatest stress came between the submission of the draft treaty on May
7 and the signing of the final treaty on June 28. Although the Germans
used the three weeks allotted to them in May to write a voluminous
critique of the draft treaty, they succeeded in changing few of the original

stipulations. The most significant alteration concerned the fate of Upper Silesia, and that issue touched peripherally on the regions between Berlin and Prague. Upper Silesia had been Imperial Germany's second most important industrial area, accounting for over a fifth of the country's prewar coal production and supplying a considerable proportion of the mineral ores as well. It was part of a Central European manufacturing hub, which was divided at the close of the war among Germany, Poland, and Czechoslovakia. The situation along Germany's southeastern frontier was similar, therefore, to that in the west, where international political boundaries also fragmented a natural economic unit. With a mixed population—the 1910 German census showed a 60 percent Polish-speaking majority—Upper Silesia was an extremely valuable piece of real estate, where the principle of national self-determination could not be applied to the satisfaction of all parties. As the draft treaty became largely a collection of maximum demands against the Germans, it required Germany to cede the area to Poland. The Germans protested the decision, searched for support, and hoped to find it in Prague.

In the Teschen dispute Poland was also a rival of Czechoslovakia for some of those mines and industries that had lain at the junction of the three old Central and East European empires. Moreover, before the war, Upper Silesia had furnished much of the coal requirements for Slovakia, and the Prague authorities could not be indifferent to the fate of that source of supply. As early as February a high official in the Czechoslovak Ministry of Foreign Affairs claimed that Beneš was determined to do everything possible in Paris to prevent the Upper Silesian coalfields from going to Poland, for no one could depend on regular production from the Poles.[74] Whether those were Beneš's true sentiments, there was little that he could actually do. It was in the interests of both Poland and Czechoslovakia to preserve some semblance of cooperation in Paris, and Beneš could hardly take a strong stand for German retention of Upper Silesia when the French were doing everything possible to build up their potential allies in Central Europe. The same policy that had won the historic borders of Bohemia and Moravia for the Czechs dictated that Upper Silesia go to the Poles. It was Lloyd George who seized upon the issue of Upper Silesia and who forced Clemenceau and Wilson to agree to the holding of a plebiscite in the area.[75] That decision postponed the ultimate showdown until 1921, when the ambivalence in Czech attitudes became even more pronounced.

The months of May and June 1919 were an exceedingly grim phase in the life of the new Czechoslovak republic. Within the country, strikes protesting rising food, coal, and clothing prices turned to riots in Prague and Kladno between May 22 and 27.[76] Although successful on the diplomatic front in Paris, the country faced many hostile neighbors in

Central Europe. In addition to the conflicts—potential or actual—with Poland, Germany, and Austria, the most immediate threat came from the Bolshevik regime of Béla Kun in Hungary. The issue was the territorial boundary between Hungary and Slovakia. Although the Carpathian Mountains afforded a well-defined frontier between Poland and Slovakia, there was no similar natural boundary in the south. The great powers forced the liberal regime of Count Mihály Károlyi to evacuate the Magyar troops from Slovakia in December 1918, and Czech soldiers moved in to occupy the area. The continuing military pressure of Rumanian and Czech occupations of Hungarian territory combined with democratic pressures in Hungary to bring about the fall of Count Károlyi's government in March 1919. A socialist-communist coalition under Béla Kun then proclaimed the Hungarian Soviet Republic. Given the Magyar military weakness, Rumanian forces advanced to the Tisza river in April, and Czech legionnaires occupied territories beyond the Allied demarcation line between Slovakia and Hungary.[77]

Béla Kun's government resorted to a levée en masse and launched a highly successful attack against the overextended Czechs in the middle of May. Within a month Magyar forces controlled a third of Slovakia. In Slovakia the Hungarian Red Army met with a joyous reception from the Magyars and Magyar-sympathizers who dominated in towns such as Košice (Kassa). Béla Kun's government supported the proclamation of an independent Slovak Soviet Republic. This was a frontal attack on the very existence of a Czechoslovak republic. Popular opinion in Prague blamed the military debacle on the mistakes of Italian officers commanding Czech troops in Slovakia, and the Czechoslovak government decided to put the organization and command of the army solely under the authority of high-ranking French officers.[78] French dominance of the Czechoslovak army dated to the closing year of the war and was to continue through the 1920s. Allied diplomatic pressure soon forced the withdrawal of Magyar forces from Slovakia, but the war and the diplomatic conflicts in Central Europe had underscored the domestic instability of Czechoslovakia. Not only did the national minorities look across the borders to Germany, Austria, Poland, or Hungary for support against the authority of the Prague government, but Slovak resentment of the centralizing tendencies of the Czechs was also becoming apparent. The Czech-Slovak rivalry was the potentially fatal threat to a state that justified its own existence by the right of self-determination of those two groups. Any conflict with a foreign power would further exacerbate the national and social tensions at home. In this situation, it appeared that the Czechoslovak government might be asked to participate in forcing Germany to accept the Treaty of Versailles.

Before the outbreak of hostilities with the Hungarians Beneš informed Clemenceau at the beginning of May that Prague was making military preparations in case Germany should refuse to sign the treaty.[79] On May 20 Foch sent an order to the Allied officers commanding the Czechoslovak army to get ready for action against Germany. The French command in Prague formulated two operational plans for the Czech army in the event of a resumption of hostilities. One plan called for an invasion of Germany in the Bayreuth-Bamberg area in order to link up with French troops operating along the Main River Valley. That action would split Germany into northern and southern halves. The other plan envisaged an immediate move toward the north in order to occupy Berlin. As the text of the second plan related, this strategy "would present more difficulties than the preceding one but on the other hand it could lead to more decisive results."[80]

The Germans were not oblivious to Czech military capabilities. In late May Saenger in Prague was warning Berlin that the build-up of Czech troops along the Bavarian border resulted from orders from the Entente to be prepared militarily if a diplomatic break with Germany should come.[81] A German military memorandum of early June estimated that fifty thousand Czech troops could march with the Poles from the east and indicated that the invasion route would probably be along the Main River Valley in order to combine with the French. This memorandum also revealed a healthy respect for Czech military capabilities, which the Germans did not doubt would be employed in the event of a resumption of hostilities.[82] The German army could not hope to stand against the Western powers; the added threat of Czech and Polish troops only cemented the issue. General Groener had the common sense and courage to admit that, and a reluctant Weimar National Assembly accepted the Treaty of Versailles.

It should be emphasized that the appraisals of Czech military capabilities were made before the collapse on the Slovak front and that the purely military estimates failed to evaluate fully the potential disruptiveness of foreign adventures on the domestic scene in Czechoslovakia. Beneš understood the desirability of making his country appear as stable and reliable as possible, and his offer to help the Western Allies impose the treaty on the Germans was a diplomatically astute policy. His promises involved a calculated risk, however, and it was a fortunate circumstance for the Czechs that they did not actually have to participate in military action against Germany. Another possibility that worried the German representative in Prague was the threat that the Czech government might confiscate Reich-German property in Czechoslovakia if Berlin refused to sign the Treaty of Versailles. Although the Czechs had previously seemed reluctant to take that step, Saenger feared a possible change of attitude and sought to mobilize German-Bohemian influence to dissuade Prague authorities from any property confiscations.[83] Although the Czechs never exercised their rights in that regard, Saenger's actions were an early tangible example of the use of German-Bohemians to further Reich-German interests in Czechoslovakia.

After the signing of the Treaty of Versailles, it was still necessary to make peace with Austria. The Austrian government naturally accepted the responsibility of representing the claims of the German-Bohemians and the German-Moravians, as they had previously been part of the Habsburg Empire. The leaders of the exile governments became members of the official Austrian delegation at the peace conference. Beneš tried to prevent the appearance of Lodgman and his cohorts at Paris by threatening to prosecute them for treason should they return to Czechoslovakia, but the Entente powers refused to take note of his protest.[84]

The method by which the peace conference dealt with Austria was the same as that employed with Germany. The Entente presented a draft treaty to the Austrians, who were allowed to submit written observations on the conditions of peace. In mid-June Lodgman, Seliger, and Freissler, together with representatives from the Bohemian Forest District and German Southern Moravia, submitted a memorandum in which they presented their maximum demands—self-determination for all the Germans in Bohemia, Moravia, and Silesia.[85] This was the first time that representatives of the Germans in the Czech lands officially presented their claims to the peace conference. They did so after the decisions concerning the main body of Germans, those in the north and west, had already been made. After submitting their requests they returned to Vienna, understandably dissatisfied with the results of their efforts. Another memorandum in a conference already flooded with paper was not likely to make much impression, especially when it concerned a problem that the Entente powers considered to be settled.

The Czechoslovak-Austrian boundary, formulated by the Commission of Czechoslovak Affairs, accepted by the Big Four in early May, and presented in the draft treaty of June 2, followed essentially the historic boundary with minor modifications in favor of Czechoslovakia.[86] The Austrians had a chance to affect the decision of the peace conference only in relation to the German areas in southern Czechoslovakia along the Austrian border. It was not likely that they could succeed even there, for not only was the Entente unfavorably inclined, but also the Germans in the south had never formed so strong a separatist movement as those in the north. In Linz the governors of Upper Austria showed no inclination to welcome the Bohemian Forest Germans into their state.[87] There was more support in Lower Austria for the Southern Moravian Germans, but the main activity emanated from the Foreign Ministry in Vienna.[88] In a series of letters exchanged between Renner and the peace conference from June to September, Renner continued to press the claims for border rectifications according to national self-determination.

As in the case of the German peace settlement, it was the Americans who were the most susceptible to claims based on self-determination. After the signing of the Treaty of Versailles, Wilson left Paris, accompanied by many American experts from the various commissions. At this time Professor Coolidge replaced Charles Seymour on the Commission for Czechoslovak Affairs. Whereas Seymour had recognized the necessity of including many German areas in Czechoslovakia in order to make it a viable state, Coolidge had already written a memorandum from Vienna in March in which he had advocated giving the Germans almost all their claims.[89] With Wilson and Seymour gone, Lansing and Coolidge worked to modify at least the Czechoslovak-Austrian border along the lines of self-determination. Wilson put a stop to this in a message from his ship and showed himself once more to be more flexible in applying his principle than was his secretary of state.[90] The final boundary as it appeared in the Treaty of St. Germain of September 10, 1919, was essentially the one originally proposed by the commission. Czechoslovakia emerged from the peace negotiations at Paris as an economically prosperous and militarily defensible state. In every important territorial issue Czechoslovak diplomacy won the battle, but a price of victory was that German, Magyar, and Polish minorities dominated most of the borderlands of the country. According to the 1921 census, of a total population of 13,374,000 Czechoslovak citizens, there were 3,124,000 Germans, 745,000 Magyars, and 76,000 Poles. All together, national minorities, including Ruthenians and Jews, made up slightly more than one-third of the entire population of the country.[91]

In an effort to safeguard the interests of the various national minorities throughout Central and Eastern Europe, the peacemakers forced Czechoslovakia and other successor states to sign special treaties that allowed the minorities to appeal to the League of Nations if they felt that their rights were being violated.[92] Liberal use was made of that privilege in the 1920s but with little practical result. In the case of Czechoslovakia, Beneš's influence in Geneva was such that he could neutralize complaints before they embarrassed his country. The charges brought against the Czechoslovak government were usually insignificant, and they primarily served the function of harassment. In addition to the minorities treaty, the disarmament decisions at the peace conference also had significance for the subsequent development of Czechoslovak-German relations. In May 1919 there was an attempt at Paris to limit the armies of the successor states proportionally to those of the defeated powers in Central Europe. The Treaty of Versailles imposed a ceiling of one hundred thousand men on the German army, and initial proposals would have limited the Czechoslovak army to twenty-two thousand. The efforts to curtail the armies of the successor states foundered on the opposition of their diplomats, however, and only the defeated powers were forced to disarm to low levels. In the early 1920s Czechoslovakia maintained an army of one hundred fifty thousand men, half again as large as the German Reichswehr.[93]

ESTABLISHING THE CZECHOSLOVAK STATE

With the signing of the peace treaties, the fate of the Germans in Bohemia, Moravia, and Silesia was finally and definitely sealed. The long process of gradual accommodation to the Czechoslovak state began already in the summer of 1919 when it became apparent that the Germans would remain in Czechoslovakia. The transition was not an easy one for either Czechs or Germans, yet despite many incidents the general trend, at least until the time that the Great Depression struck Central Europe, was toward diminution of friction between the two nationalities. In the years between 1919 and 1921 the process was slow and halting at best.

The Germans were not willing to give up their claim to the right of national self-determination, but, because it was obvious that this right could not be exercised at least in the immediate future, German leaders adopted a new policy that called for the political autonomy of the German areas in Czechoslovakia. In order to promote the policy of a united, autonomous German area they began to regard themselves in a new light. Before the revolution the Germans had felt relatively secure despite growing fears of Slav influence within the Austrian half of the empire. Because there was no special need, there was no special connection among the Germans of the old Czech crown lands. The separatist movement after October 28, 1918, never aimed at establishing a permanently united country but rather at creating a temporary state that would last only until the German areas could join their neighboring states within the Reich or Austria. When the decisions of the peace conference were published and the Germans realized that they were indeed to be a minority in the new Czech state, there began a movement to close ranks and to make themselves a united people. If they could successfully promote the idea of a unified German folk, they thought that they could more easily attain their goal of an autonomous state within the Czechoslovak republic.

The choice between the old and the new could be expressed as "German Bohemians or Sudeten Germans." Quickly after the signing of the Treaty of St. Germain, the Czechoslovak government allowed the German exile leaders to return from Vienna. Upon his arrival in Czechoslovakia Lodgman continued his political agitation in a speech to a German crowd at Ústí nad Labem (Aussig) in early October. There he proclaimed that there could no longer be a German-Bohemian policy but only a Sudeten-German one, for which the closest unity of all German

parties was necessary.[94] The old name that had always been used was
"German Bohemian" (*Deutsch-Böhmisch*). The German newspapers had
continued to use the term during the revolution and the peace conference,
but by the summer of 1919 they began increasingly to adopt the
expression "Sudeten German" (*Sudetendeutsch*). Geographically, the term
was no more accurate than the old one as a designation for all the Germans
of Bohemia, Moravia, and Silesia. The only real Sudeten Germans were the
ones who lived in the Sudeten Mountains along the Silesian border. But
the new term changed the emphasis between two concepts that were
interwoven in a romantic ideology that found strong although not
exclusive expression in Central Europe.

⌐One idea was that of the *Heimat*, or the homeland, which nourished its
people, furnished the setting for their joys and sorrows, and sheltered a
man's descendants even as it had his forebears. The Heimat was much
more than simply a place of residence; it signified almost a mystical union
between a people and their land. This attitude helps to explain the
extreme rivalries for the slightest bit of territory in Central and Eastern
Europe after the war. The other idea was that of the *Volk*, or the nation.
This meant a nation not in a political but in an ethnic sense, and it is not
insignificant for the different outlooks of German-speaking and English-
speaking persons that whereas *Volk* in German is singular, *people* in
English is normally plural. The Germanic emphasis on the group rather
than the individual when thinking of human beings was succinctly
expressed by Thomas Mann in his *Betrachtungen eines Unpolitischen*.

> And it is German above all not to confound the *Volk* with the
> individual atoms that compose the mass.[95]

When the Volk became something more than the sum of its parts and
assumed a romantic existence of its own, the way was open for policies
that slighted the interests of the "individual atoms" in the name of the
common good. The very grammar of the language influenced the thought
patterns of people and their susceptibility to certain types of political
propaganda. And it should be noted that, whereas the concepts of Heimat
and Volk lose much of their romantic content when translated into
English, one has no trouble finding their equivalents in the Czech language.
Vlast and *Národ* aroused the same impulses among Czechs that Heimat and
Volk did among Germans. Despite their rivalries Czechs and Germans had
much more in common than most of them realized. They thought alike,
and their conflicts were therefore that much more bitter.⌐

These two concepts, Heimat and Volk, complemented and supported
each other among the Germans within the Reich. There, loyalty to the
homeland and loyalty to the nation were the same. But for the Germans
who were cut off from the Reich by the peace treaties and placed as

minorities in foreign states, the two concepts were no longer completely
harmonious. For them it became a question of competing loyalties. For
the Germans in Czechoslovakia the choices were: Were they primarily
people of Bohemia, Moravia, and Silesia? If so, should they not
accommodate themselves to the Czechoslovak republic? Or were they first
and foremost members of the German nation? If so, how could they be
loyal citizens in a foreign state? The term "German Bohemian" placed the
emphasis on the homeland, and it was largely for this reason that the
German nationalists promoted the new expression "Sudeten German."
The change of terms had more than simply semantic significance. To the
extent that the Germans thought of themselves as members of the German
nation rather than as residents of their homelands in Bohemia, Moravia,
and Silesia, and hence citizens of the new Czechoslovak state, to that
extent it was more difficult for them to accommodate themselves to the
new political system.

Insofar as the governments of early Weimar Germany actually had a
policy toward the Germans of Czechoslovakia, it was one of detachment
and watchful waiting. Within weeks of the signing of the Treaty of
Versailles, the German plenipotentiary in Prague counseled loyal observance of the treaty and encouragement of the Sudeten Germans to
cooperate with Czech authorities. He emphasized that, by signing the
treaty, Berlin had recognized the Sudeten-German problem to be an
internal matter of Czechoslovakia.[96] Although Saenger was prone to
irritate his superiors in the German Foreign Office, there is no evidence of
any basic disagreement in Berlin with his advice.

The need for a moderating influence on the Sudeten Germans became
evident upon Lodgman's return to Czechoslovakia in the autumn. At the
close of October and the beginning of November, the leader of the
Sudeten-German "bourgeois" bloc developed his ideas for the benefit of
the German diplomatic representative in Vienna and for Saenger in Prague.
Lodgman wanted financial support for the campaigns of the Sudeten-
German political parties. He maintained that the Reich should support the
Sudeten Germans in resisting Prague's efforts to consolidate its control
over the Sudeten areas. If that resistance were successful the Czechoslovak
republic would inevitably dissolve, and the Sudeten areas would be able to
join the rest of Germany. Anticipating for the spring of 1920 a war by the
Poles and the Hungarians against the Czechs, Lodgman argued:

> Should it come to that, he hopes that the Reich government would
> support the German-Bohemians in their simultaneous war of liberation
> at least by winking at private weapons shipments and by allowing,
> despite energetic protests, without however resorting to force, parts of
> the Polish contingents to march through German territory on their way
> to the Sudeten-German areas of settlement.[97]

In view of the armed clashes between Germans and Poles in Upper Silesia, the notion that Berlin would allow Polish troops to march through German territory was more than adequate basis for Saenger's euphemistically expressed judgment: "In general, the limited amount of Dr. Lodgman's political and sociological training is striking."[98] In language hauntingly suggestive of tactics twenty years later, Lodgman's "sole mission" was summed up by Saenger as:

> the concentration of all German Nationalist elements under one point of view, namely, in the struggle with the Czechs to obtain the right of national self-determination by whatever means necessary, and, for this purpose, to bring the German Nationalist opposition gradually to the boiling point with irredentist demands never satisfied by small concessions.[99]

Saenger summarized his report about Lodgman with the remark: "it is not completely impossible that his policies could become a source of danger for the German Reich."[100] Not until Hitler did Berlin espouse the policies advocated by Lodgman and his cohorts. Throughout the 1920s, the universal opinion—held not just by Czech political leaders but also by German officials in Prague and Berlin and by foreign diplomats as well—was that most Sudeten-German leaders displayed little or no political ability. Ironically, the most simplistic policies of the most benighted eventually triumphed at Munich.

If German diplomats desired to see the Sudeten Germans make their peace with the Czechoslovak authorities and work from within to influence Czechoslovak foreign policy in a pro-German direction, French diplomats foresaw with apprehension that same possibility. The Sudeten Germans posed a dilemma for French diplomacy. It has been seen that at the peace conference the French were determined that the Sudeten Germans should not join the Reich. Within Czechoslovakia, however, they were a potential source of disruption, and French observers therefore hoped that the Czechoslovak government could pacify the Sudeten Germans with minor concessions and keep them quiescent.[101] But the French ministers in Prague feared any modus vivendi between Czechs and Sudeten Germans that would give the Sudeten Germans significant political influence in the new republic. For that reason Masaryk's occasional remarks about a reconciliation among the nationalities created anxiety in the French legation in Prague.[102] From the French diplomatic documents it is clear that, in the early postwar years in particular, French diplomats dreaded the possibility of a gradual reassertion of traditional ties in Central Europe and a drift of Czechoslovak foreign policy into a German orbit. In French eyes the nationality conflict within the republic was the best guarantee against a rapprochement between Prague and Berlin.[103] The intricacies of French policy toward the Sudeten Germans were well summarized in a report by the French minister in August 1919. After discussing the need to pacify the Sudeten Germans, Clemént-Simon observed:

> But, on the other hand, we must not forget . . . that the Germans of the Czechoslovak republic can only be opposed to the new state becoming the champion of the Entente against Germany, as is our hope. We must therefore try to see to it that, without being persecuted and forced into perpetual revolt, the German-Bohemians exercise only a very restricted influence here.[104]

The goal of simultaneously pacifying the Sudeten Germans while limiting their political influence remained a central part of French policy toward Czechoslovakia at least through the 1920s.

In early July Kramář had to resign as a result of losses suffered by his National Democratic party in the communal elections in June. Vlastimil Tusar became the new premier. As a leader of the Czech Social Democrats, he was one of the more moderate Czech politicians. From his years in the Austrian Reichsrat and as the Czech diplomatic representative in Vienna, he had good personal connections with both the Austrians and the Sudeten Germans. He brought to Prague a greater willingness to compromise differences than had been manifested by Kramář. In June the Germans participated in the communal elections held throughout Czechoslovakia. By doing so they maintained their control over the local government in their districts and demonstrated their political strength. But their dilemma was the same as had confronted Czech politicians in the years after 1867. The Germans refused formally to recognize the legality of the regime, yet their participation in elections conducted by the Czechoslovak government was in itself a de facto recognition of the new state. The Social Democrats emerged from the elections as the strongest German party, with almost 50 percent of the German vote.[105] They were also the most cooperatively inclined of the German parties, and with one of the leaders of the Czech Social Democrats as premier there was a real chance for improvement in the political relations between the two nationalities. Tusar publicly avowed that he hoped to attain the support of the German Social Democrats for his new government.[106] This co-operation did not mean that they would enter the cabinet, for the Czechoslovak National Assembly, in which the Germans were not included, was still dealing with the task of drawing up the basic constitutional laws of the new state.

Only Czechs and Slovaks actually participated in writing the constitution of Czechoslovakia. When the National Assembly was formed in November 1918, the Sudeten German leaders refused to participate in it, for their own separatist movement was then at its height. Nor was the National Assembly the result of a popular election, which the Czech

National Council considered impossible in the conditions of the autumn of 1918. By common agreement Czech political leaders apportioned seats among the various Czech political parties according to the percentages won by them in the last Austrian parliamentary elections of 1911. As a result, representatives of various socioeconomic classes and ideological currents—including the Catholic parties, the Agrarians, the Social Democrats, and the assorted middle-class parties—coalesced in order to establish the constitutional foundations of the state.[107] Rule by a multiparty Czech national coalition remained essentially intact until 1926.

In the interests of Czechoslovak unity it was essential to include Slovak representatives in the National Assembly as well. Inasmuch as the prewar party structure was not so well developed in Slovakia as in the Czech lands, the Slovak provisional government under the leadership of Vavro Šrobár shouldered the responsibility for appointing Slovak representatives to the National Assembly. Eventually one-fifth of the seats in the assembly were reserved for Slovak delegates. The particular Slovak representatives were carefully chosen in order to harmonize with the constitutional conceptions dominant among the Czech parties. By 1918 Šrobár was the leading Slovak advocate of the Czechoslovak orientation. Although formally a Catholic himself, Šrobár considered Slovak Protestants to be more reliable supporters of Czechoslovak centralism. His appointments both to the National Assembly and in local government in Slovakia overwhelmingly favored Protestants over Catholics despite the fact that Catholics outnumbered Protestants more than four to one. In view of the dearth of nationally reliable officials and teachers in Slovakia, Šrobár's administration began importing Czechs in the course of 1919. The newcomers often failed to exhibit either a sensitivity to Slovak cultural and religious values or an appreciation for the unique characteristics of the Slovak language. Moreover, Czechs began to fill jobs for which little special training was necessary and for which there was an adequate number of Slovaks readily available. As a result, anti-Czech attitudes began to mount in Slovakia at the same time as Slovak representatives were participating in the constitutional deliberations in Prague.[108]

Slovak hostility toward the Czechs soon became focused in the Catholic political movement. Šrobár's religious discrimination exacerbated his personal rivalries with Father Andrej Hlinka, who reorganized his Slovak People's party after the war and made it the leading advocate of Slovak political and cultural autonomy. Hlinka managed to travel to Paris on a Polish passport in 1919 in an unsuccessful effort to obtain a guarantee of autonomy for Slovakia similar to the one for Sub-Carpathian Ruthenia. Upon returning to Czechoslovakia in October 1919, Hlinka received somewhat harsher treatment than did the Sudeten German leaders and was interned for almost six months. Simultaneously, his companion on the trip to Paris, František Jehlička, helped to establish a Slovak Council in Geneva that agitated in the interwar years for a reunion of Slovakia with Hungary.[109]

The murky situation in Slovak politics did not allow active and sustained political cooperation between Slovaks and the minority nationalities. Yet on specific issues there was often agreement between the minority nationalities and a faction of the Slovaks. Probably the most significant agreement was their common desire for local political and cultural autonomy. The debate about the basic nature of the state came to be expressed in the alternatives: a "nation-state" or a "nationalities state." The former choice implied a much closer political union among a people who were essentially in agreement concerning the fundamental structure and policy of the state. The responsible Czech political leadership was determined to establish this sort of Czechoslovak nation-state. These leaders tended to consider Czechs and Slovaks as essentially one nation whose differences were the result of historical accidents. Once united in the same political entity, they reasoned, Czechs and Slovaks could gradually obliterate those differences. On the other hand, the Sudeten Germans sought a "nationalities" state, which would be a close confederation of autonomous areas where local authorities would have paramount influence. In this policy the Sudeten Germans had the support of the other national minorities and a significant proportion of the Slovaks as well.

The Czech political leaders took advantage of their control of the National Assembly to establish a Czechoslovak national state. In so doing, they gave ammunition to the minority groups, who consistently but vainly opposed the attempt to create a highly centralized administrative system in Prague. Yet Czech leaders were justifiably apprehensive about the centrifugal forces within the country. They feared that local political autonomy could lead to a dissolution of the state, with the various nationalities joining their fellow nationals across the borders or establishing their own independent rump states. It is instructive to note that officials in Berlin sympathized with and supported Sudeten German demands for political autonomy even while stoutly resisting similar movements in the Rhineland, East Prussia, and Bavaria. Weimar German leaders opposed political autonomy within their own country for the same basic reason as the Czech leadership did in Prague—all feared for the unity of their states. One of the primary arguments for political autonomy was that the various nationalities in Czechoslovakia could thereby safeguard their own particular cultures. The National Assembly did indeed adopt laws that had fundamental cultural, social, and economic bearing as well as political significance. Those laws had a combined effect of creating what the Germans labeled a "czechizing" policy and what the Czechs defended as simply an effort to give the Czechs and Slovaks that which was rightly theirs.

Among the cultural changes wrought by the Czechs, one of the most significant was the new school policy. The law adopted by the National Assembly stipulated that a national minority was entitled to a school if it could put at least forty students in a class.[110] Since there were already German schools in districts where Germans were sparsely settled and since some Czech students transferred from German to Czech institutions, the law led to the closing of a number of German schools. The Germans protested bitterly against this policy and conducted school strikes as demonstrations. Concurrently with the closing of German schools there were openings of Czech schools, often in areas that the Germans regarded as purely German. The government defended its policy on the grounds that it was simply rectifying an unjust situation inherited from the Austrian monarchy. It produced figures to show that on the basis of student-teacher ratios the Germans still had better educational opportunities than the Czechs.[111] Regardless of these arguments, the Germans were embittered at the sight of German schools being closed, and they suffered from fears that the children would lose their cultural heritage.

Related to the dispute over the schools was the decision of the National Assembly on January 13, 1920, to establish the Czech university in Prague as the only heir of the old Charles University.[112] That university, founded by Charles IV in 1348, was the oldest in Central Europe, a fact that had led many Germans to regard it as the "oldest German university." In 1882 the institution had been divided into a German and a Czech university as a reward to the Czechs for participating in the governing coalition of Count Taaffe. It was in the Czech university that Masaryk had taught for years before the war. The law of 1920 gave to the Czech university the insignia of the old Charles University. Once again the Germans protested, but they themselves had weakened their position by a campaign to relocate the German university in the border regions, probably in Reichenberg. There had been a long time in the immediate postwar months when a German professor could not safely speak out for keeping the university in Prague although the cultural and intellectual advantages of the city were obvious. The rector of the German university was a strong nationalist and had been the leader of the relocation movement.[113] By the time that the National Assembly adopted its law, this movement had largely subsided, but the Czechs were able to remark that the Germans must not care very much for the name of the "Charles University" anyway. The "German University in the Czechoslovak Republic" fell into a decidedly inferior position.

The law that affected the daily lives of people more than any other was the language law. Passed by the National Assembly on February 28, 1920, it made "Czechoslovak" the official language of the country. In their comments on the law, officials claimed that they were not seeking to take sides in the philological debate about whether Czech and Slovak were separate languages or simply dialects of the same language. They explained their terminology by saying that sometimes the laws and decrees would be in Czech, sometimes in Slovak, without any definite pattern emerging. This was part of the general policy of deemphasizing differences between Czechs and Slovaks and attempting to make them a united nation.[114]

All correspondence among government offices was to be conducted in "Czechoslovak." All citizens had to use it in dealing with authorities, unless they were members of a minority that composed 20 percent or more of the population of a district. If, for example, the Germans had more than 20 percent of the population of an administrative area, they could use German, and authorities would have to answer them in German. If not, the Germans had to use Czech. The law had a particularly harsh effect on the Germans, for whereas most Czechs spoke German, relatively few Germans spoke Czech. Most Germans had long regarded Czech as an inferior language that did not merit the trouble required to master it. Hence when German officials were given two years to learn it or lose their jobs in the administration of their towns, there went up a cry that reverberated throughout the country—just as had been the case with the Badeni reforms in 1897. The loss of bureaucratic positions was one of the harsher results of the national revolution. Between 1921 and 1930 almost half of the Sudeten German state employees, excluding teachers, lost their positions, and after the language law went fully into force in 1926 some 33,000 German bureaucrats were left without jobs.[115] Although the percentage of Germans active in state service equaled the proportion of state employees among the Czech population, the diminishing prospects for a civil service career and the displacement of people from socially prestigious positions doubtlessly had sharp psychological effects among the Sudeten German population. Besides its impact on the bureaucracy, the language law also affected daily events in the lives of people. For example, if the law were strictly adhered to, no letter could be delivered in Prague unless it had a Czech address. No telegram could be sent from Prague in a text other than Czech. No one could use a language other than Czech in speaking with an operator on the telephone. The Foreign Ministry received so many complaints from foreigners that the postal administration directed its employees not to adhere to the law.[116]

The laws of the National Assembly affected not only the cultural and educational opportunities of people but their pocketbooks as well. The keystone of the social changes in the agricultural sector was the land reform. The advent of the republic effectively destroyed the political power of the Austrian nobility in the Czech lands and created a resentful but essentially impotent group of old aristocrats.[117] The land reform measures broke up the old landed estates of the nobility and put a limit of 150 hectares (371 acres) on the holdings of any individual. The laws assumed national as well as social significance. The aristocrats whose property was being seized were popularly regarded simply as the heirs of the old foreign nobility brought in by the Habsburgs after the battle of the White Mountain. Although German and Hungarian peasants participated in the land reform, the vast majority of the new landowners were Czechs and Slovaks. Former legionnaires were particularly favored in the distribution of land. The principal goal of the land reform was the creation of a large class of small farmers loyal to the new republic.[118] Sudeten Germans charged that the land reform was used to bring Czech settlers into previously German areas, and indeed the military value of populating the border territories with Czech peasants was significant. The actual extent to which the land reform was used to settle Czech farmers into predominantly German areas is still a topic of historical debate, but it does not appear to have been great.[119] Of greater military significance was the fact that the state confiscated and retained under its own direction much of the forest lands along the frontier. No one disputed the legality of the land reform, but foreign governments did defend the rights of their own nationals, who owned estates in Czechoslovakia, to receive adequate compensation. Negotiations between Reich-German landowners and the Czechoslovak government lasted for at least a decade.

Whereas the land reform directly affected only a small group of landowners, the capital levy and the war bonds issue were subjects of concern for almost the entire German bourgeoisie. In February 1919 the borders were closed for a week, and the Austrian currency in circulation was stamped in order to transform it into Czech crowns. Part of the currency was withheld by the state as a capital levy. Inasmuch as the Sudeten Germans were relatively more prosperous, they were hurt more than other nationalities by the special tax. The war bonds issue caused an extended debate. In order to finance its military effort during the war, the Austrian government had sold bonds that were to be redeemed after the close of hostilities. The Germans, from the smallest shopkeeper to the largest financial institutions, had continued to invest heavily in these bonds right up until the disintegration of the empire. They were caught in the new republic with much of their resources in bonds that the Czechs might refuse to honor. In this highly embarrassing and extremely weak position the Germans launched a campaign as early as the summer of 1919 to persuade the government to honor the Austrian debts.[120] They enlisted the support of those Czechs who had also bought the bonds. They argued that the economy of the country would be drastically hurt if the Germans as individuals and their banks were brought to financial ruin. That was clear enough. The Czechs never seriously planned to refuse all recognition of the bonds, and the debate centered around just what percentage of the debt the government would assume. Here of course the Germans demanded a full valuation of the bonds. After much debate, parliament passed a compromise law on June 19, 1920, against the opposition of the Germans on one side and Kramář's National Democrats on the other. The Germans were bitter about the measure, for although the Czechs claimed that the bonds were receiving 75 percent valuation, the Germans protested that it was in reality much less.[121] In the late 1920s the valuation of Austrian debts remained a serious diplomatic issue between Prague and Berlin.

As the Germans continued to press for political representation, the National Assembly adopted the constitution in February 1920 and called elections for April. The returns clearly demonstrated the fairness of the electoral system. In the 300-member Chamber of Deputies there were 199 Czechs and Slovaks and 72 Germans. In the 150-member Senate there were 102 Czechs and Slovaks and 37 Germans.[122] These proportions corresponded almost exactly with the population figures established by the Austrian census in 1910 and later confirmed in the Czechoslovak census of 1921. After the elections the German bourgeois parties, except, at first, for the National Socialists, formed a parliamentary union and elected Lodgman as its leader.[123] Thus the leader of the German separatist movement in 1918 and 1919 became the German bourgeois parliamentary leader in the first Chamber of Deputies of the National Assembly. The German Social Democrats refused to join this union. As the strongest single German party they pursued an independent policy that was more moderate in opposition to the Czechoslovak government than was the activity of the German bourgeois bloc.[124]

The first meeting of the new National Assembly reelected Masaryk as the president of Czechoslovakia.[125] Masaryk commanded enough personal popularity and respect that only the most rabid Germans ever dared to attack him directly. On the other hand, the Germans could not bring themselves to vote for him for president. The bourgeois group voted for the rector of the German university, and the Social Democrats abstained. The first meeting of the Assembly hardly augured well for the establishment of a democratic process. The German National Socialists continually interrupted the Czech-language proceedings with demands that the Czechs speak German. In the roll call someone substituted the Czech equivalents for the given names of the German delegates, to which the angered Germans responded with comments such as: "You have stolen our homes, and now you are stealing our names!" or "I was baptized a German, and my name is Franz!"[126] These petty frictions at the highest governmental level mirrored daily experiences among the population.

Occasionally there were open conflicts between Germans and Czechs that resulted in injuries and deaths. One such incident occurred in the Moravian city of Jihlava (Iglau) in late June 1920. There a torchlight parade by some Germans led to a fight with Czech legionnaires, in which several Germans were injured and one legionnaire was killed.[127] The worst series of disturbances came at the time of the second anniversary of Czechoslovak independence. On October 28, 1920, and the days thereafter, Czech legionnaires and Sudeten Germans rioted in Teplice (Teplitz) and Reichenberg, and these incidents led to tumultuous scenes in the Chamber of Deputies during which some Germans rose and sang the "Watch on the Rhine."[128] The parliamentary excesses only aggravated the situation, and there was more fighting not only in the German border areas but in Prague as well. In Prague the violence in the streets assumed an anti-Semitic as well as an anti-German character with the ransacking of the Old Jewish Town Hall.[129] There were moments in mid-November when the Czechoslovak authorities simply did not have control of the situation. At the same time a group composed largely of Germans and Magyars met in Karlovy Vary (Karlsbad) to form what they called a "League of Nations Union" as a division of the Union of Democratic Control, which had its seat in London. By proclaiming their allegiance to the liberal principles of the League of Nations, they hoped to get special consideration for their minority complaints against the Czech authorities. A government representative closed the constitutive meeting of the organization.[130]

The tendency for anti-German demonstrations to assume an anti-Semitic character underscored the anomalous position of the Jews in Czechoslovakia. Their national identification was highly uncertain. One of the census reforms of the Czechoslovak government allowed citizens the right to declare themselves to be of Jewish nationality rather than forcing them to decide among Czechoslovak, German, Magyar, or Ruthenian nationality. In the 1921 census there were 354,000 people who said that they adhered to the "Israelite" religion, yet only 181,000 of those claimed to be of Jewish nationality. From west to east across the country the pattern was striking. National assimilation was far advanced in Bohemia, where only one "Israelite" in seven designated his nationality as Jewish. The proportion climbed to 40 percent in Moravia, 50 percent in Silesia, 52 percent in Slovakia, and finally 86 percent in Subcarpathian Ruthenia.[131] It was therefore the Jews (in a religious sense) of Bohemia that were most closely identified with the competing nationalities. It has been seen that already at the turn of the century a slight majority of Prague Jews designated themselves as Czech nationals. In 1921 in the country as a whole, of all the 354,000 members of the "Israelite" religion, 73,000 called themselves Czechoslovaks and 19,000 chose German nationality.[132] But in the capital city a sizable proportion of the German colony was Jewish, and among Jews it was particularly the more visible and influential upper classes that identified with German culture. They tended to perpetuate the image of Jewish germanophilism that many Czechs had imbibed across the decades, and Prague's Jews therefore became easy targets of nationalist demonstrators who thought with their fists.

Diplomatic relations between Berlin and Prague could never be harmonious so long as public opinion in both countries was aroused periodically by disturbances between the Sudeten Germans and the Czechs. German public opinion put pressure on foreign ministers in Berlin to say something about the events in Czechoslovakia, yet they were officially the internal affairs of a sovereign state. Particularly in the early postwar years German diplomats had to be careful not to appear to be reviving a pan-German policy that included a militant protection of German minorities in other countries. They therefore usually remained silent in public, or issued only bland statements, and cautiously used their private meetings with foreign diplomats to mention Berlin's concern for the welfare of the German minorities. The riots of October and November 1920 were particularly inopportune, for a Czechoslovak-German commercial treaty was then coming up for ratification in the Reichstag. In the debate on the ratification Foreign Minister Walter Simons warned that the suppression of German minorities by other governments could not fail to affect diplomatic relations with Germany, yet he added a plea to the Sudeten Germans to remove the points of friction with the Czechs and to cooperate with the rest of the population of Czechoslovakia.[133] Beneš, for his part, remarked privately to reporters trusted by him that Czechoslovakia needed nothing so much as peace, that the street excesses were therefore regrettable, and that he hoped to allay German grievances insofar as possible.[134] The conflicts in the streets and the parliamentary excesses were at cross purposes with the policies of both governments.

As in the days of the Habsburg Empire, the best means of overcoming national hostilities lay in the promotion of mutual economic interests of various social classes. At the time of the discussion of the land reform, the German and the Czech landowners tried to band together to resist the law.[135] The Czech and the German holders of the Austrian war bonds cooperated in trying to get government recognition of the full value of the bonds. The German industrialists, as has been seen, were inclined to accommodate themselves to the Czechoslovak government for the benefit of their own economic interests. There was at various times talk of cooperation between the Czech and the German Social Democrats. Thus, people of various nationalities and socioeconomic classes remained subject to conflicting loyalties. At a time when nationalism reached its peak in Central Europe an individual was acutely conscious of his own nationality, yet in a highly stratified society with a modern economy he could often more easily identify with people of other nationalities in his own class than with his fellow nationals in other classes. As the First World War had demonstrated, the general tendency in a period of crisis was to close ranks with one's fellow nationals. But if the confrontation of nationalities was a liability for the Czechoslovak republic, the hope for its viability lay in the gradual reassertion of group interests in a pluralistic society.

In September 1920 rumors began to appear in the newspapers that the Tusar cabinet would be reformed to include the German Social Democrats and that the new government would adopt a radical socialist program. The left wings of both the Czech and the German Social Democrats were pushing for such an event. But the moderate majorities of both parties, led respectively by Tusar and Seliger, were as yet unwilling to subordinate their national interests to a common socialist program, and they also refused the left-wing demands that the parties declare allegiance to the Third International.[136] The crisis within the Czech Social Democratic party forced Tusar to resign the premiership, and in September 1920 Masaryk appointed a new "cabinet of experts," headed by Jan Černý, to become a caretaker government.[137] The autumn meetings of the parties only postponed a complete and final break with their left wings. As an outgrowth of the power struggle within the Czech Social Democratic party, the radicals attempted to stage a general strike in December 1920, but it was broken by energetic government action and the opposition of the moderate socialists.[138] In March 1921 the Germans formed their own Communist party, the Czechs followed suit in May, and the two united in October and November 1921 to form the Communist party of Czechoslovakia. The Černý government, which originally was intended to exist for only three months, continued to govern for a year, until September 1921. During its life, nationality animosities and class conflicts remained much as they had been during the Tusar period, but gradually the violent manifestations of national and social friction began to subside as people adjusted to a new order in Central Europe.

NEW COOPERATION BETWEEN PRAGUE AND VIENNA

One of the most surprising developments of postwar Central European diplomacy was the rapid establishment of close and indeed friendly relations between Austria and Czechoslovakia. For the year between the dissolution of the Austro-Hungarian Empire and the Treaty of St. Germain the two states had been sharp competitors for the spoils of the old empire, and the German-Bohemian question had been the core of the dispute. With the signing of the peace treaties, however, there rapidly developed a new atmosphere in which the countries sought to reestablish the economic relations that had developed naturally over the centuries. In this process the Austrians were definitely the suppliants for the favor of the Czechs, who controlled the coal supplies upon which Vienna was dependent. The Czechs were responsive to the Austrian initiatives for both political and economic reasons. These common interests prompted the rapid improvement of relations between the two governments.

Within a week of the signing of the Treaty of St. Germain in September 1919, the new tone was set in a meeting between the Czechoslovak premier, Vlastimil Tusar, and the Austrian plenipotentiary in Czechoslovakia, Dr. Ferdinand Marek. In that meeting Tusar promised an amnesty for the Sudeten German exile leaders that, as has been seen, permitted them to return to Czechoslovakia and continue their political activities. Tusar emphasized his desire to establish friendly political relations with the Austrians and affirmed his belief that it was time to open discussions on matters of mutual economic interest.[139] Shortly thereafter, the Austrians began to receive some of their earliest firsthand impressions of Beneš upon his return to Prague from Paris. In a conversation with Marek at the close of October 1919, Beneš struck some themes that were to remain among his leitmotivs throughout the interwar years. First and foremost, the peace treaties had to be loyally accepted and adhered to. A political confederation among the Danubian states was unacceptable, but special economic ties could be created through a "system of treaties." Despite minor liabilities the Czechoslovak republic was strong, stable, and intent upon peaceful development. With elections approaching, the German question would be quickly solved, and the Germans would be invited to participate in the government "very soon." (It was not until 1926 that German ministers actually entered the cabinet, although there were serious discussions about the possibility in the early 1920s.) The minority question was an internal matter for Czechoslovakia, however, and Beneš could not permit any meddling from Germany or Austria, just as he would not intervene to protect the Czech population of Vienna. With Germany, he was gladly willing to enter into negotiations about the possible cession of border areas such as Asch, Rumburg, or Schluckenau. Finally, the strength of his diplomacy lay in its agreement with the ideals of Masaryk. Claiming to reject any form of secret diplomacy, he renounced all political intrigues (which in his opinion had evidently found a new center in Warsaw). He wanted to consider himself a progressive, democratic, and socialist-thinking politician.[140]

Building on the basis of that program, Austrian and Czech diplomats prepared for a visit to Prague by Chancellor Karl Renner in January 1920. Renner's primary purpose was to get badly needed deliveries of coal and foodstuffs from Czechoslovakia. Beneš came under increasing pressure from the West to help the Austrians out of their plight, and the British were particularly ostentatious in their friendliness toward Austrian diplomats in Prague.[141] The Czechs willingly cooperated. There were political agreements that Beneš wanted from the Austrians; a visit to Prague by the Austrian chancellor would inflate Czech pride and self-esteem; and, in any case, Austrian economic difficulties must not be allowed to come to the point of threatening Czechoslovakia's own welfare. The outward appearances during Renner's visit on January 10-13, 1920, were cordial. The two Social Democratic heads of government, Tusar and Renner, greeted one another with "Du"; and they formally established diplomatic relations between their two countries. News reports indicated that Renner was unable to attain increased commitments for coal deliveries to Austria but that the two sides had agreed to resist any attempt to reestablish the old political order (that is, a Habsburg restoration) in Central Europe.[142] In the public view the visit seemed to have gone well enough although nothing particularly outstanding had occurred.

But Beneš and Renner had actually concluded secret agreements that were of fundamental importance for Central Europe. In a series of three protocols signed by the two men, they established a diplomatic alliance against Hungary. Austria and Czechoslovakia agreed to support one another in the former Habsburg lands. Promising one another political and diplomatic support in the case that either were threatened by the Magyars, they undertook to hinder further delivery of military supplies to Hungary and, if necessary, to establish "a certain kind of very strict blockade" against the country. The Austrians promised the Czechs preference in the liquidation of military supplies left over from the war, and the Czechs in turn "guaranteed" compliance with the article of the Treaty of St. Germain giving West Hungary, or the Burgenland, to Austria. Emphasizing that these arrangements were of an "exclusively defensive character," Beneš and Renner agreed that, if one of the countries were attacked by Hungary, the way was to be left open for consultations about joint military action. With both states basing their mutual relations and their entire foreign policy on the "full, loyal, and correct" observance of the Treaty of St. Germain, the Czechoslovak government committed itself to pay special attention to the economic necessities for Austrian survival. The two states pledged to cooperate in economic matters and to conclude special treaties promoting commerce and trade between them. Finally, the issue of the national minorities was for both states a "purely internal question," about which it was possible to have "friendly discussions."[143]

The minutes of the political discussions between Beneš and Renner illuminate the reasons for their agreements. As of January 1920, Hungary was still an enemy state, and both men feared that the Hungarians might again resort to arms before agreeing to the peace terms formulated in Paris. Renner believed that the conservative social classes ruling in Budapest since the fall of Béla Kun had to maintain the territorial integrity of the old kingdom of Hungary or see their regime break apart. But it was not just Hungarian irredentism that was a potential concern. Beneš confided that he had already agreed with Rumanian and Yugoslav representatives in Paris that the three states would afford one another defensive military support in case of a threat from Hungary. (This was long before the formal conclusion of the treaties establishing the Little Entente.) Efforts to restore a Habsburg monarch in Budapest threatened both the Czechoslovak and the Austrian republics, and the two men agreed to instruct their intelligence services to cooperate in exchanging information about the restoration movements. Their spy services were evidently quite good, for Renner claimed to have infiltrated the court of former Emperor Charles in Switzerland, and Beneš quoted extensively from the minutes of the last meeting of the Hungarian council of ministers. Renner hinted that Austria might be a more effective partner against Hungary if it could be freed of the St. Germain restrictions imposing a thirty-thousand-man limit on its army, but Beneš sidestepped that particular issue. Among the foreign countries that were potential liabilities for their Hungarian policy, the two men singled out Poland, Italy, and Britain. Beneš tried to pretend that understanding between Warsaw and Prague was growing and that their initial difficulties had been exacerbated by the radicalism of Kramář. Beneš attached little importance to Italy, but both men were concerned about evident support for the Hungarians by British officers and diplomats. In regard to Germany, Renner assured Beneš that Berlin supported Czechoslovakia in the Teschen dispute and that the Germans had nothing against Renner's trip to Prague. Beneš responded that it was in Prague's own interest to keep the Sudeten Germans pacified, for, except for Austria, Czechoslovakia was surrounded by "openly imperialistic states."[144]

The prospect of a Habsburg restoration in Hungary posed internal dangers for both Austria and Czechoslovakia. Renner's Social-Democratic government represented essentially the city of Vienna, against which was aligned a clerical and a conservative countryside. The Habsburgs were Europe's traditional defenders of political Catholicism, and it was still easy for many Austrians in the small towns and the countryside to equate loyalty to the Habsburgs with devotion to the church. If Vienna's socialists wanted no more of the Habsburgs, it was not clear that other Austrians agreed. Czechoslovakia confronted the same kind of geographical and ideological divisions. Indicative of the atmosphere in Prague in the early days of independence were proposals to emblazon the Hussite chalice on the national flag.

The anniversary of Hus's execution became the occasion for national demonstrations and eventually led to an open break between the Vatican and the Czechoslovak government. Masaryk was widely regarded as a freethinker.[145] Yet 75 percent of the population was at least nominally Catholic. Catholicism was stronger in Moravia than in Bohemia, and

Catholic piety was deeply rooted among Slovak peasants in particular. Not yet educated to be republicans—when Masaryk traveled through the countryside he instructed the children: "Do not kiss my hand, but give me yours"—the peasantry was still fascinated by the panoply of monarchism. On the walls of some peasant homes a portrait of Masaryk simply took its place beside an older one of Francis Joseph. The magyarization policies in Slovakia had had their effect, and popular opinion in Slovakia was not so anti-Magyar as Prague wished the outside world to believe. A restored Catholic Habsburg dynasty in Budapest could exercise a magnetic appeal on Slovakia. Both Beneš and Renner had reason to fear a Habsburg restoration.

Relations between Czechoslovakia and Austria developed on the basis of the agreements of January 10, 1920. There was little or no open interference from Berlin. Samuel Saenger, still the German plenipotentiary in Prague, declared in a newspaper interview that Germany supported any policy that might ease Austria's economic plight and establish it as a viable country on the basis of the Treaty of St. Germain.[146] For his efforts he received a remonstrance from Foreign Minister Hermann Müller, who, while agreeing that Austro-Czechoslovak economic cooperation was momentarily in German interests, opposed any public pronouncements that might dampen Anschluss sentiments within Austria.[147] Sudeten German political leaders were miffed by Renner's failure to consult with them while in Prague. Lodgman warned Marek that the Austrian government could not ignore the Sudeten Germans in its relations with Prague, and he seemed to know a considerable amount about the anti-Hungarian nature of the agreements.[148]

With the Czechoslovak-Austrian rapprochement, the evidence of a diplomatic triangle between Prague, Vienna, and Berlin became increasingly obvious. Each of those capitals had special interests in the other two, and the three-cornered game that developed in their relations explained much about Central European diplomacy in the interwar years. From the viewpoint of the Czechoslovak leaders, despite their occasionally misleading statements, it was imperative to prevent a union of Austria and Germany. In 1921 40 percent of Czechoslovak exports went to Austria and Germany, and 35 percent of Czechoslovak imports came from those two countries. Throughout the 1920s Germany and Austria continued to account for up to half of Czechoslovak foreign trade. Given the geographical position of the country and the fact that Czechoslovakia's political allies were not its natural trading partners, it seemed difficult, if not impossible, to most commercial experts, Czech and foreign alike, for the country to redirect its trade in other directions. If Germany annexed Austria, therefore, Berlin would be likely to have a virtual stranglehold on the foreign trade of Czechoslovakia. From a military standpoint the defense of Bohemia and Moravia was already sufficiently difficult, and if Austria were added to the Reich the Germans might easily cut Czechoslovakia asunder by offensives from Silesia and Lower Austria. Moreover, an Anschluss would probably encourage the Sudeten Germans to renew their agitation for inclusion in Germany. The Czechoslovak government was therefore highly receptive to the argument that Austria must be made capable of an independent existence. That explains Prague's willingness to make economic concessions to the Austrians even though the average Czech regarded Vienna as a parasite that had too long exploited the riches of Bohemia and Moravia.

While Czechoslovak leaders worked to maintain the independence of Austria, the directors of German policy feared Austrian dependence on Czechoslovakia. In 1920 Germany was too weak to give ample economic aid to Austria, and the German leadership was therefore unable to protest the Austrians' seeking support elsewhere. Nevertheless, the Germans were acutely sensitive to any special arrangements between Czechoslovakia and Austria. Vienna possessed the historical, economic, and cultural ties with the Danube Valley that Berlin did not, and it was through Vienna that the Germans could most easily reestablish their influence in the area. For the Germans, the essential precondition was that Austria avoid constrictive attachments with the other successor states that could curtail or eliminate its usefulness to Berlin. On the other hand, an Anschluss was not indispensable. Throughout the Weimar years opinion was sharply divided among both German and Austrian leaders about the advisability of actually incorporating Austria into Germany. But widespread desire among the Austrian population to be included in Germany was a political asset that all German governments through the 1920s sought to retain whether or not those governments themselves actually desired an Anschluss. It was to Berlin's advantage to keep alive the hopes for an Anschluss even though German diplomacy did little to bring those hopes to fruition.

After the peace conference refused to allow an Anschluss with Germany, the Viennese government confronted the task of making Austria a viable state. The problem was basically one of finding economic support for the city of Vienna. In 1919 it seemed that the vast majority of Austrians wanted to join Germany, and in 1921 local states within the republic conducted plebiscites that returned overwhelming decisions for an Anschluss.[149] Vienna retained close diplomatic ties with Berlin, and the two capitals could usually rely on one another for an exchange of information. But the other main thrust of Austria's foreign policy in Central Europe was toward the states of the old empire, particularly Czechoslovakia. Already in the early 1920s Vienna developed the practice of playing Berlin and Prague against each other. By keeping fears of an Anschluss alive in Prague and by hinting of a possible rapprochement with

Czechoslovakia in Berlin, the Austrians attempted to garner economic concessions in both capitals. Despite the bitterness of domestic political rivalries in Austria, that strategy remained essentially unaltered regardless of the coalition in power.

The two primary factors influencing Austro-Czechoslovak relations in 1920 and 1921 were the threat of Hungarian revisionism and the need to reconstruct economic ties in the Danubian region. In their isolation and weakness the Reich Germans remained interested but passive observers of events in the area, but the influence of French, British, and even Italian diplomacy was considerable.

The Hungarian problem divided the Allies in 1919 when Italian diplomacy started to defend Hungarian interests in the hope that the country would be a natural ally of Italy. The Béla Kun episode and the continuing fears of Bolshevik expansion in Central Europe also sensitized British and French diplomats to the need for a stable regime in Budapest. After the fall of Béla Kun and the brief rule of Archduke Joseph, conservative forces under Admiral Nicholas Horthy soon assumed direction of the country. Not only did British circles show signs of sympathy for the new regime, but in the winter and spring of 1920 there was evidence of a rapprochement between Paris and Budapest as well. Maurice Paléologue, the new secretary-general at the French Foreign Ministry, hoped to bring Hungary into the French sphere of interest and voiced a willingness to make territorial concessions to Hungary for that purpose. Relations between Poland and Hungary were hearty as well. No peace treaty with Hungary had yet been signed. The Hungarian peace delegation that received the peace terms in Paris in February 1920 worked assiduously to salvage as much formerly Hungarian territory as possible. In relation to Czechoslovakia, Hungarian territorial claims included Subcarpathian Ruthenia, Eastern Slovakia, the island of Grosse Schütt, and the cities of Košice (Kassa, Kaschau) and Bratislava (Pozsony, Pressburg). Beneš was sensitive to the Hungarian diplomatic advances, and in 1920-21 he embarked on an effort to create a counterbalance capable of containing Hungary within the frontiers tentatively drawn in Paris in 1919. Those boundaries were confirmed in the Treaty of Trianon of June 4, 1920. The constellation of political forces still seemed to offer prospects for territorial revisions, however, and the Hungarian government cultivated sympathies in the West by offering military aid to Poland during the Soviet-Polish war.[150]

Already at the time of Renner's visit in Prague in January 1920 Beneš had offered to conclude anti-Hungarian alliances with Rumania and Yugoslavia. The negotiations that led to the creation of the Little Entente continued intermittently for more than a year and a half and eventually reached fruition because of periodical threats from Hungary.

Czechoslovak-Austrian relations in 1920-21 were characterized by Beneš's repeated efforts to draw Austria into closer association with the emerging Little Entente. When Beneš was journeying to Belgrade in early August 1920 in order to conclude the first of the treaties that established the Little Entente, he tried to persuade the Austrians to establish closer political ties with Czechoslovakia.[151] Back in Prague in September Beneš emphasized his friendliness in a conversation with the Austrian minister by claiming that he had always favored an Anschluss of Austria with Germany, which he still considered the best solution for Austria's problems; but, as the Allies had decided otherwise, he considered it his moral duty to help assure an independent existence for Austria.[152] (The archival documents do not corroborate Beneš's claim to have favored an Anschluss at the peace conference, and all his later statements and policies show quite clearly that the threat of an Anschluss quickly became his bête noire.)

The Austrians responded to Beneš's overtures by requesting a trade treaty favorable to Austrian commercial interests. They also had their own reasons to fear Hungarian revisionism, however, for the territory of West Hungary, or the Burgenland, was still a matter of hot dispute between the two countries. In a newspaper interview in October, Foreign Minister Renner claimed that Austria could not join the Little Entente because of stipulations in the Treaty of St. Germain. He welcomed the existence of the alliance, however, insofar as it was dedicated to the preservation of peace in Central Europe.[153] It therefore became Austrian policy to show sympathy for the goals of the Little Entente while maintaining a safe distance from the alliance itself. The Austrian government hoped thereby to avoid arousing the ire of the German nationalists at home or the leaders of the Reich, who were jealous of Austria's allegiance.

Intertwined with the efforts to contain Hungary were the hopes of overcoming the trade barriers that had arisen along with the national boundaries in the Danubian region. Whereas Czechoslovakia inherited a well-balanced economy and important natural resources, the city of Vienna emerged from the war as an industrial, commercial, and financial center severed from its economic hinterland. Influential circles in the West, particularly in Britain, had from the end of the war decried the "Balkanization of Central Europe." The British and the French governments feared that national jealousies and high tariff walls would ruin the economy of the region and leave it an easy field for Bolshevik expansion or a Germanic Mitteleuropa. The Western powers included in the Treaties of St. Germain and Trianon articles that left open the possibility of a Danubian preferential tariff system. Recognizing Beneš's diplomatic abilities, Western statesmen put pressure on him to take the lead in promoting commerce among the successor states. The Austrians always maintained that the peace treaties left their country in an impossible economic situation, and they tried to exploit Western pressure in order to get special trade concessions among the successor states.

Beneš found himself in a difficult position as a result of the pressure from his allies. He had no intention of establishing or even of allowing anything like a customs union in Central Europe, for he believed the axiom of statecraft that political bonds follow economic ties. The leaders of the successor states were too proud of their independence, however young and frail it was, to allow it to be threatened by a supranational economic organization. On the other hand, Beneš always had to appear reasonable and willing to compromise with the desires of the Western allies. He therefore devised the idea of a series of bilateral trade treaties that would set up a preferential tariff system among the Central European states. Such a system would not impair the sovereignty of the countries involved since there would be no single agreement or administrative organization, yet by keeping down tariff barriers it could promote the trade vital for the economic health of the region. Beneš publicly explained his plan in a speech in the Czechoslovak Chamber of Deputies on January 27, 1921.[154] The basic idea of constructing a preferential tariff system through a series of bilateral treaties had long been a part of Beneš's thinking, for he had alluded to it as early as his conversation with Marek in October 1919.[155] For years it remained his prescription for the promotion of regional commerce in Central Europe.

The two themes of economic rapprochement and containment of Hungary dominated Austro-Czechoslovak relations through 1921. Beneš liked to pose as a public defender of Austrian financial interests.[156] Although officials in the Austrian Foreign Ministry were deeply skeptical about the sincerity of Beneš's claims of goodwill, they did believe that circumstances were forcing him toward a more cooperative attitude.[157] Negotiations for a commercial treaty began in March. The first attempt of former Emperor Charles to return to Hungary and to reclaim his throne provoked a menacing reaction from Hungary's neighbors in late March. It led to the conclusion of a treaty of alliance between Czechoslovakia and Rumania that was an essential link in the Little Entente. In August Beneš delicately sounded out Chancellor Schober about the possibility of Austria's joining the Little Entente and declared: "We would scarcely watch for more than three days an attempt to restore any member of the Habsburg dynasty to the Hungarian throne."[158] Finally in the autumn the long struggle between Austria and Hungary for the Burgenland reached a climax, and Beneš attempted to mediate between the two countries in Austrian interests.[159] The issue was finally resolved in December 1921 when the inhabitants of Sopron (Oedenburg) voted in a plebiscite to remain part of Hungary while the rest of the Burgenland joined the

Austrian republic. At the end of October the second attempt of Charles to reclaim his throne in Budapest brought the Habsburg issue to a solution. The united opposition of the Western powers and the Little Entente forced the government of Count Stephen Bethlen to make Charles abdicate and denounce the Pragmatic Sanction of 1722, which had made the Hungarian throne hereditary in the House of Habsburg. Charles was exiled to Madeira, where he died five months later.[160] The resolution of the Habsburg and Burgenland issues removed the Hungarian question from its central role in Austro-Czechoslovak affairs, but economic relations were becoming ever more important for the two countries.

Austro-Czechoslovak cooperation reached a new plateau with the signing of the Treaty of Lány on December 16, 1921. The occasion was a state visit of President Hainisch and Chancellor Schober to Czechoslovakia. The real goal of the Austrians was to ensure a major loan from the Western powers. Particularly the French had made it clear that Austria must first come to a political understanding with Czechoslovakia, and the Austrians regarded Beneš as a "superbly appropriate intermediary for Paris and London."[161] In the preparatory memoranda for the conference, experts of the Austrian Foreign Ministry theorized that an Austro-Czechoslovak treaty would be merely the first step toward a reconsolidation in the Danubian area, and they considered it essential that Austria not be left out. In regard to the Sudeten Germans, they pointed out that the policy of diplomatic intervention in 1919 had hurt the Sudeten Germans more than it had helped them, and the experts therefore hoped that more was to be gained for the various German minorities by coming to agreements with the rulers of the successor states. In the Austrian view, no serious objection could be raised by Berlin, for the Reich Germans were in no position to aid Austria, and they therefore could not criticize the Austrians for doing that which was necessary to survive. Moreover, the government of Chancellor Joseph Wirth had claimed to be in outright opposition to an Anschluss, and it was obvious in any case that an Anschluss was not a short-term possibility. In a larger view, however, a union not just of Austria but also of Czechoslovakia with Germany would be in everybody's interest and would hardly be anything new in European history.[162]

In the political discussions the Austrians continued to reject any formal identification with the Little Entente, with the justification that the neutrality imposed upon them by the Treaty of St. Germain made it impossible for them to enter such an alliance. But the treaty that they signed at the presidential estate of Lány was nevertheless a far-reaching instrument. Austria and Czechoslovakia pledged to carry out completely the provisions of the Treaties of St. Germain and Trianon, and they guaranteed one another's territorial integrity and promised much political and diplomatic support to that end. Each vowed to maintain neutrality in case of an attack on the other by a third power. In addition, they promised not to permit within their borders any political or military organization that might endanger the other, and both governments were to cooperate in combatting any attempt to restore the "old regime." After settling current questions between them, they pledged to bring any future dispute that they could not solve directly to an arbitration tribunal or to the Permanent Court of International Justice.[163] The Treaty of Lány contained provisions to which Berlin was never willing to agree in its own relations with Czechoslovakia. Most significant was the mutual guarantee of territorial integrity, for by this agreement Vienna voluntarily recognized its territorial losses to Czechoslovakia in a formal treaty concluded directly between the two states. It was just such a treaty to which Stresemann subsequently refused to agree at Locarno. The provision about combatting private organizations was aimed at the irredentist groups that had sprung up in Austria, as well as in Germany, with the purpose of agitating for support of the Sudeten Germans. Although those organizations were not completely quelled, they subsequently fared better in Germany than in Austria. In exchange for his political concessions Schober won the promise of a loan of 500 million Czechoslovak crowns.

From the standpoint of Austrian domestic politics, it was significant that the policy of rapprochement with Czechoslovakia, which had started under the Social Democrat Karl Renner, was continued by Schober's coalition of Christian Socials and pan-Germans. To be sure, Schober's government informed Prague that it considered the treaty to have supplanted the Beneš-Renner secret protocols of January 1920. Beneš quickly agreed.[164] The anti-Hungarian basis for cooperation between Prague and Vienna was therefore deemphasized, for the immediate threat from Budapest had effectively vanished with the settlement of the Burgenland dispute and the failure of the Charles putsches. But in place of those contingency agreements, aimed at a particular threat, came a broader understanding regulating the general political questions between Austria and Czechoslovakia. Concluded for a period of five years, the treaty possessed higher legal status than the protocols. In getting the treaty ratified, Schober faced criticism from extreme nationalist circles at home and among the Sudeten Germans as well. (According to an Austrian intelligence report, a protest demonstration in Vienna at the end of December included "the representative of the National-Socialist Party from Munich, Adolf Hitler," who regarded the Treaty of Lány as just another link in the encirclement of Germany.)[165] But the German leaders themselves were not so upset. From conversations with President Ebert and the two state-secretaries in the Foreign Office, the Austrian minister reported that Schober's action had met with basic understanding in Berlin.

There was some concern that the affirmation of the peace treaties would prejudice future revisionist efforts, and the Germans hoped that the treaty did not signify a general turning away from the Anschluss idea in favor of cooperation with the Little Entente. Assuring the Germans that the Anschluss remained the ultimate goal of Austrian foreign policy, the minister suggested that Berlin might take more steps to support the Austrian economy by promoting trade between the two countries, by advancing a loan, and by encouraging German private investment in Austria. The German response seemed to be positive.[166]

If the Austrians were content with the agreement, Beneš had reason to be satisfied as well. The Austrians had paid the political price necessary for economic assistance, and Beneš realized that economic cooperation was important for Czechoslovakia as well. Three days after the signing of the treaty, his remarks to the British minister were paraphrased in the following manner:

> There were difficult days coming for the succession States. Germany must sooner or later again become great and prosperous, and it seemed inevitable to Dr. Beneš that Germany and Russia would come together. Unless the succession States were prepared to meet that combination of forces, the outlook would be most serious. His object was therefore to build up an economic group of States which could hold its own, no matter what might be the development of relations between Germany and Russia. He wished to develop, not only in the little *Entente,* but also in Austria and Hungary and Poland, a community of economic interest which would make them realize that they were mutually necessary to one another, if they were to attain the full development of their freedom and independence. It was in this spirit that in his negotiations with Dr. Schober he had done all he could by concessions to make things easy for Austria.[167]

However much he may have been catering to British opinion, Beneš showed remarkable prescience in predicting the German-Russian rapprochement just four months before the Rapallo agreements. Much more important, his remarks reflected a clear understanding of the basic political and economic realities in Central Europe. The question that remained was whether Beneš had the determination and the ability to translate knowledge into action.

GERMANY AND CZECHOSLOVAKIA IN INTERNATIONAL RELATIONS

The early years after the Paris peace conference were a period of transition and attempted stabilization in international affairs. The impact of the First World War had so thoroughly shaken the old diplomatic system and altered the world power structure that an extended period of adjustment was essential. The Paris peace treaties represented an attempt to establish both a new set of power relationships and a new body of diplomatic rules, at least ostensibly in accord with the principles of the "New Diplomacy" that had been popularized by Wilson. That was a Herculean undertaking, and much was left unfinished. Whereas the peace treaties were the launching point of interwar diplomacy, statesmen and diplomats still had to formulate the policies of their countries on many problems arising out of the peace settlements in the years after 1919. The early relations between the Weimar and the Czechoslovak republics were therefore conducted in a fluid international situation. Only gradually did their respective positions in international debates become fully visible.

Between 1919 and 1921 the newly established Czechoslovak republic commanded little attention in Berlin. Political decision-makers in Germany confronted many problems of greater immediate significance. The task of establishing a republican form of government in place of an authoritarian monarchy consumed the energies of the Weimar National Assembly from January to August 1919, and the constitutional debate continued long after the formal adoption of the constitution itself. The resurgence of conservative sentiment was manifest in the abortive Kapp putsch in March 1920 and the Reichstag elections of June. Social class conflict, geographical suspicions and rivalries, inflation and unemployment created a climate in which radical political movements flourished and political assassinations became commonplace. In the first three years of its existence the Weimar republic had no fewer than five governments. With the time that Weimar governments could devote to foreign affairs they had to concentrate on their relations with the victorious Western powers. Negotiations concerning German disarmament, reparation payments, the Allied occupation of the Rhineland, the plebiscites in disputed territories, and the trials of German wartime leaders overshadowed local matters in Central Europe. The frequent changes of government contributed to the absence of a general strategy in German foreign policy. A pariah among nations, Germany remained on the defensive and undertook few if any initiatives abroad.

Yet a German policy toward Czechoslovakia did slowly emerge. In its broad outlines German policy aimed at the maintenance of order and stability in Central Europe while German governments wrestled with their domestic problems and their negotiations with the Western powers. At the same time German policymakers hoped to prevent the rise of alliances or commitments that would be inimicable to the reassertion of German interests in Central Europe once Germany had recovered from the war. Berlin's policy toward both the Sudeten German question and the issue of Austria's relationship with the other successor states was in accord with those more general aims. Caution and uncertainty characterized early

Weimar diplomacy toward Czechoslovakia. The young Czechoslovak republic owed much to the Western powers, yet the traditional associations of the Czech and Slovak lands were in Central Europe. The Germans could not be certain in what direction Czechoslovak diplomacy would develop. They were therefore close observers of the positions that Czechoslovak policy took on international issues in the early 1920s. Professor Samuel Saenger was sent to Prague in 1919 as the German representative largely because of his good personal relations with Masaryk. He became the German minister to Czechoslovakia when full diplomatic relations were formally established in April 1920.[168] Although the affable and unprofessional Saenger tended to forget his reserve and undertake unauthorized initiatives, he did serve the useful function or projecting an image of goodwill in the early years of the republics.[169]

In contrast to the situation in Berlin, Czechoslovak policy toward Germany developed as part of a general diplomatic strategy conceived by an able political leadership. Edvard Beneš fully deserved the triumphant reception accorded him upon his return to Prague from the Paris peace conference in late September 1919. Fresh from his victories in Paris, Beneš aspired not only to maintain his direction of Czechoslovak foreign policy but also, with the support of Masaryk, to exercise influence in Czechoslovak domestic affairs as well. That was the impression that he left with General Pellé, the commander of the Czechoslovak army, who reported to Paris on September 28, 1919, "According to what M. Beneš told me yesterday, he goes early every morning to the president, who discusses with him all the questions of the day. When there is a cabinet meeting, Beneš arrives knowing the opinion of the president and certain of his support."[170] Although Beneš's influence tended to fluctuate in domestic affairs, he remained the chief determiner of Czechoslovak foreign policy until the aftermath of the Munich conference. On September 30, 1919, in his first parliamentary speech on foreign affairs, he expressed the basic tenets of the foreign policy that he was to follow for almost two decades. Freely admitting that Czechoslovakia was the ally of the Western powers in upholding the peace treaties, he called for a "correct and loyal" policy toward Germany. Beneš remarked that Germany would probably be involved in its internal affairs for a number of years to come but that it would eventually again play a dominant role in European diplomacy. In anticipation of that time he emphasized that Czechoslovakia must make it clear that it would never become dependent on any neighbor and that it would always oppose any revival of a pan-German policy.[171] Thus it was that both the need to live in peace with Germany and the fear of a new German dominance in Central Europe determined Czechoslovak attitudes from the beginning of the republic.

Czechoslovakia was a status quo power. In alliance with Rumania and Yugoslavia, Czechoslovakia had enough strength to thwart any revisionist efforts of the Hungarians. But for protection against German revisionism Czechoslovakia needed the support of great powers. In the early 1920s these could be only Britain and France. The major objective of Czechoslovak diplomacy in those years was to remain in alliance with a united Entente. Given the growing divergence of British and French postwar policies and Czechoslovakia's own peculiar interests in Central Europe, that was no easy task. Widespread concern in London about a potential French political, military, and commercial dominance over the continent opened fissures in the Western alliance. Whereas British policy aimed increasingly at political and social stabilization in Germany and the revival of international commerce, French policy consistently tried to weaken Germany in every way possible. The Czechs found themselves in a difficult situation, and they struggled against having to make a clear choice between the two Western allies. So long as they might safely rely on both powers, they would not become completely dependent on either. Beneš traveled and talked untiringly in an effort to preserve the unity of the Entente. Masaryk and Beneš, as the real architects of Czechoslovak foreign policy, fully shared French anxiety about a revival of German power, but they also realized that the anarchical conditions in Germany could have disastrous consequences throughout Central Europe.[172] One of their arguments for the preservation of the Entente was that British policy could restrain some of the more dangerous ideas of the French. Yet the British already showed signs of disengaging themselves from Central European affairs. The basic fact was that France was the only country with military forces on the continent capable of coming to the aid of Czechoslovakia.

Beneš's attempt to establish "correct and loyal" relations with Germany while remaining in alliance with both Western powers proved to be a thorough test of his diplomatic ingenuity. Between 1919 and 1921 three major international disputes affected the relations between Germany and Czechoslovakia, revealing both the common interests of the two countries and the limits of their cooperation. The issues were the Soviet-Polish war, the reparations debate, and the struggle for Upper Silesia.

The climax of the Soviet-Polish war in 1920 stimulated a demonstration of similar attitudes in Germany and Czechoslovakia. Both countries were involved in territorial disputes with Poland, and both tended to look to Soviet Russia as a possible defender of their own interests. The young Bolshevik regime in Russia probably found more tolerance in Prague than in almost any other European capital. Although the Czechoslovak government dared not outpace the Western allies in establishing formal ties with the Bolsheviks, Masaryk and Beneš had concluded that the Bolshevik regime would likely endure longer than most people in the West had previously been willing to admit. In April 1920, only days before the Poles launched their offensive in an effort to detach the Ukraine from the rest of the Soviet republic, Beneš responded to a note from Foreign Commissar Georgi Chicherin in a manner that, as Beneš admitted, amounted to the practical recognition of the Soviet regime.[173] At the beginning of May, even as Polish troops were pushing toward the outskirts of Kiev, Beneš remarked to the Austrian minister that the invasion was "not only a great misfortune but also a great stupidity." He emphasized that, regardless of British and French policy, Czechoslovakia would remain absolutely neutral, for it was in the most fundamental interest of the country to maintain a friendly relationship with Russia. Russia would remain a powerful factor in Europe, and in its recovery it was bound to absorb the small Baltic states again. The Ukraine could live only in union with Great Russia, and "never ever" would Beneš recognize the existence of an independent Ukrainian state.[174]

The successful Russian counterattack in early June brought increased French pressure on the Czechs to expedite the shipment of war supplies through Czechoslovakia to Poland. Sympathy for Russia was something on which both traditional nationalists and left-wing socialists among the Czech populace could agree, however, and the government itself was none too anxious to compromise its neutrality by transporting supplies to the Poles. As Czech railway shipments ground almost to a standstill, Polish dependence on Czechoslovakia became increasingly obvious, and the French hoped to pave the way for Czechoslovak-Polish cooperation by reaching a final settlement of the Teschen dispute. Adeptly exploiting the strength of his position through astute diplomacy before and during the Spa conference in July, Beneš won Polish agreement to drop the proposed plebiscite in Teschen and to accept whatever settlement the Allies might impose. The Allied decision was immediately forthcoming, and it gave the bulk of the territory, the coal mines, and the railway to Czechoslovakia while leaving a large Polish minority under Czechoslovak rule. It had been secretly drafted by two senior diplomats, Jules Laroche and Sir Eyre Crowe, with the help of Beneš himself.[175]

But even after the victory in Teschen, Masaryk and Beneš continued to oppose Allied military assistance to the Poles. As the Red Army approached the gates of Warsaw, the two men became convinced that the Polish military situation was practically hopeless. In late July Masaryk told an Entente commission headed by Jules Jusserand and Lord D'Abernon that military intervention for a losing cause would simply result in a loss of prestige and influence for the Western powers. In his view bayonets were not the way to fight Bolshevism, for "the sight of one locomotive is worth more than the capture of a battalion of Bolshevists." Given the economic hardships in Russia, commercial relations and the resulting demonstration of Western standards of living would be much more effective than military action in combatting Bolshevik propaganda.[176] In early August Masaryk paid a visit to the British minister in Prague and repeated those same arguments. On that occasion he added that Czechoslovak intervention against the Russians or the transport of troops or munitions across Czechoslovakia to Poland would strengthen the radical (that is, communist) wing of the Czech Social Democratic party and possibly lead to an upheaval in the country. In addition he was not willing to risk giving the Red Army a pretext to attack Czechoslovakia, which could hardly defend itself, and for that reason Czechoslovak officers were replacing their French colleagues in the command of Czechoslovak army contingents along the Slovak border.[177]

Relations between France and Czechoslovakia suffered a severe strain in the summer of 1920. Not only did the Czechoslovak government resist the transport of war supplies to Poland, but the formation of the Little Entente appeared to have an anti-Polish tinge as well. The steadily improving relations between Warsaw and Budapest culminated in a Hungarian offer of military aid to Poland during the war. The Hungarian government opportunistically attempted to exploit the Bolshevik threat in order to render services that would strengthen its claim to its former territories. There was interest in both Warsaw and Budapest in establishing a common Polish-Hungarian frontier, which could occur only at the considerable expense of Czechoslovakia. Although French policy showed no signs of supporting such a scheme, the issue at hand was the survival of Poland. The formation of the Little Entente as an alliance against Hungary had negative implications for Poland, and initial French reactions were cool or hostile. French diplomacy quickly tried to transform the Little Entente into a general alliance by urging the inclusion of Poland. The Czechs stoutly and successfully resisted French pressure.[178] Another element of friction in French-Czechoslovak relations was a new commercial treaty between Germany and Czechoslovakia. In a case of poor political timing German and Czechoslovak representatives signed a treaty on June 29, 1920, in which the Czechs renounced their right under the Treaty of Versailles to liquidate Reich-German property. Czechoslovakia therefore became the first of the formerly belligerent powers to sign a formal commercial treaty with Germany after the war. The French government was displeased by the Czechoslovak action, and it applied pressure on Prague to cancel the treaty or to delay its ratification until a French-Czechoslovak commercial agreement could be concluded.[179]

In the war itself, the successful Polish counterattack in mid-August quickly removed the Bolshevik danger from Central Europe and sent the Red Army once again into full retreat. Masaryk and Beneš had obviously discounted the Polish military too soon. Although the pressure on them to come to the aid of the Poles subsided, the failure to transport war supplies to Poland was an act that Marshall Pilsudski could neither forgive nor forget. It helped to envenom the Czechoslovak-Polish relationship throughout the interwar years. The friction between Poland and Czechoslovakia had graphically demonstrated the obstacles confronting the French in building a reliable eastern alliance system.

During the Soviet-Polish war popular sympathies in Czechoslovakia and the official policies of the government actually resembled attitudes in Germany more closely than those in France, although the Germans and the Czechs had fundamentally different reasons for coming to the same conclusions. During the advance of the Red Army, popular opinion along Germany's eastern frontiers imagined that the Bolsheviks would return to Germany those territories that had been ceded to Poland in the Treaty of Versailles. The psychological effect of a conquest of Poland was almost as satisfying as a defeat of France would have been. German celebrations over a report falsely announcing the fall of Warsaw led to a major Polish uprising in Upper Silesia. Top political and military leaders in Germany debated the possibility of German reacquisition of the 1914 eastern frontiers, and they received encouragement from the Soviet government. But despite popular animosity toward the Poles it was not in German interests to see an augmentation of Soviet influence in Central Europe. The political situation within Germany was none too stable, as rightist forces were openly turning against the republic. Given the various foreign and domestic pressures, the government in Berlin had little choice but to follow a policy of strict neutrality during the war. It refused to allow the transport of soldiers or war material across Germany, and the strike by German dockworkers at Danzig crippled French attempts to send supplies to the Poles by sea.[180] In the policy of neutrality, in the resistance to the transport of war supplies, in the basic animosity toward Poland, and in the fear of the Bolshevik threat in Central Europe, the two governments in Berlin and Prague found themselves in fundamental agreement. After the conclusion of the Soviet-Polish war, the reparations question and the struggle for Upper Silesia in 1921 offered other opportunities for testing the extent of a basic community of interest between Germany and Czechoslovakia.

By the late winter of 1921 the British and the French governments decided to demand German agreement to a final sum and a permanent schedule of reparation payments. The total amount at which their experts arrived was 150 billion gold marks, a figure far beyond the Germans' own estimate of their financial capabilities. When the Germans failed to respond satisfactorily to an ultimatum, the Allies established a separate customs regime in the occupied Rhineland, and French troops crossed the Rhine and occupied the cities of Düsseldorf, Duisburg, and Ruhrort at the beginning of March 1921.[181] Thereafter, French troops were poised for the occupation of the entire Ruhr industrial area in case of further recalcitrance by the Germans, and the threat of that occupation was frequently repeated. Had there been further sanctions against the Germans, the Czechs could not have remained unaffected, yet there was an obvious reluctance in Prague to become involved in applying economic pressure on Berlin. A curtailment of trade between the two countries would have hurt the Czechs at least as badly as the Germans, for it was just at that time that Czechoslovakia was beginning to feel the effects of the postwar trade depression after two years of prosperity. Even before the occupation of the three cities, Beneš predicted an international crisis, a split between Britain and France, further economic difficulties, and the undermining of all stability in Central Europe if the French occupied more German territory.[182] In February 1921 Vlastimil Tusar, the former premier, arrived in Berlin as the new Czechoslovak minister. His prestige and ability were fitting testimony to the importance and delicacy of his mission. Even as the London reparations conference was threatening to apply further sanctions against the Germans, Tusar told Foreign Minister Simons that in his opinion Czechoslovakia would not participate in those actions, and Beneš wrote that Czechoslovakia would be hurt worse by economic sanctions than Germany would be.[183] The Czechs were never put to the test of actually refusing to cooperate with their Western allies, for the Germans capitulated to another Allied ultimatum at the beginning of May, accepted a total reparations bill of 132 billion gold marks, and made an initial payment of one billion marks that month. But the reluctance of the Czechs to become involved in sanctions against Germany was a new demonstration of the common interest of the two countries in encouraging the political and economic stabilization of Central Europe.

The Upper Silesian question was a primary consideration in motivating the Germans to accept the Allied reparation demands. German diplomats proceeded to argue that without the mines and industries of Upper Silesia Germany could not possibly fulfill its reparation obligations. For two years after the peace conference German and Polish interests had jockeyed for position in Upper Silesia in preparation for the plebiscite. The basic pattern that had emerged at the peace conference—British support for Germany and French determination that Poland acquire the mines and industries—characterized the diplomatic conflicts before and after the plebiscite. At least until the weeks just before the plebiscite in March 1921, it was not at all clear just where Czechoslovak sympathies lay. The common interests that characterized German and Czechoslovak attitudes on problems involving Poland have already been sketched, and the split between the British and the French made it desirable from Prague's standpoint not to side too strongly with either ally. Yet Czechoslovak leaders could not remain impervious to the French determination that

Germany's eastern arsenal be put into the hands of a friendly power. At the close of January 1921 Beneš finally broke his silence in a typically phrased statement before the Czechoslovak Chamber of Deputies: "In the spirit of our democratic policy we heartily desire that what is Slav remain Slav."[184] Beneš's bow to ethnic solidarity certainly did no harm to his relations with the Poles and therefore with the French, and it came at a time when Beneš was professing to fear a new Bolshevik attack on Poland. He was busily attempting to create the impression that Czechoslovakia would stand beside Poland in case of another Soviet-Polish war in a way that it had not in the summer of 1920. Immediately after his "Slavic" remark Beneš added that he hoped that Czechoslovakia's economic interests in Upper Silesia would not be harmed. One of the main elements in Czechoslovak-German trade was the exchange of hard and soft coal, and the anthracite that the Germans delivered to Czechoslovakia came largely from Upper Silesia. Beneš wanted to be sure that if the coal mines went to Poland the Poles would be willing to continue the trade. When Saenger later protested Beneš's apparent siding with the Poles, Beneš retorted that his words were largely window dressing anyway. He added that, as he had often remarked, Upper Silesia posed a problem to all of Europe and not simply to Germany and Poland.[185] No one could deny that the fate of Upper Silesia was of significance for Europe as a whole, but it was also obvious that all-European problems gave Beneš a greater latitude for diplomacy than did direct confrontations between two states or groups of states.

The only direct influence that the Czechoslovak government exercised on the outcome of the plebiscite was the decision not to allow the inhabitants of Hlučín to return and vote. According to the ruling of the plebiscite commission, people born in Upper Silesia but no longer resident there were eligible voters. This description fitted a number of Hlučíners, who harbored German loyalties. By refusing to allow them to cast ballots and then return home, the Czechoslovak government probably held down to a small extent the total German vote.[186] Actually Czechoslovakia stood to gain a small amount of territory by a Polish victory in the plebiscite. The Treaty of Versailles stipulated that the district of Leobschütz was to go to Czechoslovakia if Upper Silesia were added to Poland, for it would otherwise become a German enclave between Poland and Czechoslovakia. The Czechs never showed any serious interest in the question, for an acquisition of Leobschütz would simply have added more Germans to their state.

Beneš's "Slavic" remark and Czechoslovak policy in regard to the Hlučíners put the first real strain on the relations between Prague and Berlin. While Beneš was responding to Polish and French pressure, Tusar was attempting to neutralize the effect of Beneš's remarks on the

Germans. Less than a week before the plebiscite, Tusar told Foreign Minister Simons that he personally hoped that Upper Silesia would remain with Germany, for the Poles would ruin the industry there and, besides, they were "unpleasant neighbors." Czechoslovak army contingents were massing along the Upper Silesian border, but Tusar assured Simons that those troop concentrations were there only to protect Czechoslovak territory against any armed intervention by the Poles.[187] The plebiscite resulted in a German victory, with 60 percent of the voters opting in favor of Upper Silesia's remaining with Germany. Czech newspaper reaction, according to Saenger's analysis, envied the Germans their victory without regretting the slap at the Poles.[188] Whereas the returns easily demonstrated the German or Polish loyalties of particular agricultural districts, the industrial cities and towns with their mixed populations could be claimed by both sides. A vigorous debate ensued in the Interallied Plebiscite Commission between the French representative and the British and Italian representatives about varying boundary proposals. At the beginning of May a false report appeared that the entire industrial area would stay with Germany. Polish irregulars immediately crossed the frontier and, along with local Polish insurgents, attempted to seize and hold most of Upper Silesia. The resort to force by the Poles alarmed the government in Prague, where there were fears that the Polish bands would also attempt to occupy Teschen. Beneš told the British minister that the government was "taking measures to act energetically, should such an emergency arise."[189]

The fighting between Poles and Germans in Upper Silesia was nothing compared with the diplomatic hostilities that erupted between France and Britain after the Polish invasion. When the Poles swept through the area with French acquiescence, Lloyd George publicly advocated the use of German paramilitary forces to stop them. Despite the bitter protests of Aristide Briand, who was the French premier at the time, this was exactly what happened. After the fighting ceased in June, the final allocation of Upper Silesia still remained to be decided, and the British and the French continued to disagree on the various proposals to divide the area. For a period in the summer of 1921 it seemed as if the Entente might be on the verge of complete collapse. From the German standpoint the dissolution of the front against them had to be a welcome prospect, and German diplomats did what they could to play upon the differences between Paris and London. Masaryk and Beneš, on the other hand, feared a demise of the Entente, which could force them to choose finally and definitely between their two main Western allies. In late July, as the dispute approached its climax, Beneš tried to convince Saenger that only through the survival of the Entente could Britain exercise a moderating influence on the militarist and nationalist excesses of the French.[190] Beneš avoided such language when talking with his French allies, but his country did indeed have fundamental interest in a Franco-German modus vivendi that would stabilize conditions in Central Europe and remove points of friction between Paris and London. Beneš repeatedly urged German diplomats to come to an understanding with the French, but the implication was that the agreement was to be on French terms, which were unacceptable to the Germans.

At the beginning of August Lloyd George traveled to Paris for a meeting of the Supreme Council of the Allies at which he had a final confrontation with Briand about Upper Silesia. When the two men remained unable to agree on a boundary line that would divide the area between Germany and Poland, they decided to submit the dispute to the Council of the League of Nations and to abide by whatever solution the League proposed. The Council turned the matter over to its nonpermanent member states, which in turn appointed two experts, one of whom was a Czech, to draw an international frontier through Upper Silesia. Officials in the German Foreign Office particularly resented the activities of the Czech expert, who in their opinion scarcely met the requirement of neutrality between Germany and Poland. Through the summer Beneš had encouraged the Poles to believe that he was actively supporting their position while in reality he was doing little more than uttering platitudes sympathetic toward Poland.[191] At the same time he told Saenger that in his opinion both the western and the eastern boundaries of Poland were "provisional."[192] Beneš's favorite formulation for the problems of Danzig, the Corridor, and Upper Silesia was that they were "all-European" problems that could be settled only by general consultation sometime in the future. By holding out the possibility of revising those territorial provisions of Versailles that most rankled the Germans, Beneš was obviously trying to create some goodwill in Berlin. Yet insofar as he exercised any influence in the Upper Silesian dispute he took the side of the Poles.

In mid-September, while the matter was before the League of Nations, Beneš had a long conversation with the chief British representative in Geneva, Arthur James Balfour. Balfour's memorandum about Beneš's remarks was sent to those representatives in Geneva who were charged with proposing a boundary solution. Claiming to base his opinions on his experiences in the Teschen dispute, Beneš argued that neither the French proposal to give the industrial area to Poland nor the British-Italian desire to give it to Germany was wholly fair. It was possible to draw a boundary line through the industrial area, being as true as possible to ethnic considerations and letting industrial interests make the necessary adjustments.[193] The final solution that was adopted by the League and accepted by the Western powers in October did indeed divide the industrial area essentially along ethnic lines, but the result was that the vast majority of the mines and industries thereby went to Poland. Although it was impossible to gauge the degree of Beneš's direct influence on the outcome, German leaders suspected his activities in Geneva and assigned to him a considerable share of the blame for the unfavorable decision by the League. In a speech before the Chamber of Deputies in November Beneš denied having any influence on the League decision; but from Berlin's perspective it seemed that Beneš increasingly demonstrated his negative attitudes as he continued to take stands on issues involving Germany.[194]

In April 1921 the *Bohemia* had reported that Samuel Saenger was to be recalled to Berlin in order to assume a post specially created for him in the German Foreign Office. It added that the Saxon minister in the Reichsrat in Berlin, Walter Koch, had been approached about the Prague assignment but that he had refused the job.[195] If Koch initially refused, he reconsidered, for in October he replaced Saenger as German minister in Prague. With him began at least a new tone in the conduct of Czechoslovak-German relations. Saenger had been sent to Prague because the Foreign Office had hoped to use his personal friendship with Masaryk to establish good relations with the Czechoslovak government. After almost three years in Prague the professor had outlived his usefulness, and he was called home ostensibly to reorganize the diplomatic schooling in the Foreign Office. Koch, in his initial report from Prague, stated: "The desire to come to an understanding seems to me to have been demonstrated by Germany sufficiently well. It is advisable now for a while to match reserve with reserve."[196] The personal friendliness of Saenger was replaced with the formal correctness of Koch, and in this way Koch personified the relations between Germany and Czechoslovakia.

3   "Correct Relations," 1921–1925

Walter Koch remained the German minister in Prague for almost fourteen years. During that time he saw the gradual but steady improvement in Czechoslovak-German relations until the death of Stresemann and the Great Depression; then he witnessed the increasingly precipitous decline as Hitler successfully campaigned for the chancellery. A native of Saxony, Koch had been a member of the National Liberal party in Imperial Germany and had held various posts in the state bureaucracy in Dresden. Although not a professional diplomat, he had been chosen in the first weeks after the armistice to travel to Prague as the special plenipotentiary of the Saxon government in order to conclude provisional trade agreements with the Czechs. While in Prague he had cooperated closely with the German consulate, and upon his return home he had emphasized the danger for the Reich as a whole of sending diplomatic representatives from local German states to foreign capitals.[1] His loyalty understandably had made a good impression on the Foreign Office in Berlin. After serving in the Weimar National Assembly, Koch had become the Saxon member of the Reichsrat in Berlin. From there he was persuaded in 1921 to return to Czechoslovakia as the German minister, and he stayed there until he reached retirement age in 1935. Prague was his first and only diplomatic assignment for the German Reich.

In the early years of the Weimar republic the political instability in Berlin made it possible for German diplomatic representatives abroad to exercise an unusual amount of influence. The constantly changing cabinets produced nine foreign ministers from the time of the peace conference until August 1923. The permanent state secretaries in the Foreign Office gave some continuity to foreign policy, but their responsibility was more the routine conduct of diplomacy than the formation of policy. In that situation the advice coming in from the diplomatic posts abroad was more likely to be followed than if a strong central government had been pursuing an overall policy of its own. Koch was quickly recognized as one of Germany's leading experts on Czechoslovakia, and his advice was heeded even after Stresemann took control and gave direction to German foreign policy. Koch was quiet, conscientious, straightforward—he was also unimaginative and prone to pessimism. Rather than hoping for a quick reconciliation between Germans and Czechs, Koch regarded his assignment as one of methodically cultivating acceptable relations between nationalities that were historical enemies.

THE DIPLOMACY OF CONSOLIDATION

In late 1921 and 1922 there was a relatively quiet interlude in the relations between Berlin and Prague. From May 1921 to the close of 1922 Chancellor Joseph Wirth and his cabinets attempted to "fulfill" Allied reparation demands, and in foreign capitals Wirth was considered to be the most cooperative of Germany's postwar chancellors. Through the very policy of "fulfillment" the Germans hoped to demonstrate the impossibility of fully meeting the reparations demands. Seeking to avoid conflicts with Czechoslovakia, the Wirth government faced difficulties in Bavaria. Rumors of an imminent Czechoslovak military attack abounded in Munich in late 1921. In response to a Czechoslovak diplomatic protest, the state secretary in the German Foreign Office dismissed the rumors, but the incident was important in demonstrating a divergence in attitudes towards Czechoslovakia between the Prussian north and the Bavarian south.[2] While the Prussians concentrated on problems along the Polish frontier, the Bavarians worried more about their own border areas and resented Berlin's dominance in German foreign policy. Despite the disturbing influence from Bavaria, relations between Germany and Czechoslovakia were sufficiently harmonious for the German state secretary to consider seriously an exchange of border territories between the two countries.[3] The atmosphere in Berlin improved even more with the appointment of Walther Rathenau as German foreign minister in February 1922. Conciliatory and cooperative, he issued an invitation for Beneš to visit Berlin, but that was a demonstration for which the Czechs were not yet prepared.[4]

In Czechoslovakia during the year 1921 the resignation of the nonpolitical "cabinet of experts" under Jan Černý was frequently predicted. Antonín Švehla, the leader of the Czech Agrarian party, appeared to be the most likely successor, but Švehla liked best to remain behind the scenes, and he hesitated openly to assume political leadership. Parliamentary support for Černý's bureaucratic cabinet was organized by a group that became popularly known as the "Pětka" (the Five). Emerging in the course of 1921, it included one representative from each of the five major Czechoslovak political parties—the Social Democrats, the National Socialists, the Agrarians, the Populists (Catholics), and the National Democrats.[5] The Pětka was therefore a Czech national coalition covering an ideological range from Catholics to Marxists and including spokesmen for small farmers, industrial workers, and urban commercial and financial interests. It did not include representatives of the minority nationalities, the communists, or the Slovak autonomists. The Pětka was essentially a coalition of the so-called "state-creating" parties. It served as the parliamentary basis for a new cabinet, with Edvard Beneš as premier and foreign minister, that emerged in September 1921. While the party politicians concentrated on domestic affairs, Beneš continued to devote most of his time to foreign policy. Toward Germany his statements were friendlier than ever before.[6] He obviously hoped to maintain formally good relations with Germany, while simultaneously working to secure Czechoslovakia's position in Central Europe while Germany was still recovering from the war.

The primary focus of European diplomacy in 1922 was on international economic problems. Of particular significance for Czechoslovak-German relations were diplomatic agreements involving Soviet Russia and Austria. The dichotomy between the British desire to restore European trade and commerce and the French fear of a German resurgence characterized both the Cannes conference in January 1922 and the Genoa economic conference in April and May. At Genoa Bolshevik representatives participated for the first time in a postwar international meeting. French insistence that the Bolshevik regime assume responsibility for the old tsarist debts and the Allies' continuing demand for reparation payments from the Germans prepared the way for the Treaty of Rapallo, which torpedoed the conference. In the treaty the Germans and the Russians reestablished formal diplomatic relations, mutually renounced all financial claims against one another, and laid the foundation for a revival of trade between the two countries. That Rathenau, a "Westerner" in his orientation, agreed to the treaty, was a sign of Germany's diplomatic isolation and fear of potential reparation claims by the Russians. The agreement established a diplomatic climate favorable to the secret military cooperation between Berlin and Moscow, which had already started. Although historians have debated the wisdom from the German viewpoint of concluding the Treaty of Rapallo, the treaty did have fundamental significance for Czechoslovakia. As in 1920, during the Soviet-Polish war, the Czechs were reluctant to follow French policy to the point of alienating the Russians. An apparently government-inspired article in the *České slovo*, the chief newspaper of the Czechoslovak National Socialist party, pointed out that

> France is in a position to isolate herself economically from Russia, at least for the near future, but Czechoslovakia, which in this respect is in rather the same position as Great Britain, must come to terms with Russia, as she vitally depends on the Russian market. On this point, Czechoslovak interests are not identical with those of France.[7]

Even more important than the opening of the Russian market was the undying vision in Prague of eventually relying on the Russians for political and military support against the Germans. But the Czechs were in a peculiarly difficult situation. Poland, Rumania, and Yugoslavia supported French policy toward Russia, and Beneš felt unable to extend de jure recognition to the Soviets as long as the Western powers held back. Domestic political opposition, particularly by Kramář's National Democrats, was also a barrier to diplomatic recognition of the Soviets. Czechoslovak diplomacy was immobilized. The leaders in Prague impotently witnessed German diplomacy establishing a relationship with Moscow that they secretly desired for themselves.

If Czechoslovak diplomacy could do little about Russia, the year 1922 did mark the culmination of Beneš's efforts to build barriers between Germany and Austria. The political understandings between Czechoslovakia and Austria that were formalized in the Treaty of Lány of December 1921 bore fruit in the form of extensive economic credits to Vienna during the following year. The Czechoslovak crown was one of the world's strongest currencies, and Beneš's government was determined to pursue a deflationary policy at home in order to support the rapidly increasingly value of the crown on international monetary exchanges. Beneš explained the political purpose of his financial policies to the British commercial attaché, R. H. Bruce Lockhart, at the beginning of January 1922. According to Lockhart's memorandum,

> Dr. Beneš's chief object in maintaining the improvement of the krone is to separate that unit definitely and finally from the German mark. This is merely a part of his general policy which is governed by his desire to free Czecho-Slovakia as far as possible from economic dependence on Germany. At the present moment, between forty and fifty per cent of the foreign trade of the Czecho-Slovak Republic is with Germany. Dr. Beneš wishes to reduce this figure to at least twenty-five per cent. As long as the mark and the Czech krone have approximately the same value it is impossible to force even patriotic Czechs to refrain from exporting goods or raw materials to Germany and to abandon markets to which they have been accustomed all their lives. If, however, a wide disparity can be created between the mark and the krone, Czech merchants will no longer be able to export their goods to Germany and will be forced to seek fresh markets. These markets Dr. Beneš proposes to find in Poland, Austria, Hungary and the Balkans. His aim is to keep Germany in a weak and helpless state as long as possible in the hope that in the interval before she has regained her strength the economic independence of Czecho-Slovakia will be firmly established. In order to achieve this aim, not only is he prepared to do everything he can to improve the currency of all the neighboring Succession States (his recent offer of financial credits to Austria is apparently only part of a general plan to be applied to all the Succession States), but he is also anxious that Germany should be forced to pay such reparations as will at any rate ensure the mark being kept at as low a level as possible.[8]

The liabilities for Beneš's policy, as analyzed by Lockhart, were (1) the difficulties of constructing "a solid economic bloc composed of the Succession and the Balkan States"; (2) the possibility of early German competition in the areas where Beneš wanted to expand Czechoslovak export trade; and (3) the desire of the British government not "to keep the mark in a state of perpetual depreciation." Beneš tried to convince Lockhart that "whatever may be the interests of Great Britain in Germany itself, His Majesty's Government can never desire any great expansion of German commerce and German influence in Central Europe and in the Balkans."[9] The development of British attitudes through the interwar period concerning a German-dominated Central Europe was indeed of crucial significance for the independent existence of the Czechoslovak republic.

At the beginning of February 1922 the semiofficial *Prager Presse* reported that the Czechoslovak government had agreed to extend to Austria a 500-million-crown credit for the purchase of Czechoslovak goods.[10] When that credit came up for approval in the Czechoslovak Chamber of Deputies in June, the German Nationals and the National Socialists refused to vote for it on the grounds that the Treaty of Lány was the political price that the Austrians had had to pay for Czechoslovak economic assistance.[11] Their analysis of the situation was correct, but the financial plight of the Austrians was such that they had to find help wherever it was available. As the inflation in Austria reached catastrophic proportions, Ignaz Seipel succeeded Johann Schober as chancellor at the end of May and quickly began a campaign for a new international loan. A prelate and the politically gifted leader of the Christian Social party, Seipel was less enthusiastic about an Anschluss than were the leaders of the Austrian Social Democrats or the pan-Germans. He was quite willing to exploit the threat of an Anschluss for diplomatic purposes, however. In response to Austrian diplomatic initiatives for an international loan, Beneš repeated his arguments against an Anschluss, which he characterized as an "appeasement of Prussian imperialism." Neither Masaryk nor Beneš ruled out the possibility of a new loan, but they did insist on a thorough reorganization of Austrian finances, including even the imposition of foreign financial control.[12] In an effort to publicize Austrian problems, Chancellor Seipel undertook a trip to Prague, Berlin, and Verona in mid-August. In each city he explored the possibility of closer economic relations, attempting to play one country against the other. In Berlin, although the German government could not offer promises of economic aid, Chancellor Wirth strongly opposed closer Austrian economic ties with Czechoslovakia or the Little Entente.[13] Seipel's visit to Prague, immediately followed by his trips to Germany and Italy, spurred Masaryk into action also. In a specially arranged meeting with the British minister,

Masaryk noted Seipel's assertion that Austria must seek to lean (*Anlehnung*) on some neighboring state or group of states and that a solution of Austria's economic problems presupposed a political agreement as well. As illustrated by Seipel's journeys, Masaryk thought that there existed three potential solutions for Austria: union with Germany, with Italy, or with Czechoslovakia. In arguing against a union with Germany, Masaryk stressed the religious and temperamental differences between Austrians and Prussians as well as their divergent historical experiences. The possibility of Austrian inclusion in Italy he summarily dismissed.

Masaryk then weighed the feasibility of a union of Austria and Czechoslovakia even while emphasizing the tentativeness of his ideas. He remained extremely vague concerning the precise nature of such a combination and acknowledged the difficulties posed by the Sudeten Germans for any union of the two countries in which—it was understood—the Czechs would be the dominant partner. Masaryk's own summary of the crux of his argument was:

> But from our point of view I declare honestly that—although unwillingly and constrained by events—we prefer our union with Austria to the union of Austria with Germany or Italy. This I think follows logically from the world's situation, from history and especially from the world war: it cannot be our task and that of the Allies to encourage in one form or another the realisation of the Pan-German programme, Berlin-Bagdad. . . .
>
> . . . We do not wish to be taken by surprise and to find that by some solution of the Austrian crisis our independence and that of the neighboring states would be endangered and the peace settlement of Central Europe so changed that perhaps the whole terrible war would have been waged uselessly and in vain.[14]

Masaryk paralleled his initiatives with the British minister by conversing along the same lines with the American minister as well. From his talks with Louis Einstein it appeared that Masaryk looked to the precedent of the old Dual Monarchy as a way of effecting a practicable union of Czechoslovakia and Austria. According to Einstein, Masaryk "believed that it would mean a common foreign policy, customs and monetary union and also an army uniformly equipped and able to work in cooperation."[15] Although Masaryk believed that Austria's economic sickness did not yet necessitate such strong medicine, he was obviously willing to go to great lengths to prevent German or Italian domination of Austria. Masaryk's attitude was not just episodic, for a year later he reverted to the idea of a union between Austria and Czechoslovakia in a conversation with the French general, Pellé.[16] Hard documentary evidence of Masaryk's advocacy of a Czechoslovak-Austrian union under certain circumstances therefore exists in the diplomatic archives of the three major Western countries. In Masaryk's judgment, the independence of Czechoslovakia required an Austria free of German or Italian control.

When Seipel arrived in Geneva at the beginning of September, he found a more sympathetic attitude at the meeting of the Assembly of the League of Nations than had existed earlier. Quickly there was negotiated an international loan of 650 million gold crowns in return for which Austria promised to institute financial reforms and to submit to the supervision of a League commissioner. The agreement was embodied in the Geneva protocols of October 4, 1922, and the four powers that guaranteed the loan were Britain, France, Italy, and Czechoslovakia. Those countries promised not to violate Austrian sovereignty in any way, and Austria in turn undertook not to make any political or economic agreement that might infringe upon its independence.[17] The common interpretation of those provisions was that they strengthened the prohibition of an Anschluss, which was already part of the Treaty of St. Germain. It was for that reason that most of the Sudeten-German parties in the Czechoslovak Chamber of Deputies opposed ratification of the protocol.[18] The Geneva protocol represented the culmination of Beneš's policy of using Czecho-slovak financial strength and Austrian weakness to erect more safeguards against an Anschluss. In the protocol Czechoslovakia assumed a portion of the financial liability equal to that agreed to by each of the great powers. Coming only a few months after a credit of 500 million crowns, that additional Czechoslovak financial support for Austria was all the more striking in view of the popular resentment of Vienna among the Czechs. The international loan enabled the Austrian government to stabilize its currency and reestablish some measure of domestic political stability. The threat to the independent political existence of Austria was once again averted, at least temporarily.

During the summer and autumn of 1922 the Germans remained passive observers of the efforts to sustain Austria's existence, and even their ability to make perceptive observations was curtailed by the fact that they had just lost one of their most intelligent political authorities. When young assassins from a rightist organization murdered Walther Rathenau in June, the reaction among German-Jewish circles in Prague was one of shock and chagrin. The anti-Semitism that characterized the assassination and the growing strength of reactionary forces in Germany had a sobering effect, as was manifest in the headlines of Prague's newspapers—"Ein Opfer der Erfüllungspolitik," "Diktatur oder Bürgerkrieg."[19] Beneš's semiofficial *Prager Presse* proclaimed a "Mordatmosphäre über Deutschland," and the Czechoslovak press in general emphasized that the murder organization was headquartered in Munich.[20] In Czech eyes Munich and Budapest were the primary centers for intrigues against the Czechoslovak republic.

After a tenure of just over a year Beneš resigned as premier at the beginning of October 1922 but retained his post of foreign minister. If the purpose of Beneš's holding the premiership had been to acquaint him more closely with domestic problems and to afford him a broader identification in the minds of the public, the attempt had been futile, for foreign affairs had continued to demand the greater share of his attention. At long last, the leader of the Czech Agrarians, Antonín Švehla, accepted the premiership and retained that position, except for a few months in 1926, until he had to resign because of ill health in 1929. Švehla commanded respect as a consummate party politician who, in an often turbulent parliamentary atmosphere, wrung cooperation from the various parties of his coalition governments.

A month after the change of governments in Prague, Chancellor Wirth resigned and turned his office over to Wilhelm Cuno. The major foreign problem that Cuno inherited was the continuing dispute over reparations. At the beginning of December the Czechoslovak minister in Berlin confirmed the reports that Beneš had tried to persuade Raymond Poincaré, the French premier, to relax the demands against the Germans and to agree to a moratorium on reparation payments. Tusar was pessimistic about the situation, however, because all shades of political opinion in France seemed to be pushing Poincaré toward ever more stringent measures.[21] In an effort to relieve the tension between France and Germany, Cuno made the first German offer for a Rhineland Pact by which the Western powers and Germany would guarantee the border between Germany on the one side and France and Belgium on the other. Poincaré refused to consider such a pact, saying that Germany could still continue to endanger the Danish, Polish, and Czech borders. In a discussion with Tusar on January 6, 1923, State Secretary Ago von Maltzan drew Tusar's attention to Poincaré's statement. Tusar responded that Poincaré's mixing in German-Czechoslovak relations had been embarrassing previously and that it was especially so at the current time. Tusar added that Beneš had instructed him to express Prague's complete trust in the forthrightness of the German proposals.[22] Beneš may have taken that position for tactical reasons. When Stresemann revived the offer in 1925, Beneš justifiably feared that Czechoslovakia might become increasingly isolated in Central Europe as a result of the Rhineland Pact. When the idea was originally broached in 1922, however, the Czechs gave no overt sign of fearing such an agreement. Their more immediate anxiety was a Franco-German showdown about reparations.

THE RUHR EPISODE

On January 11 French and Belgian troops marched into the Ruhr in an action that climaxed the debate over the reparations payments and brought an open break between the French and the British. The Germans adopted passive resistance and sought moral support of foreign countries.

Throughout the year and into 1924 the Ruhr occupation and the effort to find a workable reparations program constituted the central problem in European diplomacy. For Czechoslovak foreign policy, diplomatic events in 1923 posed a challenge to the freedom of movement for which Beneš had worked since the peace conference. When international affairs had been relatively calm, Beneš had been able to maintain the appearance of independence, but as the crisis mounted through 1923 Paris began to exert pressure on the Czechs to make an agreement on the order of the Franco-Polish alliance of 1921. In the early months of the Ruhr episode Paris wanted no military support from the Czechs, a situation for which the Czechs were profoundly glad, and Beneš tried his hand at mediating in the dispute. As the result of real and imagined dangers from Germany by the end of 1923, however, Beneš gave up his mediatory role and allied firmly with the French. For Czechoslovak diplomacy the result of the Ruhr episode and its aftermath was a formal treaty of alliance between France and Czechoslovakia.

Although the actual treaty came only in 1924, the practical alliance had existed since the war. When the French occupied the Ruhr the Germans were worried that the Czechs might cooperate in military action against Germany. Three days before the occupation began, Koch reported to Berlin that it was highly probable that Czechoslovakia would intervene militarily in Germany if disturbances broke out there. Koch added that the greatest border tension was concentrated along the Bavarian boundary because of the monarchist and fascist movements in Bavaria. An invasion could well be expected along the Silesian and Saxon frontiers, however, because it was there that the Czechs might want to annex territory.[23] In the following two weeks Koch expanded his reports about military preparations in Czechoslovakia. He repeated his warnings that the Czechs would probably intervene if Berlin should lose control of the political situation within Germany. As long as there was no danger of political upheavals actually spilling across the borders into Czechoslovakia, however, he did not believe that the Czechs would actually participate with the French in applying sanctions about the reparations issue. He was inclined to put trust in Beneš's assurances that Czechoslovakia wanted to maintain good relations with Germany and that it continued to hope for a Franco-German rapprochement.[24] Finally on January 22 came the official press release in Czechoslovak newspapers that Czechoslovakia would not mobilize and that it was not obligated to support any other power in the reparations dispute. Its formulation of the country's position was: "She is the ally of France and the neighbor of Germany, whereby the general direction of her policy appears to be given in itself."[25]

The primary goal of Czechoslovak diplomacy in early 1923 was to remain free of involvement in the Ruhr dispute. Beneš attempted to ease

German fears while the Czechoslovak government worked to preserve order and stability within the country. In Prague Beneš asserted that the Czechs had no obligation to move against Germany and that they would resist any pressure on them to do so.[26] Whether or not that particular information reached Berlin, the Czechoslovak minister returned to the German capital from Paris at the end of January and gave State Secretary Maltzan further assurances that the Czechs planned no intervention in Germany. Tusar voiced his hope that the British and the Americans would soon step in and help to break the diplomatic impasse to which the French and the Germans had come.[27] What he did not say was that he had conveyed word to an associate of former Chancellor Wirth that Paris would like to see Wirth replace Cuno in the chancellorship. Tusar was acting at least in that case not only as the Czechoslovak minister in Berlin but also as a private messenger for Paris. (Wirth refused to respond to the feelers from Paris, but he did confide to officials of the Foreign Office that he feared a break-up of the Reich if the Ruhr crisis continued for long.)[28] Again on February 13 Tusar told the Germans that Prague wanted to remain neutral and uninvolved in the Ruhr dispute. He noted that Czechoslovakia had the greatest interest in the unrestricted use of the Elbe River and in a free port at Hamburg, which was guaranteed by the Treaty of Versailles. In turn, Tusar pledged that Czechoslovakia would continue to honor its coal export agreements with Germany despite some French pressure to curtail the shipments. Despite Czechoslovakia's commercial interests, however, Tusar added that his government would be put in a difficult position if war should break out between France and Germany and that even a breaking of diplomatic relations between the two countries would force Prague to reexamine its policy.[29] The warning that the Czechs would support France, if forced to make a choice, was unmistakable.

It was Berlin's policy to keep Prague from having to make such a decision. Here the interests of Germany and of Czechoslovakia coincided; the Germans did not want the French to gain more support, and the Czechs did not want to be drawn into a conflict between the two great powers. The winter of 1923 found Prague authorities still trying to establish a firm foundation for the four-year-old republic. Two widely publicized treason trials and the assassination of Alois Rašín, the minister of finance, spurred parliament to adopt a "Defense of the Realm" act, which, among other measures, gave the government extensive powers of press censorship.[30] Rašín was generally credited with being the man who had set Czechoslovakia on a firm financial footing by closing the borders in the early days of the revolution and stamping all Austrian currency in the country. He had returned to the cabinet in Švehla's government in October 1922 in order to deal with the economic problems created by the high exchange rate for the Czechoslovak crown. Czechoslovakia's export industries were finding it increasingly difficult to compete in foreign markets; factories were shutting down, and unemployment was increasing. An ardent nationalist, Rašín was second only to Kramář in the National Democratic party, and he was determined to maintain the value of the crown while promoting Czechoslovak exports by sharply deflationary policies that aroused strong opposition in working-class circles.[31] At the beginning of January 1923, a deranged and avowedly leftist youth shot Rašín, who lingered for six weeks before dying. Dramatized by Rašín's fight for life, the murder demonstrated anew the class cleavages in Czechoslovak society and prompted calls for national unity. There were domestic reasons enough for Czechoslovakia's neutral policy during the Ruhr conflict.

While Beneš worked to maintain Czechoslovakia's neutrality, Berlin confronted a difficult assignment in restraining local governments within Germany from anti-Czechoslovak policies. The first incident came shortly after the French occupation of the Ruhr when Bavarian officials detained Czech miners on their way to France. The miners were not bound for the Ruhr, and the interference with their passage through Germany was a violation of the Treaty of Versailles. Berlin heeded the protests of the French and the Czechs and forced the Bavarian government to release the miners.[32] But, as passive resistance undermined the already faltering German economy, local German governments began to expel Czech workers in an effort to create jobs for Germans. In retaliation Czechoslovak officials began expelling German workers from Czechoslovakia. A memorandum from State Secretary Maltzan to the state governments in Germany about this problem is the clearest expression of German policy toward Czechoslovakia in the spring of 1923. Maltzan stated flatly that relations with Czechoslovakia were "of the greatest foreign policy importance" and that it was Berlin's goal to cultivate the "most harmonious and best relations possible." The reasons for the importance of Czechoslovakia were: (1) its geographic position and its long border with Germany; (2) its international position as an ally of France and a neighbor of Germany; (3) the presence of the Sudeten Germans in Czechoslovakia, whose protection depended largely on good relations between Germany and Czechoslovakia; and (4) the neutral position that Prague had taken in the Ruhr conflict and that Berlin wanted to see maintained. He therefore asked the state governments to stop the expulsions of Czech workers, for continued action could only bring diplomatic countermeasures from Prague.[33] On April 28 the two countries signed a protocol in which they agreed to permit the return of all workers expelled in the previous months and not to allow expulsions in the future simply for economic reasons.[34]

Chancellor Cuno took the initiative in encouraging Beneš not only to maintain Czechoslovak neutrality but to act as a mediator between Paris and Berlin. Through an intermediary, Cuno sent Beneš word of the German willingness to enter into serious negotiations with the French, and the intermediary himself added the suggestion that Beneš seek to mediate between the two countries.[35] Beneš knew better than to get involved. On March 5 Beneš told the German minister in Prague that Germany itself ought to take the initiative in approaching France, for no other power was willing to "grasp the hot iron." Such a step by the Germans would get "the public opinion of the entire world" on their side. Besides, Beneš argued, if the French presented a plan it would simply take on the aspect of another *Diktat*.[36] While remaining on the diplomatic sidelines, Beneš was well aware that Czechoslovakia was profiting economically from the Ruhr occupation. He noted to the British minister in early March that the country was exporting coal to France, and that Czechoslovak industries were receiving orders from countries with whom they had had no previous dealings. Although the boom might well be temporary, it was hoped that some new business connections would develop into permanent relationships.[37]

Given Czechoslovakia's earlier economic difficulties, Sudeten Germans of various social classes had considerable interest in the promotion of exports, but the tendency for nationalist sentiments to dominate in times of crisis appeared again. From the beginning of the Ruhr occupation Sudeten German parliamentary deputies assailed Beneš's foreign policy for failing more actively to encourage mediation attempts between France and Germany. By the end of April Beneš felt it necessary to respond to criticism from the Sudeten Germans. The official review of the Ministry of Foreign Affairs, *Zahraniční politika,* published an article in which it admitted the validity of the well-known German thesis that Czechoslovak policy should reflect the economic unity of Central Europe; but the article also repeated the equally familiar Czech arguments that political and cultural interests tied Czechoslovakia with France. The review contended that France's right to reparations was unassailable, even if its methods of collection aroused different reactions, and that Germany should take the initiative in settling the conflict.[38] Thus Beneš maintained his pro-French outlook while at the same time showing his lack of enthusiasm about the occupation of the Ruhr.

The longer that the confrontation between French and German policy in the Ruhr continued, the greater became the chances that Czechoslovakia would be drawn into the conflict. At the outset of the Ruhr occupation, the French had embarked on what amounted to a unilateral action, with some assistance from the Belgians. As the struggle continued, however, French representatives mounted increasing pressure on the Czechoslovak government to conclude an open military alliance between the two countries. Initially, Paris's chosen agent was General Mittelhauser, the French officer who had succeeded General Pellé in Prague as chief of staff of the Czechoslovak army. (Masaryk implied that the French minister in Prague was too stupid for the assignment.) Mittelhauser urged invitations for a state visit to Paris onto Masaryk, who disliked the prospect that the French would "make a fuss of him."[39] Despite Masaryk's coolness to the French overtures, French efforts to attain a military convention with the Czechs culminated briefly with the visit of Marshall Foch to Prague in May. Foch again suggested a military alliance between France and Czechoslovakia. Beneš was a man who could seldom give an absolute and definite answer, especially if it were negative, and he indicated interest in Foch's suggestion.[40] Beneš's response, more than any other single factor, encouraged the French government to work out a draft treaty of alliance and to communicate it to Prague in early June.

The tenor of documents in the archives of the French Ministry of Foreign Affairs indicates that the French government viewed a general military conflict with Germany by 1924 as a distinct possibility.[41] That reckoning explains the high priority given by Raymond Poincaré, as premier and minister of foreign affairs, and Ferdinand Foch, as president of the Allied Military Committee, to the efforts to achieve a formal alliance with Czechoslovakia. The treaty that was drafted by the French government and communicated to Beneš in June stipulated in Article II that "In case of unprovoked aggression of Germany against France or against Czecho-Slovakia, the high contracting parties undertake to lend one another mutual assistance and to concert together with the view of assuring the defense of their territory and the reestablishment of peace." The means of that mutual assistance were spelled out more clearly in Article III: "The duly qualified military authorities of the two countries will determine by common accord the arrangements necessary for the eventual application of the current convention. A constant understanding will be maintained to this effect between the respective general staffs."[42] The central axis of Czechoslovak foreign policy for the next six months was the French effort to draw Czechoslovakia into a formal military alliance.

There was a significant variation in the responses of Masaryk and Beneš to the French overtures. Beneš at first appeared basically receptive, and he tried to widen the alliance into a general French guarantee of Czechoslovakia.[43] He particularly wanted assurances against Hungary as well as against Germany. But Masaryk stoutly resisted any formal military alliance between the two countries and marshalled a number of reasons for his opposition. Paramount was his insistence that Czechoslovakia could, under no conditions, afford to be an enemy of Russia. He feared being drawn into a Polish-Russian struggle as a result of an alliance with France.[44] Subsequently Masaryk argued to General Pellé that a French-Czechoslovak military convention was superfluous inasmuch as the presence of the

French military mission in Prague already meant that the Czechoslovak army was permanently under the control of the French general staff. A treaty would only cause domestic difficulties for the Czechoslovak government and international embarrassment for France.[45] Given Masaryk's opposition, Beneš quickly changed his approach, and on his visit to Paris in July he tried to postpone discussion of an alliance to the indefinite future.[46] But the French were not to be so easily put off, and they maintained their pressure in the following months.

The French overtures threatened to damage Czechoslovakia's relations with Britain and Germany. On several occasions Masaryk informed the British minister about the French pressure on Prague and manifested his distaste for France's militant policies—"The French sent me their marshal; I return the compliment with my Minister." Masaryk did not want to be forced to choose between his two Western allies. Telling Clerk that Beneš and he had no choice but to accept persistent French invitations for a formal visit to Paris in October, Masaryk made clear his willingness to visit London as well.[47] An invitation was soon forthcoming from the British government. Foreign Secretary Lord Curzon's response to the idea was: "As to Dr. Beneš he turns up where he likes, and we are always glad to see him because he saves one all trouble in talking and assuming the entire responsibility."[48] Through 1923 the British government maintained a rather detached attitude toward Czechoslovakia and seemed confident that the country could resist French pressure for an alliance.

The Czechs also moved to reassure the Germans in the wake of the French diplomatic initiative. While Beneš was in Paris in July, the Czechoslovak minister in Vienna informed a German confidant that the Prague government would not strengthen its relations with the French. Kamil Krofta, who was soon to become Beneš's closest and most trusted aide, said that Czechoslovakia was opposed to the admission of Poland to the Little Entente because Prague did not want to become as dependent on the French as Poland was—he did not want to use the words "satellite" or "vassal," he said. He observed that whereas Czechoslovakia had taken no territory from Germany, the Polish acquisitions constituted a historical claim by Germany on Poland that someday would have to be settled. Concerning the Ruhr episode Krofta added that his country was vitally interested in the economic health of Germany and that it therefore opposed current French policy in the Ruhr, which he characterized as "pernicious stupidity." He concluded that he felt that Berlin was inclined to view the problem of the Sudeten Germans as an internal affair of Czechoslovakia, and he added that his ideas on these questions reflected those of Beneš.[49] It was easy to believe Krofta, for in August at the conference of the Little Entente in Sinaia Beneš once again blocked Polish admission to the alliance. Simultaneously he worked to keep the governments of the Little Entente from associating themselves too closely with French policy in the Ruhr.[50]

In May an American dollar had bought 70,000 marks, at the end of June 150,000, and by the close of July over a million. The spiraling exchange rate through the late summer and early autumn had little real significance, for the German currency had already effectively ceased to exist. Confronted with provincial separatism and the specter of class war in Germany, Cuno's government remained unwilling to abandon the passive resistance in the Ruhr, which had caused the hyperinflation. But something had to be done to break the impasse to which the French and the Germans had come, and Germany was much the weaker combatant. In August Gustav Stresemann replaced Cuno as chancellor, assuming the post of foreign minister as well, and in September he abandoned passive resistance. A courageous pragmatist, Stresemann possessed the intellectual and moral strength to take the necessary step despite the fact that passive resistance had been the only means of replying to the French, who were intensely hated throughout Germany. The Czechs welcomed the move, for Poincaré had made the abandonment of passive resistance a precondition for negotiations. But no quick and easy settlement was forthcoming. In September Beneš remarked to the German minister in Switzerland that Poincaré, more hardheaded than ever and feeling himself now the victor over both Britain and Germany, would make no agreement on reparations except on his own terms.[51] Beneš promised to continue his efforts for an understanding, however, and renewed that commitment in a conversation with Koch in early October.[52]

In mid-October Masaryk and Beneš left for their long-awaited tour through Paris, Brussels, and London, which conveniently corresponded with the fifth anniversary of Czechoslovak independence. On their first stop, in Paris, the French heaped attention on Masaryk and Beneš far beyond current diplomatic practice for representatives of a relatively small state. Masaryk had already characterized the festivities as a big "grind," but Beneš no doubt enjoyed them.[53] Behind the scenes the French renewed their attempts for a formal alliance. Beneš responded that a military convention appeared inopportune at the moment but a general political agreement might be possible. He noted that he was already attempting to persuade Masaryk.[54] Apparently the Czechoslovak leadership was trying to avoid a concrete military agreement by offering to sign a vaguely defined political accord. Masaryk himself claimed to favor a political agreement although he continued to worry about criticism from Britain and Italy.[55] The outcome of discussions in Paris was that Beneš promised to study the French draft treaty more closely and to communicate written proposals for an accord after returning to Prague.

In London, where the visit was purposely left less formal, Masaryk assured Curzon that he had once again resisted French pressure for a military convention and that any compensatory political treaty between the two countries would be platitudinous, affirming essentially their common desire for peace. Masaryk again criticized Poincaré's Ruhr policy, fully supported British attempts to attain American cooperation in a reparations settlement, and emphasized the continuing necessity of British participation in continental affairs. Curzon returned the compliments with the remark that Czechoslovakia was "the only solid element of stability in Central Europe."[56] In his own conversations Beneš continued his efforts to mediate between British and French views on the reparations issue.[57] After their return to Prague Masaryk forwarded to the British a memorandum by Beneš advocating a reparations agreement that would have assured German financing of French reconstruction.[58] Primarily because of Masaryk's and Beneš's efforts to remain free of a military alliance with France, their visit to London marked the most cordial point in the interwar relations between Britain and Czechoslovakia.

The Germans naturally paid close attention to the trip by Masaryk and Beneš. In early November, State Secretary Maltzan summarized the German diplomatic reports from Paris, London, and Prague in a memorandum in which he concluded that there was no new agreement between France and Czechoslovakia but that the two countries had nevertheless grown closer together during the preceding months. The reason that Maltzan gave for the growing dependence of Prague on Paris was the domestic trouble in Germany, which threatened to spill over into Czechoslovakia.[59] The centrifugal forces in the Reich, brought on by the passive resistance in the Ruhr and the soaring inflation, threatened in the autumn of 1923 to fragment the German state. Czechoslovakia was the foreign country most directly affected by those movements. Along its northwestern border there arose left-wing regimes in Saxony and Thuringia in October, and across the southwestern frontier Hitler's Nazis were agitating in Bavaria. Stresemann's government managed to purge the Saxon and Thuringian cabinets of their communist members, but it had little success against the rightists in Bavaria. One of the earliest editions of the *Central European Observer,* an English-language newspaper founded for propaganda purposes by the Prague government, warned against the "reactionary and revolutionary organizations" in Munich and singled out Ludendorff and Hitler by name.[60] It simply reflected the daily reports in the Czech papers concerning the situation in Bavaria.

In addition to their common concern about the Nazis, Czechoslovak authorities suspected the conservative government of Gustav von Kahr of favoring a restoration of the Wittelsbachs in an independent kingdom of Bavaria. Any monarchical restoration, and especially one that might exert a magnetic influence in Austria, created fear and opposition in Prague. In early October Beneš expressed his concern to both the German and the Austrian ministers about the monarchist movements in Bavaria and warned that the radical proceedings would play into the hands of the French, who could undertake further action in Germany while posing as the "savior of democracy."[61] From London, the German ambassador reported Beneš's comment to the British that the Czechs had no desire to see a dissolution of Germany, which might lead to closer cooperation between the Bavarians and the Hungarians.[62] Inside Czechoslovakia the government seized Hitler's "battle fund," which was to be used to support the Nazi movement there, and prohibited importation of the *Völkischer Beobachter*. As the crisis approached its climax in early November, Beneš opined that Germany was not far from a restoration, that Stresemann was already a "living corpse," and that Germany would probably come under a regime of the generals. The basic trouble, in his opinion, was that Germany had not completed its revolution. As he told the Austrian minister, he was not convinced that the Germans were even capable of making a decent revolution.[63] The climax of rightist activity in Bavaria came in the abortive putsch by Hitler and Ludendorff on November 8 and 9. Although its failure was a relief to the Czechs, the continued existence of Kahr's government worried them because of its suspected monarchist leanings.[64]

There can be no doubt that the Nazi upheavals in Bavaria drove the Czechs into closer alliance with the French. But, even more important in motivating Masaryk and Beneš to give way to French importunities, was the little-heeded event of the return of the Hohenzollern crown prince to Germany. When Crown Prince Wilhelm crossed the border in early November Beneš emphasized both publicly and in private to Koch that the Hohenzollern question was not an internal affair for Germany and neither was the return of the crown prince.[65] In the budget committee of the Czechoslovak Chamber of Deputies, Beneš stressed: "Even if the question of some kind of Hitler putsch is an internal matter, the Hohenzollern question is not in any case. That is and remains the standpoint of Czechoslovakia."[66] For him Wilhelm was the exponent of a system that he could not allow to be reestablished. When Koch reported Beneš's remarks to Berlin, Maltzan answered that the Foreign Office saw no international significance in the event because the crown prince had renounced both the Imperial and the Prussian crowns. Moreover his brothers had been allowed to remain in Germany after the war, and the rightists who were currently agitating in Bavaria were no supporters of his.[67] Beneš could not be satisfied with this answer, claiming that there was already talk in Hungary and Austria of a return of Archduke Otto and warning that if the crown prince remained in Germany sanctions would be forthcoming in which Czechoslovakia would participate. He pointedly observed that when Charles had returned to Hungary Czechoslovakia had enjoyed the support of the Entente.[68]

In the Council of Ambassadors the French and the Belgian representatives wanted to demand the expulsion of the crown prince and to employ sanctions if Berlin did not comply. The British representative refused to participate in that action, and after several days of negotiations the French and the Belgians agreed simply to hold Berlin responsible for the conduct of the crown prince in Germany.[69] When the British procrastinated even concerning that policy, Beneš's *Prager Presse* could hardly hide its disgust.[70] In Prague it was easy to think that the timing of Wilhelm's return was not purely accidental. With Germany in danger of breaking apart, a Hohenzollern restoration possibly could reunify the country and reestablish Berlin's authority. Stresemann's monarchist sympathies were well known, and he had a close personal friendship with the crown prince.[71] British policy either did not recognize the danger or—what would be worse—did not consider it to be a danger. Beneš, however, feared the imperialism of the old monarchies and realized that the republican foundations of the Czechoslovak state were not absolutely secure. Next to the Habsburgs the Hohenzollerns were his worst enemies. When London agreed to participate in the warning to Berlin, something was salvaged from the situation, but for Beneš the British attitude was simply another indication that the French understood the Czechoslovak position in Central Europe much better than the British.

On November 22 Beneš had to explain to the foreign affairs committee of the Chamber of Deputies what had happened. There he described the agreement among the powers that the return of the crown prince was an international issue and not simply an internal affair of Germany. This being true, the method of sanctions was immaterial. Some statesmen, he observed, had advocated making a demand for the expulsion of the crown prince, whereas others had said that Germany would have to be held responsible for any consequences that might ensue. As far as he was concerned, Czechoslovakia was united with France in the belief that a simple protest would not suffice, since it must be made clear that this was a serious matter that could involve the preservation of the peace.[72] That statement was a fine example of Beneš's ability to put a good face on diplomatic disappointments. He was the statesman who had most wanted to demand the expulsion of the crown prince from Germany. No such policy was forthcoming from the West, and Beneš had to settle for what he could get. What that amounted to was not much more than keeping an eye on the situation.

Despite the lack of Entente action, reports filtered into Berlin about new political and military agreements between France and Czechoslovakia. In mid-November Maxim Litvinov told the German ambassador in Moscow, Brockdorff-Rantzau, of his understanding that the French had promised Lusatia to the Czechs.[73] From Prague Koch confirmed plans by the Czechs and the French to intervene if a revolution broke out in Germany. He sent Berlin information that the military strategy to be employed called for the French to group troops around Mainz and the

Czechs to mass in Eger. They would proceed down the Main River line, turning north after they met. The French were to supply two-thirds of the troops, the Czechs the other third.[74] Germany confronted an ominous situation.

The German Social Democrats brought about the fall of Stresemann's government in November, but Stresemann remained the real director of German diplomacy as foreign minister under Chancellor Wilhelm Marx. Stresemann tried to calm fears concerning the crown prince's return. He remarked, accurately enough, to the British ambassador that the crown prince was more interested in women and horses than in politics.[75] In a conversation with the French ambassador he contended that Wilhelm was actually a counterweight rather than a tool of the nationalistic and monarchist movements, as Wilhelm's wartime efforts for peace as well as his enmity with Ludendorff demonstrated. If the Bavarian monarchists were aiming at a Wittelsbach restoration, they could hardly be enthusiastic about the return of a Hohenzollern prince.[76] Ambassador De Margerie's noncommittal response demonstrated again that the French were not so interested in the affair as the Czechs were. For months Poincaré had been resisting any compromise in the Ruhr dispute, and had he really been concerned about Wilhelm's return he would not have agreed to the essentially innocuous policy devised at the Council of Ambassadors. Monarchist movements in Central Europe were Beneš's bugbear, however, and he was willing to buy support in combatting them. France was his only likely source of aid.

In December Beneš traveled again to Paris for the meeting of the Council of the League of Nations, to which Czechoslovakia had been elected in September. Beneš's primary interest was in further discussions about the projected treaty with the French. On the thirteenth he submitted his "project for a treaty of alliance and friendship" with France. All that remained of the original French proposal was a mutual obligation to consult together in cases where the two nations felt their common interests to be menaced. But Beneš also added provisions aimed at maintaining Austrian independence and forbidding a Habsburg restoration in Budapest, and he inserted an article stipulating that France and Czechoslovakia would continue to pursue the same policy toward the Hohenzollern house as that expressed in the Treaty of Versailles.[77]

The French accepted Beneš's draft with minor modifications, but in turn they insisted that the form of military cooperation be stipulated in greater detail. They sought to dispatch a French officer to Prague immediately in order to serve as a permanent liaison between the two general staffs, and they wanted a secret exchange of letters spelling out the terms of military cooperation.[78] The letters were intended to have the same effect as the military clauses of a formal treaty, with the added advantage that they would not require parliamentary ratification. Beneš responded enthusiastically because he could thereby avoid open disputes with the Sudeten Germans and the Communists at home. The letters could also be phrased so as to allow Beneš to proclaim publicly that he had entered no new obligations with France. He promised to consult Masaryk, after which, it was hoped, he could give his final consent to the entire project.[79] In agreement with Beneš the French government released the news about the projected political agreement almost immediately. Of course, no public mention was made of the secret letters formalizing the military cooperation.[80] On December 28 came the news, reported by *Temps*, that the general outlines of a Franco-Czechoslovak treaty had been agreed upon. It included provisions for maintenance of the peace treaties, establishment of a defensive alliance between the two countries, recognition of the authority of the League of Nations, cooperation for the economic reconstruction of Europe, preservation of Austrian independence, and prevention of a Habsburg or Hohenzollern restoration. There would be no military treaty between the two countries, but their general staffs were to cooperate in contingency planning.[81] In the opinion of many diplomats the chief significance of the proposed treaty was that it confirmed a relationship that had existed since the war.[82] It did not seem to create any basically new dimension in international relations. The initial reaction in Berlin was mild, but the treaty created a considerably greater stir in London, Rome, and Warsaw.

On New Year's Day, 1924, an editorial in the *Times* contended that the treaty "seems to belong to a dispensation wholly unconnected with the League of Nations and with the ideal of European unity which Czecho-Slovakia has hitherto professed to serve." The basic concern that permeated the editorial was that Czechoslovakia was abandoning its "cautious and moderating influence" in international affairs and committing itself "one-sidedly to the support of French aims in Europe."[83] The force of the negative reaction in Britain apparently caught Beneš and the Czechoslovak ministers in London and Paris by surprise, but Czechoslovak policy was already too publicly committed to allow more maneuvering.[84] Although the Czechoslovak minister in London ineffectively responded that the treaty would actually "strengthen the forces which are sincerely working for peace and reconstruction,"[85] the real rebuttal to the *Times* editorial came in the *Prager Presse* on January 3. Beneš's mouthpiece observed that "there is no state in Europe with which all the interests of our state are so closely bound as with France," but that Czechoslovakia had maintained friendly relations with London "although she has not always been able to find full understanding in England for some of her justified goals."[86] For years no one in the British Foreign Office had doubted that the Czechs would opt for France if forced to choose between the two Western powers, but neither did anyone see the necessity for making such a choice at the turn of 1924. Repeatedly, in their secret reports and memoranda, British diplomatic officials expressed the fear that Beneš had tied himself more firmly to the French than he himself perhaps realized. The universal disappointment colored the language of Clerk's dispatches from Prague, in which he decried "the feeling of self-importance of this conceited and provincial-minded people."[87]

Of potentially great significance was the effect that the alliance could have on relations between the Western powers and the Soviet Union. At the time of the announcement of the treaty, it appeared that a Labor-dominated government would soon be formed in Britain as a result of Labor's gains in the parliamentary elections of early December. A general expectation was that Labor would quickly extend diplomatic recognition to the Soviet Union, as Ramsay MacDonald's government actually did at the beginning of February.[88] In Paris, President Millerand and Premier Poincaré were not yet willing to take that step, but diplomats were already explaining Poincaré's intransigence in the Ruhr dispute by pointing to his fears concerning the approaching French parliamentary elections. Poincaré might not long remain in office; and, in any case if the British extended diplomatic recognition to the Soviets, any French government would soon have to follow suit.

The desire of the Czechs to rely on their great Slavic brothers was universally recognized. Beneš openly stated his wish to normalize relations with Moscow as soon as possible. He helped to propagate the idea that Czechoslovakia could serve as a bridge between the West and the Soviet Union, and newspapers were full of speculation that France might use the Czechs as intermediaries with the Russians.[89] In a Foreign Office minute concerning the Franco-Czechoslovak treaty, Harold Nicolson wrote:

> By using the Czechs as a trait-d'union with Moscow, the French will be able to counter the advantage which we should otherwise have gained by taking the initiative of full recognition. And we shall inevitably be obliged to seek our own trait d'union in Germany.[90]

The potential competition between Germany and Czechoslovakia for the role of intermediary between the West and the Soviet Union became another complicating factor in the relations between Prague and Berlin. But of more immediate importance was the threat that the Franco-Czechoslovak treaty posed to initiatives that were just then developing in British foreign policy.

Although the French hoped that the treaty would help consolidate their eastern alliance system, the Poles reacted to the news with bitterness and hostility. The continuing rivalry between Poland and Czechoslovakia was aggravated by repeated Czechoslovak successes. After Czechoslovakia gained a seat on the Council of the League of Nations while Poland failed to do so in September 1923, the Czechs attained in 1924 a favorable decision in the Javorina dispute at the expense of the Poles.[91] If Warsaw previously took comfort in its special treaty relationship with the French, the Franco-Czechoslovak alliance destroyed the uniqueness of the Polish position in Central Europe. Beyond psychological factors, a real and practical danger to the Poles was the possibility that the Czechs might actually help bring about a reconciliation between Paris and Moscow. Most observers did not doubt that the French would eventually abandon Poland if that were necessary to reach a reliable understanding with the Russians, and it is well known that Beneš had little faith in the permanence of the Polish boundaries. In Rome, as well, the reaction to the treaty was negative. Mussolini's government resented the demonstration of French power in Central Europe and concocted imaginary alliances under Italian aegis that would counter French influence in the area. Italian diplomats busied themselves relating stories of secret military agreements between France and Czechoslovakia.[92]

The only power whose disapproval was of fundamental concern to Beneš was Britain. In January 1924 he embarked on another trip to London, in part on League business, but more immediately in an effort to explain the treaty to the British. In an icy conversation on January 16 Curzon attempted to learn whether there actually existed secret military understandings between the two countries. Beneš informed Curzon of the proposed exchange of the secret letters detailing the nature of Franco-Czechoslovak military cooperation, but he stressed that the agreements merely confirmed existing treaties and provided for consultation between the two countries.[93] Curzon wondered why Beneš should conclude a treaty at all if it were so innocuous. "Why should she [Czechoslovakia] fall into the circle of subordinate nations who are more or less attached to the French chariot wheels?" According to Curzon's paraphrase, Beneš responded:

> The real reason for the treaty was security. Within fifteen years from now Germany might recover and be a strong menace on the north and west; Austria and Hungary were temporarily out of action, but might also revive. As for Poland, he had no confidence in her stability, and felt that she might at any time in the future go under. In these circumstances it was vital to his people to have security arising from association with a great and powerful military State. That was the real explanation why the treaty had been so necessary to them.

Unlike some of Beneš's other explanations, these remarks could be taken at face value, for they were consistent with other aspects of his foreign policy. Still hostile, Curzon "bade him adieu."[94]

Claiming for public consumption to have allayed British fears, Beneš crossed the Channel for the formal signing of the treaty in Paris. There he remarked privately that he had "fallen into the mouth of the lion" by negotiating the treaty with the French. He explained the intensity of British hostility to the treaty by pointing to British opposition to French policy in the Ruhr. Wide circles in London feared French designs for dominating the continent, but Beneš believed that the British sometimes attributed their own motives to others. He noted that he caused British government officials some embarrassment by offering to negotiate a similar treaty with them.[95] (Obviously the British were unwilling to undertake such obligations in Central Europe.) On January 25, 1924, Poincaré and Beneš finally signed the French-Czechoslovak Treaty of Alliance and Friendship, while denying the existence of a military alliance. They postponed signing the secret letters until the thirty-first. Masaryk had urged that course of action in order to avoid possible charges of duplicity. The two countries ought not to arrange the cooperation between their general staffs on the very day that they claimed not to be concluding a military convention.[96] But after six days the letters were indeed signed and deposited in the archives (from which they were removed in 1936). Although the text of the letters does not exist in the archival collections where they would logically be found, a note from Poincaré to Foch does indicate the general contents of the military agreements. In sending a copy of the letters to Foch, Poincaré wrote: "In conformity with the understanding with M. Beneš, the Minister of Foreign Affairs of Czechoslovakia, I have exchanged with him, subsequent to the signing of the treaty of Alliance and Friendship, the letters which specify the conditions in which the general staffs of the two countries will continue to collaborate in all that which concerns the establishment of concerted plans to guard against aggression directed against one of the two countries by a common enemy and in studying the respective means by which the two countries can actually provide mutual assistance in case of need."[97] The military alliance between the two countries was formalized in every way except in name.

Although Masaryk in particular had resisted a formal French-Czechoslovak alliance, Czechoslovakia was ultimately too dependent on France to refuse a treaty if the French insisted. The chaotic internal situation within Germany—and particularly the return of the crown prince, which rekindled Czech fears of a monarchical restoration—drove the Czechs into the firm alliance with France. Czechoslovakia's relations with Britain suffered in the process, and the atmosphere between London and Prague was never so cordial thereafter. Yet the Czechs could retain a measure of independence between Britain and France only so long as there was no immediate menace from Germany, and they bound themselves formally to France when the reaction in Germany appeared to them to have reached its most dangerous point.

THE FAILURE TO SECURE THE VERSAILLES SYSTEM

After the confrontations of 1923 the following months seemed to offer hope of negotiated agreements on the major issues in international affairs. In January 1924 Ramsay MacDonald became the first Labor prime minister in British history, and in May and June Edouard Herriot led his *Cartel des Gauches* into power in France. Both of these new governments embarked on an effort to improve the climate between their two countries. Both extended diplomatic recognition to the Soviet Union. Both were warmly welcomed by Masaryk and Beneš, whose political philosophy was also left of center.[98] Reparations and the security-disarmament problem were the two major challenges in international affairs. At least a temporary settlement was found for the reparations dispute in the Dawes plan, which was adopted in a conference in London in July and August. The Dawes plan and the financial arrangements growing out of it contributed more than any other single factor to the relative stability of Europe in the late 1920s. The task of ensuring the security of France and its allies while meeting the demands for international disarmament seemed to approach a solution also, in the form of the Geneva Protocol. But international conciliation did little to help Czechoslovakia, whose dependence on France and whose estrangement from Germany, Italy, and even Britain became increasingly apparent.

In the spring of 1924 an episode that became known as the *Berliner Tageblatt* affair stirred a brief but bitter dispute between Germany and Czechoslovakia. Documents purporting to be secret military agreements between France and Czechoslovakia and dating back as far as 1918 came into the hands of the German Foreign Office and of Theodor Wolff, the publisher of the *Berliner Tageblatt*. Believing the documents to be genuine, officials in the German Foreign Office permitted Wolff to publish them on March 19.[99] Before the publication Stresemann telegraphed instructions to the major German missions about the manner in which they should seek to exploit the news. Stress was to be laid on the fact that the supposed secret commitments of France and Czechoslovakia violated Article 18 of the League Covenant.[100] Beneš lost no time in responding with indignation to the accusations, even though a revelation of the existence of the secret military letters with France could have severely embarrassed him. His *Prager Presse* easily discredited the charges when it published one of the bogus documents next to an agreement signed by Bismarck and Andrássy in 1879 during the formation of the Dual Alliance. The texts were identical except for a few phrases and appropriate changes in names and dates.[101]

Calling the falsifiers "uneducated or of a criminal turn of mind," Beneš demanded to know who was behind the publication, and his questions were aimed directly at Stresemann and his assistants.[102] Denials by the German Foreign Office of any complicity in the affair naturally were unconvincing. German diplomacy suffered an embarrassing propaganda defeat.

The episode was actually Berlin's delayed reaction to the formal treaty of alliance between France and Czechoslovakia. Despite their indignation about the Hohenzollern clause, the Germans had been inclined to regard the treaty as merely a confirmation of a situation that had existed since the end of the war. When resentment about the treaty persisted in Britain and Italy, however, the bogus documents seemed to afford Berlin another means of widening the rift in the Entente. Special copies of the documents were given to D'Abernon, before their publication, and Stresemann instructed Ambassador Neurath in Rome to emphasize that the treaties contained a provision pledging French-Czechoslovak resistance to Italian influence in the Mediterranean.[103] On the day that the *Tageblatt* article appeared, Neurath reported that the revelations had created a stir in Rome, adding that Mussolini also claimed to have seen texts of the secret treaties.[104] If Wolff did in fact get his information from a British source—as he claimed—British agents themselves were involved in what the Czechs labeled "clumsy German propaganda."[105]

The aftermath of the *Berliner Tageblatt* affair cast a chill over Czechoslovak-German relations during the spring of 1924. During the height of the affair the Czechoslovak minister in Berlin collapsed and died of a heart attack. Tusar's successor in Berlin was Kamil Krofta, formerly minister in Vienna and soon to become Beneš's chief assistant. An historian of some note, Krofta attempted to continue Tusar's man-of-goodwill example in Berlin. But the *Tageblatt's* charges apparently upset Masaryk, who abandoned his usually conciliatory pronouncements and made sharp anti-German comments in newspaper interviews in late April. In a heated report to Berlin, Koch wrote that every Czech considered the Germans to be traditional enemies and that Masaryk still regarded Germany as the greatest threat to peace in Europe. He concluded that Germany in its weak postwar position would best remain silent in public, "while awaiting better."[106] Shortly thereafter, Koch used a conversation with Beneš to protest Masaryk's anti-German remarks. Beneš claimed, inaccurately and unconvincingly, that Masaryk had been talking about an authoritarian, not a democratic, Germany. He added that he would like to see an equally strong German attack on Czechoslovakia's nationalistic leader, Karel Kramář.[107] German diplomacy had many priorities ahead of Kramář, however. The negotiation of the Dawes plan and its acceptance by the Reichstag in 1924 took precedence over all else, and two parliamentary elections in Germany helped to complicate the situation. After the *Berliner Tageblatt* affair, relations between Germany and Czechoslovakia remained only coldly correct.

In May Beneš undertook a trip to Italy, primarily to persuade Mussolini that the Franco-Czechoslovak pact need not damage relations between Rome and Prague. Already in January he had encouraged the conclusion of the Italian-Yugoslav agreement on Fiume in an effort to alleviate Italian resentment of French influence in the Little Entente. But, according to the Czechoslovak minister in Rome, Beneš harbored deep suspicions of Fascist Italy and expected the fall of Mussolini's regime in the near future. Vlastimil Kybal's efforts in Rome to develop a close working relationship between Czechoslovakia and Italy put him out of step with Beneš's foreign policy and undermined Kybal's position in the Czechoslovak diplomatic service. The announcement of Kybal's recall from Rome came just before Beneš's arrival.[108] Both before and after his visit Beneš made little effort to hide the fact that he attached small importance to any treaty with Italy. Poincaré had asked Beneš not to identify Czechoslovakia with the Italian-Yugoslav agreement and had reminded him that France was the only country on which the states of the Little Entente could really rely.[109] Before his departure from Prague Beneš had explained to Koch that his trips to Paris and London necessitated one to Rome as well, adding that in all his travels he was constantly trying to improve attitudes toward Germany.[110] Although Beneš was actually more interested in creating barriers to German revisionism, the Germans had little to worry about. The Italians had already assured Berlin that they simply wanted to loosen the French hold on the Little Entente and would do nothing to harm relations with Germany.[111] In preliminary negotiations for a treaty, various proposals were rejected. The Italians apparently refused any agreement that would ban monarchical restorations in Central Europe, that would contain a commitment to uphold the Treaty of Versailles, or that would make specific mention of the German problem. Loyal to the French, Beneš refused to accede to the Italian-Yugoslav pact. Finally, Mussolini and Beneš initialed only a "Pact of Sincere Collaboration," from which the original phrase "of Friendship" had been deleted. That pact contained essentially one article, providing for mutual consultation on common interests, and it remained a dead letter almost from the time of its formulation.[112] The general reaction in European capitals was summarized in Ramsay MacDonald's comment, "Beneš is fond of treaties."[113] But even though travels and treaties did not always have much diplomatic significance, they did strengthen Beneš's political position at home by augmenting his reputation as Czechoslovakia's indispensable expert on foreign affairs.

The diplomatic atmosphere among the great powers steadily improved in the summer of 1924. The problem over which most of the postwar disputes had been fought—the payment of reparations—found a temporary solution with the acceptance of the Dawes plan in July and August. Two other problem areas then became the focus of diplomatic attention. One question concerned Germany's admission into the League of Nations. The other task involved the challenge of devising a reliable collective security system. The British Labor government under MacDonald seemed to be doctrinally committed to the idea of making the League of Nations a practical and effective instrument of international relations, and for that reason it favored the admission of both Germany and the Soviet Union to the League. Whereas the Soviets rejected the idea, the German attitude was uncertain. Most Germans had long regarded the League simply as a society of victors. The attitude had been reflected as late as 1923 in the title of a book, *Der Versailler Völkerbund,* by Bernhard W. von Bülow. Because of his seeming expertise, Bülow became the head of the division in the German Foreign Office responsible for League affairs.[114] Yet a necessary move in Stresemann's strategy for Germany's recovery and reassertion of itself as a great power was its entrance into the League. By 1924 officials in the German Foreign Office had come to the conclusion that Germany would have to enter the League sometime, and they prepared for negotiations concerning the conditions under which Germany would join. But the opposition of conservative circles in Germany and the uncertain attitude of France and its allies made the idea seem premature in the summer of 1924. Stresemann and his assistants therefore settled upon a compromise. They took no overt step toward Geneva, but neither did they discourage the discussion of the idea in the press.[115]

By 1924 Beneš had become a central figure in Geneva, and he prided himself on his reputation as one of the acknowledged experts on League affairs. Beneš was particularly active after Czechoslovakia's entrance into the Council of the League of Nations at the beginning of 1924. In July, in an interview with Vienna's *Neue Freie Presse,* Beneš declared his support for Germany's entrance into the League but warned that the problems of security and control of German armaments would first have to be settled. He added that German public opinion probably was not yet ready for an entrance into the League and that it would be better to wait for a year or so.[116] Beneš was once again acting in full accord with French foreign policy. The French did not oppose Germany's eventual admission into the League, but they did want to postpone it until a workable plan of collective security could be devised and accepted. Herriot's government was in the process of preparing such a plan, the purpose of which was the transformation of the League into an effective instrument of collective security. The French hoped that, if the plan were accepted, it would constitute a guarantee of the security of France and its eastern allies against German revisionism. Moreover, if the Germans subsequently entered the League, they would be bound by the collective security system, and they would implicitly be abandoning their revisionist policies.

Beneš heartily agreed with the calculations motivating French policy, for a reliable guarantee of Czechoslovak security in Central Europe was Beneš's central goal. Seldom was there closer cooperation between Beneš and the French than at the meeting of the League Assembly in September.[117]

At the opening of the Assembly MacDonald surprised everyone by urging the early admission of Germany into the League. He had prepared neither the French nor the Germans for his step. The Germans avoided a public reaction although they used both unofficial representatives and the German minister in Switzerland to sound out opinion among the delegates in Geneva. By the middle of September the minister, Adolf Müller, reported that the French did not want Germany in the League Council until the question of military control had been settled and that Beneš was also opposing an early German entrance. Nevertheless, by the end of the month, the German cabinet decided in principle in favor of Germany's entrance into the League, while carefully spelling out the reservations that subsequently assumed crucial importance during the pre-Locarno negotiations.[118] Whereas Herriot did not reject MacDonald's idea, he managed to divert attention to the security and disarmament question.

Herriot then suggested the formula security-arbitration-disarmament, in which the concept of compulsory arbitration of disputes apparently offered the key to the task of reconciling the French desire for security with the general insistence on disarmament. Herriot managed to win MacDonald's agreement that the proposal be submitted for study to a subcommittee for which Beneš was to act as rapporteur. From that committee emerged the "Protocol for the Pacific Settlement of International Disputes," soon to be popularly known as the "Geneva Protocol." By defining aggression as the refusal to submit to arbitration or the failure to abide by the results of arbitration, the protocol apparently provided a means of determining the aggressor at the outbreak of a conflict. It thereby offered a solution to the greatest challenge to an international security agreement. Although Beneš was generally credited with the coauthorship of the protocol, the ideas were not really original with him. He was actually acting in close cooperation with his French allies in an attempt to promote a universal security plan advantageous to both France and Czechoslovakia. The Assembly of the League unanimously endorsed the protocol. It even appeared as though MacDonald was willing to reverse the foreign policy of British governments since the end of the war by undertaking far-reaching, indeed universal obligations to help maintain peace. When Beneš returned to Prague in late October, he delivered one of his most optimistic speeches on foreign policy. Concerning the protocol he said:

It makes war less possible than before, leads the entire world to the ideal of a lasting peace, and holds back many, many warlike adventures.

It will be a tremendous moral influence and can become an actual international force.[119]

Beneš's optimism was premature. As things turned out, Czechoslovakia was the only country to ratify the Geneva Protocol.

Any plan for universal security and disarmament could founder on the opposition of one great power. In Britain, after an election campaign memorable for the controversy over the "Zinoviev letter," British voters swept MacDonald's Labor party out of power in November and reinstalled Stanley Baldwin's Conservatives with an overwhelming majority in the House of Commons. Whatever decision the Labor-Liberal government might have ultimately reached about the Geneva Protocol, the Conservatives reacted against the prospect of unlimited commitments on the European continent. The new foreign secretary, Austen Chamberlain, contended in one of his conversations with Beneš that Britain had to think in terms broader than those of a traditional European power in view of its imperial commitments around the world.[120] As previous British governments had been committed to maintaining French security vis-à-vis Germany, Conservative opposition to the Geneva Protocol actually reaffirmed Britain's refusal to undertake obligations in Central Europe, as the British minister in Prague eventually admitted.[121] The willingness of the British to extend their line of defense only to the Rhine was underlined by Chamberlain's project to replace the Geneva Protocol with a British-French-Belgian defensive pact. Beneš's ultimate objective in advocating the Geneva Protocol was to secure guarantees of the peace settlements in Central Europe, and the British refusal to become involved in the area further contributed to the growing estrangement between London and Prague. Despite some lingering hopes in Paris and Prague, the protocol was a dead letter in diplomacy weeks before Chamberlain formally announced Britain's rejection of it in March 1925.

The Geneva Protocol has been celebrated as the most realistic plan ever devised for developing a workable system of collective security through the League of Nations. Its rejection signified the failure to secure a basic tenet of the "New Diplomacy." But it should also be pointed out that the protocol was the device of those countries that viewed the League primarily as a means of preserving the status quo. Wilson and his disciples had certainly intended for the League to ensure the peace through collective security, but they had also conceived of the League as the instrument for making peaceful revisions in the treaties. The protocol pointed in the direction not of a dynamic but of a static international situation. Beneš's attempts to aid the French in pushing for the adoption of the protocol before Germany's admission to the League represented the culmination of his early postwar efforts to exploit Germany's temporary weakness in order to erect barriers against future German revisionism.

Ultimately, the failure of the Geneva Protocol meant the failure to secure the Versailles system. For the Czechs the consequences were grave.

With the return of the Conservatives to office in Britain, tension between London and Prague mounted significantly. As Conservative rejection of the Geneva Protocol strained relations, another point of dispute arose as well. In November 1924 the London *Times* revived the idea of a Danubian customs union. It advocated that British financial circles make the granting of a loan to Czechoslovakia dependent on Czechoslovak efforts to create a customs union in Central Europe, and it even broached the idea of sending a foreign financial advisor to Prague in order to oversee Czechoslovak finances.[122] Such ideas were bound to elicit retorts from Prague, especially when they came from an almost semi-official source such as the *Times*. Representative of the wave of indignation that swept the Czechoslovak press was an editorial in Beneš's *Prager Presse*, in which a "leading personality of our financial life" remarked that ever since the close of the war London had tried to couple political conditions with financial loans.[123] The *Central European Observer*, which was the Czechoslovak government's English-language newspaper, wrote that the chief exponents of a customs union in Central Europe were reactionary West European political and banking circles that desired a return to prewar conditions. It pointed to Czechoslovakia's recent commercial treaty with Austria and the upcoming negotiations with the Hungarians as evidence of the effectiveness of bilateral trade agreements in reducing tariffs. (As a matter of fact, the agreement between Czechoslovakia and Austria did lower tariffs on almost a third of the products exchanged between them.) The newspaper concluded that a supranational organization on the economic level would be antithetical to the new political system among the successor states.[124]

The newspaper debates became a topic of conversation between Beneš and the British minister, Sir George Clerk, in which both men were only moderately conciliatory. Clerk took the opportunity to complain about the "childishly naive proceedings" of the Czechoslovak minister of finance, who employed "tactics which were more suitable to chaffing in a village fair than to serious discussion with British industry and finance." For some time British officials had been growing restive about Czechoslovak manipulations in foreign trade and finance, and Prague's relations with financial circles in London were hardly cordial. In 1922 the British government had helped Beneš to negotiate a state loan from Baring Brothers, a large London banking house. Although Beneš had been criticized in the Czechoslovak parliament for accepting severe terms, Clerk claimed that the Czechoslovak government had thereby been put on "intimate terms with the soundest and highest and best financial interests in London, i.e., in the world." He was disappointed that the Czechs had subsequently neglected the relationship.[125] When the Czechoslovak finance minister then tried to obtain another loan in the City without consulting Baring Brothers or the Bank of England, he provoked the disdainful condemnation that Clerk voiced to Beneš.

Beyond the frictions in the bilateral relations between London and Prague, some British officials blamed restrictive Czechoslovak tariff and trade policies for Austrian economic problems. They particularly resented Beneš's failure to take effective action to overcome the barriers that divided the former Habsburg realm. During a meeting of the Council of the League of Nations in Rome in December, Austen Chamberlain urged Beneš to "do everything in his power to improve relations with Austria, commercially and economically, and to encourage the other succession States to do the same."[126] Although Beneš answered Chamberlain with discretion, he subsequently gave vent to his real feelings back home in Prague. When the Austrian minister asked Beneš's opinion about a customs union in Central Europe, Beneš responded that the British never really knew what they wanted. Although they were propagandizing for a customs union at the moment, they would be the first to cry out, in the case that a union were really established, that they were being excluded from the markets of Central Europe.[127] Moreover, Italy would hardly allow the establishment of a customs union unless the others agreed to Italy's inclusion, and "there doesn't exist such a fool that would do that, certainly not Austria and also not Czechoslovakia." Even the French didn't really have a clear concept of conditions in Central Europe, for their policies were too often dictated by considerations involving Germany. Neither a customs union, nor a Danubian confederation, nor an Anschluss held a solution to Central Europe's economic problems. Beneš himself had a definite plan, however, which he would advance at the right moment. When the Austrian minister pressed Beneš for details of that plan, Beneš only hearkened back to his proposed "system of treaties," by which the successor states would promote commerce in the Danubian area through a series of bilateral trade treaties among themselves.[128] Despite occasionally intense pressure from the Western powers, Czechoslovak foreign policy was never willing to venture beyond bilateral treaties, which themselves would confirm the sovereignty and independence of each individual successor state.

The dispute about a customs union in Central Europe and the British refusal to ratify the Geneva Protocol reflected the coolness between London and Prague after the conclusion of the Franco-Czechoslovak pact. Although there never had been any doubt about Czechoslovakia's ultimate dependence on France, British efforts to promote the economic revival of Germany and the British refusal to undertake guarantees for the security of the successor states drove Czechoslovak foreign policy into a thoroughly French orientation. Beneš himself was beginning to suffer from overexposure in diplomatic circles. By 1924 the head of the Central Division of the British Foreign Office rarely missed an opportunity to voice his distrust of Beneš, whom he considered a "busybody," someone "determined to have his finger in every pie." Austen Chamberlain commented of Beneš, "Il est capable de tout—and quite untrustworthy."[129] But Beneš was only continuing to pursue the same objectives that he had followed since 1918. Through incessant diplomatic activity, he strove to establish the Czechoslovak republic with a firm foundation in international law and to ensure its security and independence. In his thinking, at least, Germany was always the greatest potential enemy. As late as February 1925 he claimed to foresee dark days for Germany, where the struggles between the Right and the Left had not yet been brought to an end.[130] If he was correct in the long run, he was unaware that at the moment Stresemann's Foreign Office was offering to the Western powers a regional security pact that would aggravate Czechoslovakia's isolation in Central Europe.

THE LOCARNO REVISION

Although Britain's Conservative government refused to undertake the obligations of the Geneva Protocol, it was not unsympathetic to the French need for security. Austen Chamberlain strongly supported the idea of replacing the protocol with an Anglo-French pact guaranteeing the French and Belgian borders with Germany. Such a reconstitution of the Entente certainly was not in German interests, and Chamberlain's attitude helped to prompt the German counteroffers that eventually led to the Locarno agreements. At the end of December 1924, Lord D'Abernon performed his most signal service for the Germans, who had come to refer to him as the "Lord-Protector" of Germany. With no prior authorization from London, he urged his friends in the German Foreign Office to renew the offer for a multilateral renunciation of force along the German western boundary, an offer which Chancellor Cuno had first made two years earlier.[131] The idea was attractive to Berlin. If the British planned to undertake commitments on the continent in any case, it was better from the German standpoint to be a party to the agreements. German participation would represent a further step toward the reacceptance of Germany into the international community and a corresponding growth in its diplomatic prestige. A guarantee that worked both ways—protecting German territory, as well as French and Belgian, against invasion—would undercut the assumption that danger threatened only from the German side. It would not constitute an affront to the Germans in the way that an "anti-German defensive league" (the words were D'Abernon's)[132] between

Britain and France would do. The crucial issue for the German government was that a guarantee of the western boundary not be expanded to include the eastern one as well. Whereas most Germans could probably reconcile themselves to the loss of Alsace-Lorraine, Eupen, and Malmédy, they were never willing to accept the detachment of Danzig, West Prussia, Posnania, and the industrial portion of Upper Silesia. The German insistence on differentiating between the western and the eastern boundaries lay at the heart of diplomatic negotiations in 1925. By October the abandonment of a collective security system as envisioned by the Geneva Protocol in favor of regional guarantees in the west stamped the Locarno accords as a revisionist settlement in the eyes of the smaller and more exposed powers of Central Europe.

For Stresemann's foreign policy it was essential to continue the initiative toward an understanding with the Western powers that had begun in 1924. The basic assumption of Stresemann's diplomacy was that treaty revisions could be achieved more readily in apparent cooperation with the Western powers than in open opposition to them. After the acceptance of the Dawes plan Stresemann continued to seek an accommodation with the West despite the urgent attempts of the Soviets to prevent a realignment of German foreign policy.[133] Yet by January 1925 there were serious obstacles to the further development of Stresemann's policies. The members of the Council of the League showed no willingness to accede to the conditions that the Germans demanded as their price for joining the League. Chamberlain tried to win Cabinet support for his plan of formally reviving the Anglo-French entente. And the occupying powers in the Rhineland refused to evacuate the Cologne zone according to the timetable established by the Treaty of Versailles because of the failure of the Germans to fulfill the disarmament provisions of the treaty. It was a measure of the finesse of Stresemann's diplomacy that, aside from protesting the Allied decision, he continued the policy of rapprochement even when conditions seemed unfavorable. Yet it was probably the influence of D'Abernon that tipped the balance and prompted the Germans to come forward when they did with a proposal for a regional security system in the west. The significance of the timing was that, after the final rejection of the Geneva Protocol in early March, there already existed a German security plan to which the powers could turn.[134] By that time the Committee of Imperial Defence in London had rejected the idea of a bilateral Anglo-French defensive alliance, and the way was open for consideration of a multilateral guarantee along the Rhine.

After unofficially notifying the British in late January, Stresemann approached the French directly in a note of February 9, 1925, in which he made his offer of a Rhineland security pact.[135] The essence of the proposal had been worked out by the Foreign Office's legal expert,

Friedrich Gaus, who was one of Stresemann's closest and most trusted advisers. It called for a guarantee of the territorial status quo along the Rhine and the demilitarization of the Rhineland. In addition, Germany would be willing to conclude arbitration pacts with its neighbors, eastern as well as western, but the proposal pointedly omitted any guarantee of the German eastern boundary. Despite the offer to conclude arbitration treaties, the German Foreign Office informed neither the Poles nor the Czechs about the security proposal. Word of the German initiative came to them from the Western powers. Although the public reaction in both Poland and Czechoslovakia to the rumors that soon began to circulate was hostile, the attitude in Warsaw was more bitter than that in Prague.

Beneš naturally resisted any effort to treat Germany's western and eastern boundaries differently. In memoranda that he wrote for Herriot and Chamberlain in the first half of March, he emphasized the preferability of a universal security system over regional agreements. Still hoping for the survival of a British-French alliance, he argued that a general Rhineland pact was no adequate substitute for a specific British guarantee of the French border.[136] But Beneš's diplomatic instincts propelled him along a tactically moderate course, and he carefully avoided any absolute opposition to the German proposal. At the end of February he assured the British minister in Prague that he would exercise no pressure in Paris or London about the security proposal, as it was a matter for the Western powers.[137] In mid-March in a conversation with Herriot Beneš emphasized that he did not want to make difficulties for his French allies provided that a Western security pact would not be taken to imply that Germany had a free hand in Central Europe.[138] To the American minister Beneš remarked that the proposal was "the first intelligent step Germany had taken since the war."[139] In his various conversations Beneš often repeated his belief that Germany would need as much as twenty years to recover from the war. During that time it was advisable to encourage the democratic forces in Germany so that there would be a gradual waning of the desire for revenge. Beneš believed that Germany was in the grip of a struggle between democratic and authoritarian elements. For him the election of Field Marshal Paul von Hindenburg to the presidency in the spring of 1925 demonstrated the danger of reaction in Germany and the great distance the Germans still had to cover in order to consolidate a democratic regime.[140] His mild reaction to the German initiative may well have been motivated in part by a realistic desire to see a stable and peaceful government in Berlin. But Beneš was also sufficiently astute to recognize the revisionist nature of Stresemann's policies. Ultimately Beneš fashioned his strategy by analyzing attitudes in Paris and London, and the receptivity to the German proposal in those capitals encouraged him to be moderate and cooperative.[141]

Beneš was reasonable in his statements to German diplomatic representatives as well. In Switzerland for a meeting of the Council of the
League in March, Beneš assured an attaché of the German legation that he
was willing to conclude an arbitration treaty with Germany even as he had
previously done with Austria.[142] To Berlin this early word of Beneš's
cooperative attitude was welcome, but the Germans were adamant that
there was to be no territorial guarantee between the two countries. The
new state secretary in the Foreign Office, Carl von Schubert, informed the
German minister in Prague that if Beneš mentioned an arbitration treaty to
him, he could show Beneš Germany's arbitration treaties with Finland and
Sweden as examples.[143] The point was that those treaties contained no
territorial clauses.

Although Beneš voiced no objection to the substance of the proposed
agreements, he did take exception to the Germans' failure to approach him
directly about the arbitration treaty. Once back in Prague, he summoned
Koch in order to complain about the German tactics. Beneš repeated once
again that he saw no obstacles to an arbitration treaty with the Germans,
especially since, as he had learned from the French, the pact was not to
include the boundary question. Contrary to the French and the Poles, he
did not believe that it was necessary for Germany to join the League of
Nations before the security pact could be concluded, although he did
think that Germany's agreement to enter the League should be a necessary
condition for the conclusion of the treaties.[144] (French policy on German
entrance into the League had undergone a complete reversal since the
autumn of 1924. At the time that the Geneva Protocol was under
discussion, the French had hoped to postpone German admission until a
plan for universal security could be adopted. After the failure of the
Geneva Protocol, and with the discussions of a regional security system,
the French insisted on German entrance into the League as a way of
extending German obligations beyond a regional guarantee in the west to a
commitment to uphold the Versailles system in all its aspects.)[145] When
Koch's report reached Berlin, Stresemann immediately instructed him to
soothe Beneš's ruffled feelings as soon as possible. Stresemann wanted to
inform Beneš that Berlin had fully intended to turn to Prague after
ascertaining the mood in Paris. The reason for not approaching the eastern
states to begin with was Berlin's fear that Polish (not Czechoslovak)
opposition in the early stages could wreck the whole undertaking.
Stresemann advised Koch not to bring up the territorial issue again since
Beneš had already indicated his understanding that the boundary was not
to be guaranteed.[146]

A facet of German strategy in the early stages of the negotiations was
the attempt to encourage a sense of security in Prague. First by
implication and then by avowal, German diplomats sought to convince the

Czechs that Berlin's revisionism was directed against Poland and not against Czechoslovakia. The obvious hope was to prevent a united and coordinated opposition to the German initiative by France's eastern allies. At the same time, however, the rumors about the German initiative aroused apprehensions among the Sudeten Germans. They feared that their interests might be abandoned in the process of the German rapprochement with France. State Secretary Schubert quickly moved to calm those anxieties. He instructed Koch discreetly to inform Sudeten German leaders that they had nothing to fear from an arbitration treaty between Germany and Czechoslovakia. On the contrary, Schubert maintained, Germany's entrance into the League of Nations would allow minority complaints to be brought before League agencies in a way that was not possible without German membership. Besides, Germany could not refuse an arbitration treaty with Czechoslovakia since such an action would endanger its whole initiative in the west.[147] Keeping the Sudeten Germans assured of Berlin's continuing support of their interests was but one aspect of Germany's complicated task in preparing for Locarno.

However questionable the German attitude toward Czechoslovakia might have been in view of the private assurances to the Sudeten Germans, the Czechs were highly susceptible to Stresemann's strategy. They wanted to believe German claims that Czechoslovakia and Poland were not equal in the sight of German foreign policy. In fact, Czechoslovak diplomats worked diligently to convince the Germans that there was a fundamental difference between the two countries. Jan Masaryk, the son of the president and an attaché in the Czechoslovak legation in Brussels, told the German minister there that he was not happy about the French attempt to equate the Czechs and the Poles with regard to Germany's eastern boundary problem. Masaryk said that the Czechoslovak government was convinced that there was an essential difference between the positions of Poland and Czechoslovakia on the issue.[148] Those statements, coming from the son of the president of the republic, amplified one of the basic themes of Czechoslovak diplomacy, which was that German irredentism might be understandable against Poland but not against Czechoslovakia. At approximately the same time Beneš told the American chargé that he did "not believe in the permanence of the Polish frontiers."[149] To the British minister Beneš claimed that if he were the Polish foreign minister he would give up the Corridor while seeking to retain Poland's share of Upper Silesia and to gain access to the sea through Memel.[150] And Koch, who had good informants among the Sudeten German parliamentary delegates, twice reported to Berlin that Beneš had told Czechoslovak parliamentarians that the Poles could not retain control of their western territories indefinitely.[151] Stresemann attempted to encourage these attitudes. He sent a message to Prague implying that German strategy was identical for Poland

and Czechoslovakia only because a differentiation between the two countries would amount to an open isolation of Poland.[152] Without promising the Czechs anything of substance, he let them hope that the German refusal to guarantee the boundary portended trouble for the Poles but not for themselves.

Yet Beneš characteristically attempted to retain all his options as long as possible. Whatever the advantages, that approach to policymaking sometimes meant that his actions were inconclusive and even contradictory. At the same time that he was privately questioning the viability of the Polish western frontier, he was making preparations for a demonstrative visit to Warsaw, during which a whole battery of treaties was to be concluded between the two countries. Already in February he informed the British minister of his plans but emphasized that there was no thought of a formal political or military alliance between Poland and Czechoslovakia.[153] In the face of the German initiative, the Western powers had fully expected some kind of demonstration of Czechoslovak-Polish unity. In March Briand remarked to Chamberlain, "Beneš will work upon the Poles."[154] On April 1, in a speech in the Czechoslovak parliament, Beneš declared that the proposed treaties with Poland were designed to establish "an upright friendship between both brotherly states." With friendlier words for Poland than he had ever uttered in parliament, he added: "For our existence we need the existence of Poland even as it needs our existence. The gain will be the same for both nations."[155] After a brief visit in Prague by Polish Foreign Minister Skrzyński, Beneš traveled to Warsaw in mid-April, where he was feted with lavish diplomatic receptions calculated to emphasize the solidarity of the two countries. Events reached their climax with the initialing of a series of agreements including a treaty of arbitration and conciliation as well as a commercial convention designed to increase trade on the basis of the most-favored nation policy. The Poles seemed to attach real importance to the agreements, and Skrzyński claimed in private that the German proposals had caused the two countries to stand together in the presence of a common danger.[156] But the limited extent of the actual rapprochement between the two countries was demonstrated by the arbitration treaty itself, which did not apply to territorial issues. From Prague Beneš informed Czechoslovak legations abroad that there were no changes in the basic relationship between the two countries.[157] Beneš's visit to Warsaw certainly did not create a united front against the German proposals.

The Germans remained unimpressed by the Warsaw demonstrations. Before departing for Poland, Beneš himself had assured Koch that the arbitration treaty would lead to no deeper involvement with Poland. Koch believed that assurance, for he thought that Beneš would not let friendship with Poland reach the point of permanently damaging the chances for an eventual understanding with the Russians.[158] The Czechoslovak minister in Warsaw maintained, for the benefit of his German colleague, that the "antagonism between Poland and Czechoslovakia was almost bigger than between Poland and Germany."[159] Stresemann thought that Beneš's main goal was the creation of a united front in case Germany actually made suggestions for a territorial revision in the east.[160] Such a move was not part of Stresemann's plans for the immediate future, and he showed no great concern about the Czechoslovak-Polish agreements. In a speech before the Reichstag in mid-May, he continued his policy of encouraging divisions among France's eastern allies. His remarks about Czechoslovakia varied substantially from those about Poland. In relation to the Czechs he cited the "good relationship" that had developed since the war and the "thriving economic relations" that benefited both countries. He hoped to maintain that situation, and he said nothing about territorial issues between the two countries. His treatment of Poland was significantly different. About Germany's territorial losses he remarked:

There is no one in Germany who could acknowledge that the boundary in the east, drawn in flagrant contradiction to the right of self-determination of peoples, is an eternally unchangeable fact [heavy applause]. Therefore for Germany no regulation of the security question can be considered that would include another recognition of its boundary [renewed heavy applause].[161]

By focusing German revisionist goals on Polish territory, Stresemann encouraged the Czechs to remain at a safe distance. In the role both of victim and of victimizer in their historical experiences, the Poles understood the uses of power in seizing disputed territory. Even if there were no immediate military danger from Germany, they could take little comfort in their isolated position.

If the Poles could not depend on Czechoslovak support concerning the Polish western boundary, the Czechs could not rely on Polish sympathy in the Anschluss debate. Although Poland's official foreign policy under Skrzyński opposed a German annexation of Austria, some leftist groups and followers of Piłsudski theorized that an Anschluss would be a cheap price to pay for a German guarantee of the German-Polish boundary.[162] France's two eastern allies had their own particular fears of the Germans, and neither was willing to undertake the liabilities of the other. Although Masaryk and Beneš did not fear for the territorial integrity of Czechoslovakia, they worried that a successful Rhenish settlement might refocus German attention on Austria. From the time that they learned of the initial German proposals they made clear that there could be no thought of revising the peace settlements in Austria. Beneš emphasized to Herriot in their earliest talks about the security pact that, from the Czechoslovak viewpoint, an Anschluss meant war.[163] He was just as adamant in his remarks to Austrian diplomats. After his conversations in Geneva and Paris in March, Beneš told the Austrian minister in Prague that the Austrian question "would definitely be included in the pact with Germany." Beneš claimed that the Western powers would insist on Germany's acceptance of a clause reaffirming the treaty regulations concerning Austria.[164] Again, during the return trip from Warsaw in late April, Beneš told the Austrian minister to Poland that an Anschluss would be the "sure beginning of a new world war."[165]

Yet Austrian economic difficulties continued to cause much international concern, and the Austrians focused attention on themselves by calling for a League study of their financial problems in the spring of 1925. Particularly in London, the Czechs continued to receive a major portion of the blame for Austria's troubles and for the general stagnation of trade in Central Europe. The French mounted a campaign for a preferential customs arrangement between Czechoslovakia and Austria, based on the rights afforded the countries by Article 222 of the Treaty of St. Germain.[166] The article had left open the possibility of a preferential tariff system among Czechoslovakia, Austria, and Hungary and had allotted five years for the realization of the project. The Hungarians resolutely opposed the idea, and the Austrians ultimately engaged only in dilatory conversations about it. But from the standpoint of Paris and Prague, a special customs regime between Czechoslovakia and Austria was useful in undercutting the apparent revival of Anschluss sympathies in Austria. Beneš desired to see the adherence of the Yugoslavs, and then to include other successor states as well. In that manner, he hoped to establish the preferential tariff system in the Danubian area that Masaryk and he had advocated since the end of the war. Beneš expressly rejected the inclusion of Germany because he said that would signify the realization of Friedrich Naumann's old project of a Germanic Mitteleuropa.[167] While the Austrians maintained a studied vagueness, the Germans and the Italians resisted Austro-Czechoslovak ties for political reasons. Neither Berlin nor Rome desired to see France or its allies gain more influence in Central Europe, and Berlin always remained deeply suspicious of Austrian agreements with third powers. In London, despite the widespread criticism of Central European tariff barriers, the Board of Trade steadily opposed any preferential tariff scheme that would give Czechoslovak industrial products an advantage over British goods in the Central European market.[168] Article 222 was allowed to lapse unused. No step was taken toward a preferential tariff system.

In April Herriot's cartel dissolved, and a new cabinet under Paul Painlevé, with Aristide Briand as foreign minister, came to power. Briand was the strong man of the government and the real architect of French foreign policy. He and his chief assistant, Philippe Berthelot, felt that they could not overlook the assurance of French security that the German proposals seemed to provide. Yet they also hoped to salvage as much for their eastern allies as possible. If the Germans could not be brought to acknowledge their eastern borders, the French at least hoped to guarantee Germany's arbitration pacts with Poland and Czechoslovakia. In addition, Briand wanted to treat all the agreements, eastern as well as western, as part of one indivisible whole. He insisted that Germany agree to enter the League of Nations and to undertake the obligations imposed on members by the Covenant of the League.[169] Those were the primary considerations in the minds of the leaders of the Quai d'Orsay as they attempted between April and June to formulate an answer to the original German note and to agree with London on a common policy toward the Germans.

One of the primary factors in persuading the French to accept a differentiation between Germany's western and eastern boundaries was the unwillingness of the British to extend their commitments to the east. To be sure, the Laborites under Ramsay MacDonald continued to support the Geneva Protocol despite opposition from the Dominions and criticized the Rhineland security proposal as an inadequate substitute for it. The opposition of the Laborites was ineffective, however, for they had only a small minority in the House of Commons. In addition to the British and the German refusal to undertake guarantees in Central Europe, military considerations may have influenced the French to grasp at security for their own borders. There appears to have been considerable skepticism among French military experts in Prague concerning the extent to which they could actually rely on Czechoslovakia in the event of a military conflict between France and Germany.[170] Finally on June 16, a French note officially informed the Germans of Paris's willingness to pursue negotiations for a security pact as originally outlined in the German proposals. To that acceptance Briand attempted to attach certain conditions calculated to appease the Poles and the Czechs.

A week later Beneš attempted to explain those events in the foreign affairs committee of the Chamber of Deputies. Remarking that anyone who criticized Czechoslovakia's exclusion from the guaranty pact just did not understand the situation, Beneš reviewed the history of British unwillingness to undertake commitments in Central Europe. Because of the British attitude, he said, Czechoslovakia concluded its special agreement with France and the states of the Little Entente, for "it has always been the principle of Czechoslovak policy never to demand from others more than they can actually give." He said that Prague had indicated its support of the negotiations before the French ever sent their answer to Berlin. Given German acceptance of the French conditions, he thought that Germany and Czechoslovakia could agree on an arbitration treaty between themselves.[171] Beneš's statements were indeed moderate and reasonable, and they must have been appreciated in Paris. Actually Beneš could do nothing else if the French considered the Rhineland Pact an important guarantee of French security. His statement about not demanding of others more than they could give, although referring to the British, could have been applied to the French as well. As Beneš remarked, "Whoever would make these negotiations impossible would take a heavy responsibility on himself."[172] Even if he and the Poles could have sabotaged the negotiations, he did not want to bear the blame for doing so. He therefore consistently proclaimed his support for a western security pact while covertly attempting to arrange a private meeting with Stresemann.[173] No doubt, Beneš's prime objective in seeking direct talks with Stresemann was to insure that, despite the absence of a formal guarantee, the Czechoslovak border was as secure as the French and the Belgian. The Germans were evidently willing to give secret assurances of that kind. Masaryk told the British minister in June that a personal emissary from Stresemann had promised Beneš that "There was no idea whatever of Germany seeking any change in the Czechoslovak frontier, but the German Government had been reluctant to dot the "i's" too clearly by referring to the Polish frontier alone."[174]

But in public the German government continued to treat the Polish and the Czechoslovak questions on the same plane. In their note of July 20 the Germans raised objections to the French conditions of June 16. They claimed that Germany's entrance into the League of Nations was not necessarily connected with the security pact but that the two questions could be considered together. They added that there were still ambiguities concerning the terms under which Germany would enter the League—an obvious reference to Article 16 of the Covenant. Already in a note in December 1924 the Germans had pointed to their exposed geographical position and their military disarmament as reasons for their refusal to participate in sanctions under Article 16.[175] Actually it was clear that they did not intend to abandon their special relationship with the Soviet Union and that they would undertake no obligation to participate in sanctions against the Russians in the future. Their reservations had been unrealistic in 1924, at a time when the French did not yet want the Germans in the League, but by the summer of 1925 the position of the Germans was considerably stronger as a result of the new French drive to bring Germany into the League. The other major French desire to which the Germans objected was a French guarantee of the arbitration pacts between Germany, Poland, and Czechoslovakia. They claimed that such a guarantee would put France in the position of judging whether the arbitration treaties were ever violated and that this situation would militate against German interests. They concluded that such a guarantee was not in harmony with the spirit of the League of Nations.[176] Thus after the

French had agreed to the differentiation between Germany's western and eastern borders, the Germans resisted even the French guarantee of the eastern arbitration pacts.

In August and September European diplomacy continued to focus on the security proposals. After another exchange of notes in late August the legal experts of the powers met in London in order to make preparations for a meeting of foreign ministers. Finally, on September 15 the French proposed a conference, and Stresemann formally accepted the invitation eleven days later. Locarno was selected as the site because the Germans did not consider Geneva to be a neutral setting. During the negotiations that led to Locarno Czechoslovak and Polish diplomats were definitely on the diplomatic sidelines. For Beneš that was neither a customary place nor a welcome one. Czech newspapers betrayed fear of being abandoned by the French, and the *Central European Observer* characterized German opposition to the French guarantee of the arbitration pacts as too obvious a manifestation of German designs in the east.[177] On September 2 Krofta once more tried to arrange a formal visit by Beneš to Berlin and was again put off by the Germans.[178] For months the Germans had stoutly resisted Czech efforts to stage an open meeting between Stresemann and Beneš, and so far as was publicly known the two men had never met one another. Beneš's desire to meet publicly with Stresemann reflected his continuing efforts to chart an independent foreign policy and to make his country a participant in, and not just an object of, international negotiations. But his tactics demonstrated again the impossibility of a united Czechoslovakia-Polish policy vis-à-vis the German initiatives.

By mid-September the Czechs again showed their resolve to maintain an identity distinct from the Poles on the boundary issue. Two days after Stresemann remarked in a news conference that neither Poland nor Czechoslovakia had approached Berlin about an arbitration pact, Krofta delivered an official notification to the German Foreign Office that the Czechoslovak government was prepared to negotiate about a pact. That step was universally interpreted as a demonstration of Poland's diplomatic isolation.[179] In the conversation with Krofta, State Secretary Schubert thought that he detected a desire that Beneš participate in all the negotiations at Locarno.[180] It was already publicly known that the Germans wanted to confine Polish and Czechoslovak participation to the negotiations about the eastern arbitration pacts. On September 25 Stresemann therefore received Krofta ostensibly to thank him personally for Prague's agreement to conclude an arbitration treaty. During the conversation Stresemann noted that the initial negotiations at Locarno would concern the Rhineland Pact. Since the eastern arbitration pacts would be taken up only subsequently, he thought it better that Beneš not participate during the opening stages of the conference. To those observations Krofta could reply only that such was also Beneš's opinion.[181] As matters turned out, the Germans profited tactically from the split between Prague and Warsaw while treating the Czechs exactly like the Poles in the conference itself.

On October 5 the foreign ministers of France, Germany, Belgium, Great Britain, and Italy assembled at Locarno for the most significant diplomatic conference since the peace negotiations of 1919. Although Beneš and Skrzyński arrived on October 7 and 8 respectively, they were not allowed to enter the negotiations until October 15, the day before the signing of the final agreements. By that time all the important decisions had already been made, and the two statesmen could do little more than put their signatures to those agreements that directly concerned their countries. The most important of the accords was the Treaty of Mutual Guarantee, by which France, Belgium, and Germany pledged not to resort to military force to alter their boundaries. Britain and Italy served as guarantors of the treaty. In addition, Germany concluded arbitration pacts with four of its neighbors—France, Belgium, Poland, and Czechoslovakia. The treaties were identical except for their preambles; those with France and Belgium mentioned the Rhineland Pact whereas those with Poland and Czecho-slovakia did not. Arbitration therefore applied to territorial issues in the west but not in the east. Stresemann adamantly resisted Briand's efforts to include a French guarantee of Germany's arbitration pacts with Poland and Czechoslovakia, and after a protracted struggle Briand gave way. When Skrzyński and Beneš subsequently tried to introduce their drafts for the arbitration treaties, they were ignored. The French tried to salvage something by concluding new treaties of alliance with Poland and Czechoslovakia. Stresemann refused to take official note of those treaties, which did not form a part of the Locarno accords despite Beneš's subsequent pronouncements to the contrary. As a final measure, the British and the French handed the Germans a letter, which in effect gave assurances that Germany could enter the League of Nations on its own terms. Germany's future obligations to participate in sanctions against an aggressor power, as foreseen in Article 16 of the League Covenant, were to be determined in view of Germany's geographical position and state of military preparedness. In effect, that meant that Germany could not be forced to participate in sanctions against the Soviet Union. The irony was that the formula giving the Germans their special privilege was taken from the Geneva Protocol.[182]

It should have been clear at the time that Locarno was a great victory for German diplomacy. Stresemann and his assistants recognized the magnitude of their accomplishments, but Stresemann still had to override conservative opposition at home, where the nationalists balked at what seemed to be a final renunciation of Alsace-Lorraine. In his campaign to

sell Locarno at home, Stresemann, the party politician, made remarks
about Skrzyński and Beneš that revealed a great deal about the attitudes of
Stresemann the diplomat.

> The psychology of the gentlemen was different. Mr. Beneš, that skillful
> politician, acted after he had not accomplished anything as if he had.
> He put on a big smile and appeared to be happy. Mr. Skrzyński could
> not conceal his agitation. If you have read that the Polish Foreign
> Minister was the first to leave the hall after the signing, you should have
> seen how he left it if you wonder whether Poland considers Locarno to
> be a Polish success. . . . Mr. Beneš and Mr. Skrzyński had to sit there
> waiting in the antechamber until we let them in. That was the situation
> of the states that were previously coddled because they were the
> servants of others and that were dropped in the moment when it was
> believed that there could be an understanding with Germany.[183]

Even if he employed exaggerated rhetoric for the benefit of a nationalist
audience, Stresemann was obviously pleased with the weakening of the ties
between France and its eastern allies wrought by Locarno.

In Prague Beneš confronted an assignment similar to that of Stresemann
in Berlin. Beneš also sought to popularize the agreements among a
doubting public, for it was part of his tactics never to admit defeat. It was
particularly important for him to put a good face on events because
Czechoslovakia was in the midst of a parliamentary election campaign.
Beneš attempted to minimize the differences between the western and the
eastern agreements by emphasizing that the same spirit pervaded them all.
He claimed that the guarantors of the Rhineland Pact, Britain and Italy,
were morally responsible for the maintenance of the eastern arbitration
treaties as well, since all the agreements were part of the same general
understanding.[184] In his report to parliament Beneš gave prime attention
to the new Franco-Czechoslovak treaty while at the same time remarking
that Czechoslovakia's relations with Germany entered a new and friendlier
phase as a result of Locarno.[185] He was grasping at straws.

Despite the atmosphere of moderation and understanding that came to
be known as the "Locarno spirit," despite the four or five years of friendly
diplomacy that followed, Locarno betokened in retrospect the first step in
the change from active to passive defense in French foreign and military
policy. It helped to found the Maginot Line psychology of the 1930s. With
their own border guaranteed and eventually fortified, the French grew less
concerned about Polish and Czechoslovak defense than they had been
previously. To be sure, the Rhineland Pact allowed the French to cross the
river in defense of Poland and Czechoslovakia in case of an unprovoked
attack by Germany, but French military sanctions would henceforth be
possible only after employing the machinery of the League of Nations.
France could no longer make an immediate and unilateral decision to

come to the aid of its eastern allies.[186] Indeed, the Locarno agreements quickly led to the evacuation by the Allied occupation troops of the Cologne zone in the Rhineland. Despite the dissimilar reputations of the Locarno meetings and the Munich conference of 1938, the differences between Locarno and Munich were not absolute. The very procedures adopted by the powers in excluding the smaller eastern states from the negotiations and then confronting them with a fait accompli were comparable in both meetings. The accords in the Swiss Alps in 1925 foreshadowed in subtle but crucial ways the events in Bavaria some thirteen years later.

In the years between Versailles and Locarno Beneš had never neglected an opportunity to urge the Germans to reach an understanding with the French. In October 1925 the initial step in that rapprochement was made. It was not, however, the kind envisioned by Beneš in which Germany would enter a general security system and fulfill in good faith its obligations under the Versailles Treaty. Rather, it was a special under-standing between Berlin and Paris, promoted by the British and accepted reluctantly by the French. Beneš had not foreseen that eventuality, but, once it was accomplished, he had no other choice but to cultivate new and friendlier relations with Berlin. Even as Beneš attempted to put a good face on the Locarno settlements by discounting the differences between the western and the eastern agreements, so he abandoned his old characterization of "correct relations" and spoke only of "friendly relations" with Germany. But Germany was a great power and Czecho-slovakia a small country. With German economic recovery and new diplomatic respectability in the late 1920s, Czechoslovak diplomacy vis-à-vis Germany lost its strong position of the early postwar years. That was an inevitable development, hastened by the diplomatic revolution wrought by Locarno.

ACTIVISTS VERSUS NEGATIVISTS

In the years between 1921 and 1925 issues involving the Sudeten Germans played only a peripheral role in Central European politics. The presence of the German minority in Czechoslovakia was always a subsurface factor that could break into the open but that never actually became the focal point of diplomatic negotiations. As there was little interaction between Sudeten German grievances and international politics in those years, the disputes between the Sudeten Germans and the Czechs can best be treated as a topic in itself.

Whereas all the Sudeten German political parties had agreed on the demand for national self-determination in 1918 and 1919, the Sudeten Germans were already politically divided when they entered parliament in

1920. The German Social Democrats refused to enter a parliamentary bloc with the German "bourgeois" parties. That group, which called itself the "German Parliamentary Club," included the Agrarians, the Christian Socials, the German Democratic Freedom party, the German National party, and eventually the German National Socialist Workers party. The parliamentary club was by no means monolithic, for the first three parties became much more inclined to cooperate with the Czechs than the last two. The Agrarians, the Christian Socials, and the Democrats were increasingly attracted by the hope of participating with Czechoslovak political parties in the governing of the country; and they, like the Social Democrats, came eventually to be known as "activists." On the other hand, the German Nationals and the National Socialists formed their own *Kampfgemeinschaft* within the parliamentary club and held to the old obstructionist policy with a vehemence that became greater as their position grew weaker. Theirs was the "negativist" position. The main theme of Sudeten German politics between 1921 and 1925 was the increasingly bitter struggle between the activists and the negativists.

The hope of embarking on a new attempt to pacify the Sudeten Germans was one of the reasons given for Beneš's assumption of the premiership in the autumn of 1921. The objective quickly proved to be a formidable one. When the government issued mobilization orders in October against the Charles putsch in Hungary, many Sudeten Germans resisted the attempt to induct them into the army. Again there were riots and fatalities in the German areas of the country.[187] The demonstrations warned the Czechoslovak government that the Sudeten German population was unreliable in a conflict not just with Germany but with other states as well. Although the outbursts in the streets ceased to occur after the earliest years of the republic, nationalist rivalries continued to pervade all levels of society. When the German University in Prague conferred an honorary degree on Gerhard Hauptmann in November 1921, the academic senate stubbornly refused to invite either Masaryk or the cabinet to the ceremonies. Koch, the German minister, concluded his report about the incident with the observation: "So they isolate themselves again and again, and then bewail the limited support by the government of the German educational institutions."[188]

Parts of the German academic community aggravated the divisions within the country rather than contributing a rational willingness to alleviate nationalistic rivalries. The student fraternities were determined to retain their traditions of color-wearing, parading, and duelling, which had long antagonized the Czech population of Prague. They underscored their sympathies by making not only Field Marshal Hindenburg but also Karl Helfferich, the arch-nationalist leader and foe of Matthias Erzberger, honorary members in a student club only three months after the Erzberger

assassination.[189] The myopia of the *völkisch*-minded students was manifest again in 1922 with an open campaign against the Jewish students and
professors at the German University. For decades Jews had constituted a
significant minority in the German University, and by the postwar years
the Jewish community formed the heart of the German element in Prague.
In the minority position in which the Germans found themselves, it was
obviously desirable to have as much support as possible. Yet anti-
Semitism, which had long been a fact of life in Prague, remained at least as
strong among the Germans as among the Czechs. After the war many
Jewish students flocked to Prague from Poland and Hungary. Likelier to
understand German than Czech, they registered in the German University.
Their numbers caused the nationalistic German students to clamor for
restrictions on the number of Jewish students in Prague. Although the
demand was in vain, the students received the backing of several major
German parties as well as the sympathy of elements in the Czech
population.[190] The anti-Semitic demonstrations of the right-wing students
reached their summit with a prolonged strike in November 1922 protesting
the election of a Jewish professor as rector of the German University.[191]

Despite, or perhaps because of, the irrational elements in society,
sentiment grew among others for a reconciliation among the nationalities.
Throughout the history of the republic, President Masaryk was the chief
spokesman for that hope. In his New Year's message for 1922 Masaryk
delivered a characteristically mature and humane analysis of international
and domestic problems and their possible solutions. He distinguished
himself as one of the first European leaders to note publicly that there
could be no peace in Europe until Germany and Russia had overcome the
unhappy consequences of the war. In domestic politics he pointed to the
Czech-German rivalry as the only real question confronting the state. He
stoutly opposed the German demand for local autonomy in their own
areas and made it clear that Czechoslovakia would remain a centralized
state. Obviously, he shared the fear that decentralization would lead to the
dissolution of a country composed of so many nationalities. But he noted
that the security of a state rests on the contentment of its citizens, and he
strongly advocated German participation in the government and the
bureaucracy. The only precondition was that the Germans declare their
loyalty to the state.[192]

It is important to note that the responsible French officials looked
askance at the conciliatory attitudes of Masaryk. In commenting about the
New Year's address, the French minister in Prague wrote that Masaryk's
outlook was both idealistic and potentially dangerous for French
policy.[193] The major concern for the French was that through a political
rapprochement with the Czechs the Sudeten Germans could gradually
influence Czechoslovak foreign policy toward a pro-German direction.

French observers tended to be distrustful of the older generation of Czech politicians in general. Through their education and political experience in old Austria, they appeared to the French to be the products of German culture. Their horizons seemed limited to regional affairs in Central Europe. Masaryk was an exception, but his sympathies gravitated toward the Anglo-Saxon world much more than toward the French. But the French also thought that they discerned in the younger generation a Francophile tendency, of which Beneš was the most illustrious example. The French hoped, of course, that that generation would soon gain control of affairs in Prague.[194] Beneš was happily sensitive to the French outlook. In Paris he cultivated his image as the best friend of France among Czechoslovak leaders even to the point of contrasting himself with Masaryk.[195]

The moderate Sudeten German parties therefore posed a greater threat to French interests than the ultranationalists. And it was the moderates who enjoyed the sympathies of the German Foreign Office in Berlin. Only weeks before Masaryk's New Year's address, the German Social Democrats at their annual party congress had again refused to enter the parliamentary club of the German bourgeois parties and had called for cooperation with the Czechoslovak Social Democrats instead.[196] In January 1922 the National Assembly for the first time passed a piece of legislation introduced by a German.[197] Those events were signs of a gradual understanding between Czechs and Germans. The tensions within the German parliamentary club between the moderates and the extreme nationals mounted, and the main reason for the postponement of the ultimate break was the reluctance of either side to assume the responsibility of destroying such German political unity as still existed.

Although the German Agrarians had a larger number of deputies in parliament, the leader of the German National party functioned as the chairman of the parliamentary club. Rudolf Lodgman owed his election as chairman to his reputation as the leader of the Germans in 1918 and 1919. Agrarian leaders such as Franz Křepek and Franz Spina attempted to influence the parliamentary club toward closer cooperation with Czech political parties, but Lodgman remained recalcitrant in his opposition to any political understanding with the Czechs. Members of his party, notably Alois Baeran, delivered insulting speeches in parliament that ultimately discredited the nationalist cause. At the end of January 1922 Baeran topped all previous parliamentary excesses by hurling a stink-bomb at the president of the Chamber of Deputies. Even Lodgmann apologized for that childish prank by a man almost sixty years old, but the German Nationals soon rushed to Baeran's defense when the government investigated his activities, lifted his parliamentary immunity, and successfully prosecuted him for espionage.[198] The Baeran incident widened the growing rift among the German parties. Only the National Socialists could equal or excel the German Nationals in their inflammatory conduct, and the other parties had no desire to compete.

By the summer of 1922 the split among the German bourgeois parties was practically irreparable. In view of the diversity of opinions in the parliamentary club, it was surprising that it had held together for as long as two years. On the right stood the National Socialists, who already had contacts with Hitler's circles in Munich; on the left, the German Democratic Freedom party, which was essentially a Jewish political organization relying on the support of Prague's Jews. The cosmopolitan outlook and democratic sympathies among the Jews aroused fears and suspicions among the German nationalists. From the beginning of the republic the Jews showed that they were more willing than the Germans to compromise and to adapt themselves to new conditions. Probably the main reason for the refusal of the National Socialists to join the parliamentary club in the early months of its existence in 1920 had been their distrust of the Jews. The final crisis in the parliamentary club occurred in November 1922. During a debate about the Baeran espionage trial, Lodgman burst forth with the exclamation: "The prime duty of a German deputy in this state is to commit the crime of high treason."[199] Other German deputies condemned his remarks, and a leader of the Agrarians made a speech advocating a compromise among the nationalities in Czechoslovakia. Lodgman irately walked out of the parliamentary club and thereby destroyed the last fiction of German political unity.[200]

While the Germans became embroiled in internecine disputes, the major Czechoslovak parties were able to maintain their political alliance, albeit with some difficulty. The ruling coalition of five parties, known as the Pětka, consolidated itself in 1920 and 1921. Ranging from the Czechoslovak Social Democrats on the left to Karel Kramář's National Democrats on the right, the common denominator of the coalition was loyalty to Czechoslovak national interests. On the right, Kramář's nationalistic attitudes were at least a match for those of Lodgman, and the only real difference between the two men was that Kramář cloaked himself with the legitimacy of power while Lodgman appeared ridiculous in his political impotence. But Kramář's own political prestige and that of his party had been on the wane since 1919. The more popular Czechoslovak Agrarians and the Czechoslovak Social Democrats avoided the cruder forms of nationalistic display. During the summer of 1922 moderate German politicians hoped for a break in the Pětka such that a new coalition would have to include German parties as well. This attitude represented a distinct shift from the German refusal to consider entering a government coalition as late as 1921. But even the moderate Czechoslovak parties were not yet ready to share power with the Germans. Antonín Švehla succeeded in holding the Czechoslovak parties together when he became premier in the autumn of 1922 and thereby avoided German participation in the government. The German moderates were bitterly disappointed. There can be little doubt that representatives of some of the major German parties could have been won for ministerial positions years before they finally entered the government in 1926.[201]

There was an obvious contradiction between the actions of the Czechoslovak political parties and the words of Masaryk. Whereas Masaryk urged that Germans be brought into the government, lesser Czech politicians refused to cooperate. One reason for that refusal was the surviving resentment about the supposed German domination during the old empire, but a more immediate factor was fear of a German resurgence in the republic. The fundamental goal of the Czechoslovak coalition was to hold power long enough to ensure the Czechoslovak character of a new state. In that respect there was a parallel between the government's domestic programs and Beneš's foreign policy. In both fields there was an intensive effort to establish the national identity of the republic while consolidating its international position. If they were to succeed, the Czechs had to exploit the temporary advantages that had arisen from Germany's defeat in the war. Essentially, that meant keeping the Sudeten Germans isolated in domestic politics and Germany isolated in international affairs, in order not to worsen but to prolong the weak condition of the Germans. Masaryk often decried the lack of political statesmanship among the Czechs and the Sudeten Germans, and there is no reason to suppose that he was insincere in his advocacy of a rapprochement between Czechs and Germans. Yet he himself had done more than any other to found the new state, and the efforts of other Czech leaders to consolidate the republic followed logically from Masaryk's own wartime activities. The earliest possible reconciliation among the nationalities was the best hope for the ultimate survival of the republic; but the atmosphere of the time made that idea utopian. Masaryk himself seemed to vacillate between his idealism and his political opportunism. While he talked about understanding between Czechs and Germans, he remained the strongest domestic supporter of Beneš's foreign policy, which was universally considered antagonistic to German interests.

The Švehla cabinet, which was formed in October 1922, confronted the most serious economic problems since the founding of the republic. Aggravated in part by an excessively high currency valuation, Czechoslovak exports fell drastically in 1922, factories were idled, and unemployment tripled between August 1922 and January 1923. Only the French occupation of the Ruhr and the disappearance of German competition brought temporary relief to Czechoslovak heavy industry.[202] Švehla's minister of finance, Alois Rašín, courted unpopularity with his austerity measures, and his assassination in the winter of 1923 prompted the government to enact a law for the protection of the republic. It gave to the authorities strong emergency powers to deal with any anarchical situation. The opposition parties naturally resisted legislation allowing the government to suspend constitutional rights, and the German parties found themselves in league with the Communists and Father Hlinka's Slovak People's party.[203]

At various times in the 1920s positive cooperation between Slovaks and Sudeten Germans seemed possible. Hlinka's party was the primary heir of that tradition in the Slovak national revival that emphasized Slovak distinctiveness and uniqueness from the Czechs. In 1921 the party broke with the Czech Catholics and left the governing coalition. Although Hlinka's party never garnered an absolute majority of the votes in Slovakia, it was the strongest single political organization there. The watchcry of Hlinka's movement was local autonomy for Slovakia. Inasmuch as local autonomy was also the primary demand of the Sudeten Germans, there appeared to be a programmatic basis for a political alliance. That was only an illusion. There was no common agreement about exactly what was meant by local autonomy; reforms that might encourage autonomy for one nationality could have an opposite effect upon the other. An administrative reform that took effect in Slovakia in 1923 divided the province into six counties (*Župy*) and undermined efforts to create an autonomous government for the province as a whole.[204] On the other hand, the county system—had it ever been adopted in the western provinces—could have given the Sudeten Germans greater autonomy in their own smaller areas of settlement in Bohemia, Moravia, and Silesia.[205] By instituting the county system only in Slovakia, centralist forces in Prague were able to resist demands for local autonomy from both the Slovaks and the Sudeten Germans. Very little in fact united the two nationalities, and no fundamental collaboration developed between them until 1938. For Czechoslovak-German relations in the Weimar years, the Slovak issue was significant only insofar as it generally weakened the Czechoslovak republic.

Competition between activists and negativists among the Sudeten German parties intensified with the approach of the communal elections in September 1923. The elections were particularly important for the Germans of the border areas, for local German officials could mitigate the effect of Czech legislation emanating from Prague. Local officials were of potentially greater importance if the Germans should actually succeed in gaining political autonomy. But the greatest significance of the communal elections was that they would give some indication of the relative strength of the various Sudeten German parties. Although local problems and personalities had considerable effect on the results of the elections, at least a basic idea about popular support of the activist or the negativist policies was to be forthcoming from the elections. The results showed that the Agrarians had scored significant victories while the Christian Socials and the Democrats had gained moderately. The Social Democrats incurred some losses, but the German Nationals suffered a heavier defeat. The results therefore indicated a tendency among the German voters to support the activists.[206] Encouraged by their good showing in the communal elections, the Agrarians, the Christian Socials, and the Democrats formed a parliamentary "working bloc" (*Arbeitsgemeinschaft*) in October. The German Nationals and the National Socialists were left out.[207] Thus the German parliamentary representation in the National Assembly was broken into three main groups—the activists, the negativists, and the Social Democrats. Concurrently, the Social Democrats were pursuing initiatives of their own. An international association of socialist parties conducted negotiations at Prague in October 1923 for the purpose of unifying the Czechoslovak and the German Social Democratic parties. Although problems proved insurmountable, both groups agreed to the maintenance of the commission in order to examine their differences and to work toward an eventual union of the two parties.[208]

By the spring and summer of 1924 there was an increasing amount of discussion in the newspapers about the possible entrance of German parties into the governing coalition. That publicity was promoted by the German activists and resisted by the Czechs. In a speech in late March Robert Mayr-Harting, the leader of the Christian Socials, advocated cooperation of the Germans with the Czechs in the political life of the country as well as German entrance into the cabinet. Mayr-Harting said that he was glad that the irredentist parties were not part of the "Working Bloc" and that any thought of treaty revision could come only at some later date.[209] The initiative of the activist parties, supported particularly by the *Prager Tagblatt*, continued through the summer. By August the semiofficial organs of the Czechoslovak government were openly combatting the reports of an imminent entrance of some German parties into the government. The *Prager Presse* wrote that there were so many divisions among the Germans that the Czechs did not know with whom to negotiate, and the *Central European Observer* thought that the activist policy was simply a tactical device by the Germans in order to further their own goals. It insisted that a precondition for the participation of Germans in the government was an unconditional pledge of loyalty to the Czechoslovak state.[210] By the end of the year Beneš promised the French that no Germans would enter the government until after new elections had determined the national will.[211]

While the activists worked for their inclusion in the government, the German Nationals by no means abandoned their obstructionist policy. The party adopted a resolution in May that characterized Czechoslovakia simply as a device created by French power politics for the preservation of the Paris peace treaties. Those treaties, according to the resolution, broke apart "Germandom" in Central Europe, and the goal of any "Great-German" policy must be to eliminate them.[212] The unthinking extremism of the German Nationals played into the hands of the Czechoslovak coalition, which was not yet ready to admit the German activists but which was weakened by charges of corruption. The government focused attention on the German Nationals by prosecuting one of their deputies for irresponsible if not treasonable statements in parliament. He had threatened that German landowners would burn down their forests before permitting the state to confiscate them, and had added that in the event of another war the Sudeten Germans would not shoot at fellow Germans as they had done in 1866. In the midst of parliamentary commotion traditional on such occasions he had been temporarily expelled from the Chamber of Deputies.[213] Although it was difficult for anyone to cooperate with the German Nationals or the Nazis, the German activist parties and the Social Democrats did move toward a more strongly national policy by the close of 1924. They were probably motivated in part by disappointment over their failure to come to an agreement with the Czechoslovak parties. More significant, however, was the question of current political tactics. The government was attempting to effect necessary but unpopular reforms in the bureaucracy, and the opposition parties wanted to distance themselves from any responsibility for those measures. Moreover, the German activist parties were determined not to allow the right-wing parties to pose as the sole defenders of German national claims in the next elections.

As the Sudeten Germans wavered in their unsteady political course, the Reich German government in Berlin maintained a formally correct attitude toward the Sudeten German minority. The problem was officially an internal affair of Czechoslovakia, and Berlin undertook no active intervention on behalf of the Sudeten Germans. Their leaders did confer with Koch and other members of the German legation, but those contacts were handled circumspectly in view of the sensitivity of the Czechoslovak government. Koch shared the almost universally low estimation of the Sudeten German leaders. There were a few for whom he had real admiration, however, and those men were among the leaders of the activist movement. Koch and the top officials in the Foreign Office in Berlin strongly favored participation by the Sudeten Germans in the Czechoslovak government, but they refused to exert pressure or to become involved in the internecine political disputes of the Sudeten Germans. It was obvious that the Sudeten Germans could best exploit their natural political and economic influence through formal cooperation with the

Czechs, but Koch never believed in the possibility of a complete compromise and understanding between the two nationalities. The best that could be hoped for was a kind of "armistice," but he considered leaders on both sides so recalcitrant that even a limited agreement was difficult to achieve.[214]

The political and economic recovery of Germany in the mid-1920s put the Sudeten Germans in a stronger position within Czechoslovakia. Whereas Germany had been unable to give practical assistance to the Sudeten Germans in the immediate postwar years, Germany's economic prosperity under the Dawes plan led to the support of Sudeten German financial institutions. In the spring of 1925 the German *Kreditanstalt* in Prague found itself in difficult straits and needed a loan of five to six million marks in order to cover its indebtedness. German officials and experts blamed manipulations by Czech banks for the run on its resources. The only source from which the Kreditanstalt could get quick adequate help was the Reich, and in mid-June there were negotiations between its representatives and officials of the Foreign Office and the Ministry of Finance. A document in the archives of the Reich Chancellery reveals much about Reich-German attitudes concerning the minority problem in Czechoslovakia.

> The Foreign Office and the Prussian Bank consider support of the *Kreditanstalt* unavoidable from political and economic reasons. It is the only larger German banking undertaking that has held itself free from Czech influence. The shareholders are exclusively Germans. The business area of the bank extends throughout the entire German area of settlement along the former German-Bohemian border. The Czechs are trying urgently to destroy the *Kreditanstalt*. The last run was tracked back by different experts to manipulations of a conspiracy of banks. If the *Kreditanstalt* were to crash, the entire German middle class would be destroyed and would be thrown on Czech banks for its financial needs. This success would mean the Czechization of the formerly German areas of trade and commerce in Czechoslovakia. Some six and a half million Czechs stand there against some three and a half million Germans, who are continually being pressed back.[215]

The German government granted a credit of five million marks.[216] Despite efforts to camouflage the source of the money, Czech officials were soon aware that the support was coming from Berlin, but they made no issue of the matter. The assistance to the Kreditanstalt was only the first step in a general effort in Berlin to support Sudeten German banks.[217]

While the Reich Germans were gradually becoming more active in Czechoslovakia, the various Sudeten-German parties tried as late as the autumn of 1925 to effect some compromise so as to enter the parliamentary elections of November with a unified front. The dream of unity among the Germans in Czechoslovakia continued to live even if the reality had long since ceased to exist. By October it was clear, however, that no election coalition could be constructed. The only partnership in the campaign was the association of some splinter German and Magyar parties with the German Agrarians. The Agrarians, known as the *Bund der Landwirte,* came through with a sweeping victory, and the Christian Socials enjoyed moderate success as well.[218] In an election in which much of the working-class vote went to the Communists, the German Social Democrats lost ground, although not so badly as the Czechoslovak Social Democrats. The German Nationals and National Socialists barely held their own, and the most humiliating rebuff came to Lodgman himself. He lost his own campaign to retain a seat in the Chamber of Deputies—and lost it to one of the leading German spokesmen for an activist policy. After that debacle he retired from active political life, to reappear only as a considerably older man in vastly different circumstances.[219]

By the end of 1925 it appeared that there might indeed be a new day dawning in the relations between the Germans and the Czechs in Central Europe. Within Czechoslovakia the Sudeten Germans had shown a clear preference in the elections for the cooperative attitudes of the activists. It could be only a matter of time until the Germans would get at least token representation in a government coalition. On the international scene Locarno had wrought a diplomatic revolution that Beneš had to claim to support. The "Locarno spirit" gave rise to an optimistic mood that made it easy to forget the fundamental differences between the western and the eastern settlements. That is, it was easy for those not directly involved to forget it. But responsible leaders in Berlin and Prague knew that fundamental problems were not to be so easily solved. From the Czech viewpoint the basic task of securing the independence of the new republic vis-à-vis a large and potentially overpowering neighbor became even more difficult as a result of Locarno. On the popular level, national antagonisms subsided temporarily with the economic stabilization and prosperity of the mid and late 1920s. But in diplomacy, beneath the surface of "friendly relations," the nationality conflict continued unabated as the German and the Czechoslovak republics pursued conflicting goals in Central Europe.

"Friendly relations" was Beneš's term. He used it through the late 1920s to characterize Czechoslovak-German contacts, just as he had employed "correct relations" in the immediate postwar years. No one in Berlin openly disputed that description. It was in the interests of Stresemann's diplomacy to cultivate the "Locarno spirit" of compromise and conciliation. Germany's revisionist priorities concentrated on the Allied occupation of the Rhineland, Allied military inspections in Germany, and foreign influence over German economic policy under the Dawes plan. The central focus of German diplomacy was therefore on the Western powers, and the maintenance of the special relationship with the Soviet Union was a useful device for applying pressure on Britain and France for further concessions. Given that strategy, it was important to maintain a placid atmosphere in Central Europe. Germany's open disputes with Poland can be interpreted, in part, as a means of pacifying German nationalist opposition at home. The initiatives in the bilateral relations between Germany and Czechoslovakia came usually from Prague. Imitating the example of his French ally, Beneš sought to alleviate the problems that separated Germany and Czechoslovakia. The most volatile threat to a Czechoslovak-German understanding was the condition of the Sudeten Germans. In the months after Locarno, Czechoslovakia's foreign and domestic policies paid unprecedented attention to the 3¼ million Germans living in Czechoslovakia. At the same time the continuing efforts of the small state to secure and maintain its independence against the influence of the large one demonstrated that "friendly relations" were only a surface phenomenon.

NEW INFLUENCE FOR THE SUDETEN GERMANS

After the Locarno meeting and the Czechoslovak elections in November 1925 the Sudeten Germans were in the strongest position that they had enjoyed since 1918. The economic recovery in the Reich helped them, as did Stresemann's growing diplomatic respectability. The triumph of the German activist parties in Czechoslovakia came in the same parliamentary elections that cut the Czechoslovak coalition's majority to eighteen votes in the Chamber of Deputies. The moderate gains of the Czechoslovak Agrarians, Catholics, and the previously insignificant Traders' party were more than offset by severe losses of the Czechoslovak Social Democrats to the Communists.[1] The resultant imbalance within the coalition in favor of the bourgeois parties created additional difficulties in keeping the coalition's bourgeois and socialist wings agreed on a common policy. It appeared that there was an excellent chance for a realignment of parties according to class interests rather than along national lines. Some German parties would thereby enter the cabinet. The process by which their entrance was effected continued for almost a year after the elections.

In the winter and spring of 1926 the Czechoslovak minister in Berlin, Kamil Krofta, held conversations with Stresemann and Schubert about the treatment of the Sudeten Germans. The fact that Krofta prompted those discussions represented a new departure in Czechoslovak policy, for it had always been Prague's position that the question of national minorities was an internal problem of Czechoslovakia that could not be the subject of negotiations with foreign powers. But already at Locarno Krofta had remarked to Schubert that Berlin might act as mediator between the Czechs and the Sudeten Germans, and Beneš had indicated his willingness to exchange opinions with Stresemann about the problem.[2] On January 18, 1926, Schubert reminded Krofta anew of Berlin's interest in the welfare of the Sudeten Germans and remarked that "news comes to us again and again that this treatment [of the Sudeten Germans] is completely unjustified in many instances." The specific issues that Schubert mentioned were largely those dating from the foundation of the Czechoslovak republic—land reform, language restrictions, firing of German bureaucrats, and the school reforms. Schubert concluded that the German minority in Czechoslovakia, rather than becoming a bone of contention for the two countries, should build bridges between them.[3]

The willingness of the Czechs to enter into negotiations about the Sudeten German problem with officials in Berlin aroused the suspicions of Koch, who remarked that public opinion would drive Beneš from office if his activities were generally known. Koch warned that Beneš must have some goal in mind that would justify the risk, and he thought that actually Beneš was trying to drive a wedge between Berlin and the Sudeten Germans. He observed that the Sudeten Germans themselves were too divided even to agree on their complaints and that the German Foreign Office did not have sufficient knowledge of local problems to conduct negotiations with the Czechs. If it did, it would have to abandon some of the more extreme claims, and this the Sudeten Germans would not forgive. Koch recommended that the discussions be kept in generalities without there being actual negotiations concerning grievances in Czechoslovakia.[4] With that advice to Berlin Koch implicitly recognized that many Sudeten German protests were exaggerated and that they could not stand up in bargaining sessions. Yet some unrest and discontent among the Sudeten Germans was diplomatically useful to Berlin, and there is no evidence that German diplomacy sought to moderate Sudeten German complaints.

Berlin took Koch's advice and refrained from bargaining with the Czechs, but a conversation between Krofta and Schubert in early April was unusual in its frankness about the minority problem. Krofta admitted, according to Schubert's memorandum, that the Czechs had committed "all kinds of stupidities" and that it might be best, if there were really weighty complaints, for Germany to get the League of Nations to exercise pressure on Prague. But then Krofta drew attention to the irredentist groups in Germany that aimed at annexing the Sudetenland and, some even thought, the entire country of Czechoslovakia. Schubert quickly disavowed these ideas, claiming that no serious and influential politician in Germany espoused such a policy. Upon urging from Krofta, he agreed that Berlin might indicate to the Sudeten Germans that any annexation plans "were not very practical." Claiming that the Czechs probably exaggerated the closeness of the ties between Berlin and the Sudeten Germans, Schubert remarked that any Czechoslovak government that wanted to cultivate good relations with Germany and Austria should halt the "suppressions" of the Sudeten Germans and institute a real "policy of compromise."[5] If nothing else, the conversations were evidence of a certain improvement in the diplomatic climate between the two capitals, for the most critical issue between them—and the one that had previously been taboo—was being openly discussed.

Beneš's interest in the discussions about the Sudeten Germans could have stemmed from a desire to prevent Germany's promotion of minority complaints once it entered the League of Nations. Also, foreseeing Sudeten German participation in the government in Prague, he might have hoped to undercut the force of their complaints before they gained more political influence. After the November 1925 elections, the government parties attempted (despite their reduced majority) to govern with the same coalition. By the spring it was obvious that the Czechoslovak coalition could not long stay together. The main reason for that situation was that the impressive victory of the Communist party at the polls had so weakened the Czech Social Democrats that they could not maintain their old influence in the cabinet. With the new circumstances the Czechoslovak middle-class parties saw an opportunity for inaugurating a more conservative economic policy by cooperating with the German activist middle-class parties. Before the national coalition dissolved, it did pass a law modifying and implementing the controversial language law of 1920 that made "Czechoslovak" the official language of the state. Then in March 1926 the coalition broke up, and Jan Černý came back on a provisional basis as premier of a nonpolitical "cabinet of experts." The question that split the cabinet was the proposed increase of tariffs on agricultural imports. Promoted by the Czechoslovak Agrarians and strongly resisted by the Social Democrats, the measure was finally passed in the Chamber of Deputies by the combined votes of the Czechoslovak bourgeois parties and the German Agrarians and the German Christian Socials. The Agrarian-Catholic coalition was cemented through an arrangement whereby the Catholics voted for higher agricultural tariffs while the Agrarians reciprocated by helping to pass higher state salaries for the clergy.[6] These events heralded the approach of the new "bourgeois" cabinet.

As developments moved toward the inclusion of Germans in the government, the advocates of both the activist and the negativist approaches sought to enlist Berlin's aid. Representatives of both sides held long conversations with Koch in which they tried to get invitations to visit Stresemann in Berlin, obviously in the hope of winning official sanction for their respective lines of policy. Stresemann refused to receive any Sudeten German delegation. He cautiously ruled out even a private exchange of opinions in view of "the many surviving ambiguities between us and the Czechoslovak government."[7] It was clear that Stresemann and his subordinates favored the activist policy of cooperation with the Czechoslovak authorities, and they realized that it would be foolish to receive a deputation from the Sudeten Germans during the delicate negotiations for German entrance into the cabinet. Yet the differences between the activists and the negativists were not absolute. In the early summer the two sides concluded and signed an agreement stating that both the activist and the negativist approaches were ultimately aiming at the creating of "Ein Volk, ein Reich." That was basically the same reasoning as had been developed in the 1880s by the Old and the Young Czechs, when they too had tried to rationalize their differences about active participation in Austrian governments. Koch marveled at the political naiveté of the German activists in delivering such a document into the hands of their right-wing political opponents. If the activist policy should succeed, the German Nationals could claim that they had been in basic cooperation all the time. On the other hand, the German Nationals were in a position to undercut the activist policy at any time by showing the agreement to the Czechs.[8] The hesitance and indecision with which the German activist leaders approached their task reflected their limited political abilities.

But the real political struggles of 1926 were among the Czechoslovak party leaders, who, if more resourceful than the Sudeten Germans, were just as limited in political vision. During the spring and summer of 1926, at approximately the same time as Piłsudski's coup d'état in Warsaw, there appeared a small but noisy wave of homegrown "fascism" in Prague. The central figures in the movement were Jan Stříbrný, a leader of the Czechoslovak National Socialist Party, and General Rudolf Gajda, the chief of the general staff of the Czechoslovak army. Karel Kramář also played with the idea of a right-wing dictatorship in some of his more extreme editorializing at the time.[9] The organs of his National Democratic party unleashed virulent condemnations of Beneš, even attacking him for

"Germanophilism" at the time of Germany's entrance into the League of Nations.[10] Nor was Masaryk himself spared at least indirect attack. Conditions reached such a point that Masaryk apparently considered assuming dictatorial power himself under the emergency provisions of the constitution. In fact, Masaryk remarked to the Austrian minister that a dictatorship was not necessarily irreconcilable with democracy and that it might be possible to take advantage of dictatorial powers in order to "polish up the constitution."[11] But there was more froth than force in the nationalist wave, and it is possible that government newspapers purposely exaggerated the danger in order to discredit the men connected with it. The forces around Masaryk and Beneš were popularly known as "the Castle"—in reference to the presidential residence on Hradčany. They evidently maintained an active intelligence service that compiled detailed dossiers on various leading figures in Czechoslovak political life.[12] It was often not difficult to collect embarrassing information that could be used for political blackmail. Revelations about Stříbrný and Gajda discredited them both, forced Stříbrný out of the National Socialist party and Gajda from his post.[13] As a result, Kramář and the nationalist opposition had to moderate their attacks on the leadership of Masaryk and Beneš. Stříbrný and Gajda continued to be figures around which disgruntled elements of the extreme right could coalesce in later years of the republic. There can be no doubt that in purging them from positions of power the "Castle" forces took another step toward the consolidation of the new republic. But the methods with which Masaryk and Beneš were apparently associated in domestic politics, as in foreign affairs, did not always accord with their stated principles.[14]

Much more dangerous to Beneš than the attacks from the extreme nationalist opposition were the negotiations among the moderate parties for a new "bourgeois" cabinet. Beneš's domestic political position was never weaker than in 1926. Although never primarily interested in party politics, Beneš had joined the Czechoslovak National Socialist party in 1923 in the hope of finding protection against his domestic political critics.[15] The party embraced a mildly socialist program and stood on the moderate left of the political spectrum. With the approaching exclusion of the National Socialists from the ruling coalition, it appeared that Beneš would have to resign. Beneš's chief political rival for the post of foreign minister was Milan Hodža, who exercised great influence as leader of the Slovak wing of the Agrarian party. He was particularly important in view of Prague's need for a Slovak politician who could counter the autonomist influence of Father Hlinka's Slovak People's party. After the fall of the Czechoslovak coalition cabinet in March 1926, former Premier Švehla left Prague for an extended vacation in an attempt to recoup his health. During Švehla's absence, Hodža became the chief architect of the new middle-class cabinet, and he assumed the primary responsibility for conducting the negotiations that brought the Sudeten German activists into the government.

Hodža campaigned actively, if covertly, for the post of foreign minister. He even established clandestine ties with the German Foreign Office.[16] Hodža apparently hoped for the support of the Sudeten Germans in helping him oust Beneš from office, but his chances were never so good as to allow him to come into the open with his efforts. Stresemann and Schubert sensibly remained aloof from the political struggles in Prague. It was not clear to them or to anyone else that a change in personnel in the Czechoslovak Foreign Ministry would actually bring a reorientation of Czechoslovak foreign policy, although there were signs that circles within the Agrarian party favored redirecting Czechoslovak policy along a more pro-German course.[17] Hodža represented the conservative wing of the party, which resented the power of the Masaryk-Beneš forces and whose economic interests were largely in grain production. Whereas grain interests desired protective tariffs, the sugar industry was more dependent on international trade. It was the backbone of the more liberal group of the Agrarians that sympathized with Masaryk's and Beneš's foreign policy.[18] Hodža did not enunciate an alternative foreign policy to Beneš's, contenting himself simply with emphasizing the desirability of solidarity among the Slavic agrarian states of Eastern Europe.[19] His campaign for the post of foreign minister probably stemmed at least as much from his personal ambition as from a desire to change direction in Czechoslovakia's foreign relations. At least that was the opinion of the French minister who later wrote that he much preferred Beneš's "clear, sane, and sage ideas" to the "complicated, sophisticated, and utopian thoughts" of Hodža.[20] Revelations about a scandal in which Hodža had been involved eventually forced him to modify his ambitions in 1926, and he announced publicly that he had no interest in becoming foreign minister.[21]

Upon Švehla's return to Prague in the late summer, negotiations for the new government entered their final stage. Whereas Hodža's political machinations seldom remained secret, Švehla successfully operated behind the scenes and rarely entered the public view. (The American minister wrote that he had seen Švehla just once, from afar, in Švehla's first three years as premier.)[22] Švehla was universally recognized as the most adept manipulator of the parties, and many considered him the likeliest successor of Masaryk. In the discussions between Masaryk and Švehla during September and October, Masaryk's uncompromising insistence that Beneš remain foreign minister protected Beneš from his political opponents and kept him on the job.[23] Even at that, Beneš was forced to remain away from Prague for several months, during which the country's foreign policy drifted without direction. Masaryk and Švehla eventually reached a compromise by which Beneš retained his post in the new government as a "nonpolitical expert." In order to expedite the bargain Beneš had already resigned his seat as a National Socialist deputy in parliament. But, to complete the political gymnastics, his party had emphasized simultaneously that Beneš would continue to play a leading role in its councils.[24]

While that compromise was being worked out, the decision was made to recall Kamil Krofta from the legation in Berlin and to establish him as the number-two man in the Foreign Ministry.[25] Beneš had never been able to delegate responsibility, and there was little organization or efficiency in his ministry. When he was absent, no decisions could be made. Krofta's assignment was both to oil the bureaucratic machinery and to serve as Beneš's deputy in conferences and negotiations. It was also possible that the appointment of Krofta, who was a nominal member of the National Democratic party, represented an attempt to curb Beneš's dominance in foreign affairs and to give the conservative parties greater influence in the Foreign Ministry. Krofta did show some early signs of attempting to maintain a position independent of Beneš, but, as Beneš eventually consolidated his political position, Krofta conformed. He became and remained a loyal tool of the Masaryk-Beneš foreign policy and served as foreign minister from 1936 to 1938 during Beneš's presidency. As Krofta's successor in Berlin, the government nominated František Chvalkovský, who was the friend and closest political confidant of Premier Švehla. Chvalkovský eventually succeeded Krofta as foreign minister after the debacle at Munich in 1938. A measure of the importance that was attached to the Berlin mission was the subsequent careers of the men who served as ministers there.

One of the ironies of the political conflicts of 1926 was that Beneš almost lost his job in part because of the willingness of the Sudeten German middle-class parties to enter a coalition government. Both Masaryk and Beneš had long proclaimed their support for Sudeten German participation in the government, and the October announcement of the new government, which included two Sudeten German ministers, was universally regarded as a sign of the increasing consolidation of the new state. Traditional social and economic concerns seemed once again to be taking precedence over nationalistic rivalries. Franz Spina, leader of the German Agrarians, became minister of labor, and Robert Mayr-Harting, head of the German Christian Social party, served as minister of justice. Spina soon granted interviews to Vienna's *Neue Freie Presse,* Paris's *Matin,* and Prague's *Bohemia*—all reported by the *Central European Observer*—in which he sought to explain and justify German participation in the government. Emphasizing that cooperation was made possible by the Franco-German rapprochement since Locarno, he remarked:

We have lived for a thousand years side by side with the Czechs, and we are so closely united with them in the economic, social, and cultural spheres—and indeed in blood relationship—that we form a single whole with them. We live with the Czechs in symbiosis.[26]

Spina explicitly rejected, moreover, any notion of incorporating the Sudeten Germans into the Reich. It was never clear precisely what promises the Sudeten German activists had received in return for their cooperation in the government, but Švehla seems to have indicated that political administration in the Sudeten German areas would be conducted more to the liking of the Germans.[27]

So 1926 brought a triumph for the Sudeten German activists, a compromise among Czechoslovak political forces—and a defeat for French diplomacy. To be sure, Beneš remained in office, and for the French that was the most positive aspect of the events of 1926. In the summer when Beneš was under attack, the French minister warned that if Beneš left office even temporarily Czechoslovakia "would lose at least fifty percent of the influence and authority that he has attained for it in Europe."[28] Yet in view of earlier French anxiety about Sudeten German influence in Czechoslovakia, Couget remained strangely detached from the events that brought Sudeten Germans into the government. Although he recognized the "dangerous pretentions" of the Germans, he did not think that Spina and Mayr-Harting would "abuse" their positions or precipitate basic shifts in Czechoslovak policy.[29] But Couget's optimism served him ill, and he was recalled within a few weeks after the formation of the new government. The new French minister in Prague, François Charles-Roux, unleashed a veritable barrage of reports composed around the leitmotiv of the growing Sudeten German influence in Czechoslovakia.

Charles-Roux's conversations with Beneš offer historians new evidence for assessing Beneš's attitudes about the Sudeten German problem. Even allowing for Beneš's propensity for saying what he knew his interlocutors wanted to hear, the evidence is strong that Beneš actually viewed Sudeten German participation in the government with a great deal of skepticism. In February 1927 Charles-Roux quoted Beneš directly as saying:

I am under no illusions about what we can expect from the Germans of Czechoslovakia in the case of difficult circumstances. In no grave threat from abroad will we have them with us. That is beyond doubt, and in a case of this kind, our policy will be to stop [cooperation] and continue without them. Their entry into the ministerial coalition and into the government proceeds simply from the fact that in internal policy a constant and unvarying line of policy toward them is impossible. One cannot even conceive of a line of conduct toward them, which would consist once and for all of either a gentle or a firm manner, without taking into account either their attitude or the necessities of internal politics. In reality, the events, the conditions of our national development, and the circumstances of our international life will probably impose on us an alternation of these two methods. The situation where an external danger would loom before us, but where they would not see a threat for themselves, would necessarily break the collaboration with them.[30]

Beneš repeated the same sentiments to Charles-Roux at various times in the following years.[31] In public Beneš treated Sudeten German membership in the government as a desirable factor in the consolidation of the state. In private with his closest ally, he considered it a luxury that Czechoslovakia could afford only so long as there was no immediate threat from abroad. It appears that even in those years in which the Sudeten Germans seemed most cooperatively inclined, Beneš developed no confidence in their ultimate loyalty. Although Charles-Roux continued to worry about Sudeten German influence in Prague, he grew confident that Czechoslovakia would not alter its French alliance policy so long as "this policy is directed by M. Beneš under the auspices of M. Masaryk."[32]

While Czech and Sudeten German leaders concentrated on their own political discussions, internal problems within Germany also affected Czechoslovak-German relations. Bavaria once more became a fountain of difficulties. Both the popular press and responsible officials in Munich occasionally baited the Czechs with charges of oppressing the Sudeten German minority or of harboring designs on Bavarian territory. Such accusations prompted the Czechoslovak minister to remind the Foreign Office of the harm being done by the Bavarians, and officials in Berlin in turn put pressure on Munich to stop the attacks on the Czechs. But the traditional rivalries between north and south, as well as the right-wing particularism of the Bavarian government of the 1920s, made it difficult for Reich officials to exert much influence in Munich. Among the Bavarians there existed a strong conviction that the Reich government was dominated by Prussian interests and that the government therefore showed great concern about the Prussian-Polish borderlands without paying legitimate attention to the Bavarian-Czechoslovak frontier. There was substance for that belief inasmuch as the German National People's party represented groups with property interests in the border areas with Poland, whereas no political party took a similar interest in the regions along the Czechoslovak boundary.

In February 1926 Krofta lodged an official protest in Berlin about anti-Czech statements made by the head of the Bavarian government. In the Bavarian *Landtag* the premier, Heinrich Held, had accused the Czechs of oppressing the Sudeten Germans.[33] A public statement of that kind forced Beneš's hand, for he feared being questioned by his own nationalist critics in parliament. When Krofta admitted that Beneš might want to publish the official German response, Stresemann and Schubert worked out an answer that took up a delicate position between the Czechs and the Bavarians. They pointed out that only the Reich government could formulate and conduct foreign policy for Germany, yet they admitted that statements in the *Landtag* by the Bavarian premier could not be regarded as purely private utterances. They added that Held expressed a mood of concern for the welfare of the Sudeten Germans that was widespread in German public opinion, but they concluded that a reasonable handling of "this purely cultural problem" on both sides would prevent any disturbance in German-Czechoslovak relations.[34] The statement was a fine example of diplomatic phraseology, which could pacify the Czechs and yet protect the position of the Foreign Office domestically. The attempt to establish "friendly relations" or even the appearances thereof encountered nationalist opposition in both countries, and those in charge of diplomacy in Berlin and Prague constantly had to protect their flanks at home.

Again in the winter of 1926-27 anti-Czech propaganda from Bavaria caused Krofta to make representations to the German Foreign Office. In November the Bavarian representative in the Reichsrat complained in a debate about appropriations for Prussia's border areas that Bavaria wanted "greater consideration for its endangered eastern parts." Krofta wanted to know why the Bavarians thought they were threatened.[35] When Foreign Office personnel talked with the Bavarian minister in Berlin, he said that the Czech economic and cultural encroachment put the Germans along the border in a "difficult folkish battle."[36] Officials in Munich pointed to the loans granted by banks in Czechoslovakia to Germans in Bavaria's border territories as evidence of financial aggrandizement. Upon investigation the Foreign Office discovered that the bank making the loans was a purely Sudeten German enterprise. In remarks dripping with sarcasm officials in Berlin assured Bavarian representatives that the Sudeten Germans would recall the loans whenever Munich desired, but, they added, that would seem to work an economic hardship on the Bavarians.[37]

In the continuing discussions Munich's functionaries were pushed further and further toward admitting that they were really conjuring up a Czech danger in order to get more financial aid from the central government in Berlin. In 1926 the initial Reich appropriations for the borderlands—the so-called *Sofortprogramm*—were confined to the Prussian frontier areas, where one could make a case for special subventions in view of Polish nationalist propaganda. But the jealousies of the other German states forced the Reich government to indicate that it would consider a program of general support for all the border areas.[38] In the resulting competition for funds from Berlin the Bavarian government created the myth of the czechization of its frontier territories. In March 1927 a conversation of a Foreign Office representative with a counselor from the Bavarian State Ministry showed this quite clearly.

Herr Schmelzle responded that the Czechization in the Bavarian Forest was actually more indirect than direct. On the Bohemian side of the boundary excellent roads, schools, kindergartens, etc., etc., are being built, which cannot be the case on the Bavarian side. So the population on the Bavarian side, full of jealousy, sees how good conditions are on the Bohemian side. This they [government officials] want to get around by paying more attention to the Bavarian side than previously. On what basis they get the money is all the same to him, just so long as Bavaria gets the help.[39]

There was no evidence of any attempt by Czech authorities to encroach in any way on Bavarian territory. Insofar as the situation within Czechoslovakia was actually a matter of concern for Bavarian politicians it aroused their jealousy of the superior economic conditions across the frontier. It should be remembered that those border territories on the Czechoslovak side were inhabited largely by Sudeten Germans, who could also look across the boundary and see that circumstances in the Reich were not so good as in Czechoslovakia. This was one of the reasons that the Sudeten Germans showed a decreasing interest in the late 1920s in becoming a part of Germany.

Although domestic political developments in Czechoslovakia and Germany were of chief significance for the relations of the two countries in the year after Locarno, international questions did affect them directly. In the aftermath of the Locarno agreements, the two chief international events of 1926 were Germany's entrance into the League of Nations and the conclusion of the Treaty of Berlin between Germany and the Soviet Union. Both episodes underscored the fact that relatively little had changed in the relationship between Prague and Berlin.

At the beginning of March 1926 Chancellor Hans Luther, Stresemann, Schubert, and other high officials in the Foreign Office traveled to Geneva for a special session of the League of Nations. The purpose of the meeting was to confirm Germany's admission into the League, but difficulties quickly arose concerning the allocation of seats in the Council. The crux of the problem was the French and British attempt, promoted particularly by Briand, to secure a place for Poland in the Council. When the Germans rejected any further enlargement of the Council, the Swedish delegate offered to resign his seat in favor of the Poles.[40] But Luther, Stresemann, and Schubert—mindful of the domestic political opposition stemming particularly from the German National People's party—sharply opposed the substitution of a French ally for a country that they considered truly neutral. In a conversation with Miles W. Lampson, the head of the Central European Division of the British Foreign Office, Schubert suggested that the Czechs, and not the Swedes, should make room on the Council for Poland. Lampson immediately took up the idea and broached an alternative possibility whereby both Czechoslovakia and Sweden would

resign in favor of Poland and a neutral country.[41] Thereby the political
balance in the Council would remain intact. Stresemann took the idea to
Briand, who in turn persuaded Beneš to offer his resignation from the
Council.[42] That step polished Beneš's image as a reasonable and moderate
diplomat and earned him a great deal of praise. What was not publicly
known was that it had grown out of a German initiative. Just as the plan
appeared to be succeeding, Brazilian insistence on acquisition of a
permanent seat on the Council torpedoed the entire effort. The Germans
had to wait until September in order to gain admission. But the experience
had shown that the British attached little importance to Beneš's continued
presence on the Council despite the propaganda that extolled him as one
of the foremost experts on the League. German diplomats, in their
contacts with representatives of other great powers, continued to equate
Poland and Czechoslovakia as the mildly bothersome allies of France in
Central Europe.

Of greater significance was the dispute that arose over the conclusion of
the Treaty of Berlin between Germany and the Soviet Union in April. At
no time in their rapprochement with the West did Stresemann and his
assistants intend to forsake completely the special relationship with
Moscow that had been established in the early 1920s. Their immediate
diplomatic objectives necessitated cooperation with the Western powers,
but they simultaneously did all they could to reassure the Bolshevik
regime. Stresemann and Schubert were never so heartily sympathetic to an
eastern orientation in German foreign policy as Ago von Maltzan had been
and as General von Seeckt and Count Ulrich von Brockdorff-Rantzau still
were; but they clearly recognized the advantages of maintaining a middle
position between the Western powers and the Soviet Union.[43] After the
conclusion of the Locarno agreements they proceeded to negotiate a
neutrality pact with the Soviets, which was calculated to allay Russian
fears of a capitalist alliance against the Bolshevik regime. There were
murmurings in Berlin about Germany being a bridge between East and
West.[44] Given their own hopes, the Czechs naturally watched with jealous
eyes as the Germans cultivated their special relationship with the Soviets,
particularly as the activities of the German army in the Soviet Union
became public.

Beneš learned of the German intention to conclude the Treaty of Berlin
from the French government. He reacted with sharp criticism of the whole
project. Beneš addressed a memorandum to the Western powers in which
he envisioned a possible conflict between Germany's pledge of neutrality
in case of an unprovoked attack on the Russians and Germany's
obligations under Article 16 of the Covenant of the League of Nations.
Newspapers reported that Beneš also wanted to know if the Germans were
committed to convey to Moscow reports of confidential negotiations with

other powers. When Stresemann indignantly asked Krofta about this, Beneš sent word that the newspaper reports were pure concoctions.[45] But Beneš's own complaints to Koch about the German newspaper attacks on him and about the possible juristic contradictions between the Treaty of Berlin and the Covenant of the League were enough to anger the Germans.[46] The way in which they chose to handle the situation was indicative of their basic hostility toward Beneš and his foreign policy.

On April 22 Schubert sent information about Beneš's objections to the Treaty of Berlin to the German missions in Britain, France, Italy, and Belgium. He said that in the opinion of the German Foreign Office Beneš was mixing in negotiations that did not concern him, as Stresemann had emphasized "in all sharpness" to Krofta. Schubert advised the German diplomatic representatives not to undertake any similar steps in their capitals, for an initiative would make it appear that Berlin was unduly upset by Beneš's criticism. Instead they ought to wait for a suitable opportunity and then remark that the Germans found it unpleasant to suffer attacks that were based on confidential information supplied to the Western powers under the Rhineland agreement. Schubert concluded the instructions with the suggestion:

> In a careful way you can mention that we unfortunately have the impression that it might not be unpleasant to Mr. Beneš if our entrance into the League of Nations and the taking effect of the Locarno treaties should fall through and that he might be attempting to use our negotiations with the Soviet government to this end.[47]

In Paris Ambassador Hoesch quickly found an opportunity to express Berlin's displeasure to Beneš's friend and Briand's chief assistant, Philippe Berthelot, who responded that Beneš was "inclined by nature to legalistic polemics." Berthelot added what was obvious without being said, that the important opinions were to be found in Paris and London and that Beneš would follow French policy.[48] Beneš did just that, for by September he had Krofta apologize for the "misunderstanding" concerning the Treaty of Berlin. At the same time he offered to assist the Germans personally in Geneva as Germany entered the League of Nations.[49]

The way in which the Germans handled Czech objections to the Treaty of Berlin demonstrated their determination never to treat Czechoslovakia as anything more than a small and relatively insignificant power. Part of that strategy was Schubert's advice to the missions abroad not to act as though Berlin were upset about Beneš's criticism of the Treaty of Berlin. That faintly disdainful policy was combined with a willingness to discredit Beneš's diplomacy whenever possible. Hence the suggestions that Beneš was attempting to sabotage the Locarno agreements and German membership in the League. Whatever distrust for the Czechs that Berlin could awaken in the West, whatever rift in the alliance that the Germans might create, might be helpful in forcing Prague toward a more German-oriented policy. If Beneš would not introduce a reorientation of Czechoslovak foreign policy, perhaps a new foreign minister would. Many Germans regarded a realignment of Czechoslovak policy as simply a matter of time in view of the economic and geographic facts of life in Central Europe. They failed to understand the deep-seated determination among Czechs of all political persuasions to remain absolutely independent of all things German.

DANZIG OR VIENNA?

Beneš returned to Prague in January 1927 after a forced absence of several months during the Czechoslovak cabinet crisis. The vacation in the south of France had been good for him, for he had been showing signs of exhaustion from his years of intense activity. During Beneš's absence Czechoslovak foreign policy had been allowed to drift, and there were no initiatives forthcoming from Prague. When it became clear that Masaryk had effectively secured Beneš's position in the government, however, Beneš's return meant a new impetus in Czechoslovak foreign policy. For at least a year thereafter Beneš made his most sustained effort to overcome the political and economic barriers that had fragmented the former Habsburg lands.

In London the main criticism of the Czechs had long been that they threw up protective tariffs and pursued a narrow and rigid political policy, effectively prohibiting serious attempts at regional cooperation. There was a willingness to accept Beneš as the most influential diplomat and Czechoslovakia as the most progressive country among the successor states and therefore to blame Czechoslovak policy for failing to take the lead in overcoming an unsatisfactory state of affairs in Central Europe. It cannot be demonstrated that there was an avowedly revisionist sentiment in the Foreign Office, but the campaign that Lord Rothermere launched in the London *Daily Mail* during the summer of 1927 for a revision of the Treaty of Trianon reflected a growing disillusionment with the peace treaties among some segments of the British public. At least, so it appeared to the Czechs, who took Rothermere's pro-Hungarian campaign seriously and bitterly combatted it both in government publications and the popular press.[50] Even more effective in motivating Beneš to press for regional cooperation in Danubia was the pressure that came from Paris. By 1927 the French were clearly on the defensive in their diplomatic maneuverings with the Germans. Stresemann's foreign policy since 1924 had been one of unfolding new and successful initiatives. In 1926 alone, in addition to negotiating Germany's entrance into the League of Nations, the Treaty of

Berlin, and the withdrawal of the Interallied Military Control Commission, the Germans had made determined efforts to reacquire Eupen-Malmédy, to regain full sovereignty over the Saar, and to achieve a withdrawal of large numbers of occupation troops from the Rhineland.[51] Although Berlin was concentrating for the moment on problems along the western frontier, it seemed possible that the Germans could at any time shift their attention toward the south and the east.

After the initial attempts between 1918 and 1921 to unite Austria and Germany, popular agitation for an Anschluss subsided in both countries. But if the Reich's own economic difficulties in the early 1920s were such that the dream had to lie dormant, the German recovery in the last half of the decade encouraged new popular demonstrations for the union of the two countries. Newspapers in both countries began to revive the idea, rallies furthered the cause, and scholarly or pseudo-scholarly works involved themselves with planning details for effecting the Anschluss. Leaders in both countries knew that the diplomatic situation was not ready for such a revision of the peace treaties, and they had no intention of attempting a political union. But the governments did take practical steps, expressed in the term *Angleichungspolitik,* that sought to establish a close similarity in the domestic affairs of the two countries. Educational ties reflected their common culture. Closer trade and economic relations developed. Most important, there were successful attempts throughout the 1920s to equalize the legal codes of the two lands. The rationale for this policy was that similarity in domestic conditions in Germany and Austria would help prepare the way for an eventual political union.[52]

The spectre of an Anschluss seemed particularly foreboding in Prague during 1927. In the view of Masaryk and Beneš, the danger threatened all the non-Germanic areas of Central and Southeastern Europe. The German diplomatic victories of 1925-26 caused them grave concern. They evidently feared that the Germans might use the League of Nations as a forum for reviving the Anschluss issue in international diplomacy. In February 1927 both Masaryk and Beneš made special efforts to express their concern to the French minister in Prague. Using unusually harsh language, Beneš emphasized: "If the question of the *Anschluss* is ever brought before the League of Nations, I will declare that the annexation of Austria by Germany would render war inevitable in a short time and that, consequently, for the League of Nations to authorize this annexation would be equivalent to provoking and approving war."[53] Although the Czechs received reassurances from the French, in early May Beneš repeated the same arguments in his first political conversation with the new British minister in Prague, Sir Ronald Macleay. Macleay reported,

He [Beneš] devoted much of this time to explaining the objections to the union of Austria and Germany. I asked him if he would regard the realisation of the "Anschluss" as a *casus belli*; he replied, "Not immediately, but in six months' time." He explained that though he himself was well aware of the dangers to European peace inherent in the "Anschluss," public opinion in Europe generally was not aware of them, and he allowed it some six months to awaken to them. He said that the actual "Anschluss" of Austria to Germany would inevitably imply the moral "Anschluss" of Hungary also. This would mean that Czechoslovakia was to all intents and purposes encircled by Germany. Germany would thereby be in immediate contact with Poland, Italy, Jugoslavia and Roumania. Italy may once have been in favour of the "Anschluss," but was no longer so. All the countries named, when once they felt the German pressure upon them that would inevitably follow, would feel their life menaced, and there would again be a general conflagration.[54]

Beneš went on to urge that the British government make a declaration against an Anschluss, but Foreign Office personnel, including Austen Chamberlain, opposed any public statements about the matter.[55]

Given their fears of an Anschluss and their nagging doubts about the attitudes of the Western powers, Masaryk and Beneš tried to apply two alternative lines of policy simultaneously. The first was the more constructive. In early February Beneš had already given the British chargé d'affaires his prescription against the danger, which was "to evolve in Central Europe an economic system which should make the Little States so economically interdependent that they could not do without each other."[56] The first task was to tie Austria so closely to the other successor states, particularly Czechoslovakia, that a German annexation of Austria would become impossible. Beneš hesitated to explain the precise nature of his proposed Central European economic system; and, when British and Austrian diplomats tried to pin him down, he responded only in generalities. An observer in the British Foreign Office guessed that Beneš "probably does not know what he is driving at himself."[57] Even Krofta admitted that Beneš was not certain about the specifics of his proposals.[58] To an inquiry of the Austrian minister, Beneš responded that names such as "federation, Danubian confederation, customs union, etc." were simply "sound and fury"—the important thing was that "that which will come and must come is coming and is coming soon." But *what* was coming? Beneš broached the idea that there might be a "Central European League of Nations" in which the representatives of the sovereign states could discuss their common political and economic problems, without, however, submitting to any sort of majority vote.[59] Such a periodic diplomatic congress might have satisfied Beneš's personal predilections, but it could hardly have ensured a "Central Europe for the Central Europeans," as Beneš was wont to proclaim. It certainly could not have accomplished Beneš's purpose of preventing the meddling by the great powers—meaning, for him, Germany and Italy—in Central European affairs.

By May and June 1927 Beneš was prepared to be somewhat more specific about his ideas. At the conference of the Little Entente in May Beneš tried to win agreement for closer economic ties between the Little Entente and Austria and Hungary. Although there was no resistance concerning Austria, the Rumanians apparently vetoed any rapprochement with Hungary.[60] When reporting the events of the conference, Beneš made particular efforts to be candid with his French allies. Aware of French concern about Sudeten German influence in the new government, Beneš periodically attempted to emphasize the solidarity of Prague with Paris. In what the French minister regarded as a "very interesting and satisfying formula," Beneš assured Charles-Roux that Czechoslovak-German relations were a function of the relations between France and Germany. They would be good or bad together.[61] Beneš confided that he wanted to revive his plans for preferential tariffs among the successor states. It was the French understanding that Beneš's "essential goal for this grouping is to include Austria and to avoid an economic or political *Anschluss,* which would be an extremely grave menace."[62]

Beneš's new interest in working for preferential tariffs among the successor states received active encouragement from Paris.[63] He nevertheless confronted difficulties both in domestic politics and in international affairs that soon proved to be insurmountable. Within Czechoslovakia a governing coalition that was founded on protective tariffs resisted any effort to lower Czechoslovak duties on foreign goods. The Agrarians protected agricultural products, and the National Democrats did the same for manufactured items.[64] In international affairs the Italians automatically opposed any step toward a consolidation of French influence in the Danubian region, and a preferential tariff system under Czechoslovak guidance could have been precisely that. Austrian policy under Chancellor Seipel aimed at keeping all options open and remained noncommittal.[65] Had Beneš's plans shown any real chance of realization, the Germans would have stepped in with objections of their own. And Hungarian policy was the most immediate stumbling bloc to cooperation among the successor states.

Even the most tenuous regional cooperation was impossible until the relations between Hungary and its neighbors improved. In the late 1920s one could hear occasional hints in Prague about the possibility of border rectifications along the Slovak-Hungarian frontier. Masaryk's remarks favoring boundary changes were more than once disavowed by the Czechoslovak government. Nevertheless, Beneš spoke of "depoliticizing" the Little Entente by removing its anti-Hungarian bent.[66] The trouble was that the Little Entente had never developed beyond its original purpose of combatting Hungarian revisionism, and the common fear of Hungary remained the only real cement in the alliance. In 1927 there was a major controversy between Budapest and Bucharest concerning the Rumanian government's seizure of Hungarian property in Transylvania. The Hungarian government claimed that the Treaty of Trianon forbade any confiscation of property of its nationals. A number of large landholders in Transylvania had opted for Hungarian citizenship after 1919, and the Hungarian government argued that their property was not subject to Rumanian land reform measures. The land reform program in Slovakia threatened to create a similar dispute between Hungary and Czechoslovakia, and Beneš therefore strongly supported the Rumanian side in the optants question.[67] That was only an episode reflecting a more basic problem. The truth was that the obstacles to cooperation between Hungary and its neighbors were insurmountable for both sides. No state in the Little Entente was willing to make the kind of territorial concessions that the Hungarian government expected, nor was there any readiness to accept a Habsburg restoration in Budapest. On the Hungarian side, the diplomatic weakness of Count Bethlen's government was exceeded only by its obstinancy. Hungarian diplomats reserved their choicest invective for Beneš, for whom they could never develop the slightest trust. The Hungarians persistently sought to establish a working relationship with Italy and Germany, countries that supposedly desired to undermine French influence in the Danubian region, in order eventually to tear up the Treaty of Trianon.[68] Even if Beneš had fashioned a clear and workable scheme for political and economic cooperation among the successor states, it likely would have foundered on the intransigence of the Hungarian government.

Recognizing the growing potential for German economic penetration in the Danubian region but both unwilling and unable to fashion a supranational body capable of protecting itself, Beneš formulated an alternative line of policy. He sought to divert German attention elsewhere. In so doing he steered Czechoslovak foreign policy headlong into one of the more unsavory episodes in the diplomacy of the first Czechoslovak republic. Quite simply the goal was to persuade the Germans to concentrate on the Polish problem and to forget about Austria and the Danubian region. Beneš had Masaryk's full support and participation.

During the meeting of the Council of the League in March 1927, Masaryk traveled to Geneva, where he had long discussions with Briand and Stresemann. To Briand Masaryk repeated his fears of an Anschluss and argued that a bloc composed of Poland, Czechoslovakia, Austria, and Yugoslavia would represent a barrier against German political and economic expansion. Just how such a bloc could be formed he did not specify, but he did claim to have information that Stresemann would soon concentrate his attention on the Polish Corridor issue. Masaryk believed that Stresemann would go from one demand to another, and (in French paraphrase) he likened Stresemann "to the German student who declaims about all kinds of questions with a glass of beer in his hand." Through a cooperative stance France and Czechoslovakia would have a greater likelihood of controlling German policy than through a hostile attitude, but Masaryk urged caution about any concessions to German demands.[69]

In his talk with Stresemann Masaryk displayed not only more sympathy for the Germans but also greater hostility toward the Poles. In discussing Central European affairs Masaryk emphasized and tied together two problems—Danzig and the Corridor, and Austria and the Anschluss. About the Polish problem Masaryk remarked that "anyone who looks at the map of Europe must realize that things cannot remain as they are" and that "Poland also knows quite well that it must give way." Having implied that he would support a territorial revision of the German-Polish boundary, he cautioned that Poland must be assured access to the sea by means of railway rights and free ports. Stresemann readily agreed but added that he did not consider the situation ripe for a general settlement. Masaryk continued with sharp criticism of Piłsudski's coup d'état of 1926, which he thought could be explained only in view of the "Polish mentality." Then, according to Stresemann's paraphrase, he concluded:

> He wanted to inform me quite openly that Poland recently had turned to Czechoslovakia in order to bring about a closer relationship between the two states. He did not intend to take up the suggestion, for he did not want to pull Poland's chestnuts out of the fire whenever a conflict with Germany might develop. He trusted however that this conflict could be avoided and that the Danzig question would soon be solved.

Having disposed of Poland, Masaryk turned then to Austria.

About Austria Masaryk emphasized that it was necessary to reconstruct the economic ties that had held the old Habsburg realm together while at the same time guarding the special cultural relationship between Germany and Austria. When Stresemann tried to pin him down on how this was to be done, Masaryk stayed in generalities. He said only that the Austrian problem could easily be solved and that it was not so urgent as the Danzig question. Then at the end of the discussion, Masaryk reverted from his political to his scholarly interests and made observations about the cultural development of Greece and its influence on German literature and thought.[70]

The only conclusion that can be drawn from this conversation—and from subsequent talks on the same theme—is that the Czechs, with their president leading the way, were actively seeking to direct German revisionism against Poland in order to escape the brunt of it themselves. Either they did not care who controlled the disputed territories, or they hoped to use the issue in order to inflict a defeat on a German revisionist policy that had been all too successful in the previous two years. A week after the meeting between Masaryk and Stresemann, Masaryk's son gave word to the Germans that his father was "very gratified" about the conversation. Jan Masaryk continued the attack on Poland with charges that the Poles had conducted a "false policy of prestige" based on "historical and sentimental motives." He added that the Polish Corridor must sometime become a pressing question between Germany and Poland.[71] In Prague Krofta led the Austrian minister to believe that Stresemann himself had initiated the discussion about Poland and had given Masaryk to understand that the Germans would continually bring up the Corridor question until it was settled to their satisfaction. Although the Austrian minister thought that he sensed an uneasiness in Prague about such a revision of the peace treaties, he noted that the Czechs had little trust for Piłsudski. One could always expect surprises from the man, and it was impossible to know his real goals. Krofta believed that Piłsudski "could develop into another Mussolini."[72] At the end of April, a newspaper that was published by Beneš's arch-enemy, Jan Stříbrný, reported that Beneš had characterized Poland as the "Balkan of the North" in a confidential briefing for Prague journalists. In the furor that ensued, Beneš promptly denied that and many other accusations in the article.[73] But foreign diplomats such as the German and the Austrian ministers in Prague knew from their own conversations that the allegations, even if invented, reflected the actual thinking of the molders of Czechoslovak foreign policy.

The idea of persuading or forcing the Germans to choose between the Anschluss and the Corridor issues was alive not only in Prague. In February 1927 the French ambassador in Warsaw, Jules Laroche, reported that the idea of acquiescing to an Anschluss in return for German acceptance of Polish sovereignty over the Corridor and Upper Silesia was widespread in the Polish capital. He even noted that Foreign Minister August Zaleski had broached the idea to him.[74] Despite the Polish-German tariff war, Piłsudski evidently hoped to improve relations with Germany and undertook diplomatic initiatives to that end.[75] In Poland there was obviously little concern about the potential effect on Czechoslovakia of an Anschluss. Cropping up in the French diplomatic reports in the late 1920s were repeated statements about the special Polish antipathy—particularly Piłsudski's—for the Czechs. The reasons that were always given were the Teschen/Javorina dispute and the Czechoslovak refusal in 1920 to let military supplies pass to Poland. The Czechoslovak minister complained bitterly to Laroche about his experiences in Warsaw and spoke of Piłsudski's desire to create a common frontier between Poland and Hungary.[76] Polish cooperation with the Slovak autonomists from the time that Hlinka traveled to Paris in 1919 on a Polish passport is well documented, and so is the suspicion that pervaded Czechoslovak-Polish relations particularly after Piłsudski's coup d'état.[77] It should therefore come as little surprise that leaders in each capital contemplated turning German revisionism against the other.

While seeking to direct Berlin's interest toward the Polish problem, the Czechs made no efforts to hide their fear of an Anschluss from the Germans. When State Secretary Schubert stopped off in Prague in May 1927 on his way to visit Chancellor Ignaz Seipel in Vienna, Beneš and Krofta frankly admitted that they were worried about a possible revival of the Anschluss movement. Schubert retorted that there was no basis for that concern. As he had often said, the question was one that could not be forced. Either Germany and Austria would eventually unite, or they would not; but in any case the question could only develop naturally with time.[78] Schubert's remarks offered some reassurance to the Czechs that there was no immediate urgency about Austro-German plans, yet his comments were sufficiently transparent to reveal the Germans' confidence that time was on their side. Krofta very cautiously mentioned the possibility of a Danubian economic confederation, the details of which he did not spell out. As long as Czech plans seemed vague and tentative, the Germans could assume a rather bland attitude to the whole idea. Schubert contented himself with remarking that the various countries seemed to him too heterogeneous to make the project feasible.[79] In reality the Germans were firmly opposed to any project that would include Austria in a bloc of states of which Germany was not a member. They were not promoting a political union of Austria and Germany, but they were glad to see Southeastern Europe remain divided among small and competing states.

Apparently as part of his effort to turn the Germans toward the north, Beneš toyed with the idea of a Czechoslovak-German pact. In Switzerland in June, Beneš mentioned in the midst of a long conversation with the German minister there that he would like to see the arbitration treaty between Germany and Czechoslovakia expanded into a pact of friendship and nonaggression.[80] He brought up the suggestion in connection with other diplomatic problems, and it was difficult for the Germans to know just how much importance Beneš attached to the idea. The reaction in Berlin was best expressed in the instructions to Koch from the German Foreign Office. Koch was told to wait until Beneš mentioned the idea of a friendship and nonaggression pact between Germany and Czechoslovakia and then to express as his purely personal opinion the belief that the time for such a treaty had not yet come. As a result of the Locarno agreements, Poland and Czechoslovakia were in exactly the same position vis-à-vis Germany. It was not unreasonable to assume that a special Czechoslovak-German pact might be misinterpreted and resented by the Poles and might therefore increase the tension in Eastern Europe. These remarks were of course to be embellished with assurances of Berlin's good will toward

Prague, but the final paragraph of the instructions to Koch made for a highly interesting conclusion.

> For your personal information I might also add that the conclusion of a friendship or nonaggression pact with Czechoslovakia would be in contradiction to the entire political line that we have previously followed in Southeastern Europe and that we intend to pursue further.[81]

Beneš probably waited for the Germans to respond to his feeler, for he did not follow up on his suggestion of a pact between the two countries. Koch consequently did not have to implement his instructions in Prague, but the incident is nevertheless important for an analysis of the policies of the two countries in 1927.

Critics often accused Beneš of "pactomania," and it sometimes did seem that he emphasized the number rather than the value of his treaties. His suggestion of a friendship and nonaggression pact with the Germans can be viewed as simply part of his diplomatic style of binding Czechoslovakia in an ever-increasing number of international agreements. Yet Beneš could always defend his pacts on some practical grounds, and this one would have been no exception. Coming in the summer of 1927 when the Czechs were trying to get the Germans to turn their revisionist efforts northward, such an agreement would have indeed made a sharp difference between Poland and Czechoslovakia, as the Germans realized. This distinction was what the Czechs were working for, but from the German side it was foolish policy. Current German interest was concentrated more on the evacuation of the Rhineland and the reparation questions than on treaty revision in the east. If the long-range goals were there, the immediate ones were not. Excessive pressure against Poland at that time would have disrupted the whole "Locarno spirit" in which the Germans were attempting to make their diplomatic gains. Nor, contrary to Czech fears, were the Germans preparing to revive the Anschluss issue. As will be seen, official opinion in Berlin was severely divided about the merits of ever including the Austrians within the Reich. Without immediate plans in the east, the Germans could see no reason for needlessly arousing Polish fears by a special compact with Czechoslovakia.

If eastern questions were secondary at the time, what was "the entire political line" in Southeastern Europe to which Koch's instructions alluded? Actually there was no well-developed policy. For the Germans, time was the big factor, and their plans consisted primarily in waiting until the international political climate and the economic recovery of Germany would make possible a gradual reassertion of German influence in Central and Eastern Europe. This process would certainly have been at least initially economic; indeed the Czechs already complained in 1927 that the

Germans were taking capital in loans from America and Britain and reinvesting it in Eastern Europe. But however gradual and sophisticated the spread of German influence toward the east was to be, the fact remains that Berlin opposed any additional pact with the Czechs. Why alienate the Hungarians by concluding such an accord? Why encourage the Austrians to flirt even more with the Czechs? Why not let the Czechs worry even if there were no immediate plans involving them? In the final analysis the chasm between a desire to uphold and enforce the peace settlements and a determination to revise them always separated the two nations.

But if Stresemann and his associates rejected a nonaggression pact with Czechoslovakia, the prospect of bringing that country into a larger grouping in which Germans would be dominant met with the full approval of governmental circles in Berlin. Specifically, the idea was to establish a special tariff relationship among Czechoslovakia, Austria, and Germany. One of the earliest and most influential supporters of the project was Julius Curtius, minister of economics and one of Stresemann's closest collaborators in the German People's party. Curtius later wrote in his memoirs that he had strongly advocated the idea at the International Economic Conference in Geneva in May 1927. He claimed that he had personally tried to persuade Beneš to agree.[82] Surprisingly enough, the proposal seemed to find some acceptance in Prague, although certainly not with Masaryk and Beneš. In October 1927 Krofta spoke favorably about such a grouping to the Austrian minister, although Krofta was careful to insist that measures would have to be taken to safeguard the political independence of Czechoslovakia.[83] The Sudeten German parties in the government took up the idea and supported it in opposition to Beneš's projects to exclude Germany from any Central European grouping. Franz Spina, the minister for public works in Prague and leader of the German Agrarians, confided to the Austrian minister that the strongest advocate of closer cooperation with Germany and Austria was Premier Švehla himself.[84] Seipel passed that news on to the Germans when Chancellor Wilhelm Marx and Stresemann visited Vienna in November 1927. Seipel noted that the idea had met with a favorable response among industrial interests in Austria, and he suggested that Berlin and Vienna find out how much actual support there was for it in Prague.[85] One factor that gave the report some credibility was that Švehla represented Czech agricultural interests, which could profit from a greater access to the German and Austrian markets. But, if Švehla or any of his colleagues ever toyed with the notion, they never championed it publicly. By early November Krofta also veered away from the idea of special German-Austrian-Czechoslovak economic ties.[86]

By the autumn and winter of 1927-28 the triangular relationship among Czechoslovakia, Austria, and Germany was becoming more prominent than ever before. Philippe Berthelot appeared in Prague in early October, and, according to the highly influential director of Prague's *Živnostenská banka*, attempted to promote a customs union among Czechoslovakia, Austria, and Yugoslavia.[87] In November, as just mentioned, Chancellor Wilhelm Marx and Stresemann traveled to Vienna for talks, and in February Seipel went to Prague. Little was accomplished in those meetings except to demonstrate once again the pivotal position of Austria in the power relationships in Central Europe. One of the more bizarre episodes in the early months of 1928 was a project to move the League of Nations to Vienna. A result of such a move could have been the internationalization of the city and the dismemberment of the rest of Austria among its neighboring states. Although the plan never became the subject of serious negotiations, Seipel later attributed it primarily to Berthelot and Beneš and explained that Italian objections had torpedoed the idea.[88]

If the Austrian problem were ever to be settled, the Hungarians had to be mollified as well. After Seipel's return from Prague in early February 1928, Austrian diplomats confided to the Germans that Beneš was currently concentrating on an effort to conclude a bilateral nonaggression pact with Hungary.[89] Although Beneš had no particular love for the Hungarians, an understanding with them represented the crucial step toward the goal of creating a harmonious Danubian realm capable of resisting German encroachment. When the Germans checked with the Hungarians about the news, they found out that Beneš had indeed urged an arbitration and nonaggression treaty between the two countries. The Hungarian minister in Berlin added that Beneš had even hinted of the possibility of a boundary revision once a better atmosphere was created between Prague and Budapest.[90] But the Hungarians continued to rebuff Beneš's attempts at a rapprochement, and they had Berlin's sympathy in doing so. Beneš finally attempted to work through the League of Nations. In the Committee on Arbitration and Security, which he chaired, Beneš secured the passage of a resolution offering the good offices of the League's Council in the negotiation of regional arbitration and non-aggression pacts. The German delegates diluted the strength of the resolution by insisting that the assistance of the League had to be accepted voluntarily by all countries concerned. The Hungarians would never voluntarily acquiesce, and the Germans protected them from becoming the objects of concerted international pressure.[91] Animosity between Prague and Budapest continued unabated.

With little hope of creating a united front against Germany in Southeastern Europe, Beneš tried once again in March 1928 to turn the Germans against the Poles. In Geneva he had two long conversations about the Austrian problem with a confidant of Schubert, Max Beer. To the charge that he was attempting to create a Danubian confederation in order to prevent Austria's union with Germany, Beneš responded, according to Schubert's paraphrase, like this:

> The intention further imputed to him to use a regional system so as to bring Austria into a dependent position and prevent an Anschluss is false.
>
> It is correct that he is an opponent of an Anschluss. First because the Czechoslovak economy could not survive if Germany and Austria were amalgamated in one great economic unit. Second because Europe could not permit such a combination because a bloc of seventy million Germans would constitute a danger for Europe.
>
> Besides, in his opinion Germany cannot have any interest in an Anschluss. In his opinion the interest of Germany consists in the existence of Austria as a Germanic buffer state.
>
> Mr. Beneš then declared quite openly that in his view the question of Anschluss would have to be solved very quickly and to be sure in a negative sense.
>
> To this Mr. Beer responded that there were nevertheless very important moral imponderables that spoke for the Anschluss. In his view it would therefore be a great mistake to proclaim the final prohibition of an Anschluss.
>
> Mr. Beneš admitted this. He emphasized that this question would have to be dealt with in agreement with Germany; the suspension of the Anschluss would have to be accomplished with Germany. There did exist certain possibilities, and Germany did have undoubtedly a certain claim to the Anschluss. If Germany should therefore give up the Anschluss it would have to be given something else.
>
> Mr. Beer responded, Mr. Beneš wanted to come to the formula: Danzig or Vienna.
>
> Mr. Beneš replied, that is exactly what he wanted to say. If Germany gave up the Anschluss, it would have to receive other territorial compensations.[92]

So there was the formula: Danzig or Vienna. The idea first was broached by Masaryk in March 1927, unfolded in further discussions in succeeding months, and frankly admitted in precisely those words by Beneš in March 1928.

Along with proposals for a Danubian preferential tariff system, "Danzig or Vienna" was part of the dual response of Czechoslovak diplomacy to the threat of an Anschluss. Masaryk and Beneš's fears of imminent attempts at an Anschluss reached a peak in the spring and summer of 1927, and it was at that time they most actively attempted to erect barriers against the expected German diplomatic initiatives. Their concern about an Anschluss is documentable in the diplomatic files of Germany, Britain, France, Austria, and the United States alike. Their advocacy of Danubian preferential tariffs was a central issue in their discussions with

French, British, and Austrian diplomats. Realizing Berlin's opposition to any Central European tariff system excluding Germany, they did not emphasize the idea in their discussions with the Germans. On the other hand, their attempts to deflect German revisionism from Austria toward Poland were naturally confined to diplomatic contacts with Berlin. But the strategy could not remain absolutely secret. The Germans learned about the preferential tariff ideas, and French diplomats made pointed inquiries of Beneš about Czechoslovakia's relations with Poland. Masaryk's and Beneš's fears of a German initiative for an Anschluss subsided in the course of 1927, and by the spring and summer of 1928 they no longer actively promoted either a preferential tariff system or the "Danzig or Vienna" scheme. But their policy of 1927 and early 1928 demonstrates their deep concern about Germany's revival and accords with what is already known about Czechoslovakia's relationship with Austria and Poland. And that policy is documentable in the archives of various Western countries.

That conversation between Beer and Beneš in March 1928 contained other interesting revelations as well. Beneš emphasized that he was not at all interested in an "Eastern Locarno." (That meant a territorial guarantee between Hungary and its neighbors on the order of the Rhineland Pact. There can be no doubt that Beneš would have welcomed such an agreement, but he realized that it was an impossible hope.) Rather, Beneš insisted that he was merely trying to bring Hungary into a general understanding with the other successor states, and he revealed his acute disappointment with Hungarian intransigence. Protesting that he was not an intriguer, he called the Hungarians "idiots," "swine," and "people inimical to culture." He said that, as long as there was no democratic government in Hungary, the country would have to be treated roughly but that if a reasonable government came to power he would be willing to discuss certain boundary revisions. What those revisions might be, he did not specify. He claimed that although he wanted to see cooperation among the successor states he was not interested in any type of Danubian confederation. Finally he remarked that he had told Seipel in Prague: "Nothing can be allowed to happen between you and us about which Germany does not know." A marginal notation next to that sentence in Schubert's memorandum read: "Unfortunately Mr. Seipel does not substantiate that."[93]

Schubert attached enough importance to the conversation between Beneš and Beer to relay Beneš's remarks to the Austrian minister in Berlin.[94] From the records of the conversation between German and Austrian diplomats, as well as within German councils themselves, it is clear that neither side was pushing diplomatically for an Anschluss in the late 1920s. In Vienna, Chancellor Seipel and his Christian Social party were known to have ambivalent feelings about the idea. Seipel even tried to convince the French of his outright opposition to an Anschluss.[95] Although the Christian Socials depended on the pan-German party for support against the Social Democrats, it was the Social Democrats themselves who had been the most fervent advocates of amalgamating Austria with the Weimar republic. The Social Democrats were powerful in the city of Vienna, but they never determined Austrian foreign policy in the late 1920s. In Berlin conservative and Protestant Prussians could only look askance at the augmentation of Social Democratic and Catholic power that an Anschluss would bring. Both Hindenburg and Stresemann opposed the absorption of Austria. It is ironic that in both Berlin and Vienna during the 1920s left-of-center coalitions were potentially more sympathetic to an Anschluss than conservative governments. Had Masaryk and Beneš been sure of those sentiments, they might have refrained from at least the anti-Polish aspect of their diplomacy. But there was peril for the Czechs in the Mitteleuropa ideas that refused to die out even while German diplomacy concentrated on problems in the west.

An excellent example of Mitteleuropa thinking is to be found in a personal letter from the German minister in Bucharest, Gerhard von Mutius, to Schubert. The letter, which was written in mid-February 1928, explored the opportunities for German penetration in Southeastern Europe and declared that "for the succession states of the former Austro-Hungarian Monarchy the impulse toward the German language, economy, and culture bears the character of a geographical-historical necessity."[96] In short, the path to the outside world lay across Germany. Such ideas were obviously exerting a growing influence on Schubert's thinking when he attempted to analyze the nuances of Beneš's foreign policy for the benefit of Stresemann in mid-March. Their discussion, according to Schubert's memorandum, ended like this:

> I then told the Herr Reichsminister that an idea has occurred to me that must not yet be expressed at all and that certainly requires a very exact foundation. I am of the opinion that it might be decided to work for a close cooperation of Germany, Czechoslovakia, and Austria. Such a cooperation could occur first in the economic area. Efforts will certainly continue in this direction. Second, however, one could perhaps conceive of concluding some kind of political pact among the three states. This possibility would naturally have to be examined very closely. Probably in this case effort would have to be taken that such a pact would not contain provisions that would obstruct the Anschluss. This I regard as necessary although in the bottom of my heart I have the greatest misgivings about an Anschluss.

> The Herr Reichsminister responded that he completely shares these misgivings. The Herr Reichsminister let it further be seen that he considers my idea of a certain alliance of the three named states to be interesting.[97]

The project could have been the first step toward an extension of German influence in Central Europe. There was peril for the Czechs in the idea of special political and economic cooperation among Germany, Austria, and Czechoslovakia, an idea promoted by Curtius in May 1927, toyed with briefly by Švehla's circle in the summer and autumn, blessed by Seipel in November—and "occurring" to Schubert in March 1928. The competing Czech and German ideas about the future organization of Central and Southeastern Europe reached a temporary climax when Beneš unexpectedly arrived in Berlin in May.

BENEŠ IN BERLIN

Although Beneš was a traveler without equal among the diplomats of interwar Europe, the first and only time that he came to Berlin during the existence of the Weimar republic was in May 1928. The visit was unofficial; Beneš stopped by as a tourist on a return trip from London and spent the first two or three days sight-seeing in Berlin and its environs. By chance he witnessed the Reichstag elections of May 20, 1928, in which the socialists scored gains sufficient to put a Social Democratic chancellor into office. The victory of the moderate parties was an impressive demonstration of the stability of the Weimar republic. Then, for three days after the elections, Beneš conducted wide-ranging talks with Schubert, who was substituting for a Stresemann confined to bed. Although there were no special agreements in those meetings, the conversations clarified the relationship between the two countries and gave each side a better understanding of the policies of the other. On the surface, Beneš's presence in Berlin seemed to be a graphic demonstration of the "friendly" relationship between the two countries in the post-Locarno years. But for both sides the fundamental conflicts that became even more apparent in those conversations demonstrated the limited extent of that friendliness.

Characteristically the Germans were well prepared for the talks. The staff of the Foreign Office composed a number of background memoranda for Schubert's use; on the eve of the conversations Koch arrived secretly from Czechoslovakia for consultations; even President Hindenburg summoned Schubert to him on the day that the discussions began. Hindenburg warned Schubert that one could not trust Beneš, Briand, or the League of Nations, and remarked that there ought to be some plain speaking in diplomacy; a man ought to say what he really thought. For example, one could ask the English why they had not concluded a separate peace with Germany already in 1916 or so, or one could tell the Americans just what a "swindle" the *Lusitania* affair had been, as had their entrance into the war. Warning the old man—gently to be sure—of the dangers of venting one's feelings in diplomatic contacts, Schubert took up the criticism of Beneš, and the conversation developed in a highly significant manner.

Responding to the remark of the Herr Reichspresident about Mr. Beneš, I said to him that Mr. Beneš is pursuing certain very dangerous ideas that would result in an economic and even a political union of Central Europe. This we have to prevent.

Further, however, Mr. Beneš has a very great fear of the Anschluss. Here the Herr Reichspresident interrupted me and said to me that I probably already knew quite well his opinion about the Anschluss, which is very negative: he hoped that I shared this opinion. The Herr Reichspresident then set forth in detail his misgivings about the Anschluss. I responded that I was completely of his opinion. In my view it would be best if Austria could be attached to us to a certain extent without being included in our political union. The Herr Reichspresident agreed with me in this view.

Schubert observed to Hindenburg that the previous year had been a lost one for German diplomacy and that he had "certain vague ideas" about how to change the situation.[98] Of course his ideas were the plans for closer economic and political cooperation among Germany, Austria, and Czechoslovakia.

The talks between Beneš and Schubert opened with a general discussion of international affairs. The topic that was making headlines in May 1928 was the Franco-American plan to renounce war as an instrument of national policy. Negotiations on the project culminated in August with the signing in Paris of the Kellogg-Briand Pact. Probably no single agreement affords a better glimpse of the idealism of the "New Diplomacy," of which Beneš was ostensibly one of the most articulate advocates. Beneš informed Schubert of London's favorable attitude to the project.[99] In their second meeting they also touched upon the disarmament negotiations that were proceeding in Geneva under the aegis of the Preparatory Commission for a Disarmament Conference. Established in 1925 by the League, that commission continued its work intermittently until the end of 1930. As one of the authors of the Geneva Protocol of 1924, Beneš was active in the disarmament negotiations, but he always sympathized with the French position that security would have to precede disarmament. The question was not acute in 1928, however, and Beneš and Schubert did little more than exchange general opinions.[100]

After the broad discussions the two men got down to questions that directly concerned the relations between their countries. Schubert remarked that he wondered just what goals Beneš had in mind in promoting regional treaties in the Danubian area. After some hedging Beneš responded that his primary interest was Hungary, with which he would like to conclude a nonaggression pact and a trade agreement. However, Hungarian intransigence was insuperable. Schubert mused that Beneš might be interested in Austria as well and invited him to express his opinions about the Anschluss. Momentarily taken aback, Beneš hesitated and then responded that a sudden attempt to incorporate Austria into Germany might well unleash a war or at least create a united front of states against Germany. The Czechoslovak economy would be put in a "completely impossible situation" by their union because the majority of Czechoslovak exports went to those two countries. At all costs, Beneš warned, the Czechs had to prevent an Anschluss.

Schubert wanted to set Beneš's mind at ease about Berlin's policy toward Austria. It was primarily Beneš's fear of an Anschluss that caused him to promote political and economic ties among the successor states. Berlin opposed any impulse toward regional groupings in the Danubian area, and the best way to induce Beneš to abandon his efforts seemed to be to pacify him about the Austrian question. Schubert repeated his assurances of a year earlier in Prague that the Anschluss issue could not be forced, that it had to develop naturally with time. But he went beyond that. He said also that the technical problems of a union were not so simple as many "naive people" thought, and he emphasized that the German government had not changed and would not change its policy toward Austria. He even admitted that there was validity to Beneš's argument that it was advantageous for the Reich to have a Germanic buffer state on its border. Lest he go too far, however, he cautioned that no German government could continue in office if it took a position against Austria's eventual inclusion within the Reich. Beneš responded that he quite understood.[101] In that conversation Schubert left little doubt that Berlin had no immediate intention of trying to annex Austria, whatever public opinion might favor.

The effect of those assurances was reduced on the following day when the discussion turned from political to economic questions in Central Europe. At that point Schubert chose to introduce his new pet project, the idea of special economic cooperation among Germany, Austria, and Czechoslovakia.[102] He emphasized that it was a natural economic grouping and that it could be made open for adherence by other states whenever they might care to join. Beneš retorted that his own ideas, although they had not yet taken the form of concrete plans, went in another direction. He was not promoting a customs union, but he would like to see a system of preferential tariffs among the states of the Little Entente, Austria, Hungary, Bulgaria, and Greece.[103] (They represented all the small states of Southeastern Europe, and Beneš expressly excluded Poland from the grouping.)[104] Beneš observed that Schubert's suggestion would meet strong political opposition in Britain, France, and Italy, for it would reawaken fears of Great-German expansionism. Schubert answered that those political fears could be overcome by the logic of such an economic grouping, that Stresemann could make a great impression by presenting the idea in a speech in Geneva. Beneš contradicted this contention, remarking that his own plans had a much better chance for realization since they would encounter less political opposition. Schubert in turn disagreed and warned that, whatever other countries might do, Germany would find Beneš's project unbearable and could agree to such a grouping only if the Reich were included as well. Here Beneš responded that a great power in a bloc of small states would inevitably take over the leadership and dominate the whole association. Beneš continued that Germany and France ought to come to an "understanding of the highest order," and that, if they agreed, problems in Central Europe, even the Anschluss question, would no longer have their current importance.[105]

It is instructive that the issue of the Sudeten Germans came up only at the very end of the last discussion between Beneš and Schubert. The matter was raised late in the evening after a dinner and a discussion of several minor questions involving the two countries. Schubert introduced it by remarking that with regard to the relations between the two countries he hoped that the situation of the Sudeten Germans would continue to improve. Beneš answered that there had always been an understanding in their diplomatic contacts that this internal problem of Czechoslovakia could not be discussed, and that he might have to state upon his return to Prague that they had not talked about the German minority.[106] He said that he personally considered the issue to be settled, for the Germans were in the government and would stay there.[107] Nothing more was mentioned about the Sudeten Germans.

On the day that Beneš left Berlin, foreign envoys began appearing at the German Foreign Office to find out just what had been said by Beneš and Schubert. Schubert informed them all—in the strictest confidence—about his confidential discussions with Beneš. By his own admission, Schubert gave the fullest and most candid report to the Austrian minister, Felix Frank.[108] Schubert mentioned the suggestion of economic cooperation among Germany, Austria, and Czechoslovakia, to which the Austrian responded that it was the only correct possibility for his country. Then Schubert recounted Beneš's idea of a preferential tariff system among the Southeast European states, and Frank agreed that the project did not have much chance of realization. Frank observed that there were no conflicts between Austria and Czechoslovakia, and that any idea of a border rectification was "completely insane" although one could not tell the Sudeten Germans that. To this remark Schubert answered and Frank agreed that plans for boundary changes were still being pursued only by a small and vanishing minority of the Sudeten Germans.[109] It was plain that neither regretted the fact.

Schubert also informed the Hungarian minister about the discussions with Beneš. Summoning Baron Kálmán Kánya to the Foreign Office, Schubert reviewed the main points of those conversations, emphasizing

Beneš's goal of a regional understanding among the successor states. Kánya let it be seen that Hungary was not to be had for any such project and added that Beneš was a "horrible individual" who everywhere stirred up trouble against Hungary. Schubert answered that Beneš had been courteous in his remarks about the Hungarians, probably because he knew that he was talking to the wrong man to get a sympathetic reception to anti-Hungarian statements.[110] The conversation between Schubert and Kánya helped to maintain Berlin's middle course between the Czechs and the Hungarians. Berlin was only too happy to help the Hungarians resist any political or economic understanding among the successor states. At the same time the Germans held the Hungarians at arm's length and refused to be drawn into an aggressively revisionist policy in Central Europe.

Consistent with their long-standing policy, the Germans acted as though they attached little significance to Czechoslovak diplomacy in general or to Beneš's visit in particular. Before Beneš's arrival in Berlin, a German diplomat remarked that the government would honor Beneš with the respect that he deserved, treating him like the foreign minister of any other small state, such as Lithuania.[111] For Beneš, however, his visit became a "major political event," and he emphasized that he was the first foreign minister from the camp of the former enemy powers to visit Berlin.[112] At the same time, Beneš sought to reassure the French by informing them that he had told Schubert that Czechoslovak-German relations were a function of Franco-German relations.[113] Beneš likewise gave the Austrian minister in his capital a full and accurate report of the conversations with Schubert. Reflecting on his visit in Britain, which had preceded the stop in Berlin, he claimed that no one in London took seriously Rothermere's noisy campaign in the *Daily Mail* to revise the Treaty of Trianon. Only in Hungary did Rothermere have a following, and even there the more perceptive Hungarians had realized how unadvised Rothermere's propaganda was. Beneš called Rothermere a "fool and a simpleton," who had compromised himself through various affairs with women. Beneš noted that he dared not even repeat the expressions that King George had used about Rothermere.[114]

The essence of the confidential discussions between Beneš and Schubert soon leaked to the press. Within a matter of days both the *Daily Telegraph* and the *Neue Freie Presse* published reports about Germany's desire to form a Central European customs union with some of the successor states.[115] When Köpke questioned Chvalkovský about the reports, Chvalkovský claimed that he was fully in the dark on how the newspapers got the information, but he said that he would check with Beneš about the matter.[116] Nothing came of that promise. By early June Beneš stated in a foreign policy exposé in the National Assembly that Czechoslovakia opposed any customs union, confederation, or anything that might compromise its economic sovereignty.[117] Certainly it was not very difficult for European diplomats or even well-informed newspaper readers to guess what had been discussed in Berlin. Excessive publicity was one of the most effective ways of destroying undesirable projects in their embryonic phase.

The significance of the meeting between Beneš and Schubert for Czechoslovak-German diplomacy can hardly be exaggerated. There for the first time the issues that were to separate the two countries until Hitler's accession to power came into clear focus in frank diplomatic discussions. On the German side the interest was not so much in an Anschluss, as the Czechs had previously feared. Berlin aimed for much more, and that was the reestablishment of German authority in Central Europe and its aggrandizement to the east and southeast. The Germans knew that they could work through Austria without incorporating the country. The closer German and Austrian trade policy coincided, the more pressure they could exert on the Czechs. Those hopes for a German-Austrian-Czechoslovak economic area were only "vague ideas" in Schubert's mind in the spring of 1928, and they lay dormant for a year and a half thereafter. But they quickly became established German policy under Stresemann's successor.

For the Czechs the further that German economic recovery proceeded the greater became the potential threat to them. Prodded by the French and their own fears of an Anschluss, they had sought to establish a trade association in the Danubian region strong enough to resist German economic penetration. The Germans would have tolerated that association only if they themselves could have joined, in which case they would have acquired precisely what they were seeking. In succeeding years Beneš repeated time and again that no great power could join with small nations in an economic grouping without soon dominating it. He urged co-operation between Germany and France before there could be any special connection between those powers and the Danubian group. In that way he hoped to balance German power with French influence.

Beneš's experiences of 1927 and 1928 instilled in him an even deeper skepticism concerning the possibility or even the desirability of altering the situation in the Danubian region that had arisen from the peace treaties. After the spring of 1928 Beneš strictly curtailed his attempts to fashion closer ties among all the successor states. His traditional status quo policy progressively lost its dynamic aspects and assumed an ever more negative character. The debate between the Czechs and the Germans, in its simplest terms, was actually the one that had existed ever since the end of the war. The Germans pointed out that their plans for Central and Eastern Europe were much more realistic from an economic standpoint. The

Czechs retorted that their political and cultural independence could not survive the German projects. Both were right.

STABILIZATION

The late 1920s were a period of peace and consolidation in the relationship between Czechs and Germans. That was true both of the diplomacy between Berlin and Prague and of the associations among Czechs and Germans within Czechoslovakia. Those years were also a time of domestic political and social stability in both countries. Democratic forces controlled affairs, and the prognosis for the republican experiments appeared bright.

Despite the fundamentally different conceptions about the future of Central Europe between Berlin and Prague, there were no significant conflicts between the two capitals until the depression years. Termed "friendly" by Masaryk and Beneš in public, called "correct but cool" by Koch in private, the atmosphere remained undisturbed during the last months of Stresemann's life. Stresemann, increasingly handicapped by his physical infirmities, concentrated his fleeting time on what was, to him, Germany's most vital goal, securing the evacuation of the Rhineland, and he won Allied consent for the withdrawal of troops only weeks before his death. Along Germany's eastern and southern frontiers, problems were only of secondary importance. Stresemann's moderate policy accorded fully with the views of Hermann Müller's left-of-center cabinet, and the peaceful attitude emanating from Berlin in 1928 and 1929 seemed to herald the consolidation of the Weimar republic. The same evolution was in evidence across the border in Czechoslovakia, for the nationality conflict was subsiding. The longer the Czechoslovak republic existed and avoided political or economic crises such as those of the early 1920s, the stronger became sentiments among Czechs and Sudeten Germans for understanding and cooperation. It was easy to be at least cautiously optimistic.

The reassurances that were given to Beneš in Berlin slowly exerted a soothing influence on Czechoslovak diplomacy. If the Germans did not intend to "force" an Anschluss, there was no immediate danger. Schubert's idea of special economic cooperation among Germany, Austria, and Czechoslovakia was a potential threat to the Czechs, but he had presented it to Beneš as only a notion that had recently occurred to him. The project was not yet the established German policy, and during Stresemann's lifetime Berlin let the idea lie dormant. At a meeting of the Little Entente at Bucharest in June 1928, both Beneš and Voyislav Marinković, the foreign minister of Yugoslavia, issued statements that hinted at the possible inclusion of Austria in an economic association with the states of the Little Entente. That idea kindled a debate in the Austrian parliament in which all the parties reaffirmed their hopes for an eventual union of Austria with Germany, and Seipel declared that Austria could enter no economic association unless Germany were also a member.[118] Thereafter, in the face of the resistance from Berlin, Vienna, Rome, and Budapest, Beneš abandoned his efforts to foster a political or economic understanding in the Danubian area.[119] Beneš sarcastically observed that he was "delighted" to learn from Seipel's speech that Austria was an economically viable land.[120]

The placid state of Czechoslovak-German relations was reflected in the discussions between Masaryk and Stresemann, when they met at Karlsbad while taking their summer cures in August 1928. They talked only about general matters. Masaryk remarked that the Reich was better off by having German minorities in neighboring states than it would be by incorporating them. Stresemann did not contest that notion; rather he suggested that Czechoslovakia might copy the Swiss pattern and establish separate administrative areas according to the nationality principle. That idea had long been popular among the Sudeten Germans, for it would have given them local autonomy in their own areas of settlement. Beneš had mentioned the Swiss example as a possibility for Czechoslovakia at the Paris Peace Conference when he was fighting to maintain the historic boundaries of Bohemia and Moravia. But the idea contradicted Czech dreams of a centralized Czechoslovak nation-state, and almost until Munich the Czechs adamantly opposed any change in the constitutional structure of the country. Masaryk responded to Stresemann that the language lines in Czechoslovakia were too blurred for the system to work.[121] Local administration in Czechoslovakia was potentially an explosive issue in the relations between Prague and Berlin—as became clear in 1938—but in 1928 it was still only a general topic of conversation that did not disturb the peace of Karlsbad.[122]

The Masaryk-Stresemann conversations were a good indication that there were no current disputes between Czechoslovakia and Germany. Czechoslovak diplomats pretended that the meetings were important diplomatic events, but the Germans discounted them completely. Stresemann left Karlsbad ahead of schedule, glad, he said, to escape the high prices.[123] There were some minor questions between the two countries, mostly of an economic nature, but negotiations concerning them were left largely to lower officials or to experts in the foreign services. In November 1928 Krofta came to Berlin to conclude negotiations for a treaty that established the conditions for Czechoslovak maintenance of a free zone in the port of Hamburg.[124] The Treaty of Versailles had already insured Czechoslovakia's right of access to the sea by way of the Elbe and Oder rivers. Although the Czechs were not particularly concerned about the Oder River rights, the Elbe was crucial for them.[125] Negotiations had proceeded for several years before they were brought to their successful conclusion in November 1928, but the Czechs had been using the river since the founding of the republic.[126]

The issue that caused the most friction between the two capitals was the question of Czechoslovak handling of debts inherited from the Austro-Hungarian Empire. Reich Germans as well as other foreigners held bonds that had been issued in order to finance the building of railways within the empire, and, at independence, Czechoslovakia had taken over a portion of the debts. In response to widespread pressure the Czechoslovak National Assembly in 1928 passed a revalorization that increased the value of the debts by 2.5 percent. The holders of the bonds claimed that the measure was insufficient since it did not offset the effects of inflation, and the German Foreign Office protected their interests. The subject became a matter of discussion between Beneš and Schubert, Krofta and Köpke. But Beneš and Krofta claimed that despite their intervention with domestic officials in Prague they were unable to alter the effect of the law.[127] The Germans linked the issue with the question of a trade treaty between the two countries. Negotiations for a commercial agreement had proceeded intermittently since the mid-1920s, and for a long time the Germans refused to resume negotiations about a trade agreement until the valorization of the Austrian debts was settled. This issue served as a good pretext for avoiding the concessions that the Czechs were asking for. Within Germany the greatest opposition to a trade agreement with the Czechs came typically from Bavaria, where agricultural interests stoutly resisted any lowering of tariffs on products such as hops, malt, and rye. Negotiations for the trade treaty resumed only in the summer of 1929 after Berlin had postponed hopes for getting a new valorization of the Austrian debts, but discussions again broke down in the wake of the depression, and no treaty was ever concluded.[128]

The Czechoslovak land reform affected relations with Germany tangentially although the German Foreign Office was determined not to let it become a major issue of dispute. By the end of the 1920s representatives of both countries had successfully arbitrated over 60 percent of the claims of Reich-German landowners, and the process was continuing in good order at the time of Stresemann's death.[129] Linked to the land reform was the question of the property in Czechoslovakia owned by the Breslau archbishopric. The agreement that Krofta negotiated at the Vatican in 1927-28 (which reestablished relations broken in 1925 at the time of the papal nuncio's departure in protest against the Hussite celebrations) gave Czechoslovakia the right to force the redrawing of bishopric lines along national boundaries. In Berlin in May 1928 Beneš told Schubert that he was determined to see a redistricting carried out along the Hungarian frontier, for the Hungarian clergy was involved in nationalist propaganda in Slovakia. He said that on the German border the situation was different and that he might be able to make concessions.[130] Actually the Prague and Olomouc (Olmütz) archbishoprics extended into German Silesia, so the losses there would not have been one-sided had the church districts been redrawn in conformity with national boundaries. Nevertheless, the German archbishop in Breslau, Cardinal Adolf Bertram, was a conservative German nationalist himself, and the issue was to survive into the 1930s.[131] The bishopric boundaries were redrawn to coincide with the national frontiers only after Hitler's assumption of power.[132]

Much more important in Berlin's eyes than these technical problems was the welfare of the Sudeten Germans. Although Schubert and Beneš barely touched on the matter in their Berlin talks, Stresemann always took special interest in the German minorities in Central and Eastern Europe.[133] Besides his own sincere interest in the minorities and his appreciation of their usefulness for German foreign policy, he was politically astute enough to realize that strong interests within the Reich kept a close eye on events across the eastern frontiers. Various private organizations existed in order to support some specific German nationality group, and the Sudeten Germans had their share of protectors within the Reich. Already in 1926 a bitter dispute broke out between Berlin and Prague over the arrests of Reich Germans in Czechoslovakia who were members of the *Reichsverband der heimatliebenden Hultschiner.* The Czech authorities considered the organization subversive and its members enemies of the state, while official Berlin viewed it as a harmless cultural association. After sharp threats from Berlin, the Czechoslovak government agreed to arrest Reich Germans only for crimes actually committed in Czechoslovakia and not simply because they were members of supposedly irredentist organizations.[134]

It was also in 1926 and 1927 that the German government took additional measures to support Sudeten German financial institutions in order to prevent their going bankrupt or becoming dependent on Czech financial circles. The reasoning behind the action was succinctly explained in a paraphrase of Koch's remarks during a visit to Berlin.

> If the Agrarian and Industrial Bank goes down or falls under Czech influence, this would signify a most problematical weakening of the Sudeten German elements. The three Sudeten German financial institutions—the Agrarian Bank, the Kreditanstalt, and the Central Bank of Savings Institutions—are, to be sure, only moderately sized undertakings that play no role for Sudeten German big industry; but their great significance lies in the fact that a very considerable portion of the small and middle-sized Sudeten German business enterprises, as well as numerous individuals, do business with them. If these institutions should fail or come under Czech influence, a very great part of the Sudeten Germans would become economically dependent on the

Czechs. This would have to lead politically to the most severe stricture on the Sudeten Germans.[135]

The German cabinet appropriated the necessary funds in January 1927, and every step was taken to camouflage the real source of the money. The subventions from Berlin did not, however, remain a secret from officials in Prague, who watched with satisfaction thereafter as the Sudeten German banks became an ever-increasing burden on the German government.[136] The government channeled the funds through a company known as *Ossa*, which was only a front organization for the government's support of German minorities abroad. The men who controlled *Ossa* and directed its affairs were representatives of the major political parties in the Reichstag. In that way, the government managed to avoid public debates in the Reichstag and to maintain the relative secrecy of its operations.[137]

It was difficult for Berlin to work with the Sudeten Germans, however, for the divisions among them went so deep that the different factions were often more interested in getting support against each other than against the Czechoslovak authorities. It has already been seen that Koch warned the German Foreign Office about this situation in early 1926 during the secret talks with Krofta and that Berlin refused to support the German Nationals against the activists during the negotiations for German entrance into the cabinet. After the German Agrarians and the Christian Socials joined the government in October 1926, the other German parties soon began to accuse them of abandoning German interests in order to stay in power. A delegation of Sudeten Germans voiced that criticism to Stresemann in the summer of 1927, but their specific objections were insignificant.[138] In November the German bourgeois parties in opposition tried in vain to get Berlin's financial support against the government parties.[139] Berlin still avoided involvement in internecine disputes.

But with the consolidation of the Czechoslovak republic in the late 1920s, the negativist position of the Sudeten German rightist parties became increasingly unattractive. By late 1927 even the Nazis proclaimed their willingness to cooperate in a Czechoslovak government under the right conditions.[140] The German National party was deeply split on the same issue, for there was a movement within the party to recognize formally the existence of the state, to drop the earlier irredentist propaganda, and to cooperate in a governing coalition. In the ensuing power struggle in the party, however, the moderates lost out. In the summer of 1928, under the leadership of Alfred Rosche, they left the National party and helped to found a new Sudeten German political party called the *Deutsche Arbeits-und Wirtschaftsgemeinschaft*. In addition to the German National dissidents, the new party relied primarily on the German Democrats, whose main power base was in Prague's German Jewish circles.[141] The DAWG enjoyed the pronounced sympathies of the

Prague German legation in general and of Walter Koch in particular. It was an avowedly activist party, but it criticized the German governmental parties for failing to represent German interests effectively in the cabinet. Koch agreed with the assessment, and he regarded Bruno Kafka, the head of the German Democrats, as the Sudeten German politician "with the widest horizon."[142] In 1928 and 1929, while the activist policy was still popular, the DAWG did win significant electoral victories. But, despite hopes that the new party would help to consolidate the political interests of the Sudeten Germans, it only complicated their political fragmentation.[143]

The two German parties represented in the cabinet—the German Agrarians and the German Christian Socials—attempted to work behind the scenes and to maintain a low profile in public. Such concessions as they won in nationality matters were on the level of administrative decisions rather than legal reforms. In turn, their presence in the government enabled Czech leaders to discount minority complaints by pointing out that Sudeten Germans were already in positions of authority. As irredentism subsided through the twenties, the appeal for local political autonomy increased. Sudeten Germans, as well as Slovaks and Ruthenians, shared the desire to be more independent of bureaucratic interference from Prague.

The administrative reform of 1927, however, illustrated the conflicting interests of Slovaks and Sudeten Germans. The reform abolished the county system of the early 1920s and established four provinces—Bohemia, Moravia-Silesia, Slovakia, and Ruthenia—as the major administrative areas of the country. By establishing Slovakia as a single province instead of a loose conglomeration of county units the reform seemed to be a step toward autonomy for the Slovaks. It was a concession to Hlinka's Slovak People's party, which in turn entered the governing coalition and supplied two ministers in the cabinet. For the Sudeten Germans, however, the county system could have been a vehicle toward political autonomy in their own smaller areas of settlement in Bohemia, Moravia, and Silesia. The Prague authorities had never put the county system into effect in the western provinces, probably for fear of Sudeten German separatism. Nevertheless, the administrative reform of 1927 represented a loss for Sudeten German autonomist ambitions. It removed a law through which the Sudeten Germans could have worked for local self-government, and it confirmed the provinces of Bohemia and Moravia-Silesia as larger administrative units in which the Czechs were clearly the majority.[144]

The fact that the Sudeten German government parties supported the reform requires some explanation.[145] It would appear that they acted for party gains rather than for German national interests. The reform established provincial parliamentary bodies with limited powers in economic and cultural matters. It gave the central government in Prague the right to appoint one-third of the members of each of those parliaments. That meant, in effect, that an antigovernment vote would have to be of landslide proportions in order to wrest control of the provincial parliaments from the hands of the governing coalition in Prague. Beneš himself criticized the German parties in the cabinet for failing to oppose the administrative reform. He pointed out that had the administrative areas been divided into smaller units, the Sudeten Germans could have enjoyed semiautonomous rule in their main areas of settlement.[146] In view of Beneš's well-known convictions about the necessity for strong centralized government in Czechoslovakia, his opposition to the reform no doubt sprang more from a concern about Slovak autonomist gains and the potential losses of his own National Socialist party than from any desire to see the Sudeten Germans gain local self-rule.

The relative ineffectiveness of the German government parties appeared in matters of foreign policy as well. The most striking example concerned the bitter debate over the protection of national minorities in the successor states that broke out in Geneva in 1928 and 1929. In December 1928 Stresemann and Foreign Minister Zaleski of Poland had their famous confrontation concerning complaints from Germans in Polish Upper Silesia. Thereupon Stresemann decided to join with the Canadian representative in presenting proposals for a reform of the way in which the Council of the League of Nations handled minority petitions. The resolution was introduced in March 1929, and, although Stresemann's dispute was with the Poles, the issue involved the other states that had signed minorities treaties as well. Even before the actual introduction of the resolution, Beneš had taken the position that Czechoslovakia had more than fulfilled its obligations under the treaties. He then joined with representatives of other successor states in presenting a formal memorandum opposing Stresemann's suggestions. The final result was that only minor procedural changes were adopted by the Council in its meeting of June 1929.[147]

During the height of the dispute Berlin became incensed with the Sudeten German ministers for failing to support Stresemann's initiative by attacking Beneš. Members of the German legation in Prague made little effort to hide their disgust; and the leader of the German Agrarians, Franz Spina, claimed that Stresemann himself had demanded that the Sudeten German ministers take a public stand against Beneš's memorandum. They were reluctant to do so for domestic political reasons, and only in May did they disassociate themselves from Beneš's optimistic assessment of the minorities situation in Czechoslovakia.[148] They thereby opened themselves to an attack by some of the Czechoslovak parties and to an ultimate disavowal by the Czechoslovak premier. Moreover, Czechoslovak diplomats started making noises about interference from Berlin.[149] In attempting to tread a middle course, the Sudeten German ministers satisfied neither their Czech colleagues in the cabinet nor the Foreign Office in Berlin. The French minister in Prague noted that within the cabinet the Czechs were trying to isolate the Sudeten Germans from diplomatic and military affairs.[150]

Yet in the society as a whole the general trend was toward reconciliation between the Czechs and the Sudeten Germans. The most radically inclined members of the working classes had long since buried their national differences within the Communist party, albeit only as a result of intense pressure from Moscow in the early 1920s. The more moderate elements, as represented by the Czechoslovak and the German Social Democratic parties, moved slowly but steadily toward closer cooperation. No insurmountable difficulties separated them. In January 1928 the two parties convoked a joint congress in which speakers of both nationalities, using both languages, urged the unity of all the workers of the country.[151] Although the two social democratic parties continued to maintain their separate identities, they worked together harmoniously in matters of political and social policy. And what was good for the workers was good for the factory owners as well. In the late summer of 1928 the executive committee of the Federation of German Industrialists resolved to unite their organization with its Czech counterpart. Their reasoning was that industry in Czechoslovakia would be represented better by one central organization than by two competing national groups.[152] The Agrarians and Catholic political elements were already cooperating in governing the country, and the conservative nationalist elements were losing ground. It appeared by 1929 that the process by which nationalist sentiments would be neutralized or diluted by economic class interests or religious loyalties was finally reasserting itself.

The same year marked the strengthening of Masaryk and Beneš in Czechoslovak domestic politics. After the crisis of 1926, the forces around the "Castle" gradually reconsolidated their position. Švehla's health suffered a relapse in October 1927, and he was fully incapacitated after February 1928. Švehla's illness left a leadership vacuum in the cabinet, for it was not until January 1929 that he resigned his office. The government functioned for a year without effective leadership as potential successors jockeyed for the premiership. It was generally assumed that the replacement for Švehla would also be chosen from among the Czechoslovak Agrarians, the strongest party in parliament. But the party itself was deeply divided among "pro-Castle" and "anti-Castle" elements along the same economic lines as in 1926. According to recent research, the "pro-Castle" forces represented those agrarian groups dependent on an active export trade while the "anti-Castle" circles favored protectionist tariffs. There were also various other ambitious individuals within the party whose stances on substantive issues were largely a function of personal rivalries.[153] For a successor to Švehla Masaryk favored František Udržal, the minister of defense; Karel Viškovský, formerly head of the State Land Office; or Jan Malypetr, chairman of the Chamber of Deputies.[154] The major contender from among the "anti-Castle" forces was Beneš's old adversary, Milan Hodža, who functioned as the minister of education in Švehla's cabinet.

The year between February 1928 and February 1929 witnessed a decisive test of strength between the Masaryk-Beneš forces and their enemies. In the immediate aftermath of Švehla's relapse Masaryk worried that a new premier might not be strong enough to retain Beneš as foreign minister in the Agrarian-Catholic coalition.[155] But it soon became apparent that Masaryk's personal prestige and popularity—and hence his political power—was so great that no group could openly and effectively oppose him and his supporters. With a firm basis of support among the socialist parties, he commanded the loyalties of the majority of middle-class voters as well. Moreover, the opposition was not united behind any man or program that offered a viable alternative to the logically conceived and executed policies of "the Castle." The most worrisome phenomenon of 1928 for Masaryk and Beneš was probably the ambition of Milan Hodža to become premier. But even Hodža apparently worked for time in order to reach an understanding with Masaryk.[156] Well practiced in devious tactics, Hodža simultaneously attempted to renew his clandestine contacts with State Secretary Schubert in the German Foreign Office. Hodža's apparent objective was to gain support for his candidacy among the Sudeten Germans. In view of the experiences of 1926, however, Schubert ignored him. The German government did not foresee substantial changes in Czechoslovak foreign policy if Hodža should become premier. In reporting about a speech by Hodža in June 1928, Koch warned that Berlin could not expect an "honest, German-oriented foreign policy" from Hodža any more than it could from "any other Czech."[157] Hodža, of course, was a Slovak.

In the course of 1928 Beneš again became the image of self-confidence. That was particularly true after the provincial elections in December confirmed his prognostications of socialist successes. He accurately predicted that Udržal would replace Švehla as premier in early 1929.[158] He jauntily forecast national elections for the following autumn, almost two years ahead of schedule, and he mused that his National Socialists might replace the Czechoslovak Agrarians as the most powerful party in parliament.[159] He took over leadership of the National Socialists and immersed himself in domestic politics. Masaryk harbored doubts about Beneš's activities but continued to stand behind him. Masaryk remarked to the American minister that he had advised Beneš not to regard himself as a politician, and he compared Beneš's personality with that of President Hoover. Beneš, in short, was a good expert in his field but a poor politician.[160] But Beneš was again attempting to lay the foundation for the fulfillment of his greatest personal ambition—succeeding Masaryk in the presidency. If he were ever to win a presidential election in the National Assembly, he would need a strong constellation of parties behind him. One of the political anomalies of 1928-29 was the fact that the foreign minister in the coalition was simultaneously the active leader of one of the strongest opposition parties. That situation was possible only with Masaryk in the presidency.

Perhaps partly in frustration the "anti-Castle" forces among the Agrarians launched a bitter press campaign against Beneš and the National Socialist party in December 1928. They enjoyed the support of other disaffected persons such as Karel Kramář, who seldom shunned an opportunity to criticize Masaryk or Beneš. But the attacks quickly proved counterproductive. Negative popular reaction alarmed neutral elements among the Agrarians and drove them into alliance with the "pro-Castle" wing of the party. Not only did "the Castle's" man, František Udržal, become the new premier, but the Masaryk-Beneš forces were able to force the resignation of Hodža from the cabinet. They even attempted to destroy his position within the Agrarian party by discrediting him in various ways, but Hodža's power base in Slovakia was too strong for that effort to succeed.[161] Hodža retired temporarily to Slovakia, and when he eventually returned to the national political scene he made his peace with "the Castle."

The outcome of the struggle for the succession to Švehla represented a complete victory for the Masaryk-Beneš forces. That signified a consolidation of the republic along the lines of policy that had developed in the first decade of its existence. The next two premiers worked for almost seven years in harmony with the president of the republic. In the crucial depression years Czechoslovakia possessed a strong source of political authority dedicated to liberal democratic ideals. In a formal constitutional sense Czechoslovakia was a parliamentary democracy with only a weak president. In actual fact the country possessed a presidential democracy so long as Masaryk occupied that office. The political party leaders dominated their parliamentary delegations through such devices as their power to draw up election lists or their demand for signed pledges of obedience to party discipline.[162] In turn, Masaryk effectively commanded the loyalty or the respect of the majority of party leaders. To be sure, there were alienated elements among Kramář's National Democrats, Hlinka's Slovak populists, the Communists, or the extreme nationalists from the national minorities, but a highly efficient information system allowed "the Castle" to monitor negative currents very closely. Masaryk's power lay in the fact that the majority of citizens of diverse social stations revered him as the liberator of the country. Masaryk's countrymen were accustomed to an emperor, and he exploited their monarchical traditions in an effort to establish the new republic on firm foundations of authority.

The Udržal government survived until September 1929 when it split over the appointment of a new minister of defense. Udržal had retained that post after becoming premier, but, in the autumn when he attempted to appoint another Czechoslovak Agrarian to the position, the People's party (Czech Catholic) objected and forced the dissolution of the cabinet. Although that was the public version of the cabinet crisis, the socialist parties obviously wanted an election, and Masaryk and Beneš had been predicting one for a year. Beneš privately remarked to the French minister that it was better for the government to fall because of the Czech Catholics than because of the expected departure of Hlinka's Slovak People's party.[163] One of the leaders of the party, Vojtech Tuka, faced a trial on charges of treason in October, and it was assumed that Hlinka's party would leave the coalition if Tuka were convicted. Beneš had long been critical of the Agrarian-Catholic coalition because of its dependence on the Slovaks and the Sudeten Germans for a parliamentary majority. He favored broader coalitions (including the socialist parties) in which one could dispense with Slovak or Sudeten German support in case of need.[164] In short, Beneš wanted to assure the primacy of Czech political parties.

The parliamentary elections of October 27, 1929, laid the basis for the kind of coalition desired by "the Castle." The results showed significant gains for the Czechoslovak and the German Social Democrats and slight improvements for the Czechoslovak Agrarians and Beneš's National Socialists. The Catholic parties incurred moderate setbacks while the Communist party suffered the worst losses of all.[165] After more than a month of negotiations Udržal put together a new government that was spread on a wide base of socialist, agrarian, and Catholic parties. A grand coalition of that type left only a weak and ineffective opposition in parliament, and it meant that the real political debates occurred in the secret councils of the cabinet and not in open parliamentary sessions. But the coalition did reflect the fact that power lay in the center of the political spectrum and that there were no irreconcilable differences among the major parties. At one point in the negotiations Udržal submitted an all-Czech list of ministers, but Masaryk insisted on the presence of Sudeten Germans in the cabinet.[166] Nevertheless, their strength was diluted in the new and broader coalition. The Sudeten Germans retained two portfolios; Franz Spina moved from minister of labor to public health, and Ludwig Czech, the leader of the German Social Democrats, replaced Mayr-Harting of the Christian Socials and became minister of social welfare. That was the first time that there was a German Social Democrat in a Czechoslovak cabinet. The two Germans remained in the government until 1938.

Had the relatively prosperous and peaceful atmosphere of the late 1920s endured, it is likely that understanding and toleration between the Czechs and the Sudeten Germans would have developed further. The 1929 elections, which showed a slight movement toward the Left and away from the extremist parties on both ends of the political spectrum, were indeed a hopeful sign. The trend toward the moderate parties reflected general social and economic stability, which was the indispensable foundation for a viable republic. The Communists lost exactly a quarter of their delegates in the Chamber of Deputies, and the German Nationals failed to get the requisite number of votes to have even one representative in the Senate. After the election, both the German Nationals and the Nazis felt compelled to issue statements announcing their willingness to cooperate actively in the building of a new government.[167] Negativism and irredentism seemed to be dead. Although the National Democrats on the Czech side profited in the election, it is significant that Kramář had already publicly supported Sudeten German participation in the government.[168] The growing moderation of public opinion had forced him and other politicians to emphasize cooperation among the nationalities. Yet hard times soon furnished a setting for a revival of old nationalistic jealousies and suspicions. It is remarkable and tragic that whereas the decade of the 1920s began with open fighting between the nationalities and closed with a type of compromise, the 1930s inherited a favorable situation and saw it deteriorate to new depths of hatred and revenge.

Even in this, the most favored period in the relations between Berlin and Prague, German diplomacy continued to hold the Czechs at a certain distance while negotiating agreements with the great powers. The Germans ignored Beneš's desire to go to Berlin for talks with Stresemann and excluded the Czechs from the negotiations at the Hague in August 1929 about the evacuation of the Rhineland.[169] At the Hague Stresemann finally received the long-sought promise that Allied troops would be withdrawn from Germany. In addition, the Young plan put sole responsibility on the Germans for the transfer of reparation payments from marks into foreign currency and in so doing removed foreign regulation of the German economy. Stresemann's two immediate goals were accomplished. In the first week of September Briand came forth at the League of Nations meeting with his suggestion for a European federal union. Whatever his motives, however visionary his ideas, the very fact that a major international figure could publicly advocate such a scheme was an indication of a generally harmonious atmosphere among the powers.

In addition to the placid international situation, Germany enjoyed political and socioeconomic stability in the late 1920s similar to that of

Czechoslovakia. The fundamental difference, however, was that the democratic forces in Germany were unable to consolidate their position before the onslaught of the depression. Stresemann's achievements were in foreign policy, and he failed to construct a base in German domestic politics on which successors could continue his policies.[170] Stresemann died in early October 1929. The Wall Street crash occurred at the end of the month. The Great Depression quickly destroyed the optimistic diplomatic atmosphere and progressively disrupted the domestic economies of the European countries. For German-Czechoslovak relations the tensions between a great power and its smaller neighbor in Central Europe soon erupted again into open disputes. The conflicting interests of the two countries had survived the era of Locarno diplomacy.

5   *"Danubia" or Mitteleuropa? 1929–1933*

Optimism pervaded international politics in the autumn of 1929. The French government confidently agreed to withdraw its occupation troops from the Rhineland five years in advance. The German government projected a prosperous economy in the future and accepted the requirements in the Young plan for annual reparation payments under any and all economic conditions. The Briand-Stresemann era was reaching its climax. Yet at the time that the old rivals seemed to be overcoming their major differences, forces were already at work undermining the stability out of which those compromises were growing. Germany experienced an economic downturn already in 1929, and the Great Depression quickly gripped the country after the Wall Street crash in October. With the economic dislocations came the rapid radicalization of German political life in 1930. The demands from the political extremes brought first a change of governments and then a conviction within government circles that German policy must push for far-reaching revisions of the peace treaties. At the same time, Germany's freedom for diplomatic maneuvering was increasingly constricted by its economic vulnerability. While other major industrial nations like Britain and the United States also felt the effects of the depression, France with its more balanced and self-sufficient economy remained relatively unaffected by the international economic crisis until 1932. France's relative strength in international politics was therefore greater in the early 1930s than at any other time since 1923. The French government used its financial power to obstruct undertakings that were against French interests, but Paris was less successful in forcing the adoption of positive policies that would contribute to European economic and political stabilization.

Long before hard times fell upon the industrial nations, people in the agrarian countries of Central and Eastern Europe had been living little more than a subsistence existence. With the rapid fall of grain prices in 1930, diplomats from those countries attempted to establish price supports and trading quotas on an international level, but little could be done as nations moved toward a policy of economic autarky. In the early stages of the depression Czechoslovakia was the country in Central Europe least affected by the economic difficulties, but it was not sufficiently strong to aid even its political allies in Southeastern Europe. Agrarian interests within Czechoslovakia prevented the importation of large amounts of agricultural products, which the country could not absorb in any case. As international trade dwindled, Czechoslovak industrial exports declined precipitously in 1932, unemployment mounted, and Sudeten

German radicalization grew proportionately. But until the depression belatedly struck Czechoslovakia, the political scene in the country was stable. After the elections of 1929 Premier Udržal continued to work closely with Masaryk and Beneš, who were determined to keep the country on the course they had long since charted. At no time were there significant changes in the foreign or the domestic policies of Czechoslovakia.

Across the border, new men governed Germany under radically different conditions in the early 1930s. Upon the death of Stresemann, Julius Curtius became foreign minister. A member of the German People's party and Stresemann's heir-apparent, Curtius had been minister of economics since January 1926. As has been seen, he urged special ties among Germany, Austria, and Czechoslavakia at the International Economic Conference in May 1927, a year before Schubert toyed with the same idea. In 1929 at least one rumor appeared in the Czech press accusing him of saying that from an economic standpoint Czechoslovakia would have to disappear from the map. Although the German foreign Office denied the report, it did not enhance Curtius's popularity in Prague.[1]

There was soon a new state secretary in the Foreign Office as well, for Schubert stayed on at the Wilhelmstrasse only eight months after the passing of Stresemann. In the summer of 1930 he took charge of the embassy in Rome for a brief period before going into retirement. The post of state secretary went to Bernhard W. von Bülow, a nephew of the former imperial chancellor and a career official in the Foreign Office. An intelligent but a taciturn and rigid man, Bülow was more in tune with the conservative, nationalist sentiments that were becoming dominant in Berlin. A measure of the shift in thinking was the appointment of Heinrich Brüning to succeed the Social Democratic chancellor, Herman Müller, in March 1930. Brüning represented the right-wing of the Center party, and the avowed purpose of his government was to shore up Weimar democracy by imparting a more authoritarian character to it. Of necessity, Brüning gradually became more involved in foreign affairs than his predecessors in the chancellory had been. These three men—Brüning, Curtius, and Bülow—were the principal figures in German diplomacy in the early 1930s. They were driven to step up the pace, to show new and more striking accomplishments.

RADICALIZATION

Beneš received his first direct exposure to the new German diplomatic style during the second Hague conference in January 1930. In the hopeful atmosphere of the autumn and winter of 1929-30, European diplomats were involved in a massive effort to liquidate the economic disputes arising out of the war. After the first Hague conference in August 1929 expert committees continued to meet in order to reach definitive agreements not only about German reparations but also about the obligations of Germany's wartime allies and the "liberation payments" of the other successor states. Those "liberation payments" had been established at the Paris peace conference and were theoretically intended to cover the costs to the Allies of freeing the successor states from Austro-Hungarian rule. The Czechs had never liked the obligations, which seemed to them to constitute a "tax" on their freedom. At various times in the 1920s there was talk about canceling the debts, and by the time of the Hague conference Czechoslovakia was the only country still required to make "liberation payments."[2] At a time when the total reparations bills of Germany, Austria, Hungary, and Bulgaria were being drastically reduced or canceled altogether, pressure mounted on Beneš to win some concession for Czechoslovakia. But Beneš found no sympathy from either the Italians or the British, and it soon became obvious that the Czechs could not escape their obligations. They therefore hit upon the idea of getting a special concession from the Germans.

The Czechs requested that the German government renounce the claims of its private citizens against Czechoslovakia. Most of those claims grew out of the Czechoslovak land reform, which had confiscated the estates owned by Reich Germans. Actually Article 297 of the Treaty of Versailles had given the Czechs the right to seize without compensation all property owned by Reich Germans in Czechoslovakia, but the Czechs had voluntarily renounced that privilege during the negotiations for a trade treaty with Germany in 1920. By late 1929 most of the disputes about the land reform had been successfully arbitrated, and the Czechs estimated the value of the outstanding claims at thirteen million gold marks.[3] Since this was not a tremendous sum in international finance, it was obvious that the Czechs wanted a concession from the Germans in part for psychological motives. Inasmuch as Hungarians also had claims against Czechoslovakia because of the land reform, a German renunciation could have helped the Czechs resist Hungarian demands.

Curtius was not the man, however, to make gratuitous concessions to the Czechs. When he heard about the Czech demand, he instructed Koch to prevail upon Beneš to change Prague's policy.[4] Koch's answer that Beneš was not to be moved set the stage for a confrontation between the two foreign ministers.[5] On January 7, 1930, Beneš called upon Curtius during the second Hague conference and found the German in a completely unyielding frame of mind. When Beneš remarked that an agreement could be easily found on the remaining issues between Germany and the Western powers at the Hague, Curtius retorted that Germany could make no more compromises whatever. Then when Beneš said that he could not return home without having won a concession from the Germans, Curtius answered that he, too, had domestic responsibilities. Beneš concluded that he had really come just to pay a courtesy call and left.[6]

In the final session at the Hague the Czechoslovak delegate, Štefán Osuský, signed the reparations agreements, voicing his country's reservations all the while. Osuský continued to insist in vain that Germany renounce the claims of its citizens against Czechoslovakia. The Hague settlements were by no means popular among the Czechs, for the "liberation payments" were set to run for thirty-seven more years—until 1966—at a rate of ten million gold marks annually.[7] Still, Osuský's public complaints were contrary to Beneš's diplomatic technique, which consisted of bargaining in private, and, even if defeated, appearing happy in public. Several weeks later in Prague Krofta asked Koch about the reaction in Berlin to Osuský's reservations, and Koch observed that if people did not want to uphold agreements they should not sign them. Krofta himself indicated that Osuský was becoming too self-important.[8]

Krofta's criticism of Osuský was not free of personal bias, for the two were potential rivals for Beneš's job. As Beneš pursued the goal of succeeding his mentor in the presidency, others jockeyed for the position of foreign minister. Within the diplomatic service the two leading candidates were Krofta and Osuský. Krofta was Beneš's deputy and closest collaborator, and he could be expected to follow Beneš's lead in foreign policy. Osuský enjoyed greater independence from Beneš because of his own personal prestige arising from his wartime efforts in Geneva for Czechoslovak independence and because of strong Slovak support for him on both sides of the Atlantic. Osuský had served as Czechoslovak minister in Paris since 1919. Observing the political intrigues in the capital, Koch himself did not believe that Beneš could attain the presidency, and he wrote in 1930 that Beneš was striving "passionately but in vain" to become Masaryk's successor.[9] A few weeks later Koch reported that Beneš would like to have German support but that the Reich could have no interest in helping Beneš's candidacy among the Sudeten Germans. After all, Koch said,

It cannot be forgotten so easily by Germany that for eleven years in all vicissitudes Beneš has created difficulties for the Reich, has stood behind France as a loyal shield-bearer, and that he is now as always not only the greatest obstacle to an Anschluss but also to a Central European economic entente under the leadership of Germany.[10]

What Koch said about Beneš's policy was absolutely correct; but the remarkable thing in the light of subsequent events is that Koch chose in March 1930 to single out the Anschluss issue and the question of Central

European economic arrangements as evidences of Beneš's enmity toward Germany.

Fearing a resurgence of German power in Central Europe, Beneš warmly supported French efforts to maintain the political balance that had been established by the peace treaties. He understood and approved the tactics of Briand, including Briand's advocacy in 1929 and 1930 of European federation. For political reasons, however, Beneš muted his support for Briand's proposal. European federation was a utopian idea in 1930, and Beneš always avoided identification with losing causes. Moreover, he had to reckon with Prague's conservative nationalists, who attacked any supranational construct because they feared being drowned in a Germanic sea. But Beneš was sufficiently astute to realize that a European federation in Briand's sense accorded with his own efforts to insure Czechoslovakia's independence and sovereignty. For both men, a European federation could help preserve the status quo in two important ways. It might presuppose that long-sought understanding between France and Germany in which Germany would abandon its revisionist policies altogether, or at least agree to an extension of the Locarno formula to its eastern frontiers. On the other hand, it could involve the other European powers in maintaining order on the general basis of the peace treaties and thereby dilute German power in Central Europe. In either case, the security of the states of Central and Eastern Europe would be enhanced. Under those circumstances even the specter of an Anschluss seemed less real, for Beneš occasionally remarked that the Anschluss question would lose its significance if Germany and Austria were already members of a larger federation.[11]

A European federation theoretically afforded the best prospects for the peaceful evolution of political developments on the continent. The problem was that, while men like Briand and Beneš could diagnose the disease, they were willing to prescribe only palliatives and unable to administer even those. No European federation could be effective without compromising the sovereignty of its member states, yet the nationalist spirit across the continent was far too great to admit any diminution of the formal legal rights of the nation-states. In his memorandum of May 1930 Briand stressed that a "European federal union" must not in any way infringe on the functions of the League of Nations or the sovereignty of the individual European states.[12] Like politicians across Europe, Beneš heartily agreed with those limitations, for any other course would have meant political suicide. Both the politicians in Prague and the Czech public were far too proud of their new creation to compromise its independence. As a small and geographically exposed country, Czechoslovakia had more to gain than to lose in a multilateral limitation of national sovereignties, and perceptive men such as Masaryk and Beneš could understand that fact.

Yet they were limited by the nationalist spirits that they themselves had served. Thus, Briand and his allies were unable to give effective content to Briand's own proposals. Briand's advocacy of European federation resembled his earlier espousal of the antiwar movement, in that he was attempting to exploit the idealism of the time for the national interests of France and its allies. If all else failed, he could at least win a propaganda victory. The powers agreed to form a study committee to look into Briand's proposals, but no practical accomplishment came from Briand's intitiative.

Despite the optimism among the diplomats the Young plan was stillborn. If Europeans in general were not alarmed by the collapse on Wall Street, they should have been. That was particularly true for the Germans. They had rebuilt their economy and paid their reparation obligations in the late 1920s by means of a tremendous influx of American loans. When panic struck the American financial community, Germany's main source of credit promptly dried up; and indeed many of the loans that were granted on a short-term basis were soon recalled. By recalling those loans and by setting up a prohibitive tariff, the Americans quickly exported their depression to Europe, first and foremost to Germany. The Dawes plan had allowed for a revision of the reparation terms if Germany were confronted with unexpected financial difficulties; but the Young plan divided Germany's annuities into two parts, one of which could be postponed but the other of which had to be paid under all circumstances. Thus it was that the Young plan, which had been universally regarded as a great concession to the Germans, was actually much harsher on them under the economic circumstances of 1930 and 1931 than the Dawes settlement would have been.[13]

As financial troubles multiplied in Germany in 1930, public opinion grew increasingly more radical. Through 1930 there were irredentist demonstrations along Germany's eastern frontier. The Bavarians renewed their demands for government aid to regions along the Czechoslovak boundary.[14] In February the "Reich Fraternity of Home-loving Hultschiners" staged a mass rally in Upper Silesia in commemoration of the tenth anniversary of the cession of Hultschin to Czechoslovakia.[15] In August 1930 came the famous anti-Polish demonstration in which a member of Brüning's cabinet made a rabidly nationalistic speech.[16] Brüning found himself unable to carry a parliamentary majority in July and called elections for September. That was his first great mistake. Hitler's Nazis multiplied their representation ninefold and emerged from the radical fringe as the second most powerful party in the Reichstag. The Communists improved their already sizeable representation by 40 percent and became the third strongest party.[17] Thereafter the Nazis and the Communists tried to outdo one another in crudity and rowdyism both in and outside the Reichstag. Brüning had to rely on Hindenburg's power to rule by presidential decree, and he became dependent on an increasingly senile old man. It was exactly the situation that he had hoped to avoid by calling the elections.

A week after those elections in September 1930 there broke out in Prague the most serious ethnic conflicts since 1920. The occasion was the showing in Prague of a sound film in the German language. There can be little doubt that the situation in Germany stirred old fears and resentments among the Czechs. On first thought no one would have predicted the street riots, the sacking of the theaters showing the German films, or the cries of "Down with Germans and Jews"—all of which lasted for four days. The German language was no foreign tongue in Prague: several of Prague's daily newspapers were published in German; every day it could be heard in shops, restaurants, and trams; almost every Czech understood and spoke the language; indeed, Czech itself was permeated with Germanic influence not only in vocabulary but also in idioms and phraseology to a much greater extent than any Czech cared to contemplate. Many Czechs hated the overpowering influence of things German on their culture and history, and even as they had torn down the German shop signs in 1918 some rebelled against paying to hear the language for their entertainment in 1930. The riots pointed anew to the ill will dating from the days of the national revival, the world war, and the early days of independence. The 1920s had given them insufficient time to set aside the legacy of decades. But those riots were not spontaneous demonstrations. German sound films had been showing in Prague before packed theaters for several months, and there had been no protests. The best informed reports about the riots charged that the disturbances had been provoked by a group of ultranationalists (some called them fascists, and the Austrian minister referred to them as "political desperadoes") who were intent upon embarrassing the government and particularly Masaryk and Beneš.[18] Beneš quickly asserted that he himself was the target of the riots.[19] The ringleaders—Jiří Stříbrný, Rudolf Gajda, and Charles Pergler—were popularly known as the "three musketeers" of the Czechoslovak parliament, and their reputations for honesty were hardly above suspicion. (Rumors floated around Prague that the riots were financed by American filmmakers, who wanted to rid themselves of German competition.)[20] All three men had been politically discredited by the forces of "the Castle," and they bore bitter personal grudges against Masaryk and Beneš.

But the riots were more than just a personal vendetta. Mobs numbering into the hundreds reflected a malaise that was beginning to infect particularly the younger elements of the population. The approval that the riots found in the conservative nationalist press and the failure of the police to react with vigor demonstrated the complicity of more responsible political elements. The mayor of Prague insisted that the German films be banned from the city, and his success only complicated a difficult situation. The mayor, Karel Baxa, was himself a radical National Socialist, who had traditionally drawn his political support from low- and middle-income Czechs in the city. He was hardly elated to see Stříbrný, a former party colleague whom Beneš had tossed out of the party, capture some of the best supporters of the Czech National Socialist Party. In short, the men who were openly or covertly responsible for the riots were chauvinists who genuinely desired a more nationalistic orientation in the country's domestic and foreign policies. Some of them would have been happy to see the Sudeten German ministers resign from the government in protest, but the Germans were wise enough not to fall into that trap.[21]

The riots broke out while Beneš was attending a meeting of the League Assembly in Geneva. In that respect they were a repetition of the old pattern whereby Beneš's political enemies attempted to make trouble for him while he was out of town. Beneš of course fired off a series of telegrams demanding that the authorities control the demonstrations, but a return to normal conditions awaited his return to Prague. In Geneva Beneš emphasized to Curtius that the riots were contrary to all his policies toward Germany, and he vowed to get the ban on the German films lifted upon returning to Prague.[22] Because of the ban there began a movement in Germany to boycott all Czechoslovak goods, but Koch warned that it would hurt the Sudeten Germans more than the Czechs.[23] Thereupon the Foreign Office took steps to counter any economic boycott in the Reich while encouraging the German press to maintain a sharp tone against the Czechs.[24] The Germans attempted to sever cultural relations between the two countries by preventing the Berlin Philharmonic from fulfilling an engagement in Prague and by protesting performances of Smetana and Janáček operas in Germany and in Austria as well.[25]

On October 20, in a conversation with Koch, Beneš renewed his commitment to get a reinstatement of the German sound films in Prague, but he added that he needed some time to prepare the way since his countrymen "unfortunately had a temperament that was inclined to extremes." Calling the riots "stupidities," he even opined that he probably would have reacted as had the Germans in disrupting cultural contacts between the two countries. Koch trusted Beneš's sincerity but recommended to Berlin that pressure be kept on the Czechs.[26] Curtius was searching for ways of scoring points with the nationalists at home, and he came forth on October 30 with public remarks that exacerbated feelings between Berlin and Prague. In the foreign affairs committee of the Reichsrat he denounced the riots in Prague and indicated that there could be no more cultural exchanges between Germany and Czechoslovakia until "the significance of Germandom no longer be misjudged."[27] Such remarks forced Beneš to make a public response. Saying that Curtius was poorly informed, Beneš hinted that Curtius's remarks were an attack on the "dignity of the Czechoslovak nation."[28] Despite Beneš's rejoinder, the *Prager Presse* announced within a week that German sound films would again be shown on the following day in Prague theatres.[29] The films reappeared without incident, and Koch recommended that the Reich-German press take the line that this event "signified the victory of the European-minded Czechs over the forces of the street." A Foreign Office memorandum noted that the German newspapers were receiving that instruction.[30]

German diplomacy won a propaganda victory, but it was a petty and a pyrrhic one. It could be argued that Curtius had to take a hard line against the Czechs because of nationalist pressure in Germany. But this argument is largely undercut by the fact that the Foreign Office itself urged the press to maintain a highly critical attitude toward the Czechs. One cannot help to stir up nationalist reaction at home and then legitimately use it as a defense for an uncompromising foreign policy. Curtius's diplomacy put an unnecessary strain on the relations between Prague and Berlin. Beneš was committed from the very beginning to a reinstatement of the German sound films in Prague, and there can be little doubt that he would have succeeded. Yet Curtius made political capital out of the incident and in so doing created deep resentment among officials in Czechoslovakia. The episode was an example of his heavy-handed diplomacy, which may have proceeded more from ineptness than from ill will but which was nonetheless unfortunate for German foreign policy. The action of Curtius prompted the British minister in Prague to remark that "the German exercises the art of diplomacy as the bear understands dancing. In both cases the operation is painful, slow, clumsy and ineffectual."[31]

The film riots provided an instructive contrast between the domestic situations in the two countries. The central government in Prague was quickly able to regain control of the situation and to stifle appeals to the baser nationalistic impulses of the population. Group jealousies and authoritarian tendencies certainly existed among many elements of Czechoslovak society, but the government was able to keep them in check. Beneš did not rest content until he had run Pergler out of the country.[32] If Czechoslovak democracy could deal summarily with its opponents, resolute action was all the more necessary in Germany after the Nazi victories in the elections of September 1930. The menace posed by the Nazis was obvious to all, yet Brüning's government did not have the will, or perhaps even the power, to suppress the movement. In responding to the riots in Prague, Curtius appealed to nationalistic emotions in Germany in the vain hope that such posturing by the government could undercut the burgeoning power of the rightist movement. His tactics reflected the mistaken assumptions of Brüning's conservative authoritarian cabinet. On the one hand, in attempting to combat the depression by deflationary policies, the government heaped greater and greater economic sacrifices onto the population and radicalized political sentiment. On the other, it attempted to undercut the radical appeals of the Nazis by more moderate nationalist policies of its own. But such an approach was unable to satisfy the resentments caused in part by Brüning's own policies. The Brüning government was helping create the Nazi constituency, and it was never able to resolve the contradictions in its own programs.

Brüning had become chancellor in March 1930 essentially as a result of political intrigues in the circles around President Hindenburg. The influence of the court camarilla in the demise of Weimar has justly become infamous. But it might be instructive to emphasize that intrigue was not confined to domestic politics and that already at a relatively early date certain figures were undertaking diplomatic initiatives unbeknown to the Foreign Office.

In January 1931 a lawyer from the affluent Dahlem section of Berlin, Dr. Wilhelm Regendanz, held private and secret discussions with Beneš in Geneva. Regendanz's mission was to sound out Beneš about a possible Franco-German understanding on the basis of which there could be an international loan to Germany. When Beneš inquired as to whom Regendanz was representing, the lawyer answered obliquely by saying that if Beneš would come to Berlin he could have private conversations in Dahlem with a "member of the German Reichswehr and eventually the Reich's chancellor." Regendanz emphasized that the discussions should be kept secret from Curtius, and Beneš readily agreed by remarking that Curtius lacked "flexibility" in negotiations.[33] That member of the German Reichswehr was none other than General Kurt von Schleicher, who because of his influence with Hindenburg was rapidly becoming the king-maker in German politics. It was to Schleicher that Regendanz reported, and only from Schleicher did the Foreign Office eventually find out about Regendanz's contacts with Beneš.[34]

Beneš talked with Briand after his first conversation with Regendanz and then told the German that chances for an understanding with the French were excellent. Of course, there were certain conditions that the Germans ought to meet. They should give up their collusion with the Soviet Union and Italy, and they ought to agree to an international military control commission that could inspect and certify disarmament in Europe. In addition, Beneš made it plain that he himself would like to have Germany's vote in his campaign to be elected president of the disarmament conference.[35]

After the three conversations with Beneš in Geneva, Regendanz went home and reported to Schleicher. Then in February he traveled to Prague, where he had more secret talks with Beneš in the Ministry of Foreign Affairs and in Beneš's home. Beneš held out the possibility of an international consortium, to be supported by the French and the Czechs, that would grant a loan to the Germans. Regendanz pointed out that the Germans would want to use the money to support their eastern provinces and that the Poles might not take kindly to an international loan for this purpose. Beneš only smiled. He was using the prospects of a loan as a lure for a Franco-German understanding on French terms, and he emphasized repeatedly that he was willing to act as a mediator between the French and the Germans.[36] That had long been one of Beneš's fondest dreams.

The contacts between Beneš and Regendanz predictably came to nothing. If Berlin had accepted the French conditions, it would have consented to nothing less than a complete realignment of its foreign policy. The sacrifice of cooperation with the Russians and the Italians and the conclusion of an understanding with the French would have meant that Germany forsook the revisionist bloc and itself joined those powers that were seeking to uphold the peace treaties. Obviously no one in Berlin was willing to take such a step. But it is remarkable that influential people in Berlin—Schleicher and perhaps even Brüning himself—undercut the influence of the Foreign Office in order to deal secretly with Beneš and Briand. The financial plight of Germany was already such that drastic diplomatic action was called for, even to the point of seeking aid from the French and the Czechs. But the method by which the initiative was undertaken revealed the extent to which political intrigues were taking hold in Berlin and undermining the foundations of Weimar democracy. At the same time that Regendanz was sounding out Beneš, Curtius was perfecting a scheme of his own that was perilous to the Czechs. When it became known in March 1931, it immediately engendered the worst crisis in Czechoslovak-German relations in the history of the Weimar republic.

THE AUSTRO-GERMAN CUSTOMS UNION PROPOSAL

The sudden proposal for a customs union between Germany and Austria in March 1931 reawakened and aggravated the old fears in Prague of an Anschluss. Throughout the interwar period the Czechs believed that an economic union of Germany and Austria would quickly force Czechoslovakia either to join the association or to suffer tremendous losses in foreign trade. German diplomats and experts fully agreed with that analysis, and behind the proposal for the Austro-German customs union lurked their intention of forcing Czechoslovakia into the union as well. Even Czech adherence would not have been all, for the cooperation of Germany, Austria, and Czechoslovakia in an economic bloc would have facilitated the extension of German influence throughout Central and

Eastern Europe. For this reason Beneš warned that the customs union project represented the revival of Mitteleuropa ideas and determined to oppose it with every weapon at his command.

Actually the customs union proposal was a long time in preparation even if its announcement did catch European diplomats by surprise. As has been seen, Curtius suggested to Beneš in 1927 that Czechoslovakia cooperate in an economic association with Germany and Austria. Yet Curtius's position as minister of economics did not afford him great influence as a maker of German foreign policy, and his remarks did not carry the same weight as those of Schubert for a similar project in 1928. The situation changed in the autumn of 1929 when Curtius succeeded Stresemann as foreign minister and quickly revived the idea of a customs union between Germany and Austria.

At the second Hague conference in January 1930—where he displayed his uncompromising attitude toward Beneš—Curtius began his campaign for a customs union. He met privately with Chancellor Schober of Austria, made plans for a visit by Schober to Berlin, suggested that they obligate themselves to conclude a trade treaty quickly, and discussed the possibility of a customs union.[37] Curtius's remarks sprang largely from his own initiative. Schubert, who was still state secretary at the time, considered a customs union inopportune and called attention to Austria's obligations under the Geneva Protocol of 1922 not to undertake any action that might compromise its political or economic sovereignty.[38] Curtius did not share his deputy's caution, however, and when the Austrians arrived in Berlin in late February 1930 Curtius strongly advocated the idea of a customs union. The Germans and the Austrians agreed to launch negotiations between the economic experts of the two foreign offices, Karl Ritter and Richard Schüller.[39] In June Bülow replaced Schubert as state secretary, whereby the customs union project acquired a new and avid proponent. The idea always received more support from the German side than from the Austrian, and its main advocates in Berlin were Curtius, Bülow, and Ritter. Brüning was at most a peripheral figure. Indeed, Curtius initiated the project before Brüning even became chancellor. Brüning claimed much later, in his memoirs, that he was the victim of a policy that he inherited, one that he opposed but could not completely reverse.[40]

In September 1930 at the meeting of the League of Nations the Czechs received their first direct indication that the Germans were reviving plans for closer economic ties in Central Europe. In the discussion between Curtius and Beneš about the anti-German riots in Prague, Curtius suggested that Germany, Austria, and Czechoslovakia cooperate as a unifed market area for Southeast European agricultural products.[41] The fall of prices for agricultural products in 1930 had put the agrarian countries of Southeastern Europe in a serious financial position. In August and October there were two major agricultural conferences among the states of Eastern Europe in an effort to support prices and to expand markets. Czechoslovakia's two allies in the Little Entente, Rumania and Yugoslavia, were deeply involved in the crisis. The Czechs had significant agrarian interests of their own, but Czechoslovakia was not affected to the same degree as the more purely agricultural countries of Eastern Europe. There was a growing restlessness in Prague as the Czechs watched their allies in the Little Entente moving toward other regional groupings in an effort to overcome the economic crisis. Certainly the Rumanians and the Yugoslavs would have been interested in a Central European industrial area committed to buy large amounts of agricultural products from Southeastern Europe. Beneš could not reject Curtius's proposal outright. Beneš told Curtius that he was not fundamentally opposed to the idea and that he forsaw no insurmountable barriers to negotiations for such a project. Yet Beneš's stress on the need to consult his allies should have been a clear indication of his continued opposition to economic groupings that included Germany with the Danubian states. Curtius was determined, however, to pursue the idea further.[42] In the discussion with Beneš Curtius gave no hint of the negotiations with the Austrians about a customs union, and Beneš did not infer that there were any new plans between Berlin and Vienna.

At Geneva Curtius also talked with Schober about the reports of their economic experts.[43] In a League discussion of Briand's ideas for European union Schober suggested that closer international cooperation could best begin on a regional basis. This idea was by no means novel, and no one concluded that anything concrete lay behind Schober's remarks. Although plans seemed to be progressing, a cabinet crisis in Vienna forced Schober's resignation at the end of September, and the project lay in abeyance for the next few months. Then it acquired new life in December when Schober returned to office, and it became thereafter, according to Curtius, a central issue in German diplomacy.[44] In January 1931 Ritter journeyed to Vienna to discuss a draft treaty with Schüller, and Curtius and Schober met again in Geneva where they agreed to put the plan into its final form within the next few weeks.[45] Throughout those long preliminary negotiations great emphasis was placed on preparing the diplomatic climate for a customs union announcement. The strategy was to present it as a first step toward Briand's idea of European union and to proclaim it open for adherence by other states.

Curtius went to Vienna in the first week of March 1931 in order to make the final agreement on the customs union. It still remained a secret except to a handful of men in the German and the Austrian foreign offices. On the day that Curtius arrived in Vienna, Briand delivered a speech in the French Chamber of Deputies in which he remarked that the possibility of an Anschluss was farther away than ever.[46] As part of their strategy, Curtius and Schober agreed to sign only a protocol of intent to establish a customs union, in order, they hoped, not to give the appearance of confronting other powers with a fait accompli. They settled on March 21-23 as the time for its announcement. The newspaper press in Austria and Germany greeted the visit with only the customary articles about friendship and cooperation, but by the middle of the month rumors about a possible customs union had begun to grow. One of the first reports came in Prague's English weekly, the *Central European Observer*, whose Vienna correspondent wrote that there had probably been a "feeling out" about a customs union, which he regarded as a sensible way of overcoming the "ruinous tariff barriers in Central Europe."[47] It is remarkable that such sentiments were published in what was essentially a Czech propaganda organ, especially when an editorial in the same issue of the paper discounted the possibilities of special economic cooperation between Germany and Austria.[48] The absence of a clear editorial line was another indication that the customs union project caught the Czechs by surprise.

But somehow a real information leak occurred and prejudiced the prospects of the customs union proposal before it was even formally announced. The source or sources of that information has been debated, but the Czechs were probably among the first to find out that something was afoot.[49] On March 18 and 19 Beneš and Krofta began pressuring the Austrian minister for more information about the Curtius-Schober talks.[50] Simultaneously, the Czechoslovak minister in Vienna made formal diplomatic representations to the Austrian government. A German Foreign Office memorandum described that encounter of March 18.

> Schüller told me [Köpke] that yesterday in Vienna the Czechoslo-
> vak minister made an urgent call on Schober and asked him. Schober
> was reticent in view of the formal situation. The Czechoslovak minister
> delivered an urgent warning to the Austrian government in the case that
> it actually entertains such a plan with Germany and said that it would
> surely see what would happen.[51]

Köpke's studious care not to mention the customs union as such in this memorandum shows that the Germans were still trying to maintain secrecy within their own Foreign Office even after outsiders had become aware of the project. On March 20 the French tried to get British and Italian support in démarches in Vienna before the project could be announced. They failed in the attempt, for the British and the Italians received the news with a detached attitude and waited to find out more about the Austro-German plans.[52] The French viewed the customs union as did the Czechs—it was an economic Anschluss, which would lead to a German Mitteleuropa.

Although the French and the Czechs did not succeed in nipping the project in the bud, they did cast enough doubt on German and Austrian diplomacy to give it a very inauspicious beginning. Over a year earlier, in the first serious discussion of the project, Curtius had emphasized the necessity of preparing the European diplomatic climate for the announcement. In fact there was no preparation whatsoever except for Schober's remark in Geneva about regional treaties being stepping-stones toward European union. The original negotiations among the economic experts rested on the premise that Austria and Germany would have to be ready to take advantage of any opportunity that might arise. Nothing had happened by March 1931 to justify optimism about the prospects for a customs union, yet Curtius and Schober decided to go ahead with their plans. They claimed that the economic difficulties of both countries could be alleviated by a customs union, but this assertion carried little weight abroad. In any case, the customs union was regarded as only a screen for their real intention of effecting an Anschluss. The French and the Czechs were determined to sabotage the project, and their superior financial position in 1931 soon left little doubt about their capability of doing so.

When Ambassador Hoesch officially informed Briand and Berthelot about the proposed customs union on March 21, he discovered them in a tough frame of mind and prepared with legal and political objections.[53] The encounters between Beneš and the Austrian and German ministers were more pleasant in tone, but Beneš just as firmly opposed the Austro-German plans. Beneš did not dispute the merits of a regional economic association as such, but he emphasized that no grouping could include a great power with a small state. Rather, he said, countries should make economic alliances with others of their own approximate size. He claimed that an Austro-German customs union would violate the Geneva Protocol of 1922 and that, legalities aside, political considerations would be decisive in defeating the project.[54] Chvalovský made similar remarks to Köpke on the same day in Berlin.[55] There was nothing new in the Czechoslovak position; Beneš had promoted those basic ideas for years, and he simply adapted them to the customs union proposal. The Germans did not consider the initial response from Beneš to be particularly extreme, but they misjudged the situation. Beneš was speaking from strength, and he vehemently denounced the project in conversations with other diplomats.

The wait-and-see attitude of the British provoked intense pressure from Paris and Prague. On the twenty-fifth Beneš received the British minister and made it clear that "He, and his country, would not be a part to, and a partner in, an economic union which, in effect, implied German hegemony. This would simply mean the end of Czechoslovakia. She would be swallowed up ('engloutie') and would cease to exist as an independent nation." The realization of Germany's ambitions would "inevitably lead to another war."[56] To the Czechoslovak legation in London Beneš wrote: "Fundamentally it is the prewar concept of *Mitteleuropa*, and the form that they give to it is only a screen."[57] Such attitudes influenced British Foreign Secretary Arthur Henderson to ask Berlin and Vienna for a promise not to conclude any treaty until their project could be discussed at the meeting of the Council of the League of Nations in May. The Germans and the Austrians were able to make the pledge gracefully by claiming that in any case the negotiations about the details of the customs union would take at least that long. But they stoutly insisted that only the legal—not the political—aspects of the project could be examined. They were only whistling in the dark. Expecting opposition from Paris and Prague, they underestimated the determination in those two capitals to prevent anything resembling an Anschluss. German and Austrian diplomats themselves wanted public opinion in their countries to regard the customs union as a step toward an Anschluss, for their governments stood to win popular support as a result. At the same time they insisted abroad that the plan was purely an economic one in the general spirit of European cooperation. But they could not have the best of both worlds.

Ambitions in Berlin went far beyond a customs union with Austria. The Czechs were absolutely correct that the plan signified a revival of German Mitteleuropa ideas. As the people most directly threatened, the Czechs had the clearest perception of the danger. The economic facts of life in Central Europe were just as operative in 1931 as they had been when Prague first formulated its policy of sustaining an independent Austria in the immediate postwar years. Germany was far and away Czechoslovakia's main trade partner; Austria, the second. Annually between 1927 and 1930 about 45 percent of Czechoslovak imports came from those two countries, either in the form of goods produced in Germany and Austria or products imported by them and resold to the Czechs. In the same years Czechoslovak exports to Germany dropped from 28 to 20 percent but those to Austria remained at 14 or 15 percent of the total exports of the country. This meant that Germany and Austria took from 34 to 43 percent of the total value of the products that Czechoslovakia sent abroad.[58] If the two countries had merged into one economic unit with a common trade and tariff policy, they could have dominated Czechoslovakia's import and export trade and have forced the Czechs either to join their bloc or to suffer tremendous commercial losses.

Top officials in the German Foreign Office knew full well the significance of the Austro-German customs union project for Czechoslovakia. Bülow thought that Beneš himself realized that Czechoslovakia would eventually have to enter the customs union. In mid-April Bülow wrote to Koch that Beneš would soon have to reorient Czechoslovak foreign policy or resign. But even Czechoslovak adherence to the customs union did not represent Bülow's ultimate goal. He added:

> I consider Beneš too intelligent not to realize that an opposition to a natural economic development that is based solely on the shaky grounds of pure political ideology can nowadays no longer endure.
>
> The inclusion of Czechoslovakia in our economic system is completely harmonious with the long range foreign policy of the Reich as I view it. Once the Austro-German customs union has become a reality, I calculate that the pressure of economic necessity will force the entrance of Czechoslovakia within a few years in one form or another. I would see therein the beginning of a development that would be calculated to lead to a solution of vital political interests of the Reich, which scarcely seem soluble in any other way. I am thinking of the German-Polish boundary problem. If we succeed in linking Czechoslovakia with our economic bloc and if we shall have in the meantime created closer economic relations with the Baltic states, then Poland with its weak economic organization will be encircled and exposed to all kinds of dangers. We shall have it in a pincer that, over short or long, can bring it closer to the idea of exchanging political concessions for obvious economic advantages.[59]

Therefore Bülow viewed the Austro-German customs union as ultimately a way of forcing Poland to make territorial concessions to Germany. From that perspective it is remarkable that the Polish government maintained a neutral policy toward the customs union proposal, apparently seeing in it a way of focusing German revisionist attention on the Danubian region and away from the Polish Corridor.[60] In all likelihood the central geographical focus for Curtius was indeed the Danubian area. Only six months earlier he had urged upon Beneš the suggestion of making Germany, Austria, and Czechoslovakia a special market area for Southeast European agricultural products. Czechoslovak adherence to an Austro-German customs union would have created the unified industrial area from which the Germans could have expanded their influence among the agricultural countries.[61] If Bülow concentrated on Poland, Curtius looked more toward the southeast, but both Curtius and Bülow shared one common goal for which the Austro-German customs union was only the first step. They hoped for a new German hegemony in Central and Eastern Europe.

Koch was skeptical. On April 22 he answered Bülow's letter and cautioned against the idea that any amount of economic pressure could force Czechoslovakia into a German tariff organization.

> It is difficult for me to believe that economic difficulties could bring Czechoslovakia sooner or later to cooperate with us. If they believe that their political freedom is in danger, the Czechs are insensitive to economic hardship. As was credibly reported to me, Beneš supposedly

said a few days ago among trusted friends that Czechoslovakia would
continue its opposition to the Austro-German plans "to the point of
self-destruction."

In the many conversations that I have had here about the matter,
what has struck me most is that neither with Czech politicians nor with
diplomatic representatives, even of neutral states, can one successfully
combat the notion that the treaty with Austria is a predominantly
political matter and that it signifies the desired and decisive preparatory
step for the Anschluss.[62]

Koch called upon ten years of experience in Prague in his estimate of the
character of the Czech nation, but his conclusion was the same as should
have been obvious to the most cursory of newspaper readers. That which
the Czechs valued the most was the existence of their own state.
Sovereignty, freedom, independence—those were heady concepts that
made all Czechs nationalists, and some chauvinists. The psychological
importance of the situation was never fully understood in Berlin.

The Czechs were surprised by the customs union project, in part
because they considered Schober to be one of their best friends among
Austrian politicians. It was Schober who as chancellor in 1921 had signed
the Treaty of Lány between Austria and Czechoslovakia and had accepted
extensive financial aid from the Czechs. That treaty had firmly established
Czechoslovak-Austrian relations on a friendly basis, and it had come only
two years after their bitter rivalry at the peace conference for the German
areas of Bohemia and Moravia. But Schober was like other Austrian
leaders; he was willing to get help where he could, and in the winter and
spring of 1931 it was the Germans who showed the greatest interest in
Austria.

The surprise with which the customs union announcement caught both
Briand and Beneš weakened their positions vis-à-vis their nationalist
opponents at home. Briand's loss in the election for the French presidency
in May was widely attributed to the customs union project. Beneš was
relatively more secure in **Prague,** but he still worked hard behind the
scenes in order to defeat the Austro-German plans and reestablish his full
prestige in Czechoslovakia. The announcement of the project unleashed a
struggle in Czechoslovak domestic politics. The Agrarian party had long
maintained high protective tariffs on agricultural products over the
opposition of other parties in the coalition. Czechoslovakia had acquired a
general reputation for being a difficult country with which to have
commercial dealings. High tariffs and determined bargaining by its
negotiators had contributed to its notoriety. During April Beneš pressured
his Little Entente allies to come out publicly against the customs union.
But the Rumanians and the Yugoslavs saw little immediate threat to
themselves, and they were particularly receptive to indications from Berlin

and Vienna that the customs union area might import larger amounts of Rumanian and Yugoslav produce. Beneš had to buy their support by committing Czechoslovakia to institute preferential tariffs on agricultural produce from Rumania and Yugoslavia. In order to honor that promise he had to overcome Agrarian opposition at home. He succeeded principally because the threat to the Czechoslovak economy that was posed by the customs union isolated the Agrarians. Although the Agrarians were still Czechoslovakia's most powerful political party, there were even threats that a new coalition might be formed so as to drop them from the government.[63] Beneš's efforts culminated at a meeting of the Little Entente foreign ministers in early May at Bucharest. Beneš made the tariff concessions, and the Little Entente took a united stand against the customs union.[64]

While he was engaged behind the scenes in mobilizing opposition to the customs union, Beneš at first maintained moderate tones in his discussions with the Austrians and the Germans themselves. He attempted by persuasion to get them to abandon their plans. In early April he had another private talk with Regendanz in an effort to encourage the Germans to drop the project or to dilute it beyond recognition.[65] But when persuasion failed, Beneš spoke out publicly in a much more vehement fashion. On April 23 he delivered a major speech in parliament in which he contested almost every one of the German and Austrian claims. He insisted that the political and economic aspects of the project would have to be examined as well as the legal ones. He doubted that the Austrian economic situation could be improved by a customs union. He frankly admitted that a customs union would severely damage Czechoslovak foreign trade, but he left no doubt that Czechoslovakia would never adhere to the project. He thought that it was not only a step toward the Anschluss but toward German supremacy over the agricultural states of Southeastern Europe as well.[66] After that speech, Beneš had little to do with either the Austrian or the German minister, and relations reached their nadir. Preoccupied with the ever-recurring Austrian problem, Beneš began to urge that Austria be "Helvetianized." He evidently toyed with the idea of forcing Austria to accept permanent political neutrality.[67]

During April Vienna suffered under increasing foreign economic pressure and showed signs of losing its resolve. The Austrians wanted outside support from some quarter and hoped to find it in Italy. They tried unsuccessfully to get German approval of a plan by which Austria would offer to conclude a customs union with Italy similar to the one with Germany.[68] The suggestion was clearly impossible unless both Germany and Italy were part of a larger economic grouping, and the inclusion of Italy would have undercut the political goals that the Germans had for concluding the customs union with the Austrians. By early May both the

Italians and the British sided with Paris and Prague in opposition to the customs union proposal. Germany and Austria faced a united front of hostile powers. The collapse of the Austro-German plans was heralded by the announcement of the Austrian government of May 11 that the largest bank in the country, the *Creditanstalt für Handel und Gewerbe*, had suffered losses in 1930 almost equal to its capital reserves. With a balance **more than half that of all other Austrian banks combined**, the *Creditanstalt* could not be allowed to go into bankruptcy. The Austrian government had to raise a loan for its support somewhere, and, with Berlin able to give little help, Vienna turned to the four powers of the control commission established by the Geneva Protocol of 1922—Great Britain, Italy, France, and Czechoslovakia. Vienna's plea for help meant the end of the customs union project. The Austrians could not get financial aid from four powers, all of whom by that time opposed the customs union, and simultaneously pursue the plans with the Germans.

Although the project was doomed, it still had to have a diplomatic burial. At the meeting of the League Council in May the powers referred the question to the World Court for a decision on its legality in relation to the Treaty of St. Germain and the Geneva Protocol of 1922. Henderson elicited from Schober a public promise that there would be no more negotiations on the project until the Council had acted on the advisory opinion of the Court. In fact, there were no more negotiations at all.

By June the German financial situation was almost as desperate as the Austrian. Throughout the first half of 1931 the number of unemployed workers in Germany was never lower than four million. The collapse of the *Creditanstalt* set off a fresh flight of foreign capital from Germany as well as from Austria. Brüning issued emergency decrees in an effort to stabilize the financial situation and pleaded for relief from Germany's reparation obligations. American investors stood to lose heavily by Germany's economic collapse, and President Hoover responded in late June with his proposal for a year's moratorium on all intergovernmental debt and reparation payments. He hoped to protect American private investments by easing the panic gripping Germany, but the psychological effect of the suggestion was soon nullified by French objections. In mid-July one of Germany's largest financial institutions, the *Darmstädter und National-bank*, was forced to shut its doors, and the government ordered the closing of the other banks as well. Only in August was there some temporary relief when the powers accepted a recommendation by an international committee of experts to extend the terms of all short-term loans to Germany by six months. From that moment Germany was a technically bankrupt country, for it was unable thereafter to meet its financial obligations on time and in full.[69]

In this financial crisis that gripped Central Europe and spread far abroad, Czechoslovakia remained temporarily an island of economic stability. The situation gave many Czechs an opportunity to congratulate themselves and to observe with pleasure the misfortunes of the Germans. Popular opinion attributed the superior position of Czechoslovakia to its restraint in borrowing from abroad and to its ability to maintain a favorable balance of trade. Reports coming to Berlin from the German legation in Prague in the summer of 1931 testified to the anti-German feeling rife in Czechoslovakia. In mid-June Koch related that the tone of Czech newspapers was thoroughly vindictive against Germany. On the one side, they celebrated the blocking of the customs union; on the other, they claimed that the Germans were exaggerating their economic troubles in order to win concessions from the Western powers. Warning that Germany remained as always the real danger to the existence of Czechoslovakia, the newspapers concluded that Germany's current difficulties were the penalties of its defeat in the war that it had started almost two decades earlier.[70]

In late July one of Koch's deputies reported with obvious pique that Krofta never missed an opportunity to shed "crocodile tears" about Germany's financial woes. But Holzhausen noted that the real attitudes in the Ministry of Foreign Affairs were similar to those in the press. With the semiofficial *Prager Presse* leading the attack, the Czech newspapers were contending that Germany's troubles resulted from financial mismanagement, and the main nationalist organ was openly advocating international control of German finance. Holzhausen conceded, however, that rationality and national self-interest restrained Prague's political leadership from unmitigated rejoicing over Germany's difficulties. Government officials realized that Czechoslovakia could not long maintain its own strength if its neighbors, which normally took close to half of the Czechoslovak exports, suffered a protracted economic crisis. Moreover, officials were worried that the upheavals in Germany might sweep either the Communists or the extreme nationalists into control of the Reich, in either case creating a perilous situation for Czechoslovakia.[71] Not being sorry to witness Germany's predicament, the Czechs did not want to be affected themselves.

The Permanent Court of International Justice took the summer in its deliberations concerning the customs union, which, by the time that the court reached its decision, had become an almost forgotten issue. In the middle of August the Germans and the Austrians decided definitely to bury the project, and in the first week of September Curtius and Schober announced in the Commission of Inquiry for European Union that they were dropping their proposal for a customs union and dedicating their efforts to seeking wider international cooperation.[72] Two days later the court ruled by a vote of eight to seven that the customs union was incompatible with the Geneva Protocol of 1922. The justices could not agree on the reasons for their decision, however, and it was fortunate that their advisory opinion was already of no political significance.[73] Curtius resigned within a month; Schober was forced out of the Austrian cabinet during the winter.

Thus came to an end the Austro-German customs union proposal. It began as an effort by the Germans and the Austrians to bring off a diplomatic coup. Had it been accomplished, the governments in Berlin and Vienna could have won some popularity at home for the project was universally regarded as a first step toward a political union of the two countries. But officials in Berlin hoped for much more. They let their imaginations wander afield about subsequent accomplishments—German economic hegemony in the Danubian states, territorial concessions from Poland. Their plans were logical but not realistic. Instead of an eventual German **Mitteleuropa**, the project led to an immediate economic catastrophe. It was probably French financial pressure, created by the customs union announcement, that forced the disclosure in Vienna of the losses of the *Creditanstalt*.[74] The loss of confidence, indeed the panic among foreign creditors, that the news touched off, initiated a flight of capital from Germany that helped bring the country into bankruptcy. With Britain financially harassed as well, the Bank of England could give the Austrians only temporary support.[75] Ultimately the Austrian government had to apply for a loan to the League of Nations and that essentially meant to France. The prime requirement set by the French in the summer of 1931 was the abandonment of the customs union proposal. Vienna had no other choice but to comply.

With the balance of power being what it obviously was in the spring of 1931, Curtius and Schober made a gross miscalculation in deciding to launch the project. They were leading from weakness, hoping that they could sell the idea abroad as a means of overcoming the economic difficulties of Germany and Austria. They tried to cloak the project in pan-European garments, but they were really interested only in a regional grouping under Germanic influence in Central Europe. They underestimated the determination in Paris and Prague to block any step toward an Anschluss, and their bumbling diplomacy helped rouse opposition in Britain and Italy as well.

It has been argued that the project was one of the last opportunities to bring economic order to Central Europe and that its failure fatally weakened the domestic position of Brüning's government in Germany, thereby assisting Hitler's rise to power.[76] While there is some truth to these contentions, it is Brüning's government itself that must take the principal blame for undermining its own position within Germany. A customs union with Austria was an immoderate undertaking from the standpoint of foreign powers. But it was no radical innovation in the viewpoint of the politically unsophisticated voters in Germany, who were being beguiled by the simplistic notions of the Nazis. A customs union could hardly have fired the imagination of nationalist circles at home in the way that Nazi propaganda was doing. It was a mistake to try to compete with extremist tendencies in Germany, and it was also a mistake to try to exploit those tendencies in order to force concessions from foreign powers. To be sure, the aims of Germany's policymakers went far beyond a customs union with Austria, but they could not openly explain their strategy to the electorate, even though foreign statesmen such as Beneš recognized German goals.

German officials calculated quite rightly that the customs union would put great pressure on the Czechs. It is false to argue that the Czechs should have tolerated it so as to buttress the supposedly democratic forces in Germany. Beneš had to give precedence to the realities of the moment, not the possibilities of the future. Hitler's rise was by no means inevitable after the failure of the Austro-German plans. The customs union itself was the clear and present danger to the Czechs in 1931. Beneš subsequently claimed that he himself had initially mobilized French opposition to the plan.[77] French power, with helpful although not indispensable support from Czechoslovakia, was able to destroy the Austro-German proposal. But the fault lay in Berlin and Vienna. The German and Austrian leaders attempted a highly ambitious project without commanding the force necessary to accomplish it. They suffered an inevitable defeat.

THE DANUBIAN REALM

One of the most appealing and dangerous aspects of the Austro-German customs union proposal had been that it seemed to be a constructive move toward overcoming the economic fragmentation of Central and Southeastern Europe. It was for that reason that the British government hesitated before taking a stand against it, and on the same grounds the customs union proposal found widespread sympathy and support in the United States. The economic difficulties of the Danubian realm were very real, and they were compounded by the agricultural crisis and the Great Depression in the early 1930s. Neither the French nor the Czechs could afford to take a purely obstructionist stance against the customs union. Beneš's efforts to establish some kind of preferential tariff system among the Danubian states had failed in 1927 and 1928. Thereafter he undertook few if any initiatives in that regard. But the Western powers, notably Britain and France, remained apprehensive about the situation. Although the British thought that they could maintain an isolationist attitude toward the area, the French still considered the region vital for their own security. The main impetus in the early 1930s toward overcoming Danubian economic problems came from Paris.

In April and May 1931 the Czechs and the French responded to the customs union proposal with plans of their own, which concentrated on economic problems in Southeastern Europe. In the Czechoslovak Ministry of Foreign Affairs a project was formulated that tried to divide Europe into two separate cartels of industrial and agrarian states. The proposal was that the industrial countries would grant preferential tariffs to the agrarian states of Central and Southeastern Europe. In addition, each group of states would consult among themselves about limiting production and dividing markets. The Czechs placed Czechoslovakia in both cartels—the only country to be so honored—and they frankly stated in their internal diplomatic correspondence that their primary goal was to liquidate German influence in Southeastern Europe. "With this [Czechoslovak project] the primary reason for German influence in Southeast Europe becomes inoperative. Germany will not be able to use its greater powers of consumption and its economic dominance in order to win the agrarian countries for its plan."[78]

The French took the Czechoslovak project and made two significant modifications. They proposed that all the states in the plan grant unilateral preferences to Austrian products, and they argued that the agrarian states should also adopt preferential tariffs on the products of the industrial countries. It was this latter point that aroused opposition. To the agrarian states of Southeastern Europe, the creation of cartels and of reciprocal preferential tariffs between industrial and agrarian states threatened to perpetuate the existing division of labor. The agrarian countries might be relegated simply to supplying foodstuffs and raw materials to the industrial powers of Central and Western Europe. At the Little Entente conference in early May the Rumanian and Yugoslav foreign ministers exacted from Beneš a promise to oppose the French plan before they agreed to take a public stand against the Austro-German customs union. Their impression seemed to be that the French were treating them like a colonial area. The result was that the French were unable to force adoption of any alternative scheme to the Austro-German plans.[79]

Cartels were attractive to the French as a precondition for the elimination of protective tariffs because they also feared the potential of German industrial competition. If production quotas, prices, and marketing territories were fixed for various industries by international agreement, then the French could safely dispense with protective tariffs. But until such security existed the French resolutely refused to abandon protective tariffs, and they rejected suggestions that Germany and France form a customs union. At the time of the Austro-German announcement Beneš argued that no great power could enter a customs union with a small country without quickly dominating that country. He urged instead that the Germans come to a general understanding with the French, after which both nations could talk about closer ties with the Danubian region. According to the paraphrase of the Austrian minister, Beneš exclaimed that he would enter "with closed eyes" into a plan for economic and political cooperation among France, Germany, Austria, and Czechoslovakia.[80] But the French were afraid, and their minister in Prague had already emphasized that there could be no thought of a customs union between Germany and France even in a pan-European framework. The Germans exported twice as much to France as the French did to Germany, and "French industry would be dead if one were to open the borders to German export trade."[81] France and Czechoslovakia temporarily enjoyed a superior financial position in 1931, in part because of the protective measures they had taken, and in part because their economies were more balanced and more nearly self-sufficient. But neither country, certainly not Czechoslovakia, and not even France, was a match for a great industrial power such as Germany. Just as the French ultimately proved unable to defend the Czechs in a diplomatic and a military sense, so also were they unable to protect them economically.

Through the summer of 1931 Beneš maintained his cool and reserved attitude toward the Germans and the Austrians as they floundered in the aftermath of the customs union debacle. In regard to Austria he continued to advocate a "special relationship" between the two countries without ever specifying just what the nature of such a relationship would be. He made it clear that he was awaiting an initiative from the Austrian side. At the same time he spoke in a very pessimistic fashion about domestic political developments in Germany. He foresaw bloody confrontations between the Right and the Left in Germany (actually they were occurring at the time), and he thought that it might be unavoidable that rightist forces would take over the government in Berlin. Only then would they discover that they could do no more to improve Germany's condition than the Brüning government was attempting. Beneš also warned against the Italians and pointed to British difficulties, all in an obvious effort to woo the Austrians toward a closer identification with the Franco-Czechoslovak orbit.[82] One of Beneš's favorite ideas at the time called for special economic ties among Czechoslovakia, Austria, and Hungary, but the scheme never materialized into any tangible proposal.[83] Certainly, popular attitudes in Budapest prevented such a construct. Beneš had long been aware of that basic fact, and he could not have been sanguine about the possibility of any practical accomplishments.

The estrangement between Prague and Berlin continued until after the resignation of Curtius in early October 1931, after which Brüning himself assumed the portfolio for foreign affairs. Beneš then took steps to renew his contacts with the Germans. He liked to work occasionally through unofficial channels in dealing with Berlin, as his conversations with Beer in

1928 and Regendanz in 1931 indicate. At the end of October 1931 he arranged a meeting in his home with Baron Kurt von Lersner, who was in Prague on a private visit.[84] Beneš used the opportunity for a general review of European political problems as they affected Czechoslovak-German relations.

At the time that Beneš and Lersner conversed, the Hoover moratorium on inter-governmental payments was in effect, but the final disposition of the reparations problem was still by no means certain. Beneš remarked to Lersner that Germany's obligations ought to be cancelled except for a small token payment for the reconstruction of French territories laid waste in the war. That suggestion represented a significant concession to the Germans, and it was something that Beneš had never mentioned in his public utterances. Beneš's proposal to remove Germany's obligations anticipated the Lausanne agreement of the summer of 1932. His accuracy in forecasting the settlement of the reparations problem was a striking parallel to his suggestions in 1923 that presaged the Dawes plan. Although Beneš predicted the solution of the reparations problem, he saw little hope for positive accomplishments by the disarmament conference, which was due to convene in February 1932. Subsequent events again proved his expectations to be correct.[85]

Coming shortly after the abandonment of the customs union attempt, the most interesting of Beneš's remarks concerned Central European affairs.

> Here I am very specially interested. I fought violently against the Austro-German customs union. I want a confederation of the small states: Czechoslovakia, Hungary, Yugoslavia, Rumania, perhaps Austria. At its head this Central Europe must not have Germany, not France, not Italy, but rather it must be independent, with equal rights for all its members.—Until death I am a true friend of France. But I will not let myself be pushed into a war by means of a union in Central Europe.—I am also a friend of Germany. Why does Germany mistrust me and misjudge my good intentions?[86]

Lersner answered Beneš's question by pointing to the "oppressed Bohemian Germandom." Beneš shot back that the Sudeten Germans were not persecuted, that no other minority anywhere was treated so well, that fully two-thirds of the Sudeten Germans were completely satisfied in Czechoslovakia. Lersner pointed out that no signs in German were allowed in Prague, to which Beneš responded that the situation was stupid but that in view of the earlier germanization in Prague it was understandable.[87]

By arranging the conversation with Lersner and speaking freely, Beneš clearly hoped to revive something of the more cordial atmosphere between Prague and Berlin that had existed in Stresemann's lifetime. Yet it is worth noting that the problem areas touched upon in the conversation were the same that had troubled Czechoslovak-German relations ever since 1918. Despite the fact that feelings were much more strained by 1931, the changes in political personalities in Berlin had brought no basic shifts in policy. It was on the basis of Stresemann's accomplishments that the new directors of German foreign policy focused their attention on Central Europe in the early 1930s. Beneš, in view of his obvious pride in his own diplomatic abilities, tended to overestimate the importance of personalities in diplomacy, and he appeared to expect a more conciliatory attitude from Berlin after Curtius's resignation. According to Lersner, Beneš remarked: "I will see what I can do toward cooperation between Germany and us and how Germany can learn to understand us better."[88] But Germany had to understand Beneš on his own terms, and that meant accepting the Versailles system. Beneš emphasized his oft-repeated conviction that a permanent settlement in Europe could come about only by a general understanding between France and Germany, and he indirectly offered his services as a mediator between Paris and Berlin. Beneš had modified nothing in his own foreign policy.

The last significant effort to overcome the fragmentation of the Danubian area occurred in the spring of 1932. In January Briand finally resigned his direction of French foreign policy. Only a shadow of his former self, he died in March. With a change of cabinets André Tardieu became premier and foreign minister in February and quickly launched a proposal for the Danubian area that became known as the Tardieu plan. As it eventually developed, the plan called for the establishment of a preferential tariff system among Austria, Hungary, Czechoslovakia, Rumania, and Yugoslovia. The five Danubian states were to make reciprocal reductions of 10 percent in their tariffs; and certain other countries, the most important of which were Germany and Italy, were to grant preferential rates to Danubian agricultural products. Tardieu also suggested that an international loan be raised to support the Danubian currencies.[89] Actually Tardieu's proposal was nothing more than what Beneš had long been advocating. From the beginning it was stated that the political sovereignty of the Danubian states could in no way be compromised, and the idea of preferential tariffs was adopted as a way of avoiding any central economic organization in Southeast Europe. But, in order to make preferential tariffs possible, other powers had to be willing to waive the most-favored-nation clause, which was still a part of most commercial treaties. Tardieu therefore turned first to the three other great powers in Europe—Britain, Germany, and Italy.

None of those countries were enthusiastic about Tardieu's suggestion. Under the economic conditions of 1932, British leaders were reluctant to agree to a preferential tariff system among foreign states, which would put British exports at a disadvantage relative to the products of those countries within the system.[90] Moreover, the British were in no position to guarantee loans to the Danubian states. On the other hand, British commercial interests in the Danubian area were insignificant, and London could hardly object to the device of preferential tariffs as such, inasmuch as the British Empire itself was moving away from free trade and toward an imperial preferential system. The British government maintained a reserved attitude and let Italy and Germany take the lead in defeating Tardieu's proposal. Mussolini could always be counted upon for open displays of opposition to France, especially in Southeastern Europe. The real economic interests of Italy were not seriously affected by the Tardieu plan, but the quest for importance and prestige particularly characteristic of fascist diplomacy propelled Mussolini toward ostentatious obstructionism.

Germany had far greater interests in the Danubian region than any other great power. Even Beneš had to admit that a preferential system would disadvantage German exports to the region although he tried to minimize the extent and the duration of the losses. He tried to persuade the German minister that an economic system in Southeastern Europe would offer better markets for Germany in the long run, but in view of its economic plight in 1932 the German government was unwilling to suffer immediate losses for potential long-term gains.[91] At least as significant from the German viewpoint as the economic effects were the political implications of the project. In a grouping of the Little Entente, Austria, and Hungary the dominance would be on the side of the status-quo powers. Beneš clearly aspired to the unofficial leadership of the area just as he was *primus inter pares* within the Little Entente, and Berlin officials regarded him as simply the tool of French policy. Thus the Tardieu plan demanded economic sacrifices by the Germans for a project that threatened to solidify the paramountcy of French political influence in the Danubian realm. German government officials were sure that a Danubian preferential system would be interpreted as a diplomatic defeat for Germany, and they felt that they had to obstruct its realization for domestic political reasons.[92]

Beneš realized all too well the many difficulties confronting a preferential tariff system, and he maintained a cautious attitude toward it in public. Although Beneš had privately advocated preferential tariffs for years, he had consistently refused to make any specific proposals. Affirming that he had a very definite plan in mind, he had always claimed that the time was not yet ripe to introduce it. Beneš most likely did not welcome the intervention of the French and the negotiations among the great powers about the Tardieu proposal. He feared the dominant influence of any great power in the area, and there were some indications that the French also had in mind the establishment of a currency union or even a political confederation. Beneš opposed any such scheme that seemed to threaten Czechoslovak sovereignty.[93] Any tendency among the Western powers to consult among themselves and then force their collective will on the small states of Central and Southeastern Europe particularly aroused Beneš's ire. He feared that the French would concede too much in a conference with Britain, Germany, and Italy. For Beneš the "greatest danger" was that Czechoslovakia and the Little Entente would be left to stand alone against the agreements of those four powers.[94] He emphasized to the Austrian minister in particular that the small states of the Danubian region would have to solve their own problems among themselves so as to prevent the intervention of outside powers.[95] But from his own experience he knew the many barriers to voluntary cooperation among the Danubian states. Within his own country Agrarian interests persisted in their opposition to preferential tariffs on agricultural products. Beneš finally remarked to the Austrian minister that if anything were to be accomplished it would have to be done quickly and suddenly. Otherwise vested interests in all the Danubian countries would undermine any possibility of an international agreement.[96]

During the discussion about Tardieu's ideas the German government offered a countersuggestion that seemed to be aimed specifically against Czechoslovakia and that unleashed a storm of indignation in Prague. The German proposal was that the Danubian association be a purely agricultural one, which could be accomplished by including Bulgaria and excluding Czechoslovakia.[97] Such a realignment could tip the balance in favor of the revisionist powers. The Germans clearly intended to prevent Czechoslovakia from gaining trade advantages or exercising greater political influence in the Danubian area. And the inclusion of Rumania and Yugoslavia in a grouping of which Czechoslovakia was not a member could have a disruptive effect on the Little Entente. Beneš feared just such a possibility. In private conversations he attempted to persuade the Austrians to support Tardieu's proposals, and he became increasingly perturbed with Austrian prevarication.[98] At the same time he gave cautious public support to the Tardieu plan in a major foreign policy address to the Czechoslovak parliament, but he noted that Germany and Italy would be likely to veto the project.[99]

The debate about the Tardieu plan reached its climax when Prime Minister Ramsay MacDonald invited representatives of France, Germany, and Italy to discuss the issue in London in April 1932. Tardieu came early, and from his conversations with MacDonald it appeared that the initial British hesitation about a preferential tariff system was smoothed over.[100] Despite the appearance of a united British and French front, the German and Italian representatives demonstrated their adamant opposition to the Tardieu plan from the time of their arrival in London. The four powers could not agree even to invite representatives of the Danubian states to consult on the matter, and the London conference quickly adjourned.[101] The decision came as no surprise in Prague, but that portion of the press that was under Beneš's influence did attempt to make propaganda capital out of the conference. The *Central European Observer* editorialized that Berlin and Rome would henceforth have no right to complain about the "Balkanization" of Eastern Europe.[102]

Actually the Tardieu plan was only a sequel to the Austro-German customs union proposal. The French and the Czechs had defeated the Austro-German project, and the Germans participated decisively in the opposition to the Tardieu plan. Each side had enough power to sabotage the undertakings of the other, but nobody could accomplish anything positive. The Danubian region was left divided and weak, an easy prey for a revived and militant Germany under Hitler. But even before Hitler's seizure of power, German government and business circles were already developing the devices by which Germany's dominant influence eventually pervaded the Danubian area.

During the prosperous years of the mid-1920s the keynote of German trade policy had been its emphasis on most-favored-nation treatment. In the negotiations for trade treaties German bargainers had insisted on that clause as a sine qua non. Their policy reflected the optimistic outlook of the Stresemann years and the confidence that German products could compete effectively in the world market. But when the depression gripped Germany the trend among the Germans, as among others, was toward increased protection and an attempt to establish special trading relationships with selected foreign countries. From 1930 German trade policy moved away from the most-favored-nation policy and toward a preferential tariff system. The primary focus of those preferences was the Danubian area. During the discussions about the Tardieu proposal the Germans offered to grant unilateral preferences to Austria. At the London conference, Bülow, who was the chief German delegate, proposed an extension of those preferences to agricultural products from the rest of Southeastern Europe.[103] The proposals were clearly designed to bring the Danubian countries into a closer relationship with Germany, and the Czechs had apprehensions about that policy. With their French allies, they opposed unilateral German preferences and warned that any attempt to divide Central Europe into separate industrial and agricultural trading areas would meet Czechoslovak opposition.[104]

Nor did the leaders in Southeastern Europe want to see their countries relegated to the permanent status of supplying foodstuffs to Central Europe's great industrial power. But at the moment they had to find markets for their surplus agriculture, and Germany was the only country that showed both the interest and the capability of absorbing their products. As early as 1930, Berlin's initial efforts to extend tariff preferences to Danubian agriculture had been thwarted by other countries with whom Germany had most-favored-nation agreements. Between 1929 and 1934 German trade with the Danubian area underwent a steady decline. But already under Brüning preferential import quotas were extended and barter agreements were concluded with Southeast European states. At the same time countries in the area were adopting clearing agreements in an attempt to overcome the currency crisis and maintain international trade. Those agreements disrupted old trade patterns and propelled the countries toward a bilateralism in international trade by which they tried to balance their imports and exports with any given foreign state.[105] That system left the small states particularly vulnerable and weak before a great power such as Germany. Although Germany had maintained an active trade balance with the Danubian area throughout the 1920s, already in 1932 statistics showed an import surplus for Germany. That trend quickened under Hitler as Germany paid higher than normal prices and greatly expanded its imports from the Danubian states. Having built up a big debt in the clearing agreements with the Danubian states by the mid-1930s, the Germans used that debt as a means of pressuring those countries to import more German products. The result was that most of the small states were absorbed into the German economic sphere, and they became economic satellites of Germany long before they were military allies or victims. In this respect Hitler merely continued policies, carrying them to their extreme but logical conclusions, that he had inherited from his Weimar predecessors.[106] The use of German economic power for political purposes was a common characteristic of the Weimar republic and the Third Reich. Still, that does not mean that Weimar trade policies were formulated with the goal of preparing for the kind of militaristic expansionism that Hitler pursued.

In the wake of the economic crisis of the early 1930s the limitations of the Little Entente became increasingly apparent. Hungarian revisionism and the threat of a Habsburg restoration had furnished the only cement for the alliance of the 1920s, but by the depression years those dangers had subsided. The Little Entente was not designed as a general alliance for dealing collectively with the great powers. German diplomacy never treated the Little Entente states as a unit, although there was a general recognition that Czechoslovakia, Rumania, and Yugoslavia were in varying degrees allies of France. The diplomats from the Little Entente states distanced themselves from one another in dealing with the Germans and the Austrians. In 1931 at least one Yugoslav diplomat claimed that King Alexander favored a German orientation and that there were political struggles in Belgrade concerning a potential realignment of the country's foreign policy.[107] It has been seen that Czechoslovak leaders were uneasy about the possibility of an agrarian bloc that would divide the Little Entente and that they faced difficulties in persuading the Rumanians and the Yugoslavs to oppose the Austro-German customs union proposal. Additional tensions developed as Rumania and Yugoslavia came under authoritarian governments unsympathetic to the parliamentary methods of Prague.

The fragmentation of Southeastern Europe was a source of great weakness for Prague, and Beneš went to extreme lengths to cultivate the myth of the unity of the Little Entente as a general alliance. In May 1932, after the meeting of the Little Entente foreign ministers in Belgrade, Beneš sent a circular dispatch to Czechoslovak missions abroad claiming that agreement among the partners was complete. "The consciousness of the necessity of political cooperation was more immediate than ever, just as was the recognition of the political and also economic danger from Germany. The general political and economic policy that I have represented at all conferences since 1927 found common support." He admitted in the dispatch that he had given his agreement to bilateral preferential treaties with Germany and Italy. But he characterized them as only "a provisional and momentary solution" to Danubian economic problems that must never cause the diplomats to lose sight of "our final common goal . . . our Central Europe in which the Little Entente will be the foundation of the reorganization."[108] In that dispatch Beneš was propagandizing his own foreign service, as his secret memorandum about his conversation with King Alexander at the conference demonstrated. Alexander and Beneš agreed that Czechoslovakia and Yugoslavia made up the real core of the Little Entente and that Rumania was "something like a blind passenger" that could not be relied upon when the going got rough. Beneš characterized King Carol as a "politically inexperienced man" surrounded by "unreliable people." Carol was "sympathetic to Germany," but Beneš had tried to enlighten him about German policy.[109] Alexander and Beneš were correct about the unreliability of Rumania, but the ties between Belgrade and Prague were not so firm as the two men were pretending to one another. Beneš's public reassurances that the Little Entente was in good health were true only in relation to its original purpose of combatting Hungarian revisionism. It was not an effective alliance in dealing with the basic problems confronting its member states in the 1930s—the threat of German, Italian, and Soviet expansionism. The flame of Little Entente unity flickered brightly in 1933—but then quickly died, leaving only the memory of unrealized dreams.

The Demise of Weimar and Versailles

The maintenance of the international order that had been created by the peace treaties depended on the existence of a German government that recognized their legal validity. Every coalition during the Weimar republic worked toward a revision of the Treaty of Versailles, but revisionism itself presupposed an acceptance of the legality of that treaty. Why work to revise an agreement if one does not feel bound by it? To be sure there were numerous minor violations of the Treaty of Versailles, but their peripheral significance only emphasized the basic constraint felt by German governments to observe it. The willingness of the Western powers to enforce the treaty encouraged Weimar politicians to recognize the basic legitimacy of the diplomatic system. The Germans worked within it to alter the specific peace terms to which they most objected. But by 1932 the Weimar republic was in full dissolution. If Hitler's seizure of power was not inevitable, the demise of Weimar democracy was. Whether a democratic system could have eventually been reconstituted in Germany can be only a matter of conjecture, but the constitutional system of 1919 had ceased to function. Simultaneously, in international relations statesmen groped for agreements in the two major problem-areas—reparations and disarmament—that had been the focal point of most disputes since the peace conference. But the Versailles system was already discredited in the minds of many of these statesmen of the Western powers whose support was necessary if it were to survive. They lacked the resolve to enforce the peace treaties against a great power that was no longer willing to accept the validity of the system. Weimar and Versailles were collapsing simultaneously. The triumph of Hitler spelled the defeat of the peace-makers.

By 1932 Beneš was one of the very few statesmen in Europe who were still fully committed to the peace treaties. Under his direction Czechoslovakia remained more firmly a status-quo power than almost any other country. Beneš continued his characteristically rapid pace of diplomatic activity throughout the year, making trips to Belgrade, Paris, and London, and immersing himself in League activities in Geneva. Always he was on the opposite side from the Germans, who rightly considered him one of the biggest obstacles to their revisionist policies. Between the summers of 1931 and 1932 the Hoover moratorium on intergovernmental payments remained in effect, but a new agreement on the reparations issue was still necessary. A conference was called to meet in Lausanne in June 1932. In preparation for the meeting Beneš insisted that Germany should resume reparation payments after the moratorium. (His official position therefore differed fundamentally from the ideas that he had broached to Lersner in October 1931.) Beneš thought that if the Germans should refuse on principle to continue payments, the conference ought to be allowed to fail. Beneš conceded that the Allies could reduce the sum total of reparations and the length of time that the Germans would be held liable for reparation payments, but he opposed any concession at all unless the Germans gave assurances that they would meet their new obligations. In the case of a German refusal to make further payments he believed that "a very serious legal and political situation" would develop, the consequences of which he did not predict. He did note, however, that Czechoslovakia's position on war debts to America would be eased. If the former enemies would not pay, why should the Allies?[110]

The decisions of the Lausanne reparations conference were considerably more liberal toward Germany than Beneš had desired. The conference freed Germany of its reparation obligations. Only a small final payment was due, and, as events turned out, it was never paid.[111] Technically, the concessions to Germany were dependent on cancellation of Allied war debts by the United States, but the American Congress subsequently refused to drop the claims on the former allies. Therefore, from a legal standpoint, the Young plan should have come back into force; but after Hitler took control of Germany there was never any question of the Third Reich paying reparations. America's debtors went into default, and the reparations-war debts controversy came to an unnegotiated but natural end, leaving behind universal resentment.

The most important event for European diplomacy in 1932 was the opening of the disarmament conference in February. After years of preparation, representatives of almost every country in the world met in Geneva in an attempt to find a solution to one of the most troublesome legacies of the peace settlements. Despite various compromise proposals no reconciliation could be found between the French insistence on security and the German demand for equality in armaments. The first session of the conference adjourned in July, and the Germans refused to return until their right to equality had been recognized in principle. Only in December 1932 was a formula found under which negotiations could be resumed. The conference reconvened in February 1933, but it had long been moribund before Hitler administered the coup de grâce by announcing German withdrawal in October 1933.[112]

It has already been seen that Beneš was pessimistic about the chances of the disarmament conference as early as his talk with Lersner in October 1931.[113] In his speech in March 1932 in which he gave tepid support to the Tardieu plan, Beneš publicly expressed his skepticism about early disarmament. He completely sympathized with the French desire for security, and he claimed that the international situation was too volatile for extensive disarmament to be practicable in 1932.[114] Although Beneš had been disappointed in his efforts to become president of the disarmament conference, he did receive the important position of rapporteur to the general commission of the conference. In that capacity he was extremely active in attempting to frame agreements that could find general support and still insure the security of France and its eastern allies. His most notable effort came at the conclusion of the first session of the conference in July 1932. Beneš introduced the summary resolution, which was opposed by the German representative because it contained no recognition of equal rights for Germany and to which the Germans objected by refusing to return to the conference. Through the autumn of 1932 the German government insisted that a disarmament convention must abrogate the disarmament provisions of the Treaty of Versailles while Beneš supported the French position that the Versailles restrictions should be incorporated into a general convention.[115] In early October the British foreign secretary, Sir John Simon, invited representatives of France, Italy, and Germany to an informal conference with the British, but the powers could not even agree on a choice of site.[116] The invitation was another sign of a mounting tendency of the great powers to attempt to resolve their differences in concert among themselves and to the exclusion of the small powers. Many leaders of the smaller powers, among whom Beneš was in the forefront, were becoming increasingly apprehensive.[117]

The negotiations in Geneva kept Beneš away from Prague much of the time, but his time-honored habit was to return to his capital amidst a display of public optimism about the accomplishments that had been achieved while he was abroad. Upon his return in the autumn, therefore, his pessimism about the international situation created a sensation in the local diplomatic corps. Beneš was predicting that there would be a war within two years if Bolshevism had not by that time already spread across the continent. The European countries were plunging toward self-destruction with their autarkic economic policies. Germany was preparing to revive the Corridor question, an action which would set off the landslide.[118] About these ideas the German minister commented in his report to Berlin that only those who did not know Beneš could accept his remarks as the "confessions of an upright soul." Rather, Koch added, Beneš saw that the disarmament conference was doomed, and he was trying to lay the blame on Germany. Koch concluded: "I have the impression: Scarcely anytime has Beneš worked so unconditionally in the pay of France as now."[119] To a certain extent Koch's analysis was correct, except that Beneš was actually even less willing to seek compromises with revisionist powers than the French government was under Edouard Herriot.

Beneš admitted his grave concern about the international situation in his parliamentary exposé of November 7, which he ominously entitled, "War or Peace." He pointed to the harm being done to German democracy by the repeated elections and Hitler's growing power. He said that the Papen-Schleicher regime was mistrusted abroad because it stood under military influence, and he concluded that the peace of Europe depended on what would happen in Germany. Beneš blamed not only Germany and its revisionist friends for the difficulties in Europe but also Great Britain and the United States, who, he said, had made a continental peace system impossible by their refusal to participate in European affairs. He admitted that an extension of the Locarno guarantees to Central and Eastern Europe was impossible, but he emphasized that the British and the Americans should make it clear that they would not remain indifferent in case of a conflict in the region.[120] A few days later Beneš tried to take some of the force out of his pessimistic remarks by speaking of the good relations between Czechoslovakia and Germany since the founding of the republics.[121] But it was plain that he was worried about European affairs, and he had every right to be.

Within a few days after his speech Beneš left on another trip to Paris and London in an effort to mediate differences that had arisen between the French and the British governments about the disarmament negotiations. The central question concerned the means of insuring French security. The focus of the problem was Central Europe, and the dispute was the same that had existed since the peace conference. The French thought in terms of continental-wide defense; the British were willing to make commitments only as far as the Rhine. To Prime Minister Ramsay MacDonald Beneš emphasized that Germany could be granted equality in armaments only under certain conditions. The Germans must deliver a solemn declaration that they would never resort to force to revise the peace treaties or to solve political problems. Actual equality in armaments could be attained only by stages, and after each stage an examination should be made as to "how the Germans had conducted themselves." And equality in armaments must not mean German rearmament.[122] Beneš thought that MacDonald agreed on those conditions, and Beneš happily reported to both Prague and Paris that British opinion in general was more sympathetic to the French position and more hostile toward the Germans than it had been previously.[123] But MacDonald himself admitted that differences of opinion existed within the British cabinet, and later in the month Sir John Simon made another speech more sympathetic to the Germans than Beneš had expected.[124]

Influential people within the British Foreign Office were not simply neutral or disinterested in Central European affairs. Since the early 1920s there had been a mounting tide of suspicion and even hostility toward the successor states. Lloyd George's opposition to Poland in the Upper Silesian dispute and Rothermere's campaign for a revision of the Treaty of Trianon reflected attitudes that were widespread in important London circles. It has been seen that the cordiality in British-Czechoslovak relations was largely dissipated in 1924 with the formal conclusion of the Franco-Czechoslovak alliance and the British rejection of the Geneva Protocol. Thereafter the British diplomatic documents contained more and more negative comments about the Czechs, and the British minister in Prague in the early 1930s supplied a considerable portion of them.

Joseph Addison came to Prague from Latvia in the spring of 1930. Before his service in Riga he had been stationed at the British embassy in Berlin. Once in Prague he required only a few months to formulate very definite opinions about Czechoslovakia. In his official report for the year 1930 Addison called Beneš the "Little Jack Horner" of Europe,[125] added that militarily "the country simply could not be defended," and observed that the nationalities question was complicated by a Czech "inferiority complex" resulting from fear, insecurity, and "the instinct of centuries that the Austrians and Hungarians are superior human beings." He believed that "an English statesman would probably have realized that the wisest course lay in conciliating these minorities and in pursuing a policy of appeasement and frank friendship with these countries, constituting as they do a necessary economic complement. But moderation of character and temperance in aim are conspicuous by their absence."[126] By July 1931 Addison wrote in a private letter to Omar Sargent, an official in the British Foreign Office, that:

> Czechoslovakia is an injustice—i.e., it is a fictitious country founded on several injustices and maintained by the continuance of injustice and the apparent impossibility of putting an end to it without a convulsion which it is to the general interest to avoid.[127]

Addison could comfort himself, however, because Czechs liked the British, who seemed to be "a strong silent race of supermen," who in peacetime combined "modest stillness and humility" with "quiet dignity."[128] In November Addison finally asked:

> Can we get back to the state of affairs in which the Slovaks return to their natural job of scrubbing floors and cleaning windows, the Romanians are confined to the exercise of their only national industry (according to Lord D'Abernon's statement in an official memorandum this is fornication), the Poles are restricted to piano playing and the white slave traffic and the Serbs are controlled in their great national activity—organizing political murders on foreign territory? Can we hand Europe back to those who are competent to run it? I doubt it. If this is pessimism, then I am a pessimist.[129]

Sargent's response asked for more letters like that because "fireworks which really communicate are always welcome."[130]

Addison's reports were popular in the Foreign Office. Witty and urbane, haughty and dogmatic, he enlivened the dull days of bureaucrats with half-truths and parochial prejudices. Addison's attitudes were shared by others in the Foreign Office, whose marginal comments referred to the Czechs as "arrant prigs . . . suffering from persecution mania."[131] In 1930 officials in the Central European division successfully blocked attempts by London University to invite Masaryk to Britain and confer upon him an honorary degree. They did not want Masaryk in London, for such a demonstration of solidarity with the Czechs was not in accord with British policy.[132] To be sure, there were differences of opinion within the Foreign Office, and not everyone was anti-Czech. But the dominant tone of the documents was highly critical of the Czechs. It is also true that people in the secondary levels of the Foreign Office were not ultimately responsible for the formulation and conduct of British foreign policy. They were, however, the "experts" upon whom higher officials relied for their information about a distant and little-known country. And, given the British policy of disinterest and noninvolvement in Central Europe, it was easy enough to accept and believe the negative judgments about Czechoslovakia.

There is little wonder that Beneš oriented Czechoslovak foreign policy around Paris, but by late 1932 the French government was showing unmistakable signs of neglecting its allies in favor of new approaches for insuring French security. In October MacDonald called for a consultation of representatives from Britain, France, Italy, and Germany in order to break the deadlock in the disarmament negotiations. As has been seen, the proposal aroused Beneš's apprehensions even though it failed to materialize into any concrete action. The idea evidently inspired Mussolini, however, who quickly began to advocate a four-power directory in Europe.[133] It is likely that Mussolini hoped to play the role of mediator, along with the British, between France and Germany. He could thereby feed his appetite for prestige and perhaps undermine the French diplomatic position in Central and Southeastern Europe. Mussolini sought support for his initiatives in Austria and Hungary in particular, attempting to trade economic concessions for political support. Mussolini's diplomatic offensive placed the French in much the same position as Stresemann's had done in 1925. Possibly a four-power directory could give France added assurances for its own security. But should the French buy these advantages at the price of weakening their ties with their Eastern European allies? Moreover, the political chaos in Germany and the mounting threat of Nazism were already confronting French policymakers with a terrible dilemma. Given simultaneous aggressiveness in both Italy and Germany, should one attempt to appease the Italians in order to gain their support against the Germans? The French government subsequently elected to follow that policy during the Ethiopian conflict in 1935. In their conversations with Mussolini and his subordinates in late 1932 and early 1933 French diplomats were already moving toward that decision.

In November 1932 Beneš hopefully believed that the obstacles to a Franco-Italian rapprochement were insurmountable. He was convinced that Mussolini's foreign policy remained inimical to French interests on the continent. He anticipated that Mussolini planned to support the Germans in the Polish Corridor question and recognize Czechoslovakia as a sphere of German influence, in return for German recognition of Italian dominance in Austria and Hungary as well as a neutralization of Yugoslavia. In the meantime the Italian fascists would continue to "coquet" with the Nazis, and if Hitler should come to power he and Mussolini would launch "a grandiose system of cooperative blackmail against all others."[134] For Beneš the optimum response to such a threat was a universal security system, and he remained one of the most fervent supporters of the League of Nations. Beneš was outspoken in opposing recognition of the Japanese conquest of Manchuria because he feared the creation of an "analogue" for European affairs.[135]

But the Japanese succeeded in Manchuria and dealt the League a decisive blow. If the great powers could not or would not support collective security, Beneš was prepared to search for regional assurances for his own country. By December 1932 warnings were rife in Prague that the German government was preparing to make an immediate issue of the Corridor question. There were demonstrations of loyalty and solidarity with Poland.[136] Also in December a special conference of the Little Entente was hurriedly convoked in Belgrade in order to discuss the threat of a great-power directory of European affairs. The foreign ministers agreed to create a permanent council, which would meet at least three times a year, and to establish a permanent secretariat, which would make preparations for the meetings and encourage political and economic cooperation among the states of the Little Entente. They formalized the agreement in February 1933 in Geneva by signing a "pact of organization." Each of the member states of the Little Entente agreed to seek the approval of its partners before signing new treaties and to bring existing treaties into line with the organizational pact. The original Little Entente treaties of 1920-21 were renewed in perpetuity.[137] Diplomatic observers attributed little fresh significance to the organizational pact and believed that it simply put into force agreements that had existed for several years. Yet the pact did demonstrate that the states of the Little Entente still hoped to coalesce into a united front despite their internal differences when an outside menace arose. The threat that drove them together was not Hitler's Nazi regime, which was established only after the agreement to conclude the organizational pact. Rather the revisionist currents in general and the move toward a European great-power directory in particular again stimulated vain hopes that the Little Entente could function as a unit in European diplomacy.

Nothing demonstrated the loss of faith in the Versailles system quite so much as the negotiations for the Four Power Pact in 1932 and 1933. After Mussolini first proposed the project in October 1932, private diplomatic conversations kept the idea alive for the next several months. Then in March Ramsay MacDonald and Sir John Simon paid an official visit to

Rome and reached an understanding about the nature of the proposed agreement. Britain and Italy were to act as mediators between France and Germany; the four powers would agree on revisions in the peace treaties in order to prevent "outbreaks of violence"; and, the smaller powers were to recognize the "hierarchy of the powers" and acquiesce to the decisions of the directory.[138]

Despite some strong opposition in France to those proposals the economic crisis had finally struck the country in 1932, and the French no longer possessed the dominant position in European affairs that they had enjoyed in 1931. The governments of Edouard Herriot, Joseph Paul-Boncour, and Edouard Daladier in late 1932 and 1933 seemed more pliable than the earlier cabinets of Pierre Laval and André Tardieu. Partly in order to strengthen French resistance, Beneš and the Rumanian foreign minister, Nicolas Titulescu, issued a stern warning a few days after the Rome meeting against any attempt to revise the peace treaties without consulting all the states affected by such undertakings.[139] Weeks earlier Krofta had emphasized in a private conversation with the Austrian minister that Poland and the states of the Little Entente would not permit territorial losses to be forced upon them and that any such attempt would mean war.[140] When Beneš returned from Geneva in late March, he heatedly exclaimed to Masaryk that the whole world was a "nut house" and that he repeatedly had been forced to "thrash his way" into discussions in Geneva about the Four Power Pact.[141] A few weeks later he devoted one of his parliamentary speeches to the proposal and warned again that no group of powers could dispose of questions affecting Czechoslovakia without consulting Prague. To him the idea of a four-power directory in Europe was contrary to the fundamental principles of the League of Nations to which he remained firmly committed. He repeated publicly that the Czechs would resist with force if necessary any attempt to alter the boundaries of the country.[142]

The violent opposition of France's eastern allies caused the Four Power Pact to be diluted to the point of insignificance by the time that it was finally signed in June. But the whole idea mirrored the demise of the Versailles system. Peace was to be maintained not by upholding but by making revisions in the peace treaties. Revisions were to be made not by universal agreement but as a result of the dictates of the great powers. Faith in the philosophical foundations of the peace settlement as well as in specific decisions taken at Paris in 1919 had been undermined. In British foreign policy appeasement was already beginning. It was not a policy of grudgingly acquiescing to demands backed by superior force: there was no military threat from Hitler or anyone else in 1933. Whatever its internal debates, the British government grew receptive to the idea of taking the initiative and making changes in order to prevent future confrontations.

Appeasement became basically an aggressive and dynamic foreign policy.[143] It was ill-conceived and misapplied, and the British carried with them a France that by 1933 was already weak and wavering. The four-power directory functioned only once—to dismember Czechoslovakia at Munich in 1938. No one in 1933 could foresee that event, but Beneš did recognize from the beginning the potentially disastrous implications for Czechoslovakia of a great-power directory. The Versailles system, and with it the security of the Czechoslovak republic, was destroyed more fully by Beneš's allies than by his enemies, and the destruction was in process before Hitler controlled Germany.

Hitler's seizure of power in 1933 was therefore something of an anticlimax for the Czechs. Throughout the long ordeal the death throes of Weimar had been closely observed from Prague, and the likelihood of a Nazi regime in Germany had already been accepted. A brief survey of German politics during 1932 and the reactions in Prague to the several events can help explain the comparative equanimity with which the Czechoslovak government received the news of Hitler's appointment as chancellor.

In the spring of 1932 Hindenburg had to stand for reelection as president. He had won his first term in 1925 as the candidate of the Right, but in the run-off against Hitler in March 1932 all moderate and progressive forces supported Hindenburg in order to block Hitler's drive for power. Only with difficulty did Hindenburg win reelection. As has been seen, Chancellor Brüning was unable to command a parliamentary majority and was therefore dependent on Hindenburg's power to rule by presidential decree. In May he finally lost Hindenburg's confidence by supporting a measure to divide up bankrupt estates among small farmers in Prussia's eastern provinces. General Schleicher led the palace revolution that overthrew Brüning, who was replaced by Franz von Papen, hardly a felicitous choice. Konstantin von Neurath returned from the German embassy in London and became the new foreign minister. He remained in that position until 1938. An aristocrat by birth, a diplomat by profession, he subsequently lent some respectability to the Third Reich during its formative years.

By this juncture in their relations Beneš and the German minister in Prague did not bother to talk to one another very much. But in early June Beneš did take Koch aside at a diplomatic reception in order to quiz him about the new men in Berlin. Koch remarked that the Czechs should have waited at least until the parliamentary declaration of the new government before attacking it in the press. Beneš claimed that he had advised the Czech newspapers to stop their criticisms, but Koch could find no evidence that they were doing so.[144] Beneš remarked that it would be good for him to discuss problems directly with Neurath sometime, and Koch suggested that they talk at the Lausanne reparations conference. Koch thought that he recognized Beneš's old desire to be invited on an official visit to Berlin. (Beneš had come largely on his own initiative in 1928, and the Germans never valued his friendship enough to curry his favor by inviting him to their capital.) Koch thought that Beneš still hoped to win Sudeten German support for his presidential candidacy, but Koch once again advised Berlin that the Germans could have no interest in helping Beneš to the presidency. The two men engaged in recriminations about the antagonistic economic schemes of their countries in Central Europe. Beneš criticized the Germans for vetoing the Tardieu plan, and Koch brought up Beneš's political objections to the Austro-German customs union proposal.[145] All they did was to repeat their previous positions and to show quite clearly that they had come to a stalemate.

By the summer of 1932 the Weimar republic had dissolved into political chaos. In March and April there had been two ballotings for the presidency as well as local parliamentary elections in Prussia, Bavaria, and Württemberg. The violence, terror, and mob psychology that characterized those and ensuing campaigns destroyed the democratic process, and no political power arising from such elections could validly claim a democratic basis. In April Brüning's government had moved to control the situation by outlawing Hitler's SA and SS, but in June the Papen government weakly lifted the ban. Papen's "cabinet of barons" could depend only on a small minority of Nationalist deputies in the Reichstag, and one of Papen's first actions was to dissolve that body. During the campaign for the parliamentary elections in July Papen seized control of the Prussian government, which had been immobilized by the April elections, thereby unleashing a bitter constitutional debate. The Reichstag elections of July 31 gave the Nazis their greatest victory, with 37 percent of the vote and 230 of the 608 seats in the Reichstag. After futile negotiations with Hitler in August the new body was dissolved in mid-September within two weeks of its first meeting. New elections were called for the beginning of November.

The events of the summer and autumn confirmed the fears that Beneš had been expressing for at least a year. Since the depths of the economic crisis in 1931 Beneš had predicted bloody political struggles in Germany that could culminate in rightist control of the government. It was the demise of Weimar more than the rise of Hitler that worried him. He was pessimistic about the psychological situation within Germany, and he thought that it was high time for the Germans to come to their heads. In January 1932 he predicted that Hitler would achieve power and attempt to put his ideas into action. Who could say what would happen before Hitler had "mismanaged things to ruin"?[146] Beneš's basic attitude toward the Hitler movement was that it would discredit itself by assuming power.

The major factor contributing to the Nazi upsurge was the depression, but once in the government the Nazis would soon discover that they were impotent to improve conditions. By September 1932 Beneš thought that Nazi influence was on the wane and that the party would lose twenty to thirty seats in the November elections.[147] On November 6 the Nazis lost thirty-three seats but remained, as Beneš had also predicted, a powerful factor in view of the political fragmentation in Germany.

As Papen searched for a way to continue as chancellor after the November elections, Krofta remarked to foreign journalists in Prague that it was immaterial who the chancellor of Germany was. Brüning, Papen, or Hitler—German policy would always be revisionist. Sometime, concessions to the Germans would have to cease.[148] The equation of the foreign policies of past and future German chancellors protected the leadership in Prague from panic at the rise of the Nazis. After Papen fell in November, General Schleicher headed the government in December and January but himself fell victim to court intrigues around President Hindenburg such as Schleicher himself had so often engineered. Then came the news on January 30, 1933, that Adolf Hitler was chancellor of the German Reich.

In Prague, Beneš's subsidized press moved to calm the fears of the Czech population. On January 31 the *Prager Presse* devoted the entire front page to Hitler's takeover. The headline read simply: "Hitler is Chancellor," but that was followed by the observation: "Hitler Has Bound Hands." The front-page editorial, which likely had long been in preparation, commented that the Nazis would be unable to effect their program because of the opposition of the other members of the coalition. It contended that the National Socialist revolution could be considered past, for by sharing the responsibility of government the Nazis were pledged to uphold the Weimar constitution. It concluded: "Any violation of the constitution would call forth a storm among the republican social classes in Germany."[149] The *Central European Observer* noted that Hitler's power had long since been discounted abroad. It wrote that Hitler would have to moderate some of his more extreme ideas since what was good for vote-getting was not always good governmental policy.[150]

The general reaction in Prague to the Nazi seizure of power was strikingly similar to the responses in other European capitals. The dominant opinion across the continent seemed to be that the Nazis would quickly discredit themselves in their actual attempts to govern. But Hitler moved rapidly to consolidate his power in Germany. By the new Reichstag elections, the Enabling Act, and the dissolution of the other political parties, Hitler made himself politically supreme in Germany by the summer of 1933. And Hitler's treatment of all other significant groups and organizations in society pointed to aspirations for much more than purely political power. But in late March Beneš still believed that Hitler could not keep up the pace, and he predicted that the Third Reich would not last for four years. Masaryk agreed wholeheartedly and—observing events "dispassionately and philosophically"—he could not imagine that "a people of poets, thinkers, professors, and intellectuals would long tolerate such a suppression of the most basic freedoms."[151] For months thereafter Beneš continued to predict that the Nazis would soon fall from power, much as he had maintained through the 1920s that Mussolini was a passing phenomenon.[152]

The belief that the fascist regimes would quickly topple demonstrated that Masaryk and Beneš, like many others, failed to understand the dynamics of a mass movement and its capacity for survival and destructiveness. But the failure of the Czech leaders to discern significant differences between the foreign policy of Weimar governments and Nazi goals and methods reflected, in part, their own ambitious hopes for Czechoslovakia. Weimar foreign policy had been irreconcilable with the kind of absolute independence and freedom from German influence that Czech leaders desired for their country. But there was a vast difference between German political and economic influence in Central Europe and the forced cessions of territory, the military occupation, the massacre at Lidice, and the concentration camp at Theresienstadt, which the Nazis eventually imposed upon the Czechs. In the Weimar years Masaryk, Beneš, and other Czech leaders as well, tended to exaggerate the practical disadvantages for the daily lives of Czechs of a German recovery in Central Europe. As a result, their excessive fears of the traditional uses of power may have blurred their perception of the new and radical threat posed by Hitler in the 1930s.

ECONOMIC CRISIS AND NATIONALITY CONFLICT

As political and economic upheavals gripped other countries in the early 1930s, Beneš never tired of referring to his own nation as Central Europe's "island of stability." Czechoslovakia did indeed enjoy able political leadership, democratic freedoms, and economic prosperity at a time when those qualities were increasingly rare. Until 1932 the domestic political situation in Czechoslovakia was quite placid. The governing coalition rested upon a broad base, including agrarian, socialist, and clerical parties representing Czechs, Slovaks, and Sudeten Germans. The opposition was weak and ineffective. František Udržal remained premier from 1929 to October 1932 although he suffered from ill health and was occasionally accused of weakness and inactivity. As leader of the liberal wing of the Agrarian party, he agreed generally with the policies of Masaryk and Beneš; and he actually worked more closely with them than he did with the conservatives within his own party. The forces of "the Castle" retained

Udržal in the premiership as long as they could despite repeated attacks on him from his own party by 1932.[153]

By the early 1930s Edvard Beneš was the preeminent figure in the daily routine of Czechoslovak politics. From the nadir of his fortunes in 1926 he had rebuilt his political position, relying on Masaryk's prestige and loyalty. Masaryk, who turned eighty in 1930, had to guard his health with great care. He spent long periods of time away from Prague at his summer residence or on the presidential estate at Lány. Masaryk kept a close watch over the politics of the country, and his mind was in good condition for a man of his age. Masaryk's very existence exerted a calming and stabilizing effect on the country. But it was Beneš who on a day-to-day basis expressed the viewpoints and exercised the influence of "the Castle" in Czechoslovak politics. Beneš's foreign policy was Czechoslovakia's foreign policy. The onslaught of the international economic crisis and its impact on Czechoslovakia by 1932 only strengthened his position. It was generally conceded that in times of emergency the country ought to rely on its most gifted and knowledgeable experts. Beneš was the expert in foreign affairs, and he used his preeminence to support his role in domestic politics. By the early 1930s Beneš did not yet possess enough votes in parliament to insure his succession to the presidency, but his position was stronger than it had ever been before. He had no rivals of equal stature.

In contrast to their neighbors, the Czech population remained relatively immune to political radicalization in the early 1930s. They displayed their nationalistic attitudes most memorably in the grand Sokol festival of July 1932 to which visitors flocked from around the world. No attempt was made to conceal the basic anti-German attitudes of the leaders and participants, and a delegation of Lusatian Sorbs received special attention as "the only branch of Slavs that still lives under germanic domination."[154] But such displays served basically to vent frustrations and fears, and the government both promoted the Sokol festival and kept it strictly in check. The authorities resolutely combatted attempts to radicalize Czech politics, and they launched court proceedings against Stříbrný and the few would-be Czech fascists. Between 1930 and 1932 more respectable conservative circles, such as the National Democrats and the right-wing Agrarians, apparently tried to exploit Stříbrný and his cohorts in order to attack the government indirectly.[155] But the unwillingness of the opposition to come out into the open only demonstrated the basic strength of the coalition government.

By the summer of 1932, however, the country was suffering in the throes of the depression, and political opposition was mounting. A wave of strike activity gripped Czechoslovakia in 1931 and 1932.[156] The coalition had experienced repeated difficulties with conservative Agrarians in its efforts to increase the imports of Southeast European agricultural products. The conservatives also resented unemployment relief, which they considered extravagent particularly as applied to the Sudeten Germans.[157] During the summer Udržal suffered public attacks from his own party colleagues who accused him of subservience to Masaryk and Beneš. The right-wing Agrarians pushed for new parliamentary elections as did the German National Socialists, for both groups anticipated gains at the expense of the moderate and socialist parties. The "Castle" resolutely resisted calling elections for that very reason.[158] In confronting the economic crisis the government tried valiantly to maintain a balanced budget and to avoid inflationary devices, which were anathema to economic orthodoxy at the time. One of its most unpopular measures was the introduction of significant cuts in the salaries of civil servants in the autumn of 1932. Bureaucrats constituted an important element in the membership of the "bourgeois" parties, and their opposition was particularly felt. The cut in government salaries became the occasion for a change of cabinets in October.[159] The composition of the coalition remained the same, but the Czechoslovak Agrarian ministers were replaced by generally more conservative members of their party. Jan Malypetr succeeded Udržal as premier, and Milan Hodža reentered the cabinet as minister of agriculture. The move assuaged the Agrarians, but the change in personnel brought no basic shifts in policy. The conservative opposition among the Agrarians possessed no positive program that could win general support. A crisis atmosphere was growing, and there was a general reluctance to try experiments. In addition, the Sudeten Germans were beginning to pose a challenge greater than they had at any time since 1918-19.

The experience of the late 1920s had offered hope that the nationality differences between Czechs and Sudeten Germans would continue to subside. The parliamentary elections of October 1929 confirmed the electoral strength of the German activist parties. The new Udržal cabinet included the German Agrarians and the German Social Democrats. The Christian Socials, who had been represented in the government since 1926, went into opposition, but they did not abandon the activist ideal. Their leader, Mayr-Harting, took pains to emphasize that his party's opposition was directed only against the particular coalition in power and not against the idea of German cooperation in governing the country.[160] Even the German Nationals and the National Socialists no longer maintained the old negativist policy of refusing in theory to cooperate in a Czechoslovak government. The activist approach was based on the justification that more could be done for the Sudeten Germans by cooperation with Czechoslovak authorities than by obstruction. Yet whenever an issue directly concerning the minority problem arose, the German government parties found themselves in an embarrassing situation. Such was the case in the spring of 1930 when all the minority parties in Czechoslovakia united in a parliamentary effort to establish a special minorities commission. Their initiative failed in the face of Czech and Slovak opposition. The fact that the German government parties broke with the other members of the coalition and supported the idea of a minorities commission indicated the limitations on governmental cooperation by the Germans.[161] On nationality issues where no compromise was possible, the German activists naturally supported the claims of the minorities against their Czech and Slovak colleagues in the cabinet.

Through the summer of 1930 nationalist and irredentist agitation increased in Germany, and the election in September brought Hitler's Nazis their first great success. Within a matter of days after the election anti-German riots broke out in Prague on the occasion of the showing of a German sound film. Nevertheless, despite the reviving tension between the nationalities the Czechoslovak Social Democrats continued to show understanding for minority complaints. In their annual convention, held just after the Prague riots, they called for free cultural development for all the nationalities in the country and opposed any repressions of the minorities.[162] More remarkable still was the meeting of the German Social Democratic party in October. The head of the party, Ludwig Czech, left no doubt where the German Social Democrats stood. He sounded a warning against the growing fascist danger in Germany and Austria. He contrasted the progress of social welfare legislation in Czechoslovakia with the harsh circumstances facing workers in Germany, Austria, Poland, and Hungary. And he said that even if all the German parties in Czechoslovakia joined together they could make no progress in the nationalities question without support from the Czechoslovak Social Democrats.[163] Coming at a time when formal diplomatic contacts between Germany and Czechoslovakia were severely strained, Czech's remarks seemed to indicate that the working class among the Sudeten Germans felt more loyalty toward Prague than toward Berlin. Agricultural as well as labor interests worked toward closer cooperation with their Czech counterparts. Franz Spina, the leader of the German Agrarians, repeatedly advocated closer ties between the Czech and the German Agrarians.[164] The process of mitigating national rivalries by promoting mutual class interests still seemed a viable policy.

During the controversy over the Austro-German customs union proposal in the spring of 1931, most Sudeten Germans favored the customs union either for national or economic reasons. The nationalists supported almost any policy emanating from the Reich, and the socialists favored any move toward reducing tariff barriers; both were sympathetic to policies pointing toward an Anschluss. Of the government parties, the Sudeten German Social Democrats openly sympathized with the customs union, but the Agrarians maintained a much more reserved attitude.[165] The extreme opposition of official Czechoslovak foreign policy to the customs union placed the Sudeten German government parties in a dubious position. They received warnings from Udržal and the Czech press to fall into line with Beneš's foreign policy, and they certainly wanted to hold onto the political advantages of membership in the government coalition.[166] Yet they also needed to protect their flanks against nationalist opposition within the Sudeten German camp. Their solution was to maintain a low profile throughout the conflict. For several years there had been a growing dissatisfaction among German diplomats with the failure of the Sudeten German ministers to give effective support to Berlin's policies. Koch was not at all surprised by the political gymnastics of the Sudeten German cabinet members during the customs union controversy, for he had long since reported that they disappeared from public view whenever there was an open issue between Berlin and Prague.[167]

The maneuvering of the Sudeten German political parties as late as the spring of 1931 could occur only in a fairly stable environment where power was concentrated in the middle of the political spectrum. During the next two years, however, the economic privations that struck Czechoslovakia and the political dissolution of the Weimar republic so polarized the Sudeten Germans that normal political activity was no longer possible. Although Czechoslovakia had experienced a decline in production and a rise in unemployment from the early months of the depression, the country escaped the brunt of the economic crisis into 1931. But the impossibility of maintaining Czechoslovak foreign trade at its former level was the major factor in the onslaught of the depression. The collapse of commerce during the early depression years left the value of both exports and imports in 1933 at less than 30 percent of what they had been in 1929.[168] The most drastic losses came in 1931 and 1932. At the same time, the annual mean unemployment rate rose from 42,000 in 1929 to 738,000 in 1933. With the worst increases coming in 1931 and 1932, unemployment reached a peak of 920,000 in February 1933.[169] Unofficial estimates placed unemployment at even higher levels, this in a country with a total population less than fifteen million.[170] Approximately one-quarter of the labor force was out of work.[171] Among the nationalities of Czechoslovakia, the Sudeten Germans suffered most severely since they lived and worked in the most industrialized sections of the country. Moreover, the industries—such as textiles and glass—in which the Sudeten Germans were most heavily employed were the industries that were most dependent on the export trade. The economic difficulties and the relatively greater hardships of the Sudeten Germans exacerbated old nationalistic tensions and contributed to the political radicalization of the youth in particular. Confronted with the challenge of the depression, the Sudeten German activist parties tended to merge in practice with the Czechoslovak parties from the same social and economic classes. But the Sudeten German Nazis saw a golden opportunity to capitalize on the economic difficulties.

Nazi propaganda tried to exploit the idea that the misery was worse in the Sudeten German areas because of conscious neglect by the Czechoslovak government. It was pure and utter foolishness. The man who was directly responsible for the government's efforts to mitigate the effects of the depression was Ludwig Czech, the minister for social welfare. As head of the German Social Democratic party from 1920 to 1938, Czech had long been one of the most effective spokesmen for the Sudeten Germans. One of the main reasons for the continuation of the activist policy in the early 1930s was the desirability from the standpoint of the Sudeten Germans of having one of their own at the head of that key ministry. Czech did indeed have to struggle with conservative nationalist Czechs in order to dispense government relief to unemployed Sudeten Germans. But he succeeded, and his efforts found general recognition among the Sudeten Germans. His personal popularity was such that the Nazis hesitated to attack him directly in the early 1930s even though he was a socialist and a Jew. But they eventually sent him to the concentration camp at Theresienstadt, where he died in 1942.[172]

By the early 1930s the leaders of the Sudeten German Nazis were heavily scarred from their political wars. None of them possessed charisma or vitality. None of them could come up with a fresh idea or a new emotional appeal. The depression radicalized Sudeten Germans, but their influx into the National Socialist party in Czechoslovakia was a function of the growth of Nazi power in the Reich. The growth of the Sudeten German Nazis did not result from the inner dynamics of the group itself. Finding themselves in a bleak situation, young Sudeten Germans followed the example of their brothers across the frontier and joined up with the Nazis. The leader to whom they looked for deliverance was not Hans Krebs, Rudolf Jung, or Hans Knirsch but rather Adolf Hitler. In foreign policy the Czechs could do nothing about the turmoil in the Reich despite their fear and apprehension. The government did seek, however, to quell Nazi excesses within Czechoslovakia. In March 1932 unrest among the Sudeten Germans increased during the presidential campaign in Germany. The Prague government responded by launching judicial action against members of an auxiliary organization of the National Socialist party called the *Volkssport*. The trial culminated in August and September. Seven young Germans were found guilty of organizing and conducting military exercises for the purpose of overthrowing the government and of maintaining contacts with members of the SA, who had crossed over the border and participated in the drills.[173] Hardly had the sentences been pronounced when the same court sent eight additional young Germans to prison for their activities in another youth organization called the *Jungsturm.* The court accepted the state prosecutor's contention that the *Jungsturm* had a military character and that it was dedicated to the detachment of the German areas of Czechoslovakia and their inclusion in a Great-Germany.[174]

Apparently there were deep divisions within the Czechoslovak government about those trials. Still, as of the autumn of 1932, the Nazis were a minority element among the Sudeten Germans, and they did not constitute an immediate threat to the basic stability of the country. People in the circles around Masaryk and Beneš feared that stringent action against the Nazis would only increase Nazi popularity among the Sudeten Germans. In early October Hubert Ripka criticized the *Volkssport* trial in an article in *Přítomnost* entitled "We Cannot Govern." In his opinion the gravest mistake about the trial was that it threatened to put the Sudeten German activist parties in an untenable position between their electorate and the government.[175] But the trials did frighten the leaders of the National Socialist party, who went to great lengths in the winter of 1932-33 to proclaim their loyalty to the Czechoslovak republic and to dissociate their party publicly from Hitler's movement.[176] Their efforts were to no avail, however, for when Hitler took control in Germany the Czechs redoubled their efforts to counteract the Nazi movement in Czechoslovakia. In February 1933 all the Czechoslovak parties, both in the government and in opposition, voted to waive parliamentary immunity so that Nazi leaders in the National Assembly could be tried in public courts. The measure was fought by the Sudeten German opposition parties, but the Sudeten German parties in the government avoided taking a stand on the question by remaining absent from the sessions in which the votes were taken.[177]

The burgeoning Nazi movement quickly destroyed the old political divisions among the Sudeten Germans and substituted a dichotomy between the Nazis and the anti-Nazis. An index of Nazi popularity came in the communal elections in March 1933. In Eger, for example, the DNSAP garnered 40 percent of the vote and more than doubled its representation in the town council.[178] Although Eger had long been a strongly nationalist area—it had been a citadel of Georg von Schönerer's pan-German movement in imperial days—the results of its election were probably an accurate reflection of general Sudeten German sentiment. All reports attested to the rapid growth of Nazi popularity, irredentism, and *grossdeutsch* sentiments. By the end of 1933 the German minister in Prague, who was no friend of the Nazis himself, estimated that two million of the slightly more than three million Sudeten Germans were sympathetic to the National Socialist movement.[179]

The challenge of the Nazis forced the Sudeten German moderates to define more precisely their attitudes toward the Czechoslovak republic. For the first time many Sudeten German activists appeared to become emotionally as well as intellectually committed to the republic. In the weeks after Hitler's seizure of power both Sudeten German ministers took public stands against Hitler's regime.[180] That was the first time in memory that any Sudeten German leader had openly condemned any government in Berlin. As Hitler moved against his political opponents in Germany, Prague quickly became the primary haven for refugees from the Third Reich. Socialist leaders congregated there, and the major newspaper of the Sudeten German socialists, *Sozialdemokrat,* took the lead in attacking the nazification of Germany. One of Koch's principal activities was the delivering of protests to the Czechoslovak Foreign Ministry about the attacks from the Sudeten German activist press.[181] The Jews in Prague increasingly shifted their loyalties to the Czechoslovak government. Since the founding of the republic some of the most intelligent and articulate members of the German parliamentary delegations had been Prague Jews, but Hitler's brand of anti-Semitism finally began to frighten them from their German loyalties. The change in Jewish opinion was best demonstrated in the editorial policies of Prague's two chief German newspapers, the *Prager Tagblatt* and the *Bohemia.* The newspapers had previously defended most things German. After Hitler's seizure of power they fell silent or openly criticized events in Germany. But not all Sudeten German moderates opted for the republic. Some shifted quickly to the Nazis; many others opportunistically made their peace with Nazi rule after Munich and the invasion of Prague.

The revolution in the Reich and in Sudeten German politics placed the German minister in Prague in an extremely difficult situation. Although Koch had long been a severe critic of the Czechoslovak government, he had supported the attempts of the Sudeten German activists to improve their lot by cooperating with the Czechoslovak authorities. Among the Sudeten German leaders for whom he had the highest regard were representatives of Prague's German Jews. Koch had never approved of the National Socialists, nor had he favored an irredentist policy. After January 30, 1933, the Sudeten German press sympathetic to the Nazis began to attack him openly in articles with such titles as, "Does Germany Have a Diplomatic Representation in Prague?"[182] Koch persisted, however, with the express approval of Masaryk, who urged Koch to stay at his post "in these difficult times."[183] Although Koch instituted some adaptations in his reports to Berlin after the Nazi seizure of power, he continued to counsel—courageously but vainly—against German intervention in the internal affairs of Czechoslovakia.[184] Koch was high on the Nazis' most-wanted list in Berlin, but Neurath stoutly resisted outside efforts to intervene in his ministry. Neurath successfully protected Koch, and Koch remained in Prague until he reached retirement age in 1935.

The political radicalization of the Sudeten Germans posed difficult questions for the Czechoslovak government. There were those, like Ripka, who continued to urge moderation toward the Sudeten German Nazis in the belief that the majority of the Sudeten Germans could still be won for Czechoslovakia. Masaryk's value system disinclined him to resort to political repression. But there were many in the highest government circles, including Beneš, who felt that the Nazis would have to be suppressed with force if necessary. Just as Beneš was one of the earliest and staunchest opponents of Hitler's foreign policy, so also did Beneš advocate determined resistance to Sudeten German Nazi activity within Czechoslovakia. In the presence of Masaryk, Beneš exclaimed, "We'll grab them by the throats and destroy them totally!"[185] And for good measure Beneš told the Austrian minister, who at the time was representing Dollfuss's government in Prague, that there were only two solutions for the Nazi problem in Austria—"either they'll hang you, or you'll hang them."[186] The appeals in the *Volkssport* trial continued until the autumn of 1933. In the first weeks after becoming chancellor, Hitler complained to the Czechoslovak minister about the trial and secretly ordered that the legal defense costs of the Sudeten German Nazis be paid by the Reich.[187] In early October the Supreme Court in Brno upheld the verdict while reducing the sentences against the Nazi youths.[188] That decision paved the way for a trial of the leaders of the National Socialist party, whose parliamentary immunity had been lifted the previous February and who were regarded as the men ultimately responsible for the seditious activities of the youths.

Through most of 1933 the Nazi leaders had tried to stave off the trial and the political repression that the Czechoslovak government was preparing for them. In August and September they invented various subterfuges in an attempt to create a common front with other Sudeten German political parties, but their efforts failed. On October 3 the executive committee announced the dissolution of the National Socialist party, and one of the top Nazi leaders fled across the frontier with his family. The decision preceded by only twenty-four hours a government announcement banning the National Socialist and the German National parties.[189] The dissolution of those parties marked the culmination of the government's efforts in 1933 to prevent the political radicalization of the Sudeten Germans. Although the government did not achieve that basic goal, its failure resulted from conditions beyond its control. The Sudeten

Germans had for years taken their political cues from the Reich, and the sudden popularity of Nazism among the Sudeten Germans reflected events in Germany itself. Granted economic hardship and some legitimate grievances among the Sudeten Germans, the timing and the form of their protests were determined by the example of the Reich. As long as Hitler ruled in Germany, the Sudeten German radicals were not to be conciliated or repressed. Had Hitler's regime fallen, the movement among the Sudeten Germans would probably have dissolved overnight.

Already on October 1, 1933, a new and previously unknown personality in Sudeten German politics, Konrad Henlein, called for the establishment of a "Sudeten-German Homeland Front."[190] Henlein gave public assurances that the "Homeland Front" would not be directed against the Czechs, that it would not maintain contacts with the Nazis in the Reich, and that its aims were democratic and republican. The caution incumbent upon Henlein to maintain an identity distinct from the Sudeten German Nazis and the Third Reich has afforded his apologists an opportunity to claim that he was independent of the Nazis and that his "front" was essentially a spontaneous Sudeten German movement arising out of injustices in Czechoslovakia. Nothing could have been further from the truth. It was obvious in October 1933 that the "Sudeten-German Homeland Front" was intended to be a successor organization to the outlawed parties. A Nazi leader who fled to Germany in October, Hans Krebs, had negotiated with Henlein about assuming the leadership of the *völkish* movement; and it was completely in accord with Nazi wishes that Henlein decided to enter politics.[191] Money flowed from the Reich to members of the "Homeland Front" by 1934. Various agencies of Nazi rule financed the campaign of Henlein's party in the Czechoslovak parliamentary elections of 1935.[192] The jealousy with which some older Nazis soon came to view Henlein only confirmed the fact that Henlein was a prized member of the movement. From its inception the "Homeland Front" was a tool of Berlin.

The fact that Henlein had not been a member of the DNSAP made him all the more suited to take up the leadership of the movement in October 1933. His previous associations left no doubts about his basic loyalties and outlook. He was a functionary of the "German Turnverband," whose racism was illustrated by its Aryan paragraph. He was closely associated with the *Kameradschaftsbund*, which was a small youth organization that considered itself the elite of the nationalist movement and that was fundamentally influenced by the corporatist philosophy of the Vienna professor Othmar Spann.[193] Although there had been some rivalry between the DNSAP and the *Kameradschaftsbund*—it is difficult for one self-styled elite to tolerate another—much more united the two groups than divided them. After both organizations had been dissolved in 1933, they found a common home along with many other radical elements in the "Homeland Front." Konrad Henlein's image as a mild-mannered gymnastics teacher should have deceived no one familiar with Central European national and political movements in the nineteenth and twentieth centuries. The history of the Turnvereine and the Sokols could leave no serious doubts about the political destructiveness of that unathletic enthusiast for athletics. Both Czechs and Germans understood what Henlein represented; but many foreigners could not or would not comprehend.

6   *Constants and Variables in the Nationality Conflict*

The major events in the relations between Germany and Czechoslovakia after the demise of the Weimar republic are well known. In 1935 the growing apprehension in Prague about German expansionism culminated with the Soviet-Czechoslovak pact, which represented the last major effort by the Czechs to insure their security against Germany. Anchored in Central Europe by an alliance with France in the west and the Soviet Union in the east, Czechoslovakia appeared firmly established in international relations. Yet the spirit behind the treaties rapidly dissipated. A general malaise spread through Czechoslovakia as the Germans announced rearmament in 1935, reoccupied the Rhineland in 1936, and annexed Austria in March 1938. Within Czechoslovakia Masaryk retired, and Beneš was elected to the presidency in December 1935. Henlein's Sudeten German party emerged from the parliamentary elections of 1935 as the strongest single political unit in the country. Particularly after the Austrian Anschluss in 1938 the party functioned as a powerful fifth column for Reich-German interests in Czechoslovakia. The crisis of the summer of 1938, culminating with German annexation of the Sudeten German territories at the Munich conference in September, effectively destroyed the first Czechoslovak republic. The German occupation of Prague in March 1939 only confirmed an accomplished fact.

From the nadir of their political fortunes in the early years of the Second World War, the Czechs recovered as the military situation turned against the Germans. In 1945 President Beneš returned from exile as the head of the reconstituted republic and brought with him the agreement of the great powers to expel the Sudeten Germans from Czechoslovakia. In 1946 more than two million Germans were forced to leave the country and settle in occupied Germany.[1] The expulsions disposed of the German problem within the Czechoslovak republic, and the division of Germany among the occupying powers diminished the foreign threat to Czechoslovakia. Having emerged from the war with an industrial plant essentially intact, the country seemed to have a favorable prognosis. But the dispute among political factions in the national coalition government eventually led to the coup of February 1948 in which the Czechoslovak Communist party assumed complete control of the state. The death of Jan Masaryk and the resignation and death of Edvard Beneš followed in the next several months. The Czechs had warded off German influence only to settle firmly into the Soviet political orbit.

All those events are so familiar that a mere mention of them arouses vivid impressions in the minds of many readers. But this study of Czechoslovak-German relations concludes in 1933 not primarily because of the general familiarity of subsequent events. A discussion of the years between 1933 and 1948 would alter the focus in regard both to German foreign policy and to the international situation within which the Czechs and the Germans conducted their bilateral relations.

In the preceding chapters it should have become clear that there were salient differences between Weimar policies toward Czechoslovakia and those pursued by Hitler. Hitler's was an openly irredentist policy that relied on the threat of military force in order to acquire land and to dismember the Czechoslovak state. His concept of German expansion through Central and Eastern Europe can be labeled "settler colonialism." The land would be stocked with German farmers, who would sink their roots into the soil and transform it into part of the new German homeland.[2] On the other hand, Weimar policies toward Czechoslovakia relied on the gradual assertion of German political and economic power in order to bend Czechoslovak policy toward closer cooperation with Germany. Weimar policy in Central Europe can be termed "trading-colony colonialism."[3]

That phrase was not used by Weimar leaders themselves, and most of them would have disavowed—at least publicly—any such intent. Certainly they did not aim at establishing a formal empire in Central Europe. But it is clear from the diplomatic documents that Weimar policymakers were acutely aware of the advantages that accrued to Germany as a result of its economic potential and the fact that German language and culture supplied the common denominator for regional intercourse in Cental Europe. It seemed likely to them that able exploitation of those strengths could transform the smaller states of Central Europe into political and economic dependencies and reestablish Germany as the dominant power of Central Europe. In contrast to Hitler's later military conquests, the "trading-colony" approach could proceed by more subtle and gradual means, and it need not affect the formal sovereignty or territorial integrity of the other Central European states. Moreover, the creation of a co-prosperity sphere in Central Europe under German tutelage could appear to be in the best interests of all the people of the region. Weimar diplomacy evolved in that direction in the late 1920s and the early 1930s.

There is nothing in the German Foreign Office documents to indicate that Weimar policy aimed at an incorporation of Sudeten German territories into the Reich. Weimar governments sympathized with the Sudeten German activist parties, which sought to cooperate with the Czechs and the Slovaks in governing Czechoslovakia. In contrast, the Third Reich encouraged Henlein's movement to maintain a belligerent and hostile attitude, to remain dissatisfied with any concessions that the Czechoslovak authorities might make. Those were logical tactics for an irredentist policy. For Weimar, however, the Sudeten Germans were much more valuable in Czechoslovakia than in Germany. Their potential political and economic influence in Czechoslovakia was a great asset for Germany. Their presence in the fringe areas of Bohemia, Moravia, and Silesia made the German frontier territories with Czechoslovakia seem much more secure.

The fact that Weimar policymakers undertook few initiatives in Central Europe makes it possible to doubt that they even harbored hopes for the refounding of a Germanic Mitteleuropa. Weimar governments never formulated a program for the attainment of such a goal. Nor did they possess a detailed concept of the relations that would develop in a new Mitteleuropa. In the 1920s other questions absorbed the energies of Weimar diplomats. But the realization persisted that Germany remained Central Europe's most powerful state, and from that awareness sprang the assumption that the area from the Rhine to the Soviet border, stretching from the Baltic to the Balkans, was a natural sphere of German influence. The men formulating and conducting policy in the Weimar years had imbibed their values in imperial days when a Germanic Mitteleuropa had come closest to realization. Rather than being converted to new ideas after 1918, they tried to adapt their old concepts to new circumstances. In the 1920s, while Germany was recovering from the war, the task of Weimar diplomacy was to insure against the erection of obstacles to an eventual German organization of the area. German diplomats were content to see the region remain weak and divided, and they therefore noted with pleasure the fears in Prague of any supranational Danubian organization among the successor states. In 1927 and 1928, when Beneš worked avidly for a series of bilateral preferential tariff treaties among the Danubian states, they kept a wary eye on his exploratory efforts; and they helped to veto a similar scheme when it was put forward by Tardieu in 1932. Still, there were few open disputes between Germany and Czechoslovakia, and on the surface their relations appeared placid. From Berlin's standpoint, the calm atmosphere reflected the confidence that time was on the German side and that power relationships in Central Europe would eventually force the Czechs to reorient their foreign policy toward Berlin.

German policy toward Austria likewise pointed to the "trading-colony" approach. Austria's greatest value for Weimar Germany was that it could serve as the gateway to the rest of Central and Southeastern Europe. That theme was sounded in the documents repeatedly. The abortive attempt to establish a customs union between the two countries in 1931 was intended to be only a first step toward a general expansion of German influence. Although the demonstrations of public opinion in the two countries favored an incorporation of Austria into Germany, serious doubts about the wisdom of an Anschluss existed in government circles in both Berlin and Vienna. The basic German approach to the Anschluss question in the 1920s was to emphasize that the issue was not yet ripe for solution, and no one could argue with that assertion in view of the international situation. On the other hand, the Germans adamantly insisted that Austria should not enter into any political or economic association with a group of states of which Germany was not a member. The formulation of the Austrian chancellor, Ignaz Seipel, captured the essence of the German position—"Any group with Germany, no group without Germany." Thus, the reluctance by German leaders such as Hindenburg, Stresemann, and Schubert actually to incorporate Austria into Germany and the simultaneous insistence that Austria remain free of special ties with other states pointed to a desire to keep the Austrians available as a tool for the eventual expansion of German interests in the Danubian region. At least until Engelbert Dollfuss became chancellor while the Nazis were seizing control of Germany in 1932, the Austrians proved to be more or less willing accomplices.

The year 1933 marked a watershed not just in German foreign policy but also in the conduct of international relations in general. The era of the "New Diplomacy" was concurrent with the Weimar republic. In the early 1930s the demise of Weimar and the dissolution of the Versailles system proceeded simultaneously. Even before Hitler became chancellor, support for the peace treaties had declined in the Western powers. The Nazi seizure of power meant that a major country no longer recognized the legitimacy of the diplomatic system that had been constructed in 1919. Given the new challenge from Germany and the flagging dedication to the peace treaties in the Western capitals, the years after 1933 witnessed the abandonment not just of the terms of the treaties but also of the principles and the diplomatic methods of the "New Diplomacy."

If the external security of the state is the basic goal of a country's foreign policy, the heart of any system of international relations is the way in which it attempts to insure national security. In Wilsonian ideology that was to be done on a collective, or universal, basis. The League of Nations represented the attempt to create an organizational foundation for a universal security system. The principle of collective security was particularly important for the smaller European powers such as Czechoslovakia. Without it they faced the danger of becoming merely the objects of great-power diplomacy or, at most, junior partners in the alliance system of some great power. That eventually became the fate of Czechoslovakia. Collective security never actually functioned in the 1920s because of the unwillingness of some of the great powers to undertake universal commitments. Yet there was a general recognition that the smaller powers were active participants in the diplomatic system and that, however bothersome, their opinions were also to be heeded in the process of coming to international agreements. In the 1920s some of the more avid Wilsonians supported a campaign to "outlaw war." Their efforts culminated in the Kellogg-Briand pact of 1928 by which most of the countries of the world agreed to renounce war as an instrument of national policy. In theory, therefore, the small powers were protected against the threat of overwhelming force by a great power, and they could appeal to the society of nations for support against unjust demands.

Associated also with the "New Diplomacy" were commitments toward liberal democracy and national self-determination. The 1920s supplied more than enough evidence that—at least at that point in European history—the attempt to realize the democratic equality of all states in the practice of international relations was doomed to founder on the national interests and rivalries of the various powers. The liberalism of the "New Diplomacy" espoused not only the equality of states but also the political equality of individuals within those states. The "New Diplomacy" was posited on the existence of pluralistic democratic governments. It can be argued that as those governments disappeared through the 1920s the diplomatic system was progressively weakened. But Czechoslovak diplomacy emanated from a country that has been widely praised for its democratic stability, and a close study of Czechoslovak foreign policy makes it difficult to argue that the Czechs were any less nationalistic in their territorial aspirations or their attempts to insure their national security. The principle of national self-determination placed popular nationalism at the pinnacle of importance. The political expression of nationalistic emotions helped to undermine the other principles of the "New Diplomacy."

If collective security never really existed, if the pacific settlement of international disputes and the equality among states were only fond dreams, if nationalistic rivalries corroded the rest of the system—how then were the 1920s different from the years after 1933? The differences were only a matter of degree, but even that was significant. In the 1920s the fashioners of the peace treaties still believed in their handiwork, and they were prepared to enforce the terms of those treaties. The Germans made rapid strides toward winning acceptance back into the system of international relations, but part of the price of that acceptance was their acquiescence to the rules of that system. German diplomats sought concessions and revisions in the treaties through negotiation and compromise rather than through a concentrated effort to construct a huge army in order to issue ultimatums and to stage faits accomplis. From the viewpoint of Czechoslovakia, the smaller states of Central Europe appeared to have more opportunity to participate in international diplomacy and so to exercise influence over their own destinies in the 1920s than in the 1930s. Underlying those differences was the fact that the principles of the "New Diplomacy" were still officially espoused in the 1920s. However inadequately they were applied, any commitment to them at all contributed to a willingness to support the peace settlements. When the principles of the "New Diplomacy" were no longer stated in the 1930s, the directional signals were extinguished. International relations turned down the road of the pure power-politics of appeasement diplomacy.

If 1933 marked the end of an era as far as German foreign policy and the conduct of international relations were concerned, it is legitimate to treat the period of the liberal republics—the Weimar and the Czechoslovak—as a self-contained entity. On the other hand, from the perspective of nationality conflicts between Germans and Czechs in Central Europe, it quickly becomes obvious that the years between 1918 and 1933 were an integral part of a much longer process. The foreign policy of Czechoslovakia in those years convincingly illustrates the continuing national rivalries between Czechs and Germans.

Chapter titles in this book have described Czechoslovak-German relations as "correct" and "friendly" through most of the 1920s. Those were the public descriptions given by diplomats at the time. The relatively peaceful appearance of relations was important to both sides. For the Germans it reflected their preoccupation with other diplomatic problems, their desire to maintain a placid situation in Central Europe, and their confidence that time was on their side as far as the recovery of German influence in Central Europe was concerned. For the Czechs it was important to cultivate the appearance that the new order in Central Europe was a stable one and that the new states could live harmoniously as neighbors. Because of the absence of acute crises such as came after 1933 it has been generally assumed that the relations between Germany and Czechoslovakia during the Weimar years were quite good. But beneath the surface of order and calm there still ran the currents of national rivalries.

In 1930, while helping orient a new British minister to conditions in Czechoslovakia, Edvard Beneš motioned upward and remarked, "Before the war the Sudeten Germans were here," and, pointing downward, added, "and we were there." Then he exclaimed, "Now we are up here, and they are down there."[4] It was clear that he meant to keep the situation as it was. The fundamental goal of his foreign policy was to insure the security of the new Czechoslovak nation-state, and in his eyes the primary threat to that state came from the Germans, at home and across the frontier. In the Weimar years Beneš never developed confidence that even the Sudeten German activists would remain loyal citizens of the state in a time of crisis. He supported their participation in the government, realizing that it could demonstrate Czechoslovakia's liberal minority policies, but he worked to keep Sudeten German political influence strictly circumscribed. In regional affairs in Central Europe Beneš's primary worry was that Germany's eventual political and economic recovery would again allow it to extend its influence through the area. Czechoslovak foreign policy attempted to exploit the years immediately following Germany's defeat in the war in order to strengthen Czechoslovakia to the point that it could successfully resist German influence in later years. For that reason it was crucially important to prevent the union of Austria with Germany, and Beneš's determined efforts in the 1920s to raise barriers to an Anschluss demonstrated his concern about German influence in Central Europe. Finally, in the larger issues of international relations Czechoslovak policy aligned itself firmly with the status-quo powers. In the great diplomatic debates between the French and the Germans Beneš was consistently one of the most loyal and effective allies of France.

It is possible to speak of "Beneš's" foreign policy because he was the dominant figure in Czechoslovak diplomacy throughout the first republic. Obviously, behind Beneš stood a constellation of forces that supported the policies that he was implementing. The major figure among them was Tomáš G. Masaryk.

Despite Masaryk's unwavering support for Beneš, there was a generational difference between the two men in their approach to the nationality problem. Masaryk's education had come in a German milieu, and he retained a much greater affinity for German culture than Beneš ever possessed. In the early 1920s Masaryk remarked to the Austrian minister that he would gladly visit Vienna just to "catch up on the gossip" with his old friends and colleagues.[5] In the dark days of the depression in 1932 Jan Masaryk mused about his father's place in history and concluded that historians would recognize that Tomáš Masaryk had been an ardent supporter of the Habsburg monarchy until the outbreak of the war. Then, when he had seen that the course of Austrian politics was irreversible and that his advice and warnings had fallen on deaf ears, he had naturally sided with his own people and had dedicated himself to the task of delivering them from the unavoidable debacle.[6] Deliverance took the form of founding a Czechoslovak nation-state. It was that nation-state to which Beneš dedicated his life. Growing to maturity in the worst years of the rivalries between Czechs and Germans, Beneš represented a much younger generation that was committed to the self-assertion of Czech nationality and that possessed little respect for the age-old ties between Germans and Czechs in Central Europe. In his own education Beneš had substituted French influence for the Germanic that had become traditional for Czech intellectuals.

Generalizations about generations are inevitably vulnerable to many individual exceptions. Moreover, generational differences should not be overdrawn, for common enthusiasm for the new Czechoslovak nation-state united almost all Czechs and many Slovaks. Among the political parties, the forces around Masaryk and Beneš, popularly known as "the Castle," were most clearly identified with the Czechoslovak Social Democrats and the National Socialists. But agrarian, commercial, and industrial interests, loosely grouped politically under the rubric of "middle-class" parties, also supported the state and its political leadership. Conflicting economic interests never seriously damaged the national unity of the Czech and Slovak political parties. Except for the Communists and the most radical parties of the national minorities, there was no attack on the constitutional structure of the state. And there was general support among the Czechs for Beneš's foreign policy.

The founding of nation-states after the First World War institutionalized national rivalries and brought them permanently into the political process. Popular nationalism traditionally fluctuated in intensity and appeared to serve as a kind of psychological refuge for people confronted with other kinds of socioeconomic problems. The rapid industrialization and urbanization of the late nineteenth century, the sacrifices of the First World War, and the privations of the Great Depression coincided with periods of great national tension. Yet, in the lands of the Bohemian crown, Czechs and Germans had lived for centuries in a state of symbiosis, and across the generations there had been much cooperation among them. After the First World War the principle of national self-determination encouraged a tendency to ignore the bonds among the nationalities of Central Europe. It placed an exaggerated emphasis on the national element of a person's identification to the neglect of other traits such as religious loyalties or socioeconomic interests. With the founding of nation-states, national interests became translated into diplomatic policies. Both Czechoslovak and German foreign policy represented a conceptualization of assumed national interests. In contrast to the episodic nature of political nationalism on the popular level, the foreign policies of nation-states transformed national rivalries into a relatively constant and unfluctuating aspect of international relations. The demise of old multinational empires in favor of competing nation-states, far from solving the nationality problem, exacerbated it in the sphere of international relations. In Western Europe and North America nationalities have tended to grow organically out of existing states. In Central and Eastern Europe, nationalities—defined primarily in ethnic and cultural terms—have sharpened their conflicts by trying to create states.

The confrontation between Czechoslovakia and Germany in the Weimar years was the conflict between the German potential for resurgence in Central Europe and the Czech effort to establish the absolute independence and sovereignty of Czechoslovakia. From the standpoint of nationality conflict the Weimar years were an integral part of the process that began in the late eighteenth century with the first signs of the Czech national revival. The period of the liberal republics was not an oasis of reconciliation between the nationality conflicts of the late Habsburg Empire and the brutality of the Third Reich.

Although the perspective is not yet great, the nationality conflict between Czechs and Germans apparently reached its climax in the period between the Munich conference and the expulsion of the Sudeten Germans from Czechoslovakia. The impact of those years has encouraged among a younger generation the growth of a set of values espousing interchange and interaction among nationalities. It may be that as the influence of the superpowers recedes in Central Europe present and future generations will develop new political forms that can protect their interests more effectively than did the older nation-states. It may even be that historical research on past nationality conflicts will contribute to the growth of a new cosmopolitanism.

Notes

Chapter One

1. Robert Auty, "Changing Views on the Role of Dobrovský in the Czech National Revival," *The Czech Renascence of the Nineteenth Century*, eds. Peter Brock and H. Gordon Skilling (Toronto: University of Toronto Press, 1970), pp. 14-25.

2. Barbara Kohák Kimmel, "Karel Havlíček and the Czech Press before 1848," in *The Czech Renascence*, pp. 113-30.

3. Victor-L. Tapié, *Monarchie et peuples du Danube* (Paris: Fayard, 1969), pp. 235-36.

4. William E. Wright, *Serf, Seigneur, and Sovereign: Agrarian Reform in Eighteenth-Century Bohemia* (Minneapolis: University of Minnesota Press, 1966), pp. 112-29, 160-64. Robert Joseph Kerner, *Bohemia in the Eighteenth Century* (New York: The Macmillan Company, 1932), pp. 273-306.

5. Stanley Z. Pech, *The Czech Revolution of 1848* (Chapel Hill: University of North Carolina Press, 1969), pp. 14-15.

6. Jan Havránek, "The Development of Czech Nationalism," *Austrian History Yearbook* 3, pt. 2 (1967):233.

7. Kerner, *Bohemia in the Eighteenth Century*, pp. 344-52.

8. Stanley B. Kimball, "The Matice Česká, 1831-1861: The First Thirty Years of a Literary Foundation," in *The Czech Renascence*, pp. 53-73.

9. Miroslav Hroch, "The Social Composition of the Czech Patriots in Bohemia, 1827-1848," in *The Czech Renascence*, pp. 33-52.

10. Jan Havránek, "The Development of Czech Nationalism," *Austrian History Yearbook* 3, pt. 2 (1967):243-44.

11. Pech, *The Czech Revolution of 1848*, pp. 279-90.

12. Ibid., pp. 291-93.

13. Havránek, "The Development of Czech Nationalism," p. 226.

14. The Austrian censuses came under heavy attack from the Czech side inasmuch as the measurement of nationality was the language of daily usage, or *Umgangssprache*. Czechs maintained that many Czech nationals were thereby forced to register as Germans because they lived in German areas or because they worked for German firms. At the Paris peace conference in 1919 Czech representatives vigorously attacked the reliability of the Austrian census statistics. In the nineteenth century the Austrian gauge of nationality may well have worked to the disadvantage of Czechs as long as many urban and industrial areas were predominantly German. But it should be noted that the first Czechoslovak census in 1921, determining nationality by the language spoken by one's mother, yielded a similar proportion of Czechs and Germans in Bohemia and Moravia as had

the last Austrian census of 1910, based on the language of daily usage.
Österreichisches Statistisches Handbuch, 1912 (Vienna: Verlag der K.K.
Statistischen Zentralkommission, 1913), p. 13. *Manuel statistique de la
République Tchécoslovaque* (Prague: Edition de l'Office de statistique,
1928), 3:275. The Czechoslovak statistical handbooks are cited variously
in their Czech or French editions.

15. Jan Havránek, "Die ökonomische und politische Lage der Bauernschaft in den böhmischen Ländern in den letzten Jahrzehnten des 19.
Jahrhunderts," *Jahrbuch für Wirtschaftsgeschichte* (1966), pt. 2, pp.
101-7.

16. Louis Eisenmann, *Le compromis austro-hongrois de 1867: Étude
sur le dualisme* (Paris: Société nouvelle de librairie et d'édition, 1904), pp.
278-88.

17. Ibid., pp. 493-504.

18. Robert A. Kann, *The Multinational Empire: Nationalism and
National Reform in the Habsburg Monarchy, 1848-1918* (New York:
Columbia University Press, 1950), 1:178-91. Stanley Z. Pech, "Passive
Resistance of the Czechs, 1863-1879," *Slavonic and East European
Review* 36 (June 1958):434-52. Jaroslav Purš, "Tábory v českých zemích v
letech 1868-1871," *Československý časopis historický* 6 (1958):234-66,
446-70, 661-90.

19. Havránek, "The Development of Czech Nationalism," p. 246.

20. Hugo Hantsch, *Die Geschichte Österreichs*, 4th ed. (Graz: Verlag
Styria, 1968), 2:378-79.

21. *Československá vlastivěda: Dějiny* (Prague: "Sfinx" Bohumil
Janda, 1933), pp. 782-83.

22. William A. Jenks, *Austria Under the Iron Ring, 1879-1893*
(Charlottesville: University of Virginia Press, 1965), pp. 54-61, 71-89,
104-21.

23. Arthur J. May, *The Hapsburg Monarchy, 1867-1914* (Cambridge:
Harvard University Press, 1951), p. 199.

24. H. Gordon Skilling, "The Politics of the Czech Eighties," in *The
Czech Renascence*, p. 278.

25. Havránek, "Die ökonomische und politische Lage der Bauernschaft," pp. 105-12, 125-34.

26. Stanley B. Winters, "Kramář, Kaizl, and the Hegemony of the
Young Czech Party, 1891-1901," in *The Czech Renascence*, pp. 282-314.
Hantsch, *Geschichte Österreichs*, 2:436-44. See also, Berthold Sutter, *Die
Badenischen Sprachenverordnungen von 1897*, 2 vols. (Graz: Verlag
Böhlaus Nachf., 1960).

27. Kann, *The Multinational Empire*, 2:220-27.

28. Anthony Palecek, "The Rise and Fall of the Czech Agrarian
Party," *East European Quarterly* 5 (June 1971):177-82. Anthony Palecek,
"Antonín Švehla: Czech Peasant Statesman," *Slavic Review* 21 (December
1962):699-700.

29. Hans Mommsen, *Die Sozialdemokratie und die Nationalitätenfrage*

im habsburgischen Vielvölkerstaat (Vienna: Europa-Verlag, 1963), pp. 314-38. Norbert Leser, *Zwischen Reformismus und Bolschewismus* (Vienna: Europa-Verlag, 1968), pp. 249-50.

30. R.W. Seton-Watson, *The New Slovakia* (Prague: Fr. Borový, 1924), pp. 13-14.

31. L'udovít Holotík, "The Slovaks: An Integrating or a Disintegrating Force?" *Austrian History Yearbook* 3, pt. 2 (1967):375-87.

32. R.W. Seton-Watson, *A History of the Czechs and Slovaks* (London: Hutchinson & Co., 1943), pp. 173-75.

33. Ibid., pp. 175-76.

34. Ján Tibenský, "Bernolák's Influence and the Origins of the Slovak Awakening," *Studia historica slovaca* 2 (1964):152-55.

35. Václav L. Beneš, "The Slovaks in the Habsburg Empire: A Struggle for Existence," *Austrian History Yearbook* 3, pt. 2 (1967):343-47.

36. Jozef Butvin, "Martin Hamuljak and the Fundamental Problems of the Slovak National Revival," *Studia historica slovaca* 3 (1965):169-72.

37. Thomas G. Pešek, "The 'Czechoslovak' Question on the Eve of the 1848 Revolution," in *The Czech Renascence*, p. 143.

38. Pech, *The Czech Revolution of 1848*, pp. 272-74. Daniel Rapant, *Slovenské povstanie roku 1848-49*, 5 vols. (Bratislava: Vydavateľstvo Slovenskej akadémie vied, 1937-72), 3:359-60.

39. V. Beneš, "The Slovaks in the Habsburg Empire," pp. 357-63.

40. C.A. Macartney, *Hungary and Her Successors: The Treaty of Trianon and Its Consequences, 1919-1937* (London: Oxford University Press, 1937), p. 90.

41. L. Katus, "Über die wirtschaftlichen und gesellschaftlichen Grundlagen der Nationalitätenfrage in Ungarn vor dem ersten Weltkrieg," in *Die nationale Frage in der Österreichisch-Ungarischen Monarchie, 1900-1918* (Budapest: Akadémiai Kiadó, 1966), p. 166.

42. Macartney, *Hungary and Her Successors*, pp. 81-83. Seton-Watson, *The New Slovakia*, pp. 85-86.

43. R.W. Seton-Watson, *Racial Problems in Hungary* (London: Archibald Constable & Co., 1908), pp. 331-39. The young Seton-Watson graphically demonstrated his loyalties by using a photograph of Hlinka as the frontispiece of his book.

44. L. Bianchi, "Listy Milana Hodžu šéfovi vojenskej kancelárie následníka trónu Františka Ferdinanda v rokoch, 1907-1911," *Historický časopis* 18 (1970):427-47. Milan Hodža, *Federation in Central Europe: Reflections and Reminiscences* (London: Jarrolds Publishers, 1942), pp. 37-53. The idea underlying this train of thought continued to characterize Hodža's activities as one of the most powerful Czechoslovak politicians of the interwar years. In his memoirs there is a danger that he was reading too much of his subsequent thought into his prewar activities.

45. It is instructive to note that the Czechoslovak delegation at the Paris peace conference included arguments of this nature in its official memoranda laying claim to the historic frontiers of Bohemia, Moravia, and Silesia. See chapter 2, "The Peace Settlements."

46. Andrew Gladding Whiteside, *Austrian National Socialism before 1918* (The Hague: Martinus Nijhoff, 1962), p. 40. Whiteside bases his study of Czech migration patterns largely on the work of Heinrich Rauchberg, *Der nationale Besitzstand in Böhmen*, 3 vols. (Leipzig: Duncker & Humblot, 1905).

47. Erich Zöllner, "The Germans as an Integrating and Disintegrating Force," *Austrian History Yearbook* 3, pt. 1 (1967): 208.

48. Whiteside, *Austrian National Socialism before 1918*, p. 55.

49. Ibid., pp. 51-86.

50. Elizabeth Wiskemann, *Czechs and Germans: A Study of the Struggle in the Historic Provinces of Bohemia and Moravia* (London: Oxford University Press, 1938), p. 38.

51. Andrew G. Whiteside, "The Germans as an Integrative Force in Imperial Austria: The Dilemma of Dominance," *Austrian History Yearbook* 3, pt. 1 (1967): 165.

52. Hugo Hantsch, *Geschichte Österreichs*, 2: 440. Sutter, *Die badenischen Sprachenverordnungen*, 1: 237-49.

53. Sutter, *Die badenischen Sprachenverordnungen*, 2: 442-45.

54. Havránek, "Social Classes, Nationality Ratios, and Demographic Trends," pp. 199-202.

55. Stuart A. Borman, "The Prague Student Zionist Movement, 1896-1914" (Ph.D. diss., University of Chicago, 1972), pp. 55-64.

56. R.W. Seton-Watson, *Masaryk in England* (Cambridge: At the University Press, 1943), pp. 33-35.

57. Those reports were made by the district governor's office in Prague to various administrative agencies in Vienna. They have been published under the title: *Souhrnná hlášení presidia pražského místodržitelství o protistátní, protirakouské, a protiválečné činnosti v Čechách 1915-1918*, vol. 1 of *Prameny k ohlasu velké říjnové socialistické revoluce a vzniku ČSR* (Prague: Nakladatelství Československé akademie věd, 1957).

58. *Československá Vlastivěda: Dějiny*, p. 832.

59. *Souhrnná hlášení*, pp. 19-410. The statement in the text represents my interpretation of the contents of the reports. It is clear that there were many anti-Austrian comments from the beginning of the war, but organized political demonstrations against the state itself came only in the closing stages of the war.

60. Zdeněk Tobolka, *Politické dějiny československého národa od r. 1848 až do dnešní doby* (Prague: Československý kompas, 1937), 4: 216-321. Emil Strauss, *Die Entstehung der tschechoslowakischen Republik* (Prague: Orbis, 1935), pp. 135-53, 177-201. Z.A.B. Zeman, *The Break-Up of the Habsburg Empire* (London: Oxford University Press, 1961), pp. 167-76.

61. Tobolka, *Politické dějiny československého národa*, 4: 237-48. Strauss, *Entstehung der tschechoslowakischen Republik*, pp. 184-90. Zeman, *The Break-Up of the Habsburg Empire*, pp. 119-27.

62. In 1943 S. Harrison Thomson wrote: "The nation as a whole

openly resented this weakness [of the political parties], and, under the leadership of patriotic men of letters, a movement grew to repudiate these political 'leaders'." S. Harrison Thomson, *Czechoslovakia in European History* (Princeton: Princeton University Press, 1943), p. 275. In 1969 Zeman wrote: "[Czech] writers played the leading role in the building up of their national consciousness as much as of their language. In May 1917 the writers' manifesto signed the death warrant of the Habsburg Empire." Z.A.B. Zeman, *Prague Spring: A Report on Czechoslovakia 1968* (Middlesex, England: Penguin Books, 1969), p. 42.

63. *Souhrnná hlášení*, pp. 19-410.

64. The Austrian government printed Goll's address together with pictures of the meeting in a booklet, a copy of which found its way to the French Foreign Ministry. It was filed along with pamphlets published by the Czech exiles, seemingly documenting the divisions of political opinion among Czechs. Paris, MAE, Guerre, 1914-1918, Autriche-Hongrie, vol. 153. In 1930 Pekař published the text of the oration, which he had written for delivery by the Agrarian leader Antonín Švehla. Josef Pekař, "K českému boji státoprávnímu za války," *Český časopis historický* 36(1930):520-51.

65. Tomáš G. Masaryk, *Světová revoluce* (Prague: Orbis and Čin, 1925), pp. 34-35.

66. Seton-Watson, *Masaryk in England*, pp. 44-45, 133.

67. Harold Nicolson, *Peacemaking 1919* (Boston: Houghton Mifflin Company, 1933), pp. 32-33.

68. Out of deference to Italian interests Entente statesmen decided not to make specific mention of the Yugoslavs. Seton-Watson, *A History of the Czechs and Slovaks*, pp. 291-92. Masaryk attributed the Czech success largely to Beneš's diplomatic efforts in Paris. Masaryk, *Světová revoluce*, pp. 146-48.

69. A British War Office memorandum of April 1918 traced the wartime history of the Czechoslovak question and emphasized that the Entente had not committed itself to the political independence of Czechoslovakia in 1917. London, Public Records Office, Foreign Office file 371, W3/203256/64427, Memorandum entitled "The Czechoslovak Problem–Political," General Staff, War Office, April 30, 1918.

70. London, P.R.O., F.O. file 371, vol. CAB 24/50, G.T. 4414, "Notes on conversations with Representatives of the Bohemian National Council at Versailles on 22nd April 1918."

71. London, P.R.O., F.O. 371, vol. 2864, W3/207244/137254, Memorandum for Lord Hardinge by George R. Clerk, October 26, 1917. Hardinge was Permanent Under Secretary of State. Clerk was in the War Department.

72. Ibid. The note was by Hardinge.

73. London, P.R.O., F.O. 371, volume 3323, W38/84358/50420, Note from the Ministry of Shipping to the War Office, May 8, 1918. *Parliamentary Debates*, Commons, 5th series, vol. 106, 2021-22, June 11, 1918.

74. London, P.R.O., F.O. 371, vol. 3323, W38/57780/50420, Memorandum from the War Office to the Foreign Office, March 30, 1918.

75. The best secondary account about the negotiations among the Allies concerning the use of the Czech legionnaires is D. Perman, *The Shaping of the Czechoslovak State: Diplomatic History of the Boundaries of Czechoslovakia, 1914-1920* (Leiden: E.J. Brill, 1962), pp. 28-47.

76. London, P.R.O., F.O. 371, vol. 3323, W38/79525/50420, Comment by Balfour on a telegram from Robert Hodgson, the British consul in Vladivostok, May 5, 1918.

77. George F. Kennan, *Soviet-American Relations, 1917-1920* (Princeton: Princeton University Press, 1956-58), 1:458-85; 2:58-106. W.B. Fowler, *British-American Relations, 1917-1918: The Role of Sir William Wiseman* (Princeton: Princeton University Press, 1969), pp. 164-87. Richard H. Ullman, *Anglo-Soviet Relations, 1917-1921* (Princeton: Princeton University Press, 1961), 1:82-109.

78. London, P.R.O., F.O. 371, vol. 3324, W38/113393/50420, Telegram from R.H. Bruce Lockhart to the British Foreign Office, June 14, 1918.

79. London, P.R.O., F.O. 371, vol. 3323, W38/93804/50420, Letter from Clemenceau to Lord Robert Cecil, May 22, 1918. Cecil was Parliamentary Under Secretary of State and Minister of Blockade.

80. Ibid., Telegram from Cecil to the Earl of Derby, the British ambassador in Paris, May 25, 1918.

81. Kennan, *Soviet-American Relations*, 2:381-404. Victor S. Mamatey, *The United States and East Central Europe, 1914-1918* (Princeton: Princeton University Press, 1957), pp. 277-92.

82. Edvard Beneš, *Světová válka a naše revoluce* (Prague: Orbis and Čin, 1930-31), 2:214. Quoted in Perman, *The Shaping of the Czechoslovak State*, p. 35.

83. Perman, *The Shaping of the Czechoslovak State*, p. 37.

84. Ibid., pp. 46-47.

85. Ibid., p. 35. In submitting the draft letter for cabinet approval, Cecil maintained that it "will not commit us to any increased war obligation." He continued to hope for some kind of federal state in Central Europe. London, P.R.O., F.O. file 371, vol. CAB 24/52, G.T. 4647, Note from Cecil to the War Cabinet, May 23, 1918.

86. London, P.R.O., F.O. file 371, vol. 3135, W3/90524/64427, Foreign Office minutes on the Czech question, May 22-24, 1918. Harry Hanak, "The Government, the Foreign Office and Austria-Hungary, 1914-1918," *Slavonic and East European Review* 47 (January 1969):193-94.

87. London, P.R.O., F.O. 371, vol. 3135, W3/127473/64427, Note from Beneš to the Foreign Office and minutes by Foreign Office personnel, July 22-23, 1918; W3/135132/64427, "Memorandum concerning the Recognition of Czechoslovak National Sovereignty," presented by Beneš to Cecil, July 27, 1918.

88. Ibid. Z.A.B. Zeman, *A Diplomatic History of the First World War* (London: Weidenfield and Nicolson, 1971), pp. 358-59.

89. London, P.R.O., F.O. 371, vol. 3135, W3/135132/64427, Memorandum by Cecil about a conversation with Beneš, August 9, 1918.

90. Perman, *The Shaping of the Czechoslovak State*, pp. 31-32.

91. Ibid., pp. 43-44. Mamatey, *United States and East Central Europe*, pp. 300-311.

92. Helmut Rumpler, "Der Zerfall der Habsburgermonarchie—Ein Versäumnis?" in *Aktuelle Forschungsprobleme um die Erste Tschechoslowakische Republik*, ed. Karl Bosl (Munich: R. Oldenbourg, 1969), pp. 67-78.

93. In the early years of Communist rule in Czechoslovakia Marxist historians made a concerted effort to deemphasize the significance of the emigré leadership, and in the process they exaggerated the influence of the Bolshevik revolution. See, in particular: J.S. Hajek, *Wilsonovská legenda v dějinách ČSR* (Prague: Státní Nakladatelství politické literatury, 1953). L'udovit Holotík, *Štefánikovská legenda a Vznik ČSR* (Bratislava: Vydavatel'stvo Slovenskej Akadémie Vied, 1958). More recently there has appeared a work that attempts to put both the exile leadership and the Russian precedent into a proper perspective. Karel Pichlík, *Zahraniční odboj 1914-1918 bez legend* (Prague: Svoboda, 1968).

94. Masaryk, *Světová revoluce*, pp. 239-42.

95. London, P.R.O., F.O. 371, vol. CAB 24/50, G.T. 4414, "Notes on Conversation with Representatives of the Bohemian National Council at Versailles on 22nd April, 1918."

96. London, P.R.O., F.O. 371, vol. 3135, W3/135132/64427, Copy of a telegram from Masaryk to Beneš, July 15, 1918. Also see the excerpts from a memorandum by Masaryk about the Bolshevik menace that he sent to the Department of State in the late summer of 1918. Charles Pergler, *America in the Struggle for Czechoslovak Independence* (Philadelphia: Dorrance and Company, 1926), pp. 50-55.

97. London, P.R.O., F.O. 371, vol. 3293, W38/138538/383, Memorandum by Cecil about a conversation with Beneš, August 9, 1918.

98. Czech diplomatic efforts to withdraw the legionnaires from Siberia were one of the major themes that run through the British Foreign Office documents about the intervention in Russia from late 1918 to 1920. See, in particular, volumes 3525-28 and 4094-96 of Foreign Office file 371.

For assorted Czechoslovak diplomatic documents on the subject, see: *Boj o směr vývoje československého státu, Červenec 1919-květen 1921*, vol. 6 of *Prameny k ohlasu velké říjnové socialistické revoluce a vzniku ČSR* (Prague: Nakladatelství československé akademi věd, 1969).

The exploits of the Czech legion in Siberia have inspired numerous articles and books both by historians and by writers on historical topics. Those works are not cited here because the focus in this book is not on the legion itself but rather on the diplomatic results of the Siberian campaign. A brief mention of some of the literature is included in the bibliography.

99. Strauss, *Entstehung der tschechoslowakischen Republik*, pp. 98-99.

100. Mamatey, *United States and East Central Europe*, p. 131.

101. Ibid., pp. 282-84.

102. The full text of the Pittsburgh agreement appears in Thomson, *Czechoslovakia in European History*, p. 272.

103. Mamatey, *United States and East Central Europe*, p. 283.

104. Strauss, *Entstehung der tschechoslowakischen Republik*, pp. 177-84, 220-24. Jan Opočenský, *Konec monarchie rakousko-uherské* (Prague: Orbis, 1928), pp. 85-106.

105. Tobolka, *Politické dějiny československého národa*, 4:313-27, 361-95. Peroutka, *Budování státu*, 1:5-55. Strauss, *Entstehung der tschechoslowakischen Republik*, pp. 220-66. On the socialists, see particularly: Frant. Soukup, *28. říjen 1918* (Prague: Orbis, 1928), 2:889-905, 922-56.

106. Václav Chaloupecký, *Zápas o Slovensko 1918* (Prague: Čin, 1930), p. 41.

107. Tobolka, *Politické dějiny československého národa*, 4: 284-91, 399-406. Chaloupecký, *Zápas o Slovensko 1918*, pp. 19-61. Vavro Šrobár, *Osvobodené Slovensko* (Prague: Čin, 1928), pp. 105-14. Karol A. Medvecký, *Slovenský prevrat* (Trnava: Spolok Sv. Vojtecha, 1930), 1:334-58. Josef Anderle, "The Slovak Issue in the Munich Crisis of 1938" (Ph.D. diss., University of Chicago, 1961), pp. 26-30.

108. The lawyer was Robert M. Calfee. In my possession is a copy of a letter by Mr. Calfee recounting his association with Masaryk. I also have a copy of a letter in Masaryk's handwriting, written in New York on November 20, 1918. The text reads: "Dear Mr. Calfee, before I leave this country I must say you good bye & heartily thank for your help in writing the declaration: the story of this declaration is in itself the proof of the great sympathy, which our cause has found in America. I hope to see you once more in my life. Yours sincerely T.G. Masaryk." Also see, Mamatey, *The United States and East Central Europe*, pp. 331-32. J.B. Kozák, *T.G. Masaryk a vzník Washingtonské deklarace v říjnu 1918* (Prague: Melantrich, 1969).

109. Peroutka, *Budování státu*, 1:219.

110. *Československá Vlastivěda Dějiny*, p. 832.

111. Paul Molisch, *Geschichte der deutschnationalen Bewegung in Oesterreich* (Jena: Verlag von Gustav Fischer, 1926), pp. 233-52. Zeman, *The Break-Up of the Habsburg Empire*, pp. 86-87.

112. Klemens von Klemperer, *Ignaz Seipel: Christian Statesman in a Time of Crisis* (Princeton: Princeton University Press, 1972), pp. 54-73. Kann, *The Multi-National Empire*, 2:208-19.

113. Kann, *The Multi-National Empire*, 2:154-78.

114. Hantsch, *Geschichte Österreichs*, 2:535-38.

115. Besides the host of articles and convention papers spawned by the Fischer debate, the following books afford an overview of the develop-

ment of the controversy. Gerhard Ritter, *Staatkunst und Kriegshandwerk: Das Problem des "Militarismus" in Deutschland* (Munich: R. Oldenbourg, 1954-68). Fritz Fischer, *Griff nach der Weltmacht: Die Kriegszielpolitik des kaiserlichen Deutschland, 1914-1918* (Düsseldorf: Droste Verlag, 1961). Konrad H. Jarausch, *The Enigmatic Chancellor: Bethmann Hollweg and the Hubris of Imperial Germany* (New Haven: Yale University Press, 1973).

116. Jarausch, *The Enigmatic Chancellor*, pp. 185-229, 407-23. Henry Cord Meyer, *Mitteleuropa in German Thought and Action 1815-1945* (The Hague: Martinus Nijhoff, 1955), pp. 137-250.

117. In the middle of October 1918 William II still thought in terms of a German-dominated Mitteleuropa. The fundamental power relationships in Central Europe imparted to his ideas a basic long-term realism even in the face of military collapse. F. Gregory Campbell, "The Kaiser and *Mitteleuropa* in October 1918," *Central European History* 2 (December 1969):376-86.

Chapter Two

1. Ferdinand Peroutka, *Budování státu* (Prague: Fr. Borový, 1933), 1:185-203.

2. *Deutsche Zeitung Bohemia*, October 30, 1918, pp. 1-2. Hereafter cited as *Bohemia*. *Prager Tagblatt*, October 30, 1918, p. 1. All references to newspapers are to their morning editions unless otherwise noted.

3. *Bohemia*, November 1, 1918, p. 1.

4. Albert Karl Simon, "Rudolf Lodgman von Auen und das deutsch-tschechische Verhältnis," in *Beiträge zum deutsch-tschechischen Verhältnis im 19. und 20. Jahrhundert* (Munich: Verlag Robert Lerche, 1967), pp. 47-77.

5. *Bohemia*, October 30, 1918, p. 2. *Prager Tagblatt*, October 30, 1918, p. 1.

6. On the attempts to establish separate German governments in the Czech lands, see: Paul Molisch, *Die sudetendeutsche Freiheitsbewegung in den Jahren 1918-1919* (Vienna: Wilhelm Braumüller Universitäts-Verlagsbuchhandlung, 1932), pp. 6-109. Kurt Rabl, *Das Ringen um das sudetendeutsche Selbstbestimmungsrecht 1918-19* (Munich: Verlag Robert Lerche, 1958). Johann Wolfgang Brügel, *Tschechen und Deutsche, 1918-1938* (Munich: Nymphenburger Verlagshandlung, 1967), pp. 48-66. Peroutka, *Budování státu*, 1:159-62, 185-203, 359-72. Jaroslav César and Bohumil Černý, *Politika německých buržoazních stran v Československu v letech 1918-1938* (Prague: Nakladatelství Československé akademie věd, 1962), 1:37-111. Elizabeth Wiskemann, *Czechs and Germans* (London: Oxford University Press, 1938), pp. 79-84.

7. Brügel traces the term *sudetendeutsch* to the writer Franz Jesser, who first used the concept in an article in 1902. Brügel, *Tschechen und Deutsche*, p. 116. Certainly one of the first popularizers of the idea of a

sudetendeutscher Stamm was Josef Nadler, who wrote a history of German literature according to the various German tribes or _Stämme_. Josef Nadler, _Literaturgeschichte der deutschen Stämme und Landschaften_ (Regensburg: Josef Habbel, 1912-28). Before and during World War I the popular designation was _Deutschböhmen_, but _Sudetendeutschen_ replaced it in the interwar period. In this book I have used "German Bohemians" until the approximate time that "Sudeten Germans" became popular and then have switched to the latter term.

8. _Bohemia_, October 4, 1918, p. 1. _Prager Tagblatt_, October 4, 1918, p. 2. Also see the report of the German ambassador in Vienna, Count Georg von Wedel, in which he commented favorably on the formation of the German bloc. Bonn, AA, Oesterreich 95, vol. 25, Akten betr. Beziehungen Oesterreichs zu Deutschland, Report from Wedel to Prince Max of Baden, October 4, 1918. Those documents of the German Foreign Office that were not microfilmed are cited by the archival number under which they are now catalogued in Bonn.

9. For the text of the resolution see _Prager Tagblatt_, October 4, 1918, p. 1; _Bohemia_, October 4, 1918, p. 1; _Lidové noviny_, October 4, 1918, p. 1.

10. Bonn, AA, Oesterreich 101, vol. 43, Akten betr. Böhmen, Report from Wedel to Prince Max of Baden, October 14, 1918.

11. _Bohemia_, October 19, 1918, pp. 1-2.

12. _Bohemia_, October 25, 1918, p. 4. Molisch, _Sudetendeutsche Freiheitsbewegung_, pp. 35-36, 53-54, 60ff. Others have subsequently referred to the reluctance of industrial interests to be separated from Czechoslovakia, but the fact that Molisch was German and that he disapproved of the attitude of German businessmen makes him the most authoritative source.

13. For a description by the German consul-general in Prague of the food shortage among the German-Bohemians, see AA, Grosses Hauptquartier, K1151/K294644-650/xxx, Report by Baron Gebsattel to the German Foreign Office, October 11, 1918. In the references to the microfilmed documents of the German Foreign Office, the first number is the serial number of the document collection; the second set of numbers specify the frames on which the particular document is reproduced; and the third number refers to the reel on which the particular roll of microfilm is stored. (In this case, the reel number for Serial K1151 is not listed in the guides.) Invaluable guides to the Foreign Office archives are: The American Historical Association Committee for the Study of War Documents. _A Catalogue of Files and Microfilms of the German Foreign Ministry Archives, 1867-1920_ (Oxford: At the University Press, 1959), and George O. Kent, ed., _A Catalog of Files and Microfilms of the German Foreign Ministry Archives, 1920-1945_, 4 vols. (Stanford: Hoover Institution Press, 1962-72).

For a discussion of the use of food relief for political purposes, see Arno J. Mayer, _Politics and Diplomacy of Peacemaking: Containment and_

Counterrevolution at Versailles, 1918-1919 (New York: Alfred A. Knopf, 1967), pp. 253-83.

14. See especially Rudolf Lodgman, "Meine Verhandlungen mit dem Národní Výbor," *Sudetendeutsche Tageszeitung*, December 23, 1923, pp. 1-2.

15. *Prager Tagblatt*, November 12, 1918, p. 1. Rašín later claimed that Seliger quoted him out of context, but the important thing is that the Germans believed that Seliger's account was accurate. Klaus Zessner, "Die Haltung der deutschböhmischen Sozialdemokratic zum neuen tschechoslo-wakischen Staat 1918-1919," in *Die "Burg": Einflussreiche politische Kräfte um Masaryk und Beneš*, ed. Karl Bosl, vol. 1 (Munich: R. Oldenbourg, 1973):165-66.

In March 1919 French military intelligence in Prague reported to Paris that Rašín took a hard line on the nationality question. He believed that the Germans should be given a three-year grace period after the signing of the peace treaties either to emigrate or to declare themselves Czechoslovak citizens, accepting the linguistic and national consequences of that act. Paris, MAE, Europe 1918-1929, Tchécoslovaquie, vol. 31, Report of the Chief of Military Intelligence in Prague to the French Ministry of Foreign Affairs, March 3, 1919.

In September 1919 Masaryk referred to Rašín as "a Talmudic scholar of chauvinism," meaning that Rašín was an expert on nationalistic excesses. Bonn, AA, Politische Abteilung IA, Oesterreich 101, vol. 56, Akten betreffend Böhmen, Report from Saenger to the German Foreign Office, September 25, 1919.

In Rašín's defense, it should be pointed out that he had been sentenced to death during the war for his part in Maffie activities. In his comments to the German-Bohemians he was using the words of General Windischgrätz to the Czech rebels of 1848.

16. Bonn, AA, Politische Abteilung IA, Oesterreich 101, vol. 45, Akten betreffend Böhmen, Report from Gebsattel to the German Foreign Office, November 27, 1918.

17. *Lidové noviny*, December 14, 1918, p. 1. *Bohemia*, December 14, 1918, p. 1

18. Molisch, *Sudetendeutsche Freiheitsbewegung*, pp. 79-80. For a detailed description of the policies of the Austrian and the German-Bohemian governments, see Hanns Haas, "Die deutschböhmische Frage 1918-1919 und das österreichisch-tschechoslowakische Verhältnis," in *Bohemia*, vol. 13 (Munich: R. Oldenbourg Verlag, 1972), pp. 336-83.

19. *Bohemia*, December 8, 1918, p. 2. *Prager Tagblatt*, December 8, 1918, p. 2. The assumption that all of Bohemia and Moravia would remain in the Czechoslovak republic was inherent in the official Czech response to Austrian protests on December 3. Vienna, HHStA, N.P.A., Karton 861, Note from Vlastimil Tusar, the Czechoslovak plenipotentiary in Vienna, to the Austrian State Office for Foreign Affairs, December 3, 1918.

20. *Bohemia*, February 8, 1919, p. 1. *Lidové noviny*, February 8,

1919, p. 3. For a general discussion of the Berne congress, see Mayer, *Politics and Diplomacy of Peacemaking*, pp. 373-409.

21. Bonn, AA, Weimar, 4665/E219588-91/2412, Memo concerning a conversation of Legionsrat von Riepenhausen with the Landeshauptmann of German Bohemia, Dr. Lodgman, February 8, 1919.

22. Ibid., 4665/E219589-90/2412.

23. This policy was clearly expressed by Lodgman in his conversation with Riepenhausen. Bonn, AA, Weimar, 4665/E219589/2412.

24. Jewish influence was greater in the *Prager Tagblatt* than in the *Bohemia*, but the *Bohemia* was used, for example, in the successful campaign in April 1920 to win the Jewish vote for the German Democratic Freedom party. The *Prager Tagblatt* was more accommodating to the Czechoslovak republic than the *Bohemia*, and both newspapers were much more moderate than the *Reichenberger Zeitung* or later the *Sudetendeutsche Tageszeitung*. In the later 1930s, as German public opinion moved to the Right, these newspapers became increasingly more sympathetic to the Czechoslovak government.

25. Bonn, AA, Politische Abteilung IA, 7479/H187472-475/3270, Report of Wedel to the German Foreign Office, October 16, 1918. Brügel, *Tschechen und Deutsche*, pp. 54-56.

26. Bonn, AA, Politische Abteilung IA, Oesterreich 101, vol. 43, Akten betreffend Böhmen, Report from Wedel to the German Foreign Office, October 28, 1918. Brügel, *Tschechen und Deutsche*, pp. 54-56.

27. Bonn, AA, Grosses Hauptquartier, K1151/K294656-657, Telegram from Solf to General Headquarters, October 28, 1918.

28. Bonn, AA, Grosses Hauptquartier, K1151/K294659, Telegram from Hindenburg to the German Foreign Office, October 28, 1918.

29. Bonn, AA, Politische Abteilung IA, Oesterreich 101, vol. 43, Akten betreffend Böhmen, Report from Gebsattel to the German Foreign Office, October 25, 1918. Brügel, *Tschechen und Deutsche*, pp. 56-58.

30. Bonn, AA, Politische Abteilung IA, Oesterreich 101, vol. 43, Akten betreffend Böhmen, Report from Gebsattel to the German Foreign Office, October 25, 1918. Note that Gebsattel's views corroborate the historical interpretation of Peroutka on this question. See note 1 for this chapter.

31. Bonn, AA, Politische Abteilung IA, Oesterreich 101, vol. 43, Akten betreffend Böhmen, Report from Gebsattel to the German Foreign Office, October 29, 1918. Koloman Gajan, *Německý imperialismus a československo-německé vztahy v letech 1918-1921* (Prague: Nakladatelství Československé akademie věd, 1962), pp. 29-30.

32. Gajan, *Československo-německé vztahy*, p. 30.

33. That phrase was used in a telegram from the German Foreign Office to General Headquarters curiously urging that military preparations for action in Bohemia should be conducted so as not to provoke the Czechs. Bonn, AA, Grosses Hauptquartier, K1151/K294661, Telegram from Solf to General Headquarters, October 31, 1918.

34. Bonn, AA, Grosses Hauptquartier, K1151/K294682, Telegram from General Headquarters to the German Foreign Office, November 4, 1918; K1151/K294693-694, Report from Gebsattel to the German Foreign Office, November 4, 1918. Brügel, *Tschechen und Deutsche*, p. 58.

35. Bonn, AA, Politische Abteilung IA, Oesterreich 101, vol. 43, Akten betreffend Böhmen, Report of Gebsattel to the German Foreign Office, November 2, 1918.

36. Ibid., vol. 44, Akten betreffend Böhmen, Telegram from Solf to Gebsattel, November 7, 1918.

37. Ibid., vol. 45, Akten betreffend Böhmen, Report from Gebsattel to the German Foreign Office, November 27, 1918.

38. Ibid., vol. 44, Akten betreffend Böhmen, Memorandum by Dr. Schwarz enclosed in a report by Gebsattel to the German Foreign Office, November 16, 1918. Schwarz served as the German vice-consul in Prague during the autumn and winter of 1918-19.

39. Before and during the war Saenger contributed articles to the *Neue Rundschau* in Berlin and wrote the "Junius letters," which appeared in the journal. In one of these letters, in July 1914, he wrote about the political situation in Russia and based his remarks on Masaryk's book, *Russland und Europa*. Saenger remarked: "I was lucky that I began to read Masaryk, who, himself a Slav, has become a wonderfully mature European." See "Chronik: Aus Junius' Tagebuch," *Die Neue Rundschau*, (July 1914), p. 1023. Brügel, *Tschechen und Deutsche*, p. 67.

40. Vienna, HHStA, N.P.A., Karton 861, Report by Marek to the Austrian State Office for Foreign Affairs, January 7, 1919. According to Marek, however, Czech bitterness against Austria prevented Austrian inclusion in any special economic grouping of Danubian states.

41. Bonn, AA, Weimar, 4665/E219580-86/2412, Report of Saenger to the German Foreign Office, February 6, 1919. In the conversation with Saenger, Masaryk even claimed to favor the inclusion of Germany in a Danubian confederation. The word "federation" comes from Saenger's report, and the Czechs in later years were careful to avoid any such terminology. Whether Masaryk himself used the term is not clear from Saenger's dispatch, but by favoring Germany's inclusion in any Central European grouping at all, Masaryk went far beyond subsequent Czechoslovak policy. In February 1919 the situation was still fluid, and policies on many questions had not yet been formulated.

42. Gajan, *Československo-německé vztahy*, pp. 231-32.

43. Bonn, AA, Weimar, 4665/E219584/2412, Report of Saenger to the German Foreign Office, February 6, 1919.

44. Alena Gajanová, *ČSR a středoevropská politika velmocí, 1918-1938* (Prague: Academia, nakladatelství Československé akademie věd, 1967), pp. 18-32.

45. *Bohemia*, December 8, 1918, p. 2. *Prager Tagblatt*, December 8, 1918, p. 2.

46. London *Times*, January 3, 1919, p. 7. See the publicity given to comments in the *Times* in *Bohemia*, January 12, 1919, p. 2.

47. *Lidové noviny*, January 15, 1919, p. 1. *Bohemia*, January 15, 1919, p. 1.

48. *Lidové noviny*, January 15, 1919, p. 1. *Bohemia*, January 15, 1919, p. 2.

49. *Bohemia*, June 6, 1919, p. 1.

50. Wiskemann, *Czechs and Germans*, pp. 84-85.

51. D. Perman, *The Shaping of the Czechoslovak State: Diplomatic History of the Boundaries of Czechoslovakia, 1914-1920* (Leiden: E. J. Brill, 1962), p. 45. Perman quotes Charles Seymour, who attributed the remark to Wilson, but she questions the implication that Wilson was ignorant of the ethnic composition of Central Europe. Her book is the most authoritative monograph on the Czechoslovak question at the peace conference. A significant article because of his personal participation in the decisions at Paris is Charles Seymour, "Czechoslovak Frontiers,'" *The Yale Review* 28 (Winter 1939):273-91. See also Charles Seymour, *Letters from the Paris Peace Conference*, ed. Harold B. Whiteman, Jr. (New Haven: Yale University Press, 1965). A work that treats the Czechoslovak question in the larger perspective of French eastern policy is Piotr S. Wandycz, *France and Her Eastern Allies, 1919-1925: French-Czechoslovak-Polish Relations from the Paris Peace Conference to Locarno* (Minneapolis: University of Minnesota Press, 1962). On Czechoslovakia at the peace conference, see especially chap. 2 in Wandycz's work.

52. Wandycz, *France and Her Eastern Allies*, pp. 75-103. Peroutka, *Budování státu*, 2:600-18, 1257-84.

53. Paris, MAE, Europe 1918-1929, Tchécoslovaquie, vol. 31, Memorandum about a conversation between a French intelligence agent and Lodgman in Switzerland, February 28, 1919.

54. Wandycz, *France and Her Eastern Allies*, pp. 93, 101.

55. Ibid., pp. 97-98.

56. Note Beneš's own mention of this tactic as applied to the Teschen dispute. Edvard Beneš, *Problémy nové Evropy a zahraniční politika Československá* (Prague: Melantrich, 1924), p. 66.

57. Beneš had included the request for a protectorate for the Lusatian Sorbs largely in order to please Kramář, but he presented the idea in a very weak manner. He also indicated special interest in the welfare of Czechs resident in Vienna. Beneš was more concerned about the land corridor to Yugoslavia as an assurance of Czechoslovak access to the sea. The idea completely violated the principle of national self-determination, and the Adriatic ports were by no means as economically practical as Hamburg and Stettin. When the Treaty of Versailles guaranteed Czechoslovakia free zones in those harbors, and access to them by the Elbe and Oder rivers, Beneš achieved his basic aim of overcoming Czechoslovakia's landlocked position. See the discussion of this in Perman, *The Shaping of the Czechoslovak State*, pp. 121-35.

58. Congrès de la Paix. Délégation Tchécoslovaque. "Problems Touching the Germans of Bohemia," Mémoire no. 3, English translation. In this memorandum Beneš was able to minimize the number of Germans by concentrating only on Bohemia and not mentioning Moravia and Silesia. The Czechoslovak census of 1921 eventually confirmed the Austrian census of 1910, and the government never distorted the figures or attempted to conceal the fact that more than three million Germans lived in the country. But it is worth noting that misleading statements were made more than once before the final determination of Czechoslovak frontiers. A memorandum from the Czechoslovak National Council to the French Foreign Ministry on October 12, 1918, contained the estimate that there were two million Germans in Bohemia and Silesia. It included a misleading claim that the Germans of Moravia lived only in enclaves in Czech territory and were therefore politically unimportant. Paris, MAE, Europe 1918-1929, Tchécoslovaquie, vol. 31.

59. See *Bohemia*, October 10-October 19, 1920.

60. Hermann Raschhofer, ed., *Die tschechoslowakischen Denkschriften für die Friedenskonferenz von Paris, 1919-1920* (Berlin: C. Heymann, 1938).

61. The chairman of the commission was Jules Cambon, who during the war had been general secretary of the Quai d'Orsay. The other French member was Jules Alfred Laroche, Chief of the Central European Section of the Foreign Ministry. The chairman of the subcommission was also a Frenchman, General Le Rond, who was later to be the French representative on the Upper Silesian plebiscite commission. See Perman, *The Shaping of the Czechoslovak State*, p. 133. Sir Joseph Cook and Harold Nicolson for Britain and Marquis G. F. Salvago Raggi and A. Stranieri for Italy completed the membership of the commission.

62. *Foreign Relations of the United States: Paris Peace Conference*, 4:543-47. Hereafter cited as FRUS:PPC. Perman, *The Shaping of the Czechoslovak State*, pp. 153-54.

63. For the notes of this meeting see FRUS:PPC, 4:543-47.

64. Ibid., p. 546.

65. For the minutes of the meeting see Paul Mantoux, ed., *Les Délibérations du Conseil des Quatre* (Paris: Editions du Centre national de la recherche scientifique, 1955), 1:149. For an account of this meeting see D. Perman, *The Shaping of the Czechoslovak State*, pp. 169-76.

66. Mantoux, *Les Délibérations du Conseil des Quatre*, 1:149. Quoted in Perman, *The Shaping of the Czechoslovak State*, pp. 169-70.

67. Czechoslovakia's acquisition of those territories never significantly affected its relations with Germany and Austria. In the autumn of 1919 German diplomatic representatives did try unsuccessfully to persuade the Czechoslovak government to permit a plebiscite in Hlučínsko. The area with its fifty thousand inhabitants remained in Czechoslovakia until the Munich decisions. On the plebiscite question in 1919, see Bonn, AA, Politische Abteilung IA, Oesterreich 101, vol. 56, Akten betreffend

Böhmen, Report of Wever to the German Foreign Office, October 16, 1919; Report of Saenger to the German Foreign Office, October 28, 1919.

68. *Bohemia*, October 25, 1918, p. 1. Tusar remained in Vienna as the Czech diplomatic representative after the declaration of independence and told the Austrians in May 1919 that after the conclusion of the peace many Czech politicians would like to see an exchange of territories. Tusar suggested that villages along the Bohemian border, perhaps the city of Eger, and German areas in Silesia could come to Germany in return for Slavic villages in the Glatz salient and Upper Silesia. Such an agreement might have given Germany an increase of territory and population, but Czechoslovakia would have been able to reduce its German minority by an exchange of territories rather than a simple cession. Bonn, AA, Deutsche Friedensdelegation Versailles, 4662/E214468-69/2406, Report to Brock-dorff-Rantzau, May 14, 1919.

69. FRUS:PPC, 12:327.

70. For a discussion of Beneš's offer, see Wandycz, *France and Her Eastern Allies*, p. 57. Already in early February an official in the Czechoslovak Ministry of Foreign Affairs informed the German vice-consul that after the peace conference Beneš would be willing to negotiate about ceding purely German territories to the German Reich. That remark may well have been a maneuver aimed at mitigating any German opposition to Czechoslovakia's retaining the historic frontiers of Bohemia and Moravia. Bonn, AA, Politische Abteilung IA, Oesterreich 95, vol. 27, Akten betreffend Beziehungen Oesterreichs zu Deutschland, Report of Gebsattel to the German Foreign Office, Feburary 8, 1919.

71. Dr. Walter Koch expressed that negative attitude about the German-Bohemians to the Prussian representative in Dresden at the beginning of February 1919. Koch had just returned from a mission to Prague as a special representative of the Saxon government and his views reflected the prevailing climate of opinion in Dresden. Bonn, AA, Politische Abteilung IA, Oesterreich 101, vol. 48, Akten betreffend Böhmen, Report of Schwerin to the German Foreign Office, February 3, 1919.

72. Brügel, *Tschechen und Deutsche*, pp. 107-8. Vienna, HHStA, N.P.A., Karton 859, Letter from Freissler to Foreign Secretary Otto Bauer, April 5, 1919.

73. Vienna, HHStA, N.P.A., Karton 859, Letter from the district leader for the Egerland to the Austrian State Office for Foreign Affairs, August 22, 1919.

74. Bonn, AA, Politische Abteilung IA, Oesterreich 95, vol. 27, Akten betreffend Beziehungen Oesterreichs zu Deutschland, Report of Gebsattel to the German Foreign Office, February 8, 1919.

75. Wandycz, *France and Her Eastern Allies*, pp. 29-48.

76. Věra Olivová, *The Doomed Democracy: Czechoslovakia in a Disrupted Europe 1914-1938*, trans. George Theiner (London: Sidgwick & Jackson, 1972), p. 114.

77. Mayer, *Politics and Diplomacy of Peacemaking*, pp. 521-55, 716-49.

78. Bonn, AA, Politische Abteilung IA, Oesterreich 101, vol. 53, Akten betreffend Böhmen, Report from Saenger to the German Foreign Office, June 2, 1919; Telegram from German military headquarters at Kolberg to the Foreign Office, June 9, 1919; Report from Saenger to the German Foreign Office, June 12, 1919. Wandycz, *France and Her Eastern Allies*, pp. 69-73. Peter A. Toma, "The Slovak Soviet Republic of 1919," *American Slavic and East European Review* 17(1958):203-15. Eva S. Balogh, "Nationality Problems of the Hungarian Soviet Republic," in *Hungary in Revolution, 1918-19*, ed. Iván Völgyes (Lincoln: University of Nebraska Press, 1971), pp. 112-20. Peroutka, *Budování státu*, 2:983-1022, 1067-93. Martin Vietor, *Slovenská sovietska republika* (Bratislava: Slovenské vydavateľstvo politickej literatúry, 1959). Václav Král, *Intervenční válka: Československé buržoasie proti Maďarské Sovětské Republice v roce 1919* (Prague: Nakladatelství Československé akademie věd, 1954).

79 Gajan, *Československo-německé vztahy*, p. 76. Gajan bases this on a document in the Czechoslovak Ministry of Foreign Affairs. Beneš went to great lengths to portray Czechoslovakia as a reliable and valuable ally of the Western powers, and he probably entertained exaggerated notions of the stress that his country could bear.

80. Ibid. These plans are in documents in the Central Military Archive in Prague.

81. Bonn, AA, Deutsche Friedensdelegation Versailles, 4662/ E214472-73/2406, Report of Saenger to the German Foreign Office, May 23, 1919. Saenger noted that the domestic instability of Czechoslovakia made political leaders in Prague reluctant actually to engage in a military conflict with Germany.

82. Bonn, AA, Deutsche Friedensdelegation Versailles, 4662/ E214470-71/2406.

83. Bonn, AA, Politische Abteilung IA, Oesterreich 101, vol. 52, Akten betreffend Böhmen, Report of Saenger to the German Foreign Office, May 27, 1919.

84. FRUS:PPC, 4:727-28. Letter from Beneš to Dutasta, May 9, 1919.

85. For the full text of this memorandum and the accompanying note of Austrian Chancellor Renner, see *Bohemia*, June 20, 1919, pp. 2-3.

86. Perman, *The Shaping of the Czechoslovak State*, pp. 153-54, 196.

87. Molisch, *Sudetendeutsche Freiheitsbewegung*, pp. 61-62.

88. Ibid., pp. 69-78.

89. FRUS:PPC, 12:273-74, Memorandum by Professor A. C. Coolidge, "The New Frontiers in Former Austria-Hungary," March 10, 1919.

90. Perman, *The Shaping of the Czechoslovak State*, pp. 203-8.

91. Czechoslovak Republic. Státní úřad statisticky, *Manuel statistique de la République Tchécoslovaque* (Prague: Státní úřad statisticky, 1928), p. 275. This is the French version of the Czech edition cited elsewhere.

92. Harold W. V. Temperley, ed., *A History of the Peace Conference of Paris* (London: Henry Frowde and Hodder & Stoughton, 1920-24), 5:112-49. Vondracek, *Foreign Policy of Czechoslovakia*, pp. 45-47.

93. Vondracek, *Foreign Policy of Czechoslovakia*, pp. 19-20, 44-45.

94. Friedrich Purlitz, *Deutscher Geschichtskalender 1919*, pp. 694-95. *Bohemia*, October 2, 1919, p. 1. *Prager Tagblatt*, October 2, 1919, p. 3.

95. Quoted in Fritz Stern, *The Politics of Cultural Despair* (Berkeley and Los Angeles: University of California Press, 1961), p. 87.

96. Bonn, AA, Politische Abteilung IA, Oesterreich 101, vol. 54, Akten betreffend Böhmen, Letter and memorandum from Saenger to Hermann Müller, August 1, 1919.

97. Ibid., vol. 56, Akten betreffend Böhmen, Report from Riepenhausen to the German Foreign Office, October 24, 1919. The marginal comments and the question marks on the report, put there by officials of the Foreign Office, emphasized the absurdity of Lodgman's ideas. Riepenhausen himself observed: "This train of thought of Dr. Lodgman's shows probably best of all what the German-Bohemians mean by a 'loyal attitude' toward the Czechs."

98. Ibid., vol. 57, Akten betreffend Böhmen, Report by Saenger to the German Foreign Office, November 4, 1919.

99. Ibid.

100. Ibid.

101. During the peace conference, the French minister on special mission to Prague advocated far-reaching autonomy for the German Bohemians, but he soon left Prague and his recommendation was never adopted as French policy. Paris, MAE, Europe 1918-1929, Tchécoslovaquie, vol. 31, Report of Allize to Pichon, April 19, 1919.

102. Ibid., vol. 26, Report of Couget to Briand, October 10, 1921. Report of Couget to Poincaré, January 27, 1922.

103. Ibid., vol. 31, Report of Couget to Millerand, September 13, 1920. Vol. 32, Report of Pozzi to Briand, April 26, 1921.

104. Ibid., vol. 31, Report of Clément Simon to Pichon, August 5, 1919.

105. The percentages were: German Social Democrats 47.9%, German Nationals 7.6%, German National Socialists 2.9%, German Agrarians 6.9%, Christian Socials 5.6%. Representatives of splinter parties and candidates without party identification accounted for the rest of the German vote. *Statistická příručka republiky Československé*, 2, 351.

106. *Bohemia*, July 13, 1919, p. 1. The *Bohemia* quoted Tusar's interview in the *Neue Freie Presse* in Vienna on July 12.

107. Peroutka, *Budování státu*, 1:259-63. *Národní shromáždění republiky Československé v prvém desítiletí* (Prague: Státní tiskárna, 1928), pp. 17-20.

108. R.W. Seton-Watson, *The New Slovakia* (Prague: Fr. Borový, 1924), pp. 13-50. C.A. Macartney, *Hungary and Her Successors* (London: Oxford University Press, 1937), pp. 110-19. Anderle, "The Slovak Issue in the Munich Crisis of 1938," pp. 45-47.

109. Juraj Kramer, *Slovenské autonomistické hnutie v rokoch 1918-1929* (Bratislava: Vydavateľstvo slovenskej akadémie vied, 1962), pp. 7-134. Imrich Stanek, *Zrada a pád: Hlinkovští separatisté a tak zvaný slovenský stát* (Prague: Státní nakladatelství politické literatury, 1958), pp. 51-68. Anderle, "The Slovak Issue in the Munich Crisis of 1938," pp. 47-54.

110. *Lidové noviny*, April 4, 1919, p. 1. For German comments on the law, see *Prager Tagblatt*, April 2, 1919, p. 1.

111. *Statistická příručka republiky Československé*, 2:20-21. Wiskemann, *Czechs and Germans*, pp. 207-12.

112. *Sbírka zákonu a nařízení státu Československého*, 1920, pp. 319-20. The law was passed on February 19, 1920. For initial reports about the proposed law, see *Prager Tagblatt*, January 13, 1920, evening edition, p. 1. *Bohemia*, January 14, 1920, p. 4. Wiskemann, *Czechs and Germans*, pp. 212-16.

113. August Naegle was the rector of the German university in 1919. From 1920 to 1925 he was a senator for the German National party. See the *Bohemia* and the *Prager Tagblatt* during 1919 for the continuing debate about the relocation of the university.

114. *Sbírka zákonů a nařízení státu Československého*, 1920, pp. 268-69. For a German text of the law, see *Prager Tagblatt*, February 28, 1920, p. 3.

115. Ferdinand Seibt, "Zur Sozialstruktur der ersten ČSR," *Beiträge zum deutschtschechischen Verhältnis im 19. und 20. Jahrhundert*, p. 123. In looking back upon the experience of the first republic, Milan Hodža, the premier from 1935 to 1938, agreed that the Sudeten Germans had legitimate grievances about the difficulty of entering the civil service. Milan Hodža, *Federation in Central Europe* (London: Jarrolds Publishers, 1942), pp. 141-42, 217.

116. These facts came from *České slovo*, the organ of the Czechoslovak National Socialist party, in its debate with Kramář's *Národní listy*, which wanted a stronger law. See *České slovo*, May 13, 1920, pp. 5-6. The German newspapers were quick to exploit this article. See *Bohemia*, May 14, 1920, p. 1. *Prager Tagblatt*, May 14, 1920, p. 1. See also, Harry Klepetař, *Der Sprachenkampf in den Sudetenländern* (Prague: Ed. Strache, 1930), pp. 126-52.

117. Lewis Einstein, *A Diplomat Looks Back*, ed. Lawrence E. Gelfand (New Haven: Yale University Press, 1968), pp. 174-78. Einstein was the American minister in Prague from 1921 to 1930.

118. Peroutka, *Budování státu*, 2:865-89. Wiskemann, *Czechs and Germans*, pp. 147-60.

119. The historian who has done the most comprehensive recent work on the land reform wrote: "It was the goal of the Czech bourgeoisie, with the help of the land reform, to insure in a nationally mixed Czechoslovakia the ruling position to the Czech nation, that is to the Czech bourgeoisie." Milan Otáhal, *Zápas o pozemkovou reformu v ČSR* (Prague: Nakladatelství Československé akademie věd, 1963), pp. 204-5. On the other hand,

Ferdinand Seibt has produced figures that minimize the impact of Czech immigration into German lands. Ferdinand Seibt, "Die erste ČSR im Bild der Forschung," *Aktuelle Forschungsprobleme um die Erste Tschechoslowakische Republik*, ed. Karl Bosl, pp. 207-9.

120. The Germans formed organizations to agitate for recognition of the bonds and held a number of mass demonstrations. One of the first was in Reichenberg on August 17, 1919. See *Prager Tagblatt*, August 20, 1919, p. 3. *Bohemia*, August 20, 1919, pp. 4-5

121. *Bohemia*, June 20, 1920, p. 1. *Prager Tagblatt*, June 20, 1920, p. 1. Wiskemann, *Czechs and Germans*, pp. 140-47.

122. *Statistická příručka republiky Československé*, 2:347.

123. *Bohemia*, May 8, 1920, p. 1; May 14, p. 1; May 15, p. 1; *Prager Tagblatt*, May 8, 1920, p. 1; May 14, p. 1; May 15, p. 1. Lodgman's parliamentary leadership was a foregone conclusion, for the bourgeois parties had made him their leader and representative in deliberating with the German Social Democrats immediately upon his return to Czechoslovakia in October 1919. See *Bohemia*, October 4, 1919, p. 1. The National Socialists joined the bourgeois bloc in October 1920. See *Prager Tagblatt*, October 28, 1920, p. 2.

124. *Bohemia*, May 20, 1920, p. 1. *Prager Tagblatt*, May 21, 1920, p. 1.

125. *Lidové noviny*, May 28, 1920, pp. 1-2. *Bohemia*, May 28, 1920, p. 1. *Prager Tagblatt*, May 28, 1920, p. 1. *Národní shromáždění republiky československé v prvém desítiletí*, p. 193.

126. *Bohemia*, May 28, 1920, p. 1. *Prager Tagblatt*, May 28, 1920, p. 1. In parliamentary debates the deputies could use their own native languages. All spokesmen for the government were required to use Czech. Subsequently, when Sudeten Germans became ministers, they had to speak Czech or deputize a Czech assistant to talk for them.

127. For conflicting reports of the incident see *Bohemia*, June 26, 1920, p. 1. *Lidové noviny*, June 26, 1920, p. 1. *Prager Tagblatt*, June 26, 1920, p. 1.

128. *Bohemia*, November 10, 1920, p. 1. *Prager Tagblatt*, November 10, 1920, p. 1. *Lidové noviny*, November 11, 1920, p. 2.

129. On November 13 Czech legionnaires tore down a statue of Emperor Joseph II in Cheb (Eger), and on the following day the Germans retaliated by storming and looting a Czech school. When this news reached Prague, it set off riots among the Czechs, who invaded the offices of the *Prager Tagblatt* and prevented both it and the *Bohemia* from publishing for three days. As the demonstrations continued, they were also aimed at Jews, whose upper class was culturally identified with the Germans in Prague. *Lidové noviny*, November 17, 1920, pp. 1-3; November 18, p. 3. *Prager Tagblatt*, November 20, p. 1. *Bohemia*, November 20, p. 1.

130. *Bohemia*, November 14, 1920, pp. 1-2. *Prager Tagblatt*, November 14, 1920, p. 3. See the ambivalent comments on the situation in Czechoslovakia in the official organ of the Union of Democratic Control. *Foreign Affairs* (London), 2 (December 1920):95-96. A recent and

valuable work on the Union in the war years is Marvin Swartz, *The Union of Democratic Control in British Politics during the First World War* (Oxford: Clarendon Press, 1971).

131. *Manuel statistique de la République Tchécoslovaque*, 3:277. The Czech and the French versions of the official statistical manuals of the Czechoslovak government are used interchangeably in the footnotes. Often only one version can be found in Western libraries, but it is unpredictable which that may be.

132. Ibid., p. 293.

133. *Verhandlungen des Reichstags*, vol. 346, 1407-8. *Prager Tagblatt*, December 3, 1920, p. 2. *Bohemia*, December 3, 1920, p. 10.

134. Bonn, AA, Politische Abteilung II, L416/L118802-04/4412, Report of Saenger to the German Foreign Office, December 1, 1920.

135. *Bohemia*, August 17, 1919, p. 4. This news was based on information especially supplied to the *Bohemia* concerning a secret meeting of Czech and German landed interests.

136. *České slovo*, September 9, 1920, p. 1. The *České slovo* broke the news on September 9, and other newspapers picked it up on the following day. All the newspapers carried continuing reports of the government crisis during the following week.

137. *Lidové noviny*, September 14, 1920, p. 1. *Národní shromáždění republiky československé v prvém desítiletí*, pp. 229-33, 238-40.

138. Peroutka, *Budování státu*, 3:2091-2114. Olivová, *The Doomed Democracy*, pp. 130-34. Contemporary speeches by the leader of the left wing are reprinted in Bohumír Šmeral, *Historické práce 1908-1940*, (Prague: Státní nakladatelství politické literatury, 1961), pp. 137-67.

139. Vienna, HHStA, N.P.A., Karton 832, Report of Marek to Chancellor Karl Renner, September 16, 1919.

140. Ibid., Karton 821, Memorandum by Marek about a conversation with Beneš, October 30, 1919.

141. Ibid., Report by Marek to the Austrian State Office for Foreign Affairs, November 11, 1919. Gajanová, *ČSR a středoevropská politika velmocí*, pp. 60-61.

142. *Prager Tagblatt*, January 14, 1920, p. 2. *Bohemia*, January 14, 1920, p. 7.

143. The original protocols in both German and Czech texts with the signatures of Beneš and Renner are available in the Austrian archives. Vienna, HHStA, Staatsurkunde der Ersten Republik, January 12, 1920. Věra Olivová, "K historii československo-rakouské smlouvy z roku 1921," *Československý časopis historický* 9 (1961):202-4. For this and other articles Olivová had access to Czechoslovak diplomatic documents, which constitute the primary source of her information. They corroborate what I have been able to glean from other archives.

144. Vienna HHStA, N.P.A., Karton 479, Memorandum by Marek about the conversations between Beneš and Renner, January 14, 1920.

145. Anti-Catholic attitudes in the young republic are well docu-

mented. The diplomatic archives offer more evidence, of which two examples will suffice.

In a conversation on September 30, 1919, Masaryk warned German foreign minister Hermann Müller that the Vatican was the focal point of a counterrevolutionary movement that was spreading across the European continent and into Britain and the United States. Masaryk presumably believed that the German Social Democrats would share his fears of clerical politics. Bonn, AA, Politische Abteilung IA, Oesterreich 101, vol. 56, Akten betreffend Böhmen, Memorandum by Müller about a conversation with Masaryk.

In May 1920 the French minister in Prague penned a tongue-in-cheek report about the elaborate precautions to guard the statue on Charles Bridge of Saint Jan of Nepomuk against nationalist attacks. The minister recalled the destruction of a statue to the virgin at the Prague Old Town Hall in the early days of independence. Paris, MAE, Europe 1918-1929, Tchécoslovaquie, vol. 25, Report by Clément-Simon to Millerand, May 21, 1920.

146. *Bohemia*, January 21, 1920, p. 4. The *Bohemia* reprinted here part of an interview with Saenger that appeared in the *Berliner Börsen-Courier*.

147. Bonn, AA, Politische Abteilung IA, Oesterreich 95, vol. 32, Akten betreffend Beziehungen Oesterreichs zu Deutschland, Note from Müller to Saenger, January 31, 1920.

148. Vienna, HHStA, N.P.A., Karton 821, Report by Marek to the Austrian State Office for Foreign Affairs, February 12, 1920.

149. Heinrich Benedikt, ed., *Geschichte der Republik Österreich* (Munich: R. Oldenbourg, 1954), pp. 94-103.

150. Perman, *The Shaping of the Czechoslovak State*, pp. 258-66. Vondracek, *The Foreign Policy of Czechoslovakia*, pp. 162-73. Gajanová, *ČSR a středoevropská politika velmocí*, pp. 62-68. Wandycz, *France and Her Eastern Allies*, pp. 186-93.

151. *Bohemia*, August 14, 1920, p. 1. *Lidové noviny*, August 14, 1920, p. 3. *Prager Tagblatt*, August 14, 1920, p. 5.

152. Vienna, HHStA, N.P.A., Karton 822, Report of Marek to the Austrian State Office for Foreign Affairs, September 9, 1920.

153. *Bohemia*, October 3, 1920, p. 10. *Bohemia* referred to an interview given by Renner to a correspondent of the *Neues Wiener Tagblatt*.

154. Edvard Beneš, *The Foreign Policy of Czechoslovakia* (Prague: Orbis, 1921), pp. 13-14. The Czech text of the speech was reprinted in the *Lidové noviny*, January 28, 1921, pp. 2-4. Beneš, *Problémy nové Evropy*, pp. 104-11.

Most of Beneš's major parliamentary speeches on foreign affairs during the interwar period were translated into the major Western languages and printed in pamphlet form by the Czechoslovak government. Those pamphlets are widely available in research libraries.

155. Vienna, HHStA, N.P.A., Karton 821, Memorandum by Marek about a conversation with Beneš, October 30, 1919.

156. Upon returning home from a trip to Rome, Paris, and London in March 1921, Beneš claimed that one of his main purposes had been the shoring up of Austrian finances. *Lidové noviny*, March 3, 1921, p. 1. *Bohemia*, March 3, 1921, p. 2. *Prager Tagblatt*, March 3, 1921, p. 2.

157. Vienna, HHStA, N.P.A., Karton 479, Memorandum by Egger, February 4, 1921.

158. Ibid., Karton 822, Note from Schober about his conversation with Beneš to Austrian diplomatic missions abroad, August 16, 1921. Věra Olivová, "Československá zahraniční politika a pokus o restauraci Habsburků v roce 1921," *Československý časopis historický* 7(1959):685-86.

159. *Prager Abendzeitung*, September 23, 1921, p. 1; September 24, p. 1. *Prager Tagblatt*, September 24, 1921, p. 1; September 25, p. 1. See also Schober's report to the foreign affairs committee in Vienna, *Prager Tagblatt*, October 15, 1921, p. 1. Olivová, "Československá zahraniční politika a pokus o restauraci Habsburků," p. 687. Olivová, "K historii československo-rakouské smlouvy z roku 1921," pp. 210-15.

160. Beneš played a leading role in mobilizing the opposition to the Charles putsch. Olivová, "Československá zahraniční politika a pokus o restauraci Habsburků," pp. 689-95.

161. Vienna, HHStA, N.P.A., Karton 822, Memorandum by Egger, November 12, 1921.

162. Ibid., Memorandum by Egger and Bischoff, December 2, 1921.

163. Olivová, "K historii československo-rakouské smlouvy z roku 1921," pp. 216-19.
For the text of the treaty, see *League of Nations, Treaty Series* 9(1922):247-51.
The Treaty of Lány has puzzled historians. C. A. Macartney and A. W. Palmer remark in their book, *Independent Eastern Europe* (London: Macmillan, 1962), p. 271: "It has never been sufficiently explained how Schober came to go so far." The documents in the Austrian archives show that the Treaty of Lány was intended to supplant the Beneš-Renner protocol of January 1920, which had been even more anti-Hungarian. It is also clear that the Austrians felt that political cooperation with the Czechs was the price that they would have to pay for financial aid from France and Britain.

164. Vienna, HHStA, N.P.A., Staatsurkunde der Ersten Republik, January 12, 1920. The note from Beneš to Marek of March 21, 1922, is deposited with the original treaty.

165. Ibid., Karton 822, Intelligence report to the Austrian State Office for Foreign Affairs, December 29, 1921.

166. Ibid., Report by Riedl to the Austrian State Office for Foreign Affairs, January 4, 1922.

167. London, P.R.O., F.O. 371, vol. 5788, C24019/23513/3, Report by Sir George Clerk to the British Foreign Office, December 19, 1921.

168. Bonn, AA, Politische Abteilung II, L416/L118776/4412, Monthly Report concerning the Czechoslovak Republic, April 1920. In accordance with the diplomatic practice of the time, ambassadors were not named, for

Czechoslovakia was not a large enough country to rate an exchange of ambassadors with the great powers.

169. In November 1919 Saenger suggested on his own initiative that the Czechoslovak government play a mediatory role between Germany and the Western powers. When Masaryk responded with interest, the German government deflated the idea. Bonn, AA, Politische Abteilung IA, Oesterreich 101, vol. 57, Akten betreffend Böhmen, Report by Saenger to the German Foreign Office, November 19, 1919. Note and memorandum from Müller to Saenger, December 6, 1919.

170. Paris, MAE, Europe 1918-1929, Tchécoslovaquie, vol. 25, Letter from Pellé to Berthelot, September 28, 1919.

171. *Těsnopisecké zprávy o schůzich Národního shromáždění česko-slovenského v Praze*, 77th session, September 30, 1919, pp. 2311-26. Beneš, *Problémy nové Evropy*, pp. 7-32. *Lidové noviny*, October 1, 1919, pp. 1-3.

172. Bonn, AA, Politische Abteilung IA, Oesterreich 101, vol. 57, Akten betreffend Böhmen, Report from Saenger to the German Foreign Office, December 13, 1919.

173. Vienna, HHStA, N.P.A., Karton 829, Report by Marek to the Austrian Ministry of Foreign Affairs, April 16, 1920.

174. Ibid., Report of Marek to the Austrian Ministry of Foreign Affairs, May 5, 1920.

175. Wandycz, *France and Her Eastern Allies*, pp. 157-59. Olivová, *ČSR a středoevropská politika velmoci*, pp. 70-71. Soják, *O československé zahraniční politice*, pp. 69-72. Soják's account contains informative materials from the Czechoslovak Ministry of Foreign Affairs, but they do not support his argument that the Czechoslovak government was enthusiastically anti-Bolshevik in the Soviet-Polish war. Alina Szklarska-Lohmannowa, *Polsko-czechosłowackie stosunki dyplomatyczne w latach 1918-1925* (Wrocław: Zakład narodowy imienia ossolińskich wydawnictwo polskiej akademii nauk, 1967), pp. 64-70.

176. London, Beaverbrook Library, Lloyd George papers, F/57/6/8, Letter from M.P.A. Hankey to David Lloyd George, July 24, 1920.

177. London, P.R.O., F.O. 371, C3908/3309/12, Report of Sir George Clerk to the British Foreign Office, August 7, 1920.

Wandycz notes that strikes on the Czech railways paralyzed French attempts to send supplies to Poland through Czechoslovakia. It should be emphasized that those strikes served the policies of Czechoslovakia. Wandycz, *France and Her Eastern Allies*, pp. 150-53.

178. Olivová, *ČSR a středoevropská politika velmocí*, pp. 69-81. Soják, *O československé zahraniční politice*, pp. 79-82. Wandycz, *France and Her Eastern Allies*, pp. 186-207.

179. In late October Beneš told the British minister in Prague about the pressure that had been applied to him by the French. Beneš intimated that he had been forced to make concessions in a commercial treaty with the

French in return for French political support in the Teschen dispute. London, P.R.O., F.O. 371, C10099/1698/12, Report of Sir George Clerk to British Foreign Office, October 29, 1920. Clerk's report provoked Sir Eyre Crowe to comment: "It is the French government's *methods* which are so detestable. They habitually resort to blackmail in all their political dealings." Crowe was promoted from assistant under secretary of state to permanent under secretary of state at the end of November 1920.

At the beginning of November the French and the Czechoslovak governments concluded a commercial convention. Immediately thereafter the Czechoslovak-German treaty was brought up for ratification.

180. Wandycz, *Soviet-Polish Relations*, pp. 219-20. Christian Höltje, *Die Weimarer Republik und das Ostlocarno-Problem 1919-1934* (Würzburg: Holzner-Verlag, 1958), pp. 24-30. Josef Korbel, *Poland Between East and West* (Princeton: Princeton University Press, 1963), pp. 28-30, 72-75. Harald von Riekhoff, *German-Polish Relations, 1918-1933* (Baltimore: The Johns Hopkins Press, 1971), pp. 27-39.

181. David Felix, *Walther Rathenau and the Weimar Republic* (Baltimore: The Johns Hopkins Press, 1971), pp. 8-24.

182. London, P.R.O., F.O. 371, C4252/4252/12, Report by A. Francis Aveling to the British Foreign Office, February 26, 1921.

183. Bonn, AA, Politische Abteilung II, L417/L119745/4413, Memorandum by Simons concerning a conversation with Tusar, March 15, 1921. Gajanová, *ČSR a středoevropská politika velmocí*, p. 88. Koloman Gajan, "Die ČSR und die deutsche Frage, 1918-1925," in *Die Entstehung der tschechoslowakischen Republik und ihre international-politische Stellung* (Prague: Acta Universitatis Carolinae—Philosophica et Historica, 2-3 1968).

184. Edvard Beneš, *The Foreign Policy of Czechoslovakia*, p. 16. *Lidové noviny*, January 28, 1921, p. 3. *Bohemia*, January 28, 1921, p. 2.

185. Bonn, AA, Politische Abteilung II, L416/L118840-41/4412, Report of Saenger to the German Foreign Office, February 8, 1921.

186. For Saenger's report concerning Prague's policy on the Hlučíners see Bonn, AA, Politische Abteilung II, L417/L119711-12/4413, Report of Saenger to the German Foreign Office, February 24, 1921.

187. It was in this interview as well that Tusar told Simons that he personally did not believe that Czechoslovakia would participate in economic sanctions against Germany concerning the reparations issue. He added that he regarded an Anschluss of Austria with Germany as "completely unavoidable" in the long run but that currently Austria would be too much of a burden for Germany to bear. Tusar's remark about an Anschluss contradicted Czechoslovak policy both at that time and in later years. Simons could not have set much stock in it. See Bonn, AA, Politische Abteilung II, L417/L119741-46/4413, Memorandum by Simons concerning a conversation with Tusar, March 15, 1921.

188. Bonn, AA, Politische Abteilung II, L416/L118853/4412, Report of Saenger to the German Foreign Office, March 21, 1921.

189. London, P.R.O., F.O. 371, C9767/1213/12, Telegram from Sir George Clerk to the British Foreign Office, May 11, 1921.

190. Bonn, AA, Politische Abteilung II, L416/L118895-96/4412, Report of Saenger to the German Foreign Office, July 28, 1921.

191. F. Gregory Campbell, "The Struggle for Upper Silesia, 1919-1922," *Journal of Modern History* 42(September 1970):361-85. Using Czechoslovak documents, Gajan perhaps attaches more significance to Beneš's pro-Polish efforts. Gajan, "Die ČSR und die deutsche Frage, 1918-1925," p. 199.

192. Bonn, AA, Politische Abteilung II, L416/L118880/4412, Report of Saenger to the German Foreign Office, July 1, 1921.

193. London, P.R.O., F.O. 371, C18382/92/18, Memorandum by Balfour about a conversation with Beneš, September 10, 1921.

194. *Těsnopisecké zprávy*, 91st session, November 16, 1921, pp. 265-72. *Prager Presse*, November 16, 1921, evening edition, p. 2. *Lidové noviny*, November 17, 1921, p. 3. Beneš, *Problémy nové Evropy*, pp. 151-53.

195. *Bohemia*, April 7, 1921, p. 2.

196. Bonn, AA, Politische Abteilung II, L417/L119810/4413, Report of Koch to the German Foreign Office, October 30, 1921.

Chapter Three

1. Bonn, AA, Politische Abteilung IA, Oesterreich 101, vol. 48, Akten betreffend Böhmen, Report from Schwerin to Berlin, February 3, 1919.

2. Ibid., Politische Abteilung II, L417/L119815-16/4413, Memorandum by Haniel of a conversation with Tusar, November 19, 1921.

3. Haniel was prompted to make that inquiry because Tusar himself had spoken of the desirability of some frontier rectifications. Ibid., L417/L119817-19/4413, Note by Haniel to Koch, November 25, 1921.

4. Bonn, AA, Büro des Reichsministers, 3086/D617537-39/1488, Memorandum by Rathenau of a conversation with Tusar, March 13, 1922.

5. Ferdinand Peroutka, *Budování státu* (Prague: Fr. Borovy, 1933-36), 4:2158-73. Edward Táborský, *Czechoslovak Democracy at Work* (London: George Allen & Unwin Ltd., 1945), pp. 104-6.

6. See, in particular, his parliamentary speech of November 16, 1921. *Těsnopisecké zprávy o schůzích poslanecké sněmovny Národního shromáždění republiky Československé*, 91st session, November 16, 1921, pp. 265-72. *Prager Presse*, November 16, 1921, evening edition, p. 2; *Lidové noviny*, November 17, 1921, p. 3.

7. Quoted in a report from the British legation. London, P.R.O., F.O. 371, C7800/390/12, Report from Sir George Clerk to the British Foreign Office, May 23, 1922.

8. London, P.R.O., F.O. 371, C389/386/12, Report from John Cecil

and Memorandum from Bruce Lockhart to the British Foreign Office, January 5, 1922.

9. Ibid.

10. *Prager Presse*, February 5, 1922, p. 1.

11. *Těsnopisecké zprávy*, 148th session, June 20, 1922, pp. 1113-15, 1121-27. *Prager Presse*, June 21, 1922, p. 4. Purlitz, *Deutscher Geschichtskalender 1922, Ausland*, 1:425.

12. Vienna, HHStA, N.P.A., Karton 62, Report of Marek to the Austrian Ministry of Foreign Affairs, June 18, 1922. Report of Marek to the Austrian Ministry of Foreign Affairs, July 21, 1922.

13. Klemens von Klemperer, *Ignaz Seipel: Christian Statesman in a Time of Crisis* (Princeton: Princeton University Press, 1972), p. 193.

14. London, P.R.O., F.O. 371, C13124/74/3, Memorandum by Masaryk, dated August 29, 1922, enclosed in a report by Clerk to the British Foreign Office, September 12, 1922.

15. Quoted by Zygmunt J. Gasiorowski, "Czechoslovakia and the Austrian Question, 1918-1928," *Südost-Forschungen* 16 (1957):111.

16. Paris, M.A.E., Europe 1918-1929, Tchécoslovaquie, vol. 41, Letter from Pellé to Peretti, September 29, 1923. It should be noted that Beneš subsequently tried to take some of the force out of Masaryk's statements. Beneš observed that a union of Czechoslovakia and Austria was only a last resort in order to prevent an Anschluss. Letter from Pellé to Peretti, October 7, 1923.

17. Klemperer, *Ignaz Seipel*, pp. 199-207.

18. *Těsnopisecké zprávy*, 183d session, December 18, 1922, pp. 1863-92. *Lidové noviny*, December 19, 1922, p. 3. Purlitz, *Deutscher Geschichtskalender 1922, Ausland*, 2:240.

19. *Bohemia*, June 25, 1922, p. 1. *Prager Tagblatt*, June 25, 1922, p. 1.

20. *Prager Presse*, June 25, 1922, p. 1. The association was known as "O.C." or "Organization Consul," with the notorious Captain Hermann Ehrhardt as consul. After the failure of the Kapp Putsch in 1920, Ehrhardt and his men operated out of Munich. On the O.C., see Robert G. L. Waite, *Vanguard of Nazism* (Cambridge, Mass.: Harvard University Press, 1952), pp. 212-27.

21. Bonn, AA, Politische Abteilung II, L417/L119920-21/4413, Memorandum by State Secretary Rümelin of a conversation with Tusar, December 5, 1922.

22. Bonn, AA, Büro des Reichsministers, 3086/D617597-99/1488, Memorandum by Maltzan of a conversation with Tusar, January 6, 1923.

23. Bonn, AA, Politische Abteilung II, L417/L119948-51/4413, Report by Koch to the German Foreign Office, January 8, 1923.

24. Ibid., L417/L119952/4413, Telegram from Koch to the German Foreign Office, January 15, 1923. AA, Politische Abteilung II, L416/L118970-72/4412, Report of Koch to the German Foreign Office, January 16, 1923.

25. Bonn, AA, Politische Abteilung II, L417/L119988/4413, Report of Koch to the German Foreign Office, January 22, 1923. *Prager Abendblatt*, January 22, 1923, p. 2. *Prager Abendzeitung*, January 22, 1923, p. 1.

26. Vienna, HHStA, N.P.A., Karton 62, Report of Marek to the Austrian Ministry of Foreign Affairs, January 11, 1923. On Czechoslovak efforts to remain uninvolved in the Ruhr dispute at its outset, see Manfred Alexander, "Die Tschechoslowakei und die Probleme der Ruhrbestzung 1923," *Bohemia* (Munich: R. Oldenbourg, 1971), pp. 297-336.

27. Bonn, AA, Büro des Reichsministers, 3086/D617602-03/1488, Memorandum by Maltzan, January 30, 1923.

28. Ibid.

29. Bonn, AA, Büro des Reichsministers, 3086/D617609-10/1488, Memorandum by Maltzan of a conversation with Tusar, February 13, 1923.

30. For a perceptive interpretation of the measure, see London, P.R.O., F.O. 371, vol. 8574, C3592/437/12, Report of J. W. Taylor to the British Foreign Office, February 22, 1923. The phrasing of the act was sufficiently vague that the courts were given a wide latitude for interpretation, and their decisions concerning censorship could therefore be based more on political than legal considerations.

31. London, P.R.O., F.O. 371, C14268/386/12, Report by Clerk and Memorandum by Lockhart to the British Foreign Office, October 12, 1922.

32. Bonn, AA, Old Reich Chancellery, L504/L149729-30/5068, Dispatch from Mutius to Haniel in Munich, January 29, 1923.

33. Ibid., L504/L149756-62/5068, Note from Maltzan to the Prussian State Ministry and the Ministries of Foreign Affairs of Bavaria and Saxony, March 24, 1923.

34. Ibid., L504/L149770-71/5068, Unsigned memorandum dated on May 2, 1923.

35. Ibid., L504/L149735-41/5068, Letter from Gaertner to Cuno, February 20, 1923. L504/L149743-44/5068, Letter from Gaertner to Cuno, February 21, 1923. Věra Olivová, "Československá diplomacie v době rurské krise roku 1923," *Československý časopis historicky* 6 (1958):62.

36. Bonn, AA, Politische Abteilung II, L417/L120108-10/4413, Report of Koch to the German Foreign Office, March 5, 1923.

37. London, P.R.O., F.O. 371, vol. 8721, C4561/313/18, Report of Clerk to the British Foreign Office, March 8, 1923.

38. "Orientace československé zahraniční politiky," *Zahraniční politika* (April 25, 1923), 2:513-15.

39. London, P.R.O., F.O. 371, vol. 8574, C5099/437/12, Report of Clerk to the British Foreign Office, March 12, 1923.

40. Paris, M.A.E., Europe 1918-1929, Tchécoslovaquie, vol. 41, Report from Couget to Poincaré, May 23, 1923.

41. Ibid., Documents throughout the volume contain hints of precautionary preparations for war, but see particularly Letter from Foch to Mittelhauser, June 5, 1923. Letter from Foch to Beneš, July 13, 1923.

42. Ibid., Note from Poincaré to Couget, June 9, 1923.

43. Ibid., Report from Couget to Poincaré, June 20, 1923.

44. Ibid., Report from Couget to Poincaré, July 5, 1923.

45. Ibid., Letter from Pellé to Peretti, September 29, 1923.

46. Ibid., Note on a conversation between Beneš and Laroche on July 10, 1923.

47. London, P.R.O., F.O. 371, vol. 8574, C5099/437/12, Report by Clerk to the British Foreign Office, March 12, 1923. C9697/437/12, Report by Clerk to the British Foreign Office, May 25, 1923.

48. Ibid. C9697/437/12, See Curzon's minute concerning Clerk's dispatch of May 25.

49. Bonn, AA, Politische Abteilung II, L417/L120337/4413, Report of Pfeiffer to the German Foreign Office, July 13, 1923.

50. See the reports from French ministers in the Little Entente capitals in August 1923. Paris, M.A.E., Europe 1918-1929, Tchécoslovaquie, vol. 68.

51. Bonn, AA, Büro des Reichsministers, 3086/D617643/1488, Report of Adolf Müller to the German Foreign Office, September 25, 1923.

52. Bonn, AA, Politische Abteilung II, L417/L120440-41/4413, Report by Koch to the German Foreign Office, October 8, 1923.

53. In discussing his upcoming trip with the Austrian minister, Masaryk used the German word *Schinderei*. He particularly resented the physical exertion that the journey would demand of him. Vienna, HHStA, N.P.A., Karton 62, Report by Marek to Vienna, October 3, 1923. Beneš was young enough both to endure the stress and to be flattered by the special attention that the French showered upon him.

54. Paris, M.A.E., Europe 1918-1929, Tchécoslovaquie, vol. 41, Note on a conversation between Beneš and Peretti, October 18, 1923. Gajanová, *ČSR a středoevropská politika velmocí*, p. 147.

55. Paris, M.A.E., Europe 1918-1929, Tchécoslovaquie, vol. 41, Notation by President Millerand on the record of a conversation between Beneš and Laroche, October 18, 1923.

56. London, P.R.O., F.O. 371, vol. 8575, C18224/437/12, Memorandum by Curzon about his conversation with Masaryk, October 22, 1923.

57. Ibid., vol. 8658, C18459/1/18, Memorandum by A. W. A. Leeper about a conversation with Beneš, October 25, 1923.

58. Ibid., vol. 8662, C20609/1/18, Note from Masaryk to Curzon with a memorandum by Beneš, November 13, 1923.

59. Bonn, AA, Büro des Reichsministers, 3086/D617653-56/1488, Memorandum by Maltzan, November 3, 1923.

60. *Central European Observer*, August 4, 1923, pp. 1-2.

61. Bonn, AA, Politische Abteilung II, L417/L120440-41/4413, Re-

port by Koch to the German Foreign Office, October 8, 1923. Vienna, HHStA, N.P.A., Karton 62, Report by Marek to the Austrian Ministry of Foreign Affairs, October 8, 1923.

62. Bonn, AA, Büro des Reichsministers, 3086/D617650-51/1488, Report by Sthamer to the German Foreign Office, October 25, 1923.

63. Vienna, HHStA, N.P.A., Karton 62, Report of Marek to the Austrian Ministry of Foreign Affairs, November 6, 1923.

64. Newspapers in Prague, especially those that had ties with the government, published continuing reports of the unrest in Bavaria. They were only slightly less critical of Gustav von Kahr, who exercised dictatorial powers in Bavaria in the autumn of 1923, than they were of Hitler and Ludendorff. See, for example *Prager Presse*, "Kahrs Vorarbeit für König Rupprecht," September 29, 1923, p. 1.

65. Bonn, AA, Büro des Reichsministers, 3086/D617659/1488, Telegram from Koch to the German Foreign Office, November 15, 1923. AA, Büro des Reichministers, 3086/D617660/1488, Telegram from Koch to the German Foreign Office, November 16, 1923. *Prager Presse*, November 15, 1923, evening edition, p. 1.

66. Vienna, HHStA, N.P.A., Karton 62, Report by Marek to the Austrian Ministry of Foreign Affairs, November 20, 1923. Beneš had made that remark on November 14.

67. Bonn, AA, Büro des Reichsministers, 3086/D617662-63/1488, Note from Maltzan to Koch, November 17, 1923.

68. Ibid., 3086/D617665-66/1488, Telegram from Koch to the German Foreign Office, November 21, 1923. As the son of Emperor Charles, Otto inherited the Habsburg claims after his father's death in 1922.

69. Newspapers carried full details of these meetings, and of course the *Prager Presse* gave special attention to them. For reports on the decisive phases of the meetings, see *Prager Presse*, November 20, 1923, evening edition, p. 1; November 22, 1923, pp. 1-2.

70. *Prager Presse*, "England macht weitere Schwierigkeiten," November 21, 1923, p. 1.

71. Stresemann himself had actually been instrumental in making it possible for the crown prince to return to Germany. Hans W. Gatzke, *Stresemann and the Rearmament of Germany*, (Baltimore: Johns Hopkins University Press, 1954), p. 6. Gustav Stresemann, *Vermächtnis*, ed. Henry Bernhard (Berlin: Ullstein, 1932-33), 1:215-24.

72. *Prager Presse*, November 22, 1923, evening edition, pp. 1-2.

73. Bonn, AA, Büro des Reichsministers, 3086/D617664/1488, Report of Brockdorff-Rantzau to the German Foreign Office, November 19, 1923.

74. Bonn, AA, Politische Abteilung II, L417/L120477/4413, Report of Koch to the German Foreign Office. December 10, 1923.

75. Edgar Vincent D'Abernon, *An Ambassador of Peace* (London: Hodder and Stoughton, 1929-30), 2:267.

76. Stresemann Nachlass, 7165/H154916-17/3106, Memorandum by Stresemann about a conversation with De Margerie, December 11, 1923.

77. Paris, M.A.E., Europe 1918-1929, Tchécoslovaquie, vol. 41, Note on a conversation between Beneš and Peretti, December 13, 1923. Already during the November disturbances in Germany Beneš had communicated preliminary suggestions for a treaty to Paris.

78. Ibid., Note on a conversation among Beneš, Peretti, and Laroche, December 20, 1923. Olivová, "Československá diplomacie v době rurské krise," pp. 67-70.

79. Paris, M.A.E., Europe 1918-1929, Tchécoslovaquie, vol. 41, Note on a conversation among Beneš, Peretti, and Laroche, December 20, 1923. Note on a conversation between Peretti and Beneš, December 27, 1923. For Beneš's reports to Premier Švehla about the negotiations, see Alena Gajanová, "Entstehung und Entwicklung der internationalen Beziehungen der ČSR," in *Die Entstehung der tschechoslowakischen Republik und ihre international-politische Stellung* (Prague: Acta Universitatis Carolinae—Philosophica et Historica, 2-3, 1968).

80. In supplying information about the projected Franco-Czechoslovak treaty to French missions abroad, Poincaré warned: "I recommend, however, that you maintain a strictly personal and confidential character to all that which concerns the exchange of 'interpretive letters,' the existence of which you are not even to let be suspected." Paris, M.A.E., Europe 1918-1929, Tchécoslovaquie, vol. 41, Note from Poincaré to the French diplomatic missions in London, Rome, Belgrade, Bucharest, and Warsaw, January 10, 1924.

81. *Temps*, December 28, 1923, p. 1. Bonn, AA, Büro des Reichsministers, 3086/D617672-73/1488, Telegram from Heosch to the German Foreign Office, December 27, 1923.

82. Bonn, AA, Politische Abteilung II, L414/L120486-88/4414, Report by Hoesch to the German Foreign Office, December 29, 1923. London, P.R.O., F.O. 371, vol. 8583, C22432/2597/12, Minutes on a report by Crewe to the British Foreign Office, December 27, 1923.

83. London *Times*, January 1, 1924, p. 13.

84. Paris, M.A.E., Europe 1918-1929, Tchécoslovaquie, vol. 41, Memorandum of a conversation between Laroche and Osuský, December 31, 1923. Report of the French chargé d'affaires in London to Poincaré, January 9, 1924.

85. London *Times*, January 2, 1924, p. 11.

86. *Prager Presse*, January 3, 1924, p. 1.

87. London, P.R.O., F.O. 371, vol. 9673, C636/41/12, Report from Clerk to the British Foreign Office, January 10, 1924.

88. Poincaré believed that Beneš wanted to push the Franco-Czechoslovak treaty to a quick conclusion so that it would not appear to be a reaction against British recognition of the Soviet Union. Paris, M.A.E., Europe 1918-1929, Tchécoslovaquie, vol. 41, Note from Poincaré to Couget, December 31, 1923.

89. See, for example, Beneš's parliamentary statement of October 30, 1923. *Zahraniční politika* (1923), p. 1568. Quoted by Gajanová, *ČSR a středoevropská politika velmocí*, p. 151. Edvard Beneš, *Problémy nové Evropy a zahraniční politika Československá* (Prague: Melantrich, 1924).

90. London, P.R.O., F.O. 371, vol. 8583, C22432/2597/12, Nicolson's comments on a report by Crewe from Paris, December 27, 1923.

91. Wandycz, *France and Her Eastern Allies*, pp. 276-91, 310. For further archival evidence supporting Wandycz's findings, see Paris, M.A.E., Europe 1918-1929, Tchécoslovaquie, vol. 41.

92. London, P.R.O., F.O. 371, vol. 9673, C437/41/12, Telegram from Clerk to the British Foreign Office, January 8, 1924.

93. To the French Beneš defended his revelation about the letters by claiming that information leaks to the press had made it impossible to keep the letters secret. Paris, M.A.E., Europe 1918-1929, Tchécoslovaquie, vol. 41, Telegram from Saint-Aulaire to the French Ministry of Foreign Affairs, January 21, 1924.

94. London, P.R.O., F.O. 371, vol. 9673, C882/41/12, Note from Curzon to Clerk, January 16, 1924. British hostility toward Czechoslovak policy had been growing for some time. In the summer of 1923 the British government had been sharply critical of Czechoslovak opposition to a revision of Hungarian reparation obligations. Gajanová, "Entstehung und Entwicklung der internationalen Bezichungen der ČSR," pp. 156-58.

95. Paris, M.A.E., Europe 1918-1929, Tchécoslovaquie, vol. 42, Memorandum of a conversation between Beneš and Peretti, January 25, 1924.

96. Ibid., vol. 41, Report from Couget to Poincaré, January 9, 1924.

97. Ibid., vol. 42, Note from Poincaré to Foch, February 14, 1924.

98. Radko Břach, "Československá zahraniční politika v politických proměnách Evropy 1924," *Československý časopis historický* 18 (1970):49-83.

99. *Berliner Tageblatt*, March 19, 1924, p. 1. Bonn, AA, Büro des Reichsministers, 3086/D617694-95/1488, Undated and unsigned memorandum in the German Foreign Office.

100. Bonn, AA, Büro des Reichsministers, 3086/D617689-90/1488, Telegram from Stresemann to German missions abroad, March 13, 1924.

101. *Prager Presse*, March 20, 1924, evening edition, p. 1.

102. Ibid., March 19, 1924, evening edition, p. 1.

103. Bonn, AA, Büro des Reichsministers, 3086/D617689-90/1488, Telegram from Stresemann to German missions abroad, March 13, 1924.

104. Ibid., 3086/D617702/1488, Telegram from Neurath to the German Foreign Office, March 19, 1924.

105. This phrase was the title of an article about the affair in the *Central European Observer*, March 22, 1924, p. 2.

106. Bonn, AA, Politische Abteilung II, L417/L120539-42/4414, Report by Koch to the German Foreign Office, May 4, 1924.

107. Ibid., L417/L120544-45/4414, Report by Koch to the German

Foreign Office, May 16, 1924.

108. On Czechoslovak-Italian relations between 1922 and 1924, see Vlastimil Kybal, "Czechoslovakia and Italy: My Negotiations with Mussolini, Part I: 1922-1923," *Journal of Central European Affairs* 13 (January 1954):352-68. Idem, "Part II, 1923-1924," ibid. 14 (April 1954):65-76.

109. Paris, M.A.E., Europe 1918-1929, Tchécoslovaquie, vol. 42, Telegram from Poincaré to Couget, April 16, 1924.

110. Bonn, AA, Politische Abteilung II, L417/L120544-45/4414, Report by Koch to the German Foreign Office, May 16, 1924.

111. Bonn, AA, Büro des Reichsministers, 3086/D617725-26/1488, Report by Prittwitz to the German Foreign Office, May 13, 1924.

112. Kybal, "My Negotiations with Mussolini, Part II, 1923-1924," pp. 70-76. Alan Cassels, *Mussolini's Early Diplomacy* (Princeton: Princeton University Press, 1970), pp. 177-81. Olivová, *ČSR a středoevropská politika velmocí*, pp. 162-67.

113. London, P.R.O., F.O. 371, vol. 9680, C9253/8107/12, MacDonald's comments on a report by Clerk to the British Foreign Office, June 5, 1924.

114. Bülow was the nephew of Count Bülow, the former imperial chancellor. Although the subtitle of his book, *Eine vorläufige Bilanz*, reflected Bülow's claim that he was writing an impartial analysis of the League, he clearly considered the League a *Feindbund* that Germany could enter only after a basic change of attitude by the enemy powers. He warned: "More than once we [the Germans] have let ourselves be fooled into regarding pretty words and hypocrisy as authentic and real convictions. We must not experience the same disappointments in the League of Nations that we did with Wilson's points." Bernhard W. von Bülow, *Der Versailler Völkerbund*, (Berlin: W. Kohlhammer Verlag, 1923), p. 581. Bülow's attitudes were important, for he rose quickly in the Foreign Office to become state secretary in 1930. He retained that post until his death in 1936.

115. The fullest treatment of Stresemann's diplomacy concerning German entrance into the League is Jürgen Spenz, *Die diplomatische Vorgeschichte des Beitritts Deutschlands zum Völkerbund 1924-1926*, (Göttingen: Musterschmidt-Verlag, 1966).

116. This interview was reprinted in the *Prager Presse*, July 15, 1924, evening edition, p. 1. It was reported in the *Central European Observer*, July 18, 1924, p. 2. Beneš voiced the same sentiments in private to the French. Paris, M.A.E., Europe 1918-1929, Tchécoslovaquie, vol. 69, Report from Couget to Herriot, July 1, 1924.

117. The Poles also cooperated closely with the French and the Czechs at Geneva. Wandycz, *France and Her Eastern Allies*, pp. 320-21.

118. This discussion of diplomacy at Geneva in 1924 relies heavily on Spenz, *Die diplomatische Vorgeschichte*, pp. 23-57.

119. *Prager Presse*, October 30, 1924, evening edition, p. 4.

120. London, P.R.O., F.O. 371, vol. 9676, C19104/909/12, Memorandum by Austen Chamberlain about a conversation with Beneš, December 11, 1924.
121. Ibid., vol. 10674, C3050/356/12, Report by Clerk to the British Foreign Office, February 27, 1925.
122. London *Times*, November 19, 1924, p. 20.
123. *Prager Presse*, November 25, 1924, pp. 1-2.
124. *Central European Observer*, November 22, 1924, p. 2.
125. London, P.R.O., F.O. 371, vol. 9677, C18532/918/12, Report by Clerk to the British Foreign Office, December 4, 1924.
126. This was the same conversation in which Chamberlain intimated that the Conservative government would refuse to ratify the Geneva Protocol. Ibid., vol. 9676, C19104/909/12, Memorandum by Chamberlain about a conversation with Beneš, December 11, 1924.
127. There was a great deal to what Beneš said. The previous week a report from the British legation in Budapest had concluded: "As regards this question of preferential treatment between the countries above mentioned (Czechoslovakia, Austria, Hungary), it has continually been brought to my notice by British firms, their travellers or their local agents that any import reduction which might result from such a policy to the mutual advantage of those States, and of Czechoslovakia in particular, as the most progressive manufacturing unit amongst them, would be highly detrimental to British imports, which would be handicapped by the lower dues on similar articles from the neighboring States. Czechoslovakia, it must be remembered, is our rival in nearly every branch of industry. For instance, our relatively considerable import of textiles into Hungary would have to face the crushing competition of Czechoslovakia, which has already the advantage of close proximity to the market." London, P.R.O., F.O. 371, vol. 10698, C1586/1586/62, Report from Sir Colville Barclay to the British Foreign Office, January 29, 1925.
128. Vienna, HHStA, N.P.A., Karton 62, Report by Marek to the Austrian Ministry of Foreign Affairs, February 6, 1925.
129. London, P.R.O., F.O. 371, vol. 9674, C19243/119/12, Comments by W. W. Lampson and Chamberlain on a report from Maurice Peterson in Prague to the British Foreign Office, December 19, 1924. Vol. 10674, C5120/256/12, Comment by Lampson on a report by Clerk to the British Foreign Office, April 8, 1925.
130. Vienna, HHStA, N.P.A., Karton 62, Report by Marek to the Austrian Ministry of Foreign Affairs, February 6, 1925.
131. About D'Abernon's activities in Berlin see particularly F. G. Stambrook, " *'Das Kind'*—Lord D'Abernon and the Origins of the Locarno Pact," *Central European History* 1 (September 1968):233-63.
132. Ibid., p. 237. Quoted from D'Abernon's diary, *An Ambassador of Peace*, 3:21.
133. Hans W. Gatzke, "Von Rapallo nach Berlin: Stresemann und die deutsche Russlandpolitik," *Vierteljahrshefte für Zeitgeschichte* 4 (January

1956):1-29. Zygmunt J. Gasiorowski, "Stresemann and Poland Before Locarno," *Journal of Central European Affairs* 18 (April 1958):25-47. Josef Korbel, *Poland between East and West* (Princeton: Princeton University Press, 1963), pp. 152-80. Harald von Riekhoff, *German-Polish Relations, 1918-1933* (Baltimore: The Johns Hopkins Press, 1971), pp. 71-89.

134. This is the interpretation developed by Stambrook in his previously cited article, p. 263.

135. The contents of this note were not made public until June, when the German initiative and the French response were published in newspapers throughout Europe. The gist of Stresemann's proposals was public knowledge, however, as a result of debates in the French press that began in late February. For a provocative and influential analysis of Stresemann's motivations, see Annelise Thimme, "Die Locarnopolitik im Lichte des Stresemann-Nachlasses," *Zeitschrift für Politik* 3 (August, 1956):42-63. Translated in Hans W. Gatzke, *European Diplomacy between Two Wars, 1919-1939* (Chicago: Quadrangle Books, 1972).

136. The texts of his memoranda are printed in Radko Břach, "Locarno a čs. diplomacie," *Československý časopis historický* 8 (1960):694-95. Břach's article is based in large part on documents from the Czechoslovak Ministry of Foreign Affairs.

137. London, P.R.O., F.O. 371, vol. 10674, C3050/256/12, Report by Clerk to the British Foreign Office, February 27, 1925.

138. Wandycz, *France and Her Eastern Allies*, pp. 335-56. Zygmunt J. Gasiorowski, "Beneš and Locarno: Some Unpublished Documents," *The Review of Politics* 20 (April 1958):211-12.

139. Gasiorowski, "Beneš and Locarno," p. 216.

140. London, P.R.O., F.O. 371, vol. 10674, C5120/256/12, Report by Clerk to the British Foreign Office, April 8, 1925. Vienna, HHStA, N.P.A., Karton 62, Report by Marek to the Austrian Ministry of Foreign Affairs, May 18, 1925. The periodical of the Czechoslovak Ministry of Foreign Affairs also contained observations about a turn to the Right in German domestic affairs and a possible shift in German foreign policy under Hindenburg. *Zahraniční politika* (1925), pp. 561-62.

141. Beneš's realistic assessment of French and British attitudes toward the German proposals is documented in one of his informational telegrams that he did for the Czechoslovak diplomatic corps. Gajanová, *ČSR a středoevropská politika velmocí*, pp. 188-89.

This interpretation differs somewhat from that of Manfred Alexander, whose study of the German-Czechoslovak arbitration treaty of 1925 is based on the German diplomatic documents. Alexander believes that Beneš was at first favorably disposed to the German proposals, that in cooperation with the Poles he became more hostile in April, and that he again reversed himself in September by offering to negotiate a pact with the Germans. Manfred Alexander, *Der deutsch-tschechoslowakische Schiedsvertrag von 1925 im Rahmen der Locarno-Verträge* (Munich: R. Oldenbourg, 1970), pp. 44-49, 64-77, 121-29.

Given Beneš's tactical comments to the German diplomats and the analyses in the memoranda of the German Foreign Office, it is easy to derive that interpretation. From the perspective of his negotiations with diplomats of various nationalities, however, it is clear that there were no abrupt shifts in his policy. Beneš never liked the differentiation between Germany's western and eastern frontiers. He quickly discerned French and British receptivity to the proposals, however, and he therefore tried to appear cooperative and content. Moreover, he was determined never to allow so close an identification of Czechoslovak and Polish foreign policies as would be implied by Alexander's interpretation.

142. Bonn, AA, Büro des Reichsministers, 3086/D617753-54/1488, Note from Schubert to Koch about a conversation between Beneš and the German counselor to the legation in Berne. Many of the German documents for 1925 are cited in Alexander, *Der deutsch-tschechoslowakische Schiedsvertrag.*

143. Bonn, AA, Büro des Reichsministers, 3086/D617753-54/1488, Note from Schubert to Koch about a conversation between Beneš and the German counselor to the legation in Berne.

144. Bonn, AA, Büro des Reichsministers, 3086/D617762-63/1488, Report from Koch to the German Foreign Office, March 24, 1925.

145. Spenz, *Die diplomatische Vorgeschichte*, p. 66.

146. Bonn, AA, Büro des Reichsministers, 3086/D617768-70/1488, Note from Stresemann to Koch, March 31, 1925.

147. Ibid., 3086/D617755-56/1488, Note from Schubert to Koch, March 17, 1925.

148. Ibid., 3086/D617748-49/1488, Report from Keller to the German Foreign Office, March 11, 1925.

149. Gasiorowski, "Beneš and Locarno," p. 215.

150. London, P.R.O., F.O. 371, vol. 10674, C5120/256/12, Report by Clerk to the British Foreign Office, April 8, 1925.

151. Wandycz, *France and Her Eastern Allies*, p. 337.

152. Bonn, AA, Büro des Reichsministers, 3086/D617768-70/1488, Note from Stresemann to Koch, March 31, 1925.

153. London, P.R.O., F.O. 371, vol. 10674, C3050/256/12, Report from Clerk to the British Foreign Office, February 27, 1925.

154. Ibid., C5120/256/12, Comment by Chamberlain on a report by Clerk to the British Foreign Office, April 8, 1925.

155. *Zahraniční politika* (1925), p. 490. *Prager Presse*, April 1, 1925, evening edition, pp. 1-3.

156. London, P.R.O., F.O. 371, vol. 10675, C5978/257/12, Report by W. G. Max Muller to the British Foreign Office, April 30, 1925. Alina Szklarska-Lohmannova, *Polsko-czechosłowackie stosunki dyplomatyczne w latach 1918-1925* (Wrocław: Zakład Narodowy imienia Ossolińskich wydawnictwo Polskiej Akademii Nauk, 1967), pp. 156-57.

157. Bľach, "Locarno a čs. diplomacie," pp. 674-75.

158. Bonn, AA, Büro des Reichsministers, 3086/D617773-74/1488,

Report by Koch to the German Foreign Office, March 31, 1925.

159. Gasiorowski, "Beneš and Locarno," p. 213.

160. Bonn, AA, Büro des Reichsministers, 3086/D617787/1488, Memorandum by Stresemann of a conversation with Italian Ambassador Bosdari, May 8, 1925.

161. *Verhandlungen des Reichstages*, 385:1881.

162. Wandycz, *France and Her Eastern Allies*, p. 344. Wandycz points out that these views did not influence Polish foreign policy in 1925, but it is certainly possible that such ideas had effect after Pilsudski's coup d'état in 1926. At various points in the interwar period both Poland and Czechoslovakia attempted to reach separate understandings with the Germans, and the two countries never presented a united front against Germany. In the broader perspective neither country was more responsible than the other for sabotaging cooperation between them although at any given juncture one might have been more recalcitrant than the other.

163. Wandycz, *France and Her Eastern Allies*, p. 335. Edouard Herriot, *Jadis* (Paris: Flammarion, 1948-52), 2:189-90.

164. Vienna, HHStA, N.P.A., Karton 62, Report by Marek to the Austrian Ministry of Foreign Affairs, March 25, 1925.

165. Ibid., Karton 822, Memorandum by Post about a conversation with Beneš, April 25, 1925.

166. Ibid., Karton 62, Reports by Marek to the Austrian Ministry of Foreign Affairs, February 16, March 25, and May 2, 1925. London, P.R.O., F.O. 371, vol. 10660, C6027/298/3, Report by Clerk to the British Foreign Office, April 30, 1925.

167. Vienna, HHStA, N.P.A., Karton 62, Report by Marek to the Austrian Ministry of Foreign Affairs, May 2, 1925.

168. London, P.R.O., F.O. 371, vol. 10698, Letter from the Board of Trade to the British Foreign Office, April 16, 1925.

169. Wandycz, *France and Her Eastern Allies*, pp. 347-53. Błach, "Locarno a čs. diplomacie," pp. 675-76. Alexander, *Der deutsch-tschechoslowakische Schiedsvertrag*, pp. 89-95.

170. London, P.R.O., F.O. 371, vol. 10679, C4053/3525/12, Note from the War Office to the British Foreign Office, March 17, 1925. This dispatch consisted of a report from the British military attaché in Prague and a memorandum by French officers concerning "Industrial Mobilization of Czechoslovakia in War."

171. *Prager Presse*, June 23, 1925, evening edition, p. 1.

172. Ibid.

173. About the repeated efforts on the Czech side to arrange a meeting between Stresemann and Beneš in the spring and summer of 1925, see Gasiorowski, "Beneš and Locarno," p. 219. Alexander, *Der deutsch-tschechoslowakische Schiedsvertrag*, pp. 97-100. Although no meeting between the two men before Locarno was reported, the Austrian minister in Prague remained convinced that a secret consultation took place on the Bohemian-Saxon border in July. Vienna, HHStA, N.P.A., Karton 63,

Report by Marek to the Austrian Ministry of Foreign Affairs, October 7, 1925.

174. London, P.R.O., F.O. 371, vol. 10674, C8043/256/12, Report by Clerk to the British Foreign Office, June 11, 1925.

175. Spenz, *Die diplomatische Vorgeschichte*, pp. 54-55. Wandycz, *France and Her Eastern Allies*, p. 323.

176. In German text with an English translation the note was published as a British White Paper, Cmd. 2468. Macartney, *Survey of International Affairs* (1925), p. 41.

177. *Central European Observer*, July 31, 1925, p. 2.

178. Bonn, AA, Politische Abteilung II, L417/L120610/4414, Memorandum by Köpke of a conversation with Krofta, September 2, 1925.

179. Bŕach, "Locarno a čs. diplomacie," pp. 682-83. Riekhoff, *German-Polish Relations*, pp. 102-3.

180. Bonn, AA, Büro des Reichsministers, 3086/D617830-31/1488, Note by Schubert to German ministries abroad concerning a visit by Krofta, September 21, 1925.

181. Ibid., 3086/D617839-40/1488, Note from Stresemann to Koch, September 25, 1925.

182. Macartney, *Survey of International Affairs* (1925), pp. 49-66. Wandycz, *France and Her Eastern Allies*, pp. 359-68. Bŕach, "Locarno a čs. diplomacie," pp. 683-94. Alexander, *Der deutsch-tschechoslowakische Schiedsvertrag*, pp. 150-66. Riekhoff, *German-Polish Relations*, pp. 104-14.

183. Stresemann, *Vermächtnis*, 2:234, 243. That speech has recently been published in complete and uncensored form in *Akten zur deutschen auswärtigen Politik*, series B, vol. I, 1, pp. 727-53.

184. *Central European Observer*, October 23, 1925, p. 1.

185. *Zahraniční politika* (1925), pp. 1325-34. *Prager Tagblatt*, October 31, 1925, pp. 1-2.

186. Jon Jacobson, *Locarno Diplomacy* (Princeton: Princeton University Press, 1972), p. 30.

187. The worst disturbances were in Graslitz, where, according to the *Bohemia*, thirteen people were killed. *Bohemia*, November 4, 1921, p. 3. Beneš dealt with the disturbances in his parliamentary exposé on November 3. *Bohemia*, November 4, 1921, pp. 1-2. *Prager Tagblatt*, November 4, 1921, pp. 1-2.

188. Bonn, AA, Politische Abteilung II, L407/L119821-22/4413, Report by Koch to the German Foreign Office, November 18, 1921.

189. Report by Koch to the German Foreign Office of December 10, 1921, quoted in Brügel, *Tschechen und Deutsche*, p. 165.

190. In 1922 the German Nationals, the National Socialists, and the Christian Socials supported the demand for restrictions on the numbers of Jewish students and professors at the universities, but the National Assembly defeated those efforts in November. *Prager Tagblatt*, November 30, 1922, p. 4. *Bohemia*, November 30, 1922, p. 3. Purlitz, *Deutscher Geschichtskalender, 1922, Ausland*, 2, 240.

191. Brügel, *Tschechen und Deutsche*, pp. 165-66.

192. *Lidové noviny*, January 2, 1922, pp. 2-3. Purlitz, *Deutscher Geschichtskalender, 1922, Ausland*, 1:30. Concerning negotiations in the early years of the republic for German entrance into the cabinet, see Heinrich Kuhn, "Der Anteil der Deutschen an der 'Burg'," in *Die "Burg": Einflussreiche politische Kräfte um Masaryk und Beneš*, ed. Karl Bosl, vol. 1 (Munich: R. Oldenbourg, 1973), pp. 113-21.

193. Paris, M.A.E., Europe 1918-1929, Tschécoslovaquie, vol. 26, Note from Couget to Poincaré, January 27, 1922.

194. This was a recurring theme in the French documents in the early postwar years. A good example is Paris, M.A.E., Europe 1918-1929, Tchécoslovaquie, vol. 25, Telegram from Clément-Simon to Paris, July 1, 1919.

195. Beneš did note, however, that Masaryk fully understood the necessity of the French orientation in Czechoslovak foreign policy. Paris, M.A.E., Europe 1918-1929, Tchécoslovaquie, vol. 22, Note from Poincaré to Couget, July 13(?), 1923.

196. *Prager Tagblatt*, December 13, 1921, pp. 2-3. Purlitz, *Deutscher Geschichtskalender 1921, Ausland*, 2:342-43.

197. The law itself was the kind to which everybody could agree. It prohibited the sale of alcoholic beverages to children under sixteen. *Bohemia*, January 18, 1922, p. 2. Purlitz, *Deutscher Geschichtskalender 1922, Ausland*, 1:30-31.

198. *Bohemia*, January 28, 1922, pp. 1-3. *Lidové noviny*, January 28, 1922, pp. 1, 3. Purlitz, *Deutscher Geschichtskalender 1922, Ausland*, 1:31.

199. *Těsnopisecké zprávy*, 162d session, October 26, 1922, p. 337. London, P.R.O., F.O. 371, vol. 7387, C15832/390/12, Report by Clerk to the British Foreign Office, November 17, 1922.

The magnetic attraction of Hitler's movement for the German National Socialist Workers party in Czechoslovakia is described in Hans Krebs, *Kampf in Böhmen* (Berlin: Volk und Reich Verlag, 1936), pp. 136-42.

200. *Bohemia*, November 30, 1922, p. 1; December 1, 1922, p. 3. *Prager Tagblatt*, November 30, 1922, p. 1. *Prager Presse*, November 30, 1922, p. 1. *Lidové noviny*, November 30, 1922, p. 3. London, P.R.O., F.O. 371, vol. 7387, C16537/390/12, Report by Clerk to the British Foreign Office, November 30, 1922.

201. It should be remembered, however, that in April 1921 Sudeten German leaders themselves refused to conduct negotiations with the Czechs for German entrance into the government. Personal rivalries among the Sudeten German leaders played a roll in that decision, but calculations of foreign policy were also involved. The Sudeten Germans were unwilling to support sanctions against Germany in the case that the German government resisted the London ultimatum on reparations. London, P.R.O., F.O. 371, vol. 5822, C8978/739/12, Report by Clerk to the British Foreign Office, April 29, 1921.

202. Věra Olivová, "Postavení dělnické třídy v ČSR v letech

1921-1923," *Československý časopis historický*, 2(1954):193-227.

203. *Prager Tagblatt*, March 7, 1923, pp. 1-3. *Lidové noviny*, March 7, 1923, pp. 1, 2-3. Purlitz, *Deutscher Geschichtskalender, 1923, Ausland,* 1:32.

204. Ladislav Lipscher, *K vývinu politickej správy na Slovensku v rokoch 1918-1938* (Bratislava: Vydavatel'stvo slovenskej akadémie vied, 1966), pp. 83-141. R. W. Seton-Watson, *The New Slovakia* (Prague: Fr. Borový, 1924), pp. 13-31. Josef Anderle, "The Slovak Issue in the Munich Crisis of 1938" (Ph.D. diss., University of Chicago, 1961), pp. 42-43.

205. In August 1938, under the prodding of Lord Runciman, Beneš proposed to establish a county system that would give the Sudeten Germans their own local diets and a large measure of political autonomy. Anderle, "The Slovak Issue in the Munich Crisis," pp. 148-49.

206. For this analysis of the results of the elections, see César and Černý, *Politika německých buržoazních stran*, 1, 305-7.

207. *Prager Tagblatt*, October 27, 1923, p. 2. Purlitz, *Deutscher Geschichtskalender, 1923, Ausland,* 2:173.

208. *Prager Tagblatt*, October 30, 1923, p. 3. Purlitz, *Deutscher Geschichtskalender, 1923, Ausland,* 2:172.

209. *Central European Observer*, March 29, 1924, p. 2.

210. *Prager Presse*, August 9, 1924, p. 1. *Central European Observer*, August 22, 1924, p. 2.

211. Paris, M.A.E., Europe 1918-1929, Tchécoslovaquie, vol. 26, Telegram from Cosme to the French Ministry of Foreign Affairs, December 24, 1924.

212. *Bohemia*, May 13, 1924, p. 3. Purlitz, *Deutscher Geschichtskalender, 1924, Ausland,* 1:21.

213. *Bohemia*, June 27, 1924, p. 1. Purlitz, *Deutscher Geschichtskalender, 1924, Ausland,* 1:22.

214. Representative of Koch's approach to the nationality conflict was a report that he wrote in 1925, during the negotiations for the Locarno pacts and at the beginning of the campaign for the Czechoslovak parliamentary elections. Bonn, AA. Politische Abteilung II, L416/L119123/4412, Report by Koch to the German Foreign Office, May 7, 1925.

215. Old Reich Chancellery, L504/L149832-33/5068, Memorandum of a meeting of representatives of the German Foreign Office, the Ministry of Finance, and the Prussian *Zentralgenossenschaftskasse* on June 10, 1925.

216. Ibid., L504/L149846/5068, Note from the Reich Minister of Finance to the board of the Prussian *Zentralgenossenschaftskasse*, June 15, 1925.

217. After the depression struck in the early 1930's the Sudeten German banks were in need of assistance more than ever. In the early months of the Third Reich the decision was made to concentrate the support with the *Kreditanstalt der Deutschen*.

218. For the official returns of the elections, see *Statistická příručka*

republiky Československé, 3:258-60.

219. For Lodgman's statement of retirement, see *Bohemia*, November 18, 1925, p. 1.

Chapter Four

1. The seats in the Czechoslovak Chamber of Deputies were distributed as follows.

Czechoslovak parties	Before November 1925	After November 1925
Republicans (Agrarians)	42	45
People's (Catholics)	21	31
National Democrats	22	13
Trader's	6	13
Social Democrats	55	29
National Socialists	27	28
German parties		
Agrarians	13	24
Christian Socials	9	13
German-Nationals	10	10
Democrats	2	0
Social Democrats	30	17
National Socialists	5	7
Other parties		
Communists	19	41
Slovak People's	11	23

Source: *Národní shromáždění republiky československé v prvém de-sítiletí* (Prague: Státní tiskárna, 1928), pp. 327-28.

2. Bonn, AA, Büro des Staatssekretärs, 4509/E129608-09/2272, Memorandum by Schubert about conversations with Beneš and Krofta, October 13, 1925.

3. Ibid., 4582/E175567-73/2350, Memorandum by Schubert of a conversation with Krofta, January 18, 1926. *Akten zur deutschen auswärtigen Politik*, series B, volume 3, document 31.

4. Ibid., 4582/E175755-63/2350, Report by Koch to the German Foreign Office, February 20, 1926. *Akten zur deutschen auswärtigen Politik*, series B, volume 3, document 74.

5. Ibid., 4582/E175873-76/2350, Memorandum by Schubert of a conversation with Krofta, April 7, 1926. *Akten zur deutschen auswärtigen Politik*, series B, volume 3, document 109.

6. *Těsnopisecké zprávy o schůzich poslanecké sněmovny Národního shromáždění republiky Československé*, 28th-41st sessions, June 9-25, 1926. Dušan Uhlíř, "Republikánská strana lidu zemědělského a malorol-

nického ve vládě panské koalice," *Československý časopis historický* 18 (1970):195-204. For an account of the negotiations by which the Germans entered the cabinet, see Jaroslav César and Bohumil Černý, *Politika německých buržoazních stran v Československu v letech 1918-1938* (Prague: Nakladatelství Československé akademie věd, 1962), 1:358-71.

7. Bonn, AA, Politische Abteilung II, L437/L128384-85/4424, Report by Koch to the German Foreign Office, February 27, 1926. L437/L128386-91/4424, Report by Koch to the German Foreign Office, March 18, 1926. Both documents are printed in *Akten zur deutschen auswärtigen Politik*, series B, volume 3, documents 80 and 92. Büro des Reichsministers, 3086/D617932-33/1488, Note from Stresemann to Koch, May 4, 1926. *Akten zur deutschen auswärtigen Politik*, series B, volume 3, document 126.

8. Bonn, AA, Geheimakten, K91/K009189-92/3697, Report by Koch to the German Foreign Office, July 7, 1926.

9. Hans Lemberg, "Gefahrenmomente für die demokratische Staatsform der ČSR," in *Die Krise des Parlamentarismus in Ostmitteleuropa zwischen den beiden Weltkriegen*, ed. Hans-Erich Volkmann (Marburg: Verlag J. G. Herder-Institut, 1967), pp. 113-16. Vienna, HHStA, N.P.A., Karton 63, Report from Marek to the Austrian Ministry of Foreign Affairs, April 22, 1926. Marek referred specifically to an article by Kramář in the *Národní listy* of April 18. Marek believed that even Švehla might not be immune to the attractions of an extra-parliamentary party dictatorship. Marek credited Masaryk and Beneš with being the primary obstacles to a dictatorial government by the party chieftains. See also the reports by Marek and Orsini Rosenberg on May 20, May 26, and June 21, 1926. Vienna, HHStA, N.P.A., Karton 63. Alena Gajanová, *Dvojí tvář* (Prague: Naše vojsko, 1962), pp. 36-49.

10. See the report of the German chargé d'affaires on domestic political conditions in Czechoslovakia: Bonn, AA, Politische Abteilung II, L416/L119175-76/4412, Report of Heeren to the German Foreign Office, September 6, 1926.

11. Vienna, HHStA, N.P.A., Karton 63, Report by Marek to the Austrian Ministry of Foreign Affairs, March 18, 1926.

12. Ibid., Report by Marek to the Austrian Ministry of Foreign Affairs, October 6, 1926. Uhlíř, "Republikánská strana ve vládě panské koalice," pp. 207-08, 212-13. Dušan Uhlíř, "Konec vlády panské koalice a republikánská strana v roce 1929." *Československý časopis historický*, 18 (1970), 561-62.

13. Vienna, HHStA, N.P.A., Karton 63, Reports by Marek and Orsini Rosenberg to the Austrian Ministry of Foreign Affairs, July 21, August 26, and October 6 and 27, 1926.

14. Already in 1924 the British minister in Prague reported that Švehla kept the coalition together in part by collecting information on individual politicians and threatening to expose their misdeeds if they did not cooperate with his policies. Clerk considered Švehla's tactics to be "as

cynical as those of any Walpole." It would appear that Masaryk and Beneš employed similar methods. London, P.R.O., F.O. 371, vol. 9676, C5075/909/12, Report by Clerk to the British Foreign Office, March 10, 1924.

15. In his discussion with the French minister Beneš had not hidden his hope of becoming the leader of the National Socialist party. Paris, M.A.E., Europe 1918-1929, Tchécoslovaquie, vol. 26, Couget to Poincaré, January 31, 1923.

16. Hodža privately arranged for talks with Schubert through a mutual acquaintance and then discussed various aspects of Czechoslovak policy with Schubert in Marienbad and Prague in early May 1926. Apparently Hodža was seeking Berlin's support for his negotiations with the Sudeten German political leaders. Through the summer and autumn Frau Gerta von Einem, the intermediary, informed Schubert that Hodža desired another conference, but the secrecy and unorthodox nature of Hodža's maneuvers left the Germans rightly suspicious. Schubert decided to talk with Hodža only in an official capacity, and after the governmental crisis subsided in Czechoslovakia Schubert sent assurances to Beneš that he had not meant to conspire against him. Bonn, AA, Büro des Staatssekretärs, 4582/E176023-231/2350, Spezial-Angelegenheit Hodža.

17. Věra Olivová, *The Doomed Democracy*, trans. George Theiner (London: Sidgwick & Jackson, 1972), pp. 157-61. Hans Lemberg, "Die tschechischen Konservativen 1918-1939," in *Aktuelle Forschungsprobleme um die Erste Tschechoslowakische Republik*, ed. Karl Bosl (Munich: R. Oldenbourg, 1969), p. 124.

18. Uhlíř, "Republikánská strana ve vládě panské koalice," pp. 204-12.

19. That idea became a focus of Hodža's interests while he was Czechoslovak premier from 1935 to 1938. In his memoirs he traced his hopes for agrarian cooperation in Eastern Europe back to his political activities in the Hungarian half of the Dual Monarchy. See Milan Hodža, *Federation in Central Europe: Reflections and Reminiscences*, (London: Jerrolds Publishers, 1942).

20. Paris, M.A.E., Europe 1918-1929, Autriche, vol. 78, Report by Charles-Roux to Briand, June 4, 1927.

21. Uhlíř, "Republikánská strana ve vládě panské koalice," pp. 212-15.

22. Washington, National Archives, State Department file 860f.00/244, Report by Lewis Einstein to the Department of State, May 28, 1926.

23. Uhlíř, "Republikánská strana ve vládě panské koalice," pp. 209-12. Vienna, HHStA, N.P.A., Karton 63, Reports by Marek to the Austrian Ministry of Foreign Affairs, September 23, October 6, 7, and 26, and November 12, 1926. Paris, M.A.E., Europe 1918-1929, Tchécoslovaquie, vol. 27, Report of Couget to Briand, September 13, 1926. Report of Seguin to Briand, January 3, 1927.

24. Vienna, HHStA, N.P.A., Karton 63, Report by Marek to the

Austrian Ministry of Foreign Affairs, July 22, 1926. For Koch's critical analysis of Beneš's decision to enter Švehla's government, see Bonn, AA, Politische Abteilung II, L416/L119183/4412, Report by Koch to the German Foreign Office, December 16, 1926.

25. At the time of the construction of Švehla's government, Krofta actually informed the Germans that Beneš would probably resign at least for a short time and that he, Krofta, would succeed Beneš in office. Bonn, AA, Büro des Staatssekretärs, 4582/E176009-11/2350, Memorandum by Köpke of a conversation with Krofta, October 1, 1926. 4582/E176019-20, Memorandum by Köpke of a conversation with Krofta, November 6, 1926.

26. *Central European Observer*, January 1, 1927, p. 9.

27. In his initial dispatches about the agreement between the Czechoslovak and German Agrarians, Koch reported that the Germans had received promises in matters relating to school questions, land reform, the appointment of government officials, and other traditional areas of dispute. Bonn, AA, Büro des Reichsministers, 3086/D617935/1488, Telegram from Koch to the German Foreign Office, June 22, 1926.

28. Paris, M.A.E., Europe 1918-1929, Tchécoslovaquie, vol. 69, Report by Couget to Briand, June 22, 1926.

29. Ibid., vol. 27, Report by Couget to Briand, September 13, 1926. Report by Couget to Briand, October 16, 1926.

30. Ibid., vol. 33, Report by Charles-Roux to Briand, February 22, 1927.

31. Ibid., vol. 27, Report by Charles-Roux to Briand, April 4, 1927. Vol. 33, Report by Charles-Roux to Briand, October 17, 1928. Typical of Beneš's sentiments in 1928 was his statement: "I know perfectly well that with the first difficulty from abroad they will drop us."

32. Paris, M.A.E., Europe 1918-1929, Tchécoslovaquie, vol. 33, Report by Charles-Roux to Briand, July 13, 1927.

33. Bonn, AA, Büro des Staatssekretärs, 4582/E175664-67/2350, Memorandum by Schubert of a conversation with Krofta, February 9, 1926.

34. Ibid., 4582/E175565-66/2350, Note by Schubert to Krofta, February 13, 1926.

35. Bonn, Old Reich Chancellery, L504/L149868-72/5068, Note from Köpke to the representation of the Reich government in Munich, November 27, 1926.

36. Ibid., L504/L149870/5068. In December Köpke confidentially informed Krofta about Berlin's efforts to pacify the Bavarians. See Bonn, AA, Handakten Köpkes, 5138/E296928/2453, Memorandum by Köpke of a conversation with Krofta, December 23, 1926.

37. Bonn, AA, Politische Abteilung II, L417/L120751/4414, Memorandum by Zech, an official in political department two of the Foreign Office, of a conversation with the Bavarian minister in Berlin, Ritter von Preger, January 22, 1927.

38. Dieter Hertz-Eichenrode, *Politik und Landwirtschaft in Ostpreussen 1919-1930* (Cologne: Westdeutscher Verlag, 1969), pp. 181-215.

39. Bonn, AA, Politische Abteilung II, L417/L120812-13/4414, Memorandum by Zech of a conversation with Counselor Schmelzle of the Bavarian State Ministry, March 2, 1927.

40. Erik Lönnroth, "Sweden: The Diplomacy of Östen Undén," *The Diplomats, 1919-1939*, eds. Gordon A. Craig and Felix Gilbert (Princeton: Princeton University Press, 1953), pp. 86-99.

41. Bonn, AA, Büro des Staatssekretärs, 4586/E180917-19/2359. Memorandum by Schubert about a conversation with Lampson, March 14, 1926. *Akten zur deutschen auswärtigen Politik*, series B, volume I, 1, document 161.

42. Bonn, AA, Old Reich Chancellery, 3635/D804075-78/1691, Memorandum by Stresemann, March 14, 1926. *Akten zur deutschen auswärtigen Politik*, series B, volume I, 1, document 162. Spenz, *Die diplomatische Vorgeschichte*, pp. 139-51.

43. On the negotiations for the Treaty of Berlin and the disputes created by it, see *Akten zur deutschen auswärtigen Politik*, series B, volume II, 1.

44. Bonn, AA, Büro des Reichsministers, 2860/D557062-63/1411, Telegram from Schubert to the German Embassy in Paris, April 8, 1926. *Akten zur deutschen auswärtigen Politik*, series B, volume II, 1, document 114.

45. Alena Gajanová, *ČSR a středoevropská politika velmocí, 1918-1938* (Prague: Academia, 1967), pp. 202-07. Bonn, AA, Büro des Staatssekretärs, 4562/E157183-85/2316, Memorandum by Schubert about a conversation between Stresemann and Krofta, April 21, 1926. Büro des Reichsministers, 3086/D617924-26/1488, Note from Schubert to Koch, April 23, 1926. *Akten zur deutschen auswärtigen Politik*, series B, volume II, 1, documents 155 and 163.

46. Bonn, AA, Büro des Reichsministers, 3086/D617922-23/1488, Telegram from Koch to the German Foreign Office, April 22, 1926. *Akten zur deutschen auswärtigen Politik*, series B, volume 3, document 120.

47. Bonn, AA, Büro des Reichsministers, 3086/D617919-21/1488, Note from Schubert to the German representations in London, Paris, Rome, and Brussels, April 22, 1926.

48. Ibid., Report of Hoesch to the German Foreign Office, April 24, 1926. *Akten zur deutschen auswärtigen Politik*, series B, volume II, 1, document 171.

49. Bonn, AA, Politische Abteilung II, L417/L120687/4414, Memorandum by Zech of a conversation with Krofta, September 3, 1926.

50. The *Central European Observer*, as the government's chief propaganda medium in English, was primarily responsible for combatting Rothermere's claims. Its editors liked to report that the Sudeten Germans were uninterested in Rothermere's crusade for them and the Hungarians. See *Central European Observer*, September 30, 1927, p. 641; June 29,

1928, p. 400. For Czechoslovak diplomatic reports concerning pro-Hungarian attitudes in Britain, see Gajanová, *ČSR a středoevropská politika velmocí*, pp. 217-37.

51. For the documentation on German diplomatic initiatives in 1926, see *Akten zur deutschen auswärtigen Politik*, series B, volumes 1-3.

52. About German-Austrian relations and the movement toward an Anschluss, see M. Margaret Ball, *Post-War German-Austrian Relations: The Anschluss Movement, 1918-1936*, (Stanford: Stanford University Press, 1937), pp. 77-99. *Akten zur deutschen auswärtigen Politik*, series B, volume 5, document 196.

53. Paris, M.A.E., Europe 1918-1929, Autriche, vol. 78, Report by Charles-Roux to Briand, February 17, 1927. Tchécoslovaquie, vol. 39, Report by Charles-Roux to Briand, February 26, 1927.

54. London, P.R.O., F.O. 371, vol. 12097, C4331/860/12, Report by Macleay to the British Foreign Office, May 10, 1927.

55. Ibid. See the comments at the beginning of the report.

56. London, P.R.O., F.O. 371, vol. 12097, C1407/860/12, Report by Charles Dodd to the British Foreign Office, February 7, 1927. In that conversation Beneš had drawn attention to the policy of the Austrians of making their legislation conform with that in Germany. Beneš remarked that that could not be prevented, but he hoped that Austria's economic dependence on the Danubian states could prevent an Anschluss.

57. Ibid. See comments at the beginning of the report.

58. Vienna, HHStA, N.P.A., Karton 63, Report by Marek to the Austrian Ministry of Foreign Affairs, May 10, 1927.

59. Ibid., Report by Marek to the Austrian Ministry of Foreign Affairs, March 25, 1927.

60. Paris, M.A.E., Europe 1918-1929, Tchécoslovaquie, vol. 70, Briand to French missions abroad, July 20, 1927. Felix John Vondracek, *The Foreign Policy of Czechoslovakia, 1918-1935* (New York: Columbia University Press, 1937), pp. 286-91. Vondracek's necessary reliance on newspaper reports created certain misconceptions for him. For example. it was not the case that Beneš ever supported Polish inclusion in the Little Entente.

61. Paris, M.A.E., Europe 1918-1929, Tchécoslovaquie, vol. 70, Report from Charles-Roux to Briand, May 22, 1927.

62. Ibid., Autriche, vol. 78, Memorandum about a conversation between Joseph Paul-Boncour and Beneš in Geneva, June 12, 1927. Report by Charles-Roux to Briand, June 12, 1927.

63. Ibid., Autriche, vol. 79, Letter from the Ministry of Foreign Affairs to Charles-Roux, August 22, 1927. Also see volume 80 for Charles-Roux's reports through 1927 and 1928 about his efforts to encourage a Danubian preferential system.

64. By 1928 Beneš complained bitterly about the protectionism of the Czechoslovak cabinet. Charles-Roux quoted him as saying: "M. Hodža has made an oratorical specialty of an alliance between Czechoslovakia and

Yugoslavia: I can get nothing from him; he would be disavowed by his party." Paris, M.A.E., Europe 1918-1929, Tchécoslovaquie, vol. 70, Report of Charles-Roux to Briand, June 17, 1928.

65. For the most recent and authoritative interpretation of Seipel's policy on Central European alignments, see Klemens von Klemperer, *Ignaz Seipel* (Princeton: Princeton University Press, 1972), pp. 301-29.

66. Vienna, HHStA, N.P.A., Karton 63, Report by Marek to the Austrian Ministry of Foreign Affairs, March 25, 1927.

67. For a summary of the optants question, see Arnold J. Toynbee, *Survey of International Affairs, 1928* (London: Oxford University Press, 1929), pp. 168-82.

68. Those attempts are well illustrated for the year 1926 in the published documents of the German Foreign Office. *Akten zur deutschen auswärtigen Politik*, series B, volume 3. For negotiations concerning the pact of friendship, conciliation, and arbitration between Hungary and Italy, which was signed on April 5, 1927, see Italy, Commissione per la Publicazione dei Documenti Diplomatici, *I Documenti Diplomatici Italiani*, 7th series, vol. 5. Alan Cassels, *Mussolini's Early Diplomacy* (Princeton: Princeton University Press, 1970), pp. 338-48.

69. Paris, M.A.E., Europe 1918-1929, Autriche, vol. 78, Memorandum about a conversation between Masaryk and Briand, March 15, 1927. In this conversation Masaryk also let it be seen that he favored boundary revisions between Slovakia and Hungary in order to bring Hungary into closer cooperation with the states of the Little Entente. But he noted that that could happen only if Rumania and Yugoslavia also ceded Hungarian-inhabited territories, and the Rumanians and Yugoslavs were as yet unwilling to do so.

70. Bonn, AA, Büro des Reichsministers, 3086/D617949-52/1488, Memorandum by Stresemann of a conversation with Masaryk, March 13, 1927.

71. Bonn, AA, Politische Abteilung II, L417/L120847-48/4414, Report by Dieckhoff of a conversation with Jan Masaryk, March 21, 1927. Since June 1925, Jan Masaryk had been the Czechoslovak minister to Great Britain.

72. Vienna, HHStA, N.P.A., Karton 63, Report by Marek to the Austrian Ministry of Foreign Affairs, March 21, 1927.

73. Ibid., Report by Marek to the Austrian Ministry of Foreign Affairs, April 28, 1927. Bonn, AA, Politische Abteilung II, L416/L119200/4412, Report by Koch to the German Foreign Office, April 30, 1927.

74. Paris, M.A.E., Europe 1918-1929, Autriche, vol. 78, Report by Laroche to Briand, February 28, 1927.

75. Harald von Riekhoff, *German-Polish Relations, 1918-1933* (Baltimore: Johns Hopkins Press, 1971), pp. 317-26. Josef Korbel, *Poland between East and West* (Princeton: Princeton University Press, 1963), pp. 211-27. Joseph Rothschild, *Pilsudski's Coup d'Etat* (New York: Columbia

University Press, 1966), pp. 299-302.

76. Paris, M.A.E., Europe 1918-1929, Tchécoslovaquie, vol. 70, Report by Laroche to Briand, December 28, 1927.

77. Thaddeus V. Gromada, "Pilsudski and the Slovak Autonomists," *Slavic Review* 28 (September 1969):445-62. Jörg K. Hoensch, *Die Slowakei und Hitlers Ostpolitik* (Cologne: Böhlau Verlag, 1965), pp. 51-54. Jaroslav Valenta, "Československo and Polsko v letech 1918-1945," in *Češi a Polaci v minulosti* (Prague: Academia, 1967), pp. 525-40. Jerzy Kozeński, *Czechoslowacja w polskiej polityce zagranicznej w latach 1932-1938* (Poznań: Instytut Zachodni, 1964), pp. 28-39.

78. Bonn, AA, Politische Abteilung II, L417/L120868-70/4414, Report by Schubert to the German Foreign Office, May 17, 1927. Paris, M.A.E., Europe 1918-1929, Autriche, vol. 78, Report by Charles-Roux to Briand, June 15, 1927.

79. Bonn, AA, Politische Abteilung II, L417/L120869-70/4414.

80. Ibid., L417/L119204/4412, Memorandum of a conversation between Müller and Beneš, June 16, 1927.

And again in July President Masaryk tried to turn the Germans away from any idea of attaching Austria to the Reich. He told a German with good connections to the Foreign Office that Austria ought to be included in a larger economic unit by means of treaties with its neighboring states. When asked if he were talking about a Danubian confederation, Masaryk replied that names for the project were not important, just that an *Anschluss* was no way to solve the problem. Bonn, AA, Politische Abteilung II, L417/L120917-18/4414, Memorandum by Professor Caro of a conversation with Masaryk in Karlsbad on July 29, 1927.

81. Bonn, AA, Politische Abteilung II, L417/L119206/4412, Note from Köpke to Koch, July 5, 1927.

82. Julius Curtius, *Sechs Jahre Minister der deutschen Republik* (Heidelberg: Carl Winter Universitätsverlag, 1948), p. 212.

83. Vienna, HHStA, N.P.A., Karton 64, Report by Marek to the Austrian Ministry of Foreign Affairs, October 6, 1927. Krofta remarked that he was "100% more skeptical" about a system of bilateral preferential tariff treaties among the successor states than was Beneš.

84. Ibid., Report by Marek to the Austrian Ministry of Foreign Affairs, October 27, 1927.

85. Bonn, AA, Büro des Reichsministers, 3086/D617958-59/1488, Note from Köpke to Koch, November 26, 1927. Klemperer, *Ignaz Seipel*, pp. 340-41.

86. Vienna, HHStA, N.P.A., Karton 64, Report by Marek to the Austrian Ministry of Foreign Affairs, November 10, 1927.

87. Ibid., Report by Marek to the Austrian Ministry of Foreign Affairs, October 15, 1927.

88. Bonn, AA, Politische Abteilung II, K1099/K282559-562/4632, Letter from Eduard Hoffmann to Köpke, April 5, 1928. Klemperer, *Ignaz Seipel*, pp. 319-29.

89. Bonn, AA, Büro des Staatssekretärs, 4577/E174185-89/2348, Memorandum by Schubert of a conversation with Austrian Minister Frank, March 19, 1928.

90. Ibid., 4577/E174190-93/2348, Memorandum by Schubert of a conversation with Hungarian Minister, Baron Kánya, March 22, 1928.

91. Toynbee, *Survey of International Affairs 1928*, pp. 81-93. League of Nations, *Official Journal*, (May, 1928), pp. 648-50. For the diplomatic background to the documents printed in the *Official Journal*, see AA, Politische Abteilung II, L417/L121050/4414, background memorandum prepared for Schubert upon Beneš's visit to Berlin, May 1928.

92. Bonn, AA, Büro des Reichsministers, 3086/D617976-77/1488, Memorandum by Schubert of a report by Beer, March 12, 1928. Dr. Max Beer was the representative of the Wolff Telegraphic Bureau in Geneva. He maintained excellent contacts both with foreign diplomats active at the League and with German government officials. In 1932 he published a subjective account of his impressions in Geneva, entitled *Die Reise nach Genf*. The book appeared in English as *The League on Trial* (Boston: Houghton Mifflin Company, 1933).

93. Bonn, AA, Büro des Reichsministers, 3086/D617976-77/1488, Memorandum by Schubert of a report by Beer, March 12, 1928.

94. Bonn, AA, Büro des Staatssekretärs, 4577/E174185-189/2348, Memorandum by Schubert about a conversation with Frank, March 19, 1928.

95. Paris, M.A.E., Europe 1918-1929, Autriche, vol. 79, Letter of Alfred Grünberger to de Beaumarchais, July 12, 1927. Memorandum by the Political Director of the Ministry of Foreign Affairs about a conversation with the counselor of the Austrian legation, November 10, 1927.

96. Bonn, AA, Büro des Staatssekretärs, 4567/E167077-079/2336, Letter and memorandum from Mutius to Schubert, February 13, 1928.

97. Ibid., 4577/E174194-95/2348, Memorandum by Schubert of a conversation with Stresemann, March 23, 1928.

98. Ibid., 4577/E174218-21/2348, Memorandum by Schubert of a conversation with Hindenburg, May 21, 1928. (On this morning after the election Hindenburg's reaction to the results was in keeping with his political outlook. Consoling himself that in the final analysis the results were not quite so bad for the conservative parties as originally thought, he complained bitterly about what he considered to be the lack of leadership in the German National party.)

99. Bonn, AA, Büro des Reichsministers, 3086/D617995-8002/1488, Memorandum by Schubert of a conversation with Beneš, May 21, 1928.

100. Ibid., 3086/D618009-14/1488, Memorandum by Schubert of a conversation with Beneš, May 22, 1928.

101. Ibid., 3086/D618014-23/1488, Memorandum by Schubert of a conversation with Beneš, May 22, 1928.

102. After the meetings with Beneš were over, Schubert sent Koch

copies of the memoranda from the discussions and attached a note in which he said: "As you see from the memoranda I partially (and I hope cautiously) brought up the ideas about which we spoke in our last meeting. I believe this doesn't hurt anything and was also necessary." That meeting between Schubert and Koch was on the evening of May 20, the day before Schubert's conversations with Beneš. The remark shows how embryonic Schubert's ideas for special ties among Germany, Austria, and Czechoslovakia were. See Bonn, AA, Büro des Staatssekretärs, 4577/ E174287/2348, Note from Schubert to Koch, May 26, 1928. For a detailed discussion of the Beneš-Schubert meetings and Schubert's economic ideas, see Peter Krüger, "Beneš und die europäische Wirtschafts-konzeption des deutschen Staatssekretärs Carl von Schubert," in *Bohemia-Jahrbuch*, vol. 14 (Munich: R. Oldenbourg Verlag, 1973), 320-40.

103. In the midst of their discussions about various economic forma-tions Beneš revealed that "a few years" previously there had been discussions about a preferential tariff system among Czechoslovakia, Austria, and Italy, and that the Austrians had been sympathetic to the project. Beneš claimed that he had vetoed the idea since such a system would have meant the exploitation of Austria. Later memoranda in the German Foreign Office showed that this piece of information raised some eyebrows in Berlin. See Bonn, AA, Büro des Reichsministers, 3086/D618030/1488, Memorandum by Schubert of a conversation with Beneš, May 23, 1928.

104. The French documents also corroborate Beneš's failure to include Poland in his plans for a preferential tariff system. Paris, M.A.E., Europe 1918-1929, Autriche, vol. 80, Report by Charles-Roux to Briand, December 1, 1927.

105. Bonn, AA, Büro des Reichsministers, 3086/D618028-35/1488, Memorandum by Schubert of a conversation with Beneš, May 23, 1928.

106. This must have been a curious statement by Beneš in view of the fact that he had promoted Krofta's conversations in Berlin about the Sudeten Germans in the months after Locarno. It is also instructive that Schubert demonstrated a relative lack of concern for the Sudeten Germans in the same year that Stresemann and Zaleski engaged in a bitter controversy in Geneva about Polish treatment of the German minority. See F.P. Walters, *A History of the League of Nations* (London: Oxford University Press, 1952), pp. 407-8.

107. Bonn, AA, Büro des Reichsministers, 3086/D618038-39/1488, Memorandum by Schubert of a conversation with Beneš, May 24, 1928.

108. Bonn, AA, Büro des Staatssekretärs, 4577/E174286-89/2348, Note by Schubert to Koch, May 26, 1928. Frank was a member of the pan-German party and a strong advocate of close Austro-German cooperation. Klemperer, *Ignaz Seipel*, pp. 323-24.

109. Bonn, AA, Büro des Reichsministers, 3086/D618045-49/1488, Memorandum by Schubert of a conversation with Austrian Minister Frank, May 25, 1928.

110. Bonn, AA, Büro des Staatssekretärs, 4577/E174295-300/2348, Memorandum by Schubert of a conversation with Hungarian Minister Kánya, May 26, 1928.

111. Vienna, HHStA, N.P.A., Karton 64, Report by Marek to the Austrian Ministry of Foreign Affairs, May 12, 1928.

112. Ibid., Report by Marek to the Austrian Ministry of Foreign Affairs, May 31, 1928.

113. Paris, M.A.E., Europe 1918-1929, Tchécoslovaquie, vol. 39, Report of de Margerie to Briand, May 24, 1928.

114. Vienna, HHStA, N.P.A., Karton 64, Report by Marek to the Austrian Ministry of Foreign Affairs, May 31, 1928.

115. Although the *Daily Telegraph* published its reports under a by-line from Brussels, it acquired its information from its correspondent in Berlin. For the German ambassador's reports from London about the matter, see Bonn, AA, Politische Abteilung II, L417/L121122/4415, Reports from Dieckhoff to the German Foreign Office, May 26 and May 30, 1938.

116. Bonn, AA, Büro des Reichsministers, 3086/D618142/1488, Report from Köpke to Schubert in Geneva about a conversation with Chvalkovský, June 2, 1928. Köpke was Schubert's deputy and the director of political division II, which handled Czechoslovak affairs. Chvalkovský was the Czechoslovak minister in Berlin.

117. Edvard Beneš, *La Situation Internationale et la Politique Etrangère Tchécoslovaque* (Prague: Orbis, 1928), pp. 21-22. (This is a French translation, published by the Czechoslovak government, of Beneš's speech in the foreign affairs committee of the National Assembly, June 6, 1928.) See also Koch's report about the speech, Bonn, AA, Politische Abteilung II, L416/L119251/4412, Report by Koch to the German Foreign Office, June 13, 1928. Gajanová, *ČSR a středoevropská politika velmocí*, p. 239.

118. *Central European Observer*, July 6, 1928, p. 418. Klemperer, *Ignaz Seipel*, pp. 338-40.

119. The continuing determination of the Hungarians to sabotage Beneš's projects was mirrored in a visit that Baron Kánya paid to the German Foreign Office in July. Kánya expressed his happiness about Schubert's conversations with Beneš and about the negative results of the Little Entente conference. He thought it was obvious that if in the far future Germany should revive some of its claims in Central Europe it would eventually come into conflict with the Little Entente. When asked what he meant, Kánya mentioned the possibility that Germany might bring up the Anschluss issue when it had greater freedom of movement. Schubert retorted that Kánya knew that Germany had no intention of forcing the Anschluss, that over the long range Germany hoped for some kind of general "economic compromise" in Central Europe, and that for the moment Germany was simply interested in improving its trade relations in the area. Kánya answered that nevertheless Seipel's remarks constituted an obvious veto to the economic projects publicized at Bucharest. Kánya's whole approach—his smiles and insinuations—showed that he hoped for an open dispute between Berlin and Prague over Austria.

Budapest did not mind seeing other powers in conflict with the Little Entente, but Berlin did not want to furnish the spectacle. Bonn, AA, Büro des Staatssekretärs, 4577/E174337-40/2348, Memorandum by Schubert of a conversation with Hungarian Minister Baron Kánya, July 19, 1928.

120. Paris, M.A.E., Europe 1918-1929, Tchécoslovaquie, vol. 70, Report by Charles-Roux to Briand, July 13, 1928.

121. Bonn, AA, Büro des Reichsministers, 3086/D618148-49/1488, Memorandum by Stresemann of conversations with Masaryk on July 30 and August 1, 1928. In these talks Masaryk recalled Prague's willingness in 1919 to make minor territorial concessions to Germany, and it is interesting that Stresemann knew nothing at all about this. Koch had to write a background memorandum in explanation of Masaryk's remarks. See Bonn, AA, Politische Abteilung II, L417/L121182-83/4415, Report by Koch to the German Foreign Office, August 7, 1928.

122. Konrad Henlein revived the old demand for the autonomy of the Sudeten German areas as part of his "Karlsbad Program" in April 1938. Only in September 1938 did the Czechs agree to let the Germans have autonomous government in their areas of settlement, but Hitler had much more ambitious goals. See John W. Wheeler-Bennett, *Munich: Prologue to Tragedy* (London: Macmillan & Co., 1948), pp. 45-93. Boris Celovsky, *Das Münchener Abkommen 1938* (Stuttgart: Deutsche Verlags-Anstalt, 1958), pp. 164-68, 252-57, 286-97.

123. Vienna, HHStA, N.P.A., Karton 64, Report by Orsini Rosenberg, Austrian chargé d'affaires in Prague, to the Austrian Ministry of Foreign Affairs, August 27, 1928.

124. Krofta had already been in Berlin in January 1928 for negotiations that left only details to be settled. For his remarks at that time see Bonn, AA, Büro des Staatssekretärs, 4582/E176718-21/2351, Memorandum by Schubert of a conversation with Krofta and Chvalkovský, January 12, 1928.

125. The port of Stettin and the Oder River rights were of interest primarily to the Vítkovice Iron Company for its imports of iron ore from Sweden. However, the maintenance of a free zone in Stettin appeared to be too expensive, and the question was left in abeyance. See *Central European Observer*, November 16, 1928, p. 732.

126. The agreement was signed by the two governments in February 1929 and approved by an international commission consisting of British, German, and Czechoslovak delegates in October.

For Krofta's and Chvalkovský's contacts with the German Foreign Office in November 1928, see Bonn, AA, Büro des Staatssekretärs, 4582/E176889-95/2351, Memorandum by Schubert of a conversation with Chvalkovský, November 15, 1928.

127. Bonn, AA, Büro des Reichsministers, 3086/D618024-26/1488, Memorandum by Schubert of a conversation with Beneš, May 23, 1928. 3086/D617969/1488, Note from Schubert in Geneva to the German Foreign Office about a conversation with Beneš, September 23, 1928.

Büro des Staatssekretärs, 4582/E176889-95/2351, Memorandum by Köpke of a conversation with Krofta, November 3, 1928.

128. After postponing the issue of the valorization of the Austrian debts, Berlin tried to get concessions for Reich German laborers in Czechoslovakia in return for German concessions in a trade treaty. In an effort to protect the home labor market, the Czechoslovak National Assembly had passed a law in 1928 restricting the employment of foreign nationals in Czechoslovakia. See Bonn, AA, Handakten Sammlung Nachträge V.L.R. Windel, L508/L150059-60/5068, Report of Koch to the German Foreign Office, February 1, 1929. L508/L150066-68/5068, Note from Ritter to Koch, February 11, 1929.

129. Bonn, AA, Politische Abteilung II, L417/L121401-02/4415, Background memorandum by Bülow for Stresemann for discussions in Geneva, August 20, 1929.

130. Bonn, AA, Büro des Staatssekretärs, 4577/E174266-68/2348, Memorandum by Schubert of a conversation with Beneš, May 24, 1928.

131. Bertram had played a controversial role in trying to keep all of Upper Silesia under German sovereignty in 1920-21. See F. Gregory Campbell, "The Struggle for Upper Silesia, 1919-1921," *Journal of Modern History* 42 (September 1970):361-85.

132. Bonn, AA, Büro des Reichsministers, 3086/D618311/1488, Memorandum by Foreign Minister Neurath about a conversation with the papal nuncio, June 6, 1935.

133. In one of his letters to Crown Prince Wilhelm, Stresemann wrote that Germany would have to take over the "protection of the Germans living abroad, those ten or twelve million members of the race, now under a foreign yoke." On June 14, 1925, he wrote in an anonymous article in the *Hamburger Fremdenblatt*: "Germany must next of all insure its actual independence and equality of status. Germany must further become the protector of the minorities of Europe, it must be the great mother-land of German civilization, and it must be vigilant that the rights of the German minorities be protected according to the international treaties by those who have accepted those treaties." These quotations are taken from Stresemann's *Vermächtnis* and are quoted in Ludwig Zimmermann, *Deutsche Aussenpolitik in der Ära der Weimarer Republik* (Göttingen: Musterschmidt-Verlag, 1958), p. 347.

134. Bonn, AA, Politische Abteilung II, L446/L135146-147/4467, Note from Schubert to the German Legation in Prague, April 9, 1926. L437/L128569-574/4424, Letter from Zech to Koch, May 25, 1926. L446/L135194-196/4467, Note from Stresemann to Krofta, June 11, 1926. *Akten zur deutschen auswärtigen Politik*, series B, volume 3, documents 111, 138, and 148.

135. Bonn, AA, Geheimakten, K95/K010301-305/3699, Memorandum by Erich Friedrich Benndorf, November 27, 1926.

136. For a review of Reich German support of Sudeten German financial institutions during the Weimar period, see Bonn, AA, Geheimak-

ten 75a/4, Report by Koch to the German Foreign Office, January 23, 1933.

137. *Akten zur deutschen auswärtigen Politik*, series B, volume I, 1, documents 178 and 205, volume I, 2, document 280.

138. Bonn, AA, Büro des Staatssekretärs, 4582/E176459/2351, Note from Stresemann to the German Foreign Ministry in Prague, July 5, 1927. 4582/E176460-62/2351, Reports by Heeren to Stresemann, July 6 and 7, 1927.

139. Bonn, AA, Büro des Staatssekretärs, 4582/E176572-76/2351, Memorandum by Zech for Stresemann and Schubert, November 7, 1927.

140. Johann Wolfgang Brügel, *Tschechen und Deutsche, 1918-1938* (Munich: Nymphenburger Verlagshandlung, 1967), p. 182.

141. Ibid. Bonn, AA, Politische Abteilung II, L437/L129668-671/ 4426, Report by Koch to the German Foreign Office, August 7, 1928.

142. Koch used that phrase in a report to Berlin already in 1927. Bonn, AA, Politische Abteilung II, L437/L129060/4425, Report by Koch to the German Foreign Office, May 16, 1927. Koch's friendships among Prague's German-Jewish circles helped to make him one of the earliest Nazi targets in the German foreign service after the seizure of power in 1933.

The sympathies of the Prague German Legation for the "neo-activists," as the parties that coalesced to form the DAWG were known, was already creating resentment among the Sudeten German government parties in 1927. Vienna, HHStA, N.P.A., Karton 64, Report by Orsini Rosenberg to the Austrian Ministry of Foreign Affairs, September 17, 1927. Beneš also expressed high regard for the leaders of the DAWG. Paris, M.A.E., Europe 1918-1929, Tchécoslovaquie, vol. 28, Report by Charles-Roux to Briand, December 4, 1928.

143. Eventually Rosche and his lieutenant, Dr. Gustav Peters, loosed themselves from the "Jewish liberals" in 1935 in order to join Konrad Henlein's Sudeten German party. They then strove to blot out the memories of their "liberal, capitalistic, Free Mason" background. Brügel, *Tschechen und Deutsche*, p. 578.

144. Edward Taborský, *Czechoslovak Democracy at Work* (London: George Allen & Unwin, 1945), pp. 118-20. R.W. Seton-Watson, *Slovakia Then and Now* (London: George Allen & Unwin, 1931), pp. 42-44, 217-32.

145. Two German Agrarian deputies did refuse to follow the party leadership and voted against the administrative reform. They were expelled from the party. Uhlíř, "Republikánská strana ve vládě panské koalice," p. 217.

146. Vienna, HHStA, N.P.A., Karton 64, Reports by Marek to the Austrian Ministry of Foreign Affairs, November 1, 1928, and April 24, 1929.

147. Walters, *A History of the League of Nations*, pp. 406-11. League of Nations, *Official Journal*, 10th year, no. 1 (January 1929), pp. 57-71; *Official Journal*, 10th year, no. 4 (April 1929), pp. 515-32; *Official Journal*, 10th year, no. 7 (July 1929), pp. 1005-11.

148. Vienna, HHStA, N.P.A., Karton 64, Reports by Marek to the Austrian Ministry of Foreign Affairs, May 4, 1929, and May 25, 1929. London, P.R.O., F.O. 371, vol. 13579, C3559/119/12, Report by Macleay to the British Foreign Office, May 16, 1929. The British minister believed that the Sudeten Germans had few legitimate grievances and could not understand why they would revive an old controversy.

149. Vienna, HHStA, N.P.A., Karton 64, Report by Marek to the Austrian Ministry of Foreign Affairs, June 28, 1929.

150. Paris, M.A.E., Europe 1918-1929, Tchécoslovaquie, vol. 33, Report by Charles-Roux to Briand, May 18, 1929.

151. *Prager Presse*, January 28, 1928, p. 2; January 31, 1928, p. 2. Brügel, *Tschechen und Deutsche*, pp. 186-89.

152. *Central European Observer*, September 14, 1928, p. 608.

153. Uhlíř, "Republikánská strana ve vládě panské koalice," pp. 217-23.

154. Ibid. Paris, M.A.E., Europe 1918-1929, Tchécoslovaquie, vol. 28, Report by Charles-Roux to Briand, April 5, 1928. Report by Charles-Roux to Briand, September 10, 1928.

155. Kamil Krofta related this information after a conversation with Masaryk. Paris, M.A.E., Europe 1918-1929, Tchécoslovaquie, vol. 28, Report by Charles-Roux to Briand, April 6, 1928.

156. Ibid., Report by Charles-Roux to Briand, February 20, 1928. London, P.R.O., F.O. 371, vol. 12865, C6487/365/12, Report by Macleay to the British Foreign Office, August 22, 1928.

157. Bonn, AA, Politische Abteilung II, L416/L119248/4412, Report by Koch to the German Foreign Office, June 14, 1928.

158. Paris, M.A.E., Europe 1918-1929, Tchécoslovaquie, vol. 28, Telegram from Charles-Roux to the French Ministry of Foreign Affairs, December 10, 1928.

159. Vienna, HHStA, N.P.A., Karton 64, Report by Marek to the Austrian Ministry of Foreign Affairs, December 12, 1928.

160. Washington, National Archives, State Department file 860f.00/281, Report by Einstein to the Department of State, December 19, 1928.

161. Uhlíř, "Republikánská strana ve vládě panské koalice," pp. 228-33. Uhlíř, "Konec vlády panské koalice," pp. 551-59.
Washington, National Archives, State Department file 860f.00/281, Report by Lewis Einstein, the American minister in Prague, to the Department of State, December 19, 1928.
Vienna, HHStA, N.P.A., Karton 64, Report by Marek to the Austrian Ministry of Foreign Affairs, February 21, 1929.
Paris, M.A.E., Europe 1918-1929, Tchécoslovaquie, vol. 29, Reports by Charles-Roux to Briand, February 11 and 24, 1929.

162. Taborský, *Czechoslovak Democracy at Work*, pp. 42-44, 62-64, 97-98.

163. Paris, M.A.E., Europe 1918-1929, Tchécoslovaquie, vol. 29, Telegram from Charles-Roux to the Ministry of Foreign Affairs, September 30, 1929.

330 Notes to Pages 208-214

164. Ibid., vol. 28, Reports by Charles-Roux to Briand, June 18 and December 4, 1928. Volume 29, Telegram from Charles-Roux to the Ministry of Foreign Affairs, October 4, 1929.

165. For the official result of the election see *Manuel statistique de la République Tchécoslovaque*, 4:401-04.

166. Washington, National Archives, State Department file 860f.00/308, Report by Einstein to the Department of State, November 27, 1929. Brügel, *Tschechen und Deutsche*, pp. 188-89.

167. Vienna, HHStA, N.P.A., Karton 65, Report by Marek to the Austrian Ministry of Foreign Affairs, October 31, 1929.

168. In April 1929 Kramář advocated cooperation with the Sudeten Germans at a congress of the National Democrats. The party's organ, *Národní listy*, reported the speech, from whence Wolff's wire service picked it up. A copy of the dispatch reached the files of the German Foreign Office. See Bonn, AA, Politische Abteilung II, L417/L121342/4415.

169. Bonn, AA, Büro des Staatssekretärs, 4582/E177006/2352, Note from Bülow to Koch, February 8, 1929. Politische Abteilung II, L417/L121319/4415, Memorandum by Bülow for Stresemann, February 8, 1929. Büro des Reichsministers, 3086/D618171-74/1488, Note from Schubert to Koch, July 31, 1929.

170. Henry Ashby Turner, Jr., *Stresemann and the Politics of the Weimar Republic* (Princeton: Princeton University Press, 1963), pp. 263-68.

Chapter Five

1. The report appeared in *Venkov*, the major organ of the Czechoslovak Agrarians. See Koch's note about the matter in Bonn, AA, Politische Abteilung II, L417/L121343/4415, Report by Koch to the German Foreign Office, April 30, 1929. Unsigned memorandum in the German Foreign Office, May 1, 1929.

2. For a brief discussion of the "liberation payments" imposed on the successor states of the Habsburg Monarchy, see Arnold J. Toynbee, *Survey of International Affairs 1932* (London: Oxford University Press, 1932), pp. 159-65. Alena Gajanová, *ČSR a středoevropská politika velmocí, 1918-1938* (Prague: Academia, 1967), pp. 262-66.

3. Beneš used this figure in a conversation with Curtius in September 1930. See Bonn, AA, Politische Abteilung II, L417/L121497-98/4415, Note from Curtius to the Reich Chancellery, September 29, 1930.

4. Bonn, AA, Büro des Reichsministers, 3086/D618179-80/1488, Note from Curtius to Koch, November 14, 1929.

5. Ibid., 3086/D618181/1488, Report from Koch to Curtius, November 15, 1929.

6. Bonn, Politische Abteilung II, L417/L121445-47/4415, Memorandum by Curtius of a conversation with Beneš, January 7, 1930.

7. Toynbee, *Survey of International Affairs 1932*, p. 163.

8. Bonn, AA, Büro des Reichsministers, 3086/D618186-88/1488, Report from Koch to Schubert, February 27, 1930.

9. Ibid., 3086/D618188/1488.

10. Bonn, AA, Politische Abteilung II, L417/L121460-61/4415, Report from Koch to the German Foreign Office, March 17, 1930.

11. Some of these ideas were developed by the Austrian minister in Prague in his thoughtful analysis of Briand's pan-European proposals. Vienna, HHStA, N.P.A., Karton 64, Report by Marek to the Austrian Ministry of Foreign Affairs, August 4, 1929. See also Gajanová, *ČSR a středoevropská politika velmocí*, pp. 269-71.

12. Toynbee, *Survey of International Affairs 1930* pp. 137-38.

13. John W. Wheeler-Bennett, *The Wreck of Reparations* (London: George Allen & Unwin Ltd., 1933), p. 25.

14. See Haniel's report from Munich about the situation in Bavaria. Bonn, AA, Politische Abteilung II, L417/L121443-44/4415, Report from Haniel to the German Foreign Office, January 11, 1930.

15. In April Chvalkovský officially brought the demonstration to the attention of the German government. Bonn, AA, Politische Abteilung II, L417/L121463-64/4415, Memorandum by Heeren of a conversation with Chvalkovský, April 15, 1930.

16. Gottfried Treviranus demanded a radical redrawing of the German-Polish boundary. He spoke before the "Homeland-true Eastern Unions," who were commemorating the tenth anniversary of the plebiscites in West and East Prussia. See Erich Eyck, *Geschichte der Weimarer Republik* (Erlenbach-Zürich: E. Rentsch, 1954-56), 2:346-47.

17. *Schulthess' Europäischer Geschichtskalender 1930* (Munich: C.H. Beck'sche Verlagsbuchhandlung, 1931), p. 194. For Brüning's account of his policy in calling the elections, see Heinrich Brüning, *Memoiren 1918-1934* (Stuttgart: Deutsche Verlags-Anstalt, 1970), pp. 174-87.

18. Vienna, HHStA, N.P.A., Karton 66, Report by Marek to the Austrian Ministry of Foreign Affairs, October 1, 1930. The British minister believed that antiforeign demonstrations in Prague pointed to a "state of xenophobia bordering on hysteria." London, P.R.O., F.O. 371, vol. 14331, C7525/7525/12, Report by Joseph Addison, the British minister in Prague, to the British Foreign Office, October 2, 1930. About the activities of the radical right in the early 1930s, see Alena Gajanová, *Dvojí tvář* (Prague: Naše vojsko, 1962), pp. 64-74.

19. Bonn, AA, Politische Abteilung II, L417/L121547-49/4415, Report by Koch to the German Foreign Office, October 20, 1930.

20. Vienna, HHStA, N.P.A., Karton 66, Report by Marek to the Austrian Ministry of Foreign Affairs, September 25, 1930. Johann Wolfgang Brügel, *Tschechen und Deutsche* (Munich: Nymphenburger Verlag, 1967), p. 219. The government's English-language newspaper wrote: "It also became obvious that the warring American and German film interests had a finger in the recent events on the streets of Prague." *Central European Observer*, October 3, 1930, p. 354.

21. Vienna, HHStA, N.P.A., Karton 66, Report by Marek to the

Austrian Ministry of Foreign Affairs, October 1, 1930. Brügel, *Tschechen und Deutsche*, pp. 219-20.

22. Bonn, AA, Politische Abteilung II, L417/L121496-97/4415, Note from Curtius to the Reich Chancellery, September 29, 1930.

23. Ibid., L417/L121523/4415, Report from Koch to the German Foreign Office, October 9, 1930.

24. Bonn, AA, Büro des Reichsministers, 3086/D618214/1488, Note from Bülow to Koch, October 10, 1930. Politische Abteilung II, L417/L121535-36/4415, Note from Köpke to the Ministry of Economics and the Ministry for Food and Agriculture, October 16, 1930.

25. Bonn, AA, Politische Abteilung II, L417/L121524-27/4415, Memorandum by Köpke of a conversation with Austrian Minister Frank, October 13, 1930. L417/L121547-49/4415, Report by Koch to the German Foreign Office, October 20, 1930. Büro des Reichsministers, 3086/D618224-27/1488, Letters from Curtius to Baden state officials in Mannheim, November 1, 1930.

26. Bonn, AA, Politische Abteilung II, L417/L121547-49/4415, Report by Koch to the German Foreign Office, October 20, 1930.

27. Ibid., L417/L121554-56/4415, Statement by Curtius in the Foreign Affairs committee of the Reichsrat, October 30, 1930. As the archives of the German Foreign Office show, the draft of Curtius's statement went through several versions before the final one was arrived at. But given the sentiments that Curtius expressed, the careful wording meant little. The meticulous attention to detail and the failure to comprehend the broader effects of German policy were major shortcomings of Curtius's diplomacy.

28. *Prager Presse*, November 6, 1930, pp. 1-3. Purlitz, *Deutscher Geschichtskalender, 1930, Ausland* (Leipzig: F. Meiner, 1931), p. 525.

29. *Prager Presse*, November 13, 1930, p. 1.

30. Bonn, AA, Büro des Reichsministers, 3086/D618236/1488, unsigned memorandum in the German Foreign Office, November 15, 1930.

31. London, P.R.O., F.O. 371, vol. 14331, C8453/7525/12, Report by Addison to the British Foreign Office, November 12, 1930.

32. Pergler had been an American citizen until he became the Czechoslovak minister in Tokyo after the founding of the republic. In 1931 a Czechoslovak court held that Pergler had not automatically acquired citizenship merely by entering the foreign service of the country. For Beneš's unrefined comments about Pergler, see Vienna, HHStA, N.P.A., Karton 66, Report by Marek to the Austrian Ministry of Foreign Affairs, March 10, 1931.

33. Bonn, AA, Büro des Staatssekretärs, 4606/E192142-46/2375, Memorandum by Regendanz of a conversation with Beneš, January 18, 1931. Brügel is wrong in guessing that it was the German Foreign Office that sent Regendanz to Beneš. Brügel, *Tschechen und Deutsche*, p. 223.

34. Bonn, AA, Büro des Staatssekretärs, 4606/E192139/2375, Letter from Schleicher to Bülow, January 27, 1931.

35. Ibid., 4606/E192147-53/2375, Memorandum by Regendanz of conversations with Beneš, January 20 and 21, 1931. It was no secret that

Beneš wanted to become president of the Disarmament Conference, but the German government was opposed to his election on the grounds that a neutral figure should preside over the conference. London, P.R.O., F.O. 371, vol. 15701, W230/47/98, Telegram from Sir Horace Rumbold, British ambassador in Berlin, to the British Foreign Office, January 6, 1931. Ludwig Zimmermann, *Deutsche Aussenpolitik in der Ära der Weimarer Republik* (Göttingen: Musterschmidt-Verlag, 1958), pp. 459-60.

36. Bonn, AA, Büro des Staatssekretärs, 4606/E192049-57/2375, Memorandum by Regendanz of conversations with Beneš, February 19, 1931.

37. Curtius, *Sechs Jahre Minister der deutschen Republik* (Heidelberg: Carl Winter Universitäts-Verlag, 1948), pp. 119-20.

38. Bonn, AA, Büro des Reichsministers, 3086/D614644-46/1484, Note from Schubert to the German minister to Austria, Lerchenfeld, February 4, 1930. Apparently following the lead of Curtius, Schubert dropped his caution when the Austrians visited Berlin three weeks later. Büro des Staatssekretärs, 4576/E174062-66, E174116-22/2347, Memorandum by Schubert about conversations with Schober and Peters, February 23-24, 1930.

39. Bonn, AA, Büro des Reichsministers, 3086/D614740-80/1484, Memorandum concerning conversations in the Reich Chancellery during the visit of Chancellor Schober, February 22 and 24, 1930. Edward W. Bennett, Jr., *Germany and the Diplomacy of Financial Crisis, 1931* (Cambridge, Mass.: Harvard University Press, 1962), p. 44.

40. Brüning, *Memoiren*, pp. 263-70.

41. Bonn, AA, Politische Abteilung II, L417/L121498-99/4415, Note from Curtius to the Reich Chancellery, September 29, 1930.

42. Ibid.

43. Curtius, *Sechs Jahre*, p. 188.

44. Ibid., p. 189.

45. Bennett, *Diplomacy of Financial Crisis*, pp. 47-48. Bonn, AA, Büro des Reichsministers, 3086/D614923-27/1484, Note from Curtius to Bülow, January 16, 1931.

46. *Journal Officiel, Débats parlementaires*, Chambre des Députés, 2d meeting of March 3, 1931, p. 1525.

47. *Central European Observer*, March 13, 1931, pp. 159-60.

48. Ibid., pp. 157-58.

49. Walter Goldinger, "Das Projekt einer deutsch-österreichischen Zollunion von 1931," in *Österreich und Europa*, Festschrift for Hugo Hantsch (Graz: Verlag Styria, 1965), pp. 534-36.

50. Vienna, HHStA, N.P.A., Karton 66, Reports by Marek to the Austrian Ministry of Foreign Affairs, March 18 and 19, 1931. In an effort to preserve secrecy, the Austrian government left its minister in Prague uninformed about the customs union project, and Marek was able honestly to tell Beneš and Krofta that he had no information. His first concrete news came from the German minister in Prague, which helped to arouse Marek's resentment against his own government.

51. Bonn, AA, Büro des Reichsministers, 3086/D614976/1484,

Memorandum by Köpke, March 19, 1931.

52. For the reports of the German ambassadors in London and Rome about the initial reactions in those capitals, see: Bonn, AA, Büro des Reichsministers, 3086/D615008-10/1484, Report from Schubert to the German Foreign Office, March 21, 1931. 3086/D615061/1484, Report from Neurath to the German Foreign Office, March 23, 1931.

53. Bonn, AA, Büro des Reichsministers, 3086/D615002-05/1484, Report by Hoesch to the German Foreign Office, March 21, 1931.

54. Ibid., 3086/D615068-69/1484, Report by Koch to the German Foreign Office, March 23, 1931. Vienna, HHStA, N.P.A., Karton 66, Report by Marek to the Austrian Ministry of Foreign Affairs, March 26, 1931.

55. Bonn, AA, Büro des Reichsministers, 3086/D615037-40/1484, Memorandum by Köpke of a conversation with Chvalkovský, March 23, 1931.

56. London, P.R.O., F.O. 371, vol. 15158, C2140/673/3, Report by Addison to the British Foreign Office, March 25, 1931.

57. Gajanová, *ČSR a středoevropská politika velmocí*, p. 281.

58. *Manuel statistique de la République Tchécoslovaque*, 4:216-18.

59. Bonn, AA, Büro des Staatssekretärs, 4620/E199512-15/2385, Note from Bülow to Koch, April 15, 1931. This note is printed in English translation as an appendix to F.G. Stambrook, "The German-Austrian Customs Union Project of 1931: A Study of German Methods and Motives," *Journal of Central European Affairs* 21 (April 1961):15-44.

60. Jaroslav Valenta, "Československo a Polsko v letech 1918-1945," in *Češi a Poláci v minulosti* 2 (Prague: Academia, 1967):531-32. Harald von Riekhoff, *German-Polish Relations, 1918-1933* (Baltimore: Johns Hopkins University Press, 1971), pp. 335-36.

61. Schober apparently had similar ideas, which he expressed in some of the initial discussions about a customs union in Berlin in February 1930. According to Schubert's memorandum: "He [Schober] told me that if we constructed a customs union we would thereby get the entire Balkans. Vienna remains as always the distribution center for all the Balkans. Especially Czechoslovakia conducts all important business in the Balkans not from Prague, but comes for this purpose to Vienna." Bonn, AA, Büro des Staatssekretärs, 4576/E174116-22/2347, Memorandum by Schubert about a conversation with Schober, February 24, 1930.

62. Bonn, AA, Büro des Staatssekretärs, 4620/E199520-21/2385, Report by Koch to Bülow, April 22, 1931.

63. Miroslav Houštecký, "Plán rakousko-německé celní unie v roce 1931 a postoj Československa," *Československý časopis historický* 4(1956):34-39. Vladimír Soják, *O československé zahraniční politice* (Prague: Státní nakladatelství politické literatury, 1956), pp. 174-78. Houštecký also wrote this section of Soják's collective work.

64. *Prager Presse*, May 4, 1931, pp. 1-2; May 5, pp. 1-2; May 6, pp. 1-2. Arnold J. Toynbee, *Survey of International Affairs, 1931*, p. 310.

Houštecký, "Plán rakousko-německé celní unie," pp. 41-42, 48-49. Gajanová, *ČSR a středoevropská politika velmocí*, pp. 281-84.

65. By the time of the customs union announcement, officials in the German Foreign Office knew about Regendanz's contacts with Beneš. It was clear that they considered Regendanz an amateur, who would be best advised not to dabble in diplomacy. See, for example, Bonn, AA, Büro des Reichsministers, 3086/D615489-92/1485, Memorandum by Ritter of a conversation with Regendanz, April 29, 1931.

66. *Zahraniční politika*, 1931, pp. 357-61. *Prager Presse*, April 24, 1931, pp. 1-6. The speech was also printed in pamphlet form by the Czechoslovak government. See Edvard Beneš, *The Austro-German Customs Union* (Prague: Orbis, 1931).

67. Vienna, HHStA, N.P.A., Karton 66, Reports by Marek to the Austrian Ministry of Foreign Affairs, May 4 and June 30, 1931.

68. Bennett, *Diplomacy of Financial Crisis*, pp. 74-78. Goldinger, "Das Projekt einer deutsch-österreichischen Zollunion," p. 539.

69. For a more detailed discussion of Germany's role in the international financial crisis, see Bennett, *Diplomacy of Financial Crisis*, pp. 82-312. Toynbee, *Survey of International Affairs, 1931*, pp. 59-161. Brüning, *Memoiren*, pp. 263-414.

70. Bonn, AA, Politische Abteilung II, L417/L121697-99/4415, Report by Koch to the German Foreign Office, June 15, 1931.

71. Ibid., L417/L121706-10/4415, Report by Holzhausen to the German Foreign Office, July 28, 1931.

72. The Germans and the Austrians agreed on August 17 on the tactics of their announcement. Bonn, AA, Deutsche Botschaft Wien, 5002/E285331-36/2521, Memorandum of a meeting in the German Foreign Office and a covering note by Bülow, August 17, 1931.

73. Permanent Court of International Justice, *Customs Regime between Germany and Austria*, Series A/B-No. 41, Judgments, Orders, and Advisory Opinions (Leyden: A. W. Sijthoff, 1931).

74. Public opinion at the time held that the French applied financial pressure on the Austrians, and historians have generally credited the idea. For the best discussion on how the French could have put pressure on the Austrians, see Bennett, *Diplomacy of Financial Crisis*, pp. 100-104.

75. The summer of 1931 was a dark time for British finances as well. The difficulties forced the resignation of MacDonald's Labor government and the establishment of the interparty National Coalition. Britain abandoned the gold standard in September. France, which was more self-sufficient economically, remained relatively unharmed in 1931 by the depression, and its financial stability gave Paris a trump in diplomatic negotiations.

76. Oswald Hauser, "Die Plan einer deutsch-österreichischen Zollunion von 1931 und die europäische Foederation," *Historische Zeitschrift* 179 (January 1955):91-92.

77. That statement, like many others by Beneš, was probably a

mixture of truth and exaggeration. Vienna, HHStA, N.P.A., Karton 66, Report by Marek to the Austrian Ministry of Foreign Affairs, July 15, 1931.

78. Gajanová, *ČSR a středoevropská politika velmocí*, pp. 282-83.
79. Ibid., pp. 283-84. Bennett, *Diplomacy of Financial Crisis*, pp. 92-96. Houštecký, "Plán rakousko-německé celní unie," pp. 41-42. Vondracek, *Foreign Policy of Czechoslovakia, 1918-1935* (New York: Columbia University Press, 1937), pp. 321-25.
80. Vienna, HHStA, N.P.A., Karton 66, Report by Marek to the Austrian Ministry of Foreign Affairs, April 15, 1931.
81. Ibid., Report by Marek to the Austrian Ministry of Foreign Affairs, March 28, 1931.
82. Ibid., Reports by Marek to the Austrian Ministry of Foreign Affairs, July 15, September 1, October 1 and 15, 1931.
83. Ibid., Karton 67, Reports by Marek to the Austrian Ministry of Foreign Affairs, November 5 and December 18, 1931.
84. Lersner had been in the German diplomatic service before and during the war. He served as German representative at the armistice commission in Spa in 1919, and in the summer of that year he became the head of the German delegation at the peace conference. He resigned in 1920 and retired from the diplomatic service. Lersner and Beneš knew one another from the time of the peace conference.
85. Lersner's memorandum of the entire discussion of Beneš is in Bonn, AA, Politische Abteilung II, L417/L121717-21/4415, Letter from Lersner to Brüning, November 2, 1931.
86. Ibid., L417/L121719/4415.
87. Ibid., L417/L121719-20/4415.
88. Ibid., L417/L121721/4415.
89. *Temps*, March 3, 1932, p. 1. It is significant that Tardieu called for French, British, and Italian cooperation in dealing with Danubian problems but did not mention the Germans.
90. Toynbee, *Survey of International Affairs, 1932*, pp. 22-23.
91. For a belated discussion about the project between Beneš and Koch, see Bonn, AA, Politische Abteilung II, L417/L121753-54/4415, Report by Koch to the German Foreign Office, June 10, 1932.
92. Bonn, AA, Büro des Staatssekretärs, 4617/E195099-105/2379, Unsigned and undated memorandum about the Tardieu plan.
93. London, P.R.O., F.O. 371, vol. 15922, C3448/58/62, Telegram from Sir Eric Phipps to the British Foreign Office, April 28, 1932.
94. Soják, *O československé zahraniční politice*, p. 191.
95. Vienna, HHStA, N.P.A., Karton 67, Report by Marek to the Austrian Ministry of Foreign Affairs, March 11, 1932.
96. Ibid., Report by Marek to the Austrian Ministry of Foreign Affairs, April 1, 1932.
97. *Berliner Tageblatt*, March 16, 1932, evening edition, p. 2. *Prager Presse*, March 17, 1932, p. 1.
98. Vienna, HHStA, N.P.A., Karton 67, Report by Marek to the Austrian Ministry of Foreign Affairs, March 24, 1932.

99. *Prager Presse*, March 23, 1932, pp. 1-5. The speech was published in pamphlet form by the Czechoslovak government. See Edvard Beneš, *Die Probleme Mitteleuropas* (Prague: Orbis, 1932).

100. London *Times*, April 5, 1932, p. 14. *Temps*, April 5, 1932, p. 1.

101. London *Times*, April 7, 1932, p. 12; April 8, p. 14; April 9, p. 12. *Temps*, April 8, 1932, p. 1; April 9, pp. 1-2. Gajanová, *ČSR a středoevropská politika velmocí*, pp. 293-97.

102. *Central European Observer*, April 15, 1932, p. 229.

103. London *Times*, April 9, 1932, p. 12.

104. *Prager Presse*, April 15, 1932, p. 1.

105. Antonín Basch, *The Danube Basin and the German Economic Sphere* (New York: Columbia University Press, 1943), pp. 82-89. Beneš began to advocate a "clearing-house system" in the spring of 1932. London, P.R.O., F.O. 371, vol. 15923, C4248/58/62, Report by Addison to the British Foreign Office, May 12, 1932.

106. On the shifts in German trade policy toward the agrarian states of Southeastern Europe in the early 1930s see Bonn, AA, Büro des Staatssekretärs, 4617/E195244-48/2379, Memorandum by Kroll, April 1, 1932.

107. Vienna, HHStA, N.P.A., Karton 66, Reports by Marek to the Austrian Ministry of Foreign Affairs, April 4 and 30, 1931.

108. After the Nazi occupation of Prague in March 1939, selected documents from the Czechoslovak Ministry of Foreign Affairs were translated and sent to Berlin. Almost all of them dated from the years of the Third Reich, but a few came from the Weimar period. The German copies of those documents were microfilmed by the Allies after the war, and they are now available with the rest of the German Foreign Office archives. Bonn, AA, Politische Abteilung II, 2374/D497253-54/1316, Note from Beneš to Czechoslovak missions abroad, May 18, 1932. See also Soják, *O československé zahraniční politice*, p. 194.

109. Bonn, AA, Politisches Archiv und Historisches Referat, 2028/D444429/1143, Memorandum by Beneš about a conversation with King Alexander, May 14, 1932. See also Soják, *O československé zahraniční politice*, p. 197.

110. Bonn, AA, Politische Abteilung II, 2376/D497253-54/1316, Dispatch from Beneš to Czechoslovak missions abroad, May 18, 1932.

111. Within three days after the final agreement was reached at Lausanne, Krofta remarked to the Austrian minister that Germany would obviously never have to make that final payment, which was put in solely to protect French prestige. Vienna, HHStA, N.P.A., Karton 67, Report by Marek to the Austrian Ministry of Foreign Affairs, July 12, 1932.

112. Toynbee, *Survey of International Affairs, 1932*, pp. 192-300; *Survey of International Affairs, 1933*, pp. 224-317. John W. Wheeler-Bennett, *The Disarmament Deadlock* (London: George Routledge and Sons, 1934.)

113. Bonn, AA, Politische Abteilung II, L417/L121718-19/4415, Letter from Lersner to Brüning, November 2, 1931.

114. *Prager Presse*, March 23, 1932, pp. 2-3.

115. *Documents diplomatiques français*, 1932-1939, First Series, volume I, document 112, Report from Léon Noël, French minister in Prague, to the French Ministry of Foreign Affairs, August 20, 1932.

116. Toynbee, *Survey of International Affairs 1932*, pp. 267-68.

117. *Documents diplomatiques français*, 1932-1939, First series, volume I, document 227, Note from René Massigli to the French Ministry of Foreign Affairs, October 5, 1932.

118. Vienna, HHStA, N.P.A., Karton 67, Report by Marek to the Austrian Ministry of Foreign Affairs, October 26, 1932. Bonn, AA, Politische Abteilung II, L416/L119423-27/4412, Report by Koch to the German Foreign Office, November 8, 1932.

119. Bonn, AA, Politische Abteilung II, L416/L119423-27/4412, Report by Koch to the German Foreign Office, November 8, 1932.

120. It is worth noting that the British minister in Prague was sending the opposite advice to London. Several months earlier, for example, he had urged that the British government not concern itself about Central European economic problems and that it refrain from giving advice until its suggestions were likely to be heeded. London, P.R.O., F.O. 371, vol. 15923, C4248/58/62, Report by Addison to the British Foreign Office, May 12, 1932.

121. *Prager Presse*, November 8, 1932, pp. 1-5; November 10, pp. 2-4. *Central European Observer*, November 11, 1932, pp. 647-48; November 18, p. 659.

122. Bonn, AA, Politische Abteilung II, 2376/D497302-06/1316, Memorandum about a conversation between Beneš and MacDonald on November 12, 1932, from the archives of the Czechoslovak Ministry of Foreign Affairs.

123. Ibid., 2376/D497280-82/1316, Memorandum about a conversation between Beneš and Herriot on November 17, 1932, from the archives of the Czechoslovak Ministry of Foreign Affairs. 2376/D497289-90/1316, Note from Beneš to the Czechoslovak Ministry of Foreign Affairs, November 25, 1932.

124. Ibid., 2376/D497280-82/1316, Memorandum of November 17, 1932.

125. In case it has been forgotten:
Little Jack Horner sat in a corner
Eating his Christmas pie.
He stuck in his thumb and pulled out a plum
And said what a good boy am I.
There was just enough truth in that allusion to Beneš's self-righteousness to provoke belly laughs in London.

126. London, P.R.O., F.O. 371, vol. 15179, C2362/1203/12, Report by Addison to the British Foreign Office, March 28, 1931.

127. Ibid., vol. 15180, C5339/5339/12, Letter from Addison to Sargent, July 9, 1931.

128. Ibid.

129. London, P.R.O., F.O. 371, vol. 15198, C8439/172/62, Letter from Addison to Sargent, November 5, 1931.

130. Ibid., Letter from Sargent to Addison, November 17, 1931.

131. London, P.R.O., F.O. 371, vol. 14331, C7525/7525/12, Comment by Sargent on a report by Addison, October 2, 1930.

132. Ibid., vol. 14328, C7558/25/12, Letter from Addison to Stephen Gaselee, September 30, 1930. Vol. 15178, C394/394/12, Foreign Office minutes by Stephen Gaselee and Owen St. C. O'Malley, January 14, 1931.

133. Already in July the British had proposed a consultative pact in conjunction with the Lausanne reparation agreement, but the French had expanded the scheme to include the minor powers as well. Konrad Hugo Jarausch, *The Four Power Pact, 1933* (Madison: State Historical Society of Wisconsin, 1965), p. 15.

134. Bonn, AA, Politische Abteilung II, 2376/D497287-88 and D497291/1316, Note from Beneš to the Czechoslovak Ministry of Foreign Affairs, November 24, 1932. See also Věra Olivová, *The Doomed Democracy*, trans. George Theiner (London: Sidgwick & Jackson, 1972), p. 167.

135. Vienna, HHStA, N.P.A., Karton 67, Report by Marek to the Austrian Ministry of Foreign Affairs, January 3, 1933.

136. Ibid., Reports by Marek and to the Austrian Ministry of Foreign Affairs, November 19 and 28, 1932.

137. *Prager Presse*, December 20, 1932, p. 1. For the text of the pact, see *Prager Presse*, February 26, 1933, pp. 1-2. *Documents on International Affairs, 1933*, (London: Oxford University Press, 1934), pp. 415-18. Reichert, *Das Scheitern der Kleinen Entente*, pp. 6-15, Gajanová, *ČSR a středoevropská politika velmocí*, pp. 305-7. Soják, *O československé zahraniční politice*, pp. 198-200.

138. Jarausch, *The Four Power Pact*, pp. 53-62.

139. Ibid., pp. 94-99. I. M. Oprea, *Nicolae Titulescu's Diplomatic Activity* (Bucharest: Publishing House of the Academy of the Socialist Republic of Romania, 1968), pp. 116-20.

140. Vienna, HHStA, N.P.A., Karton 67, Report by Marek to the Austrian Ministry of Foreign Affairs, January 11, 1933.

141. Seeming to forget the presence of the Austrian minister, Beneš made that remark to Masaryk at a diplomatic dinner. Ibid., Report by Marek to the Austrian Ministry of Foreign Affairs, March 31, 1933.

142. *Těsnopisecké zprávy*, 263d session, April 25, 1933, pp. 3-24. For Beneš's parliamentary speech about the project, see *Prager Presse*, April 26, 1933, pp. 1-8. *Central European Observer*, April 28, 1933, pp. 147-56. Vondracek, *Foreign Policy of Czechoslovakia*, pp. 362-63.

143. In this respect, if not in others, Mr. A. J. P. Taylor is certainly correct in his revisionist critique of diplomacy in the 1930s. A. J. P. Taylor, *The Origins of the Second World War* (London: H. Hamilton, 1961).

144. The Austrian minister reported, however, that the Czech press had received instructions to write in moderate tones about the Papen government. Evidently the Little Entente partners were not sympathetic to a strong anti-German propaganda campaign. Also, one of Masaryk's and Beneš's confidants, the journalist Hubert Ripka, had just returned from

Germany with warnings about anti-Czech sentiments rife among the German population. Vienna, HHStA, N.P.A., Karton 67, Report by Marek to the Austrian Ministry of Foreign Affairs, June 6, 1932.

145. Bonn, AA, Politische Abteilung II, L417/L121751-55/4415, Report from Koch to the German Foreign Office, June 10, 1932.

146. Vienna, HHStA, N.P.A., Karton 67, Report by Marek to the Austrian Ministry of Foreign Affairs, January 30, 1932.

147. Ibid., Report by Marek to the Austrian Ministry of Foreign Affairs, September 19, 1932.

148. Bonn, AA, Geheimakten 72/5, II Ts 1158, Report by Koch to the German Foreign Office, November 21, 1932.

149. *Prager Presse*, January 31, 1933, p. 1.

150. *Central European Observer*, February 3, 1933, p. 39.

151. Vienna, HHStA, N.P.A., Karton 67, Report by Marek to the Austrian Ministry of Foreign Affairs, March 31, 1933.

152. In September 1933 Beneš observed to the American minister that Hitler would fall within two or three years when his inability to deal with Germany's economic problems became apparent. Washington, National Archives, State Department file 860f.00/349, Report by Francis White to the Department of State, September 26, 1933.

153. Vienna, HHStA, N.P.A., Karton 67, Report to the Austrian Ministry of Foreign Affairs, July 30, 1932. Dušan Uhlíř, "Konec vlády panské koalice a republikánská strana v roce 1929," *Československý časopis historický* 18 (1970):589-91.

154. Vienna, HHStA, N.P.A., Karton 67, Report by Marek to the Austrian Ministry of Foreign Affairs, July 12, 1932.

One sign of the times: during the preparations for the congress it had been agreed that no German sound films would be shown while the festival was taking place. Report by the chargé d'affaires in Prague to the Austrian Ministry of Foreign Affairs, June 24, 1932.

155. Vienna, HHStA, Karton 67, Report by Marek to the Austrian Ministry of Foreign Affairs, January 15, 1932.

156. Olivová, *The Doomed Democracy*, pp. 177-79.

157. Brügel, *Tschechen und Deutsche*, p. 193.

158. Vienna, HHStA, N.P.A., Karton 67, Reports from the Prague legation to the Austrian Ministry of Foreign Affairs, July 30 and August 20, 1932.

159. *Prager Presse*, October 30, 1932, p. 3. *Central European Observer*, October 28, 1932, p. 619.

160. César and Černý, *Politika německých buržoazních stran v letech 1918-1938* (Prague: Nakladatelstvi Československé akademie věd, 1962), 2:20-21, 66.

161. *Prager Presse*, April 4, 1930, p. 3. Purlitz, *Deutscher Geschichtskalender, 1930, Ausland*, p. 238. Bonn, AA, Politische Abteilung II, 9544/E672425/3555, Koch's annual survey of Czechoslovak political conditions, 1930.

162. *Prager Presse*, September 30, 1930, p. 3. Purlitz, *Deutscher Geschichtskalender, 1930, Ausland*, p. 381.

163. *Prager Presse*, October 18, 1930, pp. 3-4. Purlitz, *Deutscher Geschichtskalender, 1930, Ausland*, p. 525. As minister for social welfare, Czech of course had political reasons for extolling that legislation.

164. César and Černý, *Politika německých buržoaznich stran*, 2:33-43.

165. Vienna, HHStA, N.P.A., Karton 66, Report by Marek to the Austrian Ministry of Foreign Affairs, April 20, 1931. Houštecký, "Plán rakousko-německé celní unie," pp. 38-39.

166. Bonn, AA, Politische Abteilung II, 9544/E672447-48/3555, Koch's annual survey of Czechoslovak political conditions, 1931.

167. Ibid., L417/L121597/4415, Report from Koch to the German Foreign Office, December 1, 1930.

168. *Annuaire statistique de la République Tchécoslovaque* (Prague: Orbis, 1935), p. 125.

169. Ibid., p. 199. Unemployment was highest in the winter and lowest during the summer harvest season.

170. Olivová, *The Doomed Democracy*, p. 175.

171. Basch, *The Danube Basin and the German Economic Sphere*, p. 117.

172. Brügel, *Tschechen und Deutsche*, pp. 190-94.

For a short biography and testimonial articles from his friends and colleagues, see J. W. Brügel, *Ludwig Czech: Arbeiterführer und Staatsmann* (Vienna: Verlag der Wiener Volksbuchhandlung, 1960).

173. *Prager Presse*, August 9, 1932, p. 2; September 25, p. 3. *Central European Observer*, September 30, 1932, p. 561. Elizabeth Wiskemann, *Czechs and Germans* (London: Oxford University Press, 1938), pp. 137-39.

174. *Prager Presse*, November 6, 1932, p. 3.

175. Vienna, HHStA, N.P.A., Karton 67, Report by Marek to the Austrian Ministry of Foreign Affairs, October 7, 1932.

176. Bonn, AA, Politische Abteilung II, 571/1, II Ts 39, Report by Koch to the German Foreign Office, January 11, 1933. Brügel, *Tschechen und Deutsche*, p. 230.

177. *Prager Presse*, February 10, 1933, p. 1; February 24, p. 2. Bonn, AA, Politische Abteilung II, 9149/E643565-67/3523, Report by Koch to the German Foreign Office, February 25, 1933.

178. Vienna, HHStA, N.P.A., Karton 67, Report by Marek to the Austrian Ministry of Foreign Affairs, March 24, 1933. Hans Krebs, *Kampf in Böhmen* (Berlin: Volk und Reich Verlag, 1936), pp. 208-9.

179. Bonn, AA, Politische Abteilung II, 9544/E672463/3555, Koch's annual survey of Czechoslovak political conditions, 1933.

180. Vienna, HHStA, N.P.A., Karton 67, Report by Marek to the Austrian Ministry of Foreign Affairs, March 24, 1933.

181. Bonn, AA, Politische Abteilung II, 8911/E621756/I-78/3469, Report by Koch to the German Foreign Office, March 3, 1933. 8911/E621759-63/3469, Report by Koch to the German Foreign Office, May 15, 1933. L417/L121895-99/4415, Report by Koch to the German Foreign Office, November 9, 1933. Vienna, HHStA, N.P.A., Karton 67,

Report by Marek to the Austrian Ministry of Foreign Affairs, March 27, 1933.

182. Vienna, HHStA, N.P.A., Karton 67, Report by Marek to the Austrian Ministry of Foreign Affairs, March 17, 1933.

183. Bonn, AA, Politische Abteilung II, 9149/E643568-69/3523, Report by Koch to the German Foreign Office, March 20, 1933.

184. See, for example, Koch's report after the dissolution of the German National and the National Socialist parties in October 1933. Bonn, AA, Politische Abteilung II, 9149/E643586-89/3523, Report by Koch to the German Foreign Office, October 10, 1933.

185. Vienna, HHStA, N.P.A., Karton 67, Report by Marek to the Austrian Ministry of Foreign Affairs, March 31, 1933.

186. Ibid.

187. Bonn, AA, Geheimakten, 6144/E459601-02/2900, Note from Bülow to Koch, February 9, 1933, 6144/E459585-86/2900, Memorandum by Viktor von Heeren, March 31, 1933.

188. London, P.R.O., F.O. 371, vol. 16659, C8937/193/12, Report by Addison to the British Foreign Office, October 9, 1933.

189. Ibid.

190. Ibid. On Henlein, his background, and his early political activity, see Brügel, *Tschechen und Deutsche*, pp. 238-69.

191. Brügel, *Tschechen und Deutsche*, pp. 238-69.

192. Ibid., p. 259. See the receipt, signed by Henlein, for RM 331, 711.30 for the election campaign. AA, Geheimakten, 6144/E459652/2900.

193. Wiskemann, *Czechs and Germans*, pp. 134-39, 200-206.

Chapter Six

1. The best work on the subject, despite its pro-Czech sympathies, is Radomír Luža, *The Transfer of the Sudeten Germans* (New York: New York University Press, 1964).

2. Those ideas are apparent in *Mein Kampf* and in *Hitlers Zweites Buch* (Stuttgart: Deutsche Verlags-Anstalt, 1961). A.J.P. Taylor is not alone in noticing that Hitler's notions were akin to political rantings in a beer-hall. A.J.P. Taylor, *The Origins of the Second World War* (London: H. Hamilton, 1961), pp. 68-69. The sad truth, however, is that a beer-hall philosophy controlled Germany during the Third Reich. For the most succinct analysis of Hitler's ideas, see H. R. Trevor-Roper's "The Mind of Adolf Hitler," in *Hitler's Secret Conversations, 1941-1944* (New York: Farrar, Straus and Young, 1953). For the best-informed description of Hitler's foreign policy, see Gerhard Weinberg's *The Foreign Policy of Hitler's Germany* (Chicago: The University of Chicago Press, 1970).

3. The concepts of "settler colonialism" and "trading-colony colonialism" were developed by Woodruff D. Smith in his "The Ideology of German Colonialism, 1840-1918" (Ph.D. diss., University of Chicago, 1972). I am indebted to him.

4. London, P.R.O., F.O. 371, vol. 14330, C4150/4150/12, Report by Addison to the British Foreign Office, May 16, 1930.

5. The Austrian minister in Prague recounted those remarks some years later in a report to his government. Vienna, HHStA, N.P.A., Karton 67, Report by Marek to the Austrian Ministry of Foreign Affairs, September 30, 1932.

6. Ibid.

Bibliographical Essay

Archival research built the foundation for this book. The information comes largely from diplomatic archives in Western capitals and from the newspaper archives in Prague. Most of those sources have not previously been exploited for material on themes related to this topic.

DIPLOMATIC ARCHIVES AND DOCUMENT PUBLICATIONS

Most of the German diplomatic documents for the period are now stored in the Political Archive of the Foreign Office in Bonn. They were captured by Western armies at the close of World War II, taken eventually to England, and then returned to the Federal Republic in the late 1950s. Although the German Democratic Republic inherited a few collections, mostly containing documents pertaining to economic matters, the bulk of the material is in Bonn. Before returning the documents to Bonn, the Western governments completed an extensive microfilming project of the major files. Those microfilms are available for use or purchase at the Public Record Office in London and the National Archives in Washington. The footnotes in this book cite the German documents by their microfilm number because the documents are more widely available on microfilm. In those cases where a collection was not photographed, I have used the archival numbers in Bonn. Indispensable guides to the German Foreign Office archives are the American Historical Association's *A Catalogue of German Foreign Ministry Files and Microfilms, 1867-1920* (Oxford: At the University Press, 1959), and, George O. Kent, ed., *A Catalogue of Files and Microfilms of the German Foreign Ministry Archives, 1920-1945*, 4 vols. (Stanford: Hoover Institution Press, 1962-72). Selected documents are being published in *Akten zur deutschen auswärtigen Politik, 1918-1945.* For the Weimar period, six volumes of Series B, covering the months from December 1925 through September 1927, have appeared as of 1974.

Among the various files of the German Foreign Office the most significant are those of the foreign minister and the state secretary. Since only the most important of issues came to the attention of the minister and his assistant, the documents that they used are of singular interest. In addition to their files, the secret documents, or "Geheimakten," offer interesting insights into German diplomacy. The fact that attempts were made to destroy the secret documents in 1945 adds romance to using them, but copies of most of the documents can also be found in other files of the Foreign Office. The most complete collection of documents for

German relations with any given country is to be found in the departmental files. From 1920 until 1936 the German Foreign Office was organized on a geographical basis, and Czechoslovak relations came under Department Two. Interspersed with documents of fundamental significance in these files are memoranda and notes that describe almost the day-by-day development of relations between the two countries. Much of the information is not sufficiently important to be included in even a narrowly defined monograph, but it does help to ground a researcher in the atmosphere of the time.

In addition to the major files there are minor collections that afford interesting sidelights to German diplomacy. The personal documents, or "Handakten," of Gerhard Köpke and Joachim Windel are significant for Czechoslovak-German relations. Köpke was head of Department Two from 1923 until 1936, and Windel was active in economic matters. The most famous collections of private papers is the "Nachlass" of Stresemann. It should be consulted in any general study of German domestic or foreign policy during the Weimar republic. Stresemann's activities as foreign minister centered on questions other than relations with Prague, however, and the "Nachlass" was not particularly informative for this study. The papers of the German legation in Prague are now available in Bonn although little microfilming was done of those documents. They can sometimes be used to clarify technical questions, but they are usually duplicates of documents in the major collections of the Foreign Office. In addition to the Foreign Office documents, the archives of the Reich Chancellery can afford insights into the formulation of German foreign policy. Particularly significant are the minutes of the cabinet meetings, where the most difficult policy decisions were usually made. Copies of pertinent sections of the minutes can usually be found in the Foreign Office archives.

In 1972 the French government opened sections of its diplomatic archives for the 1920s. Documentation on France's relations with Germany and Czechoslovakia is now available through 1929. Inasmuch as France was Czechoslovakia's major ally, Edvard Beneš tended to speak more frankly in conversations with French politicians and diplomats than he did with those of most other nations. The French documents therefore offer a particularly valuable source for understanding Czechoslovak policy. Of central importance are the files on domestic politics in Czechoslovakia and on Czechoslovak foreign policy. In regard to domestic politics it is possible to gain insights into the electoral and coalition strategy of "the Castle," as mirrored by Beneš's remarks to French diplomats. Perhaps even more important are Beneš's observations on the Sudeten German question and his explanations of governmental policy toward the Sudeten Germans. As for Czechoslovak foreign policy, the French documents illumine the functioning of the Franco-Czechoslovak alliance and emphasize Czechoslovakia's relations with the other French allies in Central and Eastern Europe. Within the files on Czechoslovak foreign policy, there are special volumes on Czechoslovak relations with Germany. Their existence makes it largely superfluous to go through the files for Germany, which are much more voluminous. But the section of the files for Austria pertaining to the Anschluss is indeed important.

The French diplomatic documents for the First World War period have been open for historical research somewhat longer than have those for the 1920s. A subdivision of the files for Austria-Hungary concerns the "Mouvement national tchèque," but its relative dearth of material until the closing phases of the war supports the conclusion that the Czechs were of little moment in French diplomacy in the early years of the war. More important are the volumes in the file for Russia on the intervention in Siberia and the employment of the Czech legionnaires for that purpose. In contrast to the German Foreign Office archive, the French documents contain no separate files for the foreign minister or the secretary-general of the Quai d'Orsay for the 1920s that are open for historical research. But in the general files such as those on Czechoslovak foreign policy one readily finds memoranda and dispatches from the foreign minister and his chief assistants. That is particularly true for the year 1923, for example, when Poincaré's government attached great importance to the conclusion of a Franco-Czechoslovak alliance. The published series of French diplomatic documents do not cover the 1920s, but the first two volumes of *Documents diplomatiques français, 1932-1939* (Paris: Imprimerie nationale, 1964-) contain informative material for late 1932 and early 1933. The French documents provide an effective counterbalance to the German perspective.

Since the late 1960s the papers of the British Foreign Office for the interwar period have been open for historical research. Housed in the Public Record Office in London, they have attracted many historians, but the Czechoslovak files for the 1920s have not been exploited in historical publications. The British documents, like the French, are catalogued by country. Information in this book concerning British diplomacy has been gleaned from a reading of all 101 volumes on Czechoslovakia for the years from 1920 through 1933. Similar to the German and French archives, the British documents for the years of the First World War and the peace conference are arranged separately from subsequent documents. The volumes for the war are supplemented by minutes of the War Cabinet and the collections of papers related to Cabinet decisions. Both the Cabinet minutes and the Cabinet papers are also available at the Public Record Office. Parts of chapters one and two of this book rely heavily on the war documents and the War Cabinet minutes and papers. A comprehensive guide of the Foreign Office papers for the interwar years is Great Britain, Foreign Office, *Index to General Correspondence* (Nendeln, Liechtenstein: Kraus Thomson, 1969-). Eighty-seven volumes covering the years 1920-40 had appeared by 1972. The multivolume *Documents on British Foreign Policy, 1919-1939* offers an extensive selection of documents primarily concerning Britain's relations with the other great powers. Relatively few documents come from the files for Czechoslovakia, but the series is useful as a documentary of general British diplomacy.

The British Foreign Office documents were particularly instructive for an analysis of the evolution of official British attitudes toward Central European problems. From 1918 through 1923 there was general sympathy in the Foreign Office for the young Czechoslovak republic. Relations worsened noticeably in 1924 and 1925, however, with the signing of the Franco-Czechoslovak pact and the Conservative government's refusal to support the Geneva Protocol. Thereafter tension mounted in relations between London and Prague, and by the early 1930s the dominant tone of the documents was openly hostile toward the Czechs. On the other hand, suspicion of German designs in Central Europe lingered as well. The British documents therefore offer a pro-Czechoslovak viewpoint for the early 1920s, but thereafter an increasingly neutral analysis of the rivalries between Czechs and Germans. They therefore afford a perspective somewhere between the German and French diplomatic documents.

As for the personal papers of British statesmen, the most significant for this topic are the Lloyd George papers in the Beaverbrook Library in London. They supply nuances but no startling discoveries beyond what is contained in the Foreign Office documents. Papers of other British leaders at the British Museum were not particularly fruitful for this topic.

The Austrian diplomatic documents are open for historical research through 1925, and I was granted special permission to read the reports from Prague through the year 1933. The documents are housed in the Neues Politisches Archiv of the Haus-, Hof-, und Staatsarchiv in Vienna. Although records of discussions and deliberations in Vienna documented Austrian policy toward Germany and Czechoslovakia, the most significant part of the Austrian archives consisted of reports from the Austrian minister in Prague. Ferdinand Marek headed the Austrian legation throughout the period of this book, and he proved to be a keen and analytical observer of the Czechoslovak domestic scene. His dispatches offered well-informed descriptions of events in Czechoslovakia, and he maintained a neutral and professionally dispassionate tone in his reports. They are therefore a valuable source of information about political, social, and economic issues in Czechoslovakia. Given Czech fears of an Anschluss, Beneš made a special effort to cultivate good relations with Austria. In his conversations with Marek, Beneš often assumed an air of Danubian communality. Just as Beneš drew sharp distinctions between the Austrians and the Germans, it is important that historians not equate the two. The Vienna documents offer sharply different perspectives from those of Berlin. Given the traditional ties between Vienna and Prague and the many personal friendships and associations among Czechoslovak and Austrian statesmen, the Austrian documents provide one of the most valuable windows for historical research about Czechoslovakia.

Finally, the American diplomatic documents for the interwar period are available for historical research at the National Archives in Washington. Not so copious as the other diplomatic collections, the American documents reflect the fact that the primary functions of American representatives were to maintain a diplomatic presence and to engage only in general observation and reporting. But the American mission in Prague in the 1920s boasted an insightful observer of Czechoslovak affairs. The reports of Lewis Einstein offer succinct appraisals of Czechoslovak foreign and domestic policies. The two most important files in the American diplomatic documents are 760F, concerning Czechoslovakia's foreign relations, and 860F, concerning Czechoslovakia's domestic affairs. Sections from the American diplomatic archives appear regularly in *Foreign Relations of the United States*. The thirteen volumes for the Paris peace conference have long been a primary source on peace conference diplomacy. The published documents for the 1920s and 1930s concentrate on American relations with major world powers and contain little information of specific interest for Central European diplomacy.

As for the published documents of other counrties, the Italian series— *I documenti diplomatici italiani*—and the Belgian selections—*Documents diplomatiques belges, 1920-1940*—contain some reports of conversations with German and Czechoslovak diplomats. Although they corroborate other sources, those two document series are of only tangential value for this topic.

Information gleaned from these various archives makes possible a fairly detailed reconstruction of German and Czechoslovak foreign policy. Utilization of sources outside of Central Europe also encourages a broader perspective than would be likely to come from a narrow concentration on German and Czechoslovak materials alone.

The Prague Archives

In contrast with Western countries the archives of the Czechoslovak Ministry of Foreign Affairs are not generally open to historical research. Policy for all archives in Prague allows unrestricted use of documents pertaining to matters before 1918 but forbids or sharply restricts research after that date. Thus all governmental documents since the founding of

Czechoslovakia are unavailable unless one receives special permission from the authorities.

Although Western historians have confronted difficulties, some Czech and Slovak historians have gained access to selected files or documents from the archives. Their works are cited in the notes and will be discussed in another section of this bibliographical essay. After German troops occupied Prague in March 1939, German historians sifted through the Czechoslovak diplomatic archives and sent translations of selected documents back to Berlin. Those translations became part of the files of the German Foreign Office, which were captured by the Western armies at the close of the war. They are now available on microfilm in Washington and London. The interest of the German historians centered on the years after 1933, and the translations include relatively few documents prior to that time. Nevertheless, they are useful as a direct glimpse into the archives. Inasmuch as the translations were intended for the private information of German government officials and not for public propaganda, there is no serious reason for questioning their authenticity. When the Czechoslovak diplomatic archives are opened, however, it would be worthwhile to check the translations against the originals. Caution is important in view of Franz Berber's wartime edition of Czechoslovak diplomatic documents, entitled *Europäische Politik 1933-1938 im Spiegel der Prager Akten* (Essen: Essener Verlagsanstalt, 1942).

Czechoslovak governments have published selections from the archives of the Ministry of Foreign Affairs at various times. In the interwar years white books on particular diplomatic episodes appeared that were typical of their genre. Already in 1922 the Ministry of Foreign Affairs published two special collections entitled: *Documents diplomatiques relatifs aux conventions d'alliance conclues par la République Tchécoslovaque avec le Royaume des Serbes, Croates et Slovenes et le Royaume de Roumanie, décembre 1919-août 1921*, and, *Documents diplomatiques concernant les tentatives de restauration des Habsbourg sur le trône de Hongroie, août 1919-novembre 1921*. Since World War II two collections worthy of mention and specifically concerning the Czechoslovak-German problem have appeared in Prague. They are *Německý imperialismus proti ČSR, 1918-1939* (Prague: Nakladatelství politické literatury, 1962), and Václav Král, ed., *Die Deutschen in der Tschechoslowakei, 1933-1947* (Prague: Nakladatelství Československé akademie věd, 1964). Almost any collection of documents such as these will be influenced by propaganda objectives, and I have preferred to rely on direct documentation from other archives. A more useful series of documents, some of which come from the Czechoslovak Ministry of Foreign Affairs, is *Prameny k ohlasu velké říjnové socialistické revoluce a vzniku ČSR* (Prague: Nakladatelství Československé akademie věd, 1957-). Starting with the years of the First World War, it documents Czechoslovak politics into the early 1920s.

Although the government archives in Prague are closed, the newspaper archives are most helpful in portraying the major developments in Czechoslovak foreign relations as well as the domestic political background out of which Czechoslovak foreign policy was formulated. Those newspapers are almost totally unavailable in the United States. It is therefore necessary to go to Prague if one is to undertake extensive research in the Czech public press. The archives of the state and university libraries and of the National Museum contain a complete collection of Prague newspapers during the First Republic, and copies of the provincial press can be ordered for use in Prague.

The outstanding newspaper in the Czech language during the First Republic was the *Lidové noviny*. Published in Brno, it followed a semi-independent editorial policy although it maintained close ties with Masaryk and Beneš. Beneš occasionally chose to grant interviews or to provide "leaks" to the newspaper in order to publicize some diplomatic event. On the German side both of the major German dailies in Prague were officially independent. The *Prager Tagblatt* and the *Deutsche Zeitung Bohemia* exercised great influence in molding German public opinion throughout the interwar years. There was strong Jewish influence in both papers although it was more pronounced in the *Prager Tagblatt* than in the *Bohemia*. The *Prager Tagblatt* was the better edited and more respected of the two papers, but the *Bohemia* followed a stronger German nationalistic line and probably more closely represented the opinions of the majority of Germans. Among the German provincial press the *Reichenberger Zeitung* and the *Sudetendeutsche Tageszeitung* were much more nationalistically inclined than were the Prague papers.

Among the many publications of the Czechoslovak government, two were especially important for foreign relations. The *Prager Presse* began publication in 1921 and continued until 1938 as an officially independent newspaper. But it was in fact an organ of the Ministry of Foreign Affairs and the mouthpiece of Edvard Beneš. It gave Beneš an opportunity to publicize and defend Czechoslovak foreign policy in a daily newspaper printed in a major world language. The contents of the paper were almost entirely political in nature, containing by far the most thorough coverage of Czechoslovak foreign relations. The official organ of the Ministry of Foreign Affairs was a journal entitled *Zahraniční politika*. It concentrated more on analysis and comment than on reporting events in Czechoslovak foreign relations, and, as an official publication, it was more guarded in its statements. Yet occasionally there was an article significant for Czechoslovak-German relations in the journal, and it can be used as an occasional source for Beneš's statements on public affairs.

During the First Republic the Czechs maintained an extensive propaganda establishment that was aimed primarily at the Western powers. They published weekly or biweekly newspapers in English and French that explained Czech viewpoints on European political and economic affairs. The English newspaper, entitled the *Central European Observer*, can still be profitably used in historical research. It can be found in libraries in Western countries.

A major part of the press in Czechoslovakia consisted of the publications of the various political parties. For general historical research the newspapers and journals already discussed are more important than the party press. I have referred to the party newspapers only on occasion, and not all of them have been cited in the footnotes. Yet for certain political disputes that influenced foreign policy the various party newspapers are important in setting forth the different points of view. The publications of the Czechoslovak Agrarian party—the *Venkov* and the *Večer*—were among the most significant party newspapers. The Czechoslovak Agrarians were the single most powerful party in Czechoslovakia, and the premier of the country was selected from among their ranks almost exclusively from 1922 to 1938. The *České slovo* was published by the Czechoslovak National Socialist party, of which Beneš was a member. For the Czechoslovak Social Democrats the main publication was the *Právo lidu*. After the failure of the Communists to take control of the paper in 1920, they founded their own daily newspaper, the *Rudé právo*, which is the only one of all the interwar newspapers that continues to survive with its old name and with the same general character. On the other end of the political spectrum stood the *Národní listy*, the oldest of the Czech newspapers. Highly influential before the First World War, it became increasingly conservative as the mouthpiece of Kramář's National Democrats after the founding of Czechoslovakia. For the German government parties the *Deutsche Landpost* represented the German Agrarians, the *Deutsche Presse* the German Christian Socials, and the *Sozialdemokrat* the German Social Democrats. The conflicting viewpoints expressed by these newspapers afford some idea of the complicated politics of Czechoslovakia during the interwar years.

GOVERNMENT PUBLICATIONS, MEMOIRS, DIARIES, AND OTHER PRIMARY SOURCES

The works that will be cited in this and the following section represent a selection of the published sources that have been used in the research for this book. Other references have been omitted either because of their minimal importance or their tangential relevance for the topic. On the other hand, some of the sources mentioned in this essay are not in fact cited in the notes although they have been consulted. They are included in an effort to provide the reader with a reasonably complete essay on the primary and secondary source materials relevant to Czechoslovak-German diplomatic relations. Given the breadth of the topic, oversights on my part are, unfortunately, unavoidable.

Among Czechoslovak politicians the writings of Tomáš G. Masaryk and Edvard Beneš were central for this study. Masaryk's memoirs for the First World War were published under the title, *Světová revoluce* (Prague: Orbis and Čin, 1925). In addition to his memoirs the most important sources for his thought and propaganda activities during the war are his *The Problem of Small Nations in the European Crisis* (London: Council for the Study of International Relations, 1916), and *L'Europe nouvelle* (Paris: Imprimé comme manuscrit, 1918). Certain of Masaryk's speeches as president of the republic were printed in pamphlet form by Orbis. A collection of Masaryk's public statements and speeches during the first five years of the republic were printed under the title *Cesta demokracie*, 2 vols. (Prague: Čin, 1933-34). Two sources for Masaryk's thought on the nationality question deserve mention. One is his *Česká otázka* (Prague: Pokrok, 1908), and the other is *Hovory s T.G. Masarykem* (Prague: F. Borový, 1936), which was edited by Karel Čapek. Masaryk's scholarly works dating from the decades before the First World War still enjoy periodical republication, but they are not directly germane to the subject of this book.

Edvard Beneš's memoirs for the First World War appeared as *Světová válka a naše revoluce*, 3 vols. (Prague: Orbis and Čin, 1930-31). Representative of his wartime propaganda activities is his *Détruisez l'Autriche-Hongroie!* (Paris: Delagrave, 1916), which appeared in an English version as *Bohemia's Case for Independence* (London: George Allen and Unwin, Ltd., 1917). Most of Beneš's major speeches on foreign affairs between the wars were translated into English, French, or German and published in pamphlet form by the Czechoslovak government. Those speeches that were delivered before the Czechoslovak Chamber of Deputies can also be found in the parliamentary debates, *Těsnopisecké zprávy o schůzich poslanecké sněmovny Národního shromáždění republiky Československé*. Inasmuch as some of the speeches were given before only the Foreign Affairs Committee, it can be difficult to find them even in good research libraries, which normally do not acquire the committee proceedings. But it is possible to rely on the journal, *Zahraniční politika*, the published pamphlets, or the *Prager Presse*. In addition, a collection of Beneš's speeches was printed in 1924 under the title *Problémy nové Evropy a zahraniční politika československá* (Prague: Melantrich, 1924). Another followed in 1934, actually as the fourth volume of his war memoirs, *Boj o mír a bezpečnost státu* (Prague: Orbis, 1934). The latter volume contains a long and interesting interpretive introduction by Kamil Krofta.

The other major categories of Beneš's works consist of his reports at the League of Nations about the security-disarmament problem and his speeches and memoirs for the years from the Munich conference through the Second World War. During the period of the liberal republics from 1918 to 1933 occasional articles on international affairs did appear under Beneš's name. They are representative of his attempts fo cultivate a democratic image for Czechoslovakia. Examples of Beneš's articles are: "The Little Entente," *Foreign Affairs* 1 (September 1922):66-72; "After Locarno: The Problem of Security Today," *Foreign Affairs* 4 (January 1926):195-210; "Ten Years of the League," *Foreign Affairs* 8 (January 1930):212-24; "The League of Nations: Successes and Failures," *Foreign Affairs* 11 (October 1932):66-80; "The Foreign Policy of Czechoslovakia," *The Nineteenth Century and After* 95 (April 1924):483-90; "Central Europe after Ten Years," *Slavonic Review* 7 (January 1929):245-60; "Germany and Europe," *The Saturday Review* 150 (December 13, 1930):779.

Compared with the writings of Masaryk and Beneš, there is relatively little material on Czechoslovak foreign policy from other Czechoslovak diplomats and politicians in the 1920s and early 1930s. An exception was the Czechoslovak minister in Rome in the early 1920s, Vlastimil Kybal, who wrote two articles entitled "Czechoslovakia and Italy: My Negotiations with Mussolini," *Journal of Central European Affairs* 13 (January 1954):352-68, and 14 (April 1954):65-76. Karel Kramář published in Prague in 1923 a series of his lectures on foreign affairs, entitled *Pět přednášek o zahraniční politice*. There appeared in London in 1942 a book by Milan Hodža entitled, *Federation in Central Europe: Reflections and Reminiscences*. Its chief importance is the light that it sheds on Hodža's plans for a Danubian confederation in 1935-36, when he was premier of Czechoslovakia. Documentation on Hodža's political career between 1898 and 1931 appeared in Milan Hodža, *Články, reči, štúdie*, 4 vols. (Prague: Novina, 1930-31). Of chief interest on the Communist side is Václav Kopecký, *ČSR a KSČ: Pamětní výpisy k historii Československé republiky a k boji KSČ za socialistické Československo* (Prague: Státní nakladatelství politické literatury, 1960). Reportedly, Kopecký was able to draw upon the unpublished memoirs of Jiří Stříbrný in the recording of his recollections. Beneš's deputy from 1927 to 1935 and successor as foreign minister after 1935 was Kamil Krofta, an historian who in 1939 published his assessment of the First Republic under the title: *Z dob naší první republiky* (Prague: Jan Laichter, 1939). Although he concentrated on the years immediately preceding Munich, his portrayal of the "idea of the Czechoslovak state" was indicative of the philosophy that underlay the first Czechoslovak republic.

Among the general publications of the Czechoslovak government during the interwar period, the Czechoslovak parliamentary debates have already been cited. The companion series of documents is entitled *Tisky*. Laws were published in *Sbírka zákonů a nařízení státu československého*. Statistical information concerning Czechoslovak population, election results, and foreign commerce was published by the Office of Statistics of the Czechoslovak government. For the years treated by this book there are four volumes, which appeared in 1921, 1925, 1928, and 1932. The original Czech title is *Státistická příručka republiky československé*. The volumes can also be found in a French edition entitled *Manuel statistique de la République Tchécoslovaque*. A most useful volume concerning the National Assembly and the governing coalitions in the first decade of the existence of the republic is *Národní shromáždění republiky Československé v prvém desítiletí* (Prague: government publication, 1928).

On the German side, the parliamentary debates—*Verhandlungen des Reichstags*—are well known to any German historian. The papers and speeches of Gustav Stresemann were edited by Henry Bernhard and published by Ullstein in Berlin in 1932-33 as the *Vermächtnis*. That work can serve as a guide to the Stresemann "Nachlass," which is available on microfilm. One should also see Hans W. Gatzke's "The Stresemann Papers," *Journal of Modern History* 26 (March 1954):49-59. Of the writings of various Weimar personalities the most important for research on Czechoslovak-German relations are Julius Curtius, *Sechs Jahre Minister der deutschen Republik* (Heidelberg: Carl Winter Universitätsverlag, 1948); Julius Curtius, *Bemühung um Oesterreich: Das Scheitern des Zollunions-plans von 1931* (Heidelberg: Carl Winter Universitätsverlag, 1947); Heinrich Brüning, *Memoiren 1918-1934* (Stuttgart: Deutsche Verlags-Anstalt, 1970); Bernhard W. von Bülow, *Der Versailler Völkerbund: Eine vorläufige Bilanz* (Stuttgart: W. Kohlhammer Verlag, 1923).

Among the published works of foreign diplomats in Berlin and Prague, the following are worth noting. Long a favorite of historians is the diary of Lord D'Abernon—Edgar Vincent D'Abernon, *An Ambassador of Peace*, 3 vols. (London: Hodder and Stoughton, 1929-30). The memoirs of the American minister in Prague in the 1920s were published as Lewis Einstein, *A Diplomat Looks Back* (New Haven: Yale University Press, 1968).

Occasionally of tangential interest for Czechoslovak-German relations are the *Official Journal* of the League of Nations, and the judgments, orders, and advisory opinions of the Permanent Court of International Justice.

SECONDARY WORKS

General Studies

Of the general histories of modern Germany the most distinguished is Hajo Holborn's *A History of Modern Germany*, 3 vols. (New York: Alfred A.

Knopf, 1959-69). The best histories of the Weimar republic are Erich Eyck, *Geschichte der Weimarer Republik*, 2 vols. (Erlenbach-Zürich: E. Rentsch, 1954-56), and, S. William Halperin, *Germany Tried Democracy* (New York: Thomas Y. Crowell Co., 1946). The only one-volume history of Weimar foreign policy is Ludwig Zimmermann's *Deutsche Aussenpolitik in der Ära der Weimarer Republik* (Göttingen: Musterschmidt-Verlag, 1958).

During the Second World War two one-volume histories of the Czechs and the Slovaks appeared in the English language. Both books were written by historians whose sympathies for Czechoslovakia were well known. They are: R.W. Seton-Watson, *A History of the Czechs and Slovaks* (London: Hutchinson & Co., 1943), and S. Harrison Thomson, *Czechoslovakia in European History* (Princeton: Princeton University Press, 1943). Dating from the same period and reflecting the same kinds of sympathies is the collective work edited by Robert J. Kerner, *Czechoslovakia* (Berkeley and Los Angeles: University of California Press, 1940). Conscious that those works are now dated, Victor S. Mamatey and Radomír Luža have recently published a collection of essays by fifteen historians, entitled *A History of the Czechoslovak Republic, 1918-1948* (Princeton: Princeton University Press, 1973). The best contemporary history of the First Republic is Harry Klepetař, *Seit 1918: Eine Geschichte der tschechoslowakischen Republik* (M.-Ostrava:Verlag Julius Kittls Nachfolger, 1937). During the First Republic, a collaborative history of the Czechs and Slovaks until 1918 appeared in the history volumes of *Československá vlastivěda*. Since the Second World War the *Přehled československých dějin* has served much the same function of affording a condensation of historical facts together with the desired historical interpretations. In 1969 Czech and Slovak historians published a new volume in *Československá vlastivěda* with significantly different interpretive viewpoints from those that appeared either in the time of the First Republic or in the 1950s. Also worthy of note is the collective work published by the Collegium Carolinum, *Handbuch der Geschichte der böhmischen Länder* (Stuttgart: Verlag Anton Hieresemann, 1966-). Three of the projected four volumes have appeared.

Recently the first brief but judicious history of the first Czechoslovak republic appeared in the English language—Věra Olivová, *The Doomed Democracy: Czechoslovakia in a Disrupted Europe 1914-1938* (London: Sidgwick & Jackson, 1972). Another short history of Czechoslovakia is that of Jörg K. Hoensch, *Geschichte der tschechoslowakischen Republik, 1918-1965* (Stuttgart: Kohlhammer, 1966). A good summary in Czech is that of Zdeněk Šolle and Alena Gajanová, *Po stopě dějin: Češi a Slováci v letech 1848-1938* (Prague: Orbis, 1969). A fairly recent collection of essays by Czech and German historians offers well-informed perspectives on current historical work about the First Republic—Karl

Bosl, ed., *Aktuelle Forschungsprobleme um die Erste Tschechoslowakische Republik* (Munich: R. Oldenbourg, 1969). Among general histories of interwar Eastern Europe, the most recent is that of C.A. Macartney and A.W. Palmer, *Independent Eastern Europe* (London: Macmillan, 1962). Hugh Seton-Watson's *Eastern Europe between the Wars* (Cambridge: At the University Press, 1945) through its very organization places greater emphasis on nationality distinctions.

An older work on Czechoslovak foreign policy, relying largely on public sources, is Felix John Vondracek, *The Foreign Policy of Czechoslovakia, 1918-1935* (New York: Columbia University Press, 1937). Almost simultaneously there appeared in Czechoslovakia a short history by Emil Strauss, *Tschechoslowakische Aussenpolitik* (Prague: Orbis, 1936). Also relying largely on public sources, it offers a sympathetic portrait of Czechoslovak diplomacy, but it is little more than what its subtitle claims — "Eine geschichtliche Einführung." A collective work that appeared in the 1950s now seems dated in its political rhetoric, but parts of it are still useful inasmuch as they are based on documents from the Czechoslovak diplomatic archives. The book is Vladimír Soják, ed., *O československé zahraniční politice 1918-1939* (Prague: Státní nakladatelství politické literatury, 1956). Also relying on selections from the Foreign Ministry archives is the more recent work of Alena Gajanová, *ČSR a středoevropská politika velmocí 1918-1938* (Prague: Academia, 1967). In *The Diplomats, 1919-1939*, edited by Gordon A. Craig and Felix Gilbert, (Princeton: Princeton University Press, 1953), Paul E. Zinner has provided historians with a brief but well-balanced account of Beneš's diplomacy. Although quite long and dry, Francis P. Walter's *A History of the League of Nations* (London: Oxford University Press, 1952) affords background information about Beneš's activities in Geneva.

On Austria, the best general history is that of Hugo Hantsch, *Die Geschichte Österreichs*, 2 vols. (Graz: Verlag Styria, 4th and 5th editions, 1969-1970). The most serviceable history of the Austrian republic is that edited by Heinrich Benedikt, *Geschichte der Republik Österreich* (Munich: Verlag R. Oldenbourg, 1954). The socialist sympathies of Charles A. Gulick are apparent in his *Austria from Habsburg to Hitler* (Berkeley and Los Angeles: University of California Press, 1948).

Works devoted specifically to relations between Czechs and Germans have been confined largely to Germany and Czechoslovakia. A fairly recent and controversial book is that of Johann Wolfgang Brügel, *Tschechen und Deutsche 1918-1938* (Munich: Nymphenburger Verlagshandlung, 1967). Brügel's work concentrates on the relations between Czechs and Sudeten Germans within Czechoslovakia and relies mainly on the German diplomatic archives. Brügel himself was closely identified with the German Social Democratic party in Czechoslovakia in the 1930s, and

since the Second World War he has lived in exile in London. In his book he
basically defends the policies of the Czechoslovak government and of the
German Social Democrats while bitterly attacking the German nationalists.
Although his polemical style and his episodic treatment of the history of
Czech-Sudeten German relations is not characteristic of a professional
historian, his broad knowledge, based on his personal experiences and
combined with his research, makes the book worthy of note. It has
recently appeared in abridged form in English translation under the title of
*Czechoslovakia before Munich: The German Minority Problem and British
Appeasement Policy* (Cambridge: At the University Press, 1973). For the
English translation Brügel did additional research in the British Foreign
Office archives for the Munich period. An older and well-regarded
treatment is that of Elizabeth Wiskemann, *Czechs and Germans: A Study
of the Struggle in the Historic Provinces of Bohemia and Moravia*
(London: Oxford University Press, 1938). It can still be used with profit,
particularly in regard to questions of economic and cultural policy in the
Czechoslovak republic. From the perspective of more than three decades it
is easy to recognize the author's sympathies for the Czechs and her
subscription to the nationalist values of the period.

Several collections of essays by Czech and German historians on
Czechoslovak-German problems have appeared in the last fifteen years.
They provide useful information on specific monographic topics and
reflect current research interests among historians. An East German
publication of articles by Czechs and Germans is Karl Obermann and Josef
Polišenský, eds., *Aus 500 Jahren deutsch-tschechoslowakischer Geschichte*
(Berlin: Rütten & Loening, 1958). Conferences sponsored by the
Collegium Carolinum produced *Beiträge zum deutsch-tschechischen Verhältnis im 19. und 20. Jahrhundert* (Munich: Verlag Robert Lerche, 1967),
and *Die "Burg": Einflussreiche politische Kräfte um Masaryk und Beneš*, 2
vols. (Munich: R. Oldenbourg Verlag, 1973-74). An important collection
of essays by historians in Czechoslovakia commemorating the fiftieth
anniversary of independence was published under the title, *Die Entstehung
der tschechoslowakischen Republik und ihre international-politische Stellung*. The book appeared in Prague in 1968 as part of the series Acta
Universitatis Carolinae—Philosophica et Historica, 2-3. A shorter collection
is Eugen Lemberg and Gotthold Rhode, eds., *Das deutsche-tschechische
Verhältnis seit 1918* (Stuttgart: W. Kohlhammer Verlag, 1969). Reference
to specific articles from those collections is occasionally made in the notes
of this book.

Given the centrality of Czech-German relations for the history of the
Czechoslovak republic, it is natural that the problem has attracted much
attention within Czechoslovakia. Between the wars a debate raged among
Czech thinkers and scholars concerning the degree of nationality conflict

across the centuries in Bohemia and Moravia. Representative of the Palacký tradition, which emphasized the rivalries between Czechs and Germans and which was more or less official ideology in the First Republic, is Kamil Krofta's *Das Deutschtum in der tschechoslowakischen Geschichte* (Prague: Orbis, 1936). Exemplary of a more cosmopolitan interpretation is Emanuel Radl's *Válka Čechů s Němci*, translated into German as *Der Kampf zwischen Tschechen und Deutschen* (Reichenberg: Verlag Gebrüder Stiepel, 1928). Among the works that have appeared since the Second World War in Czechoslovakia, the most important general treatment is Jaroslav César and Bohumil Černý's study of Sudeten German politics in the First Republic—*Politika německých buržoazních stran v Československu v letech 1918-1938*, 2 vols. (Prague: Nakladatelství Československé akademie věd, 1962).

On the Sudeten German side the best general history is Emil Franzel's *Sudetendeutsche Geschichte: Eine volkstümliche Darstellung* (Augsburg: Adam Kraft Verlag, 2d ed., 1958). Representative of the argumentative body of literature that grew up among the Sudeten German refugees are Wenzel Jaksch, *Europas Weg nach Potsdam* (Stuttgart: Deutsche-Verlagsanstalt, 1958); Ernst Paul, *Was nicht in den Geschichtsbüchern steht*, 2 vols. (Munich: "Die Brücke," 1961-66); Wilhelm K. Turnwald, *Renascence or Decline of Central Europe* (Munich: C. Wolf und Sohn, 1954). These books are only a selection, and they are of interest primarily as an indication of Sudeten German attitudes after the Second World War. They should not be relied upon in the absence of corroborating sources for information about the interwar period.

As for handbooks and almanacs, the most useful sources on the German side were *Schulthess' Europäischer Geschichtskalender* and Friedrich Purlitz's *Deutscher Geschichtskalender*. Both handbooks offer a fairly detailed outline of the most important political events in Germany and in international affairs. On the Czech side the daily and weekly newspapers, supplemented by the *Zahraniční politika*, served much the same function. An important British publication, devoted purely to international events, is the *Survey of International Affairs*, which during the 1920s was edited by Arnold J. Toynbee. The companion volume to the *Survey* is *Documents on International Affairs*.

Before 1918

Inasmuch as the rivalries between Czechs and Germans before 1918 were confined largely to the Habsburg Empire, the sources that were used in the writing of the first chapter of this book were basically domestic histories of the Danubian monarchy. The question of the viability of the Habsburg Empire has spawned vigorous historical debates, and the following discussion includes only a portion of the available literature. It reflects an attempt, however, to include essays and articles of more recent vintage along with classical works in the field.

A congress of historians at Indiana University in 1966 inspired several important essays on the nationality problem in the Habsburg Empire. They have been published in volume 3 of the *Austrian History Yearbook* for 1967. Of particular importance for this book were essays by Jan Havránek and S. Harrison Thomson on the Czechs, L'udovít Holotík and Václav L. Beneš on the Slovaks, and Erich Zöllner and Andrew G. Whiteside on the Germans. Another collection of valuable essays, devoted specifically to the Czech revival in the nineteenth century and published in honor of Otakar Odložilík, is Peter Brock and H. Gordon Skilling, eds., *The Czech Renascence of the Nineteenth Century* (Toronto: University of Toronto Press, 1970). Various essays from this collection are cited in the notes to the first chapter of this book.

Monographic works on the early stages of the Czech and the Slovak revivals include Ján Tibenský, "Bernolák's Influence and the Origins of the Slovak Awakening," *Studia historica slovaca* 2 (1964):140-89; Jozef Butvin, "Martin Hamuljak and the Fundamental Problems of the Slovak National Revival," *Studia historica slovaca* 3 (1965):135-72; William E. Wright, *Serf, Seigneur, and Sovereign: Agrarian Reform in Eighteenth Century Bohemia* (Minneapolis: University of Minnesota Press, 1966); Robert Joseph Kerner, *Bohemia in the Eighteenth Century* (New York: The Macmillan Company, 1932); Stanley Z. Pech, *The Czech Revolution of 1848* (Chapel Hill: University of North Carolina Press, 1969); Daniel Rapant, *Slovenské povstanie roku 1848-49*, 5 vols. (Bratislava: Vyda-vatel'stvo Slovenskej akadémie vied, 1937-72).

At least from the middle of the nineteenth century a study of the Czech revival becomes inextricably intertwined with the question of the viability of the multinational empire. Among general studies of the Habsburg Empire, the two most important recent books are C.A. Macartney, *The Habsburg Empire, 1790-1918* (London: Weidenfeld and Nicolson, 1968), and Victor-L. Tapié, *Monarchie et peuples du Danube* (Paris: Fayard, 1969). Generally recognized as the fundamental study of the nationality conflict in the nineteenth century is Robert A. Kann's *The Multinational Empire: Nationalism and National Reform in the Habsburg Monarchy, 1848-1918*, 2 vols. (New York: Columbia University Press, 1950). An older but admirable analysis of the empire is Oscar Jászi's famous *The Dissolution of the Habsburg Monarchy* (Chicago: University of Chicago Press, 1929). A basically sympathetic treatment of the empire is to be found in Arthur J. May's *The Hapsburg Monarchy, 1867-1914* (Cambridge: Harvard University Press, 1951). Provocatively prejudiced is A.J.P. Taylor's *The Habsburg Monarchy, 1809-1918* (London: H. Hamilton, 1948). Barbara Jelavich's *The Habsburg Empire in European Affairs* (Chicago: Rand McNally, 1969) is a useful survey of the foreign policy of the empire. A collection of essays, most of which are by East European historians, is to be found in *Die nationale Frage in der Oesterreichisch-Ungarischen Monarchie 1900-1918* (Budapest: Akadémiai Kiadó, 1966). From another perspective, an analysis by a devoted defender of the old empire is Hugo Hantsch, *Die Nationalitätenfrage im alten Oesterreich: Das Problem der konstruktiven Reichsgestaltung* (Vienna: Verlag Herold, 1953). Papers that were presented in a large symposium in Vienna in 1968 about the dissolution of Austria-Hungary have been collected in Richard Georg Plaschka and Karlheinz Mack, eds., *Die Auflösung des Habsburger-reiches: Zusammenbruch und Neuorientierung im Donauraum* (Vienna: Verlag für Geschichte und Politik, 1970). The volume affords an introduction to the state of historical research on the topic, but the papers are quite short, and some of the authors have developed their ideas more fully in other writings.

As one focuses more narrowly on the Czech-German conflict, one should consult the best political history of the Czechs in the empire— Zdeněk Tobolka's *Politické dějiny československého národa od r. 1848 až do dnešní doby*, 4 vols. (Prague: Československý kompas, 1932-37). Among the many journal articles on Czech and Slovak history in the late Habsburg empire, the following are particularly worthy of note: Jan Havránek, "Die ökonomische und politische Lage der Bauernschaft in den bömischen Ländern in den letzten Jahrzehnten des 19. Jahrhunderts," *Jahrbuch für Wirtschaftsgeschichte* (1966), pt. 2, 96-136; Jan Havránek, "Social Classes, Nationality Ratios and Demographic Trends in Prague 1880-1900," *Historica* 13 (1966):171-208; Stanley Z. Pech, "Passive Resistance of the Czechs, 1863-1879," *Slavonic and East European Review* 36 (June 1958):434-52; Jaroslav Purš, "Tábory v českých zemích v letech 1868-1871," *Československý časopis historický* 6 (1958):234-66, 446-70, 661-90; Jaroslav Purš, "The Industrial Revolution in the Czech Lands," *Historica* 2 (1960): 183-272. Anthony Palacek, "The Rise and Fall of the Czech Agrarian Party," *East European Quarterly* 5 (June 1971):177-201; L'udovít Holotík, "Slovak Politics in the 19th Century," *Studia historica slovaca* 5 (1967):35-55. These are only a sample of the many articles in the field.

Useful monographs include Ludmila Kárníková, *Vývoj obyvatelstva v českých zemích 1754-1914* (Prague: Nakladatelství Československé akademie věd, 1965), and William A. Jenks, *Austria under the Iron Ring, 1879-1893* (Charlottesville: The University of Virginia Press, 1965). The classical work on the constitutional reforms after the Seven Weeks' War is that of Louis Eisenmann, *Le Compromis austro-hongrois de 1867: Étude sur le Dualisme* (Paris: Société nouvelle de librairie et d'édition, 1904). An equally famous work, concentrating on the Hungarian half of the empire, is R.W. Seton-Watson (Scotus Viator), *Racial Problems in Hungary* (London: Archibald Constable & Co. Ltd., 1908).

Given the importance of 1897 for German political activities in the last decades of the Habsburg Empire, one should consult Berthold Sutter, *Die Badenischen Sprachenverordnungen von 1897*, 2 vols. (Graz: Verlag Hermann Böhlaus Nachf., 1960-65). On particular parties and political movements, see Paul Molisch, *Geschichte der deutschnationalen Bewegung in Oesterreich von ihren Anfängen bis zur Zerfall der Monarchie* (Jena: G. Fischer, 1926); Paul Molisch, ed., *Briefe zur deutschen Politik in Oesterreich von 1848 bis 1918* (Vienna: Wilhelm Braumüller, 1934). Andrew Gladding Whiteside, *Austrian National Socialism before 1918* (The Hague: Martinus Nijhoff, 1962) is particularly useful for events in Bohemia. Jiří Kořalka's *Všeněmecký svaz a česká otázka koncem 19. století* (Prague: Nakladatelství Československé akademie věd, 1963) is also informative, although it suffers from an effort to force connections between the nineteenth century and the Third Reich. Of particular value for the Austrian Social Democratic party is Hans Mommsen's *Die Sozialdemokratie und die Nationalitätenfrage im habsburgischen Vielvölkerstaat* (Vienna: Europa-Verlag, 1963). The best general history of the Social Democrats in the empire and the first Austrian republic is Norbert Leser's *Zwischen Reformismus und Bolschewismus: Der Austromarxismus als Theorie und Praxis* (Vienna: Europa-Verlag, 1968).

The crucial significance of the First World War for the demise of Austria-Hungary is rightly reflected in an impressive body of historical literature. An important work by an historian particularly well informed about the Czech national movement is that of Z.A.B. Zeman, *The Break-up of the Habsburg Empire, 1914-1918: A Study in National and Social Revolution* (London: Oxford University Press, 1961). Arthur J. May has provided a longer treatment of the same theme, written in a readable style and sympathetic to the empire—*The Passing of the Hapsburg Monarchy, 1914-1918*, 2 vols. (Philadelphia: University of Pennsylvania Press, 1966). Works that are devoted to diplomatic aspects of the dissolution of the monarchy include Harry Hanak, *Great Britain and Austria-Hungary during the First World War: A Study in the Formation of Public Opinion* (London: Oxford University Press, 1962); Harry Hanak, "The Government, the Foreign Office and Austria-Hungary, 1914-1918," *Slavonic and East European Review* 47 (January 1969):161-97; Z.A.B. Zeman, *A Diplomatic History of the First World War* (London: Weidenfeld and Nicolson, 1971). The best work on American policy toward Austria-Hungary during the war is Victor S. Mamatey's *The United States and East Central Europe, 1914-1918: A Study in Wilsonian Diplomacy and Propaganda* (Princeton: Princeton University Press, 1957).

Focusing more specifically on the Czech and Slovak questions during the war, one must first note that the best diplomatic history of the origins of Czechoslovakia is D. Perman's *The Shaping of the Czechoslovak State: Diplomatic History of the Boundaries of Czechoslovakia, 1914-1920* (Leiden: E.J. Brill, 1962). Descriptive of Masaryk's work in exile and qualifying almost as primary sources are R.W. Seton-Watson's *Masaryk in England* (Cambridge: At the University Press, 1943), and Charles Pergler's *America in the Struggle for Czechoslovak Independence* (Philadelphia: Dorrance and Company, 1926). Since 1948 there has been an effort by Czech and Slovak historians to discount the significance of the activities of the exiles during the First World War. J.S. Hájek's *Wilsonovská legenda v dějinach ČSR* (Prague: Státní nakladatelství politické literatury, 1953) was a primitive attempt in that direction. Later L'udivít Holotík pursued some of the same themes in *Štefanikovská legenda a vznik ČSR* (Bratislava: Vydavatel'stvo Slovenskej akadémie vied, 1958). The most balanced and mature of the works is Karel Pichlík, *Zahraniční odboj 1914-1918 bez legend* (Prague: Svoboda, 1968). Also of interest is J.B. Kozák, *T.G. Masaryk a vznik Washingtonské deklarace v říjnu 1918* (Prague: Melantrich, 1968).

Among the avalanche of literature that appeared during the first Czechoslovak republic concerning the winning of Czechoslovak independence, the following books are among the more important. Emil Strauss's *Die Entstehung der tschechoslowakischen Republik* (Prague: Orbis, 1934) is a useful portrayal of activities by Czech leaders at home and abroad during the war. As has been noted, Strauss was a supporter of the republic, and his account is that of a friendly witness of events. On the Czech side an exhaustive work that concentrated on diplomatic events in 1918 was that of Jan Opočenský, *Konec monarchie rakousko-uherské* (Prague: Čin and Orbis, 1928). Opočenský also published a shorter work devoted specifically to the founding of nation states in the Danubian area in October 1918—*Vznik národních států v říjnu 1918* (Prague: Orbis, 1927). Both works were sponsored by the Czechoslovak Ministry of Foreign Affairs. Opočenský's books were representative of a certain trend during the First Republic to emphasize the paramountcy of the exile leadership and to neglect events within Bohemia and Moravia. That in turn strengthened the positions of Masaryk and Beneš in Czechoslovak politics. Another example is the booklet by Jaroslav Papoušek, *The Czechoslovak Nation's Struggle for Independence* (Prague: Orbis, 1928), and a French work—Madame Levée, *Les précurseurs de l'indépendance tchèque et slovaque à Paris* (Paris: Payot, 1936)—can be included in the genre.

Efforts to right the balance and to give domestic events their due importance are to be found in the fourth volume of Tobolka's *Politické dějiny* (already discussed) and Milada Paulová's *Dějiny maffie: Odboj*

Čechů a Jihoslovanů za světové války, 1914-1918 (Prague: Československá Grafická Unie, 1937). Pichlík's *Zahraniční odboj bez legend* is a more recent example of a similar effort. Part memoir and part narrative was *28. říjen 1918* (Prague: Orbis, 1928) by Frant. Soukup, one of the five members of the National Council that proclaimed independence on October 28, 1918. From the Sudeten German side came Paul Molisch's *Vom Kampf der Tschechen um ihren Staat* (Vienna: Wilhelm Braumüller, 1929). The first volume of the single most important history of the early years of the First Republic began with the events of 1918—Ferdinand Peroutka, *Budování státu: Československá politika v letech popřevratových* (Prague: Fr. Borovy, 1933-36).

The exploits of the Czechoslovak legion in Siberia between 1918 and 1920 have stirred controversy among historians and have inspired the imaginations of historical popularizers. Among the more recent serious works on the legion, the following should be noted: Ján Kvasnička, *Československé légie v Rusku 1917-1920* (Bratislava: Vydavateľstvo Slovenskej akadémie vied, 1963); J.F.N. Bradley, *La légion tchécoslovaque en Russie 1914-1920* (Paris: Centre National de la Recherche Scientifique, 1965); and Gerburg Thunig-Nitter, *Die tschechoslowakische Legion in Russland: Ihre Geschichte und Bedeutung bei der Entstehung der 1. Tschechoslowakischen Republik* (Wiesbaden: Otto Harrassowitz, 1970). During the first Czechoslovak republic the legionnaires were politically powerful, and a special journal, *Naše revoluce*, extolled their contributions to Czechoslovak independence. Examples of the hagiographic literature of the interwar years are Lev Sychrava, *Duch legií* (Prague: Strahovský klášter, n.d.); Lev Sychrava a Jar. Werstadt, *Československý odboj* (Prague: Státní nakladatelství, 1923). The memoirs of the French commander of the legionnaires appeared as Maurice Janin, *Ma mission en Sibérie 1918-1920* (Paris: Payot, 1933).

Literature on the Czechoslovak legion inevitably becomes enmeshed in the debates about the policies of Western governments toward the Bolshevik revolution and the Russian civil war. Among Western contributions to the debates, the most famous is George F. Kennan's *Soviet-American Relations, 1917-1920*, 2 vols. (Princeton: Princeton University Press, 1956-58). The literature is enriched by Richard H. Ullman's *Anglo-Soviet Relations, 1917-1921*, 2 vols. (Princeton: Princeton University Press, 1961-68), Piotr S. Wandycz's *Soviet-Polish Relations, 1917-1921* (Cambridge, Mass.: Harvard University Press, 1969), and J.F.N. Bradley's *Allied Intervention in Russia* (New York: Basic Books, 1968). The most recent Czech contribution to the question of Masaryk's policies in regard to the Siberian intervention is Vlastimil Vávra, "K historiografické interpretaci poměru T.G. Masaryka vůči sovětskému Rusku v roce 1918," *Československý časopis historický* 21 (1973):13-44.

In addition to general diplomatic and military histories of the First World War, the controversy about German war aims has spawned a wealth of historical literature. Representative of the most important work by historians and offering varying interpretations, are Gerhard A. Ritter, *Staatskunst und Kriegshandwerk: Das Problem des "Militarismus" in Deutschland*, 4 vols. (Munich: R. Oldenbourg, 1954-68); Fritz Fischer, *Griff nach der Weltmacht* (Düsseldorf: Droste, 1961); Hans W. Gatzke, *Germany's Drive to the West* (Baltimore: Johns Hopkins University Press, 1950); Konrad H. Jarausch, *The Enigmatic Chancellor: Bethmann Hollweg and the Hubris of Imperial Germany* (New Haven: Yale University Press, 1973). In view of the significance of German Mitteleuropa ideas for Czechoslovak-German relations in the interwar years, Friedrich Naumann's *Mitteleuropa* (Berlin: G. Reimer, 1915) makes fascinating reading. Henry Cord Meyer's *Mitteleuropa in German Thought and Action, 1815-1945* (The Hague: Martinus Nijhoff, 1955) is still the most informative general survey of Mitteleuropa ideas, even though there have been more recent contributions concerning the years of the First World War. For a Czechoslovak view, which is not free of propagandistic overtones, one can see Z. Jindra and J. Křížek, *Contributions à l'histoire contemporaine des peuples de l'Europe centrale* (Prague: Československá historická společnost, 1960).

1919-1925

The literature on the Paris peace conference is voluminous. In addition to the previously mentioned volumes of *Foreign Relations of the United States*, the best of the published documentation is Paul Mantoux's *Les délibérations du Conseil des Quatre, 24 mars-28 juin 1919*, 2 vols. (Paris: Éditions du Centre national de la recherche scientifique, 1955). Mantoux was the official French interpreter in the meetings of the Council of Four, and his notes corroborate the main points of the American documents while occasionally adding new and interesting sidelights. Charles Seymour's *Letters from the Paris Peace Conference*, ed. Harold B. Whiteman, Jr., (New Haven: Yale University Press, 1965) is of interest in view of Seymour's involvement with Czechoslovak questions at the conference.

Older works on the peace conference that have been consulted in the writing of this book are Harold Nicolson's *Peacemaking 1919* (London: Constable and Co., 1933), and H.W.V. Temperley, ed., *A History of the Peace Conference of Paris*, 6 vols. (London: Henry Frowde and Hodder & Stoughton, 1920-24). Of more recent vintage, from Germany, are Klaus Schwabe, *Deutsche Revolution und Wilson-Frieden: Die amerikanische und deutsche Friedensstrategie zwischen Ideologie und Machtpolitik 1918-19* (Düsseldorf: Droste, 1971); Peter Krüger, *Deutschland und*

Bibliographical Essay

Reparationen 1918-1919 (Stuttgart: Deutsche Verlags-Anstalt, 1973). The most recent provocative work in the English language is Arno J. Mayer's *Politics and Diplomacy of Peacemaking: Containment and Counterrevolution at Versailles, 1918-1919* (New York: Alfred A. Knopf, 1967). Emphasizing the concern of the peacemakers about the possible spread of Bolshevik revolutions, Mayer continues some of the same themes that he originally developed in his *Political Origins of the New Diplomacy* (New Haven: Yale University Press, 1959). The best analyses of the Czechoslovak question at the peace conference are to be found in D. Perman's *The Shaping of the Czechoslovak State* and Piotr S. Wandycz's *France and Her Eastern Allies, 1919-1925: French-Czechoslovak-Polish Relations from the Paris Peace Conference to Locarno* (Minneapolis: University of Minnesota Press, 1962). Peter Burian has contributed a brief essay on German-Czechoslovak relations in 1918-1919 in Kurt Kluxen and Wolfgang J. Mommsen, eds., *Politische Ideologien und Nationalstaatliche Ordnung* (Munich: R. Oldenbourg, 1968). Also of interest is Hanns Haas, "Die deutschböhmische Frage 1918-1919 und das österreichisch-tschechoslowakische Verhältnis," *Bohemia* 13 (Munich: R. Oldenbourg Verlag, 1972):336-83. The collective works published by the Collegium Carolinum are edited by Karl Bosl.

A considerable portion of the historical literature about the early Czechoslovak republic has a bearing on the study of the history of Czechoslovak-German relations. Ferdinand Peroutka's *Budování státu* offers a detailed history of Czechoslovak politics from 1918 through 1921 in four volumes. It remains the most reliable single source on the subject. Alois Rašín's *Financial Policy of Czechoslovakia during the First Year of Its History* (Oxford: At the Clarendon Press, 1923) is an account by the man, who, as minister of finance, molded and directed that policy. On the Czechoslovak land reform an older work is that of Lucy Elizabeth Textor, *Land Reform in Czechoslovakia* (London: George Allen & Unwin, Ltd., 1923). More recent and more exhaustive in its treatment is Milan Otáhal, *Zápas o pozemkovou reformu v ČSR* (Prague: Nakladatelství Československé akademie věd, 1963). On economic unrest in Czechoslovakia in the early 1920s, consult Věra Olivová, *Politika československé buržoasie v letech 1921-1923* (Prague: Nakladatelství Československé akademie věd, 1961). Also see her "Postavení dělnické třídy v ČSR v letech 1921-1923," *Československý časopis historický* 2 (1954):193-227. A useful introduction in English to the Czechoslovak constitutional system is Edward Taborský, *Czechoslovak Democracy at Work* (London: George Allen & Unwin Ltd., 1945). On the crucially important language question, see Harry Klepetař, *Der Sprachenkampf in den Sudetenländern* (Prague: Ed. Strache Verlag, 1930).

More specifically related to conflicts between Czechs and Sudeten Germans is the previously cited work of Jaroslav César and Bohumil Černý, *Politika německých buržoazních stran*. Another work by the same two authors is *Od sudetoněmeckého separtismu k plánům odvety* (Liberec: Severočeské krajské nakladatelství, 1960). They have repeated many of their same ideas in articles that have been translated into English. Jaroslav César and Bohumil Černý, "German Irredentist Putsch in the Czech Lands after the First World War," *Historica* 3 (1961):195-238; "The Policy of German Activist Parties in Czechoslovakia, 1918-1938," *Historica* 5 (1963):239-81; "The Nazi Fifth Column in Czechoslovakia," *Historica* 4 (1962):191-255. On the German side, one should note Paul Molisch, *Die sudetendeutsche Freiheitsbewegung in den Jahren 1918-1919* (Vienna: Wilhelm Braumüller, 1932), and Kurt Rabl, *Das Ringen um das Sudetendeutsche Selbstbestimmungsrecht, 1918-1919* (Munich: Verlag Robert Lerche, 1958). A more objective treatment can be found in the article by Arthur G. Kogan, "Germany and the Germans of the Habsburg Monarchy on the Eve of the Armistice 1918: Genesis of the Anschluss Problem," *Journal of Central European Affairs* 20 (April 1960):24-50.

Among articles and monographs on German and Czechoslovak diplomacy in the early years of the republics, the following are important for research on Czechoslovak-German relations. A well-informed introduction to the German Foreign Office can be found in Hajo Holborn's "Diplomats and Diplomacy. in the Early Weimar Republic," in *The Diplomats 1919-1939*, ed. Gordon A. Craig and Felix Gilbert. A recent work on the most accomplished of the early Weimar foreign ministers is David Felix, *Walther Rathenau and the Weimar Republic: The Politics of Reparations* (Baltimore: The Johns Hopkins Press, 1971). The most thorough study of Czechoslovak-German relations in the first three years of the republics is Koloman Gajan's *Německý imperialismus a československo-německé vztahy v letech 1918-1921* (Prague: Nakladatelství Československé akademie věd, 1962). Articles on particular episodes and problems in early Czechoslovak diplomacy include Koloman Gajan, "Spolupráce československé buržoazie s německou reakcí po první světové válce," *Československý časopis historický* 8 (1960):843-55; Zygmunt J. Gasiorowski, "Czechoslovakia and the Austrian Question, 1918-1928," *Südost-Forschungen* 16 (1957):87-122; four articles by Věra Olivová— "Československanská zahraniční politika a pokus o restauraci Habsburků v roce 1921," *Československý časopis historický* 7 (1959):675-97, "K historii československo-rakouské smlouvy z r. 1921," *Československý časopis historický* 9 (1961):198-219, "Postoj československé buržoasie k Sovětskému svazu v době jednání o prozatímní smlouvu z roku 1922," *Československý časopis historický* 1 (1953):294-323, "Československá diplomacie v době rurské krise roku 1923," *Československý časopis historický* 6 (1958):59-70; Manfred Alexander, "Die Tschechoslowakei und die Probleme der Ruhrbesetzung," *Bohemia* 12 (Munich: R. Oldenbourg Verlag, 1971):297-336; Radko Břach, "Ruský problém v čs. zahraniční politice na počátku roku 1924," *Československý časopis historický* 16 (1968):1-28. The best general account in English of early Czechoslovak diplomacy is to be found in the previously mentioned book by Piotr S. Wandycz, *France and Her Eastern Allies, 1919-1925*.

Diplomatic preparations for the Locarno agreements of 1925 were of central importance for Czechoslovak-German relations, and the following articles and books are informative on the subject. Annelise Thimme, "Die Locarnopolitik im Lichte des Stresemann-Nachlasses," *Zeitschrift für Politik* 3 (August 1956):42-63. The article has been translated into English and published in Hans W. Gatzke, ed., *European Diplomacy between Two Wars, 1919-1939* (Chicago: Quadrangle Books, 1972). Jürgen Spenz, *Die diplomatische Vorgeschichte des Beitritts Deutschlands zum Völkerbund, 1924-1926* (Göttingen: Musterschmidt-Verlag, 1966); Radko Břach, "Československá zahraniční politika v politických proměnách Evropy 1924," *Československý časopis historický* 18 (1970):49-83; Radko Břach, "Locarno a čs. diplomacie," *Československý časopis historický* 8 (1960):662-95; Zygmunt J. Gasiorowski, "Beneš and Locarno," *Review of Politics* 20 (April 1958):209-24; Manfred Alexander, *Der deutsch-tschechoslowakische Schiedsvertrag von 1925 im Rahmen der Locarno-Verträge* (Munich: R. Oldenbourg, 1970); F.G. Stambrook, " 'Das Kind'—Lord D'Abernon and the Origins of the Locarno Pact," *Central European History* 1 (September 1968):233-63.

In view of the importance of Austria and Poland for an analysis of Czechoslovak-German relations, some of the historical literature focusing on those countries has at least tangential significance for this study. For Austria, in addition to the more general histories already discussed, a recent work by Klemens von Klemperer, *Ignaz Seipel: Christian Statesman in a Time of Crisis* (Princeton: Princeton University Press, 1972) has helped to make Seipel's foreign policy less enigmatic. Specifically concerning the Anschluss question, an older work by M. Margaret Ball, *Post-War German-Austrian Relations: The Anschluss Movement, 1918-1936* (Stanford: Stanford University Press, 1937), is still of use as a general narrative.

On relations between Poland and Germany, the most exhaustive treatment is by Harald von Riekhoff, *German-Polish Relations, 1918-1933* (Baltimore: The Johns Hopkins Press, 1971). Other respectable studies that have appeared in the United States are Josef Korbel, *Poland between East and West: Soviet and German Diplomacy toward Poland, 1919-1933* (Princeton: Princeton University Press, 1963), and two articles by

Zygmunt J. Gasiorowski—"Stresemann and Poland before Locarno," *Journal of Central European Affairs* 18 (April 1958):25-47; and, "Stresemann and Poland after Locarno," *Journal of Central European Affairs* 18 (October 1958):292-317. From Poland, the major work is Jerzy Krasuski, *Stosunki polsko-niemieckie 1919-1925* (Poznań: Institut Zachodni, 1962). For a German source, one should consult Christian Höltje's *Die Weimarer Republik und das Ostlocarno-Problem, 1919-1934: Revision oder Garantie der deutschen Ostgrenze von 1919* (Würzburg: Holzner-Verlag, 1958).

Good historical research and writing by contemporary Czech and Polish historians make possible a comparison of current views about Czechoslovak-Polish relations. From the Czechoslovak side, Jaroslav Valenta's contribution—"Československo a Polsko v letech 1918-1945"—appeared in *Češi a Poláci v minulosti*, 2 (Prague: Academia, 1967). Papers presented at a conference in Prague in 1962 were published as *Z dějin československo-polských vztahů* (Prague: Universita Karlova, 1963). From the Polish side the best analyses are Alina Szklarska-Lohmannowa, *Polsko-czechoslowackie stosunki dyplomatyczne w latach 1918-1925* (Wrocław: Zakład Narodowy imienia Ossolińskich wydawnictwo Polskiej Akademii Nauk, 1967). Jerzy Kozeński, *Czechosłowacja w polskiej polityce zagranicnej w latach 1932-1938* (Poznań: Instytut Zachodni, 1964).

Although the Slovak question is not a central issue in this study, it did help to determine the limits within which the government in Prague could operate. Among older works in the English language on the Slovak issue, the two most famous are those written or edited by R.W. Seton-Watson—*The New Slovakia* (Prague: Fr. Borovy, 1924), and *Slovakia Then and Now: A Political Survey* (London: George Allen & Unwin Ltd., 1931). C.A. Macartney, *Hungary and Her Successors* (London: Oxford University Press, 1937) contains a long section on Slovakia. Macartney is a useful counterbalance to Seton-Watson, for, although both were reputable historians, Seton-Watson was clearly identified with the Czechoslovak republic while Macartney's sympathies lay more with the Hungarians. Jozef Lettrich offers a general work, *History of Modern Slovakia* (New York: Frederick A. Praeger, 1955), and the all-important issue of political administration in Slovakia during the First Republic is analyzed in Ladislav Lipscher, *K vývinu politickej správy na Slovensku v rokoch 1918-1938* (Bratislava: Vydavatel'stvo Slovenskej akadémie vied, 1966).

The years of the First World War and the early days of Slovak independence have been treated by Karol A. Medvecký, *Slovenský prevrat*, 4 vols. (Trnava: Spolok sv. Vojtecha, 1930-31). In the late 1920s a debate among Slovak politicians about their activities at the time that Slovakia separated from Hungary led to the publication of Vavro Šrobár, *Osvobodené Slovensko: Pamäti z rokov 1918-1920* (Prague: Čin, 1928), and Milan Hodža, *Slovenský rozchod s Mad'armi roku 1918* (Bratislava: Redakcie Slovenského denníka, 1929). Václav Chaloupecký's *Zápas o Slovensko 1918* (Prague: Čin, 1930) reflected the "Czechoslovak" policy of the Prague centralists, as did Ivan Dérer's *Československenksá otázka* (Prague: Orbis, 1935). One of the leading contemporary Slovak historians has written an excellent article about Slovak independence—L'udovít Holotík, "Beginnings of the Czechoslovak State in 1918 and the Slovaks," *Studia historica slovaca* 1 (1963):117-49.

Concerning the war with Hungary in 1919 and the attempts to establish a Slovak Soviet republic, one should consult Peter A. Toma, "The Slovak Soviet Republic of 1919," *American Slavic and East European Review* 17 (1958):203-15, and Martin Vietor, *Slovenská sovietska republika* (Bratislava: Slovenské vydavatel'stvo politickej literatúry, 1959). Václav Král, *Intervenční válka Československé buržoasie proti Mad'arské sovětské republice v roce 1919* (Prague: Nakladatelství Československé akademie věd, 1954), is an older attack by a Marxist historian on the first Czechoslovak republic. Eva S. Balogh offers an Hungarian perspective in her "Nationality Problems of the Hungarian Soviet Republic," in Iván Völgyes, ed., *Hungary in Revolution 1918-1919* (Lincoln: University of Nebraska Press, 1971).

Contemporary historians in Czechoslovakia have done good work on the Slovak autonomist movement. Particularly worth mention are Juraj Kramer, *Slovenské autonomistické hnutie v rokoch 1918-1929* (Bratislava: Vydavatel'stvo Slovenskej akadémie vied, 1962); Ladislav Lipscher, *L'udácka autonómia: Ilúzie a skutočnosť* (Bratislava: Slovenské vydavatel'-stvo politickej literatúry, 1957); Imrich Stanek, *Zrada a pád: Hlinkovští separatisté a tak zvaný Slovenský stát* (Prague: Státní nakladatelství politické literatury, 1958). A condensation of the Kramer book has appeared in his article "Die slowakische autonomistische Bewegung in den Jahren 1918-1929," *Historica* 5 (1963):115-43. A careful and well-informed view of the Slovak question during the First Republic can be found in the introductory section of Josef Anderle's "The Slovak Issue in the Munich Crisis of 1938," (Ph.D. diss., University of Chicago, 1961). Egbert K. Jahn's *Die Deutschen in der Slowakei in den Jahren 1918-1929: Ein Beitrag zur Nationalitätenproblematik* (Munich: R. Oldenbourg, 1971) is a competent analysis of the nationality problem and, in part, a critique of Czechoslovak minority policies.

1925-1933

Most of the sources for chapters four and five have already been discussed in previous sections of this essay. There are, however, a number of monographic works of interest particularly for this period.

Among the major figures in Czechoslovak and German diplomacy in the years between 1925 and 1933 there is still no definitive biography of Masaryk or Beneš. The best works on Masaryk are Jaromír Doležal, *Masaryk osmdesátiletý* (Prague: Státní nakladatelství, 1931), and Jan Herben, *T.G. Masaryk: Život a dílo presidenta osvoboditele*, 5th ed. (Prague: Sfinx-Bohumil Janda, 1947). *Masarykův sborník* was a journal devoted to the study of Masaryk's life and work, six volumes of which appeared in Prague between 1924 and 1931. Most of the works about Masaryk and Beneš were adulatory, as is exemplified in the titles of books about Beneš—*Un grand Européen, Edouard Beneš; "I Built a Temple for Peace," The Life of Eduard Beneš; Edvard Beneš, Filosof demokracie*. In Czechoslovak historical writing, a period of intense criticism in the 1950s has been followed by a period of general neglect, punctuated by a brief flurry of interest around 1968. As the personal papers of Masaryk and Beneš become available for historical research, it will be more nearly possible for historians to develop well-documented and balanced analyses of their careers.

In contrast, the career of Gustav Stresemann has been the subject of considerable historical debate. Hans W. Gatzke and Annelise Thimme, in particular, have been critical of the image of Stresemann as "a great European." One should consult Hans W. Gatzke, *Stresemann and the Rearmament of Germany* (Baltimore: Johns Hopkins Press, 1954); Annelise Thimme, *Gustav Stresemann: Eine politische Biographie zur Geschichte der Weimarer Republik* (Hannover: O. Goedel, 1957), and her "Gustav Stresemann: Legende und Wirklichkeit," *Historische Zeitschrift* 181 (1956):287-338. A less critical and analytical view of Stresemann is to be found in Henry L. Bretton's *Stresemann and the Revision of Versailles* (Stanford: Stanford University Press, 1953), and a sharp reaction against the criticism of Stresemann is Felix Hirsch, *Stresemann: Patriot und Europäer* (Göttingen: Musterschmidt, 1964). A recent work analyzing the influence of military considerations on German foreign policy is Gaines Post, Jr., *The Civil-Military Fabric of Weimar Foreign Policy* (Princeton: Princeton University Press, 1973). For Stresemann's role on the German domestic scene, see Henry Ashby Turner, Jr., *Stresemann and the Politics of the Weimar Republic* (Princeton: Princeton University Press, 1963).

Several important articles on Czechoslovak domestic affairs have appeared since the late 1960s. Concerning the right-of-center governing coalition between 1926 and 1929, see Dušan Uhlíř, "Republikánská strana lidu zemědělského a malorolnického ve vládě panské koalice," *Československý časopis historický* 18 (1970):195-236; Dušan Uhlíř, "Konec vlády panské koalice a Republikánská strana v roce 1929," *Československý časopis historický* 18 (1970):551-92; Vojtěch Mencl and Jarmila Menclová, "Náčrt podstaty a vývoje vrcholové sféry předmnichovské česko-

lovenské mocensko-politické struktury," *Československý časopis historický* 16 (1968):341-64; Hans Lemberg, "Gefahrenmomente für die
demokratische Staatsform der ersten Tschechoslowakischen Republik,"
and Peter Burian, "Demokratie und Parlamentarismus in der Ersten
Tschechoslowakischen Republik," both in Hans-Erich Volkmann, ed., *Die
Krise des Parlamentarismus in Ostmitteleuropa zwischen den beiden
Weltkriegen* (Marburg: Herder-Institut, 1967). On right-wing activities
within Czechoslovakia, one should also consult Alena Gajanová, *Dvojí
tvář: Z historie předmnichovského fašismu* (Prague: Naše vojsko, 1962),
and Tomáš Pasák, "K problematice NOF v letech hospodářské krize na
počátku třicátých let," *Sborník historický* 13 (1965):93-132. On the
Sudeten German side, the leader of the German Social Democrats is the
subject of a brief biography by Johann Wolfgang Brügel, *Ludwig Czech:
Arbeiterführer und Staatsmann* (Vienna: Verlag der Wiener Volksbuchhandlung, 1960).

On diplomatic themes, Jon Jacobson's *Locarno Diplomacy: Germany
and the West, 1925-1929* (Princeton: Princeton University Press, 1972)
offers a general survey of great-power diplomacy in the late 1920s. Peter
Krüger has described Beneš's visit to Berlin in May 1928 in his "Beneš und
die europäische Wirtschaftskonzeption des deutschen Staatssekretärs Carl
von Schuberts," which appeared in the fourteenth volume of the
Bohemia-Jahrbuch. On German disarmament, besides the Gatzke book,
Michael Salewski's *Entwaffnung und Militärkontrolle in Deutschland
1919-1927* (Munich: Oldenbourg, 1966) is important, and John W.
Wheeler-Bennett's *Disarmament and Security since Locarno, 1925-1931*
(London: George Allen & Unwin, Ltd., 1932) and *The Disarmament
Deadlock* (London: George Routledge and Sons, Ltd., 1934) are still
reliable sources for factual material. Wheeler-Bennett's *The Wreck of
Reparations* (London: George Allen and Unwin, Ltd., 1933) is likewise a
useful introduction to the reparations debate, but the most authoritative
treatment of at least the crisis of 1931 is Edward W. Bennett's *Germany
and the Diplomacy of the Financial Crisis, 1931* (Cambridge, Mass.:
Harvard University Press, 1962). The Austro-German customs union
proposal has attracted the interest of several historians, using varying
source material and presenting sometimes conflicting interpretations.
Concerning the customs union proposal, besides Bennett's book, one
should see F.G. Stambrook, "The German-Austrian Customs Union Project
of 1931: A Study of German Methods and Motives," *Journal of Central
European Affairs* 21 (April 1961):15-44; Walter Goldinger, "Das Projekt
einer deutsch-österreichischen Zollunion von 1931," in *Oesterreich und
Europa*, Festschrift for Hugo Hantsch (Graz: Verlag Styria, 1965); Oswald
Hauser, "Die Plan einer deutschösterreichischen Zollunion von 1931 und
die europäische Foederation," *Historische Zeitschrift* 179 (January

1955):45-93. Jan Krulis-Randa, *Das deutsch-österreichische Zollunions-projekt von 1931* (Zürich: Europa-Verlag, 1955); Miroslav Houštecký, "Plán rakousko-německé celní unie v roce 1931 a postoj Československa," *Československý časopis historický* 4 (1956):27-51. The attempt to establish a directory of Europe's great powers in 1933 is treated in a monograph by Konrad Hugo Jarausch, *The Four Power Pact 1933* (Madison: The State Historical Society of Wisconsin, 1965). Of tangential interest is I.M. Oprea's *Nicolae Titulescu's Diplomatic Activity* (Bucharest: Publishing House of the Academy of the Socialist Republic of Romania, 1968). While uncritically laudatory of Titulescu, the book is based upon Rumanian governmental archives.

Post-1933

Inasmuch as this book ends with Hitler's seizure of power in Germany, an extended discussion of bibliography for events after 1933 would border on the presumptuous. But it is possible that a brief mention of a few important books could be useful to some readers.

Concerning German diplomacy after 1933, Hans-Adolf Jacobsen in *Nationalsozialistische Aussenpolitik 1933-1938* (Frankfurt: Alfred Metzner Verlag, 1968) attempts to determine what agencies influenced Nazi diplomacy, how decisions were reached, and what the ideological bases were. Gerhard Weinberg in *The Foreign Policy of Hitler's Germany* (Chicago: University of Chicago Press, 1970) provides the most authoritative narrative and analysis currently available of German foreign policy between 1933 and 1936. Relying on the archives of the German Foreign Office, Weinberg differs sharply with the revisionist ideas of A.J.P. Taylor in *The Origins of the Second World War* (London: H. Hamilton, 1961). In *Hitlers aussenpolitisches Programm: Entstehung und Entwicklung 1919-1939* (Stuttgart: Ernst Klett Verlag, 1970), Axel Kuhn has offered an analysis of Hitler's foreign-policy strategy that emphasizes the centrality of Britain in Hitler's thinking.

The most important diplomatic history of the mid-1930s by a Czech historian is Robert Kvaček's *Nad Evropou zataženo: Československo a Evropa, 1933-1937* (Prague: Svoboda, 1966). A useful supplement about the Little Entente is Günter Reichert's *Das Scheitern der Kleinen Entente* (Munich: Fides-Verlags-Gesellschaft, 1971). Concerning German trade penetration into Southeastern Europe in the 1930s, an older work is still of use, particularly as it comes from a Czech perspective—Antonín Basch, *The Danube Basin and the German Economic Sphere* (New York: Columbia University Press, 1943).

The literature about the Munich conference and the dismemberment of Czechoslovakia in 1938 is inexhaustible. The most extensive survey of the events is offered in Boris Celovsky's *Das Münchener Abkommen 1938* (Stuttgart: Deutsche Verlags-Anstalt, 1958). As an antidote to the detail, Keith Eubank's *Munich* (Norman: University of Oklahoma Press, 1963) makes considerably easier reading. John W. Wheeler-Bennett's *Munich: Prologue to Tragedy* (London: Macmillan & Co., 1948) is still worthwhile inasmuch as he had access to Czechoslovak documentation. Hubert Ripka's *Munich: Before and After* (London: V. Gollancz Ltd., 1939) presents the viewpoint of a prominent and respected journalist in the first Czechoslovak republic. Jörg K. Hoensch offers two studies—one of Hungarian policy in 1938 in his *Der ungarische Revisionismus und die Zerschlagung der Tschechoslowakei* (Tübingen: J.C.B. Mohr, 1967), and the other of the policies of the Slovak autonomists, *Die Slowakei und Hitlers Ostpolitik: Hlinkas Slowakische Volkspartei zwischen Autonomie und Separation 1938-1939* (Cologne: Böhlau Verlag, 1965). As an epilogue to Munich, see Vojtech Mastny's *The Czechs under Nazi Rule: The Failure of National Resistance, 1939-1942* (New York: Columbia University Press, 1971). Radomír Luža's *The Transfer of the Sudeten Germans: A Study of Czech-German Relations, 1933-1962* (New York: New York University Press, 1964) offers a sympathetic portrait of the Czechs and a spirited defense of Czech policy.

Index

Activists, 155; Beneš's attitude toward, 172-73, 270-71, 318; in elections, 160-61, 164; in governing coalitions, 167-68, 208-9, 256-57, 259, 261. *See also* Agrarians; Christian Social parties; Social Democratic party (Sudeten German)

Addison, Joseph, 247, 331, 338

Adler, Friedrich, 43

Adler, Victor, 21, 58

Agrarians (Czechoslovak), 11, 111, 165, 208; divisions among, 205-06, 256; nationality attitude of, 158; and Stříbrný, 255; and tariffs, 167-68, 170, 228-29, 239

Agrarians (Sudeten German), 155, 164, 167-68, 203-05

Agricultural crisis, 10, 211, 222-23, 240-41

Alexander (king of Yugoslavia), 241-42

Andrássy, Count Julius, 41

Angleichungspolitik, 179

Anschluss, 55, 265; Austrian policy toward, 114, 268; and Austro-German customs union proposal, 221, 226, 228-29, 232-33; German policy toward, 58, 92, 267-68; and Locarno, 147-48; Masaryk's views on, 114-16, 183, 322; in 1927-28, 178-98; and Treaty of Lány, 96-98

Arbitration treaty, Czechoslovak-German, 143-44, 150-52

Army, Czechoslovak, 70-71, 118, 127-28, 155

Article 16 (League Covenant), 150, 152

Asch, 67

Ausgleich (1867), 7, 16

Austria: and customs union with Germany, 46, 221-33; and German-Bohemian exiles, 52-53; Masaryk's attitude toward, 114-16, 183, 322; pivotal position of, 91-93, 188; and relations with Czechoslovakia, 87-98, 148, 235

Austro-Marxism, 43

Austro-Slavism, 9-10

Autonomy, local, 74; Masaryk's view of, 156, 199; Reich German policy toward, 80, 199, 314, 326; and Slovak-Sudeten German ties, 80, 160, 203-04

Bach, Alexander, 7

Badeni, Count Casimir, 10, 22

Baeran, Alois, 157-58

Balfour, Arthur James, 30, 67, 108

Banks, Sudeten-German, 162-63, 201-02, 314

Baring Brothers, 139-40

Bat'a, Tomáš, 7

Bauer, Otto, 43-44, 53

Bavaria, 52, 111, 120, 173-75, 304

Baxa, Karel, 218

Beer, Max, 188-90, 323

Beneš, Edvard: and Anschluss, 147-48, 179-81, 185, 188-90, 193-94, 215; and Austria, 89-90, 96-98, 235, 239, 297, 301, 320, 324; and Austro-German customs union proposal, 222-33; and boundary revisions, 68, 88, 290; and Britain, 101, 107-08, 129-32, 141, 196; in Czechoslovak politics, 41, 100, 112, 116-17, 169-71, 206-08, 255, 265, 316-17; and Danubia, 88, 95, 139-40, 148, 180-82, 194-95, 197-99, 234, 238-40, 320-21, 337; and demise of Versailles, 242-51; and disarmament, 137-39, 220, 244-46, 332-33; in exile, 26-27, 29, 32-37; and France, 121-34, 157, 215, 234-35, 271, 303, 313; with German diplomats, 192-98, 213-14, 220-21, 229, 235-37, 311; and Germany, 86, 98, 100, 106-09, 113-14, 118, 126-27, 133-34, 136, 176-78, 185-87, 217-19, 234-35, 240, 251-54, 298-99, 309-10, 340; and Hungary, 89-91, 93-96, 188, 190, 196, 297; and Italy, 135, 254; and Little Entente, 93-96, 181, 194, 242, 249;